For Jean,
with affection &
admiration!

with best wishes,
& many thanks

Howard

Peoples
of Alberta

Peoples
of Alberta

Portraits of Cultural Diversity

Edited by
Howard and Tamara Palmer

Western Producer Prairie Books
Saskatoon, Saskatchewan

Cover photograph courtesy The Archives, Sir Alexander Galt Museum,
City of Lethbridge
Cover design by Warren Clark/GDL

Printed and bound in Canada by Modern Press ◄━►₁
Saskatoon, Canada

The publisher acknowledges the support received for this publication from the
Canada Council.

The publisher acknowledges the financial assistance provided by
Multiculturalism Canada. The views expressed in this volume do not necessarily
reflect the position or policy of the Government of Canada.

Western Producer Prairie Books publications are produced and manufactured in
the middle of western Canada by a unique publishing venture owned by a group
of prairie farmers who are members of Saskatchewan Wheat Pool. From the first
book in 1954, a reprint of a serial originally carried in the weekly newspaper,
The Western Producer, to the book before you now, the tradition of providing
enjoyable and informative reading for all Canadians is continued.

Canadian Cataloguing in Publication Data

Main entry under title:

Peoples of Alberta

Includes index.
ISBN 0-88833-151-7

1. Alberta — Population — Ethnic groups.*
2. Multiculturalism — Alberta.* 3. Alberta —
Emigration and immigration — History. I. Palmer,
Howard, 1946– II. Palmer, Tamara Jeppson.
FC3700.A1P46 1985 971.23'004 C85-091563-5
F1080.A1P46 1985

Contents

Acknowledgments

Many people have helped us in the course of research on this book. Literally hundreds of people across the province were interviewed. Their insights and hospitality made researching the book a pleasure. Many of them are acknowledged in the footnotes to individual chapters. A number of researchers helped with interviews, and with archival research. Joanna Buhr, Marianne Fedori, Norma Milton, Joanna Matejko, Betty Wulff, and Ann Sunahara all put forth a great deal of effort and did a fantastic job. Susan Soule put most of the manuscript on a word processor and completed her tasks with consistent good humor and skill. Marta Styk of the Geography Department at the University of Calgary drew the maps based on information provided by the authors.

A number of archivists at the Glenbow Archives, the Provincial Archives of Alberta, and the Public Archives of Canada were helpful with research materials and with photographs. David Goa of the Provincial Museum of Alberta was particularly helpful. We are also indebted to our friends Jean Burnet and Harold Troper for useful editorial comments on several of the chapters.

The project would not have begun without the financial support of the former Alberta minister of culture, Horst Schmid. He saw the possibilities of the project, and we gratefully acknowledge his support. Beth Bryant of the Cultural Heritage Division of Alberta also warmly encouraged and supported this project from its inception, and we owe her a debt of thanks.

Introduction

The apparent ordinariness of Alberta's towns and cities, seemingly indistinguishable from their counterparts across the great hinterland that is the North American Midwest is deceptive. For the peoples of Alberta come from a strikingly varied number of backgrounds, representing between seventy and eighty different ethnic groups. Any true appreciation of contemporary Alberta rests on an understanding of this intriguing diversity. From its beginnings, going back as far as the time when its only inhabitants were native peoples who lived on the Plains, in the northern forests, and along the Rockies, Alberta has been a diverse society. From the last quarter of the nineteenth century to the present, this diversity has been increased by successive waves of immigration. Today, not all, or even a majority of Albertans belong to the over 1,000 organizations bearing an ethnic label; but many, in their lifestyles, in their values, and even in their personalities, retain something of their cultural heritage.

The diversity of Alberta's nine Indian tribes was first augmented by the arrival of French, British, and later American traders, and by the emergence of a new people, the Metis, offspring of the intermixing of fur traders and native peoples. The agricultural boom at the turn of the twentieth century saw the rapid influx of people from eastern Canada, Great Britain, and the United States, which greatly increased the population and made the society's base solidly Anglo-Canadian. The arrival of German, Scandinavian, and central and eastern European immigrants created further diversity. Fleeing persecution elsewhere, a number of dissenting religious groups, including Mormons, Hutterites, Mennonites, and Doukhobors, came to Alberta during the same period. The province was further pluralized by the arrival of European immigrants following each of the two world wars. Then, in the late 1960s, Canada liberalized its immigration laws; consequently, boom-time Alberta, attracting skilled immigrants from around the world, became not only multi-cultural, but also multi-racial. *Peoples of Alberta* attempts to provide a portrait of these various peoples and an analysis of their impact on Alberta.

Ethnicity has played, and continues to play, an important role in the lives of many Albertans. Alberta's history is, of course, more than the sum of the histories of individual ethnic groups—the complex interaction of these peoples, the economic development of the province, and the place of Alberta within larger national and international economic and political systems are all obviously important components of a comprehensive portrait of the province. But an awareness of why people left their homelands to come to Alberta, of what attempts they made to maintain familiar cultural patterns, and of how they adapted to the geography and society they entered, is essential to an understanding of the province's dynamics, both past and present.

At the turn of the century, many rural regions of the province were settled predominantly by one ethnic group, which thereby left a firm imprint on the area. The Mormons in southwestern Alberta, the people of German background in southeastern and central Alberta, the Scandinavians in central Alberta, and the central and eastern Europeans in north central Alberta have each left a regionalized legacy of social and religious institutions. Thus the ethnic history of Alberta is more than a chronicle of groups arriving in the province and having to conform to a pre-existing pattern (though certainly there were pressures for conformity to an Anglo-Canadian pattern, particularly in the urban areas prior to 1950). Rather, it is a history which is inseparable from that of the province's mainstream development. The Mormons in Cardston, Raymond and Magrath; the German Russians in Hilda and Schuler; the Icelanders in Markerville; the Finns and the Estonians in Eckville; the Norwegians in New Norway, Bardo, and Camrose; the Dutch in Nobleford and Neerlandia; the French Canadians in Legal, Morinville, St. Paul, and Girouxville; the Ukrainians in Mundare and Vegreville, among dozens of other examples: each has had a visible impact on regional architecture, speech, and patterns of everyday life. For those parts of Alberta that were settled primarily by one group, the ethnic history and the history of the local community are virtually identical. Consequently, in telling the stories of a number of different groups, *Peoples of Alberta* is also asserting that Alberta's ethnic diversity is one of the central facts of its history.

Part of this history has been the interaction among numerous groups with widely diverse cultures; as a result, it is inevitably a history that includes both conflict and prejudice. Limits imposed by strong prejudices against them were facts of life for blacks, central and eastern Europeans, and Asian immigrants; and many nonwhite groups, including the native peoples, are still struggling against the effects of racism. Within individual groups, religious and political conflicts among various intragroup factions have sometimes been intense; and some groups have been wracked with internal strife.

Nor is the story of the settling of Alberta merely an epic of successful adaptation. The arrival of hundreds of thousands of newcomers led to the loss of the native peoples' land base, and for many, the loss of their former way of life. Only today, a century later, are the Indian tribes again regaining control over their own lives. Among the newcomers themselves some attempts at group settlement were failures, either because the group involved lacked some of the skills necessary to survive in the new environment, or because the harsh climate or isolation of a particular region proved overwhelming. But there were also many more stories of triumph and success.

Pioneering in Alberta demanded tremendous adaptability, ingenuity, and endurance, and the majority of people who came to the province at the turn of the century were able to meet these demands. They not only survived, which was often a victory in itself, but also built the institutional foundation of Alberta's diverse economy and society.

The cultural heterogeneity of the early settlers was a crucial factor in the overall success of the pioneer farming era. No group was better suited to develop irrigated farming than the Mormons, who came to southern Alberta from the irrigation-transformed deserts of Utah. Similarly, immigrants from the American Midwest could readily transfer their dryland farming skills to southern Alberta. Central and eastern Europeans and Scandinavians were experienced in the kind of mixed farming to which the central park belt region of the province was most suited. Perhaps only the self-sufficient peasants from central and eastern Europe could have survived—with virtually no government assistance—the isolation and the back-breaking work involved in clearing and settling the northern fringes of the province's park belt and the southern reaches of the boreal forest. Nor was anyone better prepared to organize the commercial and political life of this Canadian province and to make Alberta a part of the Canadian nation than early arrivals from Britain and central Canada.

Those groups who came after the early pioneer phase had ended often faced challenges different from those encountered by the earliest settlers; new economic and social conditions, like the circumstances of pioneering, often exacted a bitter toll in personal suffering. But like the pioneer settlers, the immigrants who arrived after each of the two world wars not only survived, but also made their own unique contributions to Alberta's evolution.

Clearly, then, the history of the diverse peoples who settled and developed Alberta is enormously complex; indeed, it is so massive a subject that the authors soon realized their original plan of presenting the histories of all of the province's approximately seventy to eighty ethnic groups, within the confines of one book, would be virtually impossible to carry out. Consequently, we were then faced with a number of difficult decisions as to which groups to include as being somehow representative of "the peoples of Alberta." We have made an effort to provide a balanced view by focussing on different types of groups, from the largest and the most controversial, to the smallest and the least known. Furthermore, in attempting to provide an overview of the varieties of ethnic experience in the province, we have included chapters on three major types of minorities—religious, racial, and national—from widely scattered regions of the world.

We also felt that to provide a balanced view of ethnicity in the province, our selection would have to reflect Alberta's major regions. For example, southern Alberta is portrayed in the chapters dealing with the Hungarians, the Hutterites, and the Japanese; central Alberta is described in the chapters dealing with the Estonians and the Icelanders; north central Alberta and the Peace River district are sketched in the chapters dealing with the French Canadians, the blacks, the Poles, the Romanians, and the Ukrainians. The choice of groups has also enabled us to describe the immigrant and ethnic experience in the rural areas, in the cities, and in the province's coal mining towns. However, with each of the groups discussed we have attempted to present its history throughout the province, and not solely in areas where it was most highly concentrated.

Several of the numerically large groups are included as well. Since people of British background have comprised the largest percentage of the province's population since the 1880s, we have included a chapter on the Scots. Another important component of the British-origin category were people who came to Alberta from Ontario and subsequently played a critical role in the development of the province's urban areas and in its political life prior to the 1920s. So, we have included a chapter on Ontarians: first, to explore their important influence on the province, and second to suggest the significance to Alberta's development of the migration to the province of people from other parts of Canada. Although not technically an ethnic group, Ontarians had a distinctive and important impact on the province, and must be included in any discussion of the "peoples" of Alberta.

Widespread geographical presence, large numbers, and formative institutional impact have not been the only criteria for a group's inclusion. Since little or no research has been done on many of the province's small ethnic groups, such as the Icelanders, the Estonians, and the Romanians, we felt it was time for their stories to be told. Similarly, we thought it important for *Peoples of Alberta* to represent not only founding groups, but also those which have arrived only recently, such as the Vietnamese and South Asians. We have also included many of the groups which have been most controversial in the province's history. Blacks, Ukrainians, Hutterites, Japanese, and South Asians have all been the focus of public controversy. Their inclusion suggests the limits of ethnic and racial tolerance in the province, and indicates how outside prejudice can affect the internal development of an ethnic group.

We have attempted to provide some sense of cohesion among the book's various authors by discussing similar issues. In the case of immigrant ethnic groups, each chapter deals with the group's historical background, its reasons for immigration, its settlement patterns, its growth, its occupational and class profile, its religious and secular organizations, its expressions of ethnic identity, and its patterns of assimilation. We have been interested in the impact that Alberta has had on individual groups, the impact that the group has had on Alberta, and the ways in which this two-way process of adjustment was affected by the group's particular cultural background. We also have attempted to distinguish common problems and patterns of adjustment experienced by all immigrant groups from problems and patterns of adjustment which were unique to a particular group.

To provide an overall perspective on the peoples of Alberta, we must first present an overview of the main patterns of immigration to the province from the 1870s to the present. The first chapter deals with the early period of settlement, which established and determined the basic settlement patterns and ethnic distribution in the population. The second chapter covers the period from just after the end of World War I to the present and discusses three major waves of immigration—during the 1920s, during the post-World War II era, and between 1967 and the early 1980s. Both chapters examine the international and domestic factors behind immigration in each time period, thus explaining why particular groups arrived when they did. These two initial chapters, therefore, introduce all the different ethnic groups who have come to the province, give some sense of their relative size, explain the major growth patterns within different groups, and account for the major patterns of ethnic settlement in the province. Each chapter describes the major components of Canadian immigration policy during the period analyzed, in order to explain why the government was attempting to attract particular kinds of immigrants and discourage others.

The broad sweep of these two introductory chapters enables us to discuss several groups which are not discussed in individual chapters, and gives some sense of perspective on the relative size and significance of the groups which have been singled out for individual attention in the book. In particular, large groups which have played a very important role in the overall development of the province such as the English, Americans, and Germans are given substantial attention in these two chapters.

It is our hope that *Peoples of Alberta* will be an appropriate and a fitting tribute to the variety of individuals and groups who have made Alberta what it is—a vibrant and multi-textured society in which one can experience and be enriched by the cultures and religions of peoples from every part of the world.

Birthplace of Alberta Population

	1901	1911	1921	1931	1941	1951	1961	1971	1981
% of Canadian-born	57.20	43.24	53.54	58.20	67.54	74.45	78.32	82.66	83.52
Alberta-born % of total population		19.62	33.05	41.03	53.63	56.25	59.16	61.61	54.01
Ontario-born % of total population		15.37	11.71	8.09	*	*	*	3.66	7.71
% of British-born	10.67	18.61	16.88	14.85	11.19	7.97	5.90	4.26	10.17 }
% of Europe-born	16.36	15.70	11.85	15.53	13.29	11.29	11.36	8.74	
% of Asian-born	0.34	0.59	0.67	0.56	0.40	0.39	0.45	0.84	2.82
% of United States-born	15.29	21.73	16.97	10.79	8.49	5.90	3.86	2.91	1.98
% Other	0.10	0.11	0.06	0.04	0.03	0.04	0.07	0.58	1.51
Total % Foreign-born**	42.80	56.75	46.46	41.80	32.46	25.55	21.68	17.34	16.48
Total Alberta Population	73,022	374,295	588,454	731,605	796,169	939,501	1,331,944	1,627,875	2,213,650

*Figures not available
**Rounding of numbers affects totals for foreign-born.
Source: Censuses of Canada

Ethnic Origin of the Population of Alberta

	1901	1911	1921	1931	1941	1951	1961	1971	1981
Total	73,022	374,295	588,454	731,605	796,169	939,501	1,331,944	1,627,875	2,213,650
British	34,903	215,174	351,820	389,238	399,432	451,709	601,755	761,665	962,785
French	4,511	20,600	30,913	38,377	42,979	56,185	83,319	94,660	111,865
Dutch	369	3,195	9,490	13,665	20,429	29,385	55,530	58,565	65,060
German	7,836	41,656	35,333	74,450	77,721	107,985	183,314	231,005	233,175
Italian	109	2,150	4,028	4,766	4,872	5,996	15,025	24,805	26,605
Jewish	17	1,505	3,242	3,722	4,164	3,935	4,353	7,320	9,460
Polish	470	2,297	7,172	21,157	26,845	29,661	40,539	44,325	37,655
Russian	4,822	8,033	21,212	16,381	19,316	15,353	17,952	10,235	7,715
Scandinavian	3,940	29,547	44,545	59,461	63,494	70,929	95,879	98,425	78,565
Ukrainian	634	17,584	23,827	55,872	71,868	86,957	105,923	135,510	136,710
Other European	1,409	14,117	34,696	32,797	38,174	38,527	72,274		
Asian	249	2,103	4,300	4,929	4,204	7,441	12,503	25,665	70,785
Indian and Eskimo	13,425	11,402	14,557	15,252	12,569	21,210	28,554	44,680	60,010
Others and not stated	328	4,932	3,319	1,538	10,102	14,228	15,024	101,235	140,567
Multiple Origins									272,735

Source: Censuses of Canada

Ethnic Origin of the Population of Alberta
(percentages 1901-1981)

	1901	1911	1921	1931	1941	1951	1961	1971	1981
Total	100.00	100.00	100.00	100.00	100.00	100.00	100.00	100.00	100.00
British	47.80	57.49	59.80	53.21	50.17	48.08	45.18	46.79	43.49
French	6.18	5.50	5.25	5.24	5.40	5.98	6.25	5.81	5.05
Dutch	0.51	0.85	1.61	1.87	2.57	3.13	4.17	3.60	2.94
German	10.73	11.13	6.01	10.18	9.76	11.49	13.76	14.19	10.53
Italian	0.15	0.57	0.68	0.65	0.61	0.64	1.13	1.52	1.20
Jewish	0.02	0.40	0.55	0.51	0.52	0.42	0.33	0.44	0.43
Polish	0.64	0.61	1.22	2.89	3.37	3.16	3.04	2.72	1.70
Russian	6.60	2.15	3.61	2.24	2.43	1.63	1.35	0.63	0.35
Scandinavian	5.40	7.90	7.56	8.13	7.97	7.55	7.20	6.05	3.55
Ukrainian	0.87	4.70	4.05	7.64	9.03	9.26	7.95	8.32	6.18
Other European	1.93	3.77	5.90	4.48	4.79	4.10	5.43		
Asian	0.34	0.56	0.73	0.67	0.53	0.79	0.94	1.58	3.20
Indian and Eskimo	18.38	3.05	2.47	2.08	1.58	2.26	2.14	2.74	2.71
Other and not stated	0.45	1.32	0.56	0.21	1.27	1.51	1.13	6.22	6.35
Multiple Origins									12.32

Source: Censuses of Canada

CHAPTER ONE
Patterns of Immigration and Ethnic Settlement in Alberta: 1880-1920
Howard Palmer

The settlement of Alberta has occurred in several phases. The fifteen thousand year old nomadic way of life of the Plains and Woodlands Indians began to change with the arrival of European fur traders in the 1700s and 1800s. But large-scale settlement of this vast land did not commence until the end of the nineteenth century when the area of the Northwest Territories that was to become Alberta and Saskatchewan emerged as North America's last agricultural frontier. Newcomers established the major contours of the province's ethnic mix and settlement patterns. The opportunities of the new frontier, Canadian immigration policy, and the availability of peoples seeking a new life led to the formation of a new society in Alberta. To understand this new society which emerged before the outbreak of World War I, we must return to the world of late nineteenth century Canada to examine Canadian governmental policy towards the settlement of the West, and the forces which brought together a unique mix of peoples. Each group of newcomers brought their own ideas of what this new society should look like, and the interplay and clash of their ideals and values provides much of the drama and excitement of Alberta's early history.

Part I: The Transformation of the West: Immigration to 1896

Canada could not wait. It feared an American take-over of the sparsely populated Northwest Territories, and it needed the vast region to make the New Dominion a viable entity, a transcontinental nation. The Northwest was felt to be the guarantee of Canada's future greatness. Following confederation in 1867, both the federal Conservatives and the Liberals were anxious to fill the area with white settlers as soon as possible. Despite the completion of the transcontinental railway in 1885, it would take another decade before the boom began.

When the first governmental structure was established for the Northwest Territories in the late 1870s, the position of French in the West received due recognition. Initially the Territories were organized on the pattern of Quebec with equal rights being given to English and French in the territorial assembly, the Courts, and the schools. The law reflected the linguistic reality of the early Northwest. French Canadian settlers and the French-speaking Metis, for example, outnumbered the English-speaking settlers in the Edmonton area to the mid-1880s.

The period from 1870 to 1896 was, from the white settlers' viewpoint, one of slow growth for western Canada. By 1885, the year of the Northwest Rebellion, the provisional district of Alberta, which was then part of the Northwest Territories and included most of the southern and central parts of the present province of Alberta, reported a population of only 15,533. The Indians and the Metis still outnumbered the whites. Nor did the completion of the Canadian Pacific Railway (CPR) in that same year greatly augment these numbers of white settlers, although it did promote the slow growth of Calgary, as a divisional point and shipping center. The white population of Alberta remained relatively small, settlement being concentrated around the fur trading and police outposts at Forts Edmonton and Macleod, along the foothills of southern Alberta (where a small ranching industry had begun to develop) at Lethbridge, which began to develop as a coal mining center after the mid-1880s, and around Calgary.[1]

Although the completion of the CPR did not lead immediately to large-scale migration from eastern Canada, it made it eventually possible. The year 1885 is also extremely important as it marks the end of native power in the Northwest. With the fall of the Metis stronghold of Batoche and the capture of Louis Riel, Big Bear, and Poundmaker, the Metis and the Plains Indians lost their power of resistance. The suppression of the Rebellion of 1885 by government forces was a major turning point, for no longer did the Canadian government have to worry about the threat of an armed native uprising. After 1885, the Northwest Territories could be settled on the federal government's terms.

A large number of those who did come to the Northwest Territories in the 1880s arrived from Ontario. The majority of them eventually settled in the villages and towns of the Northwest where their knowledge of the language and Canadian institutions, as well as their educational background, made it possible for them to set up small businesses and to dominate the teaching, legal, and medical professions. In the late nineteenth century, most of the politicians in the Territories were Ontarians, as they already knew the Canadian political system.

Although most Ontario settlers came west as individuals or in small groups, there were some larger group settlements. One was started around Red Deer in the early 1880s by Methodists from London, Ontario, and another near Edmonton in 1892 by farmers from Parry Sound. Though outnumbered by the British and the Americans after 1896, the Ontario settlers continued to come in sizeable numbers throughout the period until World War I. Because of Ontario's size and its interest in the West, Ontario settlers far outnumbered newcomers from other provinces; by 1911, there were twice as many Ontario-born people in Alberta as there were people from all the other provinces combined.[2]

From the late 1870s onward English-speaking settlers from Ontario had greatly outnumbered the French-speaking from Quebec. The Roman Catholic clergy in western Canada had attempted to encourage French Canadians from Quebec to migrate westward, without any real success. Instead of west the Quebecois moved southward to New England, only approximately fifty miles south of Montreal, in contrast to the 2000 miles separating Montreal from the distant Northwest. Approximately one out of eight Quebecois emigrated to New England in the decade of the 1880s—so many that the Roman Catholic Church worked to keep as many French Canadians as it could in the province. The clergy encouraged the adventuresome to homestead in northern Quebec, not in the West.[3]

Since the French Roman Catholic clergy in the Northwest Territories were so unsuccessful in attracting settlers from Quebec, they turned their attention to attracting French-speaking immigrants from the United States and, to a lesser extent, from Europe. Colonization priests were assigned the role of bringing French-speaking settlers to the West and helping them get established. These colonizing priests helped establish groups of French-speaking settlers across the Prairies, including a number of settlements in Alberta, particularly in the region around Edmonton, and St. Paul-Bonnyville. These settlements brought together repatriated French Canadians (many of whom had been living temporarily in the United States) and a small number of immigrants from France and Belgium.

The relatively small numbers of French-speaking immigrants to the Prairies threatened their language privileges in the Northwest. The Ontarians were anxious to see the West develop as an English-speaking region, British in sympathy; they immediately began to mold their new western home in the image of Ontario. In 1892 the territorial assembly, dominated by the English-speaking members, largely eliminated the legal rights of the French-speaking population. Henceforth the French-speaking community had to rely on rural isolation, large families, and strong parish organizations to keep their language and religion alive.

The two most important dates in the history of the Northwest Territories in the late nineteenth century are 1885 and 1892. After the Riel Rebellion of 1885 the area truly became a white's country, and after 1892, an English-speaking one. The immigrants, who arrived in considerable numbers at the turn of the century, came to an area clearly modelled on Ontario, and one largely governed by Ontarians. To the Ontarians, the English language was the instrument of forging a new Canadian community; and the public school was the institution by which this "Anglo-conformity" would be imposed.

Committed to maintaining the British character of the country, the federal government itself had oriented settlement policy to promote British immigration. For example, the government introduced a programme of assisted passages for British immigrants and mounted an extensive publicity campaign promoting the Canadian West in Britain.[4]

During the 1870s the response of British agriculturalists was slight. Forced to face the fact that, if it was going to be successful in settling the vast western lands it would have to look elsewhere for immigrants, the government began to encourage emigration from other parts of Europe. Mennonites fleeing a Russification campaign in Russia came to southern Manitoba in 1874. Icelanders fleeing volcanic eruptions and failing fisheries came to Manitoba in 1875, settling along the shore of Lake Winnipeg. The government encouraged both movements by granting large reserves of land and loans and, in the case of the Mennonites, guarantees of military exemption and educational rights. Similarly, during the 1880s the government encouraged the settlement of Americans, Russian Jews, Hungarians, and Germans. Nevertheless, settlement, from the government's vantage point, proceeded slowly. To pay for the CPR, and to create a market for eastern goods, hundreds of thousands of settlers were needed.[5]

There were several reasons for the slowness of settlement. Fearing the impact of farming on their enterprises, the British and Canadian ranchers in southern Alberta actively discouraged settlement. They were aided by the widespread belief that the Palliser Triangle, which included southern Alberta, was too dry for farming. This notion, coupled with agricultural depression, the Riel Rebellion, the absence of CPR branch lines, the problems inherent in farming the Canadian Prairies (including a lack of suitable crops and techniques and unfavorable markets and prices), and the general hardships of pioneering, slowed settlement before 1896. Extensive land holdings by the Hudson's Bay Company (HBC), the CPR, and colonization companies also discouraged settlement. Since land policy was almost as liberal south of the boundary, where cheap and good land was still available, most westward-moving farmers turned away from Canada to the United States.[6]

Despite these impediments to colonization, there was some noteworthy agricultural settlement during the late 1880s and early 1890s. During the middle to late 1880s, some American, German, and Scandinavian farmers settled in present day Alberta; and Chinese workers, having just completed the CPR, began looking for alternative work in the villages and towns. Most of the Americans came individually and settled after 1891 on land along the newly opened Calgary-Edmonton and Calgary-Macleod railways. However, some of those who came from the United States (such as the Icelanders, Swedes, and Norwegians) had been part of earlier minority group settlements in the United States, and came in groups to the province.

The largest single American group were Mormons from Utah. Fleeing antipolygamy laws, they came in 1887 under the leadership of Charles Ora Card and established farms in the area around Cardston in southwestern Alberta. This group, a forerunner of a much larger group of Mormons who came for economic reasons in the late 1890s, was met by considerable opposition from the local press; but the Canadian government, glad to have skilled irrigation farmers settle in an area of the Territories known for its dryness, welcomed them. After 1890 the opposition declined when the Mormon church abandoned polygamy.[7]

People of German origin also began to settle in Alberta in the 1880s. For the most part they did not come directly from Germany. Most German immigrants who settled on the Prairies came from eastern Europe and it was their religious affiliation which gave their settlements unity. Attracted by offers of land, local self-government, and linguistic freedom, German-speaking colonists had established settlements in eastern Europe in the late 1700s and early 1800s. Increasing nationalism in eastern Europe in the late nineteenth century, pressure to assimilate, and a scarcity of land prompted many to emigrate to the American and the Canadian West.[8]

German-speaking people established several settlements in Alberta during the late 1880s and early 1890s. Based on religious affiliation, these settlements were to become the nuclei for much larger German-speaking communities after the turn of the century. The first German settlers in Alberta came to the Pincher Creek area in 1883. Six years later, the first sizeable settlements were established near Medicine Hat when nearly a hundred families arrived from two neighboring German settlements in eastern Galicia in the Austro-Hungarian Empire (now part of southern Poland and the western Ukraine). These settlements were short-lived, but they were the forerunners of the large-scale immigration of German-speaking peoples which would eventually turn the Medicine Hat area, proportionately, into one of the largest concentrations of German-origin peoples in Canada.[9]

Shortly after the completion of the Calgary and Edmonton railway in 1892, thirteen German Protestant communities (Lutheran, Reformed, Baptist, and Moravian) were established within a thirty-mile radius of Edmonton. From this beginning, the rural areas south and west of Edmonton—centered around Leduc and Stony Plain—became strongholds of German settlement in the province. Even today over half of the population of these rural areas is of German origin.[10]

Since virtually all of these early settlements were founded along denominational lines, much of their early organizational life centered around their churches. In the culturally and religiously alien atmosphere of eastern Europe, where they had been living, religion and ethnicity had become completely intertwined in their attempt to remain separate from their Slavic Orthodox neighbors.

The eastern European origins of these German-speaking settlers had an important effect on the settlement patterns of Ukrainians in Alberta. The German-speaking immigrants who settled near Fort Saskatchewan at Josephburg came from the province of Galicia in the Austro-Hungarian Empire, and they were instrumental in encouraging their former Ukrainian neighbors, who with the Poles formed one of the two dominant groups in Galicia, to come to Canada and to that particular region of Alberta.[11]

Part II: The Boom Years: 1896-1914

After 1896, immigration to Alberta increased markedly, largely as a result of two factors: the ending of the agricultural depression, and the beginning of an aggressive immigration promotion campaign by Clifford Sifton, the new Liberal cabinet minister responsible for immigration. Sifton, the most powerful western voice in Prime Minister Wilfrid Laurier's cabinet, dedicated his political life to the task of peopling the West. The Manitoba lawyer's efforts were guided by the same economic and nationalistic motives which had inspired John A. Macdonald in the 1880s: immigration to western Canada would have to be encouraged to establish a market for eastern goods, to provide freight and traffic for the railways, and to secure the West for Canada. Sifton encouraged settlement by altering the land-grant system, through which speculators and colonization companies had tied up much of the best land, by simplifying the process of securing homesteads and by streamlining an organization to administer his policy. He placed new emphasis on the campaign to promote immigration which previous governments had initiated in Europe and the United States; he also provided bonuses to steamship companies and agents who secured immigrants.[12]

Sifton's immigration policy was aimed at attracting farmers, whatever their nationality. He believed that the most desirable were industrious, self-sufficient farmers and peasants capable of enduring the difficulties and isolation of the pioneering process. While the Ontario-born Sifton recognized that his fellow Anglo-Canadians on the Prairies preferred that the West be settled with people from Ontario, Great Britain, and northwestern Europe, he knew these groups could not supply enough immigrants. In view of the limited number of farmers available in Great Britain, the reluctance of the French in Europe to emigrate, the restrictive emigration laws in Germany, and the small numbers of immigrants available in Scandinavia, he attempted to attract immigrants from central and eastern Europe.

Sifton's campaign was aided by favorable economic circumstances. Canada had just emerged from a depression. The CPR needed traffic and freight. Due to the growing demand from a rapidly urbanizing Europe, the prices of western staple products rose while transportation costs to Europe fell. At this same time, new inventions in farm machinery, along with the development of mechanical grain elevators and an early maturing wheat, made it possible to cultivate, seed, and harvest vast expanses of land with speed. Most important of all, the American frontier had been largely settled by the mid-1890s. By the turn of the century, Canada's Northwest Territories were justly known as the "last best west." [13]

The number of immigrants entering Canada increased dramatically, year by year. The numbers are phenomenal. A nation of only five million in 1900 attracted over 1,250,000 immigrants in the next ten years. During the following decade, the total was over 2,050,000, despite the fact that beginning in 1914 the outbreak of the war largely curtailed immigration. As a result of this vast movement of peoples, the country's population as a whole increased by one-third between 1901 and 1911, and Alberta's population increased 5.5 times, reaching 375,000 by 1911. The Indians and Metis, who constituted the majority of the population less than thirty years before, had become a small minority numbering at most 5 percent of the population. They were groups that could safely be ignored by the majority. By 1911, 57 percent of Alberta's population were immigrants.[14]

Although the immigration boom included peoples from all over Europe and North America, over half of the population in the province were people whose roots could be traced back to Britain. They came mostly from Ontario, the United States, and of course from Britain itself. The English-speaking newcomers from Ontario, Britain, and the United States made up the largest group and also the most influential politically, economically, and culturally.

Race Theory, Public Attitudes, and Immigration Policy

Though Sifton's immigration policy was more pragmatic than that of his predecessors, there were still many built-in ethnic and racial biases. Canada's immigration policy throughout the late nineteenth century and indeed until after World War II reflected not only Canada's British colonial past but also race theories which were prevalent in the late nineteenth and early twentieth centuries in North America and Europe. These race theories reflected an attempt to apply Darwin's theories of biological evolution to human society. Paralleling Darwin's discoveries in the animal world, "races" were thought to represent different stages of the evolutionary scale. It was commonly believed that the white "race" was superior to the black, yellow, or red "races." Even European nationalities were divided into different races with teutonic northern Europeans considered superior to Slavs, Jews, or southern Europeans. These racial theories helped justify the imperial ambitions of Britain, France, Germany, and even the United States as they carved out and extended their empires in Asia, Africa, and the Caribbean. They felt it was the duty of the white race to govern the nonwhite.[15]

These widely held notions of a world-wide racial hierarchy became firmly embedded in Canada's immigration policy and influenced the public response to each immigrant group which came to western Canada. During this period of British imperial ascendancy, the British were considered best. Americans, who were predominantly of Anglo-Saxon origin, were also thought to be ideal settlers. Scandinavians, Germans, and other northern and western Europeans were thought to be desirable; hence it was thought they should be encouraged to come. Slavs, Jews, and southern Europeans were questionable. Blacks and Asians were considered inferior and undesirable; hence it was widely believed they should be kept out. These racial and ethnic prejudices were also reinforced by strong religious prejudices, with English Canada's dominant Anglo-Protestant society having grave reservations about non-Protestant immigrants. The prevailing prejudices of the day can clearly be seen as we examine whom the Canadian government encouraged to come, whom they discouraged, whom they excluded, and which groups generated the most public controversy.

Britons

Sifton made strenuous attempts to promote British immigration by sending government agents to promote immigration. While British farmers generally proved resistant, many others in Britain were not. Canada attracted the younger, unprovided-for sons of well-to-do families who were seeking adventure in the colonies. The immigrants also included coal miners, shopkeepers, and laborers from Britain's cities who saw little hope for advancement in class-ridden Britain. Between 1900 and 1914, over one million people migrated from the United Kingdom to

Group of British ranchers, Porcupine Hills, May 1894. Young Englishmen from the upper classes saw southern Alberta as a place to re-create an English life style within the context of a frontier and Empire-building adventure. (Courtesy Glenbow Archives)

Canada, and many of these went to the Prairies. By 1911, 19 percent of Alberta's population was British born.[16]

One of the largest concentrations of British immigrants on the Prairies had emerged in the 1880s and 1890s in the ranching community of southern Alberta. The possibilities of large profits and outdoor adventure attracted affluent Britishers. Several large ranches like the Oxley, Waldrond, and Quorn ranches served as a home-away-from-home for the sons of the English well-to-do, including the famous remittance men. Many of these young men had gone to private schools in England, but not being the eldest sons, could not take over their families' estates. Finding it harder and harder to be placed in the traditional professions of the army or navy, the law, the civil service, or the clergy, they came to Canada. They often received a monthly allowance or remittance.[17]

Along the foothills in Alberta, from the Priddis-Millarville area to Pincher Creek, in a few other rural areas around Pine Lake (near Red Deer), and in the Alix area east of Lacombe, these young Englishmen— for a brief historical moment—created a unique British lifestyle. While they had to make many changes to adapt to the frontier situation, they tried to reestablish traditional social pastimes such as attending formal balls, dressing in formal attire for dinner, holding fox hunts (with a coyote substitute), playing polo, cricket and tennis, and holding horse races. Some of the more successful families imported British governesses or had their children educated in private schools. They watched events in Britain closely, strongly supported the Anglican church, and backed the Conservative party (which was seen as pro-British). The intensity of the imperial orientation was no more strongly in evidence than at the time of royal visits or during wartime.[18]

The British ranching community had a strong impact on southern Alberta, particularly in the Calgary area during the 1880s and 1890s, but its influence began to decline after the Liberals came to power in Ottawa in 1896. The Liberals favored the farmers over the ranchers. As more and more farmers settled in the area, ranchers were forced to move, sell out, or decrease the size of their ranches. The British influence in the area began to decline with the influx of farmers, many of them from the United States. Their influence declined further with the outbreak of World War I, when many of the young Britons returned to fight on the side of Britain in that war; most did not return.[19]

Of all the British immigrants to western Canada, the well-to-do consti- tuted only a small fraction of the total number. Most of the skilled workers, for example, who immigrated to Canada at this time were from Britain. While the Canadian government wanted only farmers from other parts of Europe, they were glad to have anyone from Britain, regardless of their background. The British were not really immigrants like other newcomers, since it was felt they had a special place in Canada. All Canadians at that time were considered to be British subjects, and the British flag and national anthem were then their own.

Though most of the British immigrants who came to farm came as individuals, and settled in widely scattered parts of the province, some did attempt group farming. These ventures were not very successful because very few of the British immigrants had farming experience. One of the largest of these attempts was the Barr Colony, located at what is now Lloydminster on the Alberta-Saskatchewan border. Two Anglican clergymen, Isaac Barr, from Ontario, and George Exton Lloyd, an English veteran of the force sent to fight Riel in 1885, developed a plan to bring thousands of British immigrants to farm on the Prairies. Barr and Lloyd advertised the colony in English newspapers. In 1903 several thousand settlers, mostly city dwellers from the lower middle class and without farming experience, signed up. Unfortunately Barr proved to be a poor organizer, and many of the settlers felt cheated when problems developed on the ship and later on the railway journey across the country. They blamed Barr for the problems and turned to Lloyd as their leader when Barr, under heavy criticism, deserted the group. But the problems they encountered were as much a result of their own exaggerated expectations and their lack of pioneering experience as they were of Barr's mismanagement. Many of the Barr colonists, like many other English immigrants who settled on farms, moved into the towns and cities where, as native English-speakers, they were often more successful as postmasters, policemen, or shopkeepers.[20]

The British in western Canada had their greatest impact on the cities. Many of the immigrants came from the working class. They were skilled workers; they built many of the buildings and homes in the cities and did much of the skilled work on the railways. Many British immigrants, including Joseph Knight and William Irvine, played leading roles in the labor movement in Alberta. The British also played a key role among skilled workers in Alberta's coal mining industry.[21]

British workers in western Canada brought their working class culture with them. In the larger cities they had their own boardinghouses, sports clubs, men's organizations, and even some residential concentrations. In Calgary for example, Welsh families concentrated in the suburb of Manchester; many Yorkshiremen lived in nearby Parkhill, and workers from county Durham settled in the railway suburb of Ogden.[22]

Because the Canadian government, anxious to get British immigrants, did so much to encourage them, by 1911 they formed the second largest immigrant group in the province. Their influence on politics, society, religion, and the economy was very diverse since the immigrants came from many different strata of British society. It is difficult, however, to separate the influence of British immigrants on the early development of the province from the influence of people of British background who moved west from central Canada. Their influence can, however, be clearly seen. It was particularly apparent in Alberta's strong commitment in both world wars. It was evident in the creation of a skilled labor force in the urban areas before World War I, and in the early strength of labor unions and socialist parties in the cities, and mining settlements in the province. The British influence also contributed to the numerical and social prominence of the Anglican, Presbyterian, and Methodist churches, and to the imported class distinctions which some tried to introduce in a city like Calgary before World War I.

Americans

Given prevailing public attitudes, Sifton and his department made great efforts to attract American farm settlers. Not only were they predominantly of British background, English-speaking and Protestant, but also brought with them farm machinery, money, and experience with western farming in the United States. The Canadian government established agencies to promote immigration, advertised in local newspapers, sent out pamphlets extolling the virtues of the Canadian West, and arranged visits to the area for American newspapermen and farmers.[23]

Many American farmers responded. Their coming had a significant economic, social, and political impact on Alberta, particularly in central and southern Alberta. By the turn of the century in the American West, good land was becoming scarce. With the cost of land increasing, some farmers had to rent rather than buy. The price of land soared, and farmers began looking for cheap land for their sons. Between 1898 and 1914, nearly 600,000 American immigrants, mostly farmers from the midwestern states, came to western Canada. Between 1907 and 1915, American citizens took out 40 percent of the homesteads in the Northwest and by 1911, 22 percent of Alberta's population was American born, making them the largest immigrant group of all. By the mid-1920s, one of every four farms in the province was operated by someone who

American immigrants from Colorado arriving in Bassano, 1914. American immigrants who came in large numbers to central and southern Alberta played a key role in pioneer Alberta. (Courtesy Glenbow Archives)

had been born in the United States. In the southern part of the province, the percentage was highest, ranging from 30 to 50 percent.[24]

The American farmers constituted a very diverse group. Many were returning Canadians. They had left eastern Canada before the building of the CPR, moving to the United States in search of land. They now took advantage of the opportunity to return to their home country.[25]

While most Americans came individually, some ethnic and religious settlements in the United States came as groups. Perhaps as many as one-third of those coming from the United States were actually European born. They had immigrated to the United States to farm in the 1860s, 1870s, and 1880s, and now sought land for their children. Some sought a more isolated social atmosphere where they could resist American assimilative pressures. The Canadian government hired special agents in the United States to encourage group settlements of Norwegians, Danes, Dutch, Belgians, French Canadians, German Russians, and several religious minorities, including Mormons.[26]

The Canadian government did not, however, want any American black settlers to come to western Canada. When a few hundred blacks from Oklahoma, who were fleeing racial persecution, began coming to the Edmonton area in 1910 and 1911, the federal government prevented their further entry. Canada was to be a white man's country.[27]

The Mormon settlement expanded rapidly after 1898. Their abandonment of polygamy, their use of English, and their skill at farming led to their general acceptance within a generation. In response to a joint effort by the Mormon church and the Northwest Coal and Navigation Company in Lethbridge to build an irrigation system and settle hundreds of square miles of land, Mormons came northward in sizeable numbers. Land suitable for farming in Utah was scarce, and the Mormon church itself encouraged people to go to Canada. By 1911, eighteen new Mormon communities had been founded in southern Alberta, and approximately 10,000 Mormons lived in the area.[28]

Because of this sizeable influx of settlers, southwestern Alberta became an extension of the Mormon cultural region of the American West. Settlers came as an organized group with church approval and encouragement. In many areas where they settled, they lived in villages rather than isolated homesteads. Farmers lived in town and farmed the surrounding land, a settlement pattern which made possible an active cultural, social, and religious life and nourished a strong sense of group solidarity. Irrigation enabled southwestern Alberta to overcome recurring periods of drought and enabled farmers to grow crops such as sugar beets and canning vegetables. Thus, irrigation, the village settlement pattern, cooperative enterprise, an intense social and cultural life, and strong group solidarity—all interrelated economic and social patterns of the Mormon cultural area of the American West—were transferred to southern Alberta by the Mormon settlers.[29]

Although several settlements of German-Americans, Scandinavian-Americans, and repatriated French Canadians (and near Ponoka, one sizeable settlement of Welsh-Americans) were established in Alberta, most American immigrants did not constitute a closely knit group. Knowing English, their cultural background was similar to that of English-speaking Canadians. They had the farming and social skills that made it possible for them either to establish the foundations of, or to quickly blend into, rural society. Throughout central and southern Alberta, they immediately played a prominent role in local politics and society, establishing local fraternal and service organizations, and organizing sports such as baseball, basketball, and rodeo, which became community-wide institutions.[30]

American settlers had a strong and lasting impact on Alberta. Their experience in dryland farming and irrigation made them ideally suited to adapt to the dry climate of the southern section of the province. Not all were successful. Some, discouraged by severe drought, returned to the United States. But they were better suited than most immigrant groups to farm the southern Prairies. [31]

Americans also had a profound impact on the religious and political life of the province. Although most Americans joined with eastern Canadians and British immigrants to establish the major Protestant denominations such as the Methodist, Presbyterian, and Baptist churches, they also brought to western Canada the great diversity of religious groups from the American Midwest. They brought at least twenty-eight evangelical sects to the province, and helped to establish several Bible colleges which have exerted a continuing influence on religion in the Prairies.[32]

Probably the Americans' greatest impact came with the farmers' organizations and new political groups formed before World War I. Much of the ideology and many of the leaders and new agrarian organizations which emerged to effect agrarian reform came from the United States. The farmers' political revolt in the postwar years, culminating in the victory of the United Farmers of Alberta (UFA) in the provincial election of 1921, owed much to the experience and perspective of American farmers.

Western Canadian farmers had grown discontented over the operation of banks, railways, grain companies, and governments. They believed that government needed to control big business, that the people needed to control the government, and that economic groups such as farmers should cooperate rather than compete with each other. Two of Alberta's earliest farm organizations, the Society of Equity (begun in 1905) and the Non-Partisan League (begun in 1917), were brought directly from the United States. Henry Wise Wood, the most important farm leader in Alberta, had grown up in Missouri. The Carstairs farmer developed many of his ideas out of his experience with populist farm protest movements in the United States before moving to Alberta in 1905. Like Wood, many of the other directors of the UFA and the Alberta Wheat Pool were American born. Although Alberta farmers from Ontario or Great Britain also joined in the farm movement, it was the American influence which was the strongest force for change.[33]

The American farmers simply did not have any loyalties to the "old

line" political parties in Canada, and they helped to form the new political parties which developed in western Canada at the end of World War
I. The most radical solutions to the problems faced by western Canadian
farmers emerged in Alberta, where American influence was the strongest. Direct legislation (including referendums and the recall of public
officials), the single tax, free trade, prohibition, proportional representation, opposition to an appointed senate, and monetary reform were all
reforms advocated by American settlers.[34]

While their impact was most clearly felt in agriculture, Americans also
influenced business in the province. Coal mining towns such as Hillcrest
in the Crow's Nest Pass (named after Spokane, Washington entrepreneur Charles P. Hill) and Drumheller (named after Sam Drumheller who
came to the province in 1910 from Walla Walla, Washington) confirm
the early American presence in coal mining. Though far outnumbered by
British immigrants in the urban areas, many Americans were active in
real estate and investment companies. American entrepreneurs in Calgary helped turn the area of Mount Royal into Calgary's most prestigious
suburb, with its nickname, "American Hill."[35]

Scandinavians

Many migrants from the United States came from the Scandinavian
settlements in the American Midwest. Nearly 100,000 Scandinavians, in
fact, came to western Canada before World War I. Most arrived by way
of the United States, rather than directly from the Scandinavian countries. By 1911, almost 8 percent of Alberta's population was of Scandinavian origin. [36]

Just as they had in their early settlements in the late 1880s and 1890s,
Scandinavians continued to settle primarily in central Alberta along the
edge of the park belt, where they appreciated the presence of wood, wild
hay, and adequate supplies of water. Sizeable settlements of Scandinavians, however, also existed on the open prairies, such as the Danes at
Standard and Dalum, the Norwegians at Claresholm, and the Swedes at
Scandia.

While solid blocs of any one Scandinavian nationality were relatively
rare (they usually took up homestead land according to availability
rather than having the government set aside special reserves of land), a
few sizeable communities of Scandinavians were established. These concentrations made possible the development of an active community life,
usually centered on the Lutheran church. The Scandinavians also established several educational institutions connected with the Lutheran
church, such as the college at Camrose.[37]

As with other European immigrant groups, the church played more
than just a spiritual or social role within the Scandinavian communities.
Church organizations often played a part in the very foundations of the
communities, as for example in the case of the three largest Danish
settlements in the province at Dickson, Standard, and Dalum. In all three
communities, Lutheran churches or church-related organizations helped
organize the migration. Newcomers built churches soon after they

arrived, and the churches have continued to play an important role in the communities down to the present day.[38]

The Lutheran churches, however, did not have a monopoly among Scandinavians in Alberta. A variety of other religious groups had emerged in Scandinavia and the United States to challenge Lutheranism. These groups included the Swedish Baptists, the Swedish Evangelical Mission Covenant, and the Evangelical Free Church, which the new-comers brought with them. With their evangelical and missionary appeal, these churches were popular in several Scandinavian settlements in rural Alberta.[39]

The Lutherans also met challenges from secular forces. Left wing and anticlerical ideas had considerable appeal among Finnish immigrants, many of whom had come to the province from politically radical mining communities in the United States. In coal mining areas of the province such as Canmore and the Crow's Nest Pass, and in several scattered farming communities (including one large settlement west of Sylvan Lake), they established prior to World War I several branches of the Finnish Socialist Organization of Canada, and (after 1917) of the Finnish Organization of Canada, both left wing groups. In several Finnish settle-ments in the province, the socialist hall rather than the church served as the focal point for community activities. The one sizeable Icelandic com-munity in the province at Markerville included people who, like the poet-farmer Stephan Stephansson, had grown sceptical of organized reli-gion. At Markerville, cultural, literary, and educational activities replaced the church as the focal point of group life.[40]

Despite their large numbers, the Scandinavians have not been very visible. They did not develop many concentrated blocs like the Ukraini-ans. Nor were they as anxious to preserve a distinctive identity. They were readily accepted by the English-speaking settlers because they were Protestant and because they were seen as "racially" acceptable. The previous American residence of many had already accustomed them to North American living conditions. Since there was very little prejudice against them, they did not have the same need as some other groups to rely on each other. They melded quickly into rural western Canadian society.

Assimilation was not, of course, automatic. For many years, the pietis-tic attitude of several of the Lutheran synods and other churches, with their opposition to dancing, drinking, and card playing, restrained their members from mingling with some other groups. The establishment of institutions like Camrose Lutheran College helped to encourage marriage within the same faith. Nonetheless, the quick acceptance of Scandina-vian pioneers into rural community life, the small numbers of immi-grants who came from Scandinavia during the 1920s and 1930s, and the tremendous uprooting and relocation which occurred in the dry belt of southern and southcentral Alberta during the 1920s and 1930s all con-tributed to the rapid assimilation of the Scandinavians.[41]

Despite their quick assimilation, the Scandinavians who came to the province prior to the World War I left a tangible legacy. Lutheran churches and Scandinavian surnames reflect their presence. Several place names of towns and villages in central Alberta are lasting reminders of their founders: Norwegians at Bardo, Edberg, New Norway, Bergen, Sundre; Swedes at New Sweden, Malmo, Falun, and Westerose; and Danes at Dalum.

The Scandinavian economic contribution to the province was an outgrowth of the interplay between their cultural background and the geography of the province. They took advantage of the water and hay in the park belt to establish a thriving dairy industry, which still plays an important role in the region's economy. When they were founded, the Wetaskiwin and Camrose areas attracted large numbers of Scandinavians, and they are still today two of the most important dairying regions of the province. Scandinavians also contributed to the cooperative movement in the province, and helped to promote the sport of skiing.[42]

Dutch, Belgian, and French Immigrants

Scandinavians made up by far the largest number of immigrants of northern and western European origin, but Alberta also attracted some Dutch, Belgian, and French immigrants. The Canadian government and the general public considered all three groups as part of the culturally and racially desirable northern European peoples, and the government and CPR immigration agents made special efforts to attract them. Dutch farmers established a few widely scattered farming communities in the province centered around either Reformed or Catholic churches. The Belgians included both Walloons (who are French-speaking) and Flemings (whose language is similar to Dutch). Government officials recruited Walloons as farmers, and they settled among the predominantly French-speaking settlers north of St. Albert. Other Belgian Walloons came as experienced miners to the Crow's Nest Pass. In 1913, the Knight Sugar Company in Raymond also recruited Flemish Belgian laborers for the sugar beet industry. Immigrants from France were very diverse, but they formed only a few short-lived settlements, and were overshadowed by French Canadians who established the only long-term and viable French-speaking cultural institutions in the province.[43]

Few in numbers, widely scattered, and generally well accepted, the Dutch, Belgian, and metropolitan French immigrants were quickly absorbed into rural Albertan society. Only the Dutch Reformed immigrants—who clung closely to their strict Calvinist views in closely knit communities at Granum, Nobleford, Monarch, and Neerlandia—maintained a lasting Dutch presence in the province.[44]

Germans, Mennonites, and Hutterites

The pace of settlement by German-speaking settlers also accelerated after 1896, strengthening patterns which had developed in the early 1890s. People of German origin continued to establish settlements that were primarily rural and church-centered. Settlers from Germany itself were far outnumbered by German-speaking immigrants from eastern Europe, many of whom came to Alberta after having lived for a few

German immigrants in Edmonton, 1902. Most people of German origin in pioneer Alberta went to farming areas, but a small class of successful German entrepreneurs emerged in Edmonton and surrounding towns. (Courtesy Provincial Museum and Archives of Alberta)

years in the United States. Though Lutherans continued to constitute a majority of the settlers, the newcomers also brought over ten new German-American religious denominations, further complicating and fragmenting an already diverse group. German Catholics also established several settlements across the province. German immigrants continued to be attracted to the older settlements in the Stony Plain, Edmonton, Wetaskiwin, Bashaw, and Medicine Hat areas; from 1900 to the outbreak of World War I, they also opened nearly ninety previously unsettled areas, spanning the length and breadth of the province. A sizeable German-speaking working class, with its own distinct neighborhoods, also developed in several of the province's cities, particularly in Edmonton, Calgary, and Medicine Hat; and a small German-speaking entrepreneurial class emerged in these cities and in several small towns near Edmonton.[45]

Due to their high degree of religious sectarianism, their diverse origins, their geographic dispersion, and their preoccupation with pioneering, the German settlers did not constitute a real German "community." However, some attempts were made to unite the German-speaking settlers. Partly funded by the Liberal and Conservative political parties, German language papers were started in Edmonton and Calgary. However, an attempt to form a province-wide German-Canadian association failed, and the newspapers ceased publishing during World War I.[46]

Despite their isolation and religious sectarianism, the German-speaking settlers were well accepted before World War I in pioneer Alberta. Anglo-Canadians considered the Germans, like other northern Europeans, "preferred" immigrants because they were culturally similar to themselves. Some German settlers became involved at an early stage in local politics. By 1914, people of German origin had firmly established themselves across the province: one of every ten people in Alberta was of German background, and twenty-six towns, hamlets, or post offices and twenty school districts bore German names.[47]

During World War I, however, Germans who had formerly been considered among Alberta's most desirable citizens, came under intense scrutiny and suspicion. Many urban German-speaking workers were dismissed from their jobs, unnaturalized German laborers and miners were placed in internment camps, and German language schools and churches were closed. The anti-German rage led residents of Carlstadt to change their town's name to Alderson, Wittenberg became Leedale, and Little Dusseldorf simply became Freedom. In 1921, many German-Russians listed themselves in the census as being of Russian or other origins. Between 1911 and 1921 the number of people in the province reporting themselves as being of German origin dropped dramatically.[48]

Among the German-speaking settlers who came to the province before World War I were four different sects of Mennonites, an Anabaptist, pacifist, religious group that believed in plain living and remaining separate from the world by dedicating themselves to farming. Religious individualism, legalistic sectarianism, and repeated immigration had brought about a bewildering amount of fragmentation among Mennonite groups, and they brought this fragmentation to Alberta. Those Mennonites who came to Alberta prior to World War I included German-Swiss Mennonites who came from settlements in the United States and Ontario, and German-Russian Mennonites who came from Russia, by way of Manitoba. The largest settlement of Mennonites was at Didsbury, but by 1920 there were fifteen different Mennonite settlements scattered across the province. The Mennonites in Alberta were not as visible as those in Saskatchewan or Manitoba because they were fewer in number (only 1,500 by 1911). They did not settle in concentrated bloc settlements, and since most were willing to make compromises with the larger society, they did not become involved in long and protracted conflicts with the state as they did in Manitoba over such issues as the education of their children.[49]

The Mennonites in Alberta were divided on many issues. Some, like the Holdemanites at Linden, preferred not to change their traditional way of life and maintained social separateness and distinctive, conservative dress styles. Others, like the Mennonite Brethren in Christ in the Didsbury area, were willing to make many adjustments. Despite these differences, the Mennonites shared a common Anabaptist tradition of pacifism, German cultural origins, an agricultural heritage of hard work, simple modest living, and a rigorous nonconformity. Later waves of Mennonite immigration during the 1920s, and early post-World War II period, made up of religious refugees directly from Russia and other parts of the world, brought further growth and further fragmentation by bringing new Mennonite sects to the province.[50]

The Hutterites, another Anabaptist pacifist sect, came to Alberta during World War I. With their communal lifestyle, distinctive clothing, and continuing use of the German language over several generations, they went one step further than most Mennonites in their attempt to remain separate from the "world." Because of their rigid isolationism, they became, and have remained, the province's most controversial German-speaking group.

The Hutterites had come from Russia to South Dakota in 1874. They moved to Canada in 1918 because of wartime persecution in the United States. The Canadian government promised them exemption from military service and permission to live communally. By 1918, they had established ten colonies in southern Alberta, making it the area with the highest concentration of Hutterite colonies anywhere in the world. Their initial arrival sparked a flurry of protest from groups who worried about

Hutterite children at Ewelme Colony, near Fort Macleod. This colony was one of the early colonies in the province, founded in 1925. The building in the background functions as both a school and a church. (Courtesy Glenbow Archives)

their use of German, their pacifism, and their communal living. Later expansion of the Hutterite colonies aroused fears of a possible negative impact on the social and economic life of rural Alberta and some opposition to Hutterite colonies has continued to the present day.[51]

Central and Eastern Europeans

Clifford Sifton's decision to look to central and eastern Europe for farmers to settle western Canada transplanted the great ethnic, religious, and political diversity of that region to western Canada. In central and eastern Europe in the late nineteenth century, most farmers had only tiny tracts of land, too small to support their families. They were also faced with mounting debts. In addition, their sons had to do military service for alien governments, and hostile government officials often restricted the use of their mother language. Thus, the peasants of central and eastern Europe had many reasons to look for a new home. When steamship companies began circulating information about 160 acres of free land in Canada, many farmers who owned only ten acres of land, or who owned no land at all, could not resist the temptation.[52]

The central and eastern Europeans who came to Alberta made a major contribution in agriculture, developing large tracts of farmland. They also did much of the railroad building, the work in the coal mines, and the hard manual labor in the cities. Their arrival changed forever the shape of Alberta's society: adding new religions, political perspectives, and approaches. By 1911, they had arrived in such large numbers that (excluding the large numbers of German-speaking people from central and eastern Europe) one in nine people in Alberta could trace his or her roots to central and eastern Europe.

In the prewar era, the British, central Canadians, and Americans dominated Alberta's economic, social, and political life. Central and eastern Europeans, separated by language, culture, and often location from this majority, developed their own cultural, religious, and even, to some extent, political life. They usually settled together in bloc settlements, which enabled them to help each other, establish their own churches, and keep alive their culture.

The central and eastern Europeans created their own cultural patterns, which were a blend of Old World traditions and social patterns that emerged as they struggled to survive in the park belt. They maintained their own architecture in homes and churches. They also celebrated holidays and festivals associated with rural European life, and they maintained their own styles of food and clothing. Their rural bloc settlements, their cultural differences, their initial inability to speak English, and prejudice against them kept them on the margins of western Canadian society. As a result, they kept their languages and cultures alive much longer than other European immigrant groups such as the Germans and the Scandinavians who were not as highly concentrated and were more readily accepted.

By far the largest group of central and eastern Europeans to come to the Prairies were the Ukrainians who came from the provinces of Galicia

Ukrainian immigrants outside the Edmonton (Strathcona) immigration shed at the turn of the century. The arrival of large numbers of central and eastern Europeans provoked a mixed reaction among Anglo-Canadians who valued their economic role in settling the West but feared their social and political impact. (Courtesy Provincial Archives of Alberta)

and Bukovina in the Austro-Hungarian Empire. Between 1896 and 1914, approximately 170,000 Ukrainians came to Canada, the vast majority settling in the prairie provinces. Closely related to them by language and culture were the Poles, also from Galicia, who settled primarily in scattered pockets in the predominantly Ukrainian bloc. The Romanians who came from Bukovina were also closely linked with the Ukrainians by culture and religion, though their language was entirely unrelated. These immigrants from Galicia and Bukovina made up over 80 percent of the immigrants to Canada from the Austro-Hungarian Empire at the turn of the century.[53]

In addition, immigrants came to Alberta from Hungary, Bohemia, and Slovakia, other areas in the Austro-Hungarian Empire. The settlement patterns of Hungarians, Czechs, and Slovaks differed from those of the Ukrainians, Poles, and Romanians. Many of the Hungarians, Czechs, and Slovaks came to Alberta indirectly, by way of coal mining communities in the United States. Most of them settled in the coal mining centers of southern Alberta at Lethbridge, and in the Crow's Nest Pass. Here they developed their own neighborhoods, and their own mutual aid organizations to help in the case of accidents, disease, or death, all of which were common in the mines.[54] They also established a few small, scattered farming settlements in southern and central Alberta.[55]

Czarist Russia also provided sizeable numbers of immigrants to the Prairies. German-Russians constituted the largest group, but smaller numbers of other minorities — Byelorussians, Estonians, Latvians, Lithuanians, and two religious minorities, the Jews and the Doukhobors — also came to Canada. They all sought better economic conditions in Canada, and they fled Russian military conscription and persecution of non-Russian minority groups.

The central and eastern Europeans were the most visible in the bloc settlements on the northern fringe of settlement, in the coal mining camps in Alberta, and in the working class in the cities (particularly Edmonton and Lethbridge). The largest rural bloc settlement was the Ukrainian bloc, northeast of Edmonton.

Both the central and eastern European settlers themselves and government's immigration agents felt that the wooded park belt area of the prairie provinces was an ideal location for settlement. The Ukrainians, Romanians, and Poles preferred this area since it was physically similar to their homeland. The wooded and lake-dotted regions provided wood for homes and fuel, water for livestock, and the meadowland provided hay for their cattle. The area was also well supplied with fish and game which were essential sources of food if they were to survive the first few years when crops were meagre. Both the settlers and immigration agents felt it would be a good idea to establish bloc settlements which enabled the immigrants to take care of each other in case of illness, death, or accidents, and to help newcomers who could speak their language.[56]

Central and eastern Europeans also had an important impact on the coal mining camps and the largest cities in the province, where they were part of a multi-ethnic labor force. In the mines and cities, the central and eastern Europeans held the less skilled jobs. They made less money than most English-speaking workers, and generally lived in their own neighborhoods. Alienated from their fellow Albertans, and discriminated against, some of them began to support radical political and labor groups. The Russians, Lithuanians, and Ukrainians in the mining camps included some left wing political refugees from the Czarist Empire, and they helped to establish political and cultural organizations among the workers.[57]

Radical political action was urged by some ethnic organizations. Support was also given for broader-based left wing groups, such as the Industrial Workers of the World, the One Big Union, and the Socialist Party of Canada. During the 1920s and 1930s the Communist Party of Canada found their greatest support in the mining camps of the province, particularly among central and eastern European immigrants.[58]

The central and eastern Europeans faced more prejudice and discrimination than either the Scandinavians or the Germans. Many Anglo-
Canadians were ignorant of their background and thought they were
socially and culturally inferior. These prejudices became stronger with
the outbreak of World War I, since many of the central and eastern
Europeans came from the Austro-Hungarian Empire with which Canada
was at war. The government took strong measures against them, including removing their right to vote, placing some of them in internment
camps, and closing many of their newspapers and political organizations.[59]

Jews and Doukhobors

Two groups from eastern Europe whose cultural patterns differed significantly from other central and eastern Europeans in Alberta were the Jews
and Doukhobors, both of which fled religious persecution in Russia.
Prevented from being farmers, most of the Jews in Eastern Europe had
been craftsmen, teachers, or peddlers; consequently, very few had any
farming experience. While a few attempts were made, with the help of
Jewish philanthropic organizations, to establish Jewish farming settlements in the province, they were unsuccessful. But the Jews did make a
highly successful economic adjustment to urban life, predominantly in
small business. In Calgary and Edmonton, where roughly two-thirds of
the 3,200 Jews in the province lived in 1921, they developed a wide
variety of religious, cultural, and educational institutions.[60]

The Doukhobors, a rural people like the Ukrainians and Poles, came
from Russia primarily to escape religious persecution. The Doukhobors,
like the Hutterites, were pacifists and believed in the communal ownership of property.When the Russian government persecuted these non-
conformists, they decided to find a home elsewhere. Through the help of
admirers in Russia (such as the famous novelist Leo Tolstoy), England,
and Canada, over 7,000 Doukhobors came to Canada in 1899. The
Canadian government promised them blocs of land where they could
live together, exemption from military service, and religious freedom in
the public schools.[61]

When the Doukhobors first came to Canada, they went to Saskatchewan to farm. There, through their arrangements with the Canadian government, they established several agricultural villages where they had
joint ownership of property. But they came into conflict with the Canadian government on a number of issues, and in 1907 the government
took back their land. As a result, many of them left the Prairies that same
year, moving to British Columbia. [62]

The Doukhobors began their first colonies in Alberta in 1916 as offshoots of the British Columbia settlement. They were located at the
nearest points in Alberta's foothills where wheat could be grown profitably—Cowley and Lundbreck. Here, they established six communal villages and maintained close economic and cultural ties with the Doukhobors in British Columbia. Though there were two other settlements in
the Arrowwood and Mossleigh areas begun during the 1920s (by Douk-

hobors who moved there from Saskatchewan and British Columbia), the number of Doukhobors in the province remained small. With only a few hundred adherents, and only a handful of the extremist Sons of Freedom followers, the Doukhobors in Alberta avoided the raging controversies which they aroused in British Columbia and Saskatchewan.[63]

Mediterranean Groups

Three small groups from the Mediterranean region—Greeks, Arabs, and Italians—began to make their presence felt in Alberta after the turn of the century. Canadian immigration policy, their cultural background, and their settlement patterns combined to give each of them a history quite distinct from central and eastern Europeans.

Because they avoided agriculture in a predominantly agricultural province, they were perceived as being distinctive and exotic. Their avoidance of agriculture also directly affected their numbers. They did not farm because they had limited financial resources, and because they had come to North America to escape the poverty of agricultural life in their homelands. They preferred city life where they could associate with compatriots. Since Canada's immigration policy was designed to attract farmers, the Canadian government discouraged these urban-bound and racially "unpreferred" immigrants from coming to Canada. Consequently, the numbers of Greeks, Arabs, and Italians in Alberta remained small. By 1921, there were only 350 Greeks, 200 Arabs, and 4,000 Italians in the province.[64]

Each of the three groups developed its own niche in the Albertan economy. The Greeks concentrated in small businesses. Beginning with small confectionaries, candy and ice cream stores, they gradually accumulated enough capital to open restaurants. These businesses required little schooling, small investment, and a limited knowledge of English. Most of the Greeks who came to Alberta after the turn of the century lived in Calgary and Edmonton, but there were some who settled in Alberta's small towns during the 1910s, often establishing restaurants. Small in number, the Greeks often developed close relationships with English-speaking Canadians and joined community and service organizations at an early stage. The Greeks were too few to develop a highly organized cultural and religious life. It was not until 1949 that the first Greek Orthodox Church in the province was built in Edmonton.[65]

Like the Greeks, the Arabs who came to the province prior to World War I were young, mostly male, and had limited education and capital. Most came from Lebanon. They avoided farming because they lacked capital and a knowledge of Canadian farming techniques; nor did they relish the isolation of rural life. Like Arab immigrants across North America at this time, most of those who came to Alberta began as peddlers, selling dry goods from door-to-door. For most, peddling was simply a job which, though arduous, yielded good profits and required little capital, training, or proficiency in English. Just as the Greek community initiated new immigrants into the candy store or restaurant business, established Arab immigrants taught newcomers how to peddle clothing and various household wares, and to trade for furs. They usually used the profits from peddling and trading to establish dry goods and clothing stores in urban areas.[66]

Because the Canadian government was not anxious to attract either non-Europeans or nonfarmers to western Canada, the numbers of Arabs in the province remained small. The largest number lived in Edmonton, which was close to the northern fur trading empire. A few families lived in Lac La Biche, in northern Alberta, where they peddled dry goods and traded furs. These two communities have remained the major centers of Arab life in the province. It was not until 1938 that the community in Edmonton was sufficiently large and active to build a Muslim mosque, the first in Canada.[67]

Italians made up the third and by far the largest of the Mediterranean groups in the province. They began coming at the turn of the century and concentrated in railroading, coal mining, and in heavy construction jobs in the cities. The largest concentrations developed in the coal mining communities of the Crow's Nest Pass, and the Lethbridge area, and in Calgary (which was a wintering place for single men involved in the seasonal work of the railways or the mines). There were sizeable concentrations of Italians in almost all of the province's coal mining districts, where they developed strong Italian mutual benefit organizations.[68]

In the Crow's Nest Pass and Calgary (in the Riverside area), there were enough Italians to develop small neighborhoods or "little Italies" where they lived and had their own food stores. While most of those who lived in the Pass were miners, some later began small construction or logging businesses. Though the Italians often came as sojourners, intending to return to Italy, they gradually put down roots, arranged for wives or girl friends to join them, and began raising families.[69]

Though most of the Italians avoided farming, there were some exceptions. North of Edmonton, groups of Italians established two farming communities which they named Naples (begun in 1905), and Venice (started in 1914). Though the terrain in these areas was heavily wooded, through cooperative effort they carved out farms for themselves and pioneered successfully. Despite their isolation, they maintained ties with Italian communities in other parts of the province, since the men moved temporarily to the cities or mining areas in search of work to supplement their farm incomes.[70]

Each of the three Mediterranean ethnic groups began as sojourners who planned on returning to their homelands. In 1912-1913, many young Greeks returned to fight in the Balkan wars, and during World War I many Italians returned to Italy to fight on the Allied side. But the temporary character of the communities began to change by the end of World War I as the newcomers established their families and developed their businesses. The early settlements of each group provided the nucleus which attracted later immigrants—in small numbers during the 1920s (limited mostly to wives and family members) and in much larger numbers during the 1950s and 1960s.

Chinese and Japanese

Small numbers of immigrants also came to the province from China and Japan. Their numbers remained small because of tight immigration regulations aimed at keeping them out. The Chinese moved across the Rockies from British Columbia into prairie cities and small towns where they opened restaurants and laundries. There were far fewer women than men in the province, and the Chinese men did domestic work, such as laundry and cooking, that other men were not willing to do. Some started market gardens and sold vegetables in the cities. These occupations required little education, capital, or English language skills, but they did require a willingness to work incredibly long and hard hours.[71]

Very few of the Chinese had families in Canada, and this greatly affected their lives. By 1921, there were nearly 3,500 Chinese in the province, but less than 200 were women. Some had left their families at home in southern China (where the majority originated) because they planned on returning there once they had saved enough money. In addition, the Canadian government passed special laws, which did not apply to any other immigrants, that required each Chinese immigrant who came to Canada to pay a special head tax. This made it very expensive for them to bring their families. The head tax was introduced by the federal government because of anti-Chinese sentiment in western Canada. Race theory held they were inferior. It was widely felt that the Chinese could not be assimilated, and that they provided unfair competition to white workers by accepting a lower standard of living. In small prairie towns, the Chinese lived incredibly lonely lives. Occasionally they were liked and accepted, but more often their speech and dress provoked ridicule.[72]

In Edmonton, Calgary, and Lethbridge, the Chinese congregated to form Chinatowns. Here they lived together and set up clan, regional, and political organizations to provide jobs, lodging, and credit; to settle disputes, encourage Chinese economic interests, and to influence political developments in China. They lived together not only because they spoke the same language and wanted to help each other, but because of white discrimination. Prior to World War I, there were attempts in several Albertan cities to keep them residentially segregated and to prevent them from voting.[73]

There were not as many Japanese as there were Chinese in the province. The Japanese began coming to Canada later than the Chinese, and most of them remained in British Columbia where they worked as fishermen, lumber workers, and coal miners. A few came to southern Alberta, to the Lethbridge region where they worked as either coal miners or farmers. Although strong pressures developed in British Columbia to restrict Japanese immigration, there were not as many restrictions on Japanese immigrants as there were on the Chinese, making it easier for them to bring their wives and families. By 1921 one out of four of the nearly 500 Japanese in the province was a woman.[74]

Overall, there were few Chinese or Japanese in Alberta; they have

Japanese sugar beet workers, Raymond, 1911. The Japanese had been brought by the Knight Sugar Company to work on sugar beet farms in the predominantly Mormon town of Raymond in 1908. (Courtesy Provincial Museum of Alberta)

never made up more than 0.5 percent of the Alberta population. Those who came to Canada preferred to stay in British Columbia, which was closer to their home geographically and climatically. Immigration regulations made it much harder for them to come to Canada than it was for European immigrants. During the 1920s the introduction of even tighter immigration regulations brought the number of newcomers to a virtual halt. Culturally distinctive, socially segregated, and victims of white prejudice, the Chinese and Japanese remained on the fringes of Albertan society until after World War II.[75]

Conclusion

By 1920, the major contours of the ethnic mix of the population had been established. The British, Americans, Germans, Scandinavians, Ukrainians, and French made up the largest groups in Alberta. In contrast, through diseases such as tuberculosis and smallpox, the Indian population had fallen from an estimated 18,000 during the 1870s to 6,000 by the 1920s. The major settlement patterns in the province had also been established. There were some minor changes during the 1920s with the influx of new European groups, but the overall ethnic mix of the population and settlement patterns would not significantly change until after World War II. Indeed in their ethnic and religious composition, both rural and urban Alberta still show much of the impact of the boom period of immigration and settlement at the turn of the century.

CHAPTER TWO
Patterns of Immigration and Ethnic Settlement in Alberta: 1920-1985
Howard Palmer

Introduction

Immigration to Alberta resumed after World War I. This postwar movement was one of three subsequent waves of immigrants that added numbers and diversity to Alberta's population. During the 1920s, a predominantly rural-bound group of immigrants opened up the last remaining agricultural frontiers of the province, and strengthened many of the existing ethnic communities. The depression and World War II effectively halted immigration; but following war, a new wave of immigrants, still overwhelmingly European, came to the province. This wave of immigrants, being more highly educated than those who had preceded them, went primarily to the province's cities, which were booming during the 1950s. Immigration slowed during the 1960s, but a new wave of immigrants from all over the world, arrived in the late 1960s, following the federal government's decision to remove racial biases from the country's immigration policy.

The 1920s to the present has been a period of tremendous social, economic, and political change. Alberta has undergone a dramatic transformation from a predominantly rural, agrarian community to one that is now overwhelmingly urban and industrial. Oil and gas have replaced agriculture as the province's leading industry. During this same time, two political movements—the UFA and Social Credit—have suddenly risen to power, dominated politics, and then been dramatically replaced and have now faded into oblivion. These social, economic, and political changes have been accompanied by changes in the ethnic composition of the population and in the significance of ethnicity in Alberta's life.[1]

Immigration in the Interwar Years: The 1920s

Following the World War I era a new wave of immigrants came to

Alberta. They did not come in numbers as large as they had in the main settlement boom prior to World War I. The class origins of the central and eastern Europeans, who made up over one-third of the newcomers, also differed somewhat from the previous arrivals. The newcomers included not only farmers, but workers, artisans, tradesmen, and merchants. Overall, however, the new wave of immigrants confirmed existing patterns of ethnic settlement and distribution. The newcomers usually joined friends, relatives, or fellow countrymen, thus expanding existing concentrations of immigrants in many rural areas. Though the homestead land in southern and central Alberta had already been taken up, there was still CPR land available. Alternatively, homestead land was still available in the Peace River district, and many post-World War I immigrants moved into that region, which developed rapidly during the 1920s.

It was financially difficult for newcomers to begin farming on their own in the 1920s. Consequently many immigrants who had begun their lives in Canada as farm laborers left for the cities. Several groups of newcomers—Danes, Lithuanians, Croats, Hungarians, and others—began to establish the bases of community organizations in their new urban homes. Many central and eastern Europeans also worked temporarily in coal mining centers: even though the work was difficult, dangerous, and seasonal, it nevertheless provided relatively good wages to cash-short immigrants.

During the early 1920s in Alberta, the press and business interests (particularly the railways), were strong promoters of immigration. They believed that new immigrant farmers were needed to provide freight and traffic for the railways, to develop untilled farmland, and to increase the population base.[2]

During the early period of postwar economic readjustment, the federal government slowly began to permit immigration. At first it moved cautiously, opening the immigration doors only to British immigrants, farmers with the means to establish themselves, and domestic workers. Consequently, immigration to Canada during the early 1920s was relatively meagre, but there was a large pool of potential immigrants. In 1924, the United States introduced a quota system, which allocated a certain number of places each year for immigrants from particular countries. The intent of this system was to limit severely the numbers of central, eastern, and southern Europeans entering the United States. As a result, many potential immigrants, who might otherwise have gone to the United States, now wanted to come to Canada. These changes in American policy and the Canadian government's responsiveness to the pressure from business interests for a more liberal immigration policy led to a sizeable influx of immigrants from the middle to late 1920s.[3]

During the 1920s, almost 100,000 new immigrants came to the province. The Canadian government was particularly anxious to secure British immigrants since they were still seen as people who would adjust easily and help confirm the British character of Anglo-Canadian society. The Canadian and British governments cooperated to bring British immigrants to Canada through the Empire Settlement Act of 1922 which committed the British government to subsidizing half the cost of emigration schemes. The British government was willing to do this because it viewed emigration as a means of solving some of its serious economic and social problems in the postwar era. Partly as a result of these schemes, British immigrants formed the largest single group to come to the province during the 1920s, making up over one-quarter of the total number of immigrants.[4]

Many of the British immigrants came through specialized government plans such as the soldier settlement schemes, set up to help war veterans establish themselves on the land, or the Three Thousand Farm Families Scheme. The CPR also worked closely with the Catholic Scottish Immigrant Aid Society to bring over 100 Scottish families to farms which had been laid out in central Alberta. Working with women's organizations, the CPR also helped arrange to bring much-sought-after British domestics.[5] In 1923 and again in 1928, the railways and the government also recruited farm workers and miners in Britain to help in western Canada during harvest season.[6] Though for cultural reasons they remained the preferred immigrants, the British immigrants continued to have problems adjusting to rural life, and many of them soon found their way to the cities.

American immigration had been very important prior to World War I, but the movement declined dramatically during the 1920s. The returning

Scottish settlers leaving for Alberta, 1924. One hundred and twenty Scottish families came to Clandonald in the mid-1920s in an immigration scheme promoted by the CPR and the Catholic Church. (Courtesy Glenbow Archives)

migration of American farmers, who had been dried out by successive years of drought in southeastern Alberta, far exceeded the influx of newcomers. Rather than moving to Canada, farmers' sons who were looking for new opportunity in the United States either moved to newly opened irrigated land on military and former Indian reservations in the American West, or moved to the city. Some American settlers in Alberta reacted to the economic distress of the early 1920s by supporting the populist UFA; others simply returned to the United States. Thus, during the 1920s, largely because of returning migration and the relatively small number of new immigrants, the American-born proportion of Alberta's population declined steadily from 17 to 11 percent.[7]

Immigrants from northern Europe remained in a small minority during the 1920s, despite the immigration promotion efforts of the railways and the Canadian government. Since economic conditions in northern Europe were better than in central or eastern Europe, there was not as much incentive to leave. Nor did northern Europe experience the tremendous postwar political upheavals that came with the collapse of the Austro-Hungarian Empire, the emergence of new states, the dramatic shifting of borders, and rising nationalism. Those who came to Alberta from western and northern Europe included Swiss, Dutch, Danish, Swedish, and Norwegian farmers who settled mostly on CPR land in central Alberta. The Danes made up the largest of the Scandinavian groups to come during the 1920s, bringing new growth to the older Danish settlements, and developing a new settlement on CPR land in the Tilley area. Newcomers from Norway began working as farm laborers in the Norwegian settlements in central Alberta or in the predominantly Norwegian Lutheran settlement of Valhalla in the Peace River district.[8]

While continuing to emphasize its efforts to secure British and northern European immigrants, in September 1925 the federal government, in response to the pressure from the railways, entered into the "Railways Agreement" with the CPR and the Canadian National Railway (CNR), which opened Canada's doors to more central and eastern Europeans. The government authorized the railways to encourage potential immigrants from what it called the "non-preferred" countries of central and eastern Europe to emigrate to Canada and to settle as "agriculturalists, agricultural workers, and domestic servants." The agreement extended over a period of two years and was renewed for another three years in October 1927.[9]

Under this agreement, the railways brought 165,000 central and eastern Europeans and 20,000 Mennonites to Canada. The immigrants represented a variety of ethnic groups and had a diversity of reasons for emigrating. The Ukrainian and Hungarian immigrants came for economic and political reasons; Poles and Slovaks were escaping poor economic conditions; German Russians and Mennonites fled civil war, economic disaster, and the spectre of cultural annihilation in Russia.[10]

The railways established elaborate machinery for both recruiting and settling these immigrants. In southern Alberta, the immigrants were placed by the CPR through local colonization boards, which it helped establish and support with its Canadian Colonization Association. The CNR worked with colonization boards in its domain in northern Alberta. These boards put company officials in touch with prospective immigrants and sponsors and provided employment for the immigrants upon arrival. Many of these boards were established by ethnic and religious groups to sponsor their countrymen and coreligionists.[11]

After the introduction of the Railways Agreement, the total number of immigrants who gave Alberta as their intended destination increased from approximately 11,000 in 1925 to over 17,000 in 1926. The level of immigration remained high until 1930: from 1926 to 1930, over 72,000 immigrants listed Alberta as their province of intended destination. During the 1920s a total of 35,000 immigrants came to Alberta from central, eastern, and southern Europe, comprising 35 percent of the total number of immigrants during this period. Most arrived after 1925. They helped increase the total number of central, eastern, and southern Europeans to 18 percent of the total population and the total number of people of German-speaking origin to 10 percent by 1931.[12]

Most of the roughly 10,000 Ukrainians, 7,000 Poles, and 600 Romanians who came to the province during the 1920s joined their countrymen in the older ethnic settlements or opened up new land north of Edmonton and in the Peace River district. By 1931 they brought the total number of people of Polish origin in the province to over 20,000 or 3 percent of the population, those of Ukrainian origin to 56,000 or 8 percent of the population, and those of Romanian origin to nearly 5,000 or 0.6 percent of the population.[13]

The majority of the 12,000 immigrants of German origin who came to Alberta during the 1920s also came under the Railways Agreement, since they came from Poland and Russia rather than from Germany. Germany itself contributed only 27 percent of the German origin immigrants during the 1920s. Most of the Catholics and Lutherans went to newly opened farm areas of north central Alberta.[14]

The CPR provided special loans for the 2,000 German-speaking Mennonites who came to the province, thus enabling some of them to purchase irrigated land owned by the CPR in southern Alberta. In addition, Mennonites established new settlements in central Alberta and in the Peace River district. The newcomers doubled the number of Mennonite settlements in the province, from eighteen to thirty-seven.[15]

The largest single group of Mennonites took up the CPR's irrigated land in the Coaldale area near Lethbridge. Although they began establishing themselves on the eve of the depression, the hard-working immigrants were able to pay off the CPR for their transportation loans and land purchases. The newcomers were often well educated and had come from highly organized and institutionally separate Mennonite districts in Russia. When they arrived in Coaldale, they established their own network of institutions which extended beyond the church, and included a cooperative insurance scheme, the German Saturday School, the Society for the Preservation of the German Language, a library, Bible school, cheese factory, and hospital.[16]

Separated from other Albertans by their use of German, and their settlement in blocs, the Mennonites were not very popular. This had serious consequences in 1929 when the federal government urged the Alberta government to accept more Mennonite refugees from Russia. The provincial government, bowing to hostile public opinion, refused to allow more into the province, despite the entreaties of both the federal government and Mennonites in Alberta.[17]

The CPR also brought Czech, Slovak, Croatian, and Hungarian immigrants to southern Alberta as farm laborers, and it sold farm land to Hungarians, Slovaks, and Lithuanians in central and northern Alberta. The southern Alberta sugar beet industry, which had faltered just before World War I, had been reestablished in 1925 and many of the 3,000 Czechs and Slovaks and 3,500 Hungarians who came to Alberta were brought as sugar beet laborers by the CPR in cooperation with the Alberta Sugar Beet Grower's Association. In northern and central Alberta, CPR's officials relied chiefly on continental Europeans with large families to clear the CPR's land, since they assumed that British and American immigrants would be repelled by the brush covering of much of the land. The new arrivals brought the total number of Czechs and Slovaks in Alberta to nearly 6,500, the number of Hungarians to 5,500, and the number of Yugoslavs to nearly 1,400 by 1931.[18]

Several smaller central and eastern European groups—including Russians, Estonians and Lithuanians—also increased their numbers in Alberta through immigration promoted by the railways. After 1905, small numbers of left wing political refugees of Russian, Latvian, Lithuanian, and Estonian origin had come to Alberta fleeing Czarist persecution. At the end of the war, some of the Russians idealistically returned to the Soviet Union to participate in what they hoped would be a socialist experiment. But at the same time, many people in the same emerging Soviet state, and in the three newly independent Baltic states wanted to come to North America to escape existing political and economic conditions. The Russian newcomers who arrived during the 1920s were usually inclined to strong right wing anticommunist views.[19]

Among those who came to Alberta during the 1920s was a group of about 600 "white" Russians who opposed the Bolshevik regime. After the defeat of the white armies in the Russian Civil War, thousands of refugees gathered in the city of Harbin in Manchuria, hoping to escape. The Russian government applied strong pressure to have them extradited back to Russia. Consequently they desperately sought a new home. CPR's agents directed their attention to Canada. Colonel Orest Dournovo, who had been an army officer in Czarist Russia, organized groups of Russian refugees to come to Canada, mostly to Alberta. The group included people of many different professional backgrounds, including railway employees and army officers. The group also included members of a peasant-dominated conservative Russian Orthodox sect known as the "Old Believers," who had been persecuted by the Bolsheviks. From 1924-26, officials of the CPR settled the group on the railway's land west of Ponoka and Wetaskiwin.[20]

Their initial years in the area were very difficult because of the raw-
ness of the land, their lack of capital, and their inexperience. By the late
1920s, the Old Believers relocated to better homestead land near Hines
Creek in the Peace River district, where they built a small Russian
Orthodox church, and gradually established themselves as successful
farmers. The professionals and army officers had a difficult time farming,
and most left for the cities.[21]

The Estonian and Lithuanian immigrants came from republics which
had been newly established in the postwar period, and which were
facing serious economic difficulties. Upon coming to Alberta, the Estonians and Lithuanians went first to rural areas. The Lithuanians settled
northeast of Edmonton in the Elk Point-St. Paul districts, and on the
CPR's land near Brooks where they combined farming with work on the
railway. Many who originally went to northern Alberta eventually
migrated to Edmonton where there was more work. Given their background, these newcomers were inclined to be politically conservative.
Some of the contact between the older wave of immigrants and the
newcomers, whether Russian, Estonian, Latvian, or Lithuanian was
fraught with tension because of political differences.[22]

Depression, War, and Ethnic Relations

Whether from Britain, Denmark, Hungary, or Russia, the immigrants
who came to Alberta during the 1920s had no way of knowing that they
had arrived on the eve of the Great Depression. During the 1930s, many
of the newcomers had to cope simultaneously with the overwhelming
problems of economic crisis, culture shock, and family separation. Those
who had come under the Railways Agreement had usually been
separated from their families, since the men had to establish themselves
before they could bring over their families. Some of the newcomers, such
as the Poles and Ukrainians, already had ethnic associations and personal networks to rely on to help them meet their difficulties. Others,
such as the Hungarians, Russians, or Lithuanians, had to meet these
difficulties basically on their own. Their difficulties were compounded by
an often hostile public opinion and by civic government officials who,
seeing them as one of the major causes of unemployment, tried to limit
their impact on the social welfare system by discriminating against them
in relief payments, or by deporting them.[23]

Immigration ended in 1930 when the federal government virtually
closed the immigration doors. In taking this action, they were responding to the changing economic climate and to continuous pressure from
English-speaking groups who felt that the Anglo-Saxon element of the
population was being swamped by the newcomers. New government
regulations limited immigrants to farmers with substantial amounts of
capital and to British subjects and American citizens with means to
support themselves until they found employment. Immigration to Canada fell dramatically.[24]

One group anxious to come to Canada were the persecuted Jews of
Germany. Anti-Semitism prevented their entry. The federal government,

in fact, allowed in less than 5,000 Jewish refugees, most of whom went to Quebec or Ontario. Alberta played little role in the controversy over Jewish immigration, though an anti-Semitic wing of Social Credit argued against their entry, while a small urban-based association promoted the refugee cause.[25]

Given the economic collapse and the upsurge of discrimination, conditions were favorable to the development of radical political movements among immigrants. The majority of support for the Communist party in Alberta during the 1930s came from central and eastern Europeans, particularly Ukrainians and Hungarians in the mining camps and cities. Groups with a strong religious focus, such as the Mennonites, Dutch, or Danes were much more inclined to be attracted by the appeal of Aberhart and Social Credit. The Social Credit movement, which swept to power in 1935, provided an explanation and an attractive solution to the depression. Men like Aberhart and his young assistant, Ernest Manning, also placed the movement in a "Christian context."[26]

The depression was especially difficult for the newly arrived immigrants who were just beginning to establish themselves and had few resources to fall back on. Many migrated to other parts of the country, principally British Columbia and Ontario, in search of work. A few were deported to their home countries, either because of radical political activity, or even for the fact of having gone on relief. Others asked to be deported as a way of returning home.[27]

The coming of World War II aroused new issues for groups such as the Germans and Japanese who had been out of the public eye throughout most of the 1930s. Wartime nationalism spawned a number of English-speaking patriotic groups and many turned their attention to the question of the loyalty of "enemy aliens." Though anti-German sentiment was much more benign during the Second World War than it had been during the First, anti-Japanese and anti-Hutterite sentiment reached new heights. Anti-Japanese sentiment peaked after the raid on Pearl Harbor in December 1941. The federal government ordered the evacuation of the Japanese from British Columbia. Following the evacuation order, 2,600 Japanese, forced out of their homes on the west coast and moved by the federal government, arrived in the sugar beet fields of southern Alberta in the spring and summer of 1942. The war period also witnessed an upsurge of anti-Semitism within one extremist wing of the Social Credit movement, which linked Jews with a big business-socialist-communist plot to achieve world domination.[28]

Despite the growth of prejudice toward many groups during the war, some groups such as the Chinese, Ukrainians, and Poles, who had previously encountered serious problems with acceptance, achieved a new respectability through their support for the war effort. The channels for mobility which the armed forces provided, and the involvement of all levels of society in wartime industries undermined many social barriers. Many of the children of European immigrants found that the Canadian military uniform won them a new respect and acceptance.[29]

The dearth of immigrants during the 1930s meant that by the 1940s the population as a whole was becoming increasingly Canadian born. Hence social tension stemming from highly visible ethnic diversity declined. By the 1940s, almost 70 percent of the population was Canadian born and over half was Alberta born. A new generation had grown up in Alberta. Assimilation was occurring rapidly: intermarriage was becoming more common and retention of ancestral languages less common. Even some groups that were associated with the "enemy," such as the Germans and Italians, did not encounter great problems with acceptance during the war because a large proportion of each group had lived in Alberta for many decades and they were generally accepted in the communities in which they lived.[30]

For the Japanese, acceptance was slower in coming. Their arrival in 1942 initially led to great protests. They were only accepted at first because their labor was needed in the sugar beet fields, and because the provincial Social Credit government secured a promise from the federal government that the Japanese would be again removed at the end of the war. Alberta's cities heightened the injustice by passing bylaws preventing them from living within city limits during the war. However, by the end of the war, significant shifts in public opinion occurred in the province. A growing number of people felt that the federal government's attempts to deport the Japanese to Japan and the provincial government's refusal to give permission to allow the Japanese to remain in the province were unjust. Three years after the end of the war, the provincial government agreed to treat Japanese-Canadians as equals with the other residents of the province. Some discriminatory hiring practices aimed at Japanese-Canadians continued into the 1950s. However, since that time, the Japanese have broken through virtually all social and economic barriers and are now accepted as equals in the southern Alberta towns and cities where they live.[31]

Postwar Immigration, 1946-67

The postwar period brought a new wave of immigrants to the province. Made up predominantly of people fleeing a war-devastated Europe, this wave of immigrants was smaller than the major wave in the pre-World War I era; nonetheless, it had an important impact on the province. The immigrants who came were predominantly European, reflecting the continuing assimilationist and racist basis of postwar immigration policy. The postwar influx in the late 1940s and 1950s included political refugees from central and eastern Europe and thousands of German, Dutch, and British immigrants who sought better economic opportunities. Whereas the previous two waves of immigration to Alberta had been destined for rural areas, these newcomers looked for their economic opportunities in the province's rapidly expanding cities. Though some of them served a period of apprenticeship on farms, most were educated and skilled, and they went immediately to the urban areas where they could find jobs more suitable to their backgrounds.[32]

Between 1946 and 1956 over 1,200,000 immigrants, including 200,000 political refugees came to Canada. Ninety-five thousand of the total number of immigrants came to Alberta; roughly 10 percent were political refugees. By 1956, the postwar movement of refugees largely ended. Their numbers were partially replaced during the late 1950s and early 1960s by immigrants from the Mediterranean countries including Portugal, Greece, and especially Italy. While these Mediterranean immigrants went mostly to the major urban centers of Toronto and Montreal, some came to Alberta's cities, where they concentrated in the working class. Between 1956 and 1966 another 1,400,000 immigrants came to Canada and about 90,000 of them came to Alberta.[33]

Though there were many opponents of an expansive immigration program in the postwar era, the Liberal government of Mackenzie King gradually moved to a position favoring large-scale European immigration as a way of encouraging Canada's economic development. In many circles a good deal of prejudice remained against non-British immigrants and their possible negative impact on the economy. However, the King government responded positively to pressure from business interests who wanted a labor supply and from ethnic groups who were concerned about their relatives and countrymen in Europe. In 1946 the government announced emergency measures to allow the entry of Polish Armed Forces veterans who had fought against the Germans in Italy at the end of the war. Similarly, in 1947, it allowed the entry of displaced persons —people who had been taken to Germany from German occupied countries across eastern Europe during the war as forced labor, or who had fled from eastern Europe near the end of the war before the advancing Soviet armies. They had lived for years after the war in miserable, crowded conditions in displaced persons camps in western Europe. The Canadian government was under considerable pressure from other western countries and international organizations to do its part in helping to solve the refugee problem.[34]

Besides adopting these special measures to aid displaced persons, the King government in 1947 announced its general postwar immigration policy which was "to foster growth of the population of Canada by the encouragement of immigration without altering the fundamental character of the Canadian nation." A geographic bias, based on "race" and culture was clearly written into the immigration policy. Admissible categories were arranged by countries, with preference being given to residents of Britain, France, Ireland, the United States, and European-settled dominions, while Asians, Africans, and West Indians were virtually excluded. However, the repeal of the Chinese Exclusion Act in 1947 enabled Chinese-Canadians to sponsor relatives, and thereby begin to establish more normal patterns of family life. Small quotas were also introduced for the Commonwealth countries of India, Pakistan, and Ceylon in 1951 when these countries became independent states and part of the Commonwealth.[35]

The government's immigration policy of encouraging sizeable European immigration as a way of promoting economic development while at the same time severely limiting the number of nonwhite immigrants coming to the country met with the approval of most Albertans. They believed that Canada and Alberta needed a larger population and that economic conditions in Alberta were favorable to large-scale immigration. At the end of the war, there was a farm labor shortage throughout the province, particularly in the labor-intensive sugar beet industry in southern Alberta. The German prisoners of war, who had been providing labor, were being repatriated to Europe, and many of the Japanese who had been relocated during World War II were either in a position to purchase their own farms, or were leaving the province to find homes elsewhere in Canada. Government officials felt that Polish war veterans and displaced persons could help relieve this labor shortage.[36]

During the late 1940s and early 1950s, there was also increased opportunity for immigrants in urban areas. After the discovery of oil in 1947, Calgary and Edmonton became two of the fastest-growing cities in Canada. The economic boom created opportunities for skilled workmen, technicians, and professional people.

Displaced Persons

Canada's willingness to help displaced persons was based on more than humanitarianism. It was also tied intimately to its desire to have a cheap labor supply. The displaced persons came either under the sponsored labor scheme, which selected immigrants in displaced persons camps based on the numbers and type of workers needed in Canada, or under the close-relatives scheme, which enabled Canadians to sponsor their relatives. The strong economic motive behind the government's willingness to allow in displaced persons is starkly revealed in its strong preference for single men and women rather than married people for the sponsored labor scheme.[37]

When they came to Alberta, the Polish war veterans and the other displaced persons from central and eastern Europe were required to sign contracts stating that they would remain in farming, mining, domestic service, railway work, or other specified jobs for one to two years, in order to prevent potential economic competition with returning veterans. Few had any experience with farm life and most left the farms for expanding urban areas as soon as possible. Although during the late 1920s, the drift to the cities by central and eastern European immigrants had exacerbated ethnic conflict, there was little opposition to a similar drift during the early 1950s, since economic conditions in urban areas were generally good, and the immigrants often had skills which could be utilized at all levels of the urban economic system.[38]

The government policy of preference for displaced persons with a farming or working class background resulted from the stereotypes of government officials and members of the public about the proper role in Canadian society for central and eastern Europeans. Despite the government's initial preference for farmers and laborers, the displaced persons included many skilled and professional people. Their initial economic experience in Canada as farm or menial laborers was often demoralizing. Displaced persons who came to southern Alberta as farm laborers faced the difficulties of adjusting to the primitive living conditions in the shacks provided for sugar beet workers. Once they moved to urban areas, they faced difficulties in obtaining the recognition of their previous European qualifications by Canadian authorities. Many former professionals, army officers, civil servants, and skilled workers experienced demoralizing periods of downward mobility during which they were forced to take almost any job they could find.

Most of them found some solace in the wide range of ethnic organizations and churches which they established in the cities during the 1950s. The well-educated newcomers revitalized the cultural organizations of many central and eastern European groups in the province, although tension often arose between this wave of immigrants and earlier groups, based on differing class backgrounds and diverse social and political perspectives. Because the postwar immigrants were political refugees, their interests were strongly political, reflecting their dedication to the liberation of their homelands, and their determination to keep their homeland culture and language alive in Canada, uncontaminated by the influences of Soviet communism.

British, German, Dutch, and American Immigration

Despite government efforts to help resettle postwar refugees from central and eastern Europe, the prewar view generally prevailed that Britons, northern Europeans, and Americans were the most desirable immigrants, being culturally similar and readily assimilable. The federal government made special efforts to attract British and Dutch immigrants, and the provincial Social Credit government opened an office in London in 1947 to recruit British tradesmen and professionals. The number of British immigrants coming to the province fell far short of the hundreds of thousands hoped for by the Alberta government; but nevertheless, 45,000 came to Alberta between 1946 and 1966. They made up one-quarter of all the immigrants coming to the province, thus forming by far the largest single group of immigrants in the postwar period. They came seeking better economic opportunities in a country with a familiar political system, and quickly fitted into life in the urban areas of the province where they concentrated in the skilled trades and the professions. Since there was no language barrier, they felt little need to form their own organizations.[39]

Though far outnumbered by English immigrants, the Scots, Irish, and Welsh have been more determined to keep alive a distinctive sense of ethnic identity. Scots, Irish, and Welsh immigrants, with their strong sense of ethnic pride have established or joined organizations of a social nature, to pay due honor to their national patron saints such as Wales' St. David, Ireland's St. Patrick, or the famous Scottish poet Robbie Burns. The Irish have also established sports clubs to bring together those interested in rugby, field hockey, and lacrosse and cultural organizations to keep alive Celtic ballad singing and Irish dancing. The Welsh immigrants have established choirs and helped invigorate the tradition of Gymanfu-Ganu, a religious singing festival, which had first been established on an annual basis by Welsh settlers in the Ponoka area in the 1920s. The Scots have focused on a few highly visible symbols of their origins—clans, tartans, pipe bands, highland dancing, and in recent years, Scottish country dancing. Scottish traditions have so long been part of the larger Canadian identity that many of them are now shared by Albertans of many different origins who avidly participate in pipe bands and highland dancing groups.[40]

German and Dutch immigrants made up the second and third largest groups to come to the province in the early postwar era. Both groups fled war-ravaged lands, overcrowded conditions, shortages of housing and consumer goods, limited economic opportunity, and the spectre of another European war. The Canadian government cooperated with the Dutch government, and with Catholic and Reformed churches in Canada and Holland, to encourage the movement of Dutch immigrants. The Dutch and German immigrants came to both rural and urban areas of the province. In the cities, they each made up a significant sector of the skilled labor force in the construction industry.[41]

Despite wartime animosities, immigrants of German origin formed the second largest group to come to Alberta in the early postwar period, comprising almost 20 percent of those arriving. Many of these were *Volksdeutsche*, people of German background who had lived in countries bordering Germany, but who had retained their German culture. At the end of the war, they fled westward into Germany in the face of the advancing armies of the Soviet Union. As refugees, they found little place for themselves in a war-ravaged country. Being of German origin, they did not come under the mandate of the United Nations International Refugee Organization, and consequently could not come to Canada under the same provisions as other displaced persons. However, through the lobbying efforts of Mennonite, Lutheran, Baptist, and Roman Catholic churches in Canada, in 1947 the Canadian government agreed to allow many of these refugees into Canada. These churches formed the Canadian Christian Council for the Re-settlement of Refugees, which found sponsors and jobs for the newcomers. In 1950, the Canadian government also lifted its ban on immigrants from West Germany (who had previously been excluded as "enemy aliens"), and immigrants from Germany began to arrive as farm laborers, tradesmen, and workers in many other occupations. The immigrants from Germany itself often became self-employed businessmen or professionals, while the *Volksdeutsche* tended to be tradesmen. Because of their belief in hard work and their skilled and professional backgrounds, the Germans have done well economically.[42]

The postwar Germans established a variety of secular clubs and churches to aid their adjustment to Canada. The *Volksdeutsche*, having fought to retain the German language and culture for many generations in eastern Europe, have been particularly interested in keeping alive their language and culture in Canada, while immigrants from Germany itself have been less anxious to maintain their ethnic ties. In Edmonton and Calgary, the newcomers concentrated in working and lower middle class neighborhoods such as Avonmore in Edmonton and

Bowness in Calgary, where they established an institutional network of small businesses, clubs, and churches. The Baptists, Seventh Day Adventists, Lutherans, Church of God, Mennonites, Pentecostals, and Catholics have all maintained German language services in the larger urban centers. In addition, the newcomers set up German-Canadian clubs in the smaller cities such as Red Deer, Grande Prairie, Lethbridge, and Medicine Hat. In Calgary and Edmonton, they established a wide variety of cultural and sports organizations, choirs, German language schools, and soccer teams. Churches and clubs provided a place where newcomers could meet and gain support from German-speaking friends with similar problems. Through these organizations, the immigrants hoped to keep alive their language and culture. Though at first they encountered some resentment because of their German background, they were ultimately well accepted into Canadian society.[43]

Though outnumbered by British, Dutch and German immigrants during the late 1940s and 1950s, the Americans who came to Alberta at this time played a key management role in the development of the oil industry. They had a strong influence on the social climate of Calgary, the management center of the oil industry where most of them lived. The very rapid development of the oil industry in the late 1940s and early 1950s led to a shortage of skilled labor in the industry. In the early years of the postwar oil boom, a majority of the senior management of the major oil companies, most of which were American-owned, was made up of Americans from California, Oklahoma, Texas, and Louisiana.[44]

Throughout the 1960s the American oil companies attempted to Canadianize their personnel at the senior levels of management, and the number of Americans in the industry declined. Those Americans who remained usually took out Canadian citizenship so they could vote, since they often held strong views on political issues. The Americans brought their talent for involvement in volunteer organizations and helped give Calgary its dynamic "let's go do it" social attitudes which characterized postwar life in that city. Given the large amounts of money in the oil industry and the Americans' spending habits, they undoubtedly contributed to Calgary's image as a materialistic city.[45]

Though numerically small and transient—in 1961 only 8,600 of the approximately 18,000 Americans who immigrated to Alberta between 1946 and 1961 still remained in the province—they shaped the industry that dominated Alberta in the post-World War II era. However, this influx did little to reverse the overall decline in the percentage of Americans born in the province, which had declined steadily from 22 percent in 1911 to only 4 percent by 1961. [46]

Two other movements of American immigrants during the 1960s helped diversify the American impact on the province. Throughout the 1960s, sizeable numbers of American professors came to work in the province's universities at a time when there was not enough Canadian faculty available. In addition, by the late 1960s, American war resisters, opposed to the Vietnamese war, began coming to the province. Though most of the war resisters stayed only temporarily, and had a fleeting impact, many of the professors have remained, integrating fully into Canadian university life.[47]

Recent European Refugees

Throughout the late 1950s and until the major change in immigration regulations in 1967, European immigrants continued to dominate immigration to Alberta. The immigrants came primarily for economic reasons, but there were also three additional groups of European political refugees subsequent to the movement of displaced persons which ended by 1955. Following the abortive Hungarian revolution of 1956, refugees came to the province. Again in 1968, Czech and Slovak political refugees fled their homeland in the face of a Soviet invasion to end the attempt to liberalize Czechoslovakia. Unlike the pre-World War II waves of immigration from Czechoslovakia which had been made up mostly of Slovaks, this wave was predominantly Czech (mostly from the capital city of Prague). During the middle to late 1970s, Soviet Jews arrived in Canada fleeing anti-Semitism in the Soviet Union and seeking better economic opportunities in North America. All three refugee groups were composed primarily of highly skilled and educated people who have made a rapid adjustment to economic life in Alberta's largest cities. Having grown up in the secular atmosphere of postwar eastern Europe, these immigrants were less attached to organized religion than were the displaced persons. Secondly, having experience in a communist society, they had grown wary and weary of institutional involvements. They were not strongly inclined to set up or support their own ethnic organizations, but more concerned about their economic success and integration into Canadian society.[48]

Immigration and Patterns of Immigrant Adjustment: 1967-Present

After World War II, the pseudo-scientific race theory of the turn of the century was completely discredited. By the early 1960s Canada's immigration laws, which had enshrined ethnic and racial biases were becoming increasingly unacceptable. In 1967, the federal government introduced new immigration regulations which were applied to all immigrants, regardless of ethnic or racial origins. The regulations made provision for two categories—sponsored and nominated immigrants (who were relatives of people in Canada) and independent immigrants. Independent immigrants had to meet certain standards under an assessment or "points system," which placed heavy emphasis on the educational background and skills of the immigrants and the occupational demand for their skills.[49]

This new emphasis on immigrant skills and economic demand in Canada, as opposed to ethnic or racial background opened Canada's immigration doors to virtually the whole world. With European sources of immigration declining as the economies of western Europe improved, Canada turned to other parts of the world to recruit skilled immigrants.

Throughout the late 1970s, Britain and the United States remained the two leading countries of last permanent residence for immigrants coming to Alberta. But the overall percentage of immigrants coming from Europe and the United States had declined from the pre-1967 era. In any case, those coming from Europe and the United States now included many immigrants from Third World countries who temporarily lived in Europe or the United States before applying to come to Canada.[50]

Immigration now substantially increased the size of the Chinese community in Alberta, and introduced several new groups such as the West Indians, South Asians, Filipinos, Vietnamese, Koreans, and Latin Americans. While each of these groups had been represented by a handful of students and professionals during the early 1960s, their numbers increased substantially during the late 1960s and throughout the 1970s. Attracted by Canadian economic opportunities and by the buoyant Alberta economy, emigrants from the Third World had come in large enough numbers by the early 1980s that nearly one out of ten people in Edmonton and Calgary (where most of them lived) belonged to one of these groups. In 1978, 1979, and 1980, immigrants from countries out-

The Diep family, who arrived in Edmonton in 1981 after spending more than a year in Hong Kong. Thousands of political refugees from Southeast Asia came to Alberta in the late 1970s and early 1980s. Political refugees have formed a significant part of all major waves of immigration to Alberta. (Courtesy Helen FitzPatrick)

side of Europe or the United States made up 50 percent, 62 percent, and 59 percent of the immigrants coming to Alberta.[51]

Though most of the newcomers came for economic reasons, many different groups of political refugees arrived as well from many parts of the world. They included a few dozen Tibetans who had fled to India in 1959 following the Chinese invasion of their homeland. The Canadian government, for humanitarian reasons, brought them to Canada in 1970 and 1971 following their lengthy residence in refugee camps in India. The Tibetans were originally placed as laborers in sugar beet fields in southern Alberta. Here they encountered health and adjustment problems, and most soon left for the urban areas of Lethbridge and Calgary, where they concentrated in manual and semiskilled jobs. The political refugees also included Ugandan Asians, expelled from Uganda in 1972 by dictator Idi Amin, and Chileans, who were left wing supporters of the Allende regime, overthrown in a military coup in 1973. Throughout the late 1970s, Lebanese immigrants fled political chaos and civil war in their home country and responded to economic opportunity in Canada. However, the largest and most publicized group of political refugees have been those from Southeast Asia. This movement began in 1975 with the collapse of the South Vietnamese regime, backed by the Americans. By late 1978, the exodus of refugees from Vietnam, Cambodia, and Laos had grown so large, chaotic, and dangerous, that it became a major international issue. Both the Canadian government and individual Canadians did a great deal to help these refugees, popularly known as "the boat people," to adjust to life in Canada. The response to the "boat people" was unprecedented in terms of size of the refugee movement, the organized nature of the effort to help, the involvement of the general public, and the degree of generosity extended to the refugees.[52]

While economic considerations had been paramount in the government's decision to accept earlier groups of refugees such as Mormons, Mennonites, and Hutterites, the government's refugee policy had become after 1967 more genuinely reflective of humanitarian concerns. Canadian refugee policy had become nonracist and more than ever before, ideologically neutral.

The immigrants from the Third World were pioneers in their own right. With the exception of the Chinese and Lebanese, who joined already existing communities, the newcomers had to create their own institutions and support systems. They had one considerable advantage over pre-World War II immigrants though: they arrived after the Canadian welfare state had been established. Government social services were much more fully developed than before, and they could get help with jobs and English classes. They could also rely on government services in case of sickness, accident, or unemployment.

Despite tremendous differences that reflect the great diversity of cultures, languages, and races in the world, the newcomers from the Third World have many things in common. With the partial exception of some of the political refugees, the newcomers have included a very large percentage of highly trained professionals and skilled workers, including doctors, engineers, and many other professionals. Minor changes in immigration regulations in the late 1970s, which placed greater emphasis on occupational demand in Canada as opposed to simple educational background, along with the ongoing sponsorship of relatives, has recently led to a wider cross section of occupations being represented among the immigrants. Thus, tradesmen became more common among many immigrant groups by the late 1970s.[53]

Besides their common characteristics of being predominantly young and skilled, they share an urban experience, since they have concentrated primarily in the province's two largest cities, Calgary and Edmonton. Within each of these cities, there has been little ethnic concentration. The Lebanese, South Asians, West Indians, and Filipinos in Calgary have settled in the northeastern part of the city where housing prices are lower and they are nearer to industrial jobs; but on the whole there has been relatively little residential segregation. Calgary's Chinatown has grown and developed with the sizeable influx of immigrants from Hong Kong, but only a small percentage of the newcomers actually live in Chinatown. Instead, they have moved as their financial circumstances have permitted to other sections of the city.[54]

What is perhaps the most surprising is the newcomers' relative ease of adjustment, no doubt made easier by their professional and skilled backgrounds, and by the knowledge of the English language of immigrants from the West Indies, South Asia, East Africa, and the Philippines, who grew up in former British or American colonies. Language does remain a major barrier for many immigrants, whether from Hong Kong, Korea, or Chile; but the wide availability of English language classes has made the problem somewhat less difficult than it was for earlier waves of immigrants. Successful adjustment was also facilitated by the tremendous economic opportunities in Alberta during the oil boom of the 1970s.[55]

The newcomers' adjustment has also been eased by the wide variety of cultural, sports, social, and religious organizations established during the late 1960s and 1970s. Given their urban residence and geographic dispersal, they have not maintained the same degree of cultural survival which existed in many of the rural bloc settlements prior to World War I. But they have attempted to keep alive many cultural traditions, including probably the most widespread symbol of cultural maintenance and ethnic identity, their distinctive foods. West Indians have introduced the sport of netball, have established cricket teams, and have maintained their distinctive and increasingly popular West Indian music and dance. Koreans have introduced the challenging board game of "Go" and the martial arts of Tae Kwon Do; the Chinese and Vietnamese have kept alive special traditions surrounding the lunar New Year. The establishment of religious services, mosques, and temples has also been an important part of the efforts by Muslim, Buddhist, and Sikh immigrants to keep alive their own ways of understanding the world and of giving meaning to life.[56]

The relative ease of adjustment does not mean that the reception given to these new immigrants has been wholly positive. Some have experienced racism and discrimination. The group most often singled out for negative attention has been the South Asians, or people who trace their origins to the Indian subcontinent (though they may have immigrated to Canada from places as far flung as Fiji, East Africa, or the West Indies). During the peak of their immigration between 1974 and 1977, there were several incidents of assault and vandalism against them in different parts of Alberta. The other sizeable nonwhite group to come during the 1970s, the Chinese, have not encountered as much prejudice, perhaps because the existing Chinese-Canadian population is already a familiar part of Canadian society and now includes several generations of Canadian born. Immigrants from the Middle East, South America, and the West Indies have encountered less prejudice than the South Asians because of their smaller numbers.[57]

The most serious problems of adjustment have been faced by the Vietnamese and other Southeast Asian refugees. They have had to deal with a new language, climate, society, and economic system. Further, they arrived near the end of the economic boom in the early 1980s, and a large number have had difficulty finding or keeping jobs. These adjustments have been made more difficult by the fact that many lost close relatives in the hasty exodus on leaky boats and are haunted by the experience. They remain anxious about the fate of their relatives in Southeast Asia, some of whom are still in refugee camps, or in Vietnam. Once in Canada, only the Vietnamese of Chinese origin had an existing ethnic community to fall back on. Among the few resources available to them, other than their own initiative and courage, has been a concerned group of refugee sponsors who have helped them with jobs, accommodation, support, and care.[58]

For many of the new Third World immigrants, attempting to adapt to the Canadian milieu has led to increased tension in their family relationships. The newcomers come from less industrialized societies in which extended families, often share accommodation as well as mutual obligations. In more traditional and less industrialized societies than Canada, more aspects of life are regulated by the family, and feelings of family responsibility are generally stronger than they are in North America. The process of immigration has separated relatives, and the economic conditions the newcomers face in Canada have disrupted the extended family. Most immigrant families in Canada are nuclear rather than extended and include husband, wife, children, and only rarely an elderly relative.[59]

Given the strong emphasis new immigrants place on economic success, and their strong drive to acquire a home, wives usually work. This has led to some economic independence for the wives and a weakening of the power of the husbands to control family affairs. This is a significant change for many from the Third World, inevitably creating marital tensions.

Relationships with children have also occasionally proved to be problematic because Canadian society is more permissive on many social issues than more traditional societies. However, the children of the immigrants are inevitably influenced by Canadian society. Often they resent attempts by parents to enforce norms that are stricter than those required of their Canadian-born peers. Although a wide difference of opinions exist between, and within, new immigrant groups on the subject of intermarriage, many immigrant parents prefer that their children date and marry someone of their own ethnic background. Their children do not necessarily agree.

By far the largest immigrant group to come to Alberta from the Third World has been the Chinese. Recent Chinese immigrants have greatly increased the number of people of Chinese origin in the province from 7,000 in 1961 to nearly 40,000 by 1981. They have also completely changed the character of the Chinese community in Alberta.

Like the South Asians in Alberta, who come from many parts of the globe, but trace their origins to India and Pakistan, the Chinese have come to Alberta during the 1960s and 1970s from many different parts of Southeast Asia. Over centuries, people of Chinese background have moved into many regions of Southeast Asia. In addition to the large numbers of immigrants from Hong Kong, immigrants of Chinese origin have also come to Alberta from Malaysia, Singapore, Indonesia, and the Philippines. Immigration from Hong Kong has been stimulated by unstable political and economic conditions in the aftermath of the cultural revolution in China. In addition, there has been a great deal of insecurity in Hong Kong because of mainland China's determination to eventually take control of the area from Britain in 1998. The small number of universities in a city with a population of four million has also generated great pressure for students to seek an education abroad, and many have chosen to do so in Canada. Political and economic uncertainties and racial antagonism in Malaysia, Indonesia, and the Philippines toward overseas Chinese have prompted others of Chinese origin to come to Canada.[60]

Given Canada's immigration regulations, which place a premium on education and professional qualifications, the majority of the newcomers have moved into white collar occupations. Computer science and engineering have consistently attracted the largest number of Chinese students.

The size of the influx and its predominantly middle class composition, have changed the nature of the Chinese community in Alberta. Prior to the 1950s, the restrictions on Chinese immigration, language difficulties, and the hostility of the host society had created an artificial bachelor society cut off from the mainstream of Canadian life. Chinese immigrants relied for their community life on Chinatown's clan, regional and political organizations. This way of life had been changing during the 1950s and early 1960s as a result of family reunification and the emergence of a Canadian-born generation. It changed even more dramatically and in new directions with the large influx of people in the late 1960s and 1970s.[61]

The new immigrants have developed their own lifestyle, distinct from that represented by the older institutions of Chinatown. The newcomers may be Chinese, but they come from very different societies than the

China of the oldtimers, and their social patterns in Canada have been different from those of the earlier immigrants. The newcomers have been able to establish a more typical family life. Their social and political views make them feel that the traditional organizations in Chinatown are irrelevant to their needs.

The decline of prejudice against them and their economic success have made possible a much more thorough integration into Canadian society than was possible for the earlier immigrants. In the major urban areas, the Chinese now live throughout the city. They are no longer concentrated solely in service businesses such as restaurants and laundries. They have close relations with white neighbors and their children are becoming increasingly assimilated. Intermarriage between Chinese and whites, almost unheard of before the 1950s, is now increasing.

Like other immigrant groups, the Chinese are making their own adjustment to Canada. They have established their own institutions and their own ways of coping with the transition to a new society. In Calgary and Edmonton, they have established several new language schools, cultural organizations, social service agencies, and Protestant Christian churches. New leaders have emerged to challenge Chinatown's older power structures and to try to shape its future development.[62]

Conclusion

The history of Alberta is in many ways the story of each of its immigrant groups. The original peoples, the Indians, and later the Metis occupy the stage first. A little more than a century ago they welcomed the first sizeable number of white immigrants to the western section of the Northwest Territories. The French-speaking and English-speaking population were, in the opening years of the Territories, established on a plane of equality, but when the English-speaking came to outnumber the French-speaking, English became the sole language of the West. The Ontarians imposed their image on the West before the large waves of immigrants arrived at the turn of the century. Each chapter in *Peoples of Alberta* reveals the story of Alberta through the experience of the Indians, the Metis, the French Canadians, the Ontarians and the hosts of new Albertans who followed in the twentieth century.

The arrival of each new wave of immigrants in the twentieth century has been occurring against a backdrop of great changes within the lives of individual immigrant communities in the province. As each group of newcomers becomes established, and as they make their adjustments to Canada and to Alberta, their needs and perspectives change. Acculturation of the immigrant generation and assimilation of their Canadian-born children is an ongoing process within almost all immigrant groups. Why some groups want to maintain a separate identity, while others do not, and why even among those who want to maintain a distinct identity some are very successful and others are unsuccessful are questions which will partially be answered within the context of the histories of each of the individual groups in the province.

One must also realize that immigrants to Alberta have experienced the inevitable stress involved in the processes of acculturation and/or assimilation within a broader context of rapid social change. Since becoming a province in 1905, Alberta has been transformed in the mere space of a lifetime from a largely rural to a predominantly urban society. Consequently, all Albertans, whether immigrants from a distant part of the world, interprovincial migrants from Ontario, Quebec, or the maritimes, native peoples, or Anglo-Canadians born and raised in the province, have had to attempt to develop new identities and strategies to cope with a rapidly changing and increasingly complex physical, economic, and social environment. Thus the immigrant struggle, at both the individual and the group level, to achieve economic security and to create a satisfying social and cultural identity is neither exotic nor peripheral, but rather an interesting and important variation of the quest for security and identity which has been a major dimension of the common Alberta experience. The story of various groups coming to Alberta to make their homes, as explored within the individual chapters of this book, is an integral part of the larger story of Alberta in the twentieth century.

CHAPTER THREE
The Original Peoples of Alberta[1]
Donald B. Smith

Alberta's Native Groups

Alberta had already become a cultural mosaic by the moment of the European settlers' arrival a century ago. Nine different tribes belonging to three different linguistic families—Dene (or Athapaskan), Algonkian, and Siouan—occupied the area. Apart from the Indian sign language, the *lingua franca* of the Plains, the original Albertans shared no common tongue.

In the late nineteenth century the Dene-speaking tribes—Chipewyan, Beaver, Slavey—lived in northern Alberta and the Sarcee in the south. Tribes belonging to the Algonkian linguistic family, the Plains Cree and the Blackfoot-speaking tribes—Blackfoot (or in their own language, Siksika), Blood (Kainai), Peigan (Pikuni)—occupied hunting grounds in southern and central Alberta. To the north dwelt bands of Woodlands Cree. The Assiniboines (or Stoneys as they are called in Alberta), who belong to the Siouan linguistic family, lived principally along the foothills in southern Alberta.[2]

Although not formally a tribe, the Metis constituted another distinct and separate native group. Their origin dated back to the arrival of European fur traders on the Canadian Plains. The majority of the Metis, many of whom spoke Cree as their first language, had settled in the central and northern portions of the province.[3] The Metis served as the indispensable link during the fur trading, and in the early settlement period between the Indians and the Europeans.

On the eve of European settlement in present day Alberta the native peoples had two distinct ways of life: that of the Plains and that of the Woodlands. Thanks to the existence of an estimated fifty million buffalo the Indians on the Great Plains had developed a distinctive way of life.[4] The Plains people for thousands of years had used the buffalo's hide for clothing, braided ropes, and tepee covers. From its bones they made handles, needles, and other items. They took the horns and shaped them

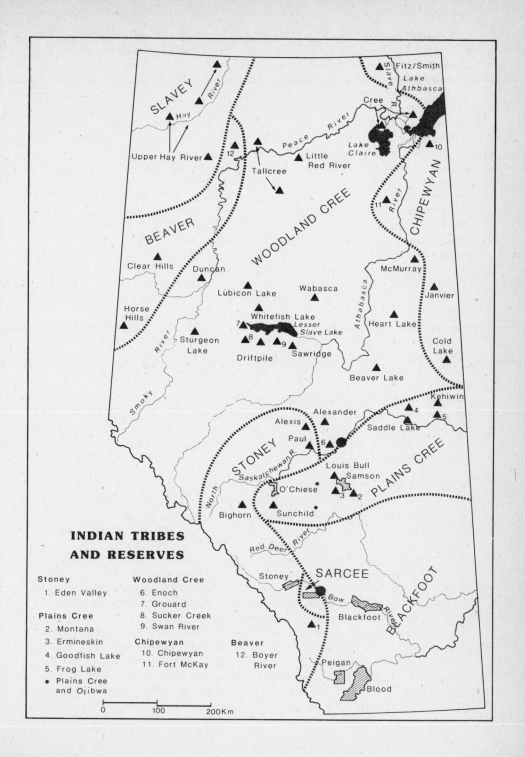

SLAVEY

Fitz/Smith

Slave River

Lake Athabasca

Cree

Hay River

Upper Hay River

12

Peace River

Little Red River

Lake Claire

CHIPEWYAN

Tallcree

10

11

River

WOODLAND CREE

BEAVER

Clear Hills

Duncan

McMurray

Lubicon Lake

Wabasca

Janvier

Horse Hills

7

Whitefish Lake

Lesser Slave Lake

Athabasca

Heart Lake

8

River

Sturgeon Lake

9

Cold Lake

Driftpile

Sawridge

Beaver Lake

Smoky

Kehiwin

Alexander

4

5

Alexis

Saddle Lake

STONEY

Paul

6

Saskatchewan R.

Louis Bull

Samson

PLAINS CREE

O'Chiese *

3   2

North

Bighorn

Sunchild *

Red Deer River

SARCEE

Stoney

BLACKFOOT

Bow

River

Blackfoot

1

Peigan

Blood

INDIAN TRIBES AND RESERVES

Stoney
1. Eden Valley

Plains Cree
2. Montana
3. Ermineskin
4. Goodfish Lake
5. Frog Lake
* Plains Cree and Ojibwa

Woodland Cree
6. Enoch
7. Grouard
8. Sucker Creek
9. Swan River

Chipewyan
10. Chipewyan
11. Fort McKay

Beaver
12. Boyer River

0   100   200Km

into spoons or drinking cups. The sinews provided thread for sewing, as well as strings for their bows.[5] They ate its nourishing meat, including its vitamin-rich internal organs.

In the northern Woodlands the Indians subsisted by hunting and fishing. They hunted over wide expanses in search of game—moose, deer, and the smaller animals—and they fished. Like the Plains tribes, they gathered berries and wild plants to supplement their diet. While supplies in the summers proved plentiful, the northern peoples experienced severe food shortages in the winter. Unlike the Indians to the south whose old way of life ended over a century ago with the extinction of the Plains buffalo, a number of the isolated northern Indians still today hunt, trap, and fish.[6]

Alberta's native peoples in the early 1980s number from an estimated 100,000 to 160,000, and constitute 5 to 7 percent of the province's total population. Approximately 40,000 are official "status" or "treaty" Indians because of their inclusion on an Indian band's membership list. The other 60,000 to 120,000 native people in Alberta are Metis (people of mixed Indian and non-Indian ancestry) and non-status Indians (Indians or children of Indian parents who have lost their band membership by voluntarily giving it up, or—in the case of Indian women who married non-Indians—being obliged, as required by the Indian Act, to surrender it). Indian reserves today occupy 1 percent (approximately 2,500 square miles) of Alberta's total land surface (approximately 255,000 square miles), and the Metis settlements are slightly less than 1 percent.[7]

The history of Alberta's native peoples roughly divides into two distinct time periods. The signing of the treaties in the late 1870s provides the best point of division. In the first period the native peoples alone occupied western Canada, and in the second they became a minority in their homeland.

Origins of Man in Alberta

Archaeologists have advanced many theories to explain how the first humans reached the Americas. Native elders remain unconvinced by their speculations. The scientists generally contend that the first Americans crossed over from Asia during the last ice ages. With so much of the earth's water locked in ice ocean levels dropped and continental shelves emerged from the sea. One area so affected was the shallow region of the Bering Strait. When the sea level fell, a broad plain emerged—a land bridge linking Alaska and Siberia. The broad land bridge became a highway for Asian animals passing into the Americas. Many archaeologists believe that an ice-free corridor also existed along the eastern slope of the Rockies providing the animals with a pathway southward. Only during the peak of glaciation did ice block this corridor. Across the Bering land bridge and down the ice-free corridor man followed the animals. Each summer, as the glacial barriers retreated, human beings advanced further into the heart of the continent.

Many older Canadian Indians, in contrast, have learned from childhood that man originated on this continent. Ancient stories and great sacred traditions confirm their opinion. From their grandparents and older relatives many young Blackfoot today are taught how Napi, or the Old Man, created the world and every living thing in it.

In the beginning water covered the entire world. One day, the ever curious Napi decided to find out what lay below. He sent first the duck, then the otter and the badger. All dived in vain. Then Napi asked the muskrat, who then plunged into the depths. He was gone so long that Napi feared that he had drowned. At last the muskrat rose, alive, holding a small ball of mud. The Old Man took this small lump, blew upon it, and magically it began to swell. It continued to grow in size until it became the whole earth. Napi then piled up rocks to make mountains, gouged out river and lake beds, filled them with water, and then covered the plains with grass. He made all the birds and animals, and finally people. Patiently he taught the men and women how to hunt and how to live. Now, his work completed, the Old Man climbed a high mountain and disappeared. Some say Napi's home lay in the Rocky Mountains at the headwaters of the Alberta river that bears his name, The Oldman.[8]

Despite their difference of opinion with the native oral tradition the archaeologists do recognize the antiquity of man in western Canada. They have provided conclusive proof that man was on the Plains at least 12,000 years ago. The hundreds of thousands of stone circles, or tepee rings—rocks placed in a circular pattern and used to cover hides—provide the most obvious sign of human occupation. It is estimated that there may have been as many as one million such rings scattered throughout Alberta. Archaeologists have also identified a number of their buffalo jumps, where Indian hunters stampeded herds down funnel-shaped runways over the edges of high cliffs. The Head-Smashed-In site near Fort Macleod was in use for at least 5,600 years and possibly as long as 9,000.[9]

The most mysterious finds of all are the two dozen "medicine wheels" found in southern Alberta. Apparently these large stone rings, with rock spokes radiating out from a stone cairn piled in the center might have had an astronomical purpose connected with the rising of one of the brighter stars. These sky calendars, constructed several thousand years ago, possibly served as indicators of the summer solstice as well as computers of the lunar month.[10]

On the basis of the weapons systems archaeologists have divided the pre-European history of the Plains Indians into three sequences. In the first or early period (12,000 to 7,500 years ago), the nomadic hunters used either a stabbing or throwing spear. Many different kinds of buffalo-kill sites utilized well into the period of European contact (jumps, traps, pounds) were developed in these years. During the second or middle period (7,500 to 1,500 years ago) a much more efficient weapon, a hand-held throwing stick (called an atlatl by the Aztecs) came into use. At this time the people constructed the first medicine wheels and large cairn sites. The extensive trade networks, along which horses and European goods would later be exchanged commercially, arose as well.

Essentially the developments of this sequence completed the Plains Indians' lifestyle. Little actually changed in the third period (1,500 years ago to about 1730 A.D.) apart from the introduction of the bow and arrow.[11]

As early as 7,500 years ago the Plains Indians practised a seasonal round of activities that lasted until the early eighteenth century. During the winter the natives gathered on the edges of the Parkland, or in the river valleys, sheltered from the blizzards and the terrible cold of the open plains. In these wooded areas the bands could find both fuel and the buffalo (which also spent the winter in protected areas). When the grass became green again, and the migrating herds could be expected, the Indians moved onto the Plains for their communal buffalo drives. The large groups dispersed in the summer into smaller bands. By fall the Indians again gathered for the communal buffalo kills during the bisons' rutting season. To operate these hunts on foot required excellent organization and daring.[12]

The Arrival of the Horse

The northern Plains culture changed dramatically in the eighteenth century. From the Spanish in Mexico the Indians in the present day southwestern United States had obtained horses, and had traded them to more northerly groups. Others were stolen or caught wild on the prairie. The Blackfoot acquired horses in the 1730s, two decades before the arrival of the European in Blackfoot country.

The Plains Indians adjusted quickly to the horse. They worked out saddles of leather bags stuffed with grass, or rode bareback guiding their horses with their knees, using a single rope of horsehair as their only rein. The horse changed their ways of hunting buffalo, and revolutionized their society.

In the "dog days" (appropriately named after the Blackfoot's only domesticated animal before the arrival of the horse) the Indians could not travel very far. A strong dog carried a load of approximately 50 pounds on its back, or dragged 75 pounds on a v-shaped drag called a travois, five or six miles a day. But a horse packed 200 pounds on its back, or 300 pounds on a travois and journeyed twice as far in a day—an efficiency, animal for animal, 8 times as great.[13] The horse ended the poverty of the "dog days."

Now the Plains Indians could have many more possessions. The Blackfoot transported extra suits of decorated clothing, as well as additional buffalo robes for the winter. Women no longer bore backbreaking burdens. They rode horseback. Since the Blackfoot now carried with them extra supplies of food, the danger of winter starvation diminished.

Literally the horse lifted the Plains Indian off his feet, extending his idea of geographical distance. The horse shortened his concepts of travel time by decreasing the difficulties of moving camp and of hunting buffalo. Life's tempo quickened becoming more exciting and, at the same time, more dangerous.

The need for swift horses for hunting buffalo and transporting baggage led to a new sport on the Plains: the capturing of horses from enemy camps. Warfare became more common after the horse's arrival, and more deadly. The mounted charge became the common form of attack. Man-to-man fighting with bow and arrow, lance, war club, and knife—and soon the gun—led to the great increase in casualties.

The horse also contributed to the development of an emerging class structure among the Blackfoot. A class system arose with rich, middle class, and poor families—all separated from each other almost solely on the basis of their wealth, or poverty, in horses.[14]

While the availability of the horse reduced the Indians' amount of walking, they remained in excellent physical condition. One of the early Europeans to reach the Plains commented on the Sioux's ability (before they obtained horses) to run so fast that they could overtake, run beside, and shoot their arrows at the buffalo. Even after becoming horse-mounted the Plains Indians kept up their extraordinary capacity for running. To cite one example, Ernest Thompson Seton, the famous Canadian naturalist, met a young Cree at Fort Ellice in 1882 (now in present day Saskatchewan); the Indian runner had just brought in dispatches from Fort Qu'Appelle, 125 miles away, in twenty-five hours. Seton remarks: "It created almost no comment. I heard little from the traders but cool remarks like, 'A good boy', 'pretty good run'. It was obviously a very usual exploit among Indians."[15]

The Impact of the European Fur Traders

The lack of written records describing the interior of western Canada makes it very difficult to describe tribal locations at the point of European contact. One must rely heavily on the records of the HBC, which established posts on Hudson Bay in 1670 and posts in the interior a century later. From the available HBC accounts it appears that by the eighteenth century a great displacement of Indians had begun. Anxious to barter for European ironware, the Indians near Hudson Bay had begun trapping. To obtain more furs, bands began intruding into other's hunting territories.

The Cree and the Assiniboine had rapidly become the middlemen of the European fur trade. They traded furs with the neighboring English traders on Hudson Bay, and with the French on Lake Superior, for the coveted iron goods with their fine cutting edge and durability. The European trade items simplified all the Indians' daily tasks, from skinning game to making toboggans and snowshoes. In addition, the European gun with its greater firepower gave the Cree and the Assiniboine a military advantage over their enemies. The interior tribes in western Canada wanted the new iron knives, axes, and chisels, but they had no direct suppliers. The shrewd Cree and Assiniboine traded their own European tools and kettles to interior bands, after marking up the original prices.[16]

Entering first as middlemen, the Cree and the Assiniboine advanced westward. When the first European fur traders arrived in present day northern Alberta, they found the Crees already established there.

This picture, taken in the late 1880s, shows a Sarcee Indian and his family in front of his lodge. The Sarcee once belonged to the Beaver tribe in present day northern Alberta, but moved out onto the Prairies, adopting the Plains Indians' culture. In 1881 they selected their reserve at Fish Creek, just south of Calgary. (Courtesy Glenbow Archives)

As the Hudson Bay Indians migrated further west along the wooded country of the North Saskatchewan River, they entered onto the Plains and into Blackfoot country. Their westward migration drove a wedge up the North Saskatchewan River to the Rockies, pushing interior tribes to the north and the south. The small Sarcee tribe was separated from its parent group, the Beaver, and the Sarcee moved onto the Plains. The Cree forced the Blackfoot tribes south from the North Saskatchewan.[17]

On the Plains the Assiniboine—and later their Cree allies—discovered the huge buffalo herds. The Assiniboine adjusted first to the horse, then taught the Cree. By the beginning of the nineteenth century the Plains Assiniboine and Plains Cree had emerged. These new Plains Indians no longer had the same need for iron axes, since their fuel usually consisted of buffalo dung or small trees from along the river banks. Similarly copper kettles, while useful for cooking meat, were by no means essential—the Plains people most often dried their meat in the sun. Pounded fine into a powder, they mixed it with melted fat and dried berries to make pemmican, which they ate uncooked. They did not need guns for the hunt. The early flintlocks, while useful in war, were difficult to load on horseback and could not be fired rapidly (repeating rifles only became available about 1870). Moreover, the noise of the guns often terrified the buffalo, prematurely stampeding the herds and thus endangering the lives of the hunters.[18]

The Cree soon established their control over a wide area north of the North Saskatchewan River. But the Crees' Assiniboine allies extended themselves too far. A violent thrust by the Blackfoot forced one group of the Assiniboine far north of the river. They escaped by going further northward, and then advancing into the southwest. These Assiniboine bands (and possibly others already in the foothills) became known as Stoneys. While a number of the Woods Cree moved southward, adopting the life of the Plains, others migrated into forested areas of northern Alberta. Their arrival led to more tribal movements.

Another Indian group, the Chipewyan (a Dene-speaking group) moved westward as well. Like the Crees they first became the Europeans' middlemen, and later used the white man's guns to expand their own hunting territory westward. Armed with their new weapons, the Chipewyan pushed the Beavers towards the headwaters of the Peace River. When the Beavers themselves obtained their first guns in the late eighteenth century, they were able to resist the Chipewyan advance from the east and that of the Woods Cree from the south. (It is said that the traders named the river "the Peace" because there the Cree and the Beaver ended their conflict.) Once armed, the Beaver in turn forced the Sekanis, another Dene-speaking group, westward from the foothills into the heights of the Rockies. The Slavey Indians retreated northward to the isolated Caribou Mountains and the Hay River, in the northwestern corner of present day Alberta.[19]

Other native groups also arrived in Alberta, but in smaller numbers. The North West Company (NWC) engaged several hundred Iroquois from the Montreal area as trappers and hunters in the 1790s. The NWC used the Iroquois to secure additional furs to those brought in by the local Indians. By 1810, the Iroquois trapped in the Lake Athabasca and Peace River regions and along the eastern slopes of the Rocky Mountains. Upon the expiry of their contracts, some Iroquois remained in the west to trade and to hunt on their own. They tended to hunt most frequently in thinly populated areas, or those not visited regularly by local Indians. A number learned the local band's languages, and married their women. Some descendants of these early Iroquois trappers eventually settled in the Lac Ste Anne area; others stayed on the eastern slopes of the Rockies, or travelled into the Peace River region of British Columbia.[20] In addition to the Iroquois, small groups of Ojibwa (Chippewa) or Saulteaux (as they are known in the West), who came originally from the Great Lakes area, traded up the North Saskatchewan River.[21]

European fur traders reached the Athabasca and the Peace River country in the last two decades of the eighteenth century. The fur trade employed thousands of Europeans in the interior of western Canada, particularly in the years of intense competition between the HBC and the NWC, its archrival. The conflict, which began in the 1780s, would only be resolved by the union of the two companies in 1821, under the name of the Hudson's Bay Company.

The Rise of the Metis

Many of the European fur traders had taken Indian wives. The traders relied on them for their survival: to make pemmican, fish, gather berries, and carry provisions. Indian wives also prepared the traders' moccasins and snowshoes and helped repair their birchbark canoes. From their women the Europeans learned the customs and languages of the tribes. Their wives also acted as guides and interpreters. On the Plains the mixed-blood children of the European traders and their Indian wives became known as Metis in French, or Half-Breeds in English.[22] (Today, since their descendants prefer the use of the word Metis in English, as well as in French, this form is followed.)

The Metis borrowed from both Indian and European cultures. Bilingual and bicultural, they became indispensable to the fur trade, acting as interpreters, traders, clerks, canoemen, fur packers, and as manual laborers around the posts. The Metis took skills from both their European and Indian parents. To the leather crafts of the Indians the Metis women added the skill of using decorative glass beads (which were sold by the trading companies) to make colorful floral patterns.[23] They used leather and furs to make their clothes in the European style, and built homes of squared logs covered with bark roofs. From their European husbands the Metis women learned to make the round and flattish Scottish loaves of bread, or bannock, still a staple food in Alberta's Metis communities.

Most important of all, the Metis brought European technology to the prairies. Making some adaptations to the small wagons used by the French Canadians in the St. Lawrence Valley, they developed the Red River cart. Their two-wheeled ox-drawn vehicles transported furs and trade goods between the Red River settlement and St. Paul, Minnesota to the south, and later between the Red River and Fort Edmonton to the west. Today modern highways follow a number of those early routes once travelled by the hard-working Metis. A cart pulled by an ox carried a load of 1,000 pounds, twenty miles a day. Several carts could be tied together and a driver could handle five at a time. As they made the carts exclusively of wood (the pieces held together by wooden wedges, pegs, and shaganappi—the raw fresh skin of buffalo or cattle), a man could make one in a week. The carts could be repaired immediately with supplies at hand. To cross a river one simply took off the wheels, strapped them underneath the cart, and used the vehicle as a raft.[24]

The number of Metis at the junction of the Red and Assiniboine Rivers increased rapidly. Each year the community went out on its two great buffalo hunts, one in the spring, and the second in the fall. Thanks to their Red River carts they could take back much of the dried buffalo meat, or pemmican which they sold to the HBC for supplies. The Red River Metis, who totalled only 500 persons in 1821, increased to 2,600 in 1843, 3,250 in 1856, and to over 12,000 by 1870.[25]

As the HBC's need for pemmican declined in the mid-nineteenth century, a number of Metis left the Red River. By 1871, from 2,000 to 4,000 Metis lived along the North Saskatchewan River between the Red River and the Rockies.[26] In present day Alberta, Metis resided at Lac la Biche, Lake Athabasca, and Lac Ste Anne, fifty miles west of Fort Edmonton. Shortly after its founding in 1862, St. Albert (just nine miles from Fort Edmonton) became one of the largest Metis communities in the West.

The Indian Tribes in the Nineteenth Century

At the very moment that the mixed-blood population rapidly increased the number of Plains Indians declined. It is believed by archaeologists that when the native peoples crossed the land bridge to the new continent, the frigid region through which they passed served as a germ filter.[27] The diseased persons perished, and the survivors' descendants spread out in small bands over two continents. Consequently, communicable Old World diseases—such as pneumonia, influenza, smallpox, measles, and tuberculosis—all became extinct in the Americas.

Indian culture insured that the Old World diseases, once introduced by the Europeans, spread rapidly. The Indians shared almost everything in common, and lived in closely packed family groups in very small living areas, as much for warmth as for friendship. The idea of a quarantine being foreign to them, they insisted on visiting the sick to help, and in doing so unknowingly contributed to spreading the epidemics.[28]

The Plains Indian suffered incredible losses from smallpox. In the epidemic of 1780-81, David Thompson, the fur trader, estimated that the Indian population decreased by 50-60 percent. According to the HBC's traders, the Blackfoot, Blood, Peigan, Sarcee, and the Assiniboine suffered losses in the smallpox epidemic of 1837-38, of up to 75 percent of their population. It wiped out whole bands. Fortunately in 1837-38, the neighboring HBC's traders vaccinated the Plains Cree before the disease spread into their hunting territory, largely sparing them.[29]

John Palliser, the leader of a British exploration party which crossed the Canadian Plains in the years 1857-59, estimated: the Plains Cree north of the United States numbered about 11,500; the Assiniboine only 1,000 (with another 4,000 on the American side of the border); and the Blackfoot, Blood, Peigan, and Sarcee, respectively 600, 2,800, 4,400, and 1,100.[30] A smallpox epidemic again hit the Blackfoot in 1869-70, carrying away more than 1,000 Peigans, 600 Blackfoot, and 600 Bloods.[31] Before the Indians recovered from their losses, white traders from Montana brought northward a new disease, one almost as lethal as smallpox.

The Blackfoot in the 1850s and the early 1860s had traded with both the HBC to the north and the American Fur Company to the south. At Fort Edmonton and Rocky Mountain House they exchanged pemmican and horses (as well as the few beaver furs they trapped) for British trade goods. They took to the Americans the bulky buffalo hides and robes which were difficult for the HBC to transport profitably in their small York boats. The American Fur Company bought all they could, shipping them down the Missouri by steamer to St. Louis. But suddenly in 1864 the American Fur Company collapsed. The buffer zone between the two long-established companies became open ground. Shortly after the conclusion of the American Civil War in 1865, American whisky traders, many of them Civil War veterans, entered southern Alberta, anxious to make their fortunes.

The market for buffalo hides seemed inexhaustible. Eastern industry could not obtain enough. It used them to make belts for power machinery, and a market existed for buffalo coats. Throughout the western United States the great herds vanished before the guns of the buffalo hunters. Scores of independent traders from Montana, loaded down with whisky, crossed into British North America.

Anxious for profits the traders stripped the Blackfoot of their possessions: robes, pelts, horses, weapons—bought and sold for a few cups of "Blackfoot milk" or watered-down liquor. Most traders simply mixed alcohol with water, then added tea leaves and tobacco. Others mixed painkiller, tobacco, and molasses with the spirits, often adding a dash of red ink to give it color.[32] The northern Plains Indians had never made, or known fermented beverages, and had no social controls for them. Formerly they had traded for alcohol a few days at a time at distant trading posts, but now the drug came right to their camps. In the winter of 1872-73, seventy Bloods died in drunken quarrels amongst themselves. Many elders believed that their whole nation would be destroyed by a combination of alcohol, murder, and disease.[33]

The North West Mounted Police (NWMP) rescued the Blackfoot.[34] Sent west in 1874 to end incidents of violence (such as the massacre in 1873 of thirty Indians in the Cypress Hills by whites from Montana), the force quickly accomplished its goal. The closure of the whisky forts led to rapid changes in the Blackfoot camps. In the place of the tattered and worn lodges new ones appeared. Harmony again reigned. Within two years the Blackfoot had purchased more than 2,000 horses to replace those sold to the whisky traders.[35]

The Signing of Treaties Six and Seven

At the very moment that the Blackfoot had begun their recovery from the ravages of smallpox and whisky, the Crees, to the north, prepared to sign a treaty with the Canadian government. The English (and later the Canadian) government had, in word and in practice, recognized the legal right of Indian tribes to the lands which they occupied. As early as 1763 the British government set down the basic principles of British Indian Policy in a royal proclamation: henceforth settlers were prohibited from settling on territory that the Indians had not surrendered. The Crown alone reserved the right to acquire Indian lands, which had to be purchased with the consent of the respective band, at a general assembly of the Indians concerned.[36] This procedure had been followed in Upper Canada and was followed, by sheer necessity, in the West.

The federal government had been reminded of the power of native groups in the West by the Indian wars in the United States and by the Red River resistance of 1869-70. In 1870 the Canadians purchased

Rupert's Land from the HBC, but only after negotiating with Louis Riel and the Red River Metis could the Canadians take possession of the Red River. Under the terms of the compromise, the Metis were conceded the right to land scrip, or title to one-seventh of the Red River, and the colony became the new province of Manitoba. On account of the royal proclamation of 1763 the Canadian government would have to deal with the Indian tribes as well, particularly if it wished to avoid the long and expensive wars of the American West.

The Canadian government's Indian policy was quite simple: sign treaties with the Indians, place them on reserves, and then work to assimilate them into Canadian society. From 1871-75, Treaties One to Five—which promised the Indians annuities, reserves, and the liberty to hunt and fish on Crown land—were signed in present day northwestern Ontario, Manitoba, and Saskatchewan. In 1876 the Treaty Commissioners came to negotiate a treaty with the Cree of central Alberta and Saskatchewan; in 1877 they approached the Blackfoot tribes, the Sarcee, and the Stoneys in southern Alberta.

The Canadian government, from its standpoint, proposed the treaties at an ideal time. First, the epidemics had seriously reduced the number of Plains warriors. Second, the tribes were divided among themselves, with the Cree fighting the Blackfoot, and the Assiniboine antagonistic to the Sioux. Among the Indians few chiefs recognized the need to form a common pan-Indian front against the white invader; tribal loyalties remained too strong. Third, even the individual tribes were split amongst themselves with the Plains Cree feeling haughty and superior to the Woods Cree.[37] Fourth, Canada also benefitted from the fact that the American Army had largely subdued its Plains Indians. Although roughly 50 percent of the Blackfoot Confederacy lived in Montana, the Canadian Blackfoot could not count on the southern Peigans (called the Blackfeet by the Americans) now under the control of the American army. Finally, the Indians were vulnerable since the mainstay of their way of life had almost vanished by the mid-1870s.

Much apprehension existed in the Treaty Six area that the buffalo soon would be extinct. At Fort Edmonton in 1871, Chief Sweet Grass of the Cree had asked the Chief HBC Factor of the district to draft up a petition on their behalf: "Our country is getting ruined of fur bearing animals, hitherto our sole support, and now we are poor and want help—we want you to pity us. We want cattle, tools, agricultural implements, and assistance in everything when we come to settle—our country is no longer able to support us."[38]

When Lieutenant-Governor Alexander Morris of the Northwest Territories and the Treaty Commissioners arrived in 1876 to negotiate the treaty, the plains Cree agreed, but only after the government promised to supply aid and rations in the event of "any pestilence" or "general famine." They also obtained the guarantee that a "medicine chest" would be kept by every Indian Agent in the Treaty Six area. These new clauses had never before been included in a treaty. The purchase dealt with the rights to 120,000 square miles of land in present day central

Saskatchewan and Alberta, an area as large as England, Scotland, Wales, and Ireland combined.

At the negotiations at Forts Carlton and Pitt the interpreters occupied by far the most important roles. They had to explain the concept of a land surrender, one completely foreign to the Indians' culture. No doubt some Plains Indians prior to 1876 did indeed see a connection between the whites' use of their land and a treaty to compensate them for such use.[39] But did they understand the European's idea of a land purchase? How could the interpreter translate sentences such as:

> The Plain and Wood Cree Tribes of Indians, and all the other Indians inhabiting the district hereinafter described and defined, do hereby cede, release, surrender and yield up to the Government of the Dominion of Canada for Her Majesty the Queen and her successors forever, all their rights, titles and privileges whatsoever, to the lands included within the following limits. . . . And also, all their rights, titles and privileges whatsoever to all other lands wherever situated in the North-west Territories, or in any other Province or portion of Her Majesty's Dominions, situated and being within the Dominion of Canada.[40]

The enormous cultural gap resulted in two totally different interpretations of the meaning of Treaty Six. The whites left with one idea of what the agreement meant, the Indians with another. As early as August 1884 an unidentified native spokesman made the following statement during an Indian council at Fort Carlton:

> The Governor Morris comes and tells the Indian we are not coming to buy your land. It is a big thing. It is impossible for a man to buy the whole country, we come here to borrow the country to keep it for you. I want my children to come here and live at peace with you, to live like two brothers.
> The Indians therefore understand that the country is only borrowed not bought.[41]

Initially not all of the chiefs made treaty. One of the Cree chiefs who freely roamed with his band over much of present day Alberta and Saskatchewan refused to sign. Big Bear saw little of value in Treaty Six. Born on the prairies around 1825, Big Bear had an illustrious war record. As a young man the Cree leader had been fearless and successful on the warpath. A stocky athletic man with a rather square face, he was a great equestrian. Within sight of enemy tribesmen he could ride, clinging spider-like to the side of the galloping horse and, while using the animal as a shield, shoot out at them from the underside of the horse's neck. A very effective orator, he spoke in a loud and deep voice. One fur trader later wrote that he reminded him of "an Imperial Caesar and one of the most eloquent and impressive speakers I have ever listened to."[42] By the mid-1870s, he had become one of the most influential Plains leaders. In 1876 Big Bear held out: he rejected the Canadian government's Treaty Six since he correctly saw it would end the Plains Crees' independence. But in 1876 only a minority of Cree warriors followed him, the vast majority allowing their chiefs to make their respective marks on the document.

To the southwest the three Blackfoot tribes—the Blackfoot, Blood, and Peigan—and the Sarcee and the Stoney, all remained outside of the Canadian government's treaty system. Largely due to their gratitude to the NWMP, however, the tribes did make treaty in 1877 at the Blackfoot Crossing in southern Alberta. Crowfoot, a leading Blackfoot chief, and Red Crow, an influential Blood chief, trusted the Red Coats who had so promptly expelled the whisky traders. They believed that Bull's Head, as they called Colonel James F. Macleod, the NWMP's Commissioner, would not support the treaty negotiations unless the terms were advantageous to the Indians.[43]

Misunderstandings resulted from both Treaties Six and Seven. A century later the elders in the Treaty Six area claim that the Indians only handed over the surface rights to the land, namely those required for farming.[44] Treaty Seven elders contend that Treaty Seven was a peace treaty, and not an instrument of land surrender at all.[45] Perhaps Father Constantine Scollen, who had been present at the Treaty Seven negotiations in 1877, provided the best summary of the treaty, when he wrote in 1879:

> Did these Indians, or do they now, understand the real nature of the treaty made between the Government and themselves in 1877? My answer to this question is unhesitatingly negative. . . . It may be asked: if the Indians did not understand what the treaty meant, why did they sign it? Because previous to the treaty they had always been kindly dealt with by the authorities (the NWMP), and did not wish to offend them; and, although they had many doubts in their mind as to the meaning of the treaty, yet with this precedent before them, they hoped that it simply meant to furnish them plenty of food and clothing. . . every time they stood in need of them.[46]

At the negotiations Crowfoot played the decisive role. Alone among the Blackfoot chiefs he had come to know well the HBC's trader Richard Hardisty, Father Albert Lacombe, and Commissioner Macleod. Born around 1830 the Blackfoot chief was Big Bear's complete antithesis. A compromiser and a conciliator, Crowfoot saw ahead to the eventual disappearance of the buffalo. Aware that thousands of white settlers would soon arrive, he wanted to make peace with the government. The whites regarded Crowfoot as the head chief of the Blackfoot Confederacy—which he was not, being only a leading chief in his own tribe. But because of his greater knowledge of the white man, the other chiefs—such as the Blood Chief Red Crow, who commanded far more warriors than Crowfoot—deferred to his judgment. Weighing the dangers for his people, and finding them outweighed by the possible benefits, Crowfoot led them into Treaty Seven.[47]

The Native Majority Becomes a Minority

At several points during the negotiation of the Treaty, Crowfoot consulted an old medicine man named Pemmican. On the first two occasions this aged man, known for his great wisdom and supernatural insight, had not answered Crowfoot's questions about the Treaty. But on this third occasion, Pemmican, in a feeble, but a still audible voice, replied:

> I want to hold you back because I am at the edge of a bank. My life is at its end. I hold you back because your life henceforth will be different from what it has been. Buffalo makes your body strong. What you will eat from this money will have your people buried all over these hills. You will be tied down, you will not wander the plains; the whites will take your land and fill it. You won't have your own free will; the whites will lead you by a halter. That is why I say don't sign. But my life is old, so sign if you want to. Go ahead and make the treaty.[48]

Pemmican's words proved prophetic. Within a year after the Indians had scrawled their large crosses on the treaty document, their way of life was completely altered. While both Indian and white realized that the numbers of buffalo had sharply declined, no one anticipated their disappearance on the Canadian side of the border in just two years. In 1877, David Laird, Morris' replacement as Lieutenant-Governor of the Northwest Territories, had himself estimated that the buffalo would last at least a decade.[49] The years 1878-80 proved ones of incredible suffering.

Faced with starvation, thousands of Canadian Indians—including Big Bear and his followers—crossed the border into Montana in search of the last great herds of buffalo. In Canada the Blackfoot and Plains Cree lived off mice and gophers, and had to pick over the putrid carcasses of dead animals left rotting on the Plains. By the winter of 1879-80 the NWMP fed 7,000 Indians every other day on their own scanty rations. Cattle thieving became common since the starving Indians were often forced to steal. In 1879 the first NWMP constable was murdered by an unknown Indian.[50]

At the treaty negotiations in 1876 and 1877, the Canadian government had promised the Indians reserves based on an allotment of one square mile for a family of five. Believing that they could continue their nomadic hunting culture for years to come, few Indians had immediately taken up their reserve land. The Canadians had also promised a small annuity, agricultural implements, and—to train them for their settled way of life—schools. Suddenly all of these pledges became significant and meaningful. But in 1879-80 the Canadian government was not ready. No one had foreseen the buffalo's sudden disappearance. The survey of the reserves on which the Indians must now settle remained uncompleted. The Department of Indian Affairs had only become a separate office in 1880. As soon as the Indians selected their reserves, the Indian Department instructed them to take up their lands. To obtain rations most of the bands did so, and by the winter of 1882-83 the majority had settled on them.[51] In 1882, Big Bear himself adhered to Treaty Six. His people badly needed the government's rations.

The final stage of the Canadian government's Indian policy began: with the treaties duly signed, and the vast majority of the Indians placed on reserves, now the third process—the assimilation of the Indian—commenced. In 1876 the Canadian Parliament passed the first Indian

Act, codifying all the existing federal Indian legislation. Under the Act (as amended in 1880) the Indian agent obtained a dictatorial control over the reserves, as did the Christian churches over the reserve schools. Together church and state would work toward the disappearance of the Indian's distinct culture, a development believed to .be to their benefit. Through education, religion, and new political and economic systems the government hoped to eradicate old values, and eventually to eliminate the Indian reserves themselves.[52] White Canadians universally supported the Indian agents and missionaries. Two world wars later intervened to shake their confidence in "civilization" and in their own western culture; but in the late nineteenth century Canadians, Americans, and Europeans had few doubts or uncertainties about their role to "raise up" the dark-skinned peoples throughout the world.

The Indians resisted the Canadian government's assimilationist policies. Crowfoot, the first important chief to support the signing of Treaty Seven, became the first to question it. He found the new Indian Department officials (to whom the NWMP transferred much of their authority in the early 1880s) to be callous in their treatment of his people. Feeling betrayed, the Blackfoot Chief defied the NWMP for the first time in 1882 when they tried to arrest a minor tribal chief.[53] Believing that the whites had broken their treaty promises, Crowfoot became distrustful of the government.

The year 1883 marks the end of the Plains Indians' independent existence in the Canadian West. With the completion of the prairie section of the CPR, built in fifteen months from the summer of 1882 to the late summer of 1883, the native peoples' isolation ended as hundreds of whites began moving westward. The Canadian government's haste to settle the West led to friction, and eventually to an armed uprising in present day Saskatchewan.[54]

The Northwest Rebellion of 1885

In retrospect the Riel Rebellion seems to have been a totally futile exercise. Only several hundred Metis around Batoche, in the South Saskatchewan River Valley, and several hundred Cree warriors living around Battleford, near the present day Alberta-Saskatchewan border, participated—against a country whose population numbered four million. But the struggle would have been far more serious if the other Metis (particularly those around Saint Albert) and if the majority of the Indians in present day Alberta had joined as well. The Indians and Metis might have kept alive a campaign of guerrilla warfare, preventing any large-scale settlement for years. The Indians and Metis, both experts in guerrilla warfare, knew the unfenced prairie, the location of fords across the rivers still unbridged, and the narrow trails through the dense forests to the north. Big Bear himself, in fact, evaded over 1,000 Canadian troops for the entire month of June 1885. They only captured him when he gave himself up on 2 July.[55]

When Louis Riel and the Metis at Batoche began their uprising in late

March 1885, Crowfoot and the Blackfoot tribe came very close to participating: half-starved, confined on their new reserve, dependent on government relief, what did they have to lose? To the north, in the distant
Frog Lake and Battleford areas, the two Cree bands of Big Bear and
Poundmaker took up arms. In the end, however, the Blackfoot and the
Indians of Alberta stayed out of the conflict. Many factors contributed to
the Indians' decision. First, the missionaries influenced their response.
Quickly Roman Catholic and Methodist missionaries travelled among
the bands urging them to stay on their reserves. Initially, a number of
the younger Cree warriors in the Battle River area (near present day
Hobbema) had favored participation. Only the tribal elders, aware of the
white man's power, had held them back.[56] Second, the prompt dispatch
from Calgary of the 1,000-man Alberta Field Force led to the pacification
of the Battle River area and the Lac la Biche district to the northeast
(where the HBC's post had been raided). While tempted to join the
rebellion the Blackfoot in the end did not. Crowfoot had lost faith in the
government, and yet he knew the strength of the Canadians. The previous year they had shown him Winnipeg, a town of 15,000 with enough
men and ammunition to defeat the entire Blackfoot tribe. The government's speedy dispatch of extra rations to the reserve, and of several
thousand troops to western Canada, also convinced him to remain at
peace. As for the Bloods, their ancestral hatred of the Metis and Cree
exceeded their dislike of the white man. Several Blood warriors, in fact,
even offered to fight on the government's behalf.[57]

While, no doubt, some support existed for Riel among the French-
speaking Metis at the mission villages of Lac Ste Anne, St. Albert, and
Lac la Biche, important differences existed between these Metis and
those around Batoche, three hundred miles to the east. First, most of the
Edmonton-area Metis had been born in the region and, unlike many of
the Metis in the South Saskatchewan Valley, had not served with Riel in
the Red River in 1869-70, or participated in the angry exodus from
Manitoba in the 1870s. Second, the surveyors had respected St. Albert's
river lots and had not resurveyed them, as had happened at Batoche,
further antagonizing the Metis. Finally, the Roman Catholic Church
(unlike that at Batoche where Riel had successfully led a revolt against
the priests) remained unchallenged in Alberta's Metis communities. The
Church's influence kept Alberta's Metis out of the struggle. The possibility of earning money by freighting and clearing bush for the Alberta
Field Force even led a number of Metis to work, and others to fight, for
the government. A militia unit, the St. Albert Mounted Rifles, sixty men
strong, left for Lac la Biche in early June.[58]

Throughout the uprising the Indians often knew of developments
before the white settlers. The rapidity by which the news travelled was
amazing. At the white settlement of Gleichen, located by the Blackfoot
(Siksika) reserve, the Indians learned of Riel's capture hours before the
whites did, even though the news came to the whites by telegraph. The
Indians could communicate over vast distances by using smoke signals,
and on bright sunny days through the use of mirrors.[59]

The Plains Indian from 1885 to the Outbreak of World War I

After the Rebellion, western settlement began in earnest. Nearly 500,000 white settlers migrated to present day Alberta from 1885 to 1914, most of them arriving after 1900. Overnight a new society arose, one which was ignorant of the area's previous history. The railway brought west people who, unlike the early Mounties, had not seen the Plains Indians before the demise of the buffalo. These newcomers had little understanding of, or respect for, Indians. Even the well-educated shared the common settlers' prejudices. In the first *History of the Province of Alberta (1912)* for example, the author, Dr. Archibald Oswald MacRae, principal of Calgary's Western Canada College, made this assessment of native character: "The Red Man of the West has always been a difficult individual, he does not care to work, to beg he is not ashamed. In consequence he tends to become shiftless and vagrant."[60]

The Plains Indian felt the reservation system's full impact at the turn of the century. Contrary to the treaty promises the Indians needed a pass, available only from the Indian agent, to leave their reserves. No longer could they wander at ease, pitch their camps wherever they pleased, take water from any stream, hunt antelope or other game wherever they wished. One of the great equestrian cultures of history had become stationary, reduced by circumstance to a welfare society, dependent on the Indian agent's rations. The assault on the existing native values was continual. Attempts, for example, were made to curtail Indian religious ceremonies, particularly the annual Sun Dances, which the Plains Indians celebrated in mid-summer to give thanks to the Great Spirit.[61]

Both the agent and the missionary worked through the schools to turn the Indians into self-reliant Christian farmers. In an age in which governmental financial support for status Indians was very slight, the churches wanted desperately for the reserves to become self-supporting. Unfortunately at no point were the Indians themselves involved in the planning—the communication was one-way.

In hindsight we understand what the older Indians, and perhaps to a lesser extent the Plains Metis, underwent in the late nineteenth and early twentieth centuries. The dominant society expected the native peoples to transform a way of life, nearly 10,000 years old, in the space of a decade or two. One wishes that the series of transformations in their society had come over a longer period of time, allowing the Plains Indians to adapt to them. The sudden immersion into a strange culture led to tremendous frustration and disorientation. It was as if the Indians and Metis were given one week to pass through the same changes that other societies had passed through in centuries.

What the Plains Indians and Plains Metis[62] experienced in the 1880s and 1890s has today been termed "future shock," the result of the far too rapid superimposition of a new culture on an old one. As one student of the phenomenon has written:

> Take an individual out of his own culture and set him down suddenly in an
> environment sharply different from his own, with a different set of cues to

react to—different conceptions of time, space, work, love, religion, sex, and everything else—then cut him off from any hope of retreat to a more familiar social landscape, and the dislocation he suffers is doubly severe.[63]

It is a credit to many of the tribespeople that their inner strength and perseverance allowed them to adjust to the new conditions as well as they did.

Treaty Eight and the Half-Breed Claims Commission of 1899-1900

The Canadian government extended its Indian policy northward in 1899-1900. At the turn of the century a few Klondike Gold Rush prospectors on their way north had entered the Athabasca and Peace River areas. Seeing the rich farm potential of the Peace, a number stayed to farm. Anxious to obtain full title to these areas of known mineral wealth and agricultural potential, the federal government sent a treaty party in 1899-1900 to negotiate Treaty Eight.[64] The Woodland Indians signed at various points in northern Alberta and Saskatchewan, and in that area of the Northwest Territories immediately south of Great Slave Lake. Again,

The Metis became indispensable to the fur trade and to the transport of goods in general in western Canada. They also proved of great assistance to the early settlers. This early photo shows Metis portaging a scow over a portage on the Slave River in 1901. (Ernest Brown photo, courtesy Provincial Archives of Alberta)

as in the south, the encouragement of the NWMP and the missionaries led the Indians to accept the treaty. In the Indians' minds the treaty only permitted the white man's use of portions of their territory. They believed that it was a friendship pact, not a land surrender, which was a concept totally foreign to their culture. The government had assured them that they had retained all their rights to hunt, trap, and fish. Their old way of life would not be restricted, and the government officials had even promised them assistance in times of need.[65]

While the treaty commissioners dealt with the Indians a half-breed commissioner met the Metis. As in Treaties One to Seven the commissioner offered the Metis who were "living like Indians" (a number of the Metis in the Treaty Eight area fell into this category, since they only spoke Cree and lived in small family groups, hunting and trapping) the choice of entering the treaty or of accepting scrip.[66] All scrip fell into one of two distinct categories. The father of each Metis family could receive land scrip (a piece of paper which he could use to claim 240 acres of land) or cash scrip (a piece of paper worth $240 for the purchase of land). Although the Roman Catholic clergy encouraged the Metis to take the treaty, many ignored their priests and took scrip. A large number did not want to be under the Indian Act and be subject to the restrictions of treaty Indians on reserves.[67]

The majority of those Metis taking scrip selected the cash scrip, the most easily transferable. Land speculators bought it up quickly for resale to settlers and to other speculators. Many of the Metis who had taken land scrip also sold it as they really had little interest in farming. Only a few knew about proper agricultural techniques. They also lacked money to buy seeds, plows, and animals to pull the plows. Many decided that it would be better to sell their bounty, take the money, and then retreat into more isolated country where fish and game still abounded.[68] As soon as the scrip had been distributed the majority of Metis gave it up for a sum lower than the scrip's face value, or were cheated out of their scrips altogether. A title worth $240 generally was bought up for $165. Some exchanged their titles for a reasonable sum of money, some for alcohol or horses, and others for mere trifles. Only a few really benefitted from the scrip granted immediately after the rebellion in 1885-87 and that given again in 1899-1900 in the Treaty Eight area.[69]

The Indians, for all of the injustices of the treaties, gained more long-term material advantages from the government than did the Metis who took scrip. Those mixed-bloods who surrendered their share in the Northwest's aboriginal title for a single payment in cash or land in most cases quickly spent it. In contrast the treaty Indians, and those Metis who signed the treaty, gained a small initial cash settlement, and thereafter, reserves, annuities, education, and eventually medical benefits. They also enjoyed a special legal protection or special status.

A Metis Reserve: St. Paul des Métis, 1896-1910

There was one attempt in the late nineteenth century to grant the Metis special status. The Roman Catholic church sponsored a Metis reserve, purchasing four townships of land, twenty-four square miles in area, near the Saddle Lake Indian reserve. In July 1896 the experiment, named St. Paul des Métis, began. The government and the church promised to make land, equipment, livestock, and schools available to the Metis settlers. But the project soon experienced considerable difficulties due to inadequate funding from the federal and territorial governments, and all of the promises could not be met. The federal government only gave an initial grant of $2,000, and the church itself and the missionaries could not provide each of the fifty Metis families with all the necessary livestock and agricultural implements. Lack of money prevented the missionaries from opening more than a day school on the farming colony.

Of those Metis attracted to St. Paul few had previously farmed. Without proper livestock and equipment they found it difficult indeed. While several families did become successful farmers, St. Paul on the whole did not prosper. The reserve simply did not produce enough to finance its schools, churches, and roads. Reluctantly in 1908 the missionaries ended the experiment, introducing French Canadian settlers to the area. In 1910—with the government's approval—the church opened up St. Paul for settlement by anyone. The missionaries, though, failed to consult the Metis at all about their decision.

Although the church gave the Metis families on the reserve title to the lands they occupied, many felt isolated and sold their farms once the whites arrived. In a short time most of the Metis families had left, moving further north and west in search of vacant land. Many departed resentful of the church and the government. For thirty years a number of them kept alive their dream of a future Metis reserve, an area to be controlled by themselves and not the church.[70]

The Native Peoples from the Outbreak of World War I to the End of World War II

In the early twentieth century, treaty Indians also faced difficult conditions. Health and education remained problem areas. Both Indians and Metis suffered greatly from infectious diseases spread by a poor diet, inadequate sewage and garbage disposal, and by their living conditions in poorly ventilated mud huts and log shanties.[71] Each year hundreds of babies died from measles, influenza, scarlet fever, and especially tuberculosis. After World War I the mortality rate remained high. At the four Cree reserves at Hobbema, about eighty miles south of Edmonton, the deadly worldwide Spanish flu epidemic of 1918 carried off 90 of the 850 Indians.[72] The Indian population of Alberta fell in a generation by two-thirds, from about 18,000 in the 1870s to less than 6,000 by the 1920s.[73]

The Indian death rate continued to be considerable until the Department of Indian Affairs began in the 1920s to establish organized health services for the status Indians. Additional hospitals, nursing care, and (particularly after World War II) improved living conditions, all helped. The opening of the Charles Camsell Indian Hospital in Edmonton in

1945 would contribute to checking the spread of tuberculosis. From the late 1920s onwards the population of the status Indians in western Canada began to rise.[74]

The education system improved much more slowly than Indian health care. At the turn of the century the churches viewed residential schools as the most effective institutions for assimilating the Indian. They separated the Indian children from their parents, banned the use of their tribal languages and the practice of their religious beliefs and rituals. The goal, as one Methodist educator had written in 1911 in his pamphlet entitled *The Indian Problem in Alberta*, remained to educate "a primitive race in the ideals of a higher form of culture."[75] The constant discouragement at school of all things culturally or religiously Indian, had a disastrous psychological effect on the students.[76] A few undoubtedly profitted from their boarding school education, leaving ready to compete in the white man's world as farmers and ranchers; but others emerged emotionally scarred by the experience, convinced of the inferiority of their native background to that of the white man. The residential schools remained the most important aspect of the Indian educational system until the 1960s.

At the very moment that their numbers declined, and the white newcomers took away their children, the treaty Indians suffered another reversal. In the early twentieth century, the government reduced the Indians' land base. Seeing the Indians' shrinking population, the federal government encouraged land surrenders. Through the sale of their "idle" lands, the Indian Department argued, the bands could improve their living conditions. Immediately before World War I, several of the bands accepted the federal government's offers. In the early twentieth century the bands ceded approximately one-sixth of the total land base of the Indians of Alberta (roughly 500 out of 3,000 square miles).[77] Tragically, however, most of the funds raised by the sales went to pay for costs normally incurred by the government, such as issuing rations and constructing agency buildings. In the long run those reserves making land surrenders showed no noticeable advancement or benefits over those which did not.[78]

Despite their difficult adjustment to a new way of life the Alberta Indians supported Canada's war effort from 1914 to 1918. The fighting spirit of the Plains Indian remained very much alive despite one generation of reserve life. A number of Alberta Indians served overseas, even though the Military Service Act of 1917 exempted treaty Indians from conscription. From the Anglican residential school on the Blood Reserve, for example, eight former students enlisted, and two died while in uniform. Corporal Norwest, an Indian from the Edmonton area, became one of the greatest snipers in the Canadian army, and was credited with 115 observed hits. At home Indians formed Red Cross societies and other patriotic organizations. Of the $44,500 contributed to patriotic organizations by Canadian Indian reserves, Alberta bands gave $8,650.[79]

The Metis, viewed as having the same responsibilities as any other Canadian citizens, were liable when Parliament introduced military conscription in 1917. A number of Metis had already enlisted voluntarily. At the end of the war, in fact, Brigadier-General H. F. MacDonald, who had Indian ancestry, commanded the Alberta Military District.[80]

A major reversal beset Alberta's Indians after the war. As late as 1923 the Calgary *Herald* could report: "It is a general belief that in the next two generations the inhabitants of the Indian reservations will be merely colonies of civilized people, principally farmers."[81] The reality turned out to be quite different. Two generations later few Albertan Indians farmed.

In the 1920s the mechanization of western Canadian agriculture quickly proceeded, and the Indians simply were not ready for the trans-formation. Very painfully many Albertan Indians had learned how to farm—to cope with the short growing season, the early frosts, the sum-mer hails, and the grasshoppers. But in the postwar era, the horse and plough style of farming ended as mechanized equipment entered Alberta. Larger acreages became necessary. The successful farmer needed to know modern business techniques, and how to secure bank loans. Not owning his farm on the reserve (held communally by the band) the Indian farmers had no collateral, and the banks could not grant them loans. In the 1920s and 1930s, and particularly the 1940s, Indian farming declined. White farmers began leasing large areas of the reserves.

On a visit to a southern Alberta reserve in the 1920s one would have found a population living poorly in contrast with the surrounding non-Indian settlements: their clothes were of a lesser quality, their homes smaller, and cars absent. Few Indians had the same amount of schooling as did their white neighbors. Only a minority spoke English. The Indians faced discrimination. In 1921 farmers around Calgary paid $4 a day to European harvesters, but to Indians working in the same fields, only $2.50. The Indians' main occupations, farming or ranching, offered little more than a bare subsistence.[82] When the Great Depression arrived in late 1929 many Indians, their lives being already so marginal, barely became aware of it.[83]

Politically, if not economically, the interwar years proved to be very important for the Alberta Indian. The first Indian political organizations in the province date back to the 1920s and 1930s. On 29 June 1922, over 1,500 Blackfoot, Stoney, Cree, and Assiniboine delegates, from across western Canada held a conference at the Samson Reserve at Hobbema. One gift of the white newcomers was prized at the meeting—English. It became the Indians' common tongue. The League of Indians led by Fred Loft, a Mohawk Indian from Ontario who had founded this organization in 1919, sponsored the meeting. At Hobbema in 1922 (as at earlier conferences in Ontario in 1919, Manitoba in 1920, and Saskatchewan in 1921), the delegates challenged the arbitrary power of the Indian Affairs Branch. Further meetings followed, and in 1929 Indians in the prairie provinces officially formed the "League of Indians in Western Canada." This new organization held conferences at the Saddle Lake Reserve near St. Paul, Alberta, in 1931 and 1932; at Paul's Band at Duffield, Alberta in 1933 and 1935; and at the Enoch Reserve near Edmonton in 1934.

Finally an Indian voice was being heard, if not yet being listened to, by the federal government. The Indians called for on-reserve schools, extra rations for the old people, an end to land surrenders, and the preservation of Indian hunting, trapping, and fishing rights.[84]

The Woodland Indians and the Metis in northern Alberta shared many of the same concerns as the Plains Indians in the interwar years. By far the most serious challenge the north faced was the decline of the area's hunting and fishing potential. After the Klondike Gold Rush, well-equipped white trappers and free traders had continued to move into the territory, making the competition for furs intense. By the 1930s outsiders flew into distant traplines. In the summer, southerners fished the lakes commercially, flying out the fish to eastern markets. The drop in fur prices, the scarcity of fur-bearing animals, and the growing number of governmental restrictions made it very difficult for many Indians and Metis to live by hunting and fishing. The provincial government (which had obtained jurisdiction of northern Alberta in 1905) had imposed fish and game restrictions on Indian trappers and fishermen, in direct violation to the promises made by the federal government in Treaty Eight.[85]

Just as the Plains Indians in the south had organized politically to fight for their rights, the Metis in the north did the same. The incentive to do so came in the late 1920s with the announced transfer, in 1930, of the Crown lands in the three prairie provinces, hitherto federal property, to the provinces. The Natural Resources Transfer Act of 1930 stipulated that only national parks and Indian reserves would remain under federal control. In essence, this decision meant that the Metis, many of whom had squatted on Crown Land for years, could now be evicted, since the province wanted to open the new lands to settlement.

To protect their native rights Joe Dion organized the Alberta Metis Association, and the Metis school teacher served as its first President.[86] Around him he gathered a group of four remarkable men—Malcolm Norris, Jim Brady, Felix Callihoo, and Peter Tomkins—all of whom were elected in 1932 to form the first executive of the L'Association des Métis d'Alberta et des Territoires du Nord Ouest (in 1940 the name of the organization changed to the Metis Association of Alberta). The Metis had many grievances: the terrible health conditions, the lack of schools and of jobs, the refusal of municipal governments to grant relief to many Metis families. The Association also spoke of the need to re-create the St. Paul des Métis experiment—to establish reserves for the Metis,[86] who needed a land base.[87] Under Dion's leadership the Association established a strong presence in Alberta. Norris and Brady did much of the planning, the public speaking, and the writing. Callihoo and Tomkins worked with local groups to help them organize. By 1934 Dion and the Executive had built up an organization of forty-one local groups, with a total membership of just over 1,200.[88] They exerted enough political pressure to convince the provincial government to appoint the Ewing Commission (named after its Chairman, J. W. Ewing, an Alberta Supreme Court Judge) to examine the Metis' grievances.

The Ewing Commission held its hearings in 1935, receiving testimony from the clergy, medical doctors, MLAs, and the Metis Association. The following year it recommended in its published report that certain of the Metis' demands for land, health, and educational services be met. In 1938 the legislature passed the Metis Population Betterment Act.[89] Six years of political pressure from the Metis Association had paid off. Under the Act, the Metis could join together and form settlement associations. Once recognized, these Associations would have land set aside for them which, like a reserve, could not be sold by the Metis (to avoid the mistake of granting scrip). In the late 1930s the government made several land allotments for the Metis. Today eight settlements or colonies exist in central and northern Alberta (originally there were nine, but the government reclaimed the Wolf Lake Settlement). They comprise about 2,000 square miles, and support 3,200 people. Since the 1940s, however, the provincial government has regarded the settlement scheme as too costly, and has not extended it to the general Metis population. The Metis feared until the summer of 1985 (when the provincial government promised them clear title to their lands) that the existing settlements themselves could be eliminated by a single act of the provincial government.[90]

Malcolm Norris, one of the organizers of the Alberta Metis Association, also contributed in the early 1940s to the founding of the first modern Indian political organization in the province, the Indian Association of Alberta (IAA), the successor to the earlier, League of Indians of Western Canada.[91] Born into a middle class Metis family in 1900, Norris had been greatly influenced by socialist thought, and had devoted his life to bettering the native peoples' position in western Canada. Norris advised John Callihoo, the organizer of the new Indian political group, and provided him with a constitution and bylaws, modelled on those drawn up by Jim Brady for the Metis Association.[92] A general convention later ratified them and also agreed upon the new name, the Indian Association of Alberta. During the war years, Norris continued to advise Callihoo and to help him build unity in the movement, particularly between the Blackfoot and the Cree.

The IAA pressed the government to curtail Indian land sales, to hire Indians in the Indian Affairs Branch, and to define reserve boundaries. The organization also passed a series of motions urging that conditions be improved on the reserves. In 1945 the IAA demanded changes in the entire system of Indian education. It sought twelve reforms including improved facilities, better textbooks, a relevant curriculum, suitably qualified teachers, and the creation of day schools.[93] The Metis Association of Alberta in the 1930s and the IAA in the 1940s both effectively made native opinions known.

The Native Peoples of Alberta from the End of World War II to the Present

Conditions improved considerably for many treaty Indians in Alberta after the war. Thousands of Canadian Indians, Metis, and nonstatus Indians had served in Canada's armed forces. The close contact this created between white Canadian soldiers and native people led to an increased concern about Indian issues. After the war Canada's social welfare system was expanded, as the idea spread of the government's responsibility to provide at least a minimum living standard for all its citizens.[94] The federal government could count after 1945 on public support to help the Indian, whose malnutrition and poor health were now publicized as a national disgrace. Throughout this period the IAA and other Indian organizations kept up the pressure on politicians. Gradually the federal government extended the entire social welfare system (family allowance, old age security, and other social welfare measures) to the Indian population.

Thanks to improved medical attention the Indian population continued to grow. Alberta's Indians benefitted from the extension of the vaccination programmes, and the better living conditions established on the reserves. Today's high birth rate, and declining death rate, prove how real the progress has been. Since 1945 the number of treaty Indians in Alberta has nearly tripled (despite the appalling infant mortality rate, which, as late as 1977, was twice that of the provincial population). In the late 1960s the birth rate of the status Indians stood at more than double the birth rate of the total provincial population. Although it declined slightly in the mid-1970s, in 1976 it remained nearly double that of the provincial population.[95] While the population grows rapidly, however, the land base remains stationary.

The federal government has also improved the education provided the treaty Indian. First, Indian students are encouraged to complete high school, and to enter technical colleges and universities. Second, in the 1960s the federal government took over control of the reserve schools from the churches, which for years had received insufficient financial assistance. The Indian students now attend better-funded federal and provincial schools. Today a number of bands have taken over control of their own school systems. In 1971 Blue Quills, established by the residents of the Saddle Lake-Athabasca Reserve located near St. Paul, became the first Indian-administered school in Canada.[96] Many Indian elders support this new approach to education. They call for truly bilingual and bicultural programmes:

> In order to survive in the twentieth century, we must come to grips with the whiteman's culture and with the whiteman's ways. We must stop lamenting the past. The whiteman has many good things . . . for example, his technology. We must take these things and discover and establish the harmonies with basic values of the Indian, and thereby forge a new and a stronger sense of identity. To be fully Indian today, we must become bilingual and bicultural.[97]

Considerable political progress has also been made since 1945. The revised Indian Act of 1951, while retaining the federal government's strong control over the bands, did give their councils increased powers. In the late nineteenth and early twentieth centuries chiefs and councils had indeed been given certain authority, but in practice, the Indian agent made all the vital decisions. A generation of Indians had grown up with little experience in managing their own affairs. After 1951 the Indian administration somewhat relaxed its paternalistic and authoritarian policies. Status Indians obtained the vote in federal elections in 1960 and in provincial elections in Alberta in 1965. In 1958 James Gladstone, a Blood Indian rancher and former President of the Indian Association of Alberta, became the first Canadian Indian appointed to sit in the Canadian Senate. Another first came in 1965 when Mrs. Lillian Pruden of the Beaver Lake band near Lac la Biche became the first woman chief elected in Alberta.[98]

Further political advances came in the 1960s. By the end of the decade, college-trained Indians began to take up positions in band administrations. Councils assumed more responsibility for their own affairs. The post of Indian agent was eliminated, and his job was taken over by superintendents who moved away to nearby centers such as Edmonton, Calgary, or Lethbridge. The powers of the chief and councillors compare today to those of a mayor and town council. The Indians in southern Alberta themselves run the public works, housing, welfare, and other services on the reserves.[99] The Department of Indian Affairs' financial control, however, remains much greater over those bands without their own oil and gas revenues.

Since 1945 perhaps the greatest development for nearly 50 percent of the forty-two Indian bands of Alberta (eighteen out of forty-two) has been the discovery of oil and gas on their reserves. In 1979 the richest group, the four wealthy Cree bands near Hobbema, obtained about $47 million (more than $10,000 per capita) from oil and gas royalties. That same year the Department of Indian Affairs also put an equal amount from oil and gas revenues in the respective bands' trust funds. Bands with resource revenue have developed commercial projects. The Samson Band of Hobbema had in 1979 their own trust company, real estate and rental properties in Edmonton, a 700-acre feed lot, thousands of head of beef cattle, and a $750,000 grain-handling system. The Ermineskin band has made investments in film productions. Near Edmonton and Calgary the Enoch and the Sarcee bands respectively have large-scale real estate development projects. The Blood tribe is developing its cattle business and a house-construction factory. [100]

In northern Alberta the status Indians face even greater challenges than those in the south. A number of remote bands still have not received their reserves. The Treaty Eight commissioners who, in 1899, had followed the Athabasca and Peace River systems, never met an estimated 500 Indians, since they did not enter the interior.[101] The landless bands in Alberta include those of Trout Lake, Peerless Lake, Loon Lake, Chipewyan Lake, and Lubicon Lake.

The example of the Lubicon Lake band, roughly 75 miles northeast of Peace River illustrates the frustrations of the landless northern Indians. In 1939 the federal government recognized them as a distinct band of Cree Indians. The following year both the federal and provincial governments agreed to grant the reserve selected by the Indians. Formal sur-

A member of the Enoch band shown in 1932 receiving his five dollar treaty money at Winterburn, west of Edmonton. This amount is given to each Treaty Indian annually. After World War II, oil was found on this Cree Indian reserve, making it one of the richest in Alberta. (Courtesy Provincial Archives of Alberta)

veying by the federal government, however, was not completed. Finally, in 1952, the Alberta government requested clarification of the status of the land set aside for a reserve. Noting that the federal government did not intend to proceed with the reserve, the province began giving out oil and gas exploration leases in the immediate area.[102] In the early 1970s, the Alberta government commenced construction of an all-weather road to open up the district to resource development. Then came the oil discoveries of 1980.[103]

The finds of the early 1980s made north central Alberta the province's hottest oil field; this has not helped the Lubicons obtain their reserve. The Natural Resources Transfer Act of 1930 stipulated that unoccupied Crown land must be surrendered by the province (upon the application of the federal government) if needed for new Indian reserves (or for extensions of old ones) to meet unfulfilled commitments to the Indians made in the treaties. In early 1985, Brian Mulroney appointed Davie Fulton, a former federal minister of justice, as his special investigator into the claims of the Cree Indians of Lubicon Lake. Mr. Fulton will recommend possible solutions to the prime minister.[104]

The deteriorating fishing and trapping economy of the entire Treaty Eight area constitutes a major problem for all of the northern bands. During the 1960s a combination of rapid native population growth, and a sudden depletion of game and fur-bearing animals led to low and declining returns. The freedom to trap has also been reduced due to stricter control over school attendance as a condition for receiving family allowances. To an increasing extent, many Indians have come to reside the year round in government-built settlements with schools, nursing stations, and trading stores. The inhabitants now depend upon relief, family allowance, old age pension, and assistance cheques for a large part of their income.[105]

The elimination of the poverty of a small percentage of Canada's population should not be insurmountable for a country with great wealth and resources. Yet the will to contribute substantially to the Indians' economic development has long been lacking,[106] and Alberta's Indian bands must become more economically self-sufficient. At present this goal seems very distant. The majority of Alberta's Indian reserves have an unemployment rate nearly 90 percent at some points in the year. It stands constantly over 50 percent.[107] In many areas no jobs exist and no opportunities of obtaining them. Most of the bands' budgets go to remedy the effects of chronic unemployment, to improve housing, health facilities, education, and provide social assistance. True, Indian Department expenditures have dramatically improved since the late 1960s; nevertheless, little money is ever left over for programmes to train band members for development and construction projects in and near their communities.[108] At the present time it appears that only those bands with adequate oil and gas revenues—and those able to settle their outstanding land claims—will be able to initiate developmental projects of their own.[109]

While conditions have improved in many respects for status Indians vast inequalities remain. In the areas of health, housing, education, and employment, the Indians throughout the province stand on a much lower scale than non-Indians. The incidence of tuberculosis among Indians in 1976, while very slight in comparison with the rate among Indians in the 1920s, was sixteen times higher than in the provincial population. Even though the retention rate for Indian students from Grades two to twelve has increased between 1966 and 1976, only 22 percent of all Indian students were retained to Grade twelve, compared to 75 percent for all students in Canada. In Alberta's Northland School Division only one out of six native students reaches high school.[110]

Some view migration off the reserve as a solution to the lack of employment at home. Presently about two out of ten treaty Indians in Alberta live in urban areas off their reserves. An estimated three out of ten will be in cities by the year 1986.[111] Many, however, have moved into the cities without any marketable skills.[112] Migration is not an answer in itself. In one year, 1974, the Department of Indian Affairs spent over $500,000 in the Treaty Seven area for urban social services.[113] As on the reserve, urban Indians need the special training that helps migrants obtain industrial jobs. Until recently, the Department had not evolved any special programming for the urban Indians; it had not increased native staff to help off-reserve Indians to adjust to city life.[114]

Reserve life is also troubled with social problems. Conditions have become intolerable to many. According to published statistics, over one-third of Indian deaths are due to accidents, poisonings, and violence (suicides, homicides, drug overdoses, motor vehicle accidents), a rate approximately three times greater than among the provincial population.[115] Alcoholism, brought on by social conditions, and a sense of helplessness, caused many of these needless deaths.[116]

Through political action the IAA has sought to improve the status Indians' social and economic situation. The IAA sees the discussions over the revision of the Indian Act and the question of aboriginal rights in the new Canadian constitution as vital to the Indians' survival. Since 1969 the IAA has struggled for an observance of the spirit of the treaties. The federal government has not accepted their position.

The "White Paper" of 1969

In June 1969 the federal government put forward a discussion paper or "White Paper," which proposed the final ending of the Indians' special status. The Department of Indian Affairs and the reserves would be abolished and the Indian Act eliminated. All federal responsibilities would be transferred from the federal to the provincial governments.[117] The goal of over one century of Canadian Indian administration would be achieved: the assimilation of the Indian. The "White Paper" created its own opposition. In Alberta the IAA, under the leadership of its young President Harold Cardinal, then twenty-four years old, became the most vocal Indian organization in Canada. Cardinal and the Indians of western Canada joined in an all-out attack on the "White Paper," calling it a blueprint for cultural genocide. In late 1969 Cardinal published *The Unjust Society*, a book which attacked the federal and provincial governments, and the churches for their manipulation of the Indian.[118] A veteran of several years with the Indian Youth Council and the Canadian Union of Students, the young Cree brought a new political sophistication to the IAA. Under his direction the organization dealt directly with the Department of Indian Affairs in Ottawa, and not with the regional office. He sought federal funding for the IAA to hire professional staff, and he obtained it. Ironically at the very moment the federal government announced its intention to abolish the reserves and the Indians' special status the government began, for the first time, to provide financial support for provincial Indian organizations. In 1970 the IAA presented its *Citizens Plus* "Red Paper," to Prime Minister Trudeau and his cabinet.[119] The "Red Paper" outlined the IAA's position. Special status had to be maintained, since the Indians were already in such an insecure economic and social position: poverty was a way of life for so many of them. It was inconceivable that their position could be further eroded through the ending of the treaties, the reserves, and their special constitutional status.[120] Instead the IAA called for the observance of the spirit of the treaties:

> The intent and spirit of the treaties must be our guide, not the precise letter of a foreign language. Treaties that run forever must have room for the

changes in the conditions of life. The undertaking of the Government to provide teachers was a commitment to provide Indian children the educational opportunity equal to their white neighbors. The machinery and live-stock symbolized economic development.[121]

Faced with the united opposition of the IAA and Indian organizations from across Canada, the federal government announced that it would not proceed with the implementation of its "White Paper."[122]

Just as the IAA serves treaty Indians, the Metis Association of Alberta acts as the provincial advocate for the Metis and nonstatus Indians. The Metis Association has publicized the Metis and the nonstatus Indians' need for education, jobs, and job-training. The Association argues that the Metis' aboriginal rights remain still in existence—that the federal government paid inadequate compensation for their land, and that it built fraud into the scrip programme, a programme which seemed designed to get the scrip out of the Metis' hands as soon as possible. The Association wants greater economic opportunities for the Metis in Alberta, and an extension of their land base. They also want to obtain the mineral rights for the land on the Metis settlements (currently the provincial government retains the oil and gas revenues).[123]

The Metis and nonstatus Indians who have not adjusted to the dominant society share many of the treaty Indians' problems. In some respects their problems are even greater for, unlike the status Indian, they are not assisted by the federal government with their education, health, and welfare. Until recently the provincial government did not supply many of these essential services because of the isolated nature of the northern Metis' communities. Furthermore, the Metis and nonstatus Indians cannot approach the Department of Indian Affairs to help them adjust to city life.[124]

Contemporary Issues

Three of the many unresolved issues for Alberta's native peoples are the question of band membership, the right to Indian self-government, and the definition of aboriginal rights. Under the Indian Act of 1876, as revised in 1951, any status Indian woman marrying a nonstatus Indian, a Metis, or any other non-Indian automatically becomes "enfranchised," which means she is no longer recognized as a status Indian—the woman must sell her property on the reserve, and can, under the present Indian Act, be refused burial there. An Indian man who marries a non-Indian, however, suffers no penalties, and as well, his wife and their children become Indians under the Indian Act.[125]

The IAA and most Alberta bands oppose any alteration in the existing procedure until there is a complete overhaul of the Indian Act with full Indian consultation, or until self-government itself is granted. Many elders fear an influx onto the already crowded reserves of formerly evicted women, their non-Indian husbands and children.[126] When the national Indian organization, The Assembly of First Nations, endorsed in May 1984 the federal government's proposal to reinstate those women and their children (who had lost their status by marrying non-Indians), the IAA, in protest, left the national body,[127] and helped to form the Prairie Treaty Nations Alliance. The federal government's reinstatement bill was accepted by Parliament and became law in late June 1985.

For status Indians the membership question raises the issue of self-government. At present band governments remain, in the Indian Department's own words, "more like administrative arms of the Department of Indian Affairs than they are governments accountable to band members.[128] Bands must operate subject to the Indian Act, the Department itself, and within the guidelines of certain federal and provincial laws and regulations. The special House of Commons' Committee on Indian Self-Government in 1983 endorsed the concept of full Indian control over matters such as education, child welfare, health care, and the whole band membership question. "Ending dependency would stimulate self-confidence and social regeneration."[129] The Committee's proposals for the achievement of Indian self-rule are currently under consideration by the status Indians, and the federal and provincial governments.

The Constitution Act (1982) affirmed existing aboriginal and treaty rights, but it did not define aboriginal rights. At a series of subsequent meetings the Prime Minister, the provincial premiers, and native representatives are to reach a definition of aboriginal rights.[130] The first meeting was held in the spring of 1983, the second in 1984, the third in 1985, and one more will be held before 1987. The Metis and the nonstatus Indians of Alberta have the most to gain from any identification of aboriginal rights. At present, the federal government has argued that any responsibilities to the Metis were extinguished by the adherence to treaty, or by the granting of land or scrip. The Treaty Indians from Alberta will be insistent that the spirit, as well as the letter of the treaties be applied—the up-dating of their terms and the inclusion of the oral promises made in 1876, 1877, and 1899-1900. Currently the federal government recognizes its responsibility only to fulfill the written texts of the agreements.

Conclusion

Paradoxically, the Albertans who have been here the longest are today the poorest, and suffer from the worst unemployment and living conditions experienced by any group in the province. Initially both the Plains, and more particularly the Woodlands, Indians benefitted from contact with the Europeans. New trade goods made their lives easier and provided them with more leisure time. With the arrival of the horse, the Plains Indians revolutionized their way of life, proving their adaptability and their responsiveness to change. But the strengthening of their culture proved only temporary, for the newcomers contributed to the extermination of the buffalo, which ended the Plains Indians and Metis' way of life.

The arrival of the Europeans led to the rise of a mixed-blood population in the West. In the early years of settlement the Metis helped the white immigrants, acting as interpreters, guides, and freighters. Years later Albert Lacombe, the veteran Roman Catholic missionary, then eighty years old, reminded his congregation: "You new-comers who come in now and spread over the lands like streams dividing, you do not know what who came first owed to the charity and goodness of these Metis who gave us so warm a welcome."[131]

Unfortunately the federal government's granting of scrip contributed little to the Metis' welfare. To some extent it may have assisted the mixed-bloods who had already adjusted to the white settler society, but it left those who had not impoverished and without any land base. Slowly, however, in the 1930s the community reorganized itself politically and regained some of its rights through the Metis Population Betterment Act of 1938.

After the treaties and the taking up of their reserves, the Indians (like the Metis after the Rebellion of 1885) lost their independence. Initially the Indian agent and the missionary spoke on the Indians' behalf. But in the 1920s Alberta's Indians developed their first political organization, the "League of Indians in Western Canada," and in the 1940s established the IAA. The Indians of Alberta now have their own spokespersons and modern political organization. Ralph Steinhauer, a treaty Indian from the Cree reserve at Saddle Lake and one of the foremost Indian leaders in western Canada, ably served as the province's Lieutenant-Governor from 1974 to 1979.

Against many obstacles Alberta's native peoples have advanced considerably. A number of Indians, Metis, and nonstatus Indians have entered the industrial economy. Indian bands have taken over control of their own tribal administration. Hundreds of native students now attend Alberta's colleges and universities. In the school systems Indian, Metis, and nonstatus Indian teachers are increasing in number.

All of this having been said, the original peoples of Alberta require and expect much more. Massive economic development must begin. There must be a real commitment by the non-Indian society to assist the Indians and Metis to create jobs for themselves by developing the reserves and Metis settlements. This commitment can begin with the recognition of the original peoples of Alberta's contributions to the province's history.

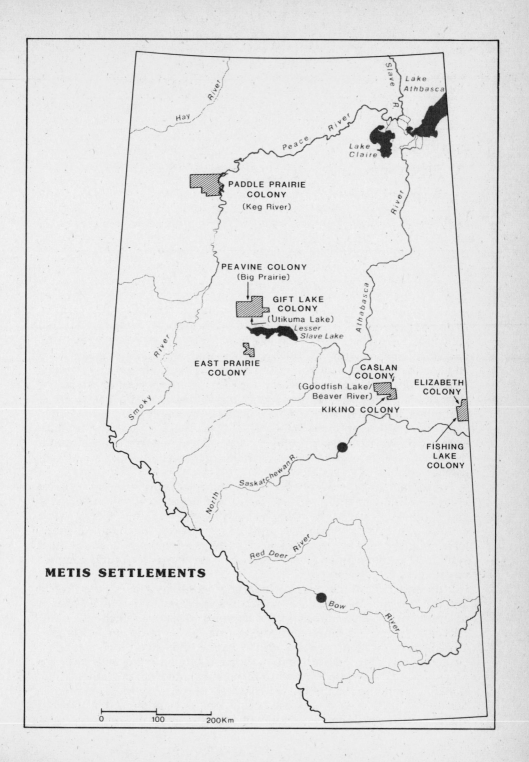

METIS SETTLEMENTS

PADDLE PRAIRIE
COLONY
(Keg River)

PEAVINE COLONY
(Big Prairie)

GIFT LAKE
COLONY
(Utikuma Lake)

EAST PRAIRIE
COLONY

CASLAN
COLONY
(Goodfish Lake/
Beaver River)

KIKINO COLONY

ELIZABETH
COLONY

FISHING
LAKE
COLONY

Lesser
Slave Lake

Lake
Athbasca

Lake
Claire

Slave R.

Hay River

Peace River

Athabasca River

Smoky River

North Saskatchewan R.

Red Deer River

Bow River

0   100   200Km

CHAPTER FOUR
A History of French-Speaking Albertans[1]
Donald B. Smith

"I do not pretend to be a prophet," Father Lacombe told his Archbishop, "but it seems to me that a big storm is brewing on the horizon. The English element, with all its fanaticism and its usual brutality, will attempt to find out whether now would not be the time to attack us frontally, with a chance of success. I expect the unleashing of the storm, both among the members of our legislature and in the press."[2] Lacombe's letter written in 1887 was indeed prophetic, for within five years the Northwest Territorial Council eliminated the French language from the territorial assembly, the courts, and—almost completely—from the schools of what today constitutes the provinces of Alberta and Saskatchewan.

The curtailment of entirely French language schools severely hurt the French-speaking community. The use of French in the school system was vital for the survival of the language, and for the teaching of the group's cultural values. For nearly a century many French-speaking Albertans have fought to have their language fully restored in the educational system. Their tenacity and perseverance to survive as a cultural community deserves recognition.

If the Indians are the original founding people of Alberta, the French and the French Canadians are the second: they have the longest history of any nonnative community in the province, a history which falls naturally into three distinct time periods. During the fur trade era, the French Canadians associated closely with the native peoples. French Canadian *voyageurs* intermarried with Indian women, originating a new race, the Metis. The arrival in the 1840s of French-speaking Roman Catholic missionaries strengthened the French character of the early Metis communities. In the 1870s a second phase began—the development of a series of viable French-speaking settlements of French Canadian emigrants from

Quebec and New England. The modern period commenced with formation of the province in 1905. For the last eighty years the French-speaking population has faced the constant threat of assimilation into the larger English-speaking community. At the time of the federal census in 1981, 29,550, or roughly one out of four franco-Albertans, or Albertans of French descent, declared that French was the language most spoken at home.[3]

The Fur Trade and the Arrival of the Missionaries

French was the first European language spoken on the Canadian Plains. Today, in the English West, Canadians and Americans still use French words such as coulee for a deep gulch or ravine; butte, for a conspicuous flat-topped hill; and, of course, the word prairie itself, derived from "pré," or meadow. French and French Canadian explorers, fur traders, and canoemen (or *voyageurs*) arrived in the West in the early eighteenth century. By the 1740s the LaVerendryes, father, sons, and nephew, were active on the North and South branches of the Saskatchewan River—the key to the interior, since it provided a transportation route for the fur trade. There may have been as many as 200 French Canadians scattered in fur-trading posts west of Lake Superior on the eve of the British Conquest in 1760. They must have been the first European group to meet the Blackfoot, for to this day the Blackfoot call "Frenchman," in their language, "real White Man." [4]

After the conquest, the French Canadian *voyageurs* continued in the West as canoemen of the newly arrived Scottish and American merchants in Montreal. They advanced further into the interior—down the Mackenzie River to the Arctic Ocean and westward across the Rockies to the Pacific. One would expect that these intrepid *voyageurs* who annually crossed half a continent would be men of heroic proportions. But actually few were taller than 5'8"; had they been any taller they would have occupied too much of the precious space in a canoe already jammed with cargo. These men, dressed in red caps, buckskins, and gaudy sashes were incredibly strong, however. Each day these *voyageurs* paddled fifteen, and on occasion eighteen, hours. They could each portage loads of over 200 pounds on their backs over rocky portage trails.[5]

French Canadians worked for both the HBC and the NWC; the latter was the HBC's bitter rival from the 1780s to their merger in 1821. The NWC counted among its employees French Canadians from nearly every parish between Montreal and Quebec. Every exploring trip in western Canada after the British Conquest made use of the French Canadian *voyageurs*.[6]

At Fort Edmonton, so many of the HBC's employees were French Canadians and Metis that French was the fort's most commonly used language until the middle of the nineteenth century.[7] Jean-Baptiste Lagimodière, whose wife, Marie-Anne Gaboury, was the first white woman in Alberta, worked for the HBC at Fort Edmonton. The Lagimodières later moved to the Red River settlement, where they raised a large family. Their daughter, Julie, born in 1822, became the mother of a man whose influence would be felt throughout the Northwest—Louis Riel.[8]

Many *voyageurs* took Indian wives, and as their mixed-blood descendants intermarried they furthered the growth of the "New Nation" of the Metis. Such Metis family names as Breland, Vandal, Desjarlais, Cardinal, Delorme, Dumont, Beaulieu, and Deschamps became well known.[9] By the beginning of the nineteenth century the Metis formed the largest French-speaking group in the Northwest.

After the union of the NWC and the HBC in 1821, the new HBC discontinued the NWC's long supply route from Montreal. It no longer recruited men on the banks of the St. Lawrence, and it also released many of the Metis.[10] To support themselves, the French-speaking mixed-bloods spread westward from the Red River, a number of them travelling to present day Alberta, where they hunted buffalo.

The arrival of French-speaking missionaries in the Red River settlement in 1818, and at Fort Edmonton in 1842, strengthened the French character of the mixed-blood communities. Until the establishment of the western missions many mixed-bloods spoke some French, and were nominally Roman Catholic, but their culture remained largely Indian. The priests and the nuns revived the Metis' Christian faith as well as their knowledge of the language and culture of their French Canadian ancestors.

Father Thibault began the Roman Catholic mission at Fort Edmonton in 1842. The following year he established a mission at Devil's Lake, later to be called Lac Sainte Anne, an excellent fishing lake forty-five miles west of Fort Edmonton. Forty Christian Metis families settled there and began farming. In 1852 Albert Lacombe, an energetic priest

Mgsr. Vital Grandin, a French-born Oblate priest, became the first bishop of the diocese of Saint Albert in 1871. He served until his death in 1902. Saint Albert (founded in 1861) had become a prosperous agricultural settlement by the late nineteenth century. Bishop Grandin appears in this photo taken in 1886 (with Saint Albert in the background). (Courtesy Provincial Archives of Alberta)

from Quebec, joined the mission. For over sixty years the popular "Black-Robe Voyageur" was the best known member of the French Canadian community in the North West.[11]

Father Lacombe soon discovered that Lac Sainte Anne's swampy land and early frosts made the area unsuitable for settlement. In 1861 he founded near Fort Edmonton a new mission, to be named Saint Albert after his patron saint. In 1871 Saint Albert became the first Roman Catholic bishopric in Alberta.

Gradually a number of the Metis marked off long narrow lots fronting on the banks of the Sturgeon River at Saint Albert, and built their log homes from 200 to 400 yards apart. To encourage agriculture in the colony, the Church imported agricultural implements and established a grist mill. The predominantly Metis settlement was organized under the direction of French Canadian and French priests of the Oblate order. French-speaking nuns also performed very important work. The sisters came from France, Belgium, or Quebec to teach the young and to care for the sick.

By the late 1880s, Saint Albert had developed into a successful agricultural community with a population of about 1,000. [12] A number of the Metis had begun subsistence farming after the extinction of the buffalo herds in the late 1870s. The government had already surveyed their long river lots. Prosperous and basically contented with the priests' role in their community, Saint Albert did not participate in Louis Riel's uprising in 1885. Unlike the Metis settlements around Batoche in the South Saskatchewan River Valley, which did take up arms, the village escaped physical destruction and military occupation by Canadian soldiers. And yet the Metis character of Saint Albert would also be altered, not by soldiers, but by the arrival of hundreds of white settlers to the area, who would soon outnumber the Metis.

The granting of scrip by the federal government in the late 1880s might have added to the land base of Metis communities like Saint Albert. With the granting of land scrip (a certificate indicating the right of the holder to receive payment later in the form of cash, goods, or land), the mixed-bloods might all have selected an additional 160 acres of land, or obtained grants of 240 acres for each of their children. Unfortunately, however, scrip was admirably suited to the quick transfer from one person to another. At Saint Albert, a large number of Metis, wanting immediate cash to buy food and other provisions, or wanting agricultural equipment for use on their river lots (to which they could also acquire title), sold their scrip for 50 percent of its value. For small sums of money, many lost rich lands in the regions of Edmonton, Lac Sainte Anne, and Saint Albert. [13]

After spending their money scrip those Metis who had never taken up river lots were as badly off as they had been before the distribution. Not having any real farming background, these former buffalo hunters, instead of filing for a homestead, retreated northward to areas still rich in fur-bearing animals, or congregated around the towns and villages where they could obtain temporary work. Father Lacombe's attempt at the turn of the century to establish a reserve for the Metis at what became known as Saint Paul des Métis, about a hundred miles northeast of the Saint Albert district, failed within fifteen years.[14] No longer would the Metis communities constitute the backbone of French-speaking settlement in the North West.

The Growth of French Canadian Settlements

A decade before the outbreak of the Riel Rebellion of 1885, a number of French-speaking farmers arrived in present-day Alberta. The two Lamoureux brothers settled in 1874 just east of Fort Edmonton at what became known as Lamoureux. As no surveys had yet been completed, they located their farms in long narrow strips leading back from the river, as at Saint Albert.[15] In 1875 the North West Mounted Police (NWMP) built a fort across from the settlement and named it Fort Saskatchewan. In the decade to follow, more farmers from Quebec came to the Lamoureux-Fort Saskatchewan area.[16] Other early French-speaking settlers migrated to Saint Albert, and to Edmonton. Of the total non-Indian population in the Edmonton area in 1885, the majority (roughly 60 percent) were of French ethnic origin (582 whites and 940 Metis out of a total population of 2,599).[17] To the south there was also a French presence. The same year that the NWMP constructed Fort Saskatchewan, 1875, they also built Fort Calgary, at the junction of the Bow and the Elbow Rivers. Inspector Ephrem Brisebois, a French Canadian, commanded the detachment that established the post. (For a few months the tiny NWMP post was actually called Fort Brisebois, until the name Fort Calgary was chosen.) A number of Metis helped to build the new fort at the junction of the Bow and the Elbow.[18]

In the Northwest Territories Act of 1875 (with its amendments in 1877), the federal government had recognised the presence of a French-speaking group in the Northwest. The Act allowed for the use of French in the legislative council and the courts, and granted the right to organize Roman Catholic schools in which French might be the language of instruction. At that time, French-speaking Roman Catholics constituted the majority of the white inhabitants in the Northwest, and the French-speaking mixed-bloods outnumbered the English-speaking.[19]

The peaceful coexistence of French and English did not last; it was ended by an influx of anglophones in the 1880s. From 1881 to 1891 the white population of the Northwest Territories jumped from 1,500 to 50,000. The reality was simply this: the Ontarians moved west, and the Québécois did not. In a letter written in 1888 to a prominent French Canadian Conservative, Prime Minister John A. Macdonald commented: "The consequence is that Manitoba and the North-West Territories are becoming what British Columbia now is—wholly English,—with English laws, English, or rather British, immigration, and, I may add, English prejudices."[20]

The English-speaking pioneers acted quickly to mold their new world in the image of the old. Only a generation earlier (from 1841 to 1867), Ontario and Quebec had been joined together in the Union of the Can-

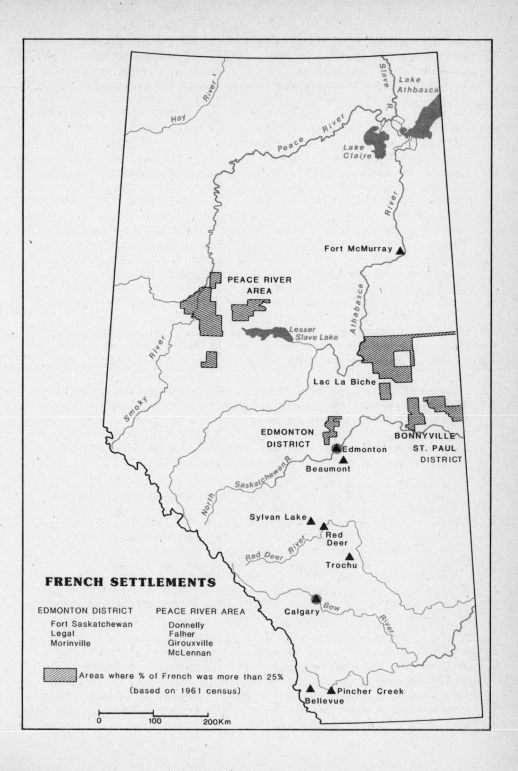

FRENCH SETTLEMENTS

EDMONTON DISTRICT

Fort Saskatchewan
Legal
Morinville

PEACE RIVER AREA

Donnelly
Falher
Girouxville
McLennan

Areas where % of French was more than 25%
(based on 1961 census)

0   100   200Km

adas. In Canada West (to become Ontario after Confederation), two political forces contested for power: the Conservatives under John A. Macdonald and the Clear Grits, or Liberals, under George Brown. Macdonald, who worked closely with George Etienne Cartier and the French Canadian Conservatives, realized that his party could not govern the Canadas without respecting the equality of both the English and French Canadians. On the other hand, the Clear Grits wanted to be free of what some of their leaders called "French domination." They still smarted from the fact that the Conservatives in the legislature of the United Province of Canada had forced upon the overwhelmingly English-speaking and mainly Protestant Canada West a state-supported Roman Catholic school system, which most of the Canada West members had voted against.

In the 1880s, the Protestant Ontarians brought westward with them the Clear Grit, not the more tolerant Conservative, tradition of the Canadas. They came to Manitoba and the Northwest Territories convinced that both areas must be made "British," and that a national state school system should be established to accomplish this goal. With this in mind, the Calgary *Herald* declared on 24 February, 1890, the "absolute necessity of securing for the English language in Canada that supremacy which British arms, British blood, British courage, British ideas, British institutions may fairly claim, at the close of the nineteenth century in a country over which the British flag has waved for a century and a quarter."

Manitoba eliminated the language and the school rights of its French-speaking population in 1890. Only two years later the Assembly of the Northwest Territories itself decided on the use of French in its debates and in their publication. Charles Nolin, a Metis and a first cousin of Louis Riel, presented, in French, the position of the French-speaking settlers. As the Regina *Leader* translated his remarks:

> He said the French Canadian people of these Territories were not asking any favour . . . every Act passed since that time by the Imperial and Canadian Parliaments had always recognized that right. Could this Assembly claim that it would act wiser than the statesmen of England and Canada? It might be said that the Germans and Swedes had the right possessed by the French Canadian people, but he said no; we were here before anybody else. We are Canadians and British subjects and what we ask for is in our capacity as Canadians. The part of the population that he represented could claim some consideration from this Assembly, because if it had not been for the fact that the Halfbreeds had been here for the last 100 years there would be no Assembly today.

But Nolin argued in vain. In 1892, by a simple vote of the assembly, English became the sole language of the chamber. Later that same year, the territorial government further reduced the use of French. Henceforth English must be the language of instruction in the Roman Catholic school system, the use of French only being permitted in a "primary course" (the first two to three years of school) for those children who spoke no other tongue.[21]

The French-speaking population, reinforced by the addition of several thousand French-speaking settlers brought West by the church, resisted the elimination of French from the assembly, and the courts, and resisted, too, its reduction in status in the schools. Energetically the church tried to build up the French-speaking population before the Territories themselves became provinces, at which time the existing legislation might be changed. The priests established offices in Montreal and organized colonization societies. The church named a number of priests, Father Lacombe being one of the first, as colonization agents (*prêtres-colonisateurs*). The agents searched out suitable areas for settlement in Alberta then returned to Quebec and New England (where many French Canadians had been migrating since the 1840s) to recruit.[22]

L'Abbé Morin brought out the first group of settlers from Quebec in the early 1890s. They began farms in the fertile lands twelve miles north of the original Saint Albert settlement and named their settlement Morinville, after their priest.

L'Abbé Morin and Father Lacombe, and other priests brought thousands of francophones to Alberta, the majority of these emigrants apparently coming from outside of Quebec. Of the 620 French-speaking families brought in the 1890s to Edmonton and the eight French settlements in the surrounding area, over half came from the United States, and only one-fifth from Quebec.[23] Once the fertile land around Edmonton had all been taken up, the colonization priests directed settlers to the newly opened Metis reserve at Saint Paul, and then to neighboring Bonnyville (named in 1907 after the area's colonizing priest).[24] The Roman Catholic fathers also directed French Canadian settlers to the Lac la Biche area, sixty miles northeast of Saint Paul, where a permanent Indian mission had been founded in 1853.[25] Other pioneers arrived on their own, attracted by the availability of free land and the opportunity to obtain a homestead for each family member.

Immediately before the outbreak of World War I, a small number of French-Canadian settlers homesteaded in the Peace River area. In 1912 French-Canadian pioneers founded Falher (named after their colonizing priest) forty miles west of Grouard. But the conditions in the Peace River district, before the railway was built there, proved too difficult to permit any large scale development at that time. The real expansion in the Peace River area did not begin until 1926, when the region became one of the major areas of French-Canadian settlement in the province.[26]

Thanks to the settlements around Edmonton, Bonnyville, St. Paul, and the Peace River, the French-speaking population did grow. But not fast enough. If the French language was to be restored to the position it enjoyed between 1877 and 1892 the number of francophones would have to grow to rival the English-speaking population, now at the turn of the century numbering—not in the thousands—but in the tens of thousands.

Distance constituted the church's major obstacle in its campaign to encourage French-Canadian settlement in the West. New England was located on Quebec's doorstep, and almost everyone in Quebec already had relatives there. Moreover, they could find jobs as factory workers or as laborers, work that they considered much easier than farming. Consequently, by 1900 over one million French Canadians lived in the United States. In contrast, the Northwest lay two thousand miles away, separated from Quebec by Protestant Ontario. It also cost a considerable sum to travel to the West by train. Railway rates, in fact, remained much higher for a Quebecer than for an emigrant from Britain or Europe who could benefit from the special fares (often only one-half of the regular price) offered to immigrants.[27]

The church's selection process also initially served to reduce the number of possible settlers. The church appealed to individuals with adequate capital, but those who were well established would be the least likely to leave Quebec, or even New England. Preference was given to married men with children, but these, too, would be unlikely to migrate. Anxious to see the settlements succeed, the priests also took special pains to emphasize the difficulties involved, which only served to limit the numbers willing to leave for the Northwest. After World War I began, they finally relaxed the conditions for selecting settlers.[28]

The fact that the Quebec clergy directed potential farmers northward in Quebec, instead of westward, also weakened the western priests' colonization movement. The Quebec clergy wanted first to ensure a French-Canadian numerical superiority in their province. Only after intense pressure from the French-speaking Roman Catholic clergy in the Northwest did the Quebec bishops finally agree to encourage westward migration—but only among those who had already decided to move to the United States.[29]

The *Census of the Prairie Provinces* of 1916 revealed the small number of French-speaking arrivals. In that year only approximately 25,000 people of French origin lived in Alberta, out of a total population of approximately 500,000.[30] Their numbers were indeed very low if they sought to have the provisions of 1877 to 1892 restored. In 1905, the Autonomy Bills by which Alberta and Saskatchewan became Canadian provinces, stipulated that French instruction was to be limited to the primary grades, and to one hour daily after the first primary school grades.[31] The French-speaking population, who at the turn of the century had imagined Confederation to have been a pact between two equal partners, now fully realized their minority status.

In their struggle to survive, the French Canadian community was strengthened by the arrival of a small number of French and Belgian immigrants in the early twentieth century. One of the most famous was Georges Bugnet (1879-1981), who came to Canada in 1905 and homesteaded at Rich Valley north of Edmonton. Later he became renowned through his novels and his poetry as Alberta's best-known author in French. His first two novels, *Le Lys de Sang* and *Nypsia*, appeared in 1923 and 1924, the third, *Siraf*, in 1934, but it was with the fourth, *La Forêt* (The Forest), published in 1935, that he established his reputation. In *La Forêt* Bugnet relates the brutal transformation of a young, urban French couple, the Bourgoins, who came to homestead in northern Alberta, and who are eventually defeated by the land. Bugnet also completed a volume of poetry, *Voix de la solitude*, in 1938.[32]

Relatively few French and Belgian immigrants came to Alberta. France had a low birth rate and a well-balanced economy providing work for its citizens. For those with a desire for adventure, France had its own colonies, so Canada was not a favored destination. Belgium, too, had a surplus French-speaking population, but many of them found work in France or in the Belgian colonies in Africa. A number of Belgians, though, did settle around Saint Albert. Switzerland had only a small number of French-speaking inhabitants, and few of them emigrated to Canada. Perhaps the most well known immigrant of Swiss French ancestry is René Richard (b. 1895) who moved with his parents to Cold Lake, Alberta in 1910. He became a successful Canadian artist, and lived at Baie St-Paul, Quebec.[33]

The French immigrants who did come to Alberta from France were scattered across the province, and the lack of large group settlements led to the rapid demise of many of the small communities that they founded. A group of former French cavalry officers established ranches north of Calgary at what became known as Trochu. Other ex-soldiers and their families followed, as well as a number of settlers from upper class and wealthy backgrounds. A group of eight French nuns, the Sisters of Charity of Our Lady of Evron, founded a convent and hospital at Trochu. A few French aristocrats also settled for a brief period south of Calgary in

Although only a small number of French settlers came to Alberta from France, among their ranks were a group of former French cavalry officers who established ranches at Trochu, north of Calgary. Several appear here in 1904 at the Ste-Anne ranch. At the outbreak of World War I the ranchers left to fight for France. (Courtesy Glenbow Archives)

the Millarville area, where they ranched and raised horses. The outbreak of war in Europe brought an end to Trochu as a French-speaking settlement, since all the French army officers left to rejoin their units. Of those who left, many were killed in France and Flanders, while many of the survivors remained in France after the war.[34]

Trochu was not the only settlement that attracted immigrants from France. Twelve Roman Catholic priests came to Alberta in 1904 after their eviction from their schools in Tinchebray, Normandy, when an anticlerical government in France assumed control of education. The Fathers of Sainte-Marie of Tinchebray began homesteading to support themselves, and attracted about 100 French and French-Canadian settlers to their two settlements of Tinchebray and Notre Dame de Savoie, north of Stettler. In 1910 the Fathers moved to Red Deer which became their new headquarters. There they built a church, a convent, a hospital and a school. By 1910, the parish counted sixty French-speaking families. The Fathers of Sainte-Marie of Tinchebray worked in the Red Deer district until 1924 when they left Alberta because of difficulties with their Irish-Canadian bishop in Edmonton.[35]

Though few in number, the French immigrants to Alberta had varied and unusual backgrounds. The early French community included the aristocratic ranchers of Trochu, the Fathers of Sainte-Marie de Tinchebray, and also the followers of Dr. Tanche of Lille, who attempted in 1906 to found a communal settlement at Sylvan Lake, just fifteen miles west of Red Deer. Thirty French families had accompanied Dr. Tanche, determined to establish a true socialist colony in the Canadian West. Everyone stayed in one large building which served as their living quarters and as their barn. Perhaps living with their livestock and fowl put everyone's nerves on edge. In any event the attempt of these former city dwellers to farm together did not succeed. The colony disbanded within two years, half the families returning to France, and the remainder taking homesteads elsewhere. Dr. Tanche himself homesteaded at Sylvan Lake until 1917, then returned to France where he died shortly thereafter.[36]

Alberta also attracted Dr. Tanche's complete antithesis: the French capitalist. The West Canadian Collieries Ltd., which operated in the Crow's Nest Pass, was French-owned and operated. In 1903 the company renamed its main settlement, then known as Frenchman's Town, Lille (after the large coal mining town in northeastern France where the company had its headquarters). West Canadian Collieries also established the village of Bellevue. While miners of all nationalities worked in their mines, the top managerial staff of West Canadian Collieries at both Lille and Bellevue was French. Business interests in France also controlled the huge Revillion Fur Company, which operated in western Canada in the early twentieth century. The company established its central warehouse for western Canada in Edmonton.[37]

Generally speaking the majority of the French and Belgian immigrants settled before World War I in the fertile and well-watered sections of central and northern Alberta. The concentrations of French-speaking settlers around Edmonton, Bonnyville-Saint Paul, and later in the Peace River country, had a real chance for linguistic survival which the small rural communities in the south never had.

Early Urban Communities

Before World War I, French-speaking communities also existed in urban centers. The French-speaking community in Calgary dated back to the freighting days of the 1870s. Many of the original members of the Roman Catholic parish were either French-speaking Metis, who worked as interpreters and bulltrain operators, or French-Canadian laborers from Quebec who had, in 1883-84 helped to build the CPR from Maple Creek to Golden. But the French-speaking population in Calgary remained small—at the turn of the century, only 125 people out of a total population of 4,400. They lived largely in the village of Rouleauville, a "little Quebec" on the banks of the Elbow River. The two Rouleau brothers, the two most prominent members of the community which bore their name, came from Isle Verte, Quebec. Charles Rouleau served as judge on the Supreme Court of the Northwest Territories, and his brother, Edouard, was the surgeon to the local NWMP detachment. After being annexed to the city in 1907, Rouleauville became known as Mission.[38]

The Saint-Jean-Baptiste Society was the leading French-Canadian patriotic organization in Canada a century ago. The first chapter in the Edmonton area dates back to 1894, the year in which this photo was taken. (Ernest Brown photo, courtesy Provincial Archives of Alberta)

Edmonton, not Calgary, always has been the real center of French-speaking life in Alberta. The community itself dated back to Fort Edmonton. Prior to 1885 the majority of Edmontonians were of French origin, and until 1916, they remained the second largest linguistic community with a total population of 2,600 in a city of 53,850. In 1894 they established their own branch of Quebec's Saint-Jean-Baptiste Society, the leading French-Canadian patriotic organization. They began publishing *L'Ouest canadien*, a weekly French language newspaper, in 1898: the first of a series of French language papers which championed French language and Roman Catholic rights in Alberta.[39]

Edmonton's French-speaking clergy, businessmen and professionals led the community. The leaders as a rule had been born and educated in Quebec, although at least one prominent member, René Lemarchand, came from France. Through his brother, an Oblate priest in Alberta, René had learned about the West and its great business opportunities. Immediately before World War I he made a fortune in real estate in Edmonton. René Lemarchand also built the first major apartment building in the city.[40]

By the beginning of the twentieth century the organization of the franco-Albertan community had been completed. The church, the most important institution, had a well-organized system of parishes throughout the French-speaking areas. The nuns (The Sisters of Assumption, the Sisters of Saint-Croix, and the Filles de Jésus being among the most active teaching orders) complemented the priests' work in the publicly supported Roman Catholic schools. French-language religious orders (in particular the Grey Nuns from Montreal and the Sisters of Charity of Our Lady of Evron from France) also founded and ran the Holy Cross Hospital in Calgary, the General Hospital and the Misericordia in Edmonton, and hospitals in Vegreville, Trochu, Saint Paul, and Bonnyville. The church, central and highly visible, exercised great power. Bishop Legal of Saint Albert, for example, exercised tremendous social influence over the development of the community. He ruled that dances and balls were sinful, and banished such activities from the church halls of his diocese.[41]

Without dances to attend, *soirées*, or social evenings, became the most popular form of entertainment in Edmonton before the war. The evening might include a card party, followed by a musical presentation and then refreshments. Occasionally it concluded with a lecture as well. Other social functions were organized to celebrate the anniversaries of important members of the French-speaking clergy such as the diamond anniversary in September 1909 of Father Lacombe's ordination in 1849. Annually the biggest event was Saint-Jean-Baptiste day, 24 June, in honor of French Canada's patron saint. At Morinville in 1907 the celebration attracted 1,500 French-speaking Edmontonians and others from the nearby French villages.[42]

Other French-speaking organizations, as well as the Saint-Jean-Baptiste Society, existed in the city. Two mutual aid associations, the *Alliance nationale* and the *Artisans canadiens-français*, organized social activities for their members, and provided them with life and accident insurance programmes. The *Société du parler français*, a national French Canadian society formed to promote the French language and those who spoke it, received franco-Albertans' support. Eight hundred delegates attended the assembly in the city in 1913. That same year the community founded two new organizations: an Edmonton branch of the *Association catholique de la jeunesse canadienne-français* (ACJC), a Roman Catholic youth organization, and the *Cercle 'Jeanne d'Arc'*, which presented French language plays in the city. For several years Edmonton's lively French community enthusiastically supported two French language weeklies, *Le Courrier de l'ouest* (1905-1916) and *Le Progrès* (1909-1913).[43]

Political Involvement in the Early Twentieth Century

French-speaking Edmontonians in the pre-World War I period knew the importance of politics. The community attempted to elect at least one French-speaking alderman in every civic election, and as many French-speaking members to the provincial legislature as possible. Predominantly rural French-speaking constituencies like Saint Paul, Saint Albert, Beaver River, and Grouard often returned French Canadians as their representatives. In 1913, five French-speaking members, all Liberals, were elected to the fifty-six seat provincial legislature. Three of those elected by northern constituencies came from Edmonton.

The French-speaking community supported the Liberals then, provincially and federally, the strongest political party. A grateful federal Liberal Party in 1905 had named Philippe Roy, an Edmonton doctor, as the senator for northern Alberta. Roy, who had arrived in Edmonton from Quebec just seven years earlier, had taken an active part in organizing the Liberal party in Alberta. After Senator Roy's appointment in 1911 as the new Commissioner General of Canada in Paris, Prime Minister Laurier named in his place another French Canadian, A. E. Forget, a former Lieutenant Governor of the Northwest Territories. From 1905 to 1958, with the sole exception of the years 1934 to 1940, a French Canadian occupied one of Alberta's seats in the federal senate.[44]

The provincial Liberal administration also rewarded the French-speaking electorate. In 1909 a French Canadian joined the provincial cabinet for the first time. P. E. Lessard, born and educated in Quebec, had come to Edmonton just eleven years earlier. The active Liberal Party organizer and member from Pakan (Saint Paul des Métis district), then just thirty-six years old, became Minister Without Portfolio from 1909-1910. Until its defeat by the UFA in 1921, the provincial Liberal administration usually included one French Canadian in the cabinet.[45] Yet despite their influence in the provincial Liberal Party, neither the French-speaking MLAs nor the Cabinet Ministers could use the French language in the legislature.

Patterns of Settlement and Growth after World War I

The war ended the migration of French-speaking settlers to Alberta just when more were badly needed to strengthen the community. While hundreds of francophones had emigrated to the province, so had tens of thousands of anglophones and non-English-speaking immigrants. Upon their arrival, the immigrants were told that English was the only language of the West. By the 1920s, English Canadian and European Roman Catholics outnumbered French-speaking Albertans in the Roman Catholic Church.[46]

After the war, only the Peace River district received a sizeable number of French-speaking settlers. Many entering the district came from the most rural areas of Quebec: Lac Saint Jean, the south shore of the Saint Lawrence, and the Gaspé districts where they had practiced a bare subsistence farming. Here on the fertile and easy-to-work lands of the Peace River, a man could still establish his sons on large homesteads. Rather than see the farmers emigrate to the United States, the majority of Quebec bishops, unable to stop the exodus (and now aware of the poverty of agricultural land in Quebec's north) supported their departure to the Canadian West.[47] Out of the approximately 200 French-speaking families attracted to Jean-Côté (one of the new French-speaking settlements in the Peace River), 75 percent came from Quebec, 15 percent from elsewhere in Canada and from Europe, and only 10 percent from the United States.[48]

Outside of the Peace River area, the French-speaking population actually diminished, and its power in the Roman Catholic Church declined. There were several reasons for this. The appointment of English-speaking bishops to the dioceses of Calgary and Saint Albert (renamed the diocese of Edmonton in 1913) ended the colonization efforts in southern and central Alberta. By the early twentieth century francophones constituted only 30 percent of the Roman Catholics in the provinces of Manitoba, Saskatchewan, and Alberta; yet before 1913 all of the bishops were French-speaking. The appointment in 1913 of John Thomas McNally as Bishop of Calgary was the church's first sign of recognition that western Canada contained a greater number of English-speaking than French-speaking Catholics. The church later appointed English-speaking bishops in Winnipeg in 1915, Edmonton in 1920, and Regina in 1930. Almost overnight, the French character of the Roman Catholic Church in western Canada disappeared.[49]

After his appointment in 1913, Bishop McNally immediately worked to reduce the number of French-speaking clergy in Calgary, who then constituted over two-thirds of the diocesan priests (twenty-five out of thirty-four). By 1916, the Irish Canadian bishop had taken the initial steps to hasten the departure of four French-language religious communities.[50]

Efforts to anglicize the Roman Catholic Church in Edmonton began with the accession in 1920 of an English-speaking bishop, Msgr. Henry J. O'Leary. The new bishop found it abnormal that a majority of the secular priests in Edmonton were francophone (sixty-four out of ninety-eight), while only a minority of Roman Catholics (18,094 out of 38,500) were French-speaking. Like Bishop McNally, he worked to alter the ethnic balance, recruiting English-speaking secular priests, mostly from the Maritime provinces. By 1931 the sixty-five French-speaking priests of 1920 had been reduced to sixteen, and the number of English-speaking ones had risen to sixty-four.[51]

In the 1920s the franco-Albertans had also lost much of their political influence. Before the war, French-speaking voters had consistently supported the provincial Liberals. But with the emergence in 1919 of a new political party, the UFA, the community split into two camps. This reduced their political power. Although two French-speaking UFA candidates won seats in the provincial election of 1924 and one in the election of 1930, none made cabinet rank from 1921 to 1935.[52]

With the demise of the UFA Party in the mid-1930s, a number of French-speaking Albertans returned to the Liberals, but others supported Social Credit, the new party of monetary reform. Lucien Maynard, a young franco-Albertan lawyer in his late twenties, became a leading spokesman for the movement. The bilingual Maynard's fluency in both French and English helped his party in northeastern Alberta, where he organized the two constituencies of Beaver River (where he himself ran) and Saint Paul for the 1935 provincial election. Thanks largely to Maynard, the two constituencies became, and remained, strong Social Credit constituencies for the next twenty years. Premier Aberhart named the newly elected member for Beaver River to the provincial cabinet in 1936, and the young franco-Albertan served until 1957.[53]

The division among the franco-Albertans between the Liberals and the UFA, and later between the Liberals and the Social Credit, weakened their political strength in the interwar years. The community also lost much of its political importance by its decline from the second to the fourth largest group in the province, behind the Germans and Ukrainians.

After World War I, a French-speaking alderman was not always elected to the Edmonton City Council. Gradually French-speaking Albertans reconciled themselves to their declining influence and power. New interests other than politics captured the young generation's attention. The post-war generation, many of whom had grown up in the West, had been in constant contact with English Canadians and recent European immigrants. Many lacked their parents' dedication to the old causes. The old feeling of franco-Albertans constituting a strong identifiable community weakened. New activities such as large dances, movies, and car trips reduced the attendance at the parishes' social activities, and at the clubs and societies which had been so active during the pre-1914 era.[54]

There appears as well to have been a general feeling of demoralization in the community. During the last years of the war, the Conscription Crisis had caused Anglo-French relations in Canada to fall to their lowest point since Confederation. Harsh criticism of Quebec and French Canadians for what was perceived as a failure to support the war effort made the community (whose members enlisted in considerable number) feel extremely insecure.[55]

When the *Association canadienne-française de l'Alberta* (ACFA) (French

Canadian Association of Alberta) was formed in 1926, one of its objectives was "to destroy the inferiority complex that exists too often among the French Canadians of Alberta, as it does among other minority groups."[56] That inferiority complex apparently arose from the awareness that they would always be a small, relatively powerless minority in Alberta unable to protect their language and culture. One hour a day in French in the primary school could not sustain a language. Franco-Albertans, taught in English, grew up without learning adequately how to write and speak their mother tongue.[57]

The community tried to improve the situation. Privately financed French language instruction had been established just before the war and (if one could afford it) a complete education could be obtained in French. Edmonton's Juniorate of Saint John the Apostle (founded by the Oblates in 1910) educated young men to become missionary priests. The other private school in Edmonton, the Jesuits' classical college (built in 1913), which led to the B.A. granted by Université Laval (Laval University) in Quebec City, received strong support in the inter-war period. The Jesuit College had 221 students in its most active year. It continued in operation until 1942, when for financial reasons it had to close.[58] The Juniorate, then known as Collège Saint-Jean was later recommended by the Commission on Bilingualism and Biculturalism to become a French language university center in the West.[59] Shortly after the recommendation was made, Saint-Jean became affiliated with the University of Alberta as Collège Universitaire Saint-Jean and is today Faculté Saint-Jean, a faculty of the University of Alberta.[60]

The Oblate and Jesuit Colleges helped to train a new franco-Albertan elite. Not all of their graduates, it is true, stayed, some preferring to work in French in Quebec.[61] But most graduates remained in the province: Henri Routhier and Lucien Maynard being two excellent examples. The grandson of Chief Justice A. B. Routhier of Quebec (who was the author of the original French version of "O, Canada"), Henri Routhier was born at Pincher Creek in 1900 and graduated from the Juniorate of Saint John in Edmonton. After studies at the Gregorian University in Rome, Father Routhier returned to Alberta. In 1949 he became the first Alberta-born bishop in the Roman Catholic Church, later serving as the Archbishop of Grouard-McLennan.[62] Similarly, Lucien Maynard remained in his native province. After graduation from the Jesuit College in Edmonton, Maynard obtained his law degree at the University of Alberta, and before his entry into politics, practiced law at Saint Paul.[63]

A third prominent member of the Franco-Albertan community is Marcel Lambert, whose father was French Canadian and his mother Belgian. Lambert was born in Edmonton in 1919. After four years overseas in World War II, he returned to the University of Alberta, becoming Alberta's Rhodes Scholar in 1947. After practicing law in Edmonton for several years he ran as a Conservative for the House of Commons in 1957, and won ten successive elections until his retirement in 1984. The fluently bilingual Lambert served as the Speaker of the House of Commons in 1962-63, and briefly as the Minister of Veterans Affairs in the last cabinet of John Diefenbaker.[64]

The training of a French-speaking elite strengthened the community, as did ACFA and the new educational organization it immediately founded in 1926, the *Association des Educateurs Bilingues de l'Alberta* (AEBA), the Alberta Association of Bilingual Teachers. For more than thirty years, AEBA organized a French language competition for schools, prepared special French language programmes, and helped to organize a number of extra-curricular activities in French for the schools: plays, Christmas concerts, choral rallies, and speaking contests.[65]

In the mid-1920s the French-speaking community also reorganized itself politically. ACFA replaced the Saint-Jean-Baptiste Society of pre-war years, becoming the new champion of the franco-Albertan. The ACFA worked to promote every possible aspect of the French-speaking community's life. On 16 November 1928, it published the first edition of *La Survivance* (Survival) which was for four decades Edmonton's most successful French language newspaper, with a circulation in the 1940s and 1950s of about 3,000. Beginning in 1930, the ACFA sponsored bimonthly concerts over the local Edmonton radio station, CJCA. ACFA also promoted in the late 1930s the development of parish-based credit unions (caisses populaires) and cooperatives.[66]

Community Survival in the Post-War Era

The ACFA's campaign in the early 1940s to secure a French language radio station for franco-Albertans, and its agitation for more French instruction, aroused great resentment among a number of English-speaking Albertans. Some of them were convinced that the French Canadian constituted a real and growing threat to Alberta, particularly in the Peace River country. An editorial in the High River *Times* in November 1944 illustrated the depth of feeling:

> The province is now confronted with the threat of a colony settlement from within Canada itself. A plan is developing in Quebec, and may be farther along than we realize, to encourage migration of French-Canadian [sic] to a specified area of Peace River country. Mention is made of whole parishes that might be transported en masse. To quote the appeal from the Peace River Colonization society (promoted from Drummondville, Quebec): "Is it not a worthy task to work for the expansion of the reign of Christ and French influence in our dear Canada? Would it not be a fine thing to see established in the Peace River valley a fine Catholic and French Canadian province? ..."
> ... Surely this cannot be regarded as a 'fine thing' but very serious in future consequences. And this is no reflection on the French Canadian as an individual. Let him come to the West as an individual as others have done, mingling with others, learning to speak the Canadian tongue, becoming a part of any community, so that he may graduate from French-Canadian to unhyphenated Canadian. Divorced from his racial obsession, he might be a real asset.[67]

A good deal of the English-speaking Canadians' resentment against French Canadians arose because of Quebec's opposition to military conscription in World War II. As in World War I, they believed the French

Canadians weakened the cause overseas. Little consideration was given to the fact that French Canadians had never viewed the war in the same way as English Canadians. Cut off from Britain and from Europe itself by over three centuries of history, the French Canadians did not see the struggle as their own. Only on the understanding that there would be no conscription had Quebec agreed to participate in the war. Prime Minister Mackenzie King and the French Canadian members of the federal cabinet had solemnly promised in 1939 that conscription would never again be introduced—yet in late November 1944, as in 1917, it was.

No doubt the animosities raised by the Conscription Crisis contributed to the strong anglophone reaction against the idea of a French language radio station in Alberta in 1945. For several years the ACFA had argued without success for the establishment of such a station by the Canadian Broadcasting Corporation (CBC). The CBC argued that funds were not available. The ACFA finally decided to incorporate itself provincially and then to apply for a licence to set up a private station. Lucien Maynard, then the Provincial Treasurer, strongly supported the bill. But in the provincial legislature in March 1945, the debate to incorporate the ACFA proved so hostile that the proposal was withdrawn by its sponsors.[68]

The franco-Albertan community was furious. Father Breton, the editor of *Survivance*, replied to the legislature and the English-language press on 28 March 1945:

> There are some among those who violently opposed the incorporation requested by the ACFA who clearly revealed their beliefs: they do not want radio in French because, as they say, this would hinder the anglicization of our population and thus be detrimental to the unification of our country. Those who hold these views would do well to remind themselves of this one thing: we are Catholic and French and, for all their opposition, we fully intend to stay this way ... We shall never allow ourselves to be treated as strangers in our house - that is, in Canada ...
>
> Last week's incident is still further evidence that we must rely upon ourselves above all else. Once again, we have seen that we cannot trust the declarations of good will, understanding and fair play, the British tenets of democracy professed by our Anglo-Saxon fellow citizens.[69]

The ACFA refused to give way: French language broadcasting was essential to the cultural survival of franco-Albertans. The establishment in 1946 of CKSB at Saint Boniface, the first French-language radio station in the West, encouraged the ACFA. Once it obtained a federal charter, the ACFA applied to the Board of Governors of the CBC for a licence to operate a private French language radio station in Edmonton. Finally, in March 1948, the Board of Broadcast Governors agreed; after raising the necessary funds (some of which were advanced by the Oblate order), station CHFA opened in Edmonton in November 1949.[70]

The years of struggle for French language broadcasting in Alberta were also marked by another campaign of the ACFA in which it stood against the amalgamation of local school districts and the adoption of large centralized units. Formerly the basic school unit had been the small, independent school district controlled by a board of trustees elected by the local ratepayers. As late as 1935 over 65 percent of Alberta's classrooms were located in one-room schools.[71] During the mid-1930s, though, many educators (supporters of the new, "progressive" movement in education) pressured the government to introduce larger, more efficient school districts, in which improved facilities could be provided. In 1936 the Alberta government introduced the appropriate legislation.

The ACFA protested that in larger units the French-speaking representatives could, in many instances, be outvoted. The government did not withdraw the legislation but thanks to ACFA's agitation, some safeguards for the small school boards were introduced. The government provided that if the board of a school district requested religious instruction, or bilingual instruction in the primary grades (in conformity with the existing regulations), the board of the large unit would hire a teacher for this purpose. The teacher would be nominated by the respective school district. In addition if three or more local school boards should disagree with the religious or bilingual instruction being offered in their large administrative unit, they could, following a majority vote of the ratepayers in a referendum supervised by the Minister of Education, withdraw from the divisional grouping.[72]

In the 1940s and 1950s other challenges arose. Franco-Albertans had little legal support in their attempt to survive as a distinctive community. Alberta had been remade into an English-speaking province. Half a century earlier the French language had lost its legal status as a language of instruction in the school system. The ACFA's call for the same privileges enjoyed by the English-speaking minority in Quebec went unheeded.[73] But in the 1960s, the climate changed. For seventy-five years French Canadians had fought to have bilingualism and biculturalism recognized across Canada, and finally in the late 1960s and the 1970s the principle was partially conceded.

The evolution in English-Canadian opinion largely came as a result of changes in Quebec itself.[74] In the early 1960s, the Liberals under Jean Lesage initiated reforms in Quebec's government, transforming the old structures into those of a modern bureaucratic state. The new Quebec became more assertive in its relations with the federal government. In the 1966 provincial elections, the Union Nationale under Daniel Johnson replaced the Liberals in power. The new government took an even stronger stand for greater provincial autonomy and for French and English linguistic equality throughout Canada. Others outside the government took a more extreme position, arguing that Quebec's demands would never be met by Canada, independence being the only answer. On the other hand, Prime Minister Lester Pearson and his federal Liberal government favored bilingualism and biculturalism. In the 1963 campaign they promised to form a Royal Commission to study English-French relations in Canada. Once elected they did.

With the publication of the preliminary findings of the Royal Commission in the mid-1960s, English-speaking Canadians learned of the extent of the growing discontent in Quebec. Many English Canadians believed that growing Quebec separatism could best be fought by granting more linguistic rights to the French Canadians outside Quebec. English Canadian opinion became even more conciliatory in the fall of 1967—immediately after René Lévesque, a former Liberal cabinet minister under Jean Lesage, left the Liberal Party to found an organization dedicated to seeking the independence of Quebec. The Parti Québécois was formed the following year.

Throughout the 1960s and 1970s, Alberta belatedly recognized a number of long-denied demands of the French-speaking population. Until 1964, the use of French in schools (where there were French-speaking students) was limited (after grade two) to approximately one hour per day. In this one hour period French grammar, reading, composition and literature were all taught. In 1964, however, the provincial government altered the School Act to allow the school board of any Alberta school district to direct that French be used as well as English as the language of instruction from grades one to nine.[75] In 1968 the School Act allowed for the extension of the use of French as the language of instruction from grades nine to twelve. It also permitted in designated bilingual schools this instruction to be up to fifty percent of the daily classroom hours.[76] Finally a regulation, adopted by the Minister of Education on 7 November 1976, authorized instruction in French "immersion schools" for all studies but English. French language instruction may now comprise 80 percent of the total instruction in this "immersion" programme.[77] By 1979, 40 percent of those Alberta children whose mother tongue was French were receiving instruction in bilingual or immersion schools.[78]

While a great step forward, the new legislation still did not recognize the right of every French-speaking child in Alberta to an education totally in his mother tongue. Bilingual or immersion schooling is designed for the anglophone student who is learning French as a second language, rather than the francophone student who enters the school speaking it as his mother tongue. The programme of the French-speaking students is delayed until the anglophone students, who enter not speaking a word of French, reach the level of the francophones. In the playground the language becomes English as the French-speaking children, for the most part, are already bilingual. Thus it has been argued, the bilingual and immersion schools still contribute to the assimilation of the French-speaking children.[79]

The new Canadian Constitution (which came into effect in April 1982) guarantees francophones, "where the numbers of those children so warrants," the right to attend publicly supported French schools.[80] The first all French language elementary schools opened in the Edmonton and Calgary separate School Boards in the fall of 1984.

In the field of communications, as in education, improvements have been made. Radio-Canada, the CBC's French language division, bought CHFA in Edmonton in 1974 and modernized it. Radio-Canada also borrowed or erected antennas permitting it to extend CHFA's broadcasting area.[81] Alberta received French language television in 1970.[82] Now linked to the Radio-Canada headquarters in Montreal, Radio-Canada in Alberta can receive directly all of the corporation's daily programming from eastern Canada.[83] But what is still lacking is a high quality service in French reflecting western Canadian interests.

Since the passage by the federal government of the Official Languages Act in 1969, federal funds totalling millions of dollars have been granted to the three prairie francophone organizations and their media (the press, radio and television). Ottawa also gives large subsidies to second official language programmes in the three prairie provinces and to social programmes. It is now in the interest of the federal government to impress upon the French-speaking Québécois the growth and the vitality of francophone communities outside of Quebec, as they want franco-phones in Quebec to believe in a bilingual Canada.[84]

A vitality certainly is visible. Cultural activities expanded in the French-speaking community in the late 1970s. In Edmonton *Le Théâtre Français d'Edmonton* produced several plays annually. A French language theatre group began meeting in Saint Paul, and a local drama circle was organized in Peace River. Throughout the province French language choral groups were active. In Saint Paul a group of young franco-Alber-tans formed *Les Blés d'Or* (The Golden Wheat), a popular dance troupe which performed French Canadian dances. Annually the *Cabane à Sucre*, or Sugar Shack, a popular get-together and cultural festival held in Edmonton, attracted 4 to 5,000 people. Nevertheless the forces of assimi-lation still weighed heavily upon the franco-Albertan community.[85]

In the 1960s and 1970s there was also evidence of a presence of the French language and of French-speaking Albertans in business. Thanks to the investment of large amounts of capital in the oil and gas industry by French and Belgian interests, a number of companies such as Aqui-taine, Elf, and Total of France have been active in Alberta. These com-panies employed a number of French personnel in the province, particu-larly in Calgary. A very prominent member of Calgary's oil and gas community has been Louis Lebel, a franco-Albertan from St. Paul, who has served as vice-president of Chevron Standard Ltd. and then presi-dent of Dome Canada Limited, as well as Chancellor of the University of Calgary. One of Alberta's wealthiest businessmen, Dr. Charles Allard of Edmonton, is of franco-Ontarian descent.[86]

Today's Challenges

As the French-speaking population becomes increasingly urbanized, the isolation of the community that once protected the rural francophones has ended. The increasing urbanization is shown by the growing number of people of French Canadian and French origin in Edmonton. In 1961 nearly 35 percent of those of French origin lived in the provincial capital, and by 1971 this percentage had risen to 41 percent.[87] Yet in Edmonton, one cannot always obtain service in stores and restaurants in French, and in other urban centers it is infinitely more difficult than in Edmonton to be served in French.[88]

Another factor which formerly helped to protect the community against assimilation was Alberta's French-speaking Roman Catholic clergy. Apart from a small French Canadian Protestant community at Bonnyville, nearly all French-speaking franco-Albertans were active members of the Roman Catholic Church, the parish church being the focal point of the community.[89] In the churches and the local schools, the cause of the French language and that of the church was traditionally presented as being the same: "If you lose your language you lose your faith." ("La langue est la gardienne de la foi.")[90] Yet in the last twenty years, a new relationship has developed between the clergy and the francophone community. Today's congregations no longer seek secular leadership from their clergy.[91] In 1970 only one out of five French Edmontonians even belonged to a French-speaking parish.[92] One wonders if the new lay elite, the business people and professionals, will be able to protect the community as effectively as the church once did.

Another challenge for the franco-Albertan community lies in its growing diversity and consequent lack of unity. No longer does the church lead the community, nor constantly remind it of the French Canadian's history in the West. Nor is the franco-Albertan community an homogenous one. From 1976 to 1981—during the province's great economic boom—a considerable number of French Canadians from Quebec, Ontario, and New Brunswick arrived in Alberta.[93] In fact the number of Albertans listing French as their mother tongue rose from 44,440 in 1976 to 62,145 in 1981 (for the first time in the history of western Canada, Alberta had a larger francophone population than Manitoba.)[94] The culture and outlook of these newcomers are quite different from those of the franco-Albertans whose roots extended back, in some cases, over a century or more in the West. The Québécois, who have lived through a period of turbulent change, have a much greater political awareness. New arrivals from France and a tiny number from former French colonies in Asia, the Middle East, Africa, and the Caribbean add to the diversity. Today, the franco-Albertan community is a small universe of its own, drawing its numbers from many social classes and from several different national backgrounds. Will a common language be a strong enough bond to unite what are really several different ethnic groups? Will newcomers join the existing French-speaking organizations?

For the young franco-Albertans, English language television and radio pose the greatest challenge of all. It has been estimated that Canadian children spend twice as much time watching television as they do sitting in school.[95] The values of an overwhelmingly English-speaking and Americanized society reach into almost every franco-Albertan home. In 1969 a researcher found that in Falher the most important French-speaking town in the Peace River district (where nearly 90 percent of the population are of French origin), "parents . . . claim their children speak French as little as possible and attribute this largely to the fact their formative years are spent watching English language television."[96] Today Falher has French language television but this in itself is not necessarily a solution. One French-language television station, and one radio station simply cannot supply the variety of programming that several English language channels can provide.

Formerly much attention was paid to the value of the family, the church, and the local community. Today, work and economic success have in many circles become paramount. Some franco-Albertans still fear that their language will work against their financial and social success.[97] In 1979, 60 percent of Alberta's francophone children attended unilingual English language schools. Nearly half of the 8,100 students in bilingual programmes in 1979 were the children of anglophones.[98]

The desire of anglophone parents to enrol their children in bilingual or immersion programmes has become intense. Bilingualism has become a job factor in politics, the civil service, and major Canadian companies. This new interest reflects the linguistic change that has taken place in Canada over the last ten years or so. In Ottawa the transformation has been dramatic. For the first time in Canadian history, Joe Clark, an anglophone prime minister and an Albertan, was able to respond to questions in the House of Commons in adequate French.[99]

What can be said of the future of the French language in Alberta? Today, while the number of native-born franco-Albertans daily using the language has declined, the number of anglophone Albertans learning it has vastly increased. In recent years, the number of students taking French as a course in school has nearly doubled in the province. Fifteen to 20 percent of the students in 1970 studied French, but in 1980 one-third took French as a second language.[100] In 1979 (the last year in which estimates of the linguistic background of the students can be obtained) four thousand anglophones were enrolled in bilingual programmes.[101] By 1980 Calgary alone claimed proportionately more students in immersion classes than any other Canadian city.[102] While losing a certain percentage of its own people, the franco-Albertan community will indeed gain additional strength from its new, English-speaking allies. Totally francophone schools will also help, giving franco-Albertan children a knowledge of their language, an opportunity to gain a better sense of their culture, and a pride in their background.[103]

Conclusion

At the turn of the century, many English-speaking Albertans insisted that their new province be entirely English-speaking. These newcomers, both Protestant and Catholic, had little understanding of, or respect for, the French language. They brought with them memories of ethnic conflict in the East. Because of these sentiments, three generations of French-speaking Albertans were deprived of a full publicly supported education in their own language.

The immigrants who later came from the United States and Europe never learned of western Canada's bilingual origins. The evidence had already been eliminated. This lack of information about the early French presence in Canada and on the plains, lies at the root of much of the misunderstanding of the French-speaking community's demands in this century.

The resurgence of a dynamic, assertive Quebec has given the franco-Albertan community a real opportunity to regain lost ground. As a partner in Confederation, the very minimum that Quebec will accept is the same respect for the rights of the French minorities in English-speaking Canada, as the English-speaking minority currently enjoys in Quebec. Restrictive though it may seem to many Albertans, Quebec's Bill 101, or Charter of the French Language, still grants to the anglophone minority in the province privileges denied elsewhere to the French-speaking minorities. The Quebec anglophones have their own entirely English-language educational system, from elementary school to university, and have the right to have their own school boards. Alberta, in contrast, while recently allowing access to entirely French language schools, denies their administration by French language boards.

CHAPTER FIVE

The Scots in Alberta
Norma J. Milton

Traditionally, Scottish immigrants to Alberta have been considered part of Canada's British-born population and little attention has been paid to the unique aspects of their culture or to the contribution they have made to the economic, political and social development of both the province and the nation. Scottish immigration to Canada began as a trickle of fur traders and explorers over 200 years ago. Gradually this immigration grew to a stream which rose and fell with the changes in economic conditions in Scotland, the opening of Canada's western frontier and the growth and diversification of the Canadian economy. In Alberta there was a relatively steady flow of Scottish immigrants who settled where farm land was available or in villages, towns and cities where their skills were in demand. They adapted to the comparatively unstructured and unsophisticated social environment, and they contributed their talents to the building of a society. At the same time, they retained several features of Scottish culture. Collectively the Scots are often viewed as being frugal in money matters, generous in hospitality, pragmatic in politics, and competitive in the pursuit of goals. That one can see these characteristics reflected in the history of Alberta's Scots could seem to suggest that this common stereotype about the Scottish character has at least some validity. Further, the ideas and skills which the Scots brought with them have been significant influences on the province's development. Whether they were farmers, tradesmen, or professionals, and whether they were from Orkney, Inverness, or Edinburgh, the Scots in Alberta have been a constant and significant presence throughout the history of the province.

Scots in the Fur Trade

The Scots first arrived in present day Alberta two centuries ago. Men such as Alexander Mackenzie and Simon Fraser came as fur traders, either in the employ of the North-West Company (NWC), based in

Montreal, or of the Hudson's Bay Company (HBC). The HBC's permanent trading posts at Fort Chipewyan and Fort Edmonton were often manned by Scottish clerks and factors recruited in the Orkney Islands and on the Scottish mainland.[1]

After the amalgamation of the HBC and the NWC in 1821, Scottish dominance of the fur trade personnel increased as the Orkney laborers of the HBC were joined with the Highlanders of the NWC. Perhaps the best known Scot who actually lived in Alberta was George Simpson. As chief factor of the Athabasca region with headquarters at Fort Chipewyan, he played a major role in the amalgamation of the rival fur trade companies.

Many descendants of those young Scottish clerks and apprentice traders who worked under Simpson and his predecessors are today Metis. The Scots often married native women in the "custom of the country." During the mid-1800s, their descendants were among the first to mine coal on the banks of the North Saskatchewan River near Edmonton, thus establishing a settlement not dependent on the fur trade for its existence. Others, known as the Scotch Metis, settled farming land in the north central and northern areas of the province. Many of the descendants of these mixed blood marriages have themselves married non-Indian Canadians and identify with their European rather than their native heritage.[2]

Scottish Participation in the Beginning of White Settlement

Canada's acquisition in 1870 of the HBC's claim to the northwest brought vast quantities of land under Canadian government control. Commissioner James Macleod of the NWMP, a Scot from the Isle of Skye, helped to facilitate the purchase of the land from the Indians. He was one of the two Commissioners for Treaty Seven, by which present day southern Alberta was transferred to the Crown.

Once the West was pacified, government officials believed a transcontinental railway and a population distributed across the prairies would ensure Canadian sovereignty. Scotsmen, such as Sanford Fleming, were among those who sought a route through the Rockies to the Pacific for the CPR, and Scottish botanist John Macoun reported that the Palliser Triangle had much greater agricultural potential than Captain John Palliser had observed. Migrants from Ontario, many of Scottish origin, pushed westward after the completion of the CPR, but they could not fill the millions of acres available for settlement. The need to bring more people to the West prompted the government and the railways to devise promotional schemes to attract immigrants from a variety of countries to the Canadian West. The federal government's immigration policy was designed to favor the British and made no distinctions among the cultural groups which inhabited the British Isles. The Scots were, therefore, among the officially preferred immigrants. Indeed, the first two prime ministers of Canada, Sir John A. Macdonald and Alexander Mackenzie (both Scottish born), were ardent supporters of British immigration.

Scottish immigrants have arrived steadily in western Canada from the 1890s to the present. By 1901 the portion of the Northwest Territories

which would shortly make up much of Alberta had a population of
73,022, of which slightly over 10 percent (9,866) were of Scottish origin
and 2 percent (1,568) were of Scottish birth.[3] Alberta's population had
grown to 374,295 by 1911, of which 16,183 were of Scottish birth and
54,866 were of Scottish origin.[4] Following World War I, the British and
Canadian governments resumed their promotion of British immigration.
In order to do so, they established a variety of assistance programmes
such as the Soldier Settlement Board, which provided British war veterans with assisted passage and homestead land, as well as with financial
assistance which enabled them to purchase the livestock and equipment
they needed to become farmers. The 1921 census shows that 96,062
Albertans, or 16 percent of the population, were of Scottish origin. Some
24,000 of these people, approximately 4 percent of the total population,
were of Scottish birth.

Scottish immigrants continued to come to Alberta until the economic
depression of the 1930s and World War II cut off immigration almost
entirely.[5] Scottish war brides, professionals and others seeking better
opportunities began arriving after World War II, thus maintaining the
Scottish component of Alberta's population in the postwar era. Changes
in Canadian immigration policy and changes in economic conditions in
both Canada and Britain have reduced the numbers of Scots arriving in
recent years. Those who have emigrated since the 1950s are mainly
skilled tradesmen, technicians, professionals (who are filling gaps in
Canada's employment market), or sponsored relatives who are joining
family members. Whether recent or pre-World War II arrivals, the Scottish immigrants who have settled in Alberta have dispersed throughout
the province in search of economic opportunities.

Scottish Bloc Settlements and Settlement in Rural Areas

While the majority of Scots who settled on farm land in Alberta arrived
as individuals or families and dispersed themselves across the province,
two group settlements were established. The Scots concentrated in the
area north of Brooks were recruited by the Duke of Sutherland's agents
following his purchase of 9,000 acres of land in Alberta in 1911. The
Duke was a wealthy Scottish aristocrat with extensive land holdings near
Golspie, Scotland, shares in the CPR and investments in South African
gold and diamond mines. He apparently planned to create in Alberta a
variation of his tenant-farmed estate in Scotland using tenant farmers
recruited from his Scottish estate and others willing to emigrate and
work for him. In 1913, thirty families and several single men, initially
agreed to come to the ready-made farms to care for the 5,000 hogs and
4,000 head of beef cattle which the Duke had purchased. These early
Scottish tenant farmers were followed by other Scottish and English
immigrants, until a thriving rural community had been established on
land owned by the Duke. In 1930 the Duke decided to sell his land in
Alberta back to the CPR. Some of the tenants purchased land they were
already living on; others chose to move to homesteads in other parts of
the province.[6]

The prefabricated log home of Murdock McKinnon, one of the Scottish settlers who came from the Hebrides to Clandonald in the mid-1920s. (Courtesy Glenbow Archives)

The second Scottish bloc settlement was started at Clandonald, north of Vermilion, during the 1920s, when Hebridean farmers and fishermen were brought to Alberta under a colonization scheme devised by a Catholic priest, Father R. A. MacDonell.[7] Father MacDonell saw group colonization as a means of preserving the Roman Catholic faith and of providing economic opportunity for the Catholic subsistence farmers and fishermen of Scotland's coastal islands. Historically, Hebrideans had migrated in large numbers because the islands' fishing-farming economy could not support large numbers of people. The 120 families recruited by Father MacDonell chose to leave when the Scottish fishing industry, the mainstay of the islands' economy, deteriorated following World War I.

The Clandonald settlement was only partially successful in supporting the families who came. The Hebrideans experienced severe hardships because of bad weather conditions following their arrival and because of initial adjustmental difficulties. An average farm in the Hebrides was five acres and the thought of farming a 160-acre homestead seemed to paralyze their first year of effort.[8] Their first three crops were damaged by rain, hail and frost before being harvested. By 1926, when undamaged, high yield crops were harvested, grain prices had begun to fall and did not recover until the mid-1930s. Consequently, though they had recovered from their initial fears and though growing conditions had improved, the Clandonald Scots fell further behind in achieving the economic stability and prosperity they sought. Several of these settlers served in the armed forces during World War II; following their discharge, they abandoned their farms for jobs in Vancouver or other coastal towns where the climate was less harsh. One resident estimated that 80 percent of the original Hebridean settlers left permanently either during or immediately following World War II.[9] Their land reverted to the Scottish Immigrant Aid Society and was later resold to post-World War II European immigrants and to some of the original settlers who chose to stay.

Scottish immigrants to Alberta generally found themselves welcome because they were among the officially preferred category of immigrants: most were Protestant, and the popular stereotype of a Scotsman—frugal, hard-working, and hardy—matched the public's image of the ideal immigrant. They were also welcomed because they were from a part of the British Isles, the motherland of Canada, and many Canadians believed that Canada should be an improved model of the motherland. Despite their easy acceptance, or at least a neutral attitude toward them, some Scottish immigrants found their new lives less rewarding than they had expected. For most, the disappointment and frustration was short-lived, but for some the struggle to adjust lasted a lifetime. Two groups of Scottish immigrants who found Alberta particularly inhospitable were those who had no previous farming skills but nevertheless settled on farms, and those who arrived in the late 1920s and almost immediately faced general economic depression while attempting to become established.

Scots in Alberta's Cities and Towns

Not all Scottish immigrants to Alberta prior to World War II chose to take up farming. Hundreds of skilled tradesmen found employment building the cities of Edmonton, Medicine Hat, Lethbridge and Calgary. Others became shopkeepers, insurance and real estate agents, livery stable owners, blacksmiths, butchers and bank clerks in the cities and small towns. Early urban police forces were frequently manned by young Scots, some with experience in Edinburgh, Glasgow, or other cities in Scotland and England. Many worked at odd jobs before finding openings in their particular trade or type of business; others found employment in their field of expertise almost immediately.

Those of Scottish descent often played important roles in their respective communities, as well as being helpful contacts for recent Scottish immigrants. Along with their wives and families, they formed the core of community volunteer organizations, such as service clubs and fraternal organizations, and the Presbyterian Church. They also organized groups to preserve the traditions of Scotland.

Early development of many of Alberta's urban centers was strongly influenced by the Scottish presence. Calgary has long been the most "British" city in the province and has always had a strong Scottish element in its business, administrative, and social life. Calgary was named in 1876 by Scottish-born Colonel James F. Macleod, who gave the city its Gaelic name because he had happy memories of a beauty spot with that name on the Isle of Mull. Calgary was influenced in its development by the British ranching community which it served.[10] Thus, Calgary eventually became known as the Scottish center of Alberta.[11]

Scotsman's Quarry (near Monarch), which operated from 1910 to 1913 with sixty Scottish stonemasons. The stone was used for the Lethbridge post office, the Banff Springs Hotel, and early CPR buildings. (Courtesy Glenbow Archives)

Residential communities in the growing city bore Scottish names such as New Edinburgh, a small area north of the Bow River in the district now known as Sunnyside.[12] The CPR shops in Calgary employed skilled and unskilled labor, including many Scottish machinists, carpenters, and other tradesmen.[13]

The Scots were also active in the city's business and professional community. Jack Gavin, who arrived in 1910, was an independent livestock commission agent and a member of the Board of Trade.[14] John Reid homesteaded near Red Deer in 1905, and later became secretary-treasurer and traffic manager for the Calgary Livestock Exchange.[15] James "Cappy" Smart was Calgary's fire chief.[16] George McGill opened a law practice in 1920 following military service in World War I.

Although Scottish influence was stronger in early Calgary than it was in other urban centers, several Scots were also represented in the business, governmental administration, and professional life of Edmonton. A. Blair Paterson, who came to Edmonton with his parents in 1910, graduated in law from the University of Alberta and established a practice.[17] Alexander Galbraith, a prominent livestock breeder who had lived in the United States from 1883 to 1915, was superintendent of agricultural fairs and institutes for the provincial government.[18] Aside from their business and professional activities, these men were also members of various volunteer fraternal and service organizations. Thus, like their Calgary counterparts, these early Scottish business and professional men and their families participated in a variety of ways in the development of their city and their province.

Scots in Alberta's Politics

The participation of Scottish immigrants in the economic and social life of Alberta's rural communities, towns, and cities was an expression of their interest in developing a successful life for themselves as well as for their community. This interest in community development was also expressed in politics. Although the typical urban, business, or professional Scottish Albertan of 1924 was a Conservative, Scots immigrants have been supporters and prominent members of a variety of national and provincial political parties.[19]

Scots in Alberta appear to have been almost evenly divided in their support for the Liberal and Conservative parties prior to World War I. However, following the social turmoil of the post-war period, the rise of the farmers' Progressive political movement was supported by Scots in rural and even in urban Alberta. Some Albertans of Scottish origin were elected to the provincial legislature and served as cabinet ministers. These politicians campaigned and were elected as UFA, Labor, or Independent candidates. The economic upheaval of the 1930s and the rise of Social Credit again saw the Scots among the political majority. Whether they were urban or rural, their economic stability had been severely eroded and they supported William Aberhart and the Social Credit movement. Businessmen, professionals and some rural Scots may have continued their support for the traditional parties, but they were a minority. Whether federal or provincial, political ideas and government policy have generally been of great interest to the Scots.

In a study of the socio-cultural characteristics of Albertan legislators from 1905 to 1970, M. L. Malliah found that of a total of 432 individuals who had been elected to the provincial legislature, 109 were of Scottish origin, but only 20 of these were of Scottish birth.[20] Three political parties dominated three well-defined periods in the sixty-five years which Malliah studied. During these periods, Scottish-born legislators represented 11.4 percent of all MLAs during the Liberal regime from 1905 to 1921; 27.7 percent during the UFA regime from 1921 to 1935; and 12.6 percent during the Social Credit regime from 1935 to 1971. During the UFA period, 4 of 9 cabinet members were of Scottish origin.[21] Yet Scottish immigrants comprised only 2.7 percent of the provincial population in 1921, 3.8 percent in 1931, and 1.5 percent in 1961.[22] Thus their representation in the government of Alberta considerably exceeded their representation in the population. Some tentative explanation of this disproportionately high representation may lie in the popular stereotype of the Scots as being frugal and hard-working or in their familiarity with the political system based as it was on the British model. Or perhaps a partial explanation may be found in the generally high level of education among Scottish immigrants.[23] To be sure, Scottish immigrants who entered politics attracted support because of the political parties they represented, but their ability to articulate these ideas and their social status undoubtedly aided their campaigns.

Many of Alberta's Scottish-born politicians entered political life as municipal councillors, school trustees, and through farm organizations. Typical of this group are Robert Gardiner and Donald Cameron. Gardiner came to Alberta in 1902 and took up land near Medicine Hat. He served as a councillor for the Municipal District of Golden Centro from 1914-1921, including one term as Reeve.[24] A popular and articulate orator, Gardiner was active in the UFA and was selected as its candidate in the 1921 Medicine Hat federal by-election. He held this seat until 1935. Cameron, who came to Alberta in 1906, was a founding member of the Alberta Non-Partisan League and an active member of the UFA in the Innisfail area. He served in the provincial legislature as a UFA member from 1921 to 1935.[25]

The Scottish-born politician who achieved the province's highest office also emerged from the farmers' movement. Richard Gavin Reid homesteaded near Mannville, Alberta in 1904. He became active in local affairs and served several terms as a municipal councillor, organizing the first municipal hospital district in the province in 1918.[26] Reid was elected as a UFA member to the Alberta legislature in 1921 and held the post of Minister of Health and Municipal Affairs until 1923. He served as Provincial Treasurer from 1923 to 1925 and held the dual portfolios of Municipal Affairs and Provincial Treasurer from 1925 to 1934. A personal scandal forced Premier Brownlee to resign in the spring of 1935, and the UFA caucus chose Reid to succeed him. Reid became

Alberta's sixth premier; however, his term in office was cut short by the landslide victory of Social Credit later that same year.

Although the majority of Alberta's Scottish-born politicians came from the ranks of the farmers' movement, some came from the labor movement and a few were professionals who represented urban constituencies. They campaigned and won election under a variety of political labels, including Labor, Independent and UFA. Among this group were: Robert C. "Bob" Edwards, editor of the *Calgary Eye Opener*, who was elected as an Independent MLA from Calgary in 1921; Arthur Smeaton, a Scottish-born steam engineer and machinist, who was elected in 1926 as a Labor representative from Lethbridge; Alexander Ross, a Scottish stonemason, who was elected as Labor MLA from Calgary Centre in 1917; William Irvine who was elected to the House of Commons in 1921 as a Labor member from Calgary East; and John F. Lymburn, a lawyer, who was elected as a UFA member for Edmonton in 1926.[27] Smeaton served two terms in the legislature. Lymburn served until the UFA government was defeated in 1935, most of that time as provincial attorney General. Alexander Ross was a leader in Calgary's construction unions and president of the Alberta Federation of Labor in 1914.[28] He was elected to the legislature in 1917. During his two terms in the provincial house, Ross was instrumental in the passage of a minimum wage bill and was Minister of Public Works.[29]

Of all the Scottish-born political representatives from Alberta, William Irvine was the most radical in his time and is perhaps the most well remembered today. He was among those who forced the breakup of the two-party system in Canada's federal politics, and was a founding member of two political parties. Born at Gletness in the Shetland Islands in 1885, Irvine came to North America in 1902 seeking work to finance a much desired education.[30] In 1904 illness forced him to return to Shetland. During that time Irvine's political philosophy was strongly influenced by the socialism of his father and by the political activism of his cousins.[31]

Following his recovery Irvine became a Methodist lay preacher and was recruited by Rev. Dr. James Woodsworth in 1907 to train as a Methodist minister in Canada. After ordination he became a supply minister in Ontario and Manitoba before being appointed full-time pastor at Emo, Ontario.[32] During his ministry there, Irvine was the subject of a heresy trial as a result of his socialist views. Though acquitted, he resigned and accepted an appointment to the First Unitarian Church of Calgary.[33]

The Calgary appointment provided Irvine with a degree of financial stability, while allowing him time to devote to a variety of social causes. He organized a People's Forum to debate current issues, started a newspaper, *The Nutcracker*, as a source of alternative opinion in the city, and became a founding member of the Non-Partisan League.[34]

Soon politics replaced religion as Irvine's prime occupation. He contested both the federal and provincial elections of 1917, but was defeated. However, four years later, he became the federal representative for Calgary East, elected as a Labor candidate. Irvine and his old friend, J. S. Woodsworth, along with Progressive members, such as T. C. Crerar and Agnes McPhail, were numerically the official opposition in the Canadian parliament. The effect of this group was to break up the tradi- tional two-party system in the House of Commons by introducing a third party which held the balance of power.

Irvine's association with the Progressives was short-lived because he felt that they were only slightly ahead of the Liberals in their thinking— thinking which Irvine believed did not include social or economic justice for all. His passionate desire to improve the living and working condi- tions of manual workers through genuine democracy placed him within a small group of radical MPs who became known as the Ginger Group. Irvine's socialist-humanist philosophy was reflected in his many parlia- mentary speeches, articles and books. His ideas brought strong reactions from admirers and detractors alike.

Before his death in 1962, Irvine had served seventeen years as a federal MP, founded a newspaper, published seventeen books, and had been a founding member of the Co-operative Commonwealth Federation (CCF) and the New Democratic parties.[35] The impact of Irvine's activi- ties and the ideas he supported significantly changed the political struc- ture of Canada and left an imprint on Alberta.

Since 1935 the number of Scottish immigrants elected to office in Alberta has declined. This decline is a result of their declining numbers in the population, a weakening of the bias against non-Anglo-Saxon candidates, and more Albertan and Canadian-born individuals becoming politically active.

Scottish Immigrants Settling In

Unlike some other ethnic groups forced to leave their homelands because of religious or political persecution or severe poverty, the major- ity of Scots arrived with both material possessions and money. Few Scots arrived without some item to remind them of Scotland and of Scottish traditions or values. Such items may have been a treasured family heir- loom, a family crest, a small piece of amber-colored stone from the Caringorm Mountains, a book of Robert Burns' poetry, a tartan shawl or a plaid blanket.[36]

A major component of the intangible cultural baggage brought by Scottish immigrants was the knowledge that Canada was an English- speaking, Christian country with institutions modelled on the British system and with citizens loyal to the British crown. Therefore, the Scots expected little difficulty in earning a living, making new friends, and establishing themselves securely in the new land. In general these expectations were fulfilled. Probably half of the new arrivals had rela- tives or friends already living in Canada (although not necessarily in Alberta) which also contributed to the ease of their adjustment.[37]

Immigrants who came to Alberta's cities and towns expecting to find surroundings similar to those they had left in Scotland soon learned that frontier towns and cities were made up of dusty, unpaved streets, board sidewalks, stores with strange goods on their racks and shelves, and people representing a variety of nationalities seeking jobs or land. Yet, those who settled in the cities or towns could easily make social contacts. However, for those who settled in the rural areas, distance and lack of transportation often meant months of isolation. Such was the experience of a pioneer woman, Mrs. MacNeill, who after seven months of seeing only her husband and his brother, eagerly looked forward to visiting her farm neighbors some distance away. When she arrived at the neighbors home she was bitterly disappointed, since the woman spoke only German and she only English. Meaningful communication was impossible, despite willingness to try and many gestures.[38]

In spite of the problems of social adjustment, adapting to Alberta's society before World War II was usually less discouraging than struggling to survive the first winter on a homestead. The Scottish immigrant who believed the glowing descriptions of the Canadian climate contained in immigration promotion literature frequently experienced discomfort and disillusionment. For example, the MacGregor family, who set off from Scotland following Mr. MacGregor's retirement from the military, came to Canada intending to create a gentle, country life growing fruit and nut trees on a homestead where a season called Indian Summer lasted well into November and spring came in March.[39] The realities of the first harsh winter at Westlock, the soon recognized possibility of snow for nine months of the year and the presence of insect pests in spring and summer made their life quite different from what they had imagined it would be.

Scottish Organizations in Alberta

The songs, dances and costumes of their homelands are often the only visible link between the old and the new world which immigrants maintain. Most Scottish immigrants and many of their descendants in the province today are associated in some way with pipe bands, highland dancing or Scottish country dancing.[40] Although Scottish country dancing may not be well known to the public, pipe bands and highland dancing have become an integral part of Alberta's culture. While deeply rooted in Scottish tradition, both pipe bands and highland dancing have become community activities in recent years. Many participants are attracted because they are interested in the music or the dance form itself, rather than because these forms are expressions of their ethnic heritage. Similarly, the thousands who regularly golf or curl are in effect playing games which were originally Scottish, but which have been absorbed into the mainstream of North American culture.

Music, dance, and athletic competitions are the major elements of the Highland Games which have been held intermittently in the province since Edmonton's first annual Caledonian Games in 1909.[41] These games included competition in pole vaulting, tossing the cabre, bagpiping, highland dancing and a game, similar to horseshoes, known as quoits. Although earlier such events may have gone unrecorded, the first Highland Games in Calgary was probably held in 1923.[42] Games were held in

A Scottish dance at Nanton in January 1918. "You're Welcome Here, Sa Mak Yersel at Hame." (Courtesy Glenbow Archives)

Banff on the grounds of the baronial Banff Springs Hotel, from 1927 to 1931 under the sponsorship of Calgary's St. Andrew's Caledonian Society, the Banff Amateur Athletic Association and the CPR. This five-year period appears to have been the apex of Highland Games in Alberta, with royalty and prominent politicians among the spectators who watched piping, drumming, and dance competitions, who heard Rev. Dr. Charles Gordon (writer, "Ralph Connor") preach, or listened to Scottish songs by one of Scotland's leading baritones.[43] The Games returned to Calgary in 1932 and were held in the less resplendant surroundings of Mewata Stadium until the beginning of World War II. The Highland Games resumed in 1946, lapsed for seven years, were revived in 1969, and have since been held annually. Most of the Highland Games held in Alberta have had as premier events competition in Highland dancing, piping and drumming, with little emphasis on traditional track and field events.

The pipe band is linked directly to our Canadian military tradition, since it came from the British Isles before Confederation. Alberta's Highland regiment, the Calgary Highlanders, evolved from the 1910 Calgary Rifles and a reorganization of the nation's military forces following World War I. The regiment was designated as a kilted unit and shortly after its formation it established formal ties with the Argyll and Sutherland Highlanders of Scotland. Known first as the Calgary Regiment and then, beginning in 1924, as the Calgary Highlanders, the regimental pipe band gained wide recognition at home during the interwar years and overseas during World War II.[44] After returning to Calgary in November 1945, the regiment became a reserve unit. The pipe band has remained active, and its members are mainly second or third generation Canadians of Scottish origin.[45] Although pipe bands are strongly linked to military tradition, the late 1960s and 1970s have seen the organization of pipe bands by several community groups.

Highland dancing is an offshoot of the traditional piping competitions held in Scotland during the late eighteenth century. Pipers waiting to compete danced to the music of the pipes. The audience apparently appreciated the dancing and demanded more of this entertainment in conjunction with piping competitions.[46] It has since evolved into a world-wide competitive activity, strictly regulated by the Highland dancing association in Scotland.

The Alberta Highland Dancing Association, formed in Edmonton in 1937, has branches across Alberta's cities and is responsible for organizing dancing competitions.[47] The members of the organization are parents of dancers and dance teachers, approximately half of whom are of Scottish birth or origin.[48] The Highland Dance Association has stronger ties with Scotland than any other of the Scottish organizations in the province because the competitions which it organizes are controlled by the international parent body in Scotland.

Although less familiar to the public than Highland dancing and pipe bands, Scottish country dancing groups in Alberta's cities also attract Scottish and non-Scottish members. These groups provide instruction in the traditional social dancing of Scotland and organize social events. Scottish country dancing is akin to North American square dancing.

While competitive piping and highland dancing have formed the basis of several Scottish organizations in Alberta, other organizations are of a social and fraternal nature. The Sons of Scotland has helped Scottish immigrants adjust to Canadian life for more than 100 years. From its origins in Ontario, this organization has spread across Canada and has provided social welfare, recreation activities and low cost life insurance to its members. Edmonton's Scottish Society, Calgary's St. Andrew's Caledonian Society, and Red Deer's Burns Club are also organizations which regularly sponsor social events to bring their members together. These contemporary associations evolved from several amalgamations and name changes of groups formed by early Scottish immigrants to these cities. A Caledonian Club existed in Edmonton in 1907 with a membership of 300.[49] A Caledonian Society and a St. Andrew's Society existed in Calgary in the years before 1920.[50] A Scottish Society existed in Red Deer in the early 1920s.[51] These groups were formed to provide social contact among Scots, to give assistance to new arrivals and to sponsor celebrations of St. Andrew's Day on 30 November and the birthday of Scottish poet Robert Burns on 25 January.

The celebration of Robert Burns' birth has been and remains the central symbol of being Scottish in Alberta. It is likely that a Burns' celebration of some type has been held somewhere in the province every year since before the turn of the century. These events were most likely small gatherings in private homes where family and friends shared a meal and a dram, and then read or recited Burns' poetry. Public Burns' dinners have been held annually in Calgary and Edmonton since at least 1909 and have usually followed a traditional form interlaced with music by a piper: dinner, including haggis, a toast to Burns, and a speaker who elaborates some aspect of Burns' writing or character. These dinners in honor of one of Scotland's most important heroes provide an important means for people of Scottish descent to reaffirm their cultural heritage.

Conclusion

The Scottish presence in Alberta has been of long duration and quiet significance. From the early fur traders to the post-World War II professionals, Scottish immigrants have participated actively in society. Scottish homesteaders opened virgin land in almost all areas of the province and helped to establish rural schools and municipalities. Skilled tradesmen built the early buildings in urban areas, mined coal, and established shops or services to serve the needs of growing communities. During the social and economic upheavals of the 1920s and 1930s, Scottish-born politicians and union leaders applied their political ideologies and knowledge to the problems which arose. These efforts modified the structure of the national government and brought about legislation which benefitted many. The popular stereotype of the Scots eased their acceptance into society and assisted them in establishing themselves in various occupations, while their humor and generosity gave them the ability to acknowledge their own humanity and that of others.

The Scots were assumed to be British; therefore, they were not subjected to the assimilative pressures experienced by other immigrant groups. Their easy acceptance made the retention of their cultural traditions simply a matter of private or public continuance of celebrations and activities held in Scotland. The variety and degree of participation in traditional Scottish culture has varied with the ebb and flow of the economy and with the demands of war, but it has never died. Post-World War II immigration and affluence have broadened the activity of some organizations and attracted an increasing number of Canadians. Discussion of Robert Burns' life and works may not be the main attraction for Scots who attend annual Burns' dinners, but their loyalty to their Scottish heritage and their desire to meet other Scots ensure that these functions are well attended.

The majority of Scottish-Albertans arrived before World War II and were engaged in establishing basic patterns of social, economic and political activity in the province. Although few in number, the dispersed nature of their settlement pattern, their determination to achieve their goals, their wide acceptance in society, and their participation in all facets of social, economic, and political life resulted in the Scots being omnipresent in the developing society. These same characteristics were brought to Alberta by post-World War II Scottish immigrants who, like their predecessors, filled shortages in the skilled labor market or carved economic niches for themselves in the professions, in commerce, and in agriculture. They too have continued to support Scottish cultural traditions and have introduced many Canadians to these traditions. Though less visible than the pre-World War II group, more recent immigrants have continued to exert a Scottish influence on the province. The Scottish presence in Alberta has left its imprint on our society in traces of determination, independence, and pride.

CHAPTER SIX

"Rural Ontario West":
Ontarians in Alberta[1]

R. Douglas Francis

Prior to 1850 English-speaking Canadians had a mental image of the Northwest as a formidable wilderness: an area with little agricultural potential, peopled by hostile Indians, and fit only for fur traders. Yet, those perceptions changed once reports reached Upper and Lower Canada in the 1850s of the true richness of the soil on the Plains. With the filling up of the Upper Canadian frontier in the 1850s, the attraction of the Northwest grew, particularly after Canada purchased it in 1870, and after the Plains Cree and Blackfoot Indians had been settled in the early 1880s on their reserves.

Tens of thousands of Ontarians migrated westward in the 1880s and 1890s.[2] They came from all areas of their native province, bringing with them the perceptions of an established English-speaking Canada. So many came, in fact, that they constituted the largest single group of people in the new province of Alberta, which some soon called "Rural Ontario West." These Ontarians played an important role in shaping the development of Alberta's economic, political and social institutions, particularly in the formative pre-World War I era.[3]

The first Upper Canadians or Ontarians (as they would be called after Confederation in 1867) came west in spite of the widely held negative view of the area. The missionaries' spiritual mission superseded material concerns. They expected hardship and deprivation. Although most of the early Protestant missionaries came from England—especially the Anglicans and Presbyterians—as part of the nineteenth-century British religious crusade to Christianize and to civilize the heathens, Ontarians constituted a significant number of the early Methodist ministers in the Northwest. The Methodist church in Canada was more independent of the home church in England and more nationalistic than either the Anglican or Presbyterian churches. From the beginning of settlement in the West, the Methodist church contributed a strong Ontarian presence.[4]

In 1854 the Canadians took over the early British Wesleyan missions and established their own in the Northwest. The first two ministers, both ordained in Ontario, arrived one year later. The Reverend Thomas Woolsey, officially stationed at Fort Edmonton, did extensive missionary work among the Crees on the Plains and the Stoneys (Assiniboines), while the Reverend Henry B. Steinhauer, a native of Lake Simcoe and a full-blooded Ojibwa, located at Whitefish Lake.[5] This Indian minister from Upper Canada established the first permanent Indian settlement in present day Alberta.

After their arrival in the 1860s, George and John McDougall expanded the missionary work.[6] George, originally from Kingston, did his initial missionary work among the Ojibwa near Sault Ste. Marie. After this apprenticeship, his church appointed him the Superintendent of Missionary Work in the Northwest in 1860. For three years, he was stationed at Norway House, the important HBC post in what is now northern Manitoba; then he moved further west, along with his eldest son, John, to begin a mission at Victoria (now Pakan), located some seventy miles downstream from Edmonton. In 1874, George McDougall established the Morleyville mission among the Stoney Indians in the foothills. After his death in 1876 his son, John, persuaded them to sign Treaty Seven in 1877.

John McDougall, who was fluent in the Cree language, carried on his father's work at Victoria near Henry Steinhauer's mission at Whitefish Lake. In 1865, he married Abigail Steinhauer, Henry's daughter, and the couple moved to Pigeon Lake where they organized another mission. One year after Abigail's death from smallpox in 1871, John McDougall met in Ontario, and married, Elizabeth Boyd of Cape Rich, Grey County. She became the first white woman and the first Ontarian woman in that southwestern area of Alberta.[7] McDougall contributed to the peaceful settlement of the West assuring the Indians in the 1870s and '80s that the influx of white farmers from Ontario and elsewhere would benefit them, leading them toward a new way of life.

A New and Positive Image of the West

A more positive view of the West developed in the East in the 1850s.[8] Perhaps the man most responsible for this change in attitude was George Brown, editor of the Toronto *Globe* and leader of the Reform movement in Ontario in the late 1850s and 1860s. Brown looked at the West solely for its potential to central Canada, and particularly to his native province, and he envisioned a number of possibilities.

Acquisition of the West, he believed, could solve the problem of political deadlock between the powerful English-speaking Protestant population of Canada West (Ontario) and the entrenched French-speaking Catholic population of Canada East (Quebec). Brown saw the West, populated predominantly by Anglo-Saxons (primarily from Ontario), as the means to tip the political scales in Ontario's favor.

Economic considerations also made expansion imperative. Ontario needed markets for its growing commercial and industrial interests.

Brown convinced businessmen in Toronto of the logic of his scheme of westward expansion and thus won over an important and powerful segment of Ontario's society. He also constantly reminded his *Globe* subscribers in the mid-1850s that the good arable farmland in the Canadas was gone.[9]

Finally, cultural consideration promoted expansion. The middle and late nineteenth century saw the rise of an imperial sentiment in Ontario, the extension of British values and ideals, which included a desire to spread "superior" Anglo-Saxon cultural and social values to less fortunate areas. Ontario's mission lay in the West. They envisioned the Northwest as an area that could be molded into another Ontario— indeed transformed into a "new Eden," superior to Ontario itself.

Early Ontario Migrants

Until Canada purchased Rupert's Land from the HBC in 1870, Ontarian migration was slight. A group of some 175 men in search of gold in the interior of British Columbia, the "Overlanders of 1862," became the first to make the trip west entirely through Hudson's Bay territory.[10] They stopped near Fort Edmonton en route and formed some very positive impressions of the area. Other Ontarians hesitated to come West, though, fearing the warlike Crees and Blackfoot. They would wait until the federal government made peace with the tribes and had surveyed the area.

In 1873 the government created the NWMP force to ensure Canadian law and order in the West. The government then obtained the purchase of central Alberta from the Crees in 1876; a year later, in 1877, the NWMP helped in securing the purchase of southern Alberta from the Blackfoot, Sarcees, and Stoneys.

Some of the first Ontarians to come to present day Alberta were NWMP (about one-half of the force's officer staff in the late nineteenth century came from Ontario). The Mounties played an important role in molding western society according to their image of what Canadian society should be, namely Ontario.[11]

A large percentage of the force stayed in western Canada after their service contracts ended. In southern Alberta, many became independent small ranchers or managers of the large ranches. Their Ontarian upbringing, their familiarity with the land, and the respect they initially enjoyed from the native population enabled them to fit easily and readily into the predominantly British ranching community.[12]

A number of the early Ontarian migrants became prominent politicians and journalists. Among them was Frank Oliver, the first Albertan newspaper editor, who played a very important role in the province's political life. A resident of Brampton, just northwest of Toronto, Oliver had apprenticed in the office of the Toronto *Globe*. In 1872 he moved to Winnipeg to work on the *Free Press*, and then in the spring of 1876 joined an oxcart brigade bound west for Fort Edmonton. For four years he worked as an itinerant trader and storekeeper before acquiring his own newspaper.[13]

Oliver never pretended that his paper, the Edmonton *Bulletin*, exemplified objective and impartial journalism. Western tradition has it that two standard reactions existed to his paper: those who swore by it, and those who swore at it. He certainly did make his own biases clear to his readers: uncompromising opposition to John A. Macdonald and the Conservative government; unrelenting support for agricultural and industrial growth in the West; and vigorous defense of western rights. Few editors in the West could match Oliver for his boundless confidence in the potential of the new territories. Oliver became one of the first of a long line of Easterners who, once in the West, became the stalwart and uncritical supporters of the region.

The young editor sought political as well as journalistic influence. In 1883 the District of Edmonton elected him to the Northwest Council, where he championed self-government for the Territories, and fought for a first-rate public school system. The ambitious Edmontonian in 1896 ran federally as a Liberal. Winning the Edmonton riding, he became in the years to follow very influential as Minister of the Interior for the Laurier government from 1905 to 1911, during which time he reorganized the Department of the Interior and pursued an aggressive policy of land settlement. Never one to forget his political powerbase, he made sure that Edmonton—not Calgary—became the capital of the new province of Alberta in 1905. He remained in federal politics until 1917.

Another Ontarian began the Calgary *Herald*. Late in July 1883, Thomas Braden arrived in the tiny frontier tent village on the east bank of the Elbow.[14] He set up his Washington press in a 12' x 24' tent with a wooden floor and began publication on 31 August 1883. His first run of 500 copies sold for $.10 each. Over a century later the *Herald* still appears, outliving the *Bulletin* which expired in the mid-1950s.

A Brampton classmate of Frank Oliver's also proved a success in Alberta's politics: Senator James Lougheed, grandfather of Premier Peter Lougheed. Trained as a lawyer in Ontario, he came to Calgary in the same year Braden began the *Herald*, 1883. Shortly afterward he married well. As his bride he selected Belle Hardisty, daughter of the wealthy William Hardisty, a chief factor for the HBC and later Conservative senator for the Territories. Advancement was quick for known Albertan Conservatives while John A. Macdonald was prime minister (he died in 1891). At the age of thirty-five, Lougheed himself became a Conservative senator in 1889 after the death of his father-in-law. His political philosophy, as expressed in his Anglo-Saxon elitist attitude toward new immigrants, his strong sense of nationalism, and his religious convictions reflected his Ontarian upbringing.[15]

The Liberal Oliver and the Conservative Lougheed joined forces with fellow Ontarian, Frederick W. G. Haultain, to fight for western rights and provincial status for the Northwest Territories. Born in Woolwich, England in 1857, Haultain grew up and received his early education in Ontario. He went to the University of Toronto before entering law at Osgoode Hall in 1879. After graduation the ambitious young barrister and solicitor emigrated to Fort Macleod, the headquarters of the NWMP, where he served as crown prosecutor. Here on the frontier, where there were few individuals with legal training, Haultain's advancement came quickly. By the 1890s he had become the leading member of the territorial Council of the Northwest Territories, the equivalent of a provincial premier.

Haultain's influence went well beyond politics. He personally invited his friend, David James Goggin of Durham (east of Toronto), to become the first Superintendent of Education and Director of Normal Schools in the Territories. Goggin had been a student, teacher, and high school principal before moving West, where he had the reputation of being "Ontario's best model school teacher." As a firm believer in the superiority of Ontario's educational system he looked to his native province for inspiration and ideas in establishing the educational program in the Northwest Territories. Thanks to Haultain and Goggin, the early schools in the Territories and later Alberta reflected Protestant Ontario's educational goals, cultural values, curricula textbooks, and standards.[16]

Both men saw the schools as instruments for perpetuating Ontario, and therefore traditional British values, and as the acculturizing agents for French Canadians and new immigrants. In a classic statement of educational goals, Goggin reiterated a belief which was accepted without question by most Anglo-Saxon settlers in the West:

> To assimilate [the] different races, to secure the co-operation of [the] alien forces, are problems demanding for their solution, patience, tact and tolerant but firm legislation. . . .
>
> Only through our schools getting an early hold of the children of these settlers can we hope to train them to live according to our social system and to understand and appreciate the institutions of the country which they are to form an integral part of. If in these respects we can place these people two generations hence where their Anglo-Saxon neighbours now are we shall have done well.[17]

Goggin could rely for support on a significant number of Ontario-educated teachers who passed through the Normal School in the Northwest Territories. If the figures available in the first Annual Report of the Minister of Education for Alberta in 1905 are any indication, then over 30 percent of the certificates granted at the Normal School went to teachers from Ontario, the largest group outside of teachers from Alberta itself. In 1906, for example, 103 of the 308, or one-third of the teachers certified in the province, had been educated in Ontario.[18] This trend continued until World War I. By 1920, the Ontario-educated teachers in Alberta had dropped to one-eighth, a reflection of the overall decline in the percentage of Ontarians in the province. Here again is evidence of the tremendous influence exerted by Ontarians in the early history of the province.

The First Boom Period: The 1880s

The 1880s ushered in Alberta's first dramatic boom period. The population expanded phenomenally from 1,000 whites in 1881 to over 17,000 in 1891, the majority coming from Ontario. By 1883, the CPR had reached Calgary, making the overland trip quicker and more comfortable, encouraging even the most hesitant traveller. By 1889, the CPR excursion trains from Ontario and Quebec served as added incentive to eastern Canadians to move West.

Ontario churches and their members played an important part in encouraging the colonization of the West in the 1880s. They wanted to ensure that the region would be provided with the proper religious institutions and Christian values. In the Red Deer and Lacombe areas, for example, local Methodists encouraged other fellow church members in Ontario to locate in the area. The importance of the Ontarian presence for the religious growth of the Northwest is evident in a speech by Reverend Rice of Winnipeg at the Methodist Church Conference in Toronto in 1881:

> Now I want Ontario to empty itself into the country. There are multitudes of English tenant farmers to whom our Ontario people could sell out their property and invest in larger farms in the North-West. We want to keep our sons in that country; we want to preserve a high ideal in regard to morality and temperance, and we want a class of men who understand what is meant by freedom—not licentiousness politically, but freedom. Give us Ontario men to lead political opinion, then let the tide come from the Old Countries and they will harmonize it, and with the establishment of schools and churches all through that land we will have one of the finest places on our earth for humanity to dwell in.[19]

Many settlers tried to convince their friends, regardless of their denomination, to join them—what excitement, they wrote home, to settle and cultivate prairie land that had never been ploughed. The following excerpt from a letter by a woman from Perth (south of Ottawa) who was the wife of one of the early Albertan ranchers, is characteristic of many of the letters by newly arrived immigrants:

> This is the only life! I have any number of troubles, in fact too numerous to mention, but I forget them all in this joyous air with the grand protecting mountains always standing around the western horizon. They seem the very spirit of the old hymn[6] "Abide with me—, Oh Thou that changest not"—and they are the dearest most constant of friends.[20]

Other Ontarians came simply on impressions of the West in letters written to local newspapers. One such letter written in 1885 by Thomas Conant, the Toronto *Globe*'s farm correspondent, began by noting the difficulties and hardships he encountered en route, especially loneliness:

> Don't for a moment suppose that the places marked on the CPR chart are towns between Moose Jaw and Calgary. Most of the places are section boss' houses and a water tank. The CPR station their men every twelve miles, and just how these fellows refrain from committing suicide is a problem I have yet to learn from them.[21]

Tongue-in-cheek, he also warned single ladies about the dangers of visiting the West alone. "The male sex so greatly predominates that our Ontario girls must take warning and keep away from the West if they would retain their liberties and single blessedness." Then came the positive endorsement—above all else this land had a terrific potential for energetic Ontarian farmers willing to give it a try. Obviously the advantages outweighed the drawbacks since Ontarians continued to come West.

The peak period of Ontarian migration to Alberta occurred at the turn of the century (1890-1910). The population of Alberta rose from approximately 25,000 to 375,000; the number of Ontario-born in the province rose proportionately from approximately 4,500 to 57,500. Some of these migrants came by way of the United States where they had gone for jobs or good land a decade or so earlier. The opening of the Canadian West during the prosperity of the early twentieth century enabled these Canadian exiles to return. Here, in the "last best West" opportunities were more readily available than in any other area of the continent.[22]

From biographical sketches and local histories a definite pattern emerges in the movement of Ontarians during this period. Not surprisingly those from Ontario's urban areas generally gravitated towards the towns and villages in Alberta, and country people went to rural areas in Alberta. This resumption of their former jobs indicates that they were not attempting to escape from them, but rather sought greater opportunities to advance. Thus the West attracted many enterprising and adventuresome individuals who could see little personal opportunity in Ontario, but unlimited possibilities in the Northwest. Oliver, Haultain, and Lougheed are all typical examples.

Ontario Migration to Rural Alberta at the Turn of the Century

Settlers from rural Ontario could be found dispersed throughout the province, from the Peace River district in the north to Pincher Creek, Cardston and Medicine Hat in the south. They congregated in the largest numbers, though, in two areas: around Calgary (particularly west to Cochrane, east to Strathmore and south to High River, Claresholm and Vulcan); and in central Alberta (extending northeast of Red Deer and southeast of Edmonton, including within its radius such towns as Vermilion, Wainwright and Castor).[23]

The region around Calgary, a mixed area of ranching and wheat farming, became one of the first areas to be settled because of the CPR. The pleasant Chinook climate made the region especially good for ranching, and the rich soil east of the town made it attractive for homesteading. This area of settlement was mainly Anglo-Saxon territory, with the American, British and Ontarian settlers providing the dominant presence. Arriving before 1910 these settlers were able to claim the region's best homestead acreage.

Many Ontarians, at the turn of the century, chose to find work in the towns and small cities rather than to homestead. Unlike many of the European immigrants, the Ontarians spoke English, some had a high school education, and others often had the capital necessary for urban success. In Claresholm, for example, the majority of the professionals were Ontarians. Two-thirds of Nanton's town councillors in 1907 came from Ontario. Anglo-Saxon settlers from Ontario, Britain and the United

States also dominated the area's societies and clubs, such as the Masons, Oddfellows, and Rebekahs, the Imperial Order of the Daughters of the Empire (IODE), the literary societies, ladies' clubs, and of course a wide variety of churches.

At the turn of the century tens of thousands of Ontarians left their crowded farms, or towns and villages (which, for many, had the same lack of economic opportunity as the tiny farms). Evidence of large-scale immigration to the West from one Ontario county is provided in a newspaper study that the Barrie *Examiner* did in 1933 of the location of the fifty students of the class of 1889 at Thornton Public School near Barrie in Simcoe County. The reporter was unable to locate ten; however, he found that twenty still resided in Ontario but that fourteen, or roughly one-third, had settled in the Canadian West.[24] Other areas had similar records. In the late 1880s and early 1890s, a wave of migrants from Glengarry County, Ontario came to the Edmonton vicinity. The familiar Scottish and Irish names in the area north and west of Edmonton (and indeed the name of one of the school districts itself, Glengarry) were the legacy of early Ontario's Scottish settlers who migrated together in those pioneer days.[25] Another example of group migration from Ontario can be found in the early settlements at Parkland just north of Claresholm. In 1904 W. J. Parkhill came with a group of settlers from Galt, Ontario to begin a new life in the West. Initially the settlers called their new community "Parkhill" in honor of their founder, but two years later changed the name to "Parkland" to avoid confusion with a Parkhill in Ontario. Initially the new name caused even more confusion than the old as bewildered settlers arrived expecting to see "parkland" rather than flat, treeless Prairie.[26]

The Parry Sound colony provides the best example of large-scale migration from a single locale in Ontario.[27] In the 1890s a group of 500–600 individuals from the rugged Precambrian Shield area of the Huntsville-Georgian Bay region of central Ontario settled northwest of Edmonton. Thomas G. Pearce of Parry Sound, Ontario, an employee of the Canada Landed Credit Company (a subsidiary of the CPR), led the settlers who had tried unsuccessfully to carve successful farms out of the Canadian Shield. After completing the preliminary organizing for the colony, Pearce arranged with the CPR to underwrite a loan for the fares and freight costs. Anxious to sell the Parry Sounders land, the CPR reduced rates on the train and colonist cars for transportation; and it issued Pearce an open ticket for himself and one other person to go west to find a suitable location for the colony. Pearce arrived in the Edmonton area in August 1891, the most favored month of the best years in that region. Greatly impressed with the area he decided to choose a site northeast of Edmonton and due east of Fort Saskatchewan. He then returned to Parry Sound, and in the winter of 1891-92 held meetings at all small villages within a fifty mile radius of Parry Sound to recruit colonists.

The first three hundred colonists left Ontario in early May of 1892 with high expectations. According to W. C. Pollard, the author of a book on the group, *Pioneering in the West,* their slogan was: "All for the West. All aboard; if you can't get a board get a slab, but go anyway and any how, ready or not ready! Everyone must go to the Promised Land!!"[28]

Like all of the early migrants at the turn of the century, the colony faced difficulties and hardships. The Canadian government had not built the promised immigration shed at Strathcona to provide for temporary accommodation until homes could be erected on their sites. The group spent their first weeks in Alberta living in the colonist cars or in make-shift buildings by the railway station. The spring thaw prevented them from crossing the North Saskatchewan River to reach their homestead sites for two weeks. When they reached their destination, they discovered that the government had not replaced missing survey stakes in the region. The settlers lost a considerable amount of time trying to discover what was HBC property, CPR land, or school sections. Discouraged and disillusioned, some members returned immediately to Parry Sound, and dissuaded other potential immigrants from going west that spring. A bitter dispute erupted between the colonists who had stayed and those who had left. But despite the initial years of hardship, the Parry Sound colony succeeded. Another 200-300 relatives and friends arrived over the next six or seven years. The result was a closely-knit community, which half-a-century later, still organized an annual Parry Sound Picnic to celebrate the anniversary of the first colonists' arrival.[29]

Ontarian Migration to Urban Alberta at the Turn of the Century

The largest migration of Ontarians came to the urban areas of Alberta. From 1901 to 1911 the population of Edmonton increased over eleven times, from 2,600 to 30,500 (including Strathcona); Calgary grew nearly tenfold, from 4,850 to 43,700. Lethbridge also rose from 2,325 to 8,050, and Medicine Hat from 1,975 to 5,600. Ontario contributed more than its share of people to this phenomenal growth.

Professionals from Ontario became numerous in Alberta's growing towns and cities. They arrived at an opportune time, just as the province was becoming crisscrossed with a network of railway lines, and just before the great waves of foreign immigrants who would soon need their services.

A statistical analysis of the biographical sketches in John Blue's two-volume, *Alberta Past and Present* (1924) a "Who's Who" of prominent Albertans, indicates the dominant role of Ontarians in Alberta's urban elite. Forty-four percent of the 750 men and women included gave Ontario as their place of origin. Seventy percent of these Ontarians lived in the three major urban centers—Edmonton, Calgary, and Lethbridge. They belonged to the important benevolent associations—Masons, Odd-fellows, and Foresters—and to the service and social clubs—Kiwanis, Rotary, and the golf and country clubs. Liberals outnumbered Conservatives in declared political affiliation. Their religious affiliation was usually Presbyterian or Methodist. Finally, an overwhelming number (nearly 70 percent) of the Ontarians included were professionals, with the largest number being doctors and lawyers. Thus, based on Blue's study, the largest percentage of Alberta's elite in 1924 had come from Ontario.

Lethbridge provides a good example of an Albertan town dominated by professionals and businessmen from Ontario. The coal mining town began in 1882 when Elliott Galt opened up the North Western Coal and Navigation Company. Galt, an English-speaking Quebecois, was the son of the famous Alexander Galt, one of the Fathers of Confederation. Elliott Galt employed many Ontarian workingmen, and the town he helped to found provided a place for many Ontarian professionals and businessmen.

Among the early residents of Lethbridge was Harry Bentley, a retail store owner from Ontario who came to Lethbridge eager to better himself economically. Arriving just prior to the town's boom years, he established a small general merchandise store, invested in a large warehouse and hotel, and within a year had become one of the wealthiest and most influential men in the area.[30] Bentley went into local politics, first serving as town councillor and eventually as mayor. Bentley's success story parallels that of other early Ontarian settlers who rose to prominence in Edmonton and Calgary.

Another notable Lethbridge pioneer arrived from Guelph, Ontario. John D. Higinbotham had settled in Fort Macleod in 1884, where he established a drugstore affiliated with the NWMP headquarters. Two years later, he moved to Lethbridge and started a large pharmaceutical business with his brother. But he found investments in the Lethbridge coal mining industry more lucrative. By 1905 he was one of the organizers and stockholders of the large Taber Coal Mining Company.

Yet another Ontarian, Charles A. Magrath, had great influence in the early economic and political life of Lethbridge. Born in North Augusta, near Ottawa, he came west as a government geological surveyor in the early 1880s. In Lethbridge he met Elliott Galt who offered him a position as land commissioner with his company. Elected in 1889 as first president of the Lethbridge Local Board of Trade and Civic Committee, Magrath convinced the committee to incorporate Lethbridge as a town in 1890. He served as the town's first mayor in 1891 and its first representative to the Territorial Assembly in 1892. In addition, the energetic Magrath helped to interest Mormons in coming to southern Alberta to build the irrigation canal from Kimball on the St. Mary's River through to Stirling, thereby helping to establish an important irrigated farming area in southwestern Alberta.

The early professional and business elite of Edmonton, like that of Lethbridge, came from Ontario.[31] Among these early migrants in the 1880s were James Goodridge, the proprietor of Jasper House (a hotel), a former cabinetmaker; John McDougall, a successful general merchant; H. L. McInnis, the government's surgeon; and D. G. McQueen, a Presbyterian minister. Other Ontarians such as K. A. McLeod rode to fame on Edmonton's real estate boom. Richard Otterwell made his Clover Bar homestead the site of such diverse enterprises as coal mining, saw milling and flour milling.

A recent study of eighty leading members of Edmonton's elite in 1898 shows that a good two-thirds were Canadian-born, and nearly half Ontario born. The majority came from respectable, lower middle class families in rural areas or villages of Ontario. Good churchgoers (most notably Presbyterian) they were well educated, one third of them having attended a professional faculty at an Ontarian university.

This early trend continued as Edmonton grew. In similar statistics for 1913 and 1921, Ontarians dominated Edmonton's social and commercial life, although their overall numbers slowly declined after increased British and American immigration. Two prominent Ontarians among many who came to Alberta at this time were W. J. Magrath, a real estate broker, and Joseph Andrew Clarke, a sports promoter.

The business community of early Calgary provides a classic example of Ontario's strong presence in Alberta cities. Of the forty wealthiest and most influential Calgarians at the turn of the century, more than half were Canadian-born, with a preponderance of them having come from Ontario.[32]

One of the best known and most colorful of these early business tycoons was Patrick Burns, a cattle king and owner of one of the largest meat-packing businesses in the world. He differed from the majority of his Calgary associates in that he was Catholic. But otherwise he fitted the stereotype. Born in Oshawa in 1856, Burns arrived penniless in Manitoba in 1878. To earn enough money to keep going on his homestead, he worked as a railway laborer. He used all his savings to buy and sell cattle, soon assembling enough to make the first shipment of western Canadian livestock to eastern markets. In 1890 this lucrative business brought him to Calgary, the heart of the cattle country. His business grew in the heady prosperity at the turn of the century. In 1931 Prime Minister R. B. Bennett appointed this railway laborer who had risen to become one of the wealthiest men in Alberta, a Canadian senator. Burns retired from the Senate at the age of eighty in 1936, one year before his death in Calgary.

Another very successful Calgary entrepreneur grew up on a farm in Ontario. William Henry Cushing moved to Calgary in 1883 where he became involved in the building trade and established a sash and door factory. His business became so large that he formed a joint stock company in 1903 under the name of Cushing Brothers Limited, with retail outlets in other prairie towns. He served as president of the board of trade, as mayor of Calgary in 1900, and as the city's representative in the first provincial cabinet of 1905. Other notable Ontario born Calgary businessmen (among many others) were Thomas Beveridge, a real estate agent; I. L. Kerr, who started the Eau Claire and Bow River Lumber Company, along with Peter Prince from Quebec in 1883, and secured a franchise from the city to supply street light for Calgarians; and Robert J. Hutchings, an early wholesaler of leather goods and the founder in 1899 of Great West Saddlery Company.

As Alberta developed, the business opportunities expanded. In 1914, businessmen in Calgary invested in a business far more lucrative than selling hogs, saddles, lumber, or even real estate—oil! At 5:00 on 14 May 1914, Dingman #1 Well had blown in at Turner Valley. The race for Albertan oil began, a race led by a number of prominent Ontarian born Albertans.

In 1901 William S. Herron, then only sixteen years old, left his home in northern Ontario to come to Okotoks, to cook in a lumber camp. Quickly he worked his way up to become a railroad contractor. One day in 1911, he noticed gas escaping from the ground near a crossing on Sheep Creek. Immediately he realized the significance of his find and bought 7,000 acres around Turner Valley for exploration purposes. Lacking capital to begin drilling he organized a fishing trip on Sheep Creek with two prominent Calgarians—R. B. Bennett (who became prime minister in 1930) and Archibald W. Dingman. Together they formed the Calgary Petroleum Products Company which drilled the Dingman #1 Well. The Board of Executives included several of Calgary's most distinguished businessmen, an amazing number of whom—men such as James Lougheed, I. K. Kerr, William Pearce, and Archibald Dingman himself—had come from Ontario. Two American companies, Imperial Oil and Standard Oil, took over the operation in 1920.[33]

Ontarian entrepreneurs in each Albertan town and city had headed west to advance economically—and socially. The majority had come from lower middle class families and seized opportunities to ascend the social ladder quickly, to easily become members of a social elite. Once established in business, these men dined with each other at the finest hotels and restaurants which Alberta had to offer; they were members of the same exclusive social clubs, such as the Ranchman's Club of Calgary or the Edmonton Club of Edmonton, which were similar to eastern clubs such as the St. James Club of Montreal or the Granite Club of Toronto which they tried to emulate. They travelled east frequently to renew their contact with mutual friends and business acquaintances and to judge their success by Ontario's standards.

This social elite of former Ontarians both molded and reflected the attitude and nature of Alberta's society in general. The familiar literary societies, debating societies, Orange Lodges, and Masonic Lodges—so evident in rural and urban Ontario—were an integral part of Alberta's society. Children used Ontario Readers at school and were often taught by teachers educated in Ontario. Many wealthy Albertan families sent their children to Ontario's private boarding schools, colleges, and universities.[34]

Even the architecture and landscaping of urban and rural Alberta reflected Ontario's influences. Early business offices duplicated the style of the head offices in Ontario, and many civic buildings used the blueprints of eastern buildings. Ontarians constructed their urban homes of familiar stone, wood frame or even brick, despite the scarcity of such building materials on the open prairies. In the farming communities most early Ontarian farmers started by necessity with wooden framed shacks or sod huts as their first home, but replaced them as soon as possible by fieldstone buildings or two-storey framed farmhouses like the ones they had known in Ontario. They also surrounded their farmhouses with protective woodlots and great banks of shelter belt trees.[35]

This importation of Ontario cultural traditions at the turn of the century had both positive and negative effects on the developing province. It helped Alberta to become part of English-speaking Canadian society much faster and more easily than it could have done otherwise. But the mental outlook of these transplanted Ontarians included as well an attitude of superiority which made it difficult for non-Anglo-Saxons to fit in. Ontarians displayed the characteristic imperial sentiments of the late nineteenth century which naturally assumed that their own ideas, values and attitudes were better than those of other cultures.[36]

Ontarians in the Political Life of Alberta

The Ontarian social and commercial elite also dominated the early political life of Alberta. Their peak of influence coincided with the era of Liberal rule from 1905 to 1921: all three premiers during this era were Ontarians, not surprising perhaps since Ontarians had a greater knowledge of the Canadian parliamentary procedure than most other immigrants. Some even had personal contacts with national politicians.

The first premier of Alberta, Alexander Cameron Rutherford (1905-1910), was raised on an Ontarian farm in the Ottawa Valley and educated in schools in Ontario, then at McGill Law School. After practising law for ten years in Kemptville, near Ottawa, he came to Edmonton in 1885 for health reasons. A few times he tried unsuccessfully to win the Edmonton seat in the Territorial Assembly from his popular opponent, Matthew McCauley, ex-mayor of Edmonton and a fellow Ontarian. When the new riding of Strathcona was formed in 1902, Rutherford became its representative. He became leader of the Liberal group in the assembly which naturally made him the logical candidate for premier when Wilfrid Laurier's Liberal government created the new province of Alberta in 1905. Rutherford won two election campaigns—1906 and 1909—before resigning as party leader in 1910.[37]

Arthur L. Sifton (1910-1917), Rutherford's successor, always lived in the shadow of his famous brother Clifford, Laurier's Minister of the Interior immediately before Frank Oliver. Born in St. John's, Ontario in 1858, the easy going, but stern-looking lawyer came to the Territories in 1889, and represented the Banff constituency from 1899 to 1903. He resigned to become a Supreme Court judge, a position he held until assuming the premiership in 1910.

The third Liberal premier, Charles Stewart (1917-1921), came from a humble family background near Trabane, Ontario. With only a public school education, he came west with thousands of other immigrants to homestead. He did a variety of additional jobs to supplement his income. In the election of 1909, he won in the Sedgewick constituency, and became one of the youngest and most dynamic members of the Legislature. He held numerous portfolios before assuming the highest elected political office in the province.[38]

A host of Ontarians sat in the Legislature; in fact eleven of eighteen

First Legislature of Alberta, 1906
Left to Right; Top to Bottom

*A. J. Robertson   *J. Simpson
*W. T. Finley   *J. R. Boyle
*W. H. Cushing   *J. R. McLeod
*A. C. Rutherford (premier)   J. R. Cowell
*C. W. Cross   *W. F. Bredin
C. W. Fisher   J. W. Woolf
C. Hiebert   *W. F. Puffer
T. A. Brick   *H. W. McKenny
*C. A. Stewart   *J. P. Marcellus
A. S. Rosenroll   *J. T. Moore
F. A. Walker   *J. A. MacPherson
*M. McCauley   *W. C. Simmons
R. T. Telford   M. McKenzie
*Born in Ontario

*Migrants from Ontario played a key role in the early political history of
Alberta. (Photo courtesy Glenbow Archives)*

cabinet ministers, and nearly 60 percent of the MLAs during the Liberal
regime were from Ontario.[39] While most Ontarians who entered Alberta
politics were respectable, middle class, and Liberals, Charles O'Brien,
from northeastern Ontario, was not. Sporting a red necktie in the House,
the first socialist elected to the Alberta Legislature proved to be a fiery,
controversial, and flamboyant MLA. In 1910, for example, during a routine vote of sympathy upon the death of King Edward VII, O'Brien

opposed the motion unless it included as well a note of condolence to the wives and families of 300 miners killed in a British mine disaster that same year. His colleagues became so upset that anyone would dare link the death of royalty with that of coal miners they fired books and inkwells at O'Brien.[40]

Influence of Ontarian Women in the West

Ontarian women also came west hoping to take up positions of leadership in Alberta's communities, in the social reform organizations: the Women's Christian Temperance Union, the Local Council of Women, the Women's Canadian Club, Women's Institute, and the various church clubs. Many of these organizations were either branches of larger organizations with headquarters in the East, usually Ontario, or else replicas of eastern institutions. Committed to the same goals they fought to rid society of its social ills, particularly drinking, gambling and prostitution. In fact, the Albertan movement had an intensity beyond that of its Ontarian counterpart because of its greater task, "the West being more sinful than the East."[41] Ontarian women saw the need to "civilize" the West by transforming it completely into "new rural Ontario west."

One reform movement of particular concern to Albertan women was female suffrage. The "Famous Five" spearheaded the fight in the province.[42] Three of the five leading Albertan women suffragettes came from Ontario: Emily Murphy, Louise McKinney, and Nellie McClung. (Of the other two, Henrietta Edwards was from Montreal and Irene Parlby from London, England.)

Emily Murphy, the "captain of the Famous Five," was a spirited woman from Cookstown, on the outskirts of Toronto. The wife of an Anglican minister, she had travelled throughout the West and had established a name for herself as "Janey Canuck," the famed writer of the West, before moving to Edmonton in 1907. In 1916 the provincial government appointed her to the Edmonton Juvenile Court as the first woman magistrate in the British Commonwealth. This honor marked the beginning of the long battle to recognize the equal rights of women, which led finally to the decision of the Privy Council of the British Empire on 28 October 1929 that women were "persons" with all the legal rights which accompanied such status, including the right to sit in the Senate of Canada.

Emily Murphy had had the support of another fiery and witty Ontarian woman, the beloved Nellie McClung, nicknamed "Windy Nellie" or "Calamitous Nell." A small but determined woman from the Bruce Peninsula, she had first moved to Manitoba where she taught school, wrote books, and fought for female suffrage in that province. After moving to Alberta she won election to the Legislature in 1921, only five years after women had gained the provincial franchise.

Louise McKinney, the third of the Famous Five from Ontario, was raised on a farm near Ottawa in a family with a strong social conscience. She maintained that social commitment during her travels through the American Midwest (where she met her husband) before coming to

Claresholm. In Alberta she became involved in the antidrink movement and became the first president of the local branch of the Women's Christian Temperance Union. In 1917 she ran as a Non-Partisan League candidate. She won the election, and along with it the recognition of being one of the first two women to take a seat in a Legislature in the British Empire. This honor she shared with Roberta MacAdams, another Ontarian from Sarnia, who became the first and only woman to be elected by the armed services to a Legislature in Canada.[43]

Decline of Ontario's Presence in the 1920s

The dominant influence of the Ontarian-born in the political, social, and commercial life of Alberta reached its peak by 1920. The census figures for 1921 and the election of the UFA over the Liberal Party both indicated the changed position of Ontarians in the province. The census of 1921 showed the largest number of Ontarian born individuals to date in Alberta (68,900). (That number has not been reached since; the 1971 census indicates only 55,640 Albertans were born in Ontario.) By the census of 1931, the number was down to 59,100 since their own children and grandchildren were recorded as Albertan born. In 1901, the Ontarians had formed 16 percent of the population and in 1911, 15 percent. By 1921, their percentage within the population had dropped to 11 percent, as the original pioneering generation died and more immigrants, especially from Britain and the United States, arrived. The British and the Americans showed the largest increase in these years. These two groups homesteaded the virgin land in larger numbers, and moved into prominent positions in urban areas previously the domain of Ontarian citizens. As a result of this change, Alberta continued to reflect its dominant Anglo-Saxon image, but Ontarians would no longer be the primary molders of that image. Clearly the incentive for Ontario people to move West declined with the end of Alberta's pre-war boom. In the towns and cities, professional, business, clerical and labor positions had been filled to the saturation point, while in the rural areas the best homestead land was long-taken.

Ontarian harvesters, though, did come in large numbers in the 1920s. They came on the harvest excursions, run by the CPR and the new CNR (formed just after World War I).[44] In 1925, the peak year, nearly 55,000 temporary workers arrived in the three prairie provinces in August, September, and October. They came from central and eastern Canada, and even Britain and the United States; but the largest number came from Ontario. Good pay, not free land, proved the incentive for this second migration from Ontario. A harvester could make twice as much as he would for agricultural work at home, and one-third more than unskilled construction workers in the cities. Few of these excursionists remained to become farm owners, since they were really a generation too late; but a number did use the greatly reduced fares on special harvest excursion trains as a cheap means to come West and find jobs.

The provincial election of 1921 which swept away the Liberal regime, inaugurated a new era dominated by a new Albertan party, the UFA.

The new government had won the support of those groups in the province who were disenchanted with the Liberals. Out with the old political
regime went many of the Ontarian born who had dominated this earlier
period.

The composition of the UFA government during its fourteen years in
power reflected the changing nature of the province. Only one of the
three premiers, John Edward Brownlee (1925-1934), came from Ontario.
His early life fitted the mold of many Ontarians in Alberta's politics.
Raised in a small town by lower middle class parents, he had attended
high school and university before coming west to begin his career.
Brownlee articled in the law firm of James Lougheed and R. B. Bennett,
and then became legal advisor to the UFA. This latter position proved to
be a springboard to a political career. During the UFA period from
1921-1935 only four cabinet ministers (compared to eleven in the Liberal
era) and only 32 percent of the MLAs were from Ontario. Clearly in one
of the main spheres of influence in a democracy—political representation—the Ontarian born were rapidly losing ground in Alberta.

The Impact of the Dirty Thirties

The stock market crash in late 1929 ushered in the worst decade in
western Canadian history. Severe drought compounded the problems of
world-wide depression, and in a few years blowing dust and idle farm
machinery symbolized a bankrupt province. Alberta was no longer "the
paradise in the West" that Ontarians had envisioned earlier. In the 1941
census, only 48,900 Albertans identified Ontario as their place of birth,
down 10,200 from 1931. Clearly some Ontario migrants who had tried
to make a go of it in Alberta had become disillusioned with the "dust
bowl" conditions, and had moved on to other provinces. The decrease
meant that by 1941 Ontario's proportion of the overall population of
Alberta reached an all-time low of only 6 percent. Some native Albertans—perhaps sons and daughters of earlier Ontarian migrants—even
reversed the earlier trend of westward migration: the census records for
Ontario indicate that some 10,870 people in that province in 1941 were
born in Alberta, up more than 6,000 from 1931.

Ontario's decline in influence was evident during the long Social
Credit regime from 1935 to 1971. Of the forty-three Social Credit cabinet
ministers, only seven were Ontarian born. And over half of these were in
William Aberhart's first cabinet. Besides Aberhart himself, as premier
and minister of education, there were W. N. Chant, minister of agriculture, who was born in Brampton; W. W. Cross, minister of health, from
Barrie; and C. C. Ross, minister of lands and mines, from Ottawa.

"Bible Bill" Aberhart, the most famous and charismatic of Alberta's
premiers, was the son of an Ontario dairy farmer from Egmondville.
His deeply religious parents often took him to local revival meetings,
where he acquired that Ontarian sense of mission which had inspired
previous Ontarian migrants. His effective technique of pounding the
table to keep control of his audience came from his early Ontario
upbringing, as he once told a political rally:

Excuse my pounding the table. It reminds me of the fact that when I was a boy we had protracted revival meetings in our district. I sat in those meetings night after night and marvelled at the power of the preacher over the people. The preacher was very emphatic and he pounded the pulpit heavily. I was so impressed that I went out into a woodlot, day after day, and practised speaking and pounding a pine stump with my clenched fists. I had discovered the power of words and gestures over the people, and I have never forgotten the power of that preacher to dominate those people.[45]

Aberhart taught school in Ontario before coming to Calgary in 1910 to take a position at the new Crescent Heights High School. To fulfill his religious calling, he became a lay preacher at Westbourne Baptist Church. In time, the local radio station, CFCN, invited him to give a Sunday afternoon sermon. An instant success, he continued to give regular radio sermons which reached an estimated 350,000 people weekly. With the money collected through voluntary contributions, he built the Prophetic Bible Institute in Calgary.

As the depression worsened, Aberhart became attracted to the Social Credit writings of Major C. H. Douglas, and began by 1932 to inject Social Credit ideas into his weekly sermons. The resulting blend of politics and religion appealed to destitute Albertans; Aberhart's popularity and that of Social Credit grew rapidly. With the provincial election approaching in 1935, Aberhart formed his own movement. It swept the province like a prairie fire. When the returns were counted on election night, the new party had won 56 of the 65 seats!

Aberhart was the last premier of the province to come from Ontario. After his death in 1943, he was succeeded by his protégé, Ernest Manning, who had grown up in Saskatchewan. Manning's various cabinets reflected his own western orientation, with the largest number of his ministers being native Albertans.

The Great Oil Boom and Another Wave of Ontarians

The slow population growth continued during World War II. From 1939 to 1945 the province's overall population grew by less than 10,000 to 803,000 people, and the number of Ontarian born declined further. Alberta's expansion appeared to be over. In 1946, few would have predicted that the greatest Albertan boom of all, and the next era of Ontarian migration would begin the following year.

Unlike the first era of prosperity and expansion, the beginning of this second boom period can be pinpointed to an exact date—13 February 1947. On that day, seventeen miles southwest of Edmonton, an oil well —Leduc #1—blew. Up with the soaring oil went the future of Alberta. Leduc was an oil field twice the size of Turner Valley. A new era of expansion was underway which created a demand for skilled and unskilled workers beyond the capacity of the province to fulfill. Once again, Alberta became what the Parry Sound settlers had called "the Promised Land." A new wave of Ontarians arrived in the 1950s; by the end of that decade 30,175 Ontarians were living in the province. The majority of them owed their livelihood either directly or indirectly to the oil industry. Most of these new jobs were in cities.

Once again Ontarians contributed to Alberta's rapid growth; but they no longer dominated it. By 1961 they formed only 3.9 percent of the total population; by 1971, their numbers represented only 3.6 percent of the population. Alberta had a large native-born population (many of whom, like Premier Lougheed himself, were grandchildren of Ontarian pioneers) which now decided its own future. No longer an "Ontario outpost," the province had grown into a mature, self-reliant entity capable of confronting Bay Street in Toronto or the politicians in Ottawa.

During the 1970s there was a renewed wave of migration from Ontario, which included professionals, skilled workers and public employees who contributed to the province's booming oil industry and its growing urban population. Statistics dated March 1981 indicated, for example, that 63,365 Ontarians moved to Alberta since 1978, while 7,955 made the reverse trek.[46]

Conclusion

During the early and formative period in Alberta's history, Ontarians constituted the single most influential group. They arrived in large numbers with firmly held cultural values, and stamped their beliefs and values on a new and impressionable settlers' society. By the late nineteenth and early twentieth centuries, Ontarians had molded the cultural context of Alberta; the new province had a reputation of being "rural Ontario west"—in some aspects, it was a miniature replica of English-speaking Canada's most established society. Other immigrant groups added their contribution, but none so strongly as Ontarians.

The cultural ethos that these Ontarians brought with them was a combination of nationalism and religious fervor. The West was seen as an essential component to the fulfillment of the dream of a nation that would stretch "from sea to sea." Many Ontarians believed they had a divine mission to bring the virgin frontier society into Canadian civilization. They felt a responsibility to implant their Anglo-Saxon values in this raw region, and their efforts to do so reflected a form of imperialism which contained a strong religious component. To some the West was seen as a "promised Eden" which had the potential for becoming a society superior even to Ontario itself. Ironically, many of these Ontarians would use this sense of superiority to protect the West against perceived eastern domination. Many Ontarians became the molders of regional consciousness and the strong defenders of western rights.

This religious fervor and nationalism were partly behind the drive to populate Alberta, and it sustained the early immigrants when they arrived. The other component was economic: this expanding region provided the opportunity for quick wealth and status. Many of the first wave of newcomers from Ontario quickly moved into leading positions in the political, social, and commercial life of the new province. They attempted to reproduce familiar physical surroundings including elements of Ontario architecture and landscape; they established replica social institutions, including social and service clubs, literary societies, and familiar eastern churches; and these individuals, essentially from the lower middle class, maintained values and ideals similar to those they had been taught in Ontario.

The importing of this Ontarian mental outlook had both positive and negative results. By participating in the early political life of the province, Ontarians enabled Alberta to become incorporated quickly into the new nation. From the beginning, Albertans were familiar with the Canadian parliamentary system and its federal nature. They would have a different perception of the nation—one molded by their own particular region—but it was a perception premised on their desire to be part of the nation. Ontarians would also ensure the continuation of those British traditions which had been so much a part of the early cultural composition of Ontario's society itself. Anglo-Saxon values dominated early Albertan society; thus British and American settlers, who also settled in large numbers in the early years, could readily adapt to that society and help to shape its ethos. The negative effects of the influence of Ontarians resulted from the weakness inherent in the cultural assumptions that they brought with them. For example, Albertans inherited some of Protestant Ontario's long-established dislike of French Canadian Catholics, along with a more general sense of Anglo-Saxon superiority to non-Anglo-Saxons. The cultural ethos of the province was established by 1920 when the Ontarian presence began to decline. Other groups, particularly the British and the Americans, but also eastern and western Europeans and Asians, added their own particular contributions to the province. But they could not succeed in destroying the imprint of the dominant group of Ontarians who had established the early political, social, and commercial institutions. Only a new generation of native-born Albertans would alter its composition and nature. Yet a large number of these individuals were sons and daughters of early Ontarians, and they often accepted implicitly many of the ideals and values of their parents and grandparents. They were strongly western in their outlook and were staunch defenders of their own particular province. But then so too were the early Ontarians who had proudly helped to share the foundations of their province of Alberta.

CHAPTER SEVEN

The Religious Ethic and the Spirit of Immigration: The Dutch in Alberta[1]

Howard and Tamara Palmer

Introduction

Most Albertans probably view the province's Dutch-origin people as a comparatively small, noncontroversial group whose history does not seem particularly compelling. To the casual student of Alberta's past and present society, the Dutch may seem all but invisible. In the past, they did not have to cope with blatant racism and discrimination or contend with divided wartime loyalties and government repression. Nor have the Dutch immigrants who settled in the province throughout its history made any highly visible attempt to preserve Dutch folk culture or to share it with their new neighbors.

However, this first impression of "the invisible Dutch" is, in many ways erroneous. First, the group is a sizeable one—the fifth largest in the province—and of the many immigrants who came to Alberta following World War II, those from Holland formed the third largest group. In relation to the total provincial population, there is a larger proportion of people of Dutch background in Alberta than in any other province. Second, if one looks at the Dutch more closely, one sees that they should be given further attention, not only because their contribution to Alberta's development has been notable, but also because in a number of significant, if subtle, ways their history in Alberta is unique.

Since the turn of the century, three main waves of Dutch immigration have arrived in Canada and Alberta. Most of these people left Holland for economic reasons and have ultimately had their decision to emigrate vindicated by the economic success they have been able to attain in Canada. While the typical non-Anglo-Saxon immigrant experience has been that only the second and third generations have been able to achieve substantial economic success, the Dutch have been able to take advantage of economic opportunity to such an extent that many of the post-World War II immigrants have achieved not only security, but affluence, despite their overwhelmingly lower and lower middle class backgrounds and limited educational levels. The paradoxical aspect of the Dutch-Canadian experience in Alberta has been that while, as a whole, the Dutch have deemphasized their ethnicity and encouraged linguistic and cultural assimilation into the Canadian mainstream, the strong religious affiliation of a majority of the Dutch immigrants has meant that in practise, they have formed a cohesive minority with many of their own institutions and a distinctive lifestyle.

Each of these facets of Dutch-Canadian history raises questions about the characteristics of both the Dutch immigrants and Alberta's society and economy, which seem to have been tailor-made for each other.

Taming the Land: Dutch Pioneers in Alberta

Near the turn of the present century, a number of economic factors combined to bring the first wave of Dutch immigrants to Alberta. The Netherlands was (and is) a small country and it could not support its burgeoning population. In addition, a revolution in agriculture had been brewing.

The Dutch farmer was faced with a combination of dilemmas which forced him to consider leaving his homeland. Industrialization in Holland and competition from other agricultural nations had precipitated a crisis. The restrictive economic policies of other European countries limited Dutch agricultural exports. At the same time, there was increased competition from North America, which led to reduced prices for agricultural products. Agricultural modernization brought labor-saving machinery, but this was a mixed blessing since it turned the permanent farmhand into a seasonal worker faced with intermittent unemployment. On the one hand, because of economic conditions, few farmers were able to expand their holdings and even fewer were able to begin on their own. On the other hand, North America was calling out for immigrants, especially experienced farmers. For many young Dutchmen to whom the land meant stability and success, emigration was the only hope for the future. [2]

In the late nineteenth century, most emigrants from Holland went to the midwestern and western American states of Michigan, Iowa, Illinois, North Dakota, South Dakota, Montana, and Washington. In several closely knit, predominantly Dutch communities, the Dutch language could be maintained, Calvinist churches could flourish, and the rural society of the Netherlands could be re-created. But by the turn of the century, land in most of these communities had been taken up. Immigrants from Holland and Dutch-Americans who wanted to stay on the land began to consider Canada as an alternative. [3]

To immigration officials and the general Canadian public the Dutch seemed ideal colonists. First of all, most had farm experience. Second, as "Nordic" northern Europeans, they were thought to be of "superior racial stock." Finally, they were predominantly Protestant and were acquainted with democratic institutions. Thus it was felt that they would fit easily into Canadian life. They had no "strange" religious or political practises or beliefs which would set them apart. Hence, both the railways and the government sought out Dutch settlers. The *Edmonton Bulletin* in 1906 described newly arrived Dutch immigrants as "splendid looking specimens" while the *Calgary Herald* described Dutch immigrant farmers as "good people to cultivate."[4]

Given these factors, the Canadian government made considerable effort to attract immigrants from Holland. Immigration organizations in Holland also became active in providing information to prospective immigrants. They offered loans to finance the immigrant's transportation, and they attempted to arrange suitable jobs for him upon arrival in Canada.[5]

At the turn of the century, Canada's prairie provinces were offering free homesteads, leading most Dutch immigrants to settle on the prairies. As their settlements were not localized in any one part of the prairies, they assimilated relatively rapidly. In 1892, the first Dutch settlers arrived in Manitoba, and in the same year a Dutch colony was started at Yorkton, Saskatchewan. During the early 1900s, groups of Dutch people settled in various parts of Saskatchewan, including Leoville, Cramersburg, Edam, and Moose Jaw.[6]

Between 1904 and 1912, Dutch immigrants established several rural settlements in widely scattered parts of Alberta. The first and largest settlement was in the southern Alberta area of Granum, Nobleford, and Monarch. This settlement began in 1904 and was composed primarily of people whose roots were in the Reformed Church. The second Dutch settlement, which was begun in 1908 near Strathmore, was founded by Dutch Catholics. A third settlement begun in 1910 at Alderson, mid-way between Brooks and Medicine Hat, proved to be shortlived, declining by the mid-1920s. Neerlandia, the fourth settlement, was begun in 1912 and was the only exclusively Dutch settlement in the province. The Dutch people who settled there were members of the Christian Reformed faith. But these Dutch-established settlements received only a minority of the immigrants from Holland; Dutch farmers homesteaded in virtually every part of the province.

Dutch families who came individually and settled where there were few other immigrants from Holland assimilated quickly. However, those who came to the rural Dutch communities established their own church institutions and, for a generation, preserved the Dutch language and some elements of Dutch culture. The rural Dutch communities also served as nuclei for subsequent waves of Dutch immigrants in the 1920s, the 1950s and the 1960s. Thus the location of these first settlements largely shaped the eventual overall distribution of Dutch in the province.

The settlements at Nobleford, Monarch, and Granum combined two streams of immigration: one directly from the Netherlands, the other from the Dutch-American settlements. Among the Dutch-American settlers from Iowa and Montana who decided to take up homesteads in this area were people who had emigrated originally from Nijverdal in the province of Overijsel. The first to come to Canada arrived in the spring of 1904 and arranged to meet a group of settlers who would be joining them from the Netherlands. Most of the newcomers soon began home-steading in the Monarch area, which they named Nieuw Nijverdal in remembrance of their home in Holland.[7]

The Dutch who settled in the nearby Granum area (then known as Leavings) were concentrated about ten miles east of the hamlet. Most of the families were from the province of Groningen in northern Holland. They were strict and devout Calvinists and maintained a closely knit, isolated community.[8]

These first settlers sought to attract other Dutch immigrants to their communities by writing letters to Dutch-American newspapers as well as by personal contacts. Some of the newcomers came directly from the Netherlands, while others came by way of brief or lengthy stays in Dutch-American settlements at Sioux City, Iowa, and Vesper, Wisconsin. By 1921 there were approximately 250 people of Dutch origin in the Nobleford and Monarch areas and 140 in Granum.[9] They came to form a sizeable minority in these areas, outnumbering settlers from the United Kingdom and rivaling those from the United States and eastern Canada. Though at first they lived almost exclusively on farms, they would even-tually play important roles in the lives of the towns themselves.

There were no shortcuts for Alberta's pioneers, and the early Dutch settlers were no exception. Once the men had put up a shack for their families to live in temporarily and had broken the required ten acres of land, they then had to make enough money to buy supplies. Many of them hired themselves out as farmhands to nearby neighbors or worked on railway construction crews. In addition to purchasing initial supplies, obtaining adequate water and fuel were two of the early problems. The cold was a serious problem in winter to all of the early settlers and they and their children all had grim experience with blizzards and frostbite.[10] These early years were particularly difficult for the pioneer women; the son of one of the pioneer families would later write, "Through these discouraging years of real hardship, mother wished many times that she was back in Holland."[11]

Religion played an important part in the settlers' lives and they soon turned their attention to establishing churches. In 1905 a congregation of the Christian Reformed Church, the first in Canada, was organized by Reverend Holwerda who had come for that purpose from the Dutch settlement at Manhattan, Montana. In 1909 the other major Reformed denomination at this time, the Reformed Church in America, formed a congregation in Monarch, also the oldest such church in Canada. Another congregation was formed further east near Burdett, to accom-modate the families who had moved into the rural area between Burdett and Foremost as land prices rose and as land became less available near Granum and Monarch.[12]

At first it was difficult for the Dutch settlers to support a full-time minister, and so they had to rely on itinerant ministers from the United

States. Neither the Christian Reformed Church nor the Reformed Church in America was able to call a minister until 1916 and neither had continuous full-time ministers thereafter. They continued to rely on lay leadership in the intervals when the congregation could not afford to pay the minister's meagre salary. At first, they conducted services in Dutch, but even from the early years of settlement, some thought that the services should be conducted in English.[13]

Religion was an integrating factor, but many challenges remained to be overcome. They were faced with numerous agricultural difficulties, particularly soil drifting because of the area's dryness and extremely high winds. The harvest of 1914 was such a disaster that the provincial government had to provide the farmers with seed grain so that they could plant a crop the following spring. By 1916, the Dutch farmers were able again to raise a successful crop, but in 1917, soil drifting in the Monarch area had become so severe that clearly a solution had to be found. Arie Koole, an imaginative settler, experimented with the idea of alternating strips of crop and summer fallow. His success encouraged other farmers to try his method, which proved so effective that by the 1930s strip farming was widely practised in southern Alberta. Strip farming would later help limit the severity of soil drifting during the "dust bowl" of the 1930s.[14]

World War I had relatively little impact on the communities of Monarch and Nobleford other than to promote higher prices for agricultural produce. The settlers had only recently arrived and had little attachment to British imperial struggles. Indeed, some carried bitter memories of the British crushing Dutch farmers in South Africa in the Boer War. As a result, most male immigrants and their sons were content to make their contribution to the war effort by growing grain. While they continued to struggle with the problems of soil drifting, calamity struck the settlers just after the war—influenza. The impact of the world-wide epidemic of 1919 was devastating to the little community of Dutch settlers. Many families lost several members to the dread virus.[15]

Although a few new immigrants arrived in the 1920s, the growth of southern Alberta's Dutch settlements in that decade was primarily the result of natural increase rather than immigration. Ten was not an uncommon number of children and many families were even larger. This proved to be a mixed blessing. Children were invaluable assets when it came to farm work, but they posed a problem when they came of age and needed to acquire their own farms. Some families found it necessary to move to other parts of Alberta in order to find enough agricultural land for all of their sons.[16]

Despite the many challenges which they had faced, Monarch and Nobleford were firmly established by 1920:

> The Dutch settlers began to achieve the economic security and independence for which they had worked so hard. Crop returns in the Nobleford area were high and good prices for their products permitted expansion and investment. More land, implements and horses were purchased and more ground was broken and seeded. The settlers abandoned their shacks to the chickens and

Dutch-Canadian threshing crew near Nobleford, 1926. Nobleford was at the center of the Dutch settlements in southern Alberta. (Courtesy Joe Koynenbelt)

built roomier, more comfortable wooden homes. Barns replaced dugouts and the community took on a prosperous look. Homesickness lessened as the community grew and conditions were bettered. The Dutch slowly began to cut their ties with the Netherlands and accommodate themselves to Canadian society.[17]

Additional Settlements

The CPR launched a recruitment drive to settle their western irrigation block near Strathmore in 1908. To facilitate this project, the railway hired special agents to attract a number of different ethnic groups in Europe and the United States; among those which they attempted to entice were the highly regarded Dutch.

Two Dutch immigrants played an important part in founding the settlement at Strathmore. Their experience illustrates how the CPR's lands were settled. George Boer had emigrated from the Netherlands in the 1890s. When appointed water inspector of the CPR's ready-made farms in Strathmore in 1908, Boer contacted Father Van Aaken, a Dutch Catholic priest in Helena, Montana. The CPR hired the priest to tour the

Catholic areas of the Netherlands in search of prospective immigrants for the irrigated farms. The success of Van Aaken's promotional tour in North Brabant, a predominantly Catholic area of southern Holland led to the enticement of almost 100 families to Strathmore, beginning in 1908.[18]

A variety of factors combined to limit the economic success and growth of the Strathmore settlement. Most of the North Brabant settlers in the end did not remain in the area. Some who came had no previous farm experience. Also, the untimely onslaught of a severe hailstorm in 1908 put the colony in serious jeopardy. In addition, the settlers soon realized that homestead land was available for the taking, whereas the CPR was selling its land. Ultimately, both the CPR and Van Aaken became focal points for the frustrations of the Dutch immigrants and the priest eventually left, along with many of the disgruntled settlers.

George Boer, however, continued to promote Dutch emigration to Canada. As a result of his efforts, a few Dutch families came to the Strathmore area in 1912 and even during the war years. But the CPR's lands and agents had begun to acquire a bad reputation, the agents being inclined to promise more than the land could deliver. This is not to say that the settlement failed completely. While the settlement did not grow to meet the high expectations of its organizers, it nevertheless became a sizeable community. At the time of the 1921 census, there were 270 people of Dutch origin in the Strathmore area.[19]

Repeating the pattern which characterized the Dutch American experience in the nineteenth century, Dutch Catholics in Alberta were more prone to assimilation than the Calvinists; thus the Dutch in the Strathmore settlement generally became involved in community activities earlier than those who had settled further south. Their Catholic affiliation united them with many of their neighbors rather than separating them, as religious affiliation did in the southern settlements. Intermarriage was more common in Strathmore than in Monarch and Nobleford. In the southern communities, the church maintained an active social life for young people which encouraged them to marry within the Reformed faith; the Dutch Catholics also married within their own faith; but this frequently meant that they married Catholics of non-Dutch background.[20]

The Neerlandia settlement eighty miles northwest of Edmonton was no larger than those in the Monarch and Nobleford areas or the one at Strathmore, but it was one of a small handful of exclusively Dutch farming communities in all of Canada. Like other ethnic colonies situated on the fringe of settlement, its isolation preserved its ethnic exclusivity. The settlement of Neerlandia was begun in 1912 by Dutch settlers who had originally come to Edmonton. Many Dutch immigrants who had first come to the city had no intention of remaining there as laborers; rather, they hoped to establish themselves as independent farmers. These people (most of whom belonged to the Christian Reformed faith) had come to Edmonton from the United States, or directly from Holland.[21]

In 1910 a group of Dutch Christian Reformed immigrants in Edmonton organized an immigration society. The organization's purpose was twofold: first, to attract other Reformed immigrants to Alberta from Holland and the United States, and second, to explore the possibilities of locating a tract of land where a Dutch Christian Reformed community could be established. The organizers wrote articles about Alberta for church newspapers in the United States and Holland. Results were almost immediate. In 1911 several Dutch families, wanting to obtain their own farms, responded to these advertisements and immigrated to Edmonton. A scouting committee soon obtained a tract of free land which boasted good soil and was large enough for at least 100 families. The only deterrent to the chosen site was its dense covering of heavy poplars and brush.[22]

In 1912, seventeen men, both married and single, took up homesteads in the district which they had chosen and named Neerlandia after their home country. More Dutch settlers followed in the next three years. By the end of 1915 there were over forty quarter sections occupied, and by the time of the 1921 census there were 168 people in the new settlement.[23]

When the settlers first arrived in Neerlandia after a week-long oxcart ride from Edmonton, their first chore was to build log cabins. It was an arduous experience, building homes and clearing the land. Isolation forced the settlers to become self-sufficient. It was not long before they could depend almost entirely on game and their own gardens for food.

Ox-drawn sleigh — Dutch immigrants en route to Neerlandia. Neerlandia was started by a group of Dutch immigrants in Edmonton who wanted to establish a Dutch-Christian Reformed settlement. (Courtesy Joe Koynenbelt)

Each pioneer had to become his own butcher, veterinarian, blacksmith, shoemaker, and carpenter since none of these services was within twenty miles of their settlement.[24]

Like other immigrants, in order to accumulate capital, the Dutch pioneers found it necessary to work outside of their settlement during part of the year. In this, as in many other aspects of pioneer life, the experiences of Ted Reitsma, one of the early settlers in Neerlandia, were typical. Reitsma had arrived in Canada in 1915, unable to speak a word of English and with only $40 in his pocket. After working briefly in Quebec, he made his way to Granum, since he knew that a friend of his family was living there. For a time he worked as a hired hand on local farms. Here, he learned about the settlement at Neerlandia from some of his fellow workers. Reitsma was intrigued by their reports and eventually decided to join the Neerlandia settlers.

After spending the winter at Neerlandia, Reitsma returned to Granum the following spring and once again worked as a hired hand. When harvest the following autumn was complete, he repeated the trek to Neerlandia to fulfill the homestead residence qualification. The following year he repeated the pattern—going south for the summer work, earning money and then going north to homestead for the winter. Reitsma sadly remembers the winter of 1918-19 when he lost his friend and partner in the disastrous flu epidemic.

Soon, the work pattern for Reitsma, and other Neerlandia settlers, began to change. Due to the growth of Barrhead, the nearest major town, there was an increased demand for lumber. Consequently, logging camps established sawmills relatively close by and stepped up production, thus providing work and wages closer to home for the Dutch pioneers at Neerlandia. One winter, Reitsma and six other settlers walked twenty miles each way in order to come home from the logging camp every weekend.[25]

In 1921, when he was twenty-seven, Reitsma married another Dutch immigrant, Ida Kampnar. After his marriage, it was still necessary for him to find outside winter employment in Edmonton as a coal miner.

Since Neerlandia was isolated and wheat was difficult to transport, the Dutch settlers, like Reitsma, concentrated on the raising of cattle, hogs, and poultry. Most of their wheat was fed to the cattle, which could be herded to the nearest railhead. During these early years, the settlers busily built their livestock herds, breaking up more land, and improving their homes.[26] They also established their community institutions: a post office, a cooperative store, and, most important of all, a church.[27]

Like many of the community's projects, the Christian Reformed church, built in 1915, was constructed with cooperative labor. The church united the settlement and boosted the morale of the pioneers, as Ted Reitsma recalls:

Snow, rain, mud, 40 or 50 below weather would never be a deterrent (to church attendance). When a familiar face was missing, everybody sought the reason and offered any help needed. In the early period of the settlement, this was the only social contact the settlers had. We were all happy to greet our neighbors and actually looked forward to these Sunday meetings as not only did we get to hear what God had to say to us but we were able to listen to all the happenings in the settlement.[28]

Once the church was built, a place where classes could be taught was available. In 1917, the provincial government insisted that the settlers organize their own school district, so a one room school was built one mile south of the church. The Christian Reformed people did not establish their own religious schools in Neerlandia (which they later did in other parts of the province); since they comprised nearly the entire community, they were able to operate the public school in conformity with their religious beliefs.[29]

The first wave of immigrants established the basic settlement pattern for Dutch immigration in Alberta which continued until the 1960s. As the Dutch were a relatively small group, their presence went almost unnoticed in Alberta. Nevertheless in their own way, they were making an important contribution to the agricultural development of the province. By 1921 Alberta's population included 9,490 people of Dutch origin who were scattered throughout its boundaries. (This number included 3,125 Mennonites of "Dutch" origin.)[30] Only at Neerlandia had the Dutch been able to establish a complete community of their own. Neerlandia continued to be dominated by people of Dutch origin, lying as it did on the fringe of the boreal parkland transition forest. This prevented expansion, and discouraged non-Dutch people from settling there.

Schoolchildren in Neerlandia, 1920. Neerlandia was the only all-Dutch settlement in the province. (Courtesy Joe Koynenbelt)

Although farmers predominated in the first wave of Dutch immigration, there were some Dutch immigrants in all of the major urban areas. They did not, however, form cohesive communities. One noteworthy urban Dutch immigrant was Pete Vandermeer, who came to Calgary from Holland in 1907. Ironically, this town dweller became a champion rodeo performer. As a young man, he worked for Burns and Company meat packing; through them he became associated with Burns Ranches and began riding the rodeo circuit. In 1923 he won the Canadian Bucking Horse Riding Championship, received an award from the Prince of Wales, and was selected to perform before the King in England where he won the World Championship. After his career as a rodeo star, Vandermeer worked in the cartage business and then as a private trucker for the city of Calgary, remaining in Calgary. The former world champion rodeo rider died, almost forgotten in his adopted city, in 1977.[31]

The Twenties Sequel: A Second Wave of Dutch Immigration

The outbreak of World War I temporarily ended the first wave of immigration from Holland. After the war, however, it resumed. Due to overpopulation, the Dutch were once again being forced to look beyond their homeland for economic opportunity.[32]

Many Dutch people in this second wave of immigration chose Canada, the United States having adopted stringent immigration restrictions. For those who could farm there were many opportunities. Urbanization and industrialization in Ontario had left rural Ontario with a severe shortage of agricultural workers. In western Canada, undeveloped farm land remained as well as a need for agricultural workers. Official encouragement also helped. The Canadian government and the major railways actively promoted immigration to Canada. Catholic and Calvinist churches in the Netherlands established competing immigration societies, and Dutch journalists came to Canada to describe the country for their countrymen. This combination of circumstances created a favorable climate for Dutch immigration to Canada during the 1920s.[33]

While the immigrants of this second wave were more inclined to settle in Ontario than to travel west, over 1,000 did come to Alberta during the 1920s. By 1931 the number of people of Dutch origin in the province rose to 13,665. This second wave of immigration did not have as profound an impact on Alberta as the first, but it did lead to the founding of two new settlements with sizeable numbers of Dutch-origin people— Lacombe and Iron Springs (which would become important nuclei for Dutch immigrants after World War II)—and to the settlement of a number of Dutch immigrants in rural areas near Rockyford and Stettler.

The existing Dutch settlements in southern Alberta did not benefit from this new influx because they were facing serious economic problems. The economic slump of the early 1920s, coupled with problems of arid land, restricted farm income to such an extent that the settlements were barely able to maintain their numbers. A number of families left Alberta for Dutch settlements in British Columbia, Washington and other parts of the United States.[34]

Dutch Reformed Church near Alderson, 1915. Dutch settlers at New Holland developed a self-contained community, complete with school and church. Most had left by 1924 because of drought and depression, taking their institutions with them. They relocated in other parts of southern Alberta, closer to the mountains, or moved to the United States. Only a few remained until the area was expropriated and turned into a military reserve in 1941. (Courtesy Glenbow Archives)

World War I had been a period of growth for the Dutch communities in Edmonton, Strathmore, and Neerlandia; but, as in Nobleford, development slowed during the 1920s. Each of these communities received a few families from Holland during the decade after the war, but most of their growth came from natural increase rather than immigration.

The Dutch who began farming during the 1920s did not settle on dryland grain farms; rather most settled either on irrigated farms near Lethbridge in southern Alberta, or on mixed farms near Lacombe in central Alberta where moisture was not a problem during the 1920s. When the Lethbridge Northern Irrigation Project was in the early 1920s, it opened previously unsettled and uncultivated land, including the Iron Springs area north of Lethbridge. Dutch settlers were among those attracted to Iron Springs in the late 1920s and early 1930s, and Dutch farm laborers were scattered throughout the irrigated areas of southern Alberta, particularly on sugar beet farms.[35]

In most of the province's areas of Dutch settlement the CPR worked closely with religious denominations to promote colonization. The Dutch settlement at Lacombe provides a typical example of this partnership. William Van Ark had been one of the original settlers at Neerlandia, having arrived there in 1914. During the 1920s, he was hired by the CPR as a travelling colonization agent to scout land settlement schemes in Alberta and to promote immigration from the Netherlands. He travelled frequently to Holland and used a number of techniques to encourage emigration. Patiently he waited outside Dutch churches, Bible in hand, to greet parishioners as they left services. Once having engaged them in conversation he told glowing stories of the wonderful opportunities available in the promised land of Canada. In promoting emigration, Van Ark worked closely with the Calvinist immigration society. The settlement which they established at Lacombe was thus composed almost exclusively of members of the Christian Reformed Church.[36]

The Dutch who settled in the Lacombe area were concentrated approximately ten miles west of the town. Lying within sight of scenic Gull Lake, the mixed farming area supported grain, grass, hogs, and dairy cattle, though it was wooded and required clearing. Some families moved to the Lacombe settlement from overcrowded Dutch settlements in other parts of the province, but the majority of new settlers came directly from Holland. The community evolved through the same stages as earlier Dutch settlements. Fortunately, however, for these later settlers conditions were less primitive due to improved transportation facilities. Many new settlers worked for established farmers nearby to earn cash.

By 1931, there were over 100 people of Dutch origin living in the new settlement near Lacombe. Their numbers were further increased during the 1930s by the arrival of family members from Holland as well as by the relocation of several families from a Dutch settlement in Saskatchewan, where severe drought was forcing people to leave their land. By 1941, the settlement had expanded to nearly 300 people. The Christian Reformed Church, built in 1935, became the focal point for community activities.[37]

Whether they lived in one of the predominantly Dutch communities or not, most Dutch-Canadians in Alberta were farmers. In 1931, 64 percent of the Dutch as compared to 51 percent of the total Alberta population were involved in farming. There were about 1,000 people of Dutch origin in each of Calgary and Edmonton, but with the exception of a small Christian Reformed church in Edmonton, there was no organized Dutch-Canadian group life in either city.[38]

Uphill Years: The Impact of Depression and War

During the depression, only the wives and children of those immigrants able to support themselves, and people with enough capital to start a business were allowed into Canada. This policy drastically reduced the number of Dutch entering Canada to a total of just over 3,000 for the entire decade. Few of these immigrants came to Alberta, one of the hardest hit provinces during the Great Depression. For many of those immigrants who had come during the 1920s, life became a struggle to survive, to stay off relief and thereby to avoid being deported.[39]

Despite their hardships the Dutch, as a group, survived the Great Depression as well as or better than most other people in the province. Since most were farmers and had settled on irrigated land or in the park belt, they had achieved a high level of self-sufficiency. They relied on their own farms for meat, milk, butter, eggs, and produce and on themselves for mechanical and blacksmithing work. In addition, the closely knit solidarity of the rural Dutch farming communities meant that those who were having serious difficulty were helped by the others.[40] Like so many other Albertans, the Dutch responded to the privations of the depression era by turning to William Aberhart and Social Credit for economic salvation. For example, in the 1935 federal election, 78 percent of the voters at Neerlandia voted for the Social Credit candidate. The religious orientation of the new movement convinced the Reformed Dutch to support Social Credit until the 1970s.[41]

For Alberta's people of Dutch origin, the 1940s marked a transition period. The war brought many changes to their lives. The wartime prosperity led to the expansion of their farms. Enlistments in the services and the movement of others to urban wartime industries necessitated increased farm mechanization. With their large families, Dutch-Canadians contributed many young men to the armed services. Some families sent as many as three or four sons to fight for the Allied cause and the liberation of their Nazi-occupied homeland.

By the end of the war, the Dutch community in Alberta was on the verge of being assimilated. There was a sprinkling of closely knit, church-oriented rural groups of Dutch people in the province, but they did not have any compelling reason to maintain the Dutch language or culture. Religion, rather than culture or language, stood as the only barrier to intermarriage. The great human mixmaster created by the war led to more intermarriage and assimilation. But just after the war ended and as urbanization threatened to further erode ethnic identity, a large wave of Dutch immigrants began arriving in the province, increasing the number of Dutch in the existing predominantly Dutch rural settlements, establishing new rural concentrations and bringing a strong Dutch-Canadian presence to all of the major urban centers.

Sharing the Boom: Postwar Dutch Immigration to Alberta

The impact on Alberta of this third and largest wave of Dutch immigrants can be seen in census statistics. In 1941, prior to the massive postwar influx, the number of Dutch-origin people in the province was 20,429. By 1961, this number had increased to 55,530. The 2,000 Dutch born who were living in Alberta in 1941 rose to over 23,000 by 1961 and the number of Dutch born among those of Dutch origin had, during the same time period, increased from 15 percent to 47 percent. Virtually all parts of the province felt the impact of this new postwar wave of Dutch immigration.[42]

A combination of forces prompted the postwar migration from Holland to Canada. Holland's perennial problem of overpopulation became even more acute in the postwar era due to high birth and low infant mortality rates. In addition, the war had devastated the Netherlands' economy. When the Germans left the country, it had been stripped of almost all movable property. Approximately 4 percent of the homes had been destroyed along with one-tenth of the agricultural land. Loss of the Dutch East Indies (Indonesia) after the war dealt the economy a further blow. Overcrowding, food shortages, unemployment, and inflation troubled postwar Holland.[43]

Three solutions to these problems had been attempted. The government promoted industrialization to invigorate the economy and create jobs. However, the program was impeded by the churches, whose leaders feared the social consequences of industrialization and urbanization.

Another attempt to ease the pressures of overpopulation involved the reclamation of land in the Zuider Zee which could then provide farmland for large families. But land could not be reclaimed fast enough to keep pace with the increase in manpower to work it. The shift of young landless farmers to farms of their own encouraged them to raise larger families, thus defeating the purpose of the program. One obvious solution—the introduction of birth control—was not even seriously considered, since it was directly contrary to the teachings of the Catholic and most of the Protestant churches in Holland.

The third response to the population problem was to sponsor emigration to countries like Canada and Australia, which still welcomed immigrants. The Dutch government became actively involved in promoting and facilitating emigration and set as its goal the departure of 10,000 farm families every year. The government used no overt compulsion, but it did do everything it could to encourage and expedite emigration. It centralized all emigration activities, provided information to emigrants on their chosen country, offered technical training, and negotiated agreements with receiving countries. The Dutch government also introduced a system of subsidies for emigrants which provided, on the average, $220 per person for transportation, board allowance, and landing money. At first, only rural workers, particularly farmers' sons who were not able to establish themselves on the land, were encouraged to leave. But by 1953 the general principle was to promote the departure of all those capable of emigrating. Approximately 85 percent of those who left were assisted by the Dutch government, which even acquired three ships and chartered other ships and aircraft to facilitate the flow of people.[44]

Emigration sentiment turned very early to Canada. Princess Juliana had lived in Canada during the war, and Canadian soldiers had liberated Holland. In addition, economic prospects looked promising in Canada's booming and labor-short postwar economy. Canada's appeal was further enhanced by its relative proximity to Holland in comparison with other potential receiving countries such as Australia.[45]

Thus the third wave of immigration from Holland to Canada was composed primarily of people who were seeking greater economic opportunity for themselves and their children. A number of other factors provided additional motivation. Many Dutch people had a strong desire to escape the endless government bureaucracy necessitated by attempts to deal with the problem of overpopulation. (Long waiting lists for employment and housing shortages—which often meant the postponement of marriages—were commonplaces of Dutch life.) Also, the cold war atmosphere of the late 1940s and early 1950s made many fear the advent of a third world war. In addition, the severe flooding of 1953 forced a number of people to leave their homes. Others wanted to leave Holland to escape what they felt was a restrictive social environment.[46]

As it had been half a century earlier Canada was favorably disposed toward these new Dutch immigrants. Immigration officials felt that they were competent farmers and would remain on the land. Also, some of the turn-of-the-century racist views continued to be reflected in the notion that the Dutch were desirable because they were of "Nordic stock." More reasonably, Canadian proponents of Dutch immigration argued that the Dutch would assimilate rapidly because of the similarities between Canadian and Dutch society.

In 1947, the Canadian and Dutch governments negotiated an agreement whereby the Canadians accepted progressively larger groups of immigrants. The two governments would determine how many people should come and they would then be placed by the Canadian Immigration Department in appropriate areas, depending on housing and job availability.[47]

Although Dutch immigrants went to many different countries in the postwar era (including Australia, New Zealand, South Africa, the United States, Brazil and Argentina), Canada was the destination of the largest number. Forty-two percent of the 250,000 Dutch who emigrated between 1945 and 1956 came to Canada, and by 1961 there were 133,500 postwar Dutch immigrants in Canada.

The first Dutch farm settlers in the third wave of immigration began arriving in Canada in June of 1947 under the arrangement known as the "Netherlands Farm Families' Movement." After 1951 immigrants also included people with business, professional, and technical backgrounds.[48]

Postwar immigration dramatically changed the size and nature of the Dutch-Canadian community. By 1961, there were 430,000 people of Dutch origin in the country. Like those who had come to Canada during the 1920s, most of the postwar immigrants chose Ontario as their destination: over 50 percent went to southern Ontario where many entered truck gardening, mixed farming and dairying. About 20,000 Dutch immigrants, or 15 percent of the total, came to Alberta. During the 1950s, Dutch immigrants made up the third largest immigrant group coming to Alberta—outnumbered only by the British and Germans. The number of people of Dutch origin in Alberta increased by 89 percent between 1951 and 1961, a figure which was more than double the growth rate for Alberta's population as a whole for those years, during a period of rapid growth in the province. The numbers of Dutch immigrants coming to the province did not diminish until 1961 when the yearly number, which had averaged about 1,000 in the late 1950s, fell to just over 200. This change was largely due to economic improvement in Holland.[49]

Beginning Anew: Settlement of Postwar Immigrants

Several features characterized the postwar wave of Dutch immigrants. It was comprised primarily of farmers, workers, and lower middle class people whose average educational attainment was limited to approximately grade six to eight. Most came in family groups under the auspices of a church organization and many were sponsored by relatives who had arrived earlier. All had a strong desire to become independent as soon as possible. Farm workers wanted to own their own farms, and tradesmen wanted to reenter their trades or establish their own businesses. Most settled in areas where the Christian Reformed Church had field men who could locate jobs and sponsors for newcomers, notably the Edmonton, Lethbridge, and Lacombe areas.

Another striking characteristic was the preponderance of farmers at a time when the agriculture in Alberta was undergoing revolutionary changes. Technological advancements were making it possible for fewer people to farm larger tracts of land. The experienced Dutch farmers successfully adapted to the changing situation by establishing mixed farms and by initiating more intensive agriculture in the irrigated areas of southern Alberta and in the central park belt. Those in central Alberta specialized in dairy and potato farming. Few became involved in dryland and wheat belt farming. The accustomed practise was to buy up existing farms and then to farm the same land more intensively. In a few cases the newcomers brought whole new areas under cultivation. By the 1970s, one out of every twenty farmers in the province was of Dutch origin. Because of their numbers, industry, and innovativeness, the Dutch have made a highly important contribution to the development of agriculture in postwar Alberta.[50]

As in earlier waves of Dutch immigration, the churches played key

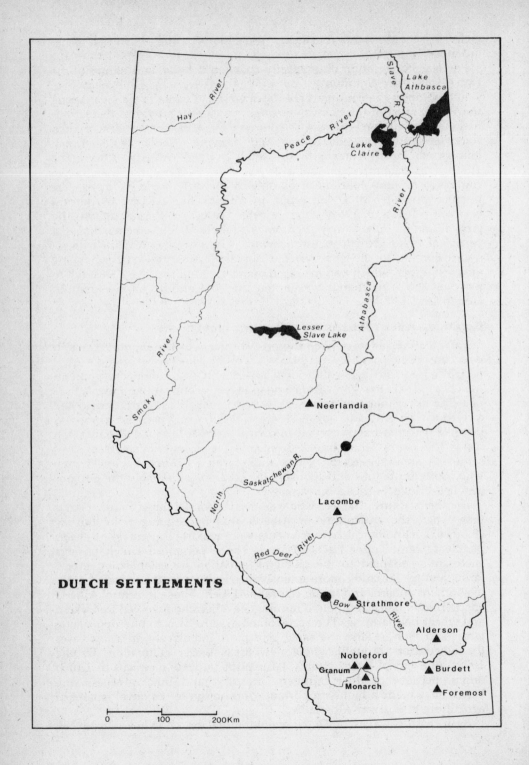

DUTCH SETTLEMENTS

Hay River

Slave R.

Lake Athbasca

Peace River

Lake Claire

River

Athabasca

Lesser Slave Lake

Smoky River

Neerlandia

North Saskatchewan R.

Lacombe

Red Deer River

Bow Strathmore

Alderson

Nobleford

Granum

Burdett

Monarch

Foremost

0   100   200Km

roles in this third wave. In effect, they took charge of the movement, partly for humanitarian reasons and partly because they were concerned with the immigrants' continued church affiliation. In Holland, prospective immigrants registered with the Immigration Society which their respective churches maintained. In Canada, the churches hired field men whose duty was to find sponsors for the immigrants, who in turn were to provide employment and housing for one year. The field men worked closely with the Canadian Settlement Service of the Department of Citizenship and Immigration in the immigrant's initial adjustment.[51]

The irrigated farmlands surrounding Lethbridge attracted the largest number of Dutch farmers. A severe labor shortage made it possible for the Christian Reformed Church field men to place hundreds of families throughout the district. By the late 1940s, many of the Japanese sugar beet workers (who had been evacuated from British Columbia during the war) had either acquired their own farms, moved to Alberta's urban centers, or left for eastern Canada. At a time when demand for sugar was strong and prices were rising, their departure left a great demand for sugar beet workers; Dutch immigrants replaced them. These experienced farmers in the prime of life worked very hard with the help of their large families: an essential asset for the labor intensive sugar beet industry.[52]

The major areas of settlement in southern Alberta were on irrigated land near Picture Butte, Vauxhall, Iron Springs, Taber, and Brooks. Other Dutch immigrants settled on dryland farms in the older communities at Granum and Nobleford and a few went to Bellevue and High River. Many who were settled in scattered areas soon moved to the major Dutch settlements, where the transition to Canadian society was much easier. In central and northern Alberta, postwar Dutch immigrants settled

Dutch farm family harvesting sugar beets, Lethbridge area, 1952. Large numbers of Dutch immigrants came as farmers to the Lethbridge area, increasing both the group's size and its degree of religious diversity.

in and around Rockyford, Sundre, Lacombe, Rocky Mountain House, Red Deer, Neerlandia, Barrhead, Edson, Peers, and Grande Prairie.

The three largest cities of the province—Lethbridge, Calgary, and Edmonton—also attracted many Dutch immigrants. Some came directly to the urban centers. Others migrated to the cities at the completion of their one-year farm labor contracts. Edmonton attracted the largest number of Dutch immigrants. By 1961, there were nearly 7,000 postwar Dutch immigrants in that city compared to less than 5,000 in Calgary and nearly 1,000 in Lethbridge. In Edmonton, the existence of a small Christian Reformed congregation served to attract a number of city-bound immigrants. The church provided them with help in finding jobs and housing.[53]

The newcomers from Holland had a difficult time during their first years in Canada. Since many of them had studied English in school, language was not as difficult a problem for the Dutch as it was for some other European immigrants; it was, nevertheless, a serious obstacle. The language barrier which existed between the Dutch immigrants and their employers was often a source of misunderstanding. Language was a particular problem for the women who were housewives and mothers of large families and who stayed at home a great deal of the time.

Some of the immigrants were disappointed with their circumstances in Canada. At first almost all of them had been forced to accept a lower standard of living than they had left in Holland. Nor did they relish the long hours of work, lack of financial security, and infrequent leisure time which their new life imposed on them. Families fulfilling sugar beet contracts, for instance, worked from dawn until dark during the busy periods. Many felt exploited by their employers. Urban immigrants were also forced to adjust to reduced living standards since their trade certificates and professional qualifications were often not recognized and their facility with English was limited.[54]

Despite their initial difficulties, the discomforts of most of the Dutch immigrants were temporary.[55] Canada was indeed the land of opportunity. Usually within three years Dutch immigrants acquired farms. A few years later, they had themselves become employers, hiring farm workers to help on their neat, efficient farms. Similarly, the urban Dutch immigrants were establishing themselves successfully in trades and small businesses, as well as in technical and professional jobs.[56]

Although the postwar influx of Dutch immigrants was sizeable, they experienced few problems of acceptance by Canadians. They had job skills badly needed in an expanding economy. They also had acquired a reputation for being hard-working, reliable, and law-abiding. Many tell stories of neighbors and employers who went out of their way to help them learn English. Nor did the immigrants' religion become a source of tension. The presence of four different Reformed churches in southern Alberta, three of which held very strong sectarian views, was scarcely noticed in an area known for its sectarian diversity. Perhaps the only negative response that the Dutch elicited was one of envy and resentment from neighbors who had struggled mightily to acquire or keep farms during the Great Depression and now found their new Dutch neighbors seeming to succeed almost overnight.[57]

The Dutch who moved to the cities arrived during a period of economic expansion. The construction booms of the 1950s put laborers and skilled tradesmen in great demand. Quickly the Dutch were able to establish a strong presence in the construction industry. Initially most lived in immigrant and working class neighborhoods. Not surprisingly, the first Christian Reformed churches appeared in these districts.[58]

While the socio-economic composition of the Dutch-Canadian communities in all of Alberta's cities was similar, there were some noteworthy class and religious differences. While the majority of Calgary's urban Dutch were tradesmen, the city also attracted a number of technicians, draftsmen, engineers, and geologists who worked in the oil industry. Some with previous experience in Indonesia's oil fields had left after Indonesia acquired independence. Many were employed by the Dutch-owned Shell Oil Company. Calgary also attracted a larger number of Catholic and nonsectarian immigrants than Edmonton where a Christian Reformed field man helped place Reformed immigrants. Lethbridge's Dutch population developed primarily as a spillover from the surrounding rural areas; consequently the Lethbridge community, reflecting the highly religious and sectarian nature of the rural Dutch-Canadian population, ultimately had the greatest variety of Reformed denominations in the province. However, these differences are minor variations on a theme of hard work, social and political conservatism, strong, closely knit and patriarchal family life, ardent religious belief, and minimal effort to maintain the Dutch language and culture.

While the Dutch in the postwar era have remained more rural than the Alberta average, like other Albertans they have increasingly chosen to live in cities. The typical Dutch experience of the postwar years has been urban. The proportion of people of Dutch origin living in urban areas grew from 35 percent in 1951 to 71 percent in 1971. The number of Dutch people in rural Alberta decreased only slightly in the same time period, but the large growth in their total number was felt primarily in the urban centers. During a period of dramatic off-farm migration throughout the province (including most of the original Dutch settlements) the total number of rural Dutch has remained relatively constant only because of the establishment of several new rural settlements during the 1950s. The urban trend is reflected in census figures which show that the Dutch now comprise between 3 and 5 percent of the population in each of the province's major cities. Their representation among blue collar workers and the self-employed is above the provincial average, while it is below the provincial average in clerical, managerial, and professional categories.[59]

Religion and the Dutch: The Preservation of an Identity

Among the many postwar European immigrants to Alberta, the Dutch gave up their language and folk culture with the greatest speed. This was generally true, whether the immigrants were Reformed or Catholic, religious or nonreligious. However, the Reformed immigrants made strenuous efforts to erect a complete institutional structure based on their church, which is their main expression of cultural identity. They brought with them a Dutch concept of the central role religion should play in life. Their attempt to create a Christian society must, they believe, be reflected in all social institutions, including schools, trade unions, and political parties. Paradoxically, because of the energy which Reformed churches have directed toward accomplishing this goal, the churches are now the main institutions both uniting and dividing Alberta's people of Dutch origin.[60]

There are four Dutch Reformed churches in Alberta. All trace their origins to the teachings of John Calvin so their basic theological orientations are similar. However, since they are also offshoots of each other, their members maintain a strong awareness of their differences and these churches have, in reality, competed for the loyalty of the postwar Dutch immigrants and their children. While nonsectarian and Catholic Dutch immigrants have quickly assimilated into Alberta's society, the Reformed churches in the province isolated themselves to varying degrees, and their members now form distinctive and cohesive groups.

The postwar Dutch migration led to a substantial growth in the two Reformed churches which already existed in Alberta and introduced two new Calvinist sects which had stronger sectarian orientations than either of the previously established Reformed churches. The emphasis in Canada's immigration policy on Dutch farmers and farmhands and the control exercised by the churches in the immigration movement itself led to a re-creation in Canada of Dutch sectarian struggles. In Canada, the rural and church-oriented nature of the immigration movement also led to a shift in the relative proportion of various religious denominations from what it was in Holland; thus, the Christian Reformed Church, which had been in a minority position in Holland, emerged as by far the largest and strongest of the Reformed churches in Canada and in Alberta.

The third wave of Dutch immigrants was in many ways a "cultural fragment" of rural Dutch society in the 1950s. The attitudes and values still existing among the Dutch in Canada mirror those of a rural Holland twenty and thirty years ago. Most of the Dutch immigrants to Canada represented the most religiously conservative element of Dutch society. Ironically, while the Netherlands itself has become increasingly secularized in the postwar era, the Reformed churches have continued to flourish among postwar Dutch immigrants in Canada and in Alberta.

Religious institutions have served as a concrete link with the past and have fulfilled an important social function for Dutch immigrants. The church became the place where they could feel comfortable and where they could unite with like-minded people to meet the challenges of their uprooting and resettlement. And yet, the goal of the majority of people involved with the Reformed churches is something greater. They seek not to cling to ways of life brought with them from the Netherlands; rather, they hope to change the broader Canadian society, which they see as now being threatened by secularism.

With thirty-six congregations in twenty-four communities and over 13,000 members, the Christian Reformed Church is the largest and most influential denomination among Alberta's Dutch. It originated during the nineteenth century as a break-away from the Reformed denomination, Holland's quasi state church, which the dissidents viewed as being too formal and too liberal. Although members of the Christian Reformed Church share many beliefs and social values with North American fundamentalists, their theological orientation is conservative rather than fundamentalist. The reasons for the Christian Reformed dominance in Alberta are readily apparent. The Christian Reformed Church made up only 10 percent of the population in Holland, but in the early years of Dutch migration (1948-1952) 41 percent of the Dutch immigrants belonged to it. People who belonged to this church in Holland were mainly farmers, and a large portion of the Dutch immigrants coming to Canada at the time were farmers.[61]

The Christian Reformed Church has developed a wide range of interlocking organizations and institutions, all aimed at providing mutual assistance and developing an integrated Christian life. Edmonton, which has the most highly developed Christian Reformed institutional structure in the province, boasts an immigrant aid society, a Christian Labor Association, a senior citizens' home, several private Christian schools, and King's College which is loosely affiliated with the University of Alberta.

While Christian Reformed churches elsewhere in Alberta do not have as many institutions as in Edmonton, they try, where at all possible, to establish Christian schools. These schools have absorbed considerable time and energy from their supporters, and while they do receive some financial assistance from the provincial government, parents still have to pay high fees for their children to attend. As the Dutch community in Alberta has become increasingly affluent, the Christian schools are expanding. Critics of the schools, both Dutch and non-Dutch, contend that they unnecessarily isolate children from the rest of society. Recently, however, a growing number of members of the various evangelical denominations have come to share Christian Reformed reservations about public schools. Some are enrolling their children in these Christian schools.[62]

As part of its effort to have Christianity permeate all aspects of life, the Christian Reformed Church has also helped establish the Christian Farmers Federation (CFF), the Committee for Justice and Liberty (CJL), and the Christian Labor Association of Canada (CLAC). The CFF is concerned with ecologically responsible agriculture and with the best usage of agricultural land. The CJL concerns itself with broad social and political issues facing Canadian society, and the CLAC attempts to introduce Christian principles into labor relations. The latter opposes the "closed shop," or compulsory unionism and attempts to concern itself with the spiritual as well as the economic needs of its members.

Some Christian Reformed clergy and lay leaders (in addition to their reservations about public schools and labor unions) feel that none of the Canadian political parties is based on Christian principles. They look to the day when a truly Christian political party can be established. Not all Christian Reformed people support the parallel institutions discussed above; but the clergy and many lay people ardently and enthusiastically advocate them as the basis necessary for a totally Christian way of life.

Throughout the province, members of the Christian Reformed Church form a distinctive subculture within the larger Dutch-Canadian community. Their institutional completeness encourages maintenance of social relations within the group, and the social needs of members are met almost exclusively within their own church community. Although intermarriage rates differ in various parts of the province, most members marry within their group. In fact, only about 10-20 percent of the Christian Reformed youth (depending on the community) marry outsiders. The group is not particularly concerned about interethnic marriage. Their concern is to insure that their children marry within their faith. The Christian Reformed community also has maintained some beliefs and practices which have distinguished it from more secular Dutch-Canadians as well as from most other Canadians. Opposition to dancing, card playing, and other "worldly" amusements form part of the group's historical tradition. Christian Reformed families have traditionally been large and patriarchal. Few women work outside the home since they believe that the nurturing of children is the most important task of both father and mother. They feel that the mother should be at home during the child's formative years.

All of these social patterns characteristic of Christian Reformed people have been eroded somewhat in recent years. Mobility has increased interaction with outsiders, social conservatism has relaxed somewhat, and families have become smaller and less patriarchal. Nevertheless, the average Christian Reformed family remains more traditional than others.

The rapid growth of the Christian Reformed Church during the 1950s and 1960s and its continued growth into the 1970s and 1980s has not been totally painless. Congregations have been divided on such issues as language, the acquiring of Dutch- or American-trained ministers, conservatism versus ultraconservatism; and whether or not there is a need to support a parallel set of educational, social, and political institutions. However, such divisions are natural in immigrant churches faced with the conflicting needs and perspectives of people from different generations and different waves of immigration. Despite these stresses, the strong discipline of the Christian Reformed Church has enabled its continued growth during a time when many of the large Protestant denominations have experienced a significant decline.[63]

The second largest Reformed church, the Reformed Church in America has had Alberta congregations since the early years of settlement in the Monarch area. In Canada as a whole there are now about 7,500 people who belong to the church, with 880 of these in Alberta, divided among three congregations in Monarch, Calgary, and Edmonton. Historically and doctrinally, the Reformed Church in America is a branch of Holland's state-supported Reformed Church. Although its members constitute one-third of Holland's population, this Reformed Church contributed only one-fourth of the postwar Dutch immigrants to Canada. This was due to its being largely an urban church. Since most of the Dutch emigrants who came to Canada were from rural areas, the presence of the more establishment-oriented Reformed Church was muted in Alberta. Nor were most of its members ardently bent on re-establishing the denomination on North American soil.[64]

As a result of the large postwar influx of Dutch immigrants, two new Reformed sects have been transplanted to Canada—the Canadian Reformed and the Netherlands Reformed churches. The Canadian Reformed Church is a branch of a Dutch church which broke away from the equivalent of the Christian Reformed Church in Holland in 1944. Since this schism occurred just prior to the emigration to Canada, the controversy was fresh in the minds of many and they naturally trans-planted the dispute to Canada. The theological origin of the rupture seems minor, since it revolves around differing interpretations of the significance of infant baptism. However, the roots of the dispute went deeper, extending backwards to a theological controversy at the turn of the century and reflecting latent conflict between young farmhands (who comprised the majority of the Canadian Reformed supporters) and more prosperous Christian Reformed farmers. In Alberta, the Canadian Reformed Church has established five congregations, the first Canadian church having been founded near Lethbridge in 1950. The total member-ship is now 1,300, and the largest congregations are located in the areas of Dutch settlement at Neerlandia, Edmonton, and near Lethbridge where the immigrants were first placed in jobs when they came to Canada.[65]

Because the Canadian Reformed group broke away from the Christian Reformed church and because they are only one-tenth as large as the Christian Reformed community, they find themselves in an ambivalent position with regard to the larger church. On the one hand, they share the Christian Reformed conviction about the need to build a truly Chris-tian society and so they support the idea of Christian schools and organi-zations such as the CLAC; but their small numbers make it difficult for them to sustain their own parallel set of institutions. On the other hand, they feel that the Christian Reformed Church has gone astray and find it difficult to cooperate with it. The Canadian Reformed stance toward Christian schools, which have been primarily established by Christian Reformed people, has been a divisive issue within their community. In places where they are sufficiently concentrated to establish their own school, they have done so; however, in places where their numbers are small, some send their children to the Christian school, others do not.

Despite its small numbers, the Canadian Reformed Church's sectarian stance and community solidarity has kept marriage outside of the group at a minimum. Members are characterized by a generally conservative stance, with many opposing such secular activities as dancing and higher education. Canadian Reformed families tend to be patriarchal and larger than average. The group has avoided contact with other like-minded fundamentalists who share a similar literal interpretation of the Bible and a conservative social stance, because fundamentalists do not share all of the Calvinist assumptions. Although there have been tentative ecumenical contacts between the Christian and Canadian Reformed churches, the legacy of bitterness on both sides is too profound to allow a union between the two groups in the near future. Since immigration from the Netherlands has declined and since they have not been successful in proselytizing, future expansion of the Canadian Reformed denomination will likely be limited almost entirely to internal growth.

The smallest and most conservative of the Reformed groups in the province are the Netherlands Reformed Congregations. In the early 1980s there were ten Netherlands Reformed Congregations in Canada with a membership of 6,500. Four of these congregations are located in Alberta with by far the largest congregations at Fort Macleod and Lethbridge, with a combined membership of around 800. They are strictly opposed to working on Sunday and they shun television, movies, and dancing. Possession of a television can be grounds for excommunication. Also, they do not buy life insurance and are opposed to medicare, inoculation, and vaccination because they believe these practices are an affront to God's will. National attention focussed on the Netherlands Reformed people in 1978 when their opposition to vaccination resulted in an outbreak of several polio cases among their children. Considerable adverse publicity for the group followed and precipitated an internal dispute over the vaccination issue. Netherlands Reformed conservatism is also expressed in strong attachment to their group, low rates of marriage outside the denomination, large and patriarchal families, resistance to higher education and attachment to farming. Of the four Reformed churches in the province, the Netherlands Reformed is the only one which has made any effort to maintain the Dutch language.[66]

Though their conservatism is expressed in varying degrees, the Christian Reformed, Canadian Reformed, and Netherlands Reformed people share a similar conservative orientation. All three groups place a high value on hard work and rigid social standards, which fervently preclude such practices as common law living, divorce, and abortion. Some outsiders see the unswerving stance and continued sectarian strife of the Reformed churches as undesirable. Nevertheless, this reflection of dedication to principle, no matter what it may cost in time, money, or energy has been and continues to be the hallmark of the Protestant Dutch-Canadian identity in the province. The Dutch Calvinist churches have contributed to the introduction of strands of Christian thought largely absent from the Canadian religious scene.

Unlike the majority Reformed Dutch, Dutch Catholics have been underrepresented in the postwar Dutch immigration and they have not formed a separate community in Canada. In the postwar era, they comprised a disproportionately small percentage of the total number of immigrants. The absence of Catholic field men in Alberta during most of the main years of immigration meant that a disproportionately small number of the Dutch Catholics who immigrated to Canada came to this province. Consequently, although Catholics constituted 38.5 percent of the population in the Netherlands, only 24 percent of the postwar Dutch immigrants to Canada were Catholic, and in 1971, only 18 percent of Dutch-Canadians in Alberta were Catholic.[67]

The experience of postwar Dutch Catholic immigrants differed in some respects from that of Reformed immigrants. Their immigration was not organized to the same extent as that of Reformed immigrants; they came as individuals and had to find their place in the new country on their own. The Catholics tended to integrate more rapidly with the larger Canadian society than Reformed people. At the same time, however, Dutch Catholics were among the few postwar Dutch immigrants who made an organized attempt to preserve aspects of Dutch language and culture.

Advantage Through Concord, an Edmonton cooperative and social organization and the Dutch-Canadian Club of Calgary are the only major nonreligious Dutch-Canadian organizations in the province. Both clubs have active programmes—including dance groups and choirs—and frequently hold dances and other social and cultural activities; significantly, both organizations are largely composed of Dutch-Catholics. The only other nonchurch organizations which cater primarily to Dutch-Canadians in the province are credit unions, which exist in all the larger urban centers. Most of them were established by Christian Reformed people to help themselves develop farms and businesses when bank credit was difficult to obtain.[68]

Finding a Place: Patterns of Assimilation among Dutch Immigrants

Among all of the postwar European immigrant groups, the Dutch have made the most conscious effort to assimilate as quickly as possible. This effort has been largely successful. Despite the religious segregation, in all other aspects of their lives, postwar Dutch immigrants have made strong efforts to become Canadianized.

A variety of studies demonstrate the Dutch tendency toward assimilation. For example, only one in ten of Alberta's Dutch-origin people give Dutch as the language most often spoken in their homes. The most common pattern for language use is that the immigrant generation continues to use Dutch in private conversation between spouses at home, while the second generation (particularly the older children) understands Dutch but does not speak it. The third generation neither understands nor speaks the Dutch language. In emphasizing the value of learning English quickly, the immigrant generation provided little opportunity or encouragement for their children to learn Dutch well and to use it. While it is true that the Dutch have a lower percentage of marriage outside the group than many other ethnic groups in the province, this is primarily the result of the large percentage of immigrants who brought their spouses with them when they came to Canada or who married within their community shortly after arriving (and of the religious solidarity of the Reformed people), rather than of any desire to preserve a Dutch-Canadian community. Indeed, many people of Dutch origin object to the very notion of their being considered an ethnic group, since they feel such a label connotes "foreignness." Many Dutch-Canadians have little or no awareness of or interest in the various dimensions of the Dutch-Canadian community in Alberta or in Canada; some even deliberately avoid associating with other people of Dutch origin since they have no desire to be labelled as Dutch-Canadians themselves. They consider themselves Canadians.[69]

For Dutch immigrants, assimilation has been facilitated by the similarity of their northern European culture to Canadian culture. In addition, their churches encouraged Dutch immigrants to identify with Canada as quickly as possible. Another factor contributing to their early assimilation was that the rural, lower middle class people who constituted a majority in each of the waves of Dutch immigration to Canada, had little or no exposure to the sophisticated, urban traditions of Dutch "high culture," and so did not bring this aspect of Dutch life with them. Indeed, the Reformed Dutch people had few visible signs of Dutch culture to retain, and only a few subtle decorative domestic items such as Delft china, lace half curtains, and heavy dining room rugs have been retained. Nor did their numbers include political refugees who might have added a strong national consciousness and a desire to return to the homeland. The Dutch also found that Canadian attitudes toward them facilitated an easy acceptance. For many immigrants, a Dutch accent eventually became the only identifiable reminder of their immigrant past.

One indication of the degree to which Dutch-Canadians have committed themselves to Alberta and been accepted by Albertans has been the successful political involvement of several Dutch immigrants in the province's small towns. Politics at the provincial and federal levels has seldom been either attractive or open to immigrants and, since there is such a large percentage of immigrants among the Dutch population in the province, it is not surprising that few have become visibly involved at these levels. However, at the local level of politics, Dutch-Canadians have been surprisingly active. During the 1970s, Lacombe, Sundre, Redcliff, and Nobleford all elected Dutch immigrants as mayors. There has also been some involvement at the provincial and federal levels by Canadian-born people of Dutch descent. For example, Gerry Amerongen, an Edmonton lawyer and Progressive Conservative member for Edmonton-Meadowlark, has served as speaker of the Alberta legislature since 1972; and Peter Elzinga, a farmer from Sherwood Park, has been member of Parliament for the Pembina constituency since 1974.[70]

This general pattern of rapid assimilation among the Dutch does not, however, mean that all ties with Holland have been severed. Reciprocal letters and visits with relatives in Holland are frequent. The Reformed groups have retained some religious ties with groups in the Netherlands, necessitating minimal retention of the language for religious purposes.

Contemporary Trends

In the postwar era, Dutch-Canadians created a solid niche for themselves in Alberta's economy, especially in mixed farming and in the skilled trades. Throughout their history in the province, a major, recurring pre-occupation among the Dutch has been the desire to become financially independent. Despite their predominantly rural backgrounds and limited educational levels, the majority of Dutch immigrants have attained in one generation the economic goals which brought them to Canada. It has been a common experience for Dutch tradesmen to eventually become independent businessmen, owning contracting businesses, machine shops, or service stations. Dutch immigrants in cities and towns across the province, but particularly in the Medicine Hat and Redcliff area, have combined agricultural and business skills in the pioneering and development of flourishing greenhouses. Although they started with almost nothing when they first arrived in Canada, through their hard work and tenacity most Dutch immigrants have reached or exceeded the average provincial income level. A few immigrant farmers and busi-nessmen have become millionaires.

Prior to the 1970s, there was (with the small exception of a few professionals in the oil industry in Calgary) virtually no managerial or professional class among Dutch-Canadians. This pattern is now chang-ing, for two reasons. The children of the postwar generation are now coming of age; while some remain in farming or the trades, many have branched out into other occupations including the professions and other white collar jobs. Second, there has recently been a new type of Dutch immigrant coming to Alberta. Though their numbers are few, the newly arrived Dutch include young professionals looking for economic oppor-tunity and wealthy, retired businessmen looking for a secure investment climate. These new immigrants are urban, educated and aggressive and most have little or no interest in either the Dutch-Canadian clubs or the Reformed churches which they regard as anachronistic. The Dutch-Canadian community was momentarily diversified by the arrival of Dutch-Canadians from Ontario who came to participate in Alberta's economic boom in the late 1970s. Given this diversification, the stereo-type of the Dutch farmer or tradesman will become increasingly out-moded in the future and Dutch-origin people will be involved in all aspects of Alberta's economy and society.

Conclusion

Alberta's Dutch-origin population is diverse, scattered, and split along religious lines. It includes people who represent a wide range of life-styles, from the urban, cosmopolitan, and nonsectarian to the rural, con-servative, and sectarian. It is not, however, simply a cross section of Holland's population; rather, it reflects a selective migration of some of the most conservative elements of Dutch society.

The social and economic climate of Alberta has been, in many respects, tailor-made for conservative Dutch immigrants. The values of each have been mutually complementary. Most of the newcomers from Holland have been staunch believers in the virtues of the free enterprise system and have united with the majority of Albertans in their support first for the Social Credit and then for the Conservative party. Also, the traditional views of Reformed immigrants with regard to social issues and family life have been in harmony with the consensus in a province long renowned for its "Bible belt" conservatism. The similarity between the beliefs of Reformed people and the dominant values in Alberta has made their adjustment a relatively easy one, even if the more religious among the Dutch have not recognized these common grounds.

Each of the three waves of Dutch immigrants has contributed substantially to Alberta and to each other. In contrast with many other immigrant groups, there have been relatively few differences among the various waves of Dutch immigration. The social and religious backgrounds of people in each wave have been similar, thus greatly minimizing time-of-arrival conflict within the Dutch community. The first wave of immigrants was more oriented to the United States than later arrivals, since many of them had lived there before coming to Canada and consequently had developed links with the Dutch-American settlements; but in general, social and religious patterns have been similar for Dutch people coming to Alberta throughout the present century.

The early pioneer communities eased the adjustment of later immigrants by helping them find jobs and housing, giving them essential knowledge about Canadian life and providing them with established churches where they could worship and meet each other in a familiar setting. During the postwar period, the early settlements at Nobleford, Monarch, Neerlandia, and Lacombe acted as magnets for attracting immigrants. Certainly many Dutch immigrants would have come to Alberta during this time whether or not there had been earlier settlements, but their presence increased the numbers of Dutch people who chose Alberta as their destination. The postwar immigrants in turn also had an impact on the rural settlements by reinforcing or reviving their strong Dutch flavor and invigorating community and church organizations.

While all three waves of Dutch immigrants who came to Alberta have made successful adjustments to Canadian society, the third and largest group, building on the foundation laid by those who came earlier and applying an ethic of hard work to ample postwar opportunity, have exemplified the classical immigrant success story.

The Dutch success story is not, however, simply an advertisement for the virtues of hard work and the free enterprise system. From the early days at Neerlandia, Dutch immigrants have acted out their belief in the importance of cooperation and various forms of mutual helpfulness, including cooperatives and credit unions. This Dutch emphasis on cooperative endeavor has been an important ingredient in their economic success. Nor has the Dutch experience in Alberta been completely free of hardship and disappointment. It has been marked by problems of initial adjustment to Canadian culture, generational conflict, and sectarian strife. For the Reformed community, there has been considerable disappointment in their failure to effect, in their perception, a dramatic "Christianization" of Alberta's society.

While it is difficult to predict future trends among the Dutch in

Alberta, it would seem reasonable to suggest that the values of the Reformed Dutch will become increasingly unusual in a society which is undergoing rapid secularization. Since World War II, and particularly in recent years, Alberta has experienced massive urbanization and an accompanying liberalization of social attitudes. But the majority of Dutch Reformed immigrants and their children have not been part of this trend to the same extent as the general population. Consequently, the Reformed presence in the province will likely become more noticeable in the future. If one assumes that immigration from Holland will remain small in the foreseeable future and that present overall patterns of assimilation will continue, it would seem that the long term impact of Dutch immigration to Alberta will be reflected primarily in the continued and more visible presence of the Reformed churches.

CHAPTER EIGHT

The Icelandic Experience in Alberta
Howard and Tamara Palmer

Introduction

The Icelanders have a fascinating history in Canada and Alberta. They came from a small island nation, just below the Arctic Circle in the North Atlantic Ocean, which had been cut off from Europe for centuries. This nation of striking contrasts—of glaciers, geysers, and volcanoes— had been settled between 870 and 910 A.D. by 400 Norwegian Viking settlers. Iceland received almost no subsequent immigration and though it was dominated politically and economically for long periods by Denmark, it developed in virtual isolation from the rest of Europe. This isolation enabled the Icelanders to maintain the Old Norse language with few changes from the ninth century. Few in number and forced to eke out a bare existence from fishing and livestock raising, the Icelanders were hardy and self-sufficient. While they lacked educational institutions, they valued books and education and developed a rich literary heritage, in which poetry and versifying were not only greatly admired, but were practised by large segments of the population; they could also boast one of the highest literacy rates in the world.

Over the centuries of their development, the Icelanders nurtured a strong love for their language, history, and literature which was passed on from generation to generation and was brought by the first Icelanders who came to Canada in the 1870s. The Icelanders were a paradox: they were insular and poor, yet they were devoted to education and literature.

All these characteristics were brought by the Icelanders to Alberta in the 1880s, 1890s, and 1900s during the first and only wave of Icelandic immigration to the province. The Icelanders established only one major area of settlement in Alberta at Markerville (in 1888, near what was to become the town of Innisfail) in central Alberta. They met the same challenges faced by other pioneers at the turn of the century, but their response to those challenges was conditioned by their Icelandic culture and traditions. This made their pioneering experience somewhat different from that of other groups. Their cultural background fitted them to cope with the challenge of surviving in the pioneer conditions of central Alberta.

The Icelanders in Alberta have been a very small group—considerably fewer than in Manitoba or Saskatchewan. Despite its small size, the settlement of Markerville was known to Icelanders not only throughout western Canada, but in Iceland as well. This is partly because Icelanders had a great interest in family ties and were very much aware of the whereabouts of other Icelanders. Also, Markerville was the home of Stephan Stephansson, a political and religious radical and writer who was considered by many Icelanders to be the greatest Icelandic poet of the twentieth century. Stephansson not only homesteaded and farmed in pioneer fashion, but also authored six large books of poetry and 1,400 pages of articles.

Although the Icelanders are the smallest of the Scandinavian groups in the province, they have been the most tenacious in preserving their identity. To understand the roots of Icelandic settlement in Alberta, one must return to the Iceland of the 1870s and to the Icelandic settlements in Manitoba and the United States.

Conditions in Iceland and the Origins of Icelandic Settlements in North America

The original Icelandic settlers in the Markerville area did not come directly from Iceland, but from Pembina County, North Dakota. For many, the Markerville experience was their third attempt at pioneering since most had first settled elsewhere in Wisconsin or "New Iceland," an Icelandic bloc settlement in the Interlake area of Manitoba before moving to the Icelandic settlements in North Dakota.

These initial settlements in Manitoba and Wisconsin had been established in the early 1870s by people fleeing deteriorating economic condi-

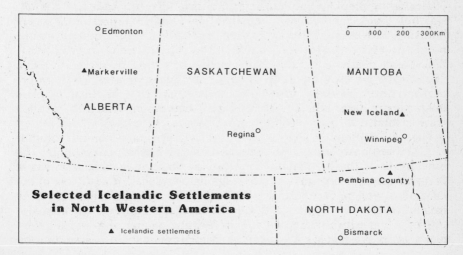

**Selected Icelandic Settlements
in North Western America**

▲ Icelandic settlements

tions in Iceland. Because of its geography, Iceland has been able to support only a small population; it has few natural resources and only about 1 percent of the land can be used for farming. Consequently, Icelanders traditionally combined fishing and livestock raising. Most farmers grew only hay which was used to feed sheep (for wool, meat, and skins) and cattle (for dairy products). In 1870, the total population of Iceland was just 70,000, but even this was too many people for the island to sustain.[1]

The Icelanders who established settlements in North America looked upon Iceland as a place where they could no longer eke out a living. Many were tired of a system where Icelanders were tenant farmers, renting their land from the Danish crown, which had gained control of their country in 1380. Epidemics of sheep diseases in the 1850s, a series of crop failures from 1865 to 1874 and volcanic activity which spread volcanic ash over the island: these combined to force Icelandic farmers to look elsewhere for a home. A few went to Brazil, but most looked to North America. The first Icelandic settlement in North America began in 1855-56 at Spanish Fork, Utah and was made up of Mormon converts from Iceland.[2]

However, the first sizeable group of Icelandic settlers to North America left Iceland 5 August 1873, and included Stephan G. Stephansson (then twenty years old), his parents and family, along with 165 other Icelanders. They went by ship from Iceland to Scotland and then on to Quebec. Lord Dufferin, the Governor General at the time, who had travelled in Iceland during the 1850s and had been impressed by its people and so influenced the Canadian government's decision to encourage Icelandic settlers to settle in Canada.[3]

The Canadian government offered the group free passage from Quebec City to their destination, and 200 acres of free land. Succumbing to this offer, 115 people who had originally intended to go to the United States decided to settle in the Muskoka region of central Ontario, while 50, including Stephan Stephansson and his family, proceeded to Wisconsin. But the Icelanders who remained in Ontario experienced severe hardship. Government promises went unfulfilled, and they had almost no money and very little food. As a consequence, there was considerable illness and death. Ultimately, their settlement did not succeed and in 1875, with government help, a group of approximately 200 people moved to the Interlake area of Manitoba, just north of the province's existing boundary, where they founded a settlement which they called New Iceland.[4]

The new settlement soon became the largest rural Icelandic community in North America. Although New Iceland was placed under the jurisdiction of the Lieutenant Governor of Manitoba, the settlement at first was given a constitution to manage its own local affairs. Most of the Icelanders who came to Canada between 1876 and 1887 settled in New Iceland where they hoped to combine fishing and farming. The area also offered wood which could be used for fuel and shelter; this was a particularly attractive feature for Icelandic immigrants used to depending on driftwood, since trees were so scarce in their homeland. The Icelanders also felt that the large reserve of land which was set aside for them would enable them to maintain a cohesive Icelandic community where they could retain their traditions and language.[5]

Conditions in New Iceland were, however, far from ideal. In 1876 approximately 100 of the 1,400 to 1,500 settlers died in a smallpox epidemic; (one-third to one-half of the settlers had contracted the disease). One hundred more died from other causes—mainly malnutrition. There was a perennial food shortage due to poor crops and limited success in fishing.

Dissatisfaction grew and although New Iceland retained a sizeable number of Icelanders, by 1878-79 some began to leave. They departed to establish new settlements in southwestern Manitoba, in the Wynyard area of the Northwest Territories (in what was later to become Saskatchewan), or to work and live in Winnipeg. Winnipeg soon became the unofficial Icelandic-Canadian capital—the main center for Icelandic newspapers, churches, and cultural organizations in North America. Several families of settlers followed Pall Thorlakson, a Lutheran minister, to establish a new Icelandic settlement in Pembina County, North Dakota in 1878. They were soon joined by several more families, including that of Stephan Stephansson, from the Icelandic settlement in Wisconsin.[6]

Pioneering in North Dakota

The early years in the Dakota settlement were not easy. Due to the lack of transportation, the majority of the Icelanders were compelled to walk 160 miles from New Iceland to their new home. The men who came from Wisconsin herded their cattle 850 miles to reach the new settlement. The pioneers soon came face-to-face with the familiar problems of little outside employment, scarce food, and intense winter cold. However, in the North Dakota settlements the initial difficulties were gradually overcome, and by the 1880s the communities were fairly well established: they had their own Lutheran churches, post offices, schools, ladies aid societies, and literary societies. One of the reading/debating clubs was the Icelandic Cultural Society, founded on 4 February 1888, at the home of Stephan Stephansson.[7]

Stephansson's background provides an insight into the origins of the Icelandic community at Markerville. As a boy he received no formal education, but learned to read at the nightly readings that were common in Icelandic families. Stephansson soon absorbed his family's love of books and poetry. Before leaving Iceland, he had begun composing poetry and continued to do so in Wisconsin, despite the time-consuming hardships of pioneering. He had learned some English from his church minister before leaving Iceland. Once in Wisconsin, where there were many Scandinavians, Stephansson taught himself to read and write both Danish and Norwegian.

The Wisconsin settlers, including Stephansson, had to cope with several serious problems. The land they had acquired was covered with giant hardwood trees and the soil was sandy; thus clearing was difficult and yields disappointing. After five years of work establishing himself in the area, Stephansson married his young cousin, Helga Jonsson. Soon the combined pressures of poor economic conditions and a growing family led the Stephanssons, along with all the other Icelanders in the Wisconsin community, to pull up stakes and move to the North Dakota settlement, which had been founded by their former pastor, Pall Thorlaksson.[8]

The Icelandic Cultural Society of North Dakota which Stephansson established gave evidence not only of the Icelanders' love of books, but also of the strong religious ferment in the Icelandic settlements. During the 1880s and 1890s, the Icelandic communities in North America split into three religious factions—liberal and conservative Lutherans and the more liberal Unitarians. In Iceland, most of the people belonged to the Lutheran church, which was the state church, and they retained this attachment in North America. But Unitarian influences had reached Iceland from Great Britain, and some of the Icelanders in North Dakota became interested in America Unitarianism. Through the influence and energetic work of Bjorn Petursson, an Icelandic farmer in North Dakota who became a Unitarian minister, Unitarianism gradually began to make inroads into almost all the Icelandic settlements in Canada.[9]

Stephansson had joined the Lutheran church in his community in North Dakota when it was formed, but he objected to both its theological conservatism and its exclusion of women from church government. By the late 1880s he had dropped his Lutheran affiliation. Stephansson was attracted to liberal religious thinking in the United States, and the Icelandic Cultural Society was composed of a group of like-minded Icelanders who shared his quest for truth, his love of knowledge, and his independence. Stephansson's record of the objectives of the Literary Society indicates the extent to which the liberal and rationalist religious thought of Unitarianism and the late nineteenth century Ethical Culture movement had influenced his thinking and that of other Icelanders in the area:

> Humanity, Research, Freedom. The objectives of this organization are to support and promote culture and ethics, that ethics and that faith which is based upon experience, knowledge and science. In place of ecclesiastical sectarianism it seeks humanitarianism and fellowship; in place of unexamined confessions of faith, sensible and unfettered research; in place of blind faith, independent convictions; and in place of ignorance and superstition, spiritual freedom and progress on which no fetters are placed.[10]

The activities of the Cultural Society reveal a good deal about the religious and cultural concerns of the Icelanders who eventually came to Alberta. The thirty-four male members of the association, all impoverished immigrant farmers, took turns giving talks to each other on such topics as natural history, comparative religion, and the history of religion. The Society was attacked in the pages of a Lutheran magazine as godless and dangerous, and the North Dakota settlement was enlivened by the conflict between liberals and conservatives which occurred in almost all the Icelandic settlements in the United States. The

Society disbanded in the early 1890s—not because of outside criticism or wrangling within the Icelandic community, but simply because several of the leading members moved away, including several like Stephansson who went to Alberta.[11]

Although by the mid-1880s the Icelanders in North Dakota felt they were well on the way to being established, they soon found themselves on the downward edge of one of the boom-bust cycles which have plagued prairie farmers for decades. Population growth in the area led to rising land prices and to inflated prices for farm machinery and other goods. Many of the Icelanders went heavily in debt. When livestock and wheat prices slipped significantly, they found that the only way they could pay their debts was to sell their land. Beginning in the mid-1880s, poor financial conditions were exacerbated by dust storms, drought, and prairie fires. When they came to Alberta, the Icelanders brought with them an intense dislike of loan companies, banks, railway companies, and grain companies since they felt that these institutions had all conspired with the weather to force them off the land. In addition, they also brought experience in American farm protest groups. Before deciding to emigrate, some of the Icelanders participated in the Dakota Farmers Alliance, a populist, anti-big business organization, in an attempt to confront their problems.[12]

By the 1880s, yet another problem plagued the Icelanders in North Dakota—land pressure. The continued influx into the settlement of families from Iceland and the desire of some second generation Icelanders to establish their own farms meant that the best land was soon taken up; consequently, it readily became apparent that those who wanted land would have to look elsewhere.

The Beginnings of Icelandic Settlement in Alberta

The decision to settle in Alberta was accidental. In March 1888, a meeting was called to discuss prospects for resettlement elsewhere. Three of the leading people behind the movement were Olofur Olafson Espiholi, Einar Jonasson, and Sigurdur J. Bjornson. The settlers were convinced that they should move, but they were not sure just where. Some wanted to move to the Pacific coast where they envisioned a scenic panorama, a temperate climate, and abundant fishing and agricultural opportunities. The meeting selected Sigurdur Bjornson to go as a scout to select a site and make preliminary preparations for a group settlement. He travelled to British Columbia and scouted Vancouver Island, but was unable to locate a suitable place.[13]

On his return, Bjornson came on the CPR which had been completed through Calgary just five years before. In Calgary, he met Oliver Goodman, an Icelander who had arrived the previous year. Goodman and his father had previously filed on land near the Red Deer River. Bjornson decided to look at the land and travelled there in the company of Oliver Goodman's brother, Sigfus. Bjornson liked the land and decided to reserve townships for the Icelandic immigrants in North Dakota. In a letter to one of the prospective immigrants, Bjornson explained his choice:

> I like the country north of the Red Deer River, the soil is good and lots of grass alternatively plow land and hay meadows with clumps of trees here and there. Good fishing in the lakes and rivers, the winters are said to be shorter and milder than in Manitoba and North Dakota.[14]

Three of the main factors in this choice of land related to previous experience in Iceland. The area was chosen not primarily for its grain-growing potential, but because water and fish were readily available and there was feed for livestock, which in turn would provide food and dairy products. The presence of wood, which could be used for homes and fuel, also helps explain why the Icelanders chose this area on the southern edge of the park belt instead of the plentiful unsettled prairie land which they encountered on their trek north from Calgary.

Bjornson convinced some of the Icelanders in North Dakota to sell their farms and livestock and to come north. On 24 May 1888, a group of fifty, which included eleven families and four single men, began their journey to Alberta. The group travelled by wagon to the border, then by train to Winnipeg where they were joined by two more families. After making some purchases of cookstoves and utensils, the group left by train for Calgary.[15]

When they arrived in Calgary in June, Oliver Goodman advised them to work in the city temporarily to accumulate cash, but they decided to push on to their new home. The group was delayed by rain, but in the middle of June, after purchasing four teams of horses in Calgary, the cavalcade set off for their new home, approximately eighty miles to the north.

When the Icelanders arrived in the territory that would become Alberta, the central portion of it was still almost completely uninhabited, and there was no railway north from Calgary. Indeed, there were only five stopping houses along the way from Calgary to what is now Innisfail.[16]

The group's journey north from Calgary was slow and difficult because rain had made the trail north almost impassable. Finally, on the sixth day, they reached the Red Deer River. This presented the most difficult challenge to them so far since the river was in flood. The river was to continue to be a source of difficulty for the Icelandic settlers. It isolated them from the main north-south lines of transportation and communication in the province until a bridge was built across it at the turn of the century.

After further delay, while they tried to decide how to get across the river and a near fatal attempt to cross the swollen waters, the group built a flat boat for ferrying across the river. Finally on 27 June, people, luggage, and wagons were loaded aboard and taken across. The settlers then moved on to take up their homesteads along the banks of the Medicine River, which flowed into the Red Deer River. In 1889, several more families arrived from North Dakota, including that of Stephan Stephansson.[17] Given the scarcity of settlers in Alberta and the public preference for northern Europeans over eastern or southern Europeans, it is not surprising that the local press welcomed the Icelanders.[18]

For most of the settlers this would be the third and last time they would pioneer in North America. The pioneering experience at Markerville would not be an easy one, but conditions would prove to be more suitable than they had been in New Iceland, Wisconsin, or North Dakota. Most of the settlers would make Alberta their permanent home, where they would live out their lives and raise their families.

Pioneering, Icelandic Style

The pioneering experience of the Icelanders was similar to the pioneering experience of other immigrants in Alberta, but their response to the challenges of the frontier had a uniquely Icelandic flavor. Their first task, of course, was to build shelter. Most of the settlers made homes of logs chinked with moss and clay with roofs of prairie sod.[19]

Food was not a serious problem because the Icelanders knew how to live off the land. The Medicine River was full of fish and there was ample prairie chicken, partridge, and rabbit in the surrounding area. Burnt Lake and Sylvan Lake, near Markerville, also provided fish. Fish were not eaten fresh, but were dried after the Icelandic custom, thus providing protein throughout the lean winters. The settlers also tried to grow gardens, but some of the soil around Markerville was like gumbo and even potatoes and turnips were hard to grow. However, in season, wild berries were an important addition to their diet. As the settlers established themselves and built up their herds, they were able to add pork, beef, mutton, and poultry to their diet.[20]

The Icelanders turned early to the raising of sheep since they were familiar with sheep raising in Iceland and since sheep had so many uses. Mutton was a food staple, tallow was used for candles, and the wool was used to make clothing. A number of the women had been able to bring spinning wheels with them. As they had done in Iceland, the women washed the wool, carded, and spun it into yarn, which they then used to knit warm woolen garments, including underwear, sweaters, socks, and mittens. Extra garments were used as barter for groceries and other necessary goods, and some of the women were able to sell their woolen products outside of the settlement.[21]

Besides raising sheep, Icelanders also concentrated on livestock and dairying, just as they had in Iceland. Grain growing was not attempted successfully until the early 1900s; early frosts in the area were a continual problem, particularly in an era when early maturing grains were still being developed and transportation of grain out of the settlement was, in any case, extremely difficult. There was no railway until 1891 and when it was built, it bypassed the area where they had settled and went through Innisfail, fifteen miles distant.[22]

Dairying formed the main economic staple of the area prior to World War I. During the 1890s, Icelanders established three cheese factories in the Markerville area. However, the major economic mainstay of the community was the creamery, which bought out the three cheese factories in 1899, and continued as a major economic activity until the early 1970s. The federal government played a role in the development of the creamery by financing and supervising its initial operation. On 23 September 1899, a government appointed manager and the producers formed a joint stock company, incorporated as "The Tindastoll Butter and Cheese Manufacturing Association," to run the creamery. The new company had thirty-five members and all but two of them were Icelanders. The creamery soon became known for its high quality product and it helped put the Icelanders on their feet financially. The Markerville Icelanders helped to establish the Innisfail area as one of the earliest and most important dairying centers in the province.[23]

However, the development of dairying was a gradual process and in the early years, the Icelandic men had to leave their wives and families for periods of time to find work outside in order to get enough cash to buy food, machinery, and livestock. They trapped, did harvesting and sheared sheep on southern Alberta ranches at a rate of $.03 per head.[24]

Transportation and communication continued to be difficult problems for the Markerville pioneers throughout the early years of settlement. The railway's bypassing the community was a hard blow since the Icelanders had expected that it would come nearer the settlement. In addition, they had to contend with the perpetual struggle of fording the Red Deer and Medicine rivers until bridges were built in 1901 and 1902. Almost all the settlers experienced dunkings, and there were some near drownings during the times of spring runoff.[25]

Once a post office was established in 1890, the Icelanders were able to maintain contact with friends and family in Manitoba, North Dakota, and Iceland. The post office—the first west of the Red Deer River—was named "Tindastoll," an Icelandic name suggesting the new geographic setting. "Tinda" is a ridge of mountains and "stoll," a chair. The settlement was located on rolling land within sight of the mountains. The Icelandic community as a whole was also known as Tindastoll until 1899 when the townsite was renamed in honor of C.P. Marker, a Danish immigrant and the Dairy Commissioner of the Northwest Territories who had been responsible for the establishment of the government-supported creamery.[26]

The early adjustment of the Icelanders to the area was conditioned by the interplay of local economic and geographic conditions and the Icelanders' own traditions. Their experiences in Iceland had particularly suited them to survive the pioneering struggle for existence; they were highly self-sufficient and willing to work together for common goals.

Establishment of Community Institutions

The Icelanders established a number of community institutions, both to help them adjust to the new land and to enable them to maintain their cultural traditions. Community cooperation was essential for meeting the challenges of pioneering and overcoming their almost overwhelming isolation. Many of the Icelanders who came to Alberta had previously made attempts to establish bloc settlements in Manitoba, North Dakota, or Wisconsin where they could maintain their language and culture. They called themselves "West Icelanders"—not because they were from western Iceland (most came from northern Iceland), but because they felt themselves to be Icelanders living in the West. That they named their Manitoba settlement "New Iceland" is suggestive of their original intentions when they came.[27]

Among the first community institutions to be established were the rural schools, which served not only as educational institutions for the young, but as social centers for the districts they included. During the early 1890s, the settlers built the Tindastoll and Hola schools, the latter one on Stephan Stephansson's farmland. Stephansson was the first chairman of the Hola school board, while the first teacher was Jon Gudmundson who, like most of the Icelandic immigrants, had little formal schooling, but was nonetheless strongly devoted to education. The school did not function as an agency for the quick assimilation of the immigrants' children since not only were some of the first teachers Icelanders, but the school year was short; there was also a high turnover of teachers and almost all the children in these two schools were of Icelandic descent.[28]

The Markerville settlers formed a literary society in 1892 called Ithunn, sixteen years before they opened a church. Money from memberships bought books, and eventually a substantial library of Icelandic books was housed in Markerville. The founders of the society included several of the people who had been associated with Stephansson in the

The home of Icelandic-Canadian poet Stephan Stephansson (far left) and family members, Markerville, ca. 1907. Stephansson's home reflected the Gothic-revival style of Victorian architecture. The home has now been restored as a provincial historic site and is open to the public. (Courtesy Provincial Museum of Alberta)

Icelandic Society of North Dakota. Controversy surrounding the political and religious beliefs of those involved in the reading society eventually led to disbanding of the discussion groups connected with it, though the library that the society had established continued to play an important role in the community until the 1930s.

Monday was cream and library day in Markerville—the day when settlers took their cream to the creamery and picked up books at the library. Discussions were sometimes heated when participants clashed over religious questions. The library also housed copies of the two major Icelandic-Canadian newspapers, the Conservative weekly *Heimskringla* and the Liberal *Logberg*. Both were published in Winnipeg and they kept the Icelanders in touch with events and debates in Manitoba and in Iceland. Stephansson was a frequent contributor to both papers. During the cold winter evenings, the settlers kept alive their love for literature. Following the Icelandic tradition, the family would gather around the stove and the men read books aloud while the children would card the wool and the mother would spin and knit it into mitts and sweaters. Thus, though Stephansson was the only poet in the community, he was not alone in his passion for books.[29]

One of the oldest organizations in the community was the Icelandic Ladies' Aid which was first established in 1891 by Icelandic women who were living in Calgary while their husbands built homes for them in the new settlement. Revealingly, they called their group *Vonin* meaning hope. The group has continued to the present day and, until 1978, kept its records in the Icelandic language. The organization sponsored social events, such as the annual *Tombola*, or bazaar, which helped to unite the community. In 1903, the Ladies' Aid played an important part in the building of the Markerville Community Hall, named *Fensala* (a name from Icelandic mythology) and in organizing social events connected with the Lutheran church.[30]

The Icelandic picnic, which was held in Markerville on 2 August, an Icelandic national holiday, was the most important social event in the community; it eventually attracted many people, including non-Icelanders, who travelled considerable distances to attend. At its peak during the late teens and the 1920s, the picnic was attended by 800 to 1,000 people. The program included speakers, sports events, ball games, a tug of war while the day concluded with a dance. Several Icelandic meat dishes, sweet cheese, and pastries also made an appearance at this and other social events.[31]

Unlike many other ethnic settlements in Alberta, social life in Markerville did not revolve around the church. While the vast majority of the Icelanders were Lutherans and they did establish a church, they were not noted churchgoers. After the first few years, use of the church gradually dwindled until it was used only at Christmas, Easter, weddings, and funerals.

Nevertheless, the Lutheran church was the only one in the settlement. Beginning in 1898, Icelandic student ministers from Manitoba visited the settlement and, in February 1900, some of the settlers established a

Confirmation class, Markerville Lutheran Church, ca. 1914. Rev. Petur Hjalmsson stands third from right. The Icelanders were divided into Lutherans and Unitarians. Organized religion, however, did not play a major role in the Icelandic settlement at Markerville. (Courtesy Provincial Museum of Alberta)

Lutheran congregation. The first minister to be engaged was Rev. Petur Hjalmsson, who was hired in 1902, but he had a short and controversial career. He was dismissed in 1909, partly because of lack of funds and partly because of the settlement's divided religious opinion. Hjalmsson continued to serve the needs of the settlement at major ceremonial occasions, but devoted most of his life while in Markerville to farming. Although the church building itself is now little used, it remains a handsome landmark.[32]

Undoubtedly the free-thinking and Unitarian influence which developed among the Icelanders in North Dakota and which was brought by many to Alberta, played a role in the Lutheran church's limited success in the settlement. The Icelanders of Unitarian persuasion were never numerous enough or committed enough to the idea of institutional, organized religion to establish a Unitarian church, but their presence meant that the Lutheran church could enjoy only limited success, even though the majority of the settlers were Lutherans.

While the Icelanders may have been divided on religious and political questions, they nonetheless formed a closely knit community. Paradoxically, conflict probably even served to unite them since it delineated community boundaries and heightened their awareness of each other. Despite the group's small numbers (there were about thirty-five Icelandic families in the settlement at the turn of the century), bloc settlement made it possible for them to develop distinctive Icelandic institutions.

While their position among the first pioneers of central Alberta made their initial pioneering experience even more difficult than that faced by many later arrivals, at the same time it made possible the development of one homogeneous bloc settlement, since there were so few other settlers coming into the area until the turn of the century.

The Icelanders were a proud and independent people who had shared both a common poverty, which had led to their migration to Alberta, a common pioneering experience, and a common culture. They possessed the ability and the will to work together to improve their lot and soon gained a reputation as honest and progressive farmers.[33]

The Impact of the Settlement Boom

The settlement boom from 1900 to 1914 brought many changes to the Markerville area. New districts were opened up as newcomers from Icelandic settlements in the United States, Saskatchewan, and Manitoba and from Iceland arrived and homesteaded. The Burnt Lake area northeast of Markerville had first attracted individual Icelanders in 1891, when Sigurdur Grimson settled there. The road from Red Deer west (known as the Burnt Lake trail) at that time passed through both Burnt Lake and Markerville and when the Burnt Lake area opened up at the turn of the century; several Icelandic families, including those of Johan Sveinson, Sam Johnson, Fred Johnson, and Gudmundur Gudmunsson settled there. Other rural areas near Markerville which opened up at this time included the school districts of Happy Hill, New Hill, and Heckla. Several Icelandic families from either Iceland or Manitoba settled in each of these places.[34]

But the Icelanders in all of these new regions were in a minority. The immigration boom at the turn of the century brought in large numbers of Americans, Danes, Swedes, and Norwegians who were rapidly transforming west central Alberta from a frontier into a settled area. For a time, Markerville was able to preserve its Icelandic character—but the area's Icelanders were quickly becoming a minority. Not only were they being greatly outnumbered by other settlers, but their overall proportion was gradually diminishing as newcomers of other backgrounds continued to come into the area, as the children of the original Icelandic settlers moved away, and as people of Icelandic origin ceased to come there after the immigration boom ended around 1910. At the time of the 1916 census, the first census where the people of Icelandic background were enumerated separately from other Scandinavians, there were 700 people of Icelandic descent in Alberta, approximately one-third of whom had been born in Iceland. Four hundred of the 700 people of Icelandic descent lived in the Markerville and Burnt Lake areas.[35]

The period from 1900 to 1910 was a period of significant and dramatic change in the area. The building of roads and bridges and the introduction of grain farming, which the influx of settlers facilitated, increased their links with the outside. The introduction of early maturing grain made growing feasible, and the building of a better transportation system made it much easier to market the grain. The Icelanders were becoming commercial rather than self-sufficient farmers. While the new settlers still had to endure at least some of the difficulties of the pioneering stage, the older settlers entered a phase of consolidation and expansion. The hamlet of Markerville itself reached the height of its activity between 1910 and 1925; it was the outpost for the "west country" of west central Alberta, and its creamery attracted commerce from farmers for miles around. Livery stables, hotels, general stores, and blacksmith shops were built to accommodate the needs of the small, but bustling settlement.

Ethnic relations in the area were never a significant problem despite the influx of new settlers; the Icelanders had something in common, not only with the Danes, Swedes, and Norwegians, all of whom formed sizeable groups in the area, but also with the Americans, because of the experience of many of the Icelanders in North Dakota. The large group of Danes who settled in nearby Dickson beginning in 1902 were staunchly Lutheran and were, therefore, not always compatible with the Icelanders. The Danes thought the Icelanders were much too liberal and lax in their religious beliefs and social practices, while the Icelanders felt the Dickson Danes were too strict and conservative. However, the two groups, realizing that all of them were newcomers to Canada and that they were all in need of helpful and friendly neighbors, gradually accepted each other and were able to live together harmoniously.[36]

Markerville was undergoing gradual changes which were making it more and more similar to other rural hamlets in Alberta. Perhaps the

The Markerville Brass Band, photographed at an Icelandic picnic on August 2, 1912. The annual picnic was a major social and cultural event that attracted hundreds. The picnic has recently been revived as an annual event and attracts people of Icelandic descent from across western Canada. (Courtesy Provincial Museum of Alberta)

most basic change was the diminishing use of Icelandic for commerce in the community, as the Icelanders accommodated themselves to the realities of living in a multi-ethnic region. Social and cultural patterns were also shifting. Although the soccer and baseball teams, the fraternal lodges and the regionally famous Markerville brass band—all of which were an important part of the community's social life—were composed primarily of Icelandic-origin people, these activities were shared with non-Icelanders and they provided important links between Markerville and the larger rural society of west central Alberta.[37]

World War I brought a growing commercialization of agriculture in the Markerville area, a continuing shift to grain raising, and more evidence of the integration of Icelanders into western Canadian society. Many of the sons of the Icelandic settlers served in World War I, forming part of the 964 Icelanders from western Canada who served in the armed forces at a time when there were approximately 16,000 people of Icelandic descent in Canada (including 12,000 in Manitoba, 3,200 in Saskatchewan, and 700 in Alberta).[38]

Although the war effort received the support of the majority of the Canadian born—most of the Icelandic press in Winnipeg and the churches, all of whom wanted to prove the loyalty of Icelanders to Canada—it had its critics within the Icelandic community. Stephan Stephansson was a pacifist and a political radical, closely akin to the socialists, though he never joined a political party. Like socialists across Canada, he was bitterly critical of the war, which he saw as another British imperialistic adventure (he had also denounced Canada's involvement in the Boer War in South Africa in 1899). He lashed out at World War I in his series of poems *Vigslodi (The Trail of War)*. His poem "In War Time" read:

> In Europe's reeking slaughter-pen
> They mince the flesh of murdered men,
> While swinish merchants, snout in trough,
> Drink all the bloody profits off!

In a similar tone, he mocked the sentimental tributes to the Unknown Soldier:

> In Paris was my burial Number One;
> My Second was in London; and now vex'd
> By vaunting hands,
> I'm lugg'd to Washington
> —Where next, O lord, where next?

Stephansson's pacifist views did not win him many friends during a period of extreme patriotism, particularly when some of his neighbors had lost sons during the war.[39]

The Work of Stephan Stephansson

Stephansson played an active part in community affairs, but was unique among the Icelanders because of his creative energy. Stephansson was a prolific poet whose published work ran to six volumes and who was heralded in Iceland as one of its foremost poets. Noted literary critic, Watson Kirkconnell, has given an assessment of his significance:

> His breadth of literary knowledge, his historical sense, and his philosophical wisdom, all give him an assured place in modern Scandinavian literature and a permanent claim on the regard of Canadians . . . it is quite possible that he will some day be acknowledged as the earliest poet of the first rank, writing in any language, to emerge in the national life of Canada.

What is remarkable about Stephansson is not only his creative output, but his producing it while at the same time raising a family of eight

Stephan G. Stephansson, photographed in 1923 at seventy years of age. (Courtesy Glenbow Archives)

children and struggling with all the difficulties of pioneering in Markerville.[40]

Stephansson worked hard on his farm and participated in community
projects (as chairman of the Hola School Board, secretary-treasurer of the
Creamery Association, and the introducer of grain growing in the Markerville area), but he spent his nights writing and composing poetry by
the light of a coal-oil lamp. The house which he built on a knoll over-
looking the Medicine River and facing the majestic Rockies, was unusual
among prairie farm homes in that one of the main rooms was Stephansson's study where he did his writing. Though without formal education,
Stephansson was an avid reader and he built up a large personal library
of books on Scandinavian literature, language, and history, and of general works in philosophy, history and economics. Although he had very
few English-Canadian friends and no English-speaking contacts with
whom he corresponded, he subscribed to free-thought American religious publications and read contemporary left wing Canadian political
works. Some of his poetry drew its inspiration from Norse sagas, but
much of it arose as a response to the natural landscape of Alberta and to
the community and family life which were so important to him. His six
volumes of collected verse are aptly titled *Andvokur (Sleepless Nights)*
indicating when he found time for his prodigious writing. This self-
trained poet was acclaimed in Iceland and in 1917, the Icelandic government invited him to Iceland to give readings from his work. Stephansson
continued to write until his death in 1927 at the age of 74. Posthu-
mously, he was declared Poet Laureate of Iceland.[41]

The Interwar Years: 1920-1940

The Icelanders experienced all the vicissitudes of Alberta's boom-bust
economy during the 1920s and 1930s. The effects of the economy's
crests and peaks were buffered marginally by the Icelanders' mixed
farming practises, which prevented them from becoming as dependent
as most prairie farmers on one crop—wheat. Their location in the park
belt, which did not experience the severe ravages of drought during the
depression, also made their life relatively easier than it was in many
parts of Alberta, though of course there was no real escape from the
depressed economy of the 1930s.

In the late 1920s and the 1930s, Markerville gradually lost both its
economic viability and its distinctively Icelandic character. As the major
transportation routes bypassed the hamlet and as better roads and the
use of cars and of trucks became almost universal, thus widening mobility, the town's businesses gradually declined. With farm mechanization,
farms had to become bigger to remain economical. The rural population
peaked and in some areas declined. The hamlet of Markerville itself
maintained its population of about fifty, but commerce diminished markedly.

The increased economic and geographic mobility also contributed
to the growing assimilation of Icelanders in central Alberta. As the pioneer generation passed away, Icelandic was spoken by fewer and fewer

people, the activities of the Icelandic organizations dropped off, the annual Icelandic day festivities came to an end (during the 1930s), and intermarriage gradually became the rule rather than the exception. The establishment of the Good Neighbor Club in 1935, a women's organization which drew its members from the whole community, was a strong indication of shifting social patterns in the area—it was established because of the need for a ladies group other than the Icelandic Club, *Vonin*. By the end of the 1930s, the Markerville area was almost indistinguishable from other districts in rural central Alberta.

Increased geographic mobility promoted assimilation, but there were also a number of other causes. By the 1930s, most of the original generation of pioneers had passed away. Unlike many other ethnic groups in the province, during the 1920s the Icelanders did not receive a new wave of immigrants. Assimilation was also facilitated by the esteem in which Icelanders were held in the area. Since the majority of the settlers in the area were Scandinavian and Lutheran, there were few cultural or religious barriers to intermarriage. Given generally weak ties to Lutheranism, marriages outside the faith were seen as neither disastrous nor regrettable and such unions became common. The Canadian born felt some outside pressure to identify themselves as *Canadians*, rather than Icelandic-Canadians, and this encouraged their assimilation. But these assimilative pressures were certainly not felt as strongly by Icelanders as by central and eastern European immigrant groups. Nor did the Icelanders generally experience the personal traumas which led to name changing in order to hide their origins.[42]

Urbanization and the Ethnic Revival

By the 1930s, a new constellation was emerging among Icelanders in Alberta. Calgary and Edmonton were gradually becoming the centers of Icelandic concentration in the province. The 1930s, 1940s, and 1950s saw the continued erosion of the Icelandic presence in the Markerville area.

The initial growth of the Icelandic communities in Edmonton and Calgary was slow. Calgary had been the jumping off point for Markerville in the 1890s, and some Icelanders had remained to work for the Eau Claire Lumber Company. Some of the Icelanders who settled in Calgary also established themselves in trades, such as carpentry, and many worked for the CPR. The Icelanders were basically working class; however, one enterprising Icelander, Sigurdur Sigurdson, who arrived in Canada in 1904, built up the Alberta Furniture Company (started in 1919) into one of the major furniture stores in Calgary.[43]

Icelanders first began moving into Edmonton at the turn of the century. Several became successful in the real estate and construction business. Many Icelanders had established successful construction and real estate firms in Winnipeg during the 1880s and 1890s and it was natural that they would make their living in the same way when they moved to other urban centers in western Canada.

The number of Icelanders in each city grew slowly but steadily; by

1936 there were 167 people of Icelandic descent in Calgary and 148 in Edmonton, together comprising 30 percent of the 1,033 Icelanders in the province. The urban Icelanders were residentially scattered and their only links with Icelandic culture were informal friendships or personal ties with people in the Markerville district.[44]

This trend toward urbanization among the Icelanders accelerated during the war and postwar period. The Icelanders' strong belief in education led many of the second and third generation to seek higher education; numerous graduates then, not only from the Markerville area but from the Icelandic settlements in Manitoba and Saskatchewan, moved to Calgary and Edmonton during the postwar era. Those who came to Calgary included several oil industry engineers, geologists, and physicists, as well as other professionals, whose presence gradually changed Calgary's Icelandic community from a mainly working class group to a relatively wealthy and overwhelmingly professional population.[45]

Although there were some organized Icelandic activities in Edmonton beginning in the 1930s, most organizational activity in Calgary and Edmonton developed during the 1960s and 1970s. The unique characteristic of the Icelandic clubs in Edmonton and Calgary has been the paucity of recent Icelandic immigrants among their memberships, in direct contrast to most ethno-cultural organizations which are usually comprised predominantly of immigrants. Ninety percent of the members in both clubs are second and third generation people of Icelandic background, most of whom came originally from Icelandic settlements in Manitoba and Saskatchewan and most of whom are married to non-Icelanders.

The small numbers of immigrants in the Icelandic clubs of both Calgary and Edmonton is not surprising since between 1946 and 1980, according to immigration department statistics, only sixty-one gave Alberta as their destination. However, despite their small numbers, the new immigrants have injected an element of vitality into the Icelandic organizations. The newcomers are young, educated, middle class urbanites who have come to Canada in search of better economic opportunities than they had in Iceland. They have formed close ties with many of the second and third generation—some of whom are distant relatives—and their awareness of the contemporary culture and society of Iceland has given firsthand authenticity to the maintenance of Icelandic customs and language.[46]

In both Calgary and Edmonton, the Icelandic clubs cooperate to maintain the Scandinavian centers which provide facilities for all Scandinavian groups. Recent impetus for these clubs has come from the heightened ethnic consciousness which emerged in North America in the late 1960s and 1970s.

The Icelandic clubs in Calgary and Edmonton played a key role in reawakening ethnic consciousness in the Markerville area during the 1960s. Contact between these organizations and the hamlet's remaining Icelanders gradually expanded and they revived the Annual Icelandic Picnic, established a Stephan Stephansson Icelandic society and Icelandic language classes, and helped develop Stephansson's home as a provincial historic site.[47]

Conclusion

The two key factors affecting the future of Alberta's Icelandic community are its small size and its lack of recent Icelandic immigrants. In 1971, there were only 2,620 people of Icelandic descent in the province and only 100 of them had been born in Iceland. Even if, given these statistics, one cannot expect high visibility from the group, the future of Icelandic identity in Alberta is not completely bleak. The changed social climate of the 1960s, 1970s, and 1980s has helped make ethnic identity a source of pride, and international travel has facilitated much closer contacts with Iceland. For the Canadian-born generations, travel to Iceland has played an important part in awakening their own sense of ethnic identity. It has made them more aware of their relatives and roots in Iceland and has given them a sense of personal responsibility for the preservation of an age-old culture and language which is maintained by a small and ecologically fragile island.

Despite their small numbers, the Icelanders have been among the most tenacious of Alberta's Scandinavian groups in preserving a sense of ethnic identity. Their overall pattern of adjustment has been similar to Alberta's other Scandinavian groups; it has been characterized by initial migration by way of the United States, relatively small numbers of immigrants during the interwar and post-World War II period, a concentration occupationally in agriculture and geographically in central Alberta, a relative absence of prejudice from the larger community, a strong attachment to education, high rates of intermarriage, and post-World War II rural to urban shifts in the centers of group life. But the Icelanders' attachment to literature, their relative indifference to the church, and their tenacity in preserving their identity over several generations have distinguished them to some degree from the Swedes, Danes, and Norwegians.[48]

It is difficult to predict how long Icelanders will retain a distinct sense of group identity. Already, for some, being of Icelandic descent has ceased to have any significant impact on their lives. For others, it may simply mean retaining the double "s" spelling of their names, remembering a few Icelandic customs at Christmas time, and occasionally enjoying Icelandic dishes.

The Icelanders have played their part in the pioneer development of the province: they helped to demonstrate how mixed farming and dairying could provide a strong economic base for central Alberta, and their descendants contributed to Alberta in a variety of ways. The Icelanders' previous background of self-sufficiency in Iceland, their prior experience with homesteading elsewhere in North America, the relative absence of prejudice towards them, and the similarity of their political and religious background to the prevailing English-Canadian one enabled them to adjust to Albertan society with less difficulty than many other groups. A strong sense of pride in the contribution Icelanders have made to the

Markerville area remains. The more tangible reminders of the past—the Markerville creamery, the Fensala Hall, the Lutheran church, the Hola school, the Stephan Stephansson home, and the Tindastoll Cemetery—all suggest images and echoes of a bygone era, an era of struggle, challenge, cooperation, and creativity that deserves to be remembered.

CHAPTER NINE

Estonians in Alberta
Howard and Tamara Palmer

Introduction

"Estonia" has never been a household word in Alberta; nor have most Albertans been aware of the Estonian presence in the province. Nevertheless, Estonians have been a small but significant part of Alberta's development since before the turn of the century. The relative obscurity of Alberta's Estonian community is partly due to the small size of its ancestral country. Estonia is one of three small Baltic nations—Estonia, Latvia and Lithuania—situated on the eastern shore of the Baltic Sea in northern Europe. Albertans have not been alone in their general ignorance of this tiny country; it has never had a high international profile.

Estonia's size and location have meant that throughout its history it has been dominated by other European powers. From the thirteenth to the early eighteenth centuries, Estonia's development was largely shaped by western European culture. In the early 1700s, Sweden lost Estonia to Russia and it became part of the Russian Empire. Estonians chafed under the political domination of the Russian Czars and the economic domination of German landlords and by the late nineteenth century their irritation, spurred by rising educational levels in Estonia and by burgeoning nationalism in western Europe, had grown into a strong national consciousness.

The effects of these developments in Estonia would ultimately be felt in that part of the Northwest Territories which was destined to become Alberta. In 1899 two Estonian brothers, Hendrik (Henry) and Kristjan Kingsep, and their young families immigrated to Canada and settled in central Alberta, just east of Sylvan Lake. Their arrival was important, both to the overall history of Estonians in Canada, as well as to the development of parts of central and southern Alberta. The settlements that the Kingseps and other Estonians founded at the turn of the century in Alberta were the only significant concentrations of Estonians in Canada until after World War II. In large part, the history of the organized

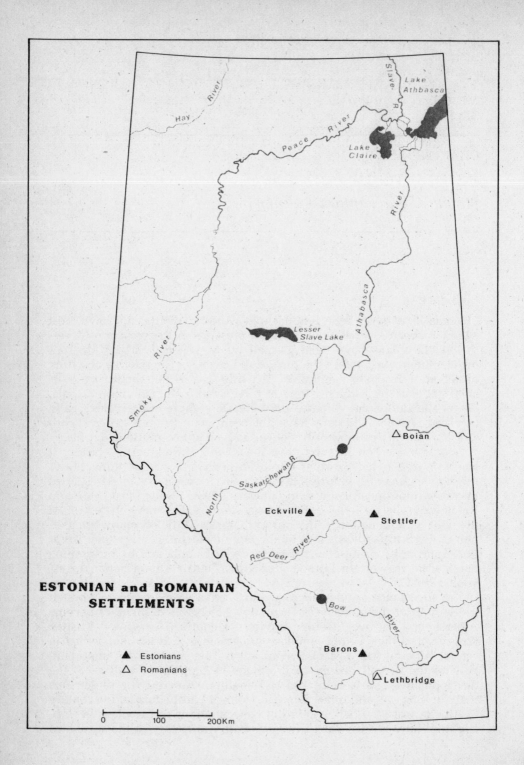

ESTONIAN and ROMANIAN
SETTLEMENTS

▲ Estonians
△ Romanians

Estonian community in Canada prior to World War II is a history of Estonians in Alberta. Though small in numbers, the Estonians were able to make a notable contribution to the development of several communities in Alberta through their agricultural and technological inventiveness, their strong interest in cooperatives, and their emphasis on music and education.

Estonians came to Alberta in three waves of immigration: from the turn of the century until World War I, during the 1920s, and after World War II. The first and third waves were the most substantial, but neither was numerically large. Many in the first wave, and all of those in the third, came for political rather than economic reasons; but the political background of the two groups was quite different. The early refugees were left wing opponents of the czarist regime, while the post-World War II refugees fled Russian communism. The political views, settlement patterns, and occupations of the two largest waves of Estonian immigrants to Alberta were quite different, yet there were common threads which link their history.

The Old World Background

When the Kingsep families decided to emigrate from Estonia, they left behind a country of about one million people which was under the control of the Russian Czarist regime and which faced many economic, political, and social problems. For the rural sector of Estonia's population, economic conditions throughout the nineteenth century had been harsh. Serfdom of the peasants had been abolished prior to 1820, but their working conditions were difficult, their wages were low, and they had to pay high rent to German landlords for use of the land they tilled. One of the few ways to achieve their dream of independence was to emigrate. During the mid-1800s, many did so, moving to southern Russia where people were needed to colonize the vast, empty lands of the Crimea. But by the late 1800s, those who had emigrated to the Crimea were equally dissatisfied with conditions there; consequently, like many of those who had remained in Estonia, they were eager for new opportunities. Nor were conditions favorable for Estonia's aspiring urbanized middle class. Increasing numbers of young Estonians were graduating from universities in the late 1800s with aspirations of social and economic advancement, but their mobility was often blocked by the powerful presence of the Baltic Germans, who owned the land, the factories, most of the businesses, and also dominated the professions.

In addition to general economic hardship, by the late 1800s, Estonians were also faced with the Czarist policy of Russification—a heightened attempt by the Russian regime to assimilate them. These policies were very unpopular in a region which was in the throes of a national awakening. Dissatisfied with their situation, a number of Estonians, like the Kingsep families, decided to emigrate and some were attracted to the free homestead lands of western Canada.

Around the turn of the century, opposition to the Russian Czarist government took the form of both Estonian nationalism and socialism.

Social and economic tensions made the country receptive to revolutionary ideology and Marxism spread among the intelligentsia, the landless peasants, and the workers. The year 1905 was particularly explosive, with the Japanese defeat of Russia and the Russian revolution spurring a revolt in Estonia against the Czarist regime and the German landlords. Suppression of this revolt and subsequent Czarist persecutions led to the exit of a wave of political refugees, many of whom made their way to North America, including Alberta. The combination of political and economic factors motivating their emigration meant that there was a wide cross section of occupations among the migrants. They included sailors, industrial workers, tradesmen, several teachers, and a few peasants. But despite their varied backgrounds, they all settled on the land when they arrived in Alberta.[1]

The Pioneering Years

Henry Kingsep was born in the district of Vōru, Estonia in 1870 to a farm family of comfortable means. As a young man, he graduated from the University of Tartu and went on for postgraduate studies at the University of St. Petersburg in Russia, where he became fluent in several languages and trained to become a teacher. He also became involved with a group of radical students who were plotting to overthrow the Czar. Later when he was twenty-four and teaching school, he married Emilie Saar, daughter of the village shoemaker. But Henry was dissatisfied with conditions in Estonia and he also feared reprisals for his political activities. He had read and heard about freedom and vast lands in North America and his brother, Christian, had visited Montreal as a sailor. Henry became convinced that the best future for himself and his young family lay in Canada and he began to learn English and make other preparations for the long voyage to North America.[2]

In 1899 the Christian and Henry Kingsep families set sail for New York and continued their journey to Canada by train. The two brothers decided to settle in the Sylvan Lake area and took up adjoining land in the virgin bush and forest. Two factors were probably involved in their choosing this particular land. Like other Nordic people coming from wooded countries with access to water, the Kingseps were sensitive to the need for land which could provide both ample timber and water. There were also a few Finnish settlers in the area, and the Kingseps may have been aware of this. Though they were not Finns, the Estonian and Finnish peoples are closely related both linguistically and culturally.[3]

When Henry and Emilie Kingsep finally arrived at their remote destination, they were faced with the formidable task of making a living for themselves in a virtual wilderness. The only clearings in the densely wooded landscape were those that had been made by forest fires. Roads were nonexistent.

The Kingsep families were not to remain alone for very long. They were soon joined by other Estonians, many of them friends and acquaintances from the old country, and by 1903 they and the other settlers had partially cleared sixteen farms and had named the area

Mr. and Mrs. Henry Kingsep and children, ca. 1899, just before their departure for Canada. The Kingseps were one of the first Estonian families in Alberta and played a leading role in the Medicine Valley Estonian community. (Courtesy Nick Kingsep)

"Livonia" in remembrance of their homeland. Even the topography reminded them of their homeland.

Clearing the land was an enormous task: raising crops in the area's cool, wet climate was beset with difficulty, and the isolation and loneliness were at times overpowering. In these difficult pioneering circumstances, it soon became clear that cooperation was essential to survival. This inescapable fact, combined with the left wing sympathies of many of the early Estonian settlers, prompted them to attempt cooperative farming. In the plan which they formulated, households and gardens were individually owned, but the land was used collectively. Besides growing vegetable gardens, the settlers raised flax and wheat and established dairy herds. Because of the uncertainties of the early years, hunting and fishing were essential to the group's survival.[4]

Gradually the little settlement near Sylvan Lake assumed an appearance of permanency. By 1903, it boasted twenty-two Estonian families, a new school and an English-speaking teacher. However, "Livonia" was not to remain the major Estonian settlement in Alberta. The area was quickly being settled by people of various nationalities. It was soon obvious that "Livonia" could not expand to accommodate further Estonian settlement. Consequently, Henry Kingsep began looking elsewhere for land that would be suitable for additional Estonian settlers. He chose land in the Medicine River Valley, near what was to become the town of Eckville, and in 1903 he and his family moved to this new site. The Kingseps were soon joined by other Estonian families from the Sylvan Lake area. Still others from the original "Livonia" settlement moved east to Stettler, founding what was to become another sizeable Estonian settlement.[5]

Medicine Valley, with its deep black soil and treed hilly landscape, also reminded them of their homeland and appealed to the Estonians. The first settlers in the Medicine River area were joined in 1904 by 25 people directly from Estonia, and between 1905 and 1914, 40 more came to the area to make their homes. Several families immigrated to Canada with their brothers' or sisters' families; when they arrived in Alberta, they settled together, developing large extended family networks. Many of the new immigrants, like Kingsep, were politically radical, and disillusioned with the Czarist regime. By 1920, there were 187 people of Estonian origin living in the Eckville area and approximately forty farms had been established.[6]

The pioneering years near Eckville were difficult. The Estonians first dwellings were log cabins with sod roofs and clay floors, which were characteristic of their homeland. At first only cattle, chickens, and vegetable gardens were raised and dairying was the main source of farm income. Wheat varieties had not yet been developed to withstand the area's cool, wet summers and limited number of frost-free days. Gradually, however, they began to grow barley, oats, and rye. Prior to World War I, the amount of cleared and cultivated land remained small because of the type of mixed agriculture which the Estonians practised and the area's lack of transportation facilities. Writing about the early years, Erna

Doig, one of the daughters of Adam and Anna Matteus, emphasized her parents' self-sufficiency:

> On part of the homestead there were spruce and tamaracks and they cut down enough of the bigger timbers to build themselves a one-room cabin before winter set in again. The cabin had a sod roof and earthen floor and the logs were caulked with moss and clay. A stove was made of rocks, which were plastered with clay. This was used for cooking, heating and baking. A heavy table and a few benches were shaped from logs. Also the beds were shaped from logs and the pieces were held together with wooden dowels. The mattress bags were filled and stuffed plump with dried, fresh hay. To Adam and Anna this was luxury—a home of their own![7]

Gradually, the isolation and pioneer conditions of the settlement were overcome and it became increasingly integrated into the economic life of central Alberta. After a long delay, two competing railways were constructed through the area and between 1910 and 1914 this provided temporary work and facilitated commercial development. For the first time, pig and cattle raising became commercially viable. The small hamlet of Gilby and the nearby town of Eckville developed sufficiently to become merchandising centers for the Estonians. By 1911 there was sufficient grain growing for John Kinna to build the area's first water-driven flour mill. However, grain growing did not become a major economic enterprise until World War I generated record grain prices.[8]

With the most difficult stage of pioneering behind them, the Estonian settlers turned their attention to the establishment of organizations to meet their social, economic, and educational needs. Central to all of these endeavors was the cooperative ethic which they had brought with them to Canada. Realizing the need for their children to learn English and to obtain an education, the Estonians, joined by a few Finnish and Scandinavian settlers in the area, united in 1909 to establish Estonian School District #1760. The school board was made up mostly of Estonians who were strongly committed to education.[9]

The second major community project was the Estonian society, which they established in April 1910.[10] The Medicine Valley Estonian Society was to play a key role in the community's social and cultural life for decades. The minutes of the first meeting, chaired by Henry Kingsep, report that the pioneers debated the question of whether the objectives of the association were primarily social or economic. They concluded that both objectives were essential. The group eventually built its own hall in 1918.[11]

The groups' social activities included dramatic productions, a mixed choir and a string ensemble which performed at concerts and dances. Choirs and singing festivals were an important aspect of life in Estonia and the settlers in Alberta continued this musical tradition. Kingsep had experience in Estonia as a choir master, so it was he who organized and directed the choir.[12]

Adult education and political concerns were also important to the group. The society maintained a library of books on politics, economics, history, and literature. Using their own group as a source of talent and information, the community also heard lectures on education, literature, farming, and politics. As with other aspects of community life, Kingsep, being widely read and fluent in five languages (German, Russian, Estonian, Finnish, and English), was very much involved; he gave lectures on subjects as varied as education, the cooperative movement, the plight of native Indians in Canada, and "The Harmful Effects of Alcohol and Tobacco." Many other settlers were also actively involved. In the winter of 1910-1911, the following talks were given: Henry Kingsep—Farm Organizations and Farm Management; Henry Kinna—Alberta Politics; Peter Kost—Socialism; August Posti—Estonian Literature; Sam Kinna— The Russian Parliament, and K. Onton—Scientific Discoveries. The subjects reflected both their Old and New World interests. By 1912, speakers were being warned to keep their speeches to one-half hour, since meetings which included programs and entertainment were lasting until 3:00 a.m. Talks in the winter of 1912-1913 included "Blacks and Socialist organizations in the U.S.," "German Landlords in Estonia," and "St. Augustine." After the outbreak of World War I in 1914, several members of the organization gave talks denouncing the war as resulting from the ruling class' desire for profits. Not all of the Estonian settlers in the community were left wing politically, but the main community leaders were, and the activities of the Estonian society had a definite left wing orientation.[13]

The settlers kept in touch with the Estonians elsewhere in North America and with political events in their homeland through the New York-based left wing weekly newspaper *Uus Ilm (New World)*. Kingsep was a frequent contributor to the paper, commenting on political issues and reporting Estonian activities in Alberta. During the war years, *Uus Ilm* was forbidden by the Canadian authorities because of its radical point of view, and settlers caught with it by the NWMP were arrested and fined.[14]

For Alberta's Estonian community, cooperation was an economic as well as a cultural matter and the society developed several projects on a cooperative basis. Their cooperative efforts included the Eckville and Gilby cooperative company, a mutual fire insurance company, a cattle sale cooperative and a savings and loan cooperative bank.[15] They also strongly supported the UFA and the wheat pool movement. In the 1921 federal election when the UFA first entered the political arena, the UFA candidate received 102 of the 107 votes cast at Gilby, in the heart of the Estonian district. Cooperatives have played an important role in Estonia throughout the twentieth century, and they were also important among Estonian immigrants in Canada.[16]

In the early years of the Estonian society, the educational, political, and cooperative aspects of the organization were dominated by men; women were limited to the role of food suppliers and providers of entertainment, but there are also early indications of the women becoming more vocal. As early as 1912, the group discussed women's rights and the impact of socialism on marriage.[17]

In addition to their noteworthy penchant for cooperative endeavor, the

Estonians who settled in Medicine Valley, like the Estonians who settled in other parts of the province, were also innovative and self-reliant. They did not allow a lack of technology to hinder their progress; when they faced a technical problem, they simply built their own machines. Henry Kingsep attached his horse and oxen to a power shaft to create the power for sawing lumber and milling grain; he also built his own threshing machine and designed the community's first horse-drawn brush cutter. With equal ingenuity, Martin Sestrap organized twenty families into a barbed wire telephone system. Thus, with its gardens and livestock, its wealth of practical skills, and its inventiveness, the Medicine Valley community was remarkably self-sufficient.[18]

The women in the settlement were equally self-reliant and adaptable; they worked closely with their husbands in the pioneering venture. During harvest season when the men were busy in the fields, the women would hitch up the family buggy and go to town to transact business. They used spinning wheels to spin wool for homemade woolen clothing and bedding, they made pillows and quilts from goose feathers, and they devoted many hours to preparing and preserving food for their large families. During the early years, the women also assumed reponsibility for handling medical problems. At childbirth, they depended on those among them who were experienced midwives, such as Emilie Kingsep.[19]

One notable aspect of the Eckville settlement was the absence of an Estonian church and minister. Though other Estonian settlements in Alberta were smaller, they received regular visits from an Estonian Lutheran minister. At Eckville, however, the radical political backgrounds of many of the settlers made them reluctant to establish a church. In June 1916, the Estonian society held a debate over whether or not the ruling classes used organized religion as a means of enslaving the masses. One account of an early visit by the Lutheran minister, John Sillak, to the settlement tells of the minister arriving on a Saturday night to a gathering of the Estonian society, and being angered that the settlers would dance the night before they were supposed to take Communion. When his scolding only served to irritate the dancers, "who danced even more wildly," he collected his things, denounced the dancers, and departed. Despite their economic problems and growing discontent with Canada's political system, for most of the settlers strong family ties, self-sufficiency, community cooperation, and a variety of cultural activities provided a rich and purposeful life.[20]

The Linda Hall Settlement

The second major settlement in Alberta was located just south of Stettler and was composed primarily of people who had previously left Estonia for the Tver region in the Russian Empire. But the Estonian settlers had found the economic conditions difficult and the climate particularly harsh in this region of Russia, so when they learned about free homesteads and political freedom in Canada, they decided to emigrate. In 1901, three men—John Neithal, John Oro, and Mike Rahu—left for Canada, where they joined Estonian settlers at Sylvan Lake. Their numbers were soon bolstered by other Estonian immigrants from the Tver region and they began looking elsewhere for a place to settle. In 1903, some of the men located land ten miles south of what would later become the town of Stettler. Shortly thereafter, they were reinforced by other families from Sylvan Lake and two years later by refugees from the 1905 Russian revolution. By late 1905, there were sixty Estonian households in the area, divided into two groups, the largest being located just south of Stettler in an area which they named "Linda," the other at "Kalev" which was further south near Big Valley. Both areas were named after legendary Estonian figures.[21]

The early settlement, like the one at Eckville was isolated. The town of Stettler did not come into being until 1905 with the arrival of the CPR; consequently, in the early years, settlers had to carry supplies on their backs from Red Deer, eighty miles distant. The men worked outside the community on railway construction, in logging camps, and in coal mines to obtain cash; and they worked cooperatively in establishing their farms.[22]

Like their countrymen at Eckville, the Stettler area Estonians were strong supporters of the UFA and the wheat pool movement. But for the Estonians in Stettler, religion was more important. Most of the early settlers were devout Lutherans and in 1906, they built a small, simple chapel. They had no resident minister, but a travelling Estonian pastor, John Sillak, presided over their religious services (which were held in

Rev. John Sillak, Estonian Lutheran minister. Though unpopular with some of the Estonians, Sillak was an important visitor for scattered Estonian Lutherans in Alberta, as well as other Baltic immigrants in both western Canada and the western United States. (Courtesy Joe Tipman)

An early Estonian gathering in the Linda Hall district, near Stettler. The Estonian settlers' social activities included picnics, dances, Estonian plays, and concerts. The Estonians in this area, as elsewhere in the province, placed a strong emphasis on music, education, and cooperative activities. (Courtesy Joe Tipman)

Estonian). Pastor Sillak, who had a Ph.D. in philosophy and spoke several languages, travelled over an enormous area, serving scattered Estonians and other Baltic immigrants from California to Manitoba.[23]

Cultural and social activities were also important to the Stettler area Estonians. In 1910 they organized an agricultural club and the following year they built Linda Hall in the center of the settlement. They used the hall for social and farm meetings, dances, Estonian plays, concerts, weddings, and various other community gatherings. They also established their own brass band and developed a large library. Initially, activities were limited to Estonians, but as the first generation acquired greater fluency in English, members of the surrounding community began to participate in their Saturday night socials. During special celebrations, such as the annual St. John the Baptist Day festivities, which were held in the spring, the Stettler community was joined by Estonians from Eckville.

The Estonian pioneers were anxious to have their children learn the Estonian language and keep up their traditions, but use of Estonian was forbidden by teachers in the public schools which they attended. The second generation, anxious to overcome the stigma of being considered "foreigners," learned English quickly and used Estonian only with their parents.[24]

Unlike the Eckville settlement, the Stettler area community did not experience continued growth. As early as 1913, fifteen families left for the United States and Australia, hoping to find better economic conditions. Until World War II, the Linda Hall area retained its Estonian-Canadian identity, since many second and third generation descendants of the original pioneers remained; but with their increased assimilation Linda Hall gradually came to be used as a community center by people of many different backgrounds.[25]

Additional Settlements

The third largest Estonian settlement in Alberta was located at Barons, in the heart of the province's southern wheat growing plains. The Estonian settlers who came to Barons had first settled in the Crimea, where they were engaged in mixed farming before migrating to South Dakota at the turn of the century and from there to Canada. Lisa Silverman, one of the daughters of Jacob Erdman, a Barons' pioneer, later described their coming to Alberta:

> It was 1901 in May, when we landed in New York. From there, by railroad, we went to Fort Pierre, South Dakota. We were met there by our old friends ... In this group of ours were Jacob Erdman and family of eight persons; Anton Kulpas and a family of four persons; Peter Lentsman and wife; Mrs. Reinstein (a widow) and two daughters.
>
> We stayed in South Dakota one and one-half years. Then we decided to look for a better place to live. Four of the men went to look for better homesteads. They were: J. Erdman, G. Erdman, A. Kulpas and P. Lentsman. None of these men could speak any English, so they asked Mr. John Kewe to accompany them as an interpreter. They went by train to Oregon, but the land there was already settled. There they met a Finlander who knew that in

The Jacob Erdman family, one of the first Estonian families to settle in Barons, in Crimea before emigration, ca. 1894. The Erdman family played an important role in the development of the Barons area. (Courtesy Ellen Johnson)

Alberta, Canada there was still good land available for homesteads, so they travelled to Claresholm, where they were met by eager land agents who drove them out eastward.[26]

By 1908 twenty-six Estonian families, most of them from the Crimea, had settled in Barons. They were soon able to become large-scale farmers, specializing in grain growing and cattle raising. The Estonians at Barons formed a tightly knit community, with many of them connected by family ties. They organized church services to keep alive their Lutheran heritage, and they were noted for their musical abilities, their support of the cooperative movement, their emphasis on education, and their technological inventiveness.[27]

There were two other Estonian settlements in southern Alberta, but due to unfavorable climatic conditions, they were short-lived. Like those who settled near Barons, the seven (mostly related) Estonian families who homesteaded in the Foremost area southeast of Lethbridge beginning in 1906, had originally come from the Crimea and had lived temporarily in South Dakota. But these families, including the Meers, Lindermans, Krasmans, and Mursas, were not as fortunate as the Barons settlers had been in their choice of land; the area they chose was dry and rocky and a homestead and preemption were much too small to support a farm in an arid area. During the 1920s there was a general exodus from the area. Twelve Estonian families settled at Walsh, east of Medicine Hat, between 1904 and 1906, but that area was also too arid and the settlement was soon abandoned.[28]

A Second Wave of Immigrants

The first of the three waves of Estonian immigration to Alberta was the largest and had the greatest impact on the province: by 1916, there were approximately 500 Estonians in Alberta, living in several small, scattered rural settlements. During the interwar years, a second and smaller wave of Estonian immigration arrived from a newly independent Estonia and was, for the most part, absorbed into the existing settlements. This wave was smaller than the first since the establishment of an independent Estonian nation in the aftermath of World War I and the success of the communist revolution in Russia had fulfilled both the nationalistic and the political aspirations of Estonians who might otherwise have considered emigration. Most of the newcomers were young, single males, and their primary motivation was economic.[29]

For those Estonians who did emigrate to Canada in an effort to escape the economic uncertainty of the new Estonian republic, Canada's eastern urban centers were more attractive than the prairie settlements. Of the approximately 650 Estonians who came to Canada during the 1920s, less than 100 made their way to Alberta, where they began work as farm laborers or domestics.[30]

Forty-six immigrants came to the Eckville area during the 1920s and 1930s. Some of those who came at this time married children of the pioneers. Those who were not able to earn enough to establish their own farms, but remained in Alberta, fell into a pattern of working as farm laborers during the summer and fall, then leaving for the cities, where, during the winters of the depression years, they subsisted on relief. The newcomers had arrived just before the outbreak of the Great Depression, and it was extremely difficult to purchase and establish farms of their own during the depression years. A few of the newcomers were able to establish their own farms with help from newly acquired wives and fathers-in-law and endless work. Most, however, left for other parts of Canada; by the early 1940s, twenty-nine of the forty-six who had arrived in the Eckville area in the interwar years had left.[31]

Radical political activity among Estonians in the Eckville area began to decline by the late 1920s. Among the reasons were the improving economic conditions of late 1920s (many of the pioneers could now afford to hire farm laborers), the growing impact of the new immigrants (most of whom were "white" or anticommunist), and the passing of some of the early community leaders (Henry Kingsep for example died in 1929).

Radicalism also declined in the wake of disillusionment over the failure of the communal experiment of seven families who returned to Russia from Eckville in the early 1920s. Fired by the utopian ideals of Russian communism and disillusioned by economic and political conditions in Canada, the group returned to Russia in 1923 to establish a commune, taking farm equipment with them. However, within two years, all but two of the families were back in Eckville, impoverished and somewhat disillusioned. With the decline of radicalism, the Estonian society gradually lost its political orientation and became primarily a cultural organization.[32]

The Second Generation Comes of Age

The major demographic and social change among Estonians in Alberta during the 1920s and 1930s resulted not from the arrival of new immigrants, but from the dispersal, urbanization, and assimilation of the second generation. Estonian activities continued to flourish in the main rural settlements; indeed, the Estonian Young People's Society at Eckville reached its peak of activity during the Great Depression, when many young people had ample free time because of restricted economic opportunities. But those who left the settlements to further their education or pursue economic interests usually intermarried and lost touch with Estonian activities. Many of Eckville's young Estonian-Canadians left their parents' farms and moved to other parts of central or southern Alberta where they opened small businesses, such as general stores, construction companies, or repair shops. Others became electricians, machinists, welders, or tradesmen.[33]

By the time of World War II, the organized Estonian community in Alberta was in decline. Many of the pioneer generation had passed away during the 1930s and 1940s. The Estonians' small numbers and scattered settlements, their emphasis on education and minimal prejudice against them led to assimilation. This process was given added impetus during World War II when many young men from the Estonian settlements joined the armed forces. However, the arrival after the war of a new wave of Estonian immigrants injected new vigor into Estonian activities in southern and central Alberta and led to the first significant concentrations of Estonians in Edmonton and Calgary.

Postwar Immigration

As a small country, with a population of just over one million in 1939, Estonia was caught between Germany and the Soviet Union during World War II and experienced harsh occupations by both powers. In June 1940, the Soviet Union occupied Estonia and incorporated it as a republic of the Soviet Union. During the brutal Soviet rule from 1940-41, 19,000 Estonians, including most of the national leadership, were forcibly resettled to the Soviet Union or executed for political reasons.[34]

In August 1941, the German army invaded Estonia and began a harsh three-year occupation. Although some Estonians fled to Finland to avoid compulsory German military service, the major exodus of people from Estonia escaped in the autumn of 1944 as the Soviet Army approached Estonia from the east and the German army retreated westward. Nearly 72,000 refugees (or 9 percent of the total population) left, many escaping to Sweden in small boats; but the majority crossed Latvia and Lithuania to Germany under very arduous conditions.[35]

The refugees then began their long wait in Sweden or in the refugee camps of Germany, hoping to obtain immigration visas to other countries. In 1947, the United Kingdom began accepting Estonian refugees, many of whom ultimately moved to Canada. However, the Canadian government did not take an active interest in the plight of the Estonians until the fall of 1948. In the meantime, as early as 1945, the Soviet government began pressing the western powers to extradite Estonian army officers, some of whom had been drafted into the German army as Soviet citizens, during the wartime occupation of Estonia by Germany. Well aware of the fate which awaited them at the hands of the Soviets, they desperately tried to emigrate elsewhere. When it appeared that the Swedish government, under pressure from the Soviet Union, might extradite Estonians and other Baltic refugees (and with Canadian officials incapable of helping since they were enmeshed in their own red tape), some of the Estonians had little choice but to set out for North America in small 30' to 40' vessels. Thirty-five boats made this voyage between 1945 and 1951; nine of the boats and 987 Estonian refugees arrived in Canada. The Canadian government's response to the arrival of Canada's first "boat people" was basically generous. All normal immigration procedures were waived, and all but 12 of the immigrants were allowed to remain in Canada. Eventually the Canadian government unravelled the red tape, and a total of 5,000 Estonians came to Canada from Sweden.[36]

However, it was not easy for Estonians to come to Canada immediately after the war. During this period, the Canadian government preferred single, unskilled immigrants who would be suitable for manual labor and farm jobs which were difficult to fill with Canadian workers. Under these circumstances, one of the few ways for Estonians to emigrate as families was to come under the sponsorship of Canadian citizens. In response to this need, members of Alberta's existing Estonian community sponsored a number of families; consequently, many of the Estonians who came to Alberta at this time worked first on farms at Eckville, Barons, or Stettler. Others found sponsors on sugar beet farms in the Lethbridge area. Because of their hasty flight from Estonia, some arrived with little more than the clothes they were wearing.

Thus, fleeing the political upheaval precipitated by World War II, 13,521 Estonians immigrated to Canada between 1946 and 1955. Although the majority settled in Ontario, approximately 400 came to Alberta, helping to push the number of people of Estonian origin in the province from 819 in 1951 to 1,115 in 1961.[37]

The social and professional composition of the Estonian refugees was diversified, but most were from middle class backgrounds and many were professionals. Among those who came to Alberta were engineers, architects, veterinarians, medical doctors, dentists, clerks, tradesmen, army officers, lawyers, and teachers, some of whom had been prominent personalities in Estonia. Although most were originally placed as farmhands, few had any direct farming experience. As with other postwar refugees, most abandoned Alberta farms after their one-year contracts and looked for more suitable employment in the cities. For example, only two of the thirteen Estonian families who came to the Eckville area after the war remained in the area. In Calgary and Edmonton, they found jobs relatively easily, but mostly as blue collar workers. Later some tried to reestablish themselves in their professions.[38]

Both men and women worked after they arrived in Alberta. Women had trained in Estonia for careers; several Estonian women were professionals in veterinary medicine, accounting, medicine, dentistry, or in academic fields. The exceptions were able to contribute to Alberta society in these capacities, but most followed the pattern of Estonian men and took any work at first including jobs as seamstresses, cleaners, kitchen helpers, or hospital workers. This disruption of their careers and expectations was inevitably painful for both men and women. For some, because their Canadian work experiences did not provide sufficient challenges or status, there was a strong stimulus to maintain an intellectual life at home and within Estonian socio-cultural circles.[39]

Society, Culture, and the Postwar Immigrants

Soon after their arrival in Alberta, Estonians organized social, cultural, and political activities. Estonia's turbulent history bred an intense nationalism. These sentiments were heightened for many of the postwar immigrants, who had been deeply committed to their country's independence and then had been forced to flee by wartime events. Consequently, some have maintained a "refugee mentality," marked by a persistent desire to hope and fight for an independent, noncommunist Estonia to which they can someday return.

Estonians in both Calgary and Edmonton began organizations in 1949 and both groups were affiliated with national organizations. The focus of organizational activity in the urban centers was the celebration of Estonian Independence Day, but the groups also initiated displays of ethnic arts and crafts, and held concerts featuring the performance of national dances and songs. Each summer during the 1950s, Estonians from across the province gathered in Eckville for a traditional midsummer festival which included bonfires, dancing, and singing. In Edmonton the society organized recreational and sports trips, which the refugees welcomed as opportunities to escape from their crowded apartments. Several times a year, the organizations also invited travelling Lutheran ministers from eastern centers to provide religious services. The newcomers gave strong financial support to the Toronto-based Estonian National Committee and the Estonian Relief Committee. The community activities provided a place where Estonians could meet and discuss their common problems.[40]

Organized Estonian activities began to decline during the 1960s as a result of the loss and aging of members, and the assimilation of the Canadian born. Many Estonians moved from Alberta to other Canadian centers, particularly Toronto, where over half of Canada's approximately 19,000 people of Estonian origin now reside and which boasts a very active Estonian-Canadian cultural and political life. Between 1961 and 1971, the number of people of Estonian background in Alberta decreased to 845. The last large-scale event involving Estonians was the Baltic Festival held in Edmonton in October of 1967 to celebrate Canada's Centennial Year.[41]

The postwar displaced persons and the second generation Estonian-Canadians from the rural communities had little in common, and the latter generally did not participate in the activities of the newly founded urban Estonian societies. However, the Medicine Valley Estonian Society provided a point of contact for the different waves of immigrants. Differences in perspective between the Canadian born and the newcomers created misunderstandings. The new arrivals suspected the existing Estonian community of having communist sympathies, while the Canadian born, who were committed to complete integration into Canadian society could not understand and at times resented the intense nationalism of the newly arrived political refugees.[42]

For a variety of reasons, Alberta's Estonians have now largely disappeared as a distinct part of the provincial mosaic. The second and third generation offspring of both the pioneer generation and the postwar refugees are now almost completely integrated into Alberta's society. Estonian clubs in Edmonton and Calgary each have less than one hundred members and activities have declined to only a few meetings during the year (the major one being the 28 February celebration of the Independence of the Estonian Republic). After years of declining activity, the Medicine Valley Estonian society disbanded in 1979.

Among all of the postwar refugees from eastern Europe, the Estonians have integrated most quickly into Alberta's society. This is partly due to the group's small size, its unique language, and its multilingual heritage. In addition, Estonians' relatively high educational level facilitated their economic and social integration at a time when many of their most active community leaders were leaving for other Canadian centers, thus weakening the group's organizational capacity.

Conclusion

The Estonian experience in Alberta has had much in common with that of many other small immigrant groups, but it has also been distinctive in a number of ways. There were numerous parallels between the Estonian pioneers and their Scandinavian and Finnish counterparts. Like the Finns who were their neighbors at Eckville and Barons, the Estonians had nearly all grown up in the Lutheran faith. Also like the Finns, a sizeable number of Estonians were attracted to the ideals of socialism or communism.

The Eckville area's Estonian and Finnish peoples were linked not only by a similar linguistic and cultural background, a similar farming experience, and a similar division of political opinion within each community, but also by their commercial associations through the coop. Like Scandinavians throughout central Alberta, Estonians were not illiterate or semiliterate peasants; most had been educated in Estonia (some were university graduates) and they placed a strong emphasis on education. Estonians and Scandinavians both assimilated rapidly.

There have also been points of similarity between Estonians and immigrants from central and eastern Europe; however, most of these similarities are to be found in the experiences of post-World War II immigrants. The Estonians who came to Alberta in the aftermath of the war often shared the problems and the mentality of other refugees from central and eastern Europe, such as Latvians, Lithuanians, Poles, and Ukrainians. This new wave of Estonian immigrants had less in common with postwar Scandinavian immigrants than with those from central and eastern Europe, with whom they shared the experience of being "displaced persons"—the trauma of sudden uprooting, and the uncertainty of refugee camps or temporary residence in various European countries. When they arrived in Canada, refugees shared the common problem of status dislocation caused by their being forced to accept menial labor jobs. That their homeland is still under Soviet rule has prompted Estonian immigrants to assume the anticommunist, anti-Soviet stance characteristic of most central and eastern European immigrants and has fueled the ever present hope that someday, somehow their homeland will be liberated.

Despite these similarities with other immigrant groups, there are several themes which emerge repeatedly throughout the history of Estonians in Alberta which seem to be an expression of Estonian cultural traditions. The themes of technological inventiveness, emphasis on cooperation, belief in education, and love of music, emerge repeatedly through the history of Estonians in Alberta.

While the Estonian presence and identity in Alberta is not readily apparent, it has not completely disappeared. Numbers and organizational activity may be limited, but there are still many Estonian immigrants and people of Estonian origin whose frames of reference and world views include an awareness of developments in Estonia and of the presence and concerns of Estonians around the world. Even among the Canadian born who are completely removed from organized Estonian-Canadian life, there is often an awareness of and interest in their cultural roots which finds visible expression in their homes in artifacts, handicrafts, and cuisine. This interest is often both symbolized and strengthened by visits to Estonia, which inevitably heighten awareness of Estonian history and culture.

Like other groups from small countries of which Canadians have been only barely aware, Estonians have faced an uphill and largely unnoticed struggle for recognition. As with many other immigrant groups who helped to settle rural Alberta, their contribution is not highly visible; besides the Estonian family names, the only tangible signs of their presence are roadside and community plaques and rural cemeteries near the sites of early settlements. In one such roadside cemetery near Linda Hall, beneath rows of wrought-iron crosses lie sixty-nine Estonian settlers who were members of the Estonian Evangelical Lutheran congregation, providing mute testimony to the early Estonian presence in the area. But the struggles and contributions of the pioneer Estonians are alive in the memories of their children and grandchildren and should become part of the awareness of all Albertans seeking to understand the many strands which have come together to make today's Alberta.

CHAPTER TEN
The Ukrainians in Alberta[1]
Frances Swyripa

Some 100 kilometers east of Edmonton a gigantic metal Easter egg proclaims the Ukrainian influence in the town of Vegreville, home of the annual Ukrainian "Pysanka" Festival. Further west the Ukrainian Cultural Heritage Village portrays the history of the people who settled the area at the turn of the century. In Edmonton itself one can buy a local specialty, "kovbasa on a stick," or attend Ukrainian dance and choral performances in the Jubilee Auditoriun. Now the third largest ethnic group in Alberta, the Ukrainians have not always enjoyed such recognition.

Immigration

The present Ukrainian Canadian population is the result of three distinct immigrations. The first, the largest and most significant, formed the backbone of the Ukrainian group in Canada and included the ancestors of most Alberta Ukrainians. The two smaller and subsequent waves had less impact.

The first immigration (1891-1914) was primarily a movement of peasants from the provinces of Galicia and Bukovyna in the Austro-Hungarian Empire. During this period few Ukrainians immigrated to Canada from the Russian Empire, which claimed approximately four-fifths of ethnic Ukrainian territory. Over 75 percent of the immigrants came from eastern Galicia, dominated politically and economically by the Poles; fewer came from Bukovyna, where local power and influence lay in Romanian hands. Galician Ukrainians were Greek Catholic, members of a hybrid church combining the Eastern rite with Roman Catholic doctrine that had been imposed on Ukrainians in the Polish-Lithuanian Commonwealth in 1596. Bukovynians, untouched by this church union, had remained Orthodox. While some Ukrainians emigrated for political reasons or to escape compulsory military service, the majority were fleeing poverty. Shrinking landholdings, rural overpopulation, malnutrition, primitive farming methods, widespread illiteracy, and increasing indebtedness with loss of their plots, were the peasants' unenviable lot. For many, working for the local manor or temporary migration to Prussia or the coal mines of Pennsylvania to supplement their income gave way to permanent emigration abroad.

Interest in Canada was aroused by two Galician peasants, Ivan Pylypiw and Vasyl Eleniak, who visited the country in 1891. The colony established east of Edmonton as a result of their activity became the nucleus of Ukrainian settlement in Canada. In 1895 the way was paved for large-scale immigration when Dr. Josef Oleskiw, an agricultural expert in Galicia, toured the Dominion, meeting with government officials, and subsequently publicized western Canada in two popular booklets distributed throughout Galicia.[2] Oleskiw's proposal for the controlled immigration of peasants with means was ignored, however, and the movement remained unregulated as it assumed mass proportions. Canada itself was in the throes of nation building and needed manual labor, particularly to open up the West; Ukrainian peasants gladly exchanged their tiny plots for 160 acres, "free" for a $10 registration fee. In spite of Minister of Interior Clifford Sifton's enthusiastic endorsement of the "men in sheepskin coats" however, Ukrainian immigrants were greeted with mixed emotions by the dominant Anglo-Celtic society in Canada.

Approximately 170,000 Ukrainians immigrated to Canada before World War I. Most settled in the three prairie provinces, and by 1921 Manitoba could boast the largest Ukrainian community in Canada, followed by Saskatchewan and Alberta.[3]

With the collapse of the Austro-Hungarian and Russian empires during World War I, the peoples of eastern Europe asserted often conflicting claims to statehood. Ukraine also declared its independence, but proved unable to withstand the designs of its neighbors. In 1921 with the Treaty of Riga, the new Polish and Soviet states divided the bulk of the fledgling Ukrainian People's Republic between them; Czechoslovakia and Romania received Carpatho-Ukraine and Bukovyna respectively. As stability returned to eastern Europe, emigration resumed. The old provinces of Galicia, now in Poland, and Bukovyna supplied the majority of immigrants in the second immigration as they had in the first, although other non-Soviet areas also contributed. Poland's oppression of its Ukrainian citizens was one factor behind emigration, but economic conditions remained the primary motive; interwar Poland faced massive rebuilding and was unable, in spite of manpower losses, to satisfy the demand for land.

The new immigrants were often more nationalistic and worldly than their predecessors; in general, they tended to be better educated and more inclined to urban living. They came to a Ukrainian-Canadian community prepared to receive them, and were morally and financially assisted by Ukrainian immigrant aid societies in both Canada and Poland. As Canada continued to prefer British, American, and northern European immigrants, as well as immigrants with capital, Ukrainians

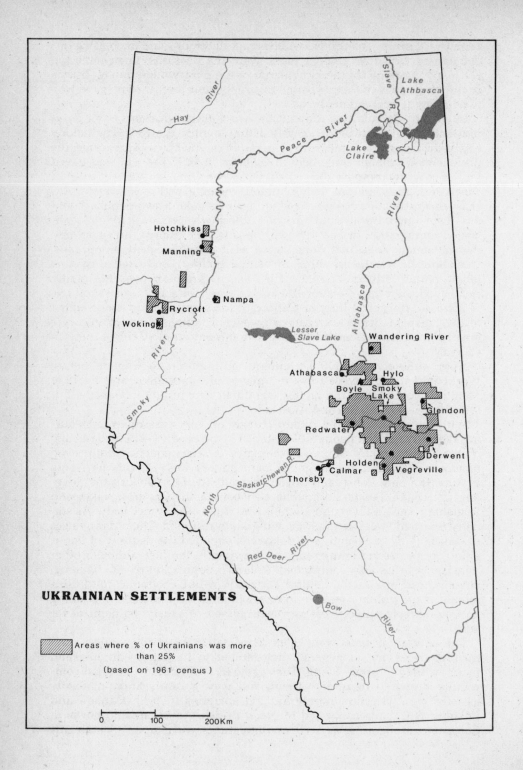

Hotchkiss

Manning

Nampa

Rycroft

Woking

Wandering River

Athabasca
Boyle
Hylo
Smoky
Lake
Glendon

Redwater

Derwent

Holden
Calmar
Vegreville
Thorsby

UKRAINIAN SETTLEMENTS

Areas where % of Ukrainians was more
than 25%

(based on 1961 census)

0   100   200Km

were relegated to "non-preferred" status. In the 1930s Ukrainian immigration dropped dramatically; with widespread unemployment in Canada, nativist hostility and deportation plagued recent arrivals who lacked economic security.

Almost 68,000 Ukrainians immigrated to Canada between the world wars. Alberta's Ukrainian population, through immigration and natural increase, rose to 71,868 by 1941 and was exceeded only by Manitoba and Saskatchewan.

The third wave of Ukrainian immigration to Canada coincided with the international resettlement of displaced persons after World War II. Thousands of Ukrainians deported to concentration camps, labor farms, or German war industries in western Europe refused to return to the Ukrainian Soviet Socialist Republic, which now included all Ukraine. When forced repatriation was halted, the remaining refugees were granted "displaced person" status and resettled abroad. The Ukrainian-Canadian community, with the exception of the communist minority which denounced the refugees as fascist traitors fleeing Soviet justice, urged the Canadian government to accept Ukrainian immigrants. Some 34,000 Ukrainians came to Canada as displaced persons, the majority arriving between 1947 and 1953. In spite of the wave's small size, all ethnic Ukrainian territories were represented. Many immigrants were well educated or trained professionals, although ignorance of English retarded many careers and created a certain amount of frustration. The bulk of the third wave settled in Ontario, particularly in the Toronto area.

By 1981 the number of people of Ukrainian origin in Alberta (a high percentage of them Canadian-born) had risen to 136,710 and had eclipsed both Manitoba and Saskatchewan.[4] More Ukrainians now live in Ontario than in any other province except Alberta, but they form less than 2 percent of its population. In the prairies where they first settled, Ukrainians constitute a significant 10 percent of the residents. Unlike their agricultural, "foreign," pioneer-immigrant ancestors, Albertan Ukrainians in the early 1980s are predominantly urban, Canadian-born, and largely indistinguishable from their neighbors.

Settlement and Distribution

Perhaps the most conspicuous development among Albertan Ukrainians has been their dispersal from one cohesive area of settlement throughout the entire province. Future population shifts in response to economic change will further affect their demographic distribution.

The first Ukrainian settlement in Canada was founded at Edna-Star, east of Edmonton, between 1892 and 1894.[5] The site of the colony, in which both Pylypiw and Eleniak eventually homesteaded, was determined by the presence of a group of Galician Germans that included one of Pylypiw's former schoolmates. Its subsequent growth rested on two factors—the natural wish of later immigrants to settle among their own kind and the promotion of the area by Oleskiw, who had been favorably impressed during his Canadian tour. With the unprecedented growth of

Ukrainian immigrants outside Edmonton (Strathcona) immigration shed, turn of the century. Immigration sheds temporarily housed the newcomers until they could begin their trek by wagon, on foot, or sometimes even by raft to their new homes. (Ernest Brown photo, courtesy Provincial Archives of Alberta)

the Albertan colony after 1896, the Liberal government faced strong Conservative and public opposition to the possibility of a solid bloc, impervious to Canadian influences, stretching from Edmonton into Saskatchewan. To check expansion around Edna-Star and diffuse the Ukrainian impact, yet respect the immigrants' desire for Ukrainian neighbors, several smaller settlement nuclei were established across the prairie provinces.[6]

In spite of the fragmentation of the bloc concept, the Vegreville colony (as it was eventually called after its major urban center) continued to flourish. By 1905 its core was well defined around the original area of settlement along the Star-Vegreville axis. Settlement south of the North Saskatchewan River had been essentially achieved; preliminary inroads in the direction of present-day Two Hills and Myrnam had been made and the first settlers had ventured north of the river.[7] A smaller second settlement nucleus lay southwest of Edmonton at Rabbit Hills, near Leduc. Expansion continued through the interwar years, and during the 1940s and early 1950s the bloc reached its maximum extension. Ukrainian settlement in the east central Albertan parkland extends from Fort Saskatchewan, outside Edmonton, to Vermilion, sixty kilometers from the Saskatchewan border. Its southern limits lie around Holden and Round Hill, while to the north and east expansion into new pioneer areas after World War I brought the peripheries of the bloc to Athabasca, Lac la Biche, and Bonnyville. Ukrainian concentration has always been less on the fringes than in the center.

The early Ukrainian settlers unconsciously divided the bloc according to village and district of origin as they chose homesteads near friends and neighbors or those speaking the same dialect.[8] Although overwhelmingly Galician, the bloc also contains a large Bukovynian settlement—a pocket between Krakow and Kaleland extending north to Smoky Lake and from there east toward Vilna. Even in the early years, the bloc was never wholly Ukrainian. Polish and Romanian settlers, for example, came with the Ukrainians and formed distinct enclaves. Other nationalities—Scandinavian, British, German and French—had settled in parts of the bloc before the Ukrainians arrived and were not displaced on any scale until the interwar years.

Beginning in the 1920s, Ukrainians moved into new areas of the province. Not only did they push the boundaries of the original bloc outward, but they also created new settlements separated from the parent colony. Ukrainians helped pioneer the Peace River district in northwest central Alberta, and by 1941 formed 7.8 percent of the region's population.[9] The Peace River bloc now constitutes a significant secondary area of Ukrainian settlement in the province. Expansion was due to several factors. First, prosperity from high wartime wheat prices enabled Ukrainian farmers to buy additional land, both from non-Ukrainians within the bloc and beyond its fringes. Second, as unoccupied land in the original bloc disappeared, the second generation looked elsewhere to new frontiers. Finally, during the 1920s and 1930s Alberta attracted Ukrainians from submarginal lands in Manitoba and drought-plagued farms in Saskatchewan.

The basic pioneering experience, with individual variations depending on material circumstances, was common to all settlers in the Vegreville bloc regardless of nationality. Local Anglo-Canadian homesteaders, teachers and townspeople, however, had their own formal and informal social networks—picnics, church gatherings, sports days, clubs—that by and large excluded their often more numerous Ukrainian neighbors. The "society columns" of the Vegreville and Lamont newspapers, for example, focussed on the Browns and the Smiths, not the Melnyks and the Sawchuks, while friendly rivalry among local centers often took the form of deriding the "Ukrainianness" of each others' communities.[10] As Ukrainian activities crept into local newspaper columns written by Anglo-Canadians, however, more generous views of Ukrainian lifestyles gradually prevailed:

> The Ruthenian (Ukrainian) Christmas has been celebrated here by the holding of numerous parties, and visiting together of relatives and friends. A large group of young men formed themselves into a choral choir on the night of

the seventh and went about from home to home singing sweet carols and bringing greetings. It is somewhat surprising that such a beautiful practice has not been adopted in this new land more than it has.[11]

Obviously, Christmas carolling in the Ukrainian settlement had existed long before it came to the attention of that particular correspondent and would continue long after. It was but one of many customs transplanted from Galician and Bukovynian villages onto Canadian soil. Within the bloc a distinctive way of life emerged—one that absorbed features of the larger Canadian society, but also preserved centuries-old Ukrainian traditions. Typical of peasant agricultural communities, Ukrainian life revolved around all-important natural and seasonal cycles, as well as the religious calendar. The rituals celebrating these events incorporated pagan customs reaching back over 1,000 years with later practices adopted with Eastern Christianity. Religious holidays, one's saint's day, weddings and even funerals broke the monotony of homestead life and provided eagerly welcomed opportunities for socializing.

Not unexpectedly, many Ukrainian traditions changed in the Canadian environment. The white wedding dress and ready-made clothes bought from Eaton's catalog, for example, slowly replaced the Ukrainian peasant costume. Gradually, some customs were abandoned altogether as the modernized North American descendants of the Ukrainian pioneers lost their peasant roots and the traditions of their ancestors became inapplicable. Others have been retained out of symbolic significance, although no longer daily relevant to Ukrainians in a suburban bungalow or a downtown condominium: wheat, for example, the symbol of life, remains an integral part of the Ukrainian Christmas celebration.

A physical Ukrainian imprint was also made on the landscape in northeast central Alberta. Traditional Ukrainian peasant cottages—plastered, whitewashed, thatched-roofed—became a common sight on the Canadian prairies. Their decaying remains still dot the countryside, lying in fields or huddled beside the shingled frame houses that replaced them. More impressive were the churches the pioneers and their descendents raised to the glory of God. With their distinctive cross-topped onion domes reaching skyward, many of these rural churches still stand. They often mark the spot where once-flourishing, rural crossroads communities bearing such Ukrainian names as Buczacz, New Kiew, Sich-Kolomea, and Zawale dominated the social lives of the Ukrainians who lived nearby. For many years these crossroads communities of post office-general store, school, church(es) and often *narodnyi dim* or national hall constituted the major focal point in local Ukrainian society. Here the Ukrainians went to collect their mail, buy basic supplies, exchange gossip, worship, attend plays or concerts, hear the news of the old country, and read Ukrainian-Canadian newspapers.[12]

Three railway lines, giving rise to a new series of urban service centers along their tracks, were built through the Vegreville bloc between 1905 and 1928. Each of them affected Ukrainian social patterns and radically altered transportation and communication routes within the bloc and with the outside world. Mundare, for example, came into being because

John Gavinchuk reading a newspaper outside his thatched, plastered cottage near Hilliard in 1917. These whitewashed cottages were common in north central Alberta until the 1920s and 1930s, when they were replaced by larger, more conventional structures built of lumber. (Courtesy Provincial Archives of Alberta)

of the CNR, while the CPR line that gave birth to Two Hills, Willingdon, and Hairy Hill contributed to the decline of neighboring rural communities. Paved highways and automobile travel that brought Edmonton and larger towns within easy reach continued to erode physical and cultural isolation in the bloc.

Rural-urban migration within the Vegreville bloc, beginning seriously in the interwar years, accelerated after World War II. As towns and villages assumed a more Ukrainian character, the rural crossroads communities serving the pioneer immigrants declined. Mass media, higher education, agricultural technology, upward social mobility, and the rise of a Ukrainian entrepreneurial middle class and wage employees have had a profound impact. Together they have destroyed the cohesiveness of the bloc, raised its standard of living and expectations, and contributed to Ukrainian outward migration. While the proportion of Ukrainians compared with other ethnic groups is declining in the original area of settlement north and east of Edmonton, numbers are increasing in other parts of Alberta, particularly the major urban centers.

Ukrainian urban life in Alberta is not new. Many early immigrants, arriving without the ready cash to begin farming, became low-paid, unskilled laborers. Edmonton absorbed some of these workers; others went to mining centers in the Crow's Nest, Drumheller, and Lethbridge. Perhaps a majority intended to remain only temporarily, but others became permanent members of the urban labor force. The latter, the more stable element, included families, while the former was a fluid group of single males or men separated from their homesteads and families, as well as single girls working to supplement the family coffers. They formed the nuclei of Ukrainian urban communities in Alberta, crowded in tenements around a rudimentary institutional network near the city core. Edmonton's equivalent to Winnipeg's celebrated North End lay north of Jasper Avenue in a corridor between Ninety-fifth and

Ninety-eighth streets. Residentially, later immigrant groups and native Canadians have largely displaced the Ukrainians, but the area still houses a profusion of Ukrainian churches, organizational headquarters, and businesses.[13]

Concentration in the original inner city immigrant reception area in Edmonton eventually gave way to housing in working class districts close to places of employment. Nearby railway yards and meat-packing plants, for example, made the Calder and Norwood areas of the city attractive to Ukrainian workers. Most recently, reflecting affluence and the adoption of dominant middle class values, Ukrainians have begun the move to suburbia. The dispersion of Ukrainians throughout Edmonton has destroyed the physical neighborhood community of home, church, clubs and ethnic shops, since most institutions failed to follow. Immigrants from the second and third waves, as well as migrants from rural Alberta and other parts of Canada, have added to Ukrainian populations in Edmonton and other urban centers in the province. From small numbers contemporary with the period of pioneer settlement, Edmonton's Ukrainian population mushroomed to the point where in 1971 Ukrainians comprised 12.6 percent of the city's residents.[14]

"Foreigner" and "Alien"

Convinced of their own natural superiority, Anglo-Canadians at the turn of the century tended to judge immigrant groups according to the distance between their traditions and institutions and those of the British. Ukrainians, made highly visible by their curious peasant dress and customs, their clannishness, and their "questionable" standard of living, lay near the bottom of the scale. A negative public stereotype of Ukrainians as a dirty, immoral, unintelligent, and unenterprising people, overly fond of alcohol and fighting, placed Anglo-Canadians in a dilemma.[15] While they valued the Ukrainians' physical role in building the country, they feared their socio-political impact. Thus they believed that assimilation was mandatory if British democratic traditions, ideals, and way of life were to survive. "The close relations into which we are brought with these people who are now vicious and degraded," one minister warned, "ought to force us to do them good in self-defense. Either we must raise them or they will lower us."[16]

Public Schools and Protestant Missions

The public school, one of the few nonindigenous institutions to penetrate a Ukrainian community successfully in the pioneer era, was the primary Canadianizing body. The education of the "foreigner" aimed not simply at teaching the English language but at producing useful and patriotic citizens as well. Motivated by the social gospel, evangelical dislike of "authoritarian and ritualistic" religion, and self-interest, the Methodist and Presbyterian churches were also active among the Ukrainians.

In 1897, as a concession to French Canadians and Mennonites, Manitoba permitted bilingual instruction in English and any other language.

Ukrainians eagerly exploited the law and a Ukrainian training school provided bilingual teachers with special certificates valid in Ukrainian districts. In the Territories, which were to form Alberta and Saskatchewan, second language instruction was limited to the last hour of the school day. After 1905 bilingual schools operated unofficially in Saskatchewan, but Alberta kept a tight rein on "foreign" education. Although not escaping repercussions from the bilingual schools issue, it imposed uniform instruction and teacher standards throughout the province and ensured that Ukrainian was taught only at the end of the school day.[17]

Education in pioneer communities was hampered by scattered, isolated populations, poor communications and often material poverty that precipitated a dim view of school taxes. Difficulties were compounded in "foreign" settlements where the people understood little English and were unfamiliar with British forms of government or the operation of a school district. To facilitate matters in the Ukrainian bloc east of Edmonton, the Department of Education in Alberta appointed Robert Fletcher as Supervisor of Schools for Foreigners. Under his watchful eye, 130 schools were established among the Ukrainians by 1915.[18]

Not all Ukrainians approved of Fletcher's paternalistic approach. Peter Svarich of Vegreville, self-appointed school organizer among his people, characterized Fletcher's term of office as marked by "a great deal of misunderstanding and trouble."[19] Between 1909 and 1912 Svarich obtained some twelve Ukrainian bilingual teachers with "second-class" certificates from Saskatchewan and Manitoba for Ukrainian schools in Alberta. When they began to teach in both English and Ukrainian, a crisis in "foreign" education in Alberta crystallized around the 1913 provincial election.[20]

Led by a nationally conscious leadership, Alberta Ukrainians resented the prohibition of bilingual schools under teachers of their own nationality and had repeatedly requested a Ukrainian training school, a Ukrainian school organizer and inspector, and a Ukrainian translation of the School Act. In 1913, frustrated by government inaction, they nominated independent candidates in five provincial ridings. Although all were defeated, the Minister of Education was convinced that the imported Ukrainian teachers lay behind this attempt to promote Ukrainian educational aims in Alberta through political agitation. Insisting on "English only," the Department of Education refused to recognize their certificates, cancelled their permits, and forbade any school board to pay them salary. Fletcher took over rebellious school districts. Tempers flared and violence erupted as school boards refused to release their Ukrainian teachers, and students boycotted classes where Fletcher's replacements taught.[21] Ultimately, the revolt failed and Ukrainian school boards bent to departmental regulations.[22]

Convincing qualified "English" teachers to accept the physical and cultural isolation of pioneer immigrant communities, however, was not always easy. In spite of public campaigns advising the teaching profession of its patriotic duty, teachers were reluctant to accept a Ukrainian school if more lucrative or congenial positions existed elsewhere. Never-theless, many Anglo-Canadians teaching among the Ukrainians in Alberta did subscribe to the view that theirs was a great national service. Not only were they introducing the Ukrainians to British ways and ideals, but their own example was influencing the outlook and lifestyle of Ukrainian youth.[23]

Emphasis on anglicizing and assimilating gradually subsided as educa-tors turned to practical problems facing teachers in Ukrainian districts.[24] For their part, by the end of World War I the Ukrainians were turning to private educational institutions to preserve their language and culture, impossible in the public school. Ukrainian did not return to Alberta's schools until 1959, and then only as a high school subject.

Presbyterian and Methodist missions, established by the Home Mis-sion Boards of their respective churches, were the second assimilatory force in the Ukrainian bloc in Alberta.[25] For in spite of its being under-taken in the name of Christ, evangelization of the Ukrainians became identified with the sentiment that Canada was to be a British country. The actual programs of the two churches were similar, with school homes, hospitals, and religious work complementing each other. Not infrequently, educational and medical activities were viewed as means to an end—ways to break down suspicion and prejudice and gain entry to Ukrainian homes, thereby paving the way for "more distinctly aggres-sive work of an evangelistic character."[26]

In spite of the valuable educational and medical services they pro-vided, the Methodist and Presbyterian missionaries remade few Ukraini-ans in their own image or converted them to Protestantism. The two churches suffered from the inadequacy of their workers, in number and frequently in attitude.[27] It also proved wrong to assume that the Ukraini-ans would not resist absorption by Anglo-Canada, or that western evan-gelical Christianity would quickly supplant a hierarchical religious tradi-tion closely interwoven with daily rituals. Even without the admonitions of their priests, most Ukrainians were kept at a distance by the social ostracism facing potential converts. Then, too, the crystallization of organized Ukrainian-Canadian religious life by the end of World War I resulted in growing hostility or indifference to the Presbyterian and Methodist churches.

In 1931 only 1.6 percent of Ukrainian Canadians were affiliated with the United Church of Canada, illustrating the small number of converts inherited from the Presbyterians and Methodists in 1925. By 1971 the figure had risen to 13.9 percent, and in 1981 it stood at 13.3 percent.[28] Support for the United Church among contemporary Ukrainian Canadi-ans stems from such factors as intermarriage, loss of the Ukrainian lan-guage, and Canadianization, rather than turn-of-the-century missionary activity.

World War I

When war erupted in Europe in August 1914, Canada was aligned against the Central Powers led by Germany and Austria-Hungary. Over several months the federal government enacted a number of measures to segregate and monitor the activities of immigrants from enemy countries. Official sanctions and public prejudice were felt most keenly by ethnic Germans and Ukrainians; the latter were the largest non-German minority in the Austro-Hungarian Empire to come to Canada and were already viewed with ambivalence by Canadian society.

The British Nationality and Status of Aliens Act, passed prior to the war to introduce uniform naturalization procedures throughout the Empire, was suspended for enemy aliens. New regulations required them to register and thereafter report regularly to the nearest government office; internment in camps faced those who failed to do so. Established to house enemy reservists and individuals thought to threaten national security, the camps also absorbed unemployed men and those fired from their jobs because of wartime patriotism. In 1917, when the "foreigner's traditional Liberal vote" was thought to threaten the victory of Robert Borden's conscriptionist Union government, the Wartime Elections Act disfranchised all enemy aliens naturalized after March 1902.[29] In September 1918 the last major war measure to affect the Ukrainians suspended their press, under censorship since June 1915, although the ban was soon lifted for all but organs of the recently outlawed Ukrainian socialist organizations.

Public hostility also plagued the Ukrainians. British and other "allied" miners, for example, often demanded that Germans and "Austrians" be dismissed and refused to work with them, although a growing labor

Ukrainian and other "Austro-Hungarian enemy aliens" in an internment camp at Castle Mountain, near Banff during World War I. Bitterness over the way they had been treated by the government would remain for many years. (Courtesy Glenbow Archives)

shortage as the war progressed made enemy alien workers less undesirable. In 1916 when Edmonton aldermen moved to dismiss "enemy" city employees, a local Ukrainian editor was outraged since many of the "Austrians" were Ukrainian citizens of Canada, aware of their responsibilities and deserving of better treatment. "For us Canada is first, we have sworn our loyalty to this country, and we do not see the reason why we have to be regarded as enemies!" he protested.[30] Returning veterans increased ethnic tensions. Often unable to find work, they resented the inflated wages and prices received by "enemy alien" workers and farmers. Bitterness mounted when disfranchised enemy aliens were exempted from military conscription. In January 1918, Alberta's Ukrainians were greatly alarmed when the Great War Veterans' Association in Edmonton demanded the conscription of disfranchised enemy aliens for essential industry, confiscation of enemy alien property, and restriction of their movement and acquisition of land.

The Ukrainians' reaction to the war and their treatment was not uniform. While the socialists denounced the war as an imperialistic conflict, the remainder of the community generally supported the Canadian war effort after an initial period of confusion. On 27 July 1914, after the assassination of the Austrian Archduke, the recently appointed Ukrainian Catholic bishop in Winnipeg, Nykyta Budka, had issued an unwise pastoral letter supporting Emperor Franz Joseph and encouraging Ukrainian reservists to return to defend the fatherland.[31] Although Budka reversed his stand immediately after Britain declared war against Austria-Hungary, his original statement had been damaging. Budka himself remained suspect, in spite of repeatedly urging his largely rural flock to prove its loyalty by helping to feed Canada's soldiers.[32] Ukrainian leaders generally advised their people to obey the distasteful wartime regulations, but the community did protest its treatment. Six Ukrainian newspapers, for example, issued "An Address to the Canadian People" in which they asked for sympathy and support, at one point arguing:

> Thousands of our Ukrainian boys have enlisted with the Canadian overseas force, and many have already lost their lives fighting beside their English brethren on the battlefields of France. And as the price of their blood we have the right to ask the Canadian people for better treatment of the Canadian Ukrainians.[33]

Much of the war on the eastern front was fought on their native soil, and the fate of relatives and old neighbors was unknown to Ukrainians in Canada. With the exception of the small number of Russophiles, they could only reluctantly accept Russia, for centuries the oppressor of the Ukrainian nation and now the destroyer of much of eastern Galicia, as an ally. Russophile Ukrainians in Alberta worked diligently to discredit anti-Russian Galician and Bukovynian Ukrainians as pro-German.[34] In the latter stages of the war, much of the energy in the Ukrainian-Canadian community was absorbed by the burning issue of Ukraine's independence.

Although enemy aliens could not volunteer for military service, some 10,000 Ukrainians were able to enlist, either because they were naturalized, passed as Russians, or came from the Russian Empire. The 218th Battalion or "Irish Guards" recruited in northern Alberta for construction at the front had significant numbers of Ukrainian volunteers, characterized by their Anglo-Canadian comrades as "good, strong, capable fighting men, and as thoroughly patriotic as any."[35] On the home front Ukrainians in Alberta contributed generously to the Victory Loans, the Canadian Patriotic Fund, and the Red Cross.[36]

The Ukrainians emerged from the war scarred by the enemy alien stigma and politically suspect. This image was bolstered in the immediate postwar years by their association in the public mind with labor unrest, radicalism, and Bolshevist Russia. Nevertheless, although the debate over the desirability of Ukrainians as immigrants continued, attitudes were changing. The ethnic stereotype gradually modified as Anglo-Canadians became more familiar with the Ukrainians and their history. Then, too, the group was moving out of the immigrant-pioneer stage into greater economic prosperity and adopting Canadian lifestyles and outlooks. Assimilation could work, and Anglo-Canadians were encouraged. The "foreigner" was becoming the "New Canadian."

Socio-Economic Development

Like other immigrants of the period, most Ukrainians coming to Alberta at the turn of the century settled on the land. With little cash, no experience with large-scale farming, often poor land and outdated peasant agricultural techniques, the Ukrainians underwent greater and more prolonged hardship than did some other groups. An investigation among new arrivals in the Edna-Star colony in 1897 revealed great destitution as winter approached. One man had "one horse, four children and nothing else"; another, robbed of $150 aboard ship, fed three small children from one cow.[37] Material circumstances of the first settlers had, however, improved; three years after settling at Edna-Star, Ivan Pylypiw boasted a comfortable house, several head of livestock, numerous implements (including a binder), eighty acres of land under cultivation, and 1,300 bushels of wheat in the granary.[38]

Even with material comforts, the psychological support of Ukrainian neighbors, and familiar cultural and religious rituals, life was not easy. The gulf between expectations and reality often produced great disillusionment. Years later, a woman recalled the arduous journey from Edmonton to the Ukrainian colony to the east during a snowstorm: "I wept bitterly over my fate and cursed my husband and his Canada."[39] Some found the strain of dislocation too great and returned home; one Bukovynian settler, deserting his family at the Immigration Hall in Edmonton, told his wife that the Canadian government would look after her.[40] Reports of violent death in the Ukrainian colony testified that mental and physical pressures took their toll. Woman's lot was particularly grueling and lonely. Not infrequently, together with her children, she erected the first dwelling, broke the first acres, and planted and harvested the first crop while husband and father worked elsewhere for badly needed cash.

Soaring wheat prices during World War I put Alberta's Ukrainian farmers on the road to economic prosperity. Small news items in the local press—the purchase of a phonograph or gas-powered tractor—testified to socio-economic progress and the adoption of middle class values. Relative growth continued to the 1930s, when overexpansion and overemphasis on wheat farming exacted their price during the Great Depression. Since 1945, large-scale mechanization, scientific and extensive agriculture, farm consolidation, and rural depopulation in the Ukrainian bloc have paralleled contemporary developments throughout much of rural Alberta.

The Ukrainian pioneers' lack of money made outside work imperative to buy seed, implements, livestock, and even foodstuffs. As unskilled miners and laborers on lumbering and railway crews, they encountered deplorable working conditions and exploitation rising from negative public stereotypes. The resulting anger and resentment against Canadian society radicalized many Ukrainian workers. In the 1930s the Communist Party of Canada and its affiliated organizations, the Workers' Unity League (WUL) and Farmers' Unity League (FUL), attracted a significant number of Albertan Ukrainians. The FUL received its greatest support in the Ukrainian bloc east of Edmonton where the procommunist Ukrainian Labor-Farmer Temple Association (ULFTA) also had its greatest influence. Ukrainian farmers who had operated through credit or mortgaging were hard hit by falling prices for grain and other commodities; those who defaulted on their payments or land taxes faced foreclosure and relief. "Foreign" workers were also the first to be laid off; the unnaturalized faced deportation, which affected interwar immigrants in particular, while public relief or "make-work" camps were often the only avenues open to unemployed Ukrainian-Canadian workers.

The largest protest against depression conditions occurred in December 1932 when the FUL and WUL organized a hunger march in Edmonton. Ukrainian workers and farmers, together with thousands of others from across the province, participated in the demonstration, which proceeded despite a ban and police harrassment.[41] In 1934 Ukrainian farmers again protested: grain strikes in Myrnam and Mundare under the auspices of the FUL opposed unfair grain-grading practices by local elevator agents. Although there were sympathy strikes in other districts, violence and litigation resulted when those wishing to deliver grain were forcibly prevented. However, by 1935 the influence of the FUL had declined as man-made famine and purges in Soviet Ukraine discredited communism among the eastern Europeans in Canada.[42]

Not all Ukrainians had gone to the land or joined the working class. Teaching was attractive to those wanting to improve their status, and was often seen as a stepping stone to other professions. Agricultural colleges also drew young men anxious to put Ukrainian farming on a more scientific footing. Movement into these and other occupations, however, was gradual; the first Ukrainian teacher graduated in Alberta in 1916.[43] A number of Ukrainians in Edmonton became general merchants and small businessmen, providing basic services for their Ukrainian clientele and such special establishments as bookstores and boardinghouses. Although the large-scale movement of Ukrainians into the business sections of the towns and villages of the Vegreville bloc was an interwar phenomenon, foundations were laid earlier.[44] In addition to flour mills, general stores and implement dealerships, early enterprises also included such Mundare businesses as a dressmaking and millinery establishment and a moving picture theater.

Cooperatives also appeared. By 1916 the National Cooperative Company of Vegreville, with two hundred shareholders (mostly Ukrainians), had three stores and capital stock worth $60,000.[45] Consumer cooperatives expanded between the wars largely as a reaction to the depression. In 1917 Albertan Ukrainians had their own farmers' union,[46] but with Canadianization they increasingly joined such organizations as the Alberta Wheat Pool. Ukrainian credit unions, reflecting the stimulus of the third immigration, have been confined to Edmonton and Calgary.

Over ninety years, great socio-economic changes have occurred among the descendents of the original immigrants, while two later immigrations with distinct characteristics further altered the Ukrainian group's profile. Scholars in the third immigration, for example, boosted the number of Ukrainian Canadians in academic university positions. Third wave immigrants, however, also temporarily increased the proportion of Ukrainians in blue collar occupations; because ignorance of English forced individuals into jobs incompatible with their education, the man with a university degree found himself painting cars in an Edmonton garage. The most striking trend among Ukrainian Canadians has been movement upward from overwhelmingly peasant origin, rural status and illiteracy to economic diversification and distribution throughout the socio-economic spectrum. Nevertheless, as a group they are still entrenched in the lower middle class. Their present position, when compared with Canadians as a whole or other ethnic groups, suggests imperfect integration into Canadian socio-economic life.

The Ukrainians were almost exclusively farmers when they arrived in Canada. By 1931 the proportion of Albertan Ukrainians engaged in agriculture had dropped to 72.1 percent; over the next forty years it plummeted to 16.1 percent and during the next decade to 8.7 percent, but in 1981 it still remained above the proportion of the total Albertan labor force reporting farming as its occupation.[47] Once overly prominent in blue collar jobs, Ukrainians subsequently became represented in manufacturing industries more than their numbers statistically warranted.[48] At the upper end of the scale, they remain underrepresented. For example, while the absolute number of Ukrainian-Canadian doctors, lawyers and engineers has risen dramatically over the last few decades, the proportion of Ukrainian-Canadians in these prestigious professional occupations has been below the Canadian average.[49] The average income of the Ukrainian male labor force has also compared unfavorably with that of Canadians of other ethnic groups.[50] In 1971 Ukrainian Albertans earned slightly less, on the average, than Albertans as a whole.[51] Within the Ukrainian group itself, their socio-economic position is lowest in the prairie provinces and progressively better in Ontario, British Columbia, and Quebec.[52]

Until Ukrainians' socio-economic patterns conform to those of the country in general, or compare more favorably with those of other groups, they will continue to form a separate ethnic group whose ethnicity not only rests on a cultural-lingual identity, but which is reinforced by a particular socio-economic status. Ukrainians also compete for jobs and prestige with newer, well-educated immigrant groups who have a higher "entrance status" and who therefore enter the "vertical mosaic" above many Ukrainians.

Political Activity

In addition to maintaining interest in the homeland, which can splinter it into hostile factions based on old country alignments, an immigrant group integrates into the political system of the new country. The political adaptation of the Ukrainians in Canada was understandably influenced by their political backgrounds.[53] Unlike the picture conjured up by many Anglo-Canadians, Austria-Hungary was a constitutional monarchy which guaranteed the right of assembly and freedom of expression, and in 1907 introduced universal male suffrage for elections to the *Reichsrat* or parliament in Vienna. Ukrainian political parties had multiplied in Galicia at the end of the nineteenth century, and by 1914 the balance of power in eastern Galicia was moving from Polish into Ukrainian hands. These developments, coupled with the Ukrainian national awakening sweeping the countryside and peasant unrest expressed in a series of agrarian strikes in the two decades before World War I, could not help but affect the political maturity of Galician Ukrainians, including the immigrants to Canada. Interwar and post-World War II immigrants from Poland came from a highly politicized Ukrainian community, under both parliamentary and totalitarian regimes. Only those arriving after 1945, who had spent their formative or adult years in Soviet Ukraine, had limited experience with participatory democracy or representative institutions.

Not unexpectedly, the Ukrainians received their first direct exposure to Canadian politics at the municipal level with the operation of the rural school districts that dotted the bloc settlements. It was inevitable that they would eventually control elected and administrative organs in rural municipalities, school divisions, towns, and villages where they dominated numerically. Today, for example, a majority of the councils, secretary-treasurers, and superintendents of schools in the heavily Ukrainian counties of Lamont, Two Hills, and Smoky Lake are of Ukrainian origin. To many Ukrainian Canadians, one of the people at the pinnacle of political success, in spite of scandal surrounding his career, has been businessman William Hawrelak, elected four times as mayor of Edmonton;[54] in 1983 a second Ukrainian Canadian, Laurence Decore, occupied the mayor's chair.

The Ukrainians' introduction to federal and provincial politics was at the grassroots' level and campaigns in Ukrainian districts became notorious for "buying the Galician vote." It was no secret that both Liberals and Conservatives employed various tactics—cash bribes, alcohol, premature naturalization, and the enlistment of influential Ukrainians and the Ukrainian-language press—to win Ukrainian votes at election time. Ukrainian ignorance and disregard for the obligations of Canadian citizenship were often held responsible for such chicanery, while the less prejudiced blamed unscrupulous politicians willing to abuse the democratic tradition. Independent Ukrainian activity in Canadian politics and the emergence of successful Ukrainian candidates in the 1910s gave many Anglo-Canadians a new worry: an organized Ukrainian vote in the bloc settlements could both influence an election's outcome and elect significant numbers of Ukrainian legislators.

Initially, the Ukrainians tended to vote Liberal. A Liberal government had brought them to Canada and was given credit for the gift of homestead land, while the Conservatives had opposed Ukrainian immigration and were identified with the unpopular wartime measures of the Borden government. It was not until the 1920s that the Ukrainians east of Edmonton noticeably changed their party preferences. The evidence suggests, however, that they supported both the UFA and Social Credit less than did the Anglo, German, and Scandinavian Canadians who lived in the area south of Edmonton.[55]

The first Ukrainian candidate victorious at the provincial or national level in Canada was Bukovynian-born Andrew Shandro. Elected Liberal MLA for the Ukrainian riding of Whitford in Alberta's 1913 provincial election after a heated campaign, he was a Russophile who later identified with the nationally conscious sector of the Ukrainian community. By 1975, 66 of 207 Ukrainian candidatures for the Alberta legislature had been successful: Liberal, 5; United Farmers of Alberta, 4; CCF/NDP, 3; Social Credit, 33; and Conservative, 21. Twenty-five Alberta Ukrainians had been elected to the House of Commons: UFA, 2; Liberal, 3; Social Credit, 5; and Conservatives, 15.[56]

Initially, it was inevitable that a Ukrainian MLA or MP would be regarded by his people and his party as a spokesman for the Ukrainian group. That this perception has endured to the present shows that many Ukrainian-Canadians still feel a need for a figurehead to represent their special interests. Many Ukrainian parliamentarians have welcomed this role. Among the most committed national spokesmen on behalf of Ukrainian interests have been two Albertans, Michael Luchkovich (UFA, 1926-35) and Anthony Hlynka (Social Credit, 1940-49). Luchkovich condemned anti-east-European prejudice during the interwar years and Poland's oppression of its Ukrainian citizens, while Hlynka urged Commons support for Ukrainian struggles overseas and worked actively to bring Ukrainian displaced persons to Canada. This commitment on the part of elected Ukrainian officials is now changing. Provincial cabinet posts have come to Ukrainian-Canadians only since World War II, and five of the seven ministers in Alberta by 1980 had been appointed in the 1970s. By the end of the decade, only one Ukrainian MP from Alberta had held a federal portfolio.

Ukrainian-Canadians have always publicized conditions in Ukraine and pressured Canadian governments and political parties to do likewise. Continuing political subjugation, the denial of human rights and Russification in the homeland have prompted them to seek public support for the preservation and encouragement of their language and culture in Canada.[57] Their concern made the organized community a major force behind a federal policy of multiculturalism. Alberta's Ukrainians have been the most successful to date in effecting concrete policy changes to benefit the community. In the early 1970s, the Edmonton branch of the Ukrainian Professional and Business Federation was instrumental in persuading the Alberta government to permit bilingual instruction in the province's schools; by 1980 the Ukrainian-English program in Edmonton reached the junior high level, and elementary classes had begun in Vegreville, Lamont, and Sherwood Park. When the national executive of the Ukrainian Professional and Business Federation was located in Edmonton in the early 1970s, the local club also spearheaded the drive for a publicly funded academic research and publishing institute; in 1976 the Canadian Institute of Ukrainian Studies opened at the University of Alberta. Their achievements testify to the recognition of Ukrainians as a legitimate pressure group and their penetration of the provincial political power structure.

The Ukrainian Community

Parallel to the gradual integration of Ukrainians into Canadian society was the evolution of Ukrainian-Canadian community life around religious and secular institutions and traditions. This structure has been most important to immigrants, whether from the first, second or third period of immigration, and less so to Canadian-born generations.

Historically, community life has been fraught with factionalism and dissension. While religious controversy between Catholic and Orthodox developed in Canada, most political divisions were introduced by successive immigrations fresh from a period of turmoil in Ukraine. Although the second and third immigrations fortified the Ukrainian Canadian community, friction arose as they criticized the Canadian orientation of those Ukrainians already in Canada, and the latter resented the often self-righteous and condescending attitudes of the newcomers. Antagonisms have eased considerably over the last thirty years, since few new immigrants have arrived and the declining influence of the formal community has forced greater cooperation among its component organizations.

Religious Life

While some Ukrainian peasants in the late nineteenth century had begun to question the church's wealth as well as the privileged status and autocratic actions of many of its priests, most still demurred to religious authority. Neither Greek Catholic nor Orthodox clergy accompanied the early immigrants to Canada, however, and the social and religious vacuum deprived them of centuries-old stability. They were truly "uprooted." Who would bless the Easter *paska* (bread), pray for the dead, or lead them in the observance of countless other rituals necessary to living? What would replace the village church? Letters to the old country begged for priests, and in their absence, the immigrants gathered to worship on their own. Religious holidays they observed as best they could, while important occasions—marriages, baptisms, burials—meant accepting the spiritually unsatisfactory services of clergymen of other faiths. When their own priests did come, the occasion was momentous. An Anglo-Canadian watched the worshippers at the consecration of a Ukrainian church east of Edmonton:

> Did anywhere a congregation face their priest turning to him eyes full of more pleading need? How eager they were to listen! For hours they have been standing, and they still stood, showing no sign of weariness or impatience.[58]

And turning to her in broken English, a girl expressed the feelings of them all: "It plenty much like old land. Many days we no forget. It is dobra day."[59]

Other denominations willingly tried to fill the spiritual vacuum. Besides the Presbyterian and Methodist missions and the short-lived Independent Greek Church (which was supported by the Presbyterian Church), the Russian Orthodox and Roman Catholic churches also played a role.[60]

Although the Orthodox Church in Bukovyna was administratively distinct from its counterpart in Russia, the Bukovynian Ukrainians in Alberta who appealed to their metropolitan for priests were directed to the Russian Orthodox Mission in the United States. Soon the fledgling settlement was being visited by travelling Russian Orthodox missionaries from California, as well as by Greek Catholic priests from Pennsylvania. Although both satisfied a religious need, a war for souls began as rival parishes sprang up, and opposing factions fought for title and control in others. In 1907 litigation between Catholic and Russian Orthodox supporters over the Limestone Lake church in the heart of the Vegreville colony reached the Privy Council in London.

In spite of their Russian view, Russian Orthodox missionaries were popular among many Galicians as well as Bukovynians. Not only was their form of worship familiar, but the priests demanded little for their services and interfered little in local church affairs. However, success was short-lived. The creation of a Greek Catholic hierarchy and establishment of the Ukrainian Greek Orthodox Church by 1920 were major factors. The 1917 Russian Revolution also deprived the Russian Orthodox missionaries of their financial support from the Russian government. Lastly, hostility to everything Russian increased among noncommunist Ukrainians with the founding of Soviet Ukraine under Russian domination. The Russian Orthodox Church still has some strength among Alberta Ukrainians, no doubt largely because of firm roots planted in the original Bukovynian colony. Besides St. Barbara's cathedral parish in Edmonton, where a significant proportion of members are of Ukrainian origin, there are now some eighteen rural parishes under the Patri-

Russian Orthodox Church at Smoky Lake. The cross-topped churches with their onion-shaped domes are characteristic landmarks throughout central and northern Alberta. The Russian Orthodox, Ukrainian Catholic, and Ukrainian Greek Orthodox churches vied for support among the Ukrainians. (Courtesy Provincial Archives of Alberta)

arch of Moscow, plus a handful associated with the Orthodox Church of America.

Ukrainian Catholic immigrants initially fell under the jurisdiction of the French-dominated Roman Catholic hierarchy in western Canada. Although they shared doctrine with the Roman Catholic Church, they differed in rite, and had traditionally resented the Catholic Church as an instrument of Polonization. Since the Vatican had extended the Latin rule of celibacy to Ukrainian Catholic priests in North America, the Ukrainian secular clergy, married as was the custom in the Greek rite, could not work in Canada.[61] Unwelcome Latin-rite French and Belgian missionaries took their place at first, while the task of organizing and staffing the Ukrainian Catholic Church in Canada fell largely to the Order of St. Basil the Great (OSBM), the only monastic order in Galicia. Accustomed to married priests, the Ukrainians often received the Basilians coolly.

In 1902 the first Basilian Fathers and Ukrainian Sisters Servants of Mary Immaculate arrived in Canada. They came to Alberta, to the Diocese of St. Albert where the Catholic-Russian Orthodox conflict was alarming Bishop Legal. From their headquarters east of Mundare, the Basilians and Sisters Servants began to assert their influence over a wide area, although ministering to a large, widely scattered flock in pioneer circumstances often tested them severely.[62] The head of the Ukrainian Catholic Church in Galicia, Metropolitan Andriy Sheptytsky, toured the settlements in 1910, and following his successful appeal to Rome, Nykyta Budka became the first bishop of the Ukrainian Greek Catholic Church of Canada in late 1912. He immediately set out to restore his church to its accustomed position of dominance in Ukrainian life, but in so doing alienated many Ukrainians, particularly the rising "intelligentsia."

This group, including locally influential pioneer teachers, had been touched by the nationalist-populist and anticlerical philosophy of the Galician Radical Party. They opposed the authority of the Ukrainian Catholic Church and its bishop and objected to such features in the church in Canada as the episcopal incorporation of church property, the imposition of celibacy, the use of non-Ukrainian Latin-rite priests, and the failure to guarantee that its bishop be Ukrainian. Matters first erupted in 1916 when Ukrainians from across the prairies voted, over the objections of Bishop Budka, to establish a nondenominational *bursa* or students' institute, the Petro Mohyla Institute, at Saskatoon. The climax to the ensuing dispute came in 1918, when a confidential meeting, called at the initiative of the men around the Mohyla Institute, voted to break with Budka and form the Ukrainian Greek Orthodox Church of Canada. Its priests were to marry, bishops were to be elected by a council of clergy and laymen, and congregations were to engage their priests and own church property. The new church found it comparatively easy to obtain priests, given the defection of Russian Orthodox and Independent Greek priests, and soon established a theological seminary. Its search for a suitable bishop, however, resulted in charges of canonical unorthodoxy and years of internal dissension until the election of Metropolitan Ilarion (Ivan) Ohienko in 1951 guaranteed its autonomy and hierarchy.[63]

The advent of the Ukrainian Greek Orthodox Church altered the course of Ukrainian-Canadian religious life and provoked years of strife. Many Albertan Ukrainians had supported the establishment of an independent Ukrainian national church and had participated in the events leading up to it. Within the Vegreville bloc a number of parishes—Russian Orthodox, Greek Catholic, Independent Greek—joined the new church, although litigation, violence, and burned church buildings accompanied many transfers. The stress placed on small communities by hostile churches, which were duplicating services and competing for support, persisted for decades. Although religious tensions have abated, some Ukrainian families are still reluctant to accept marriages or close friendships that cross Catholic-Orthodox lines.

Both Catholic and Orthodox churches have formalized national networks of men's, women's, and youth lay organizations with local branches in Albertan communities. Immigrants in the second and third waves joined either the Ukrainian Catholic or Ukrainian Orthodox church, although their arrival sometimes caused discord. In Edmonton, for example, certain "traditional" Ukrainian Catholic parishes have become identified with the third immigration, which objected to Latin features and modernization in the Canadian church. Today the central position the Ukrainian church once enjoyed in Ukrainian-Canadian life has eroded, and the local priest has lost much of his authority and prestige.

In 1931 the Ukrainian Catholic Church held the allegiance of 58 percent of Ukrainian Canadians compared to its Orthodox rival's 24.6 percent; by 1971 only 32.1 percent of census respondents identified with the former and 20.1 percent with the latter. In 1981, 30.0 percent and 18.6 percent of Ukrainian Canadians reported affiliation with the Ukrainian Catholic and Orthodox churches respective; the Roman Catholic Church claimed 16.8 percent and the United Church 13.3 percent. At present, the numerical strength of the two churches in Alberta is almost equal. A smaller proportion (53.9 percent) of Ukrainians in Alberta supported the two traditional Ukrainian churches in 1971 than in Manitoba (62.6 percent) or Saskatchewan (59.8 percent). The United Church of Canada (16.7 percent) was third among Alberta's Ukrainians and the Roman Catholic Church (12.9 percent) fourth.[64]

Intermarriage, loss of the Ukrainian language, and the adoption of Canadian lifestyles and values have estranged many Albertan Ukrainians from the two traditional Ukrainian churches with their nationalistic and Ukrainian cultural emphasis. Whether such measures as the introduction of the prevalent Gregorian calendar or English in the liturgy and sermon can stall or reverse the trend remains to be seen.

Secular Life

Prior to World War I, secular organizational life in the Ukrainian community existed almost solely on the local level, but Alberta's Ukrainians were not isolated from the activities of their compatriots in other provinces. An active press formed a communications link among Ukrainians in all parts of the country, and immigrants across Canada reproduced institutions they had inherited in common.

In the late nineteenth century, adult education societies (*prosvity*) and reading halls (*chytalni*), designed to combat illiteracy and raise the cultural and national awareness of the peasantry, crisscrossed Galicia.

Together with national halls *(narodni domy)*, they soon emerged in Canada; by 1917, two Ukrainian societies and six reading clubs were reported in the vicinity of Lamont, Chipman, and Mundare alone.[65] Although they frequently had a specific religious or political orientation, educational-cultural associations boasted similar programs—concerts, plays, popular and scholarly lectures, and readings for the illiterate. They maintained a lively interest in the homeland, but also instructed their members about Canada. The rural national halls and related institutions enjoyed their heyday in the 1920s and 1930s, but have largely ceased to function today.[66]

To ensure the survival of their language and culture, the Ukrainians also organized *ridni shkoly* or part-time vernacular schools, and *bursy* or student institutes. The former could and did exist wherever there were sufficient pupils and a willing instructor. The latter emerged in the cities and larger towns of the prairie provinces. They not only guaranteed a Ukrainian linguistic and cultural environment for the student residents, thus cushioning the impact of urban life, but also facilitated education beyond the rural school.

Today *ridni shkoly* reach only a fraction of Ukrainian-Canadian youth. Their main focus is in urban areas, where the children of the post-World War II immigration have provided a new group of students; enrollments have declined among third and fourth generation Ukrainian-Canadians, but some *ridni shkoly* serve mixed marriages or families who speak only English. The majority operate at the elementary level, teaching Ukrainian language, culture, and history.

Early *bursa* students tried to raise the educational level and national consciousness of their people and for many years provided community and cultural leadership. The only surviving *bursa* among several pioneer efforts in Alberta is St. John's Institute in Edmonton, opened in 1918 as the Michael Hrushevsky Institute in the euphoria surrounding the launching of the Mohyla Institute in Saskatoon. Today, although still working closely with the Orthodox community, St. John's is primarily a student residence of the University of Alberta; residents still interested in things Ukrainian can now register for language, literature, history, and political science courses on campus.

The Federation of Ukrainian Social Democrats, formed in 1909 in Winnipeg, gave the socialists an early national profile, one that leaders of the movement in Edmonton briefly but unsuccessfully attempted to rival. By 1917 the Ukrainian Social Democratic Party (USDP), as it was renamed in 1914, had become Marxist; the change was reflected in Alberta in growing radicalism among Ukrainian workers in mining communities, where the USDP was particularly strong. When banned in September 1918, the party was pro-Bolshevik.

While the Ukrainian left rejoiced in the establishment of the Ukrainian Soviet state and the cultural flowering that followed, the remainder of the community had supported the ill-fated Ukrainian People's Republic. Throughout the interwar years, Albertan money went to assist Ukrainian political movements in exile in western Europe and to aid Ukrainian veterans, war orphans, and various educational, cultural, or political causes in Poland. In the 1930s efforts were made to bring Polish atrocities in Western Ukraine and Stalinist terror in the USSR to the attention of Canadian and world leaders. Community and political groups organizing these campaigns, however, did not present a united front.

Three major Canadian-rooted organizations emerged in the interwar years.[67] The Ukrainian Catholic Brotherhood, its first concern Catholicism, was less vocal in Ukrainian secular affairs than the Ukrainian Self-Reliance League, representing the Orthodox laity. Drawing its support from the growing middle class, the latter was equally concerned with the image and status of the Ukrainians in Canada; public denunciations of the Ukrainian-Canadian left by its members attempted to assure Canadian society of the group's respectability. The last of the three, the ULFTA, was the largest ethnic organization through which the Communist Party of Canada operated. It received its greatest support during the depression in Alberta, among both Ukrainian farmers (many receiving their political training in the province's mining camps) and wage earners.[68] The ULFTA's silence regarding the intellectual purges, forced collectivization, and artificial famine in Soviet Ukraine in the early 1930s, however, hurt its image and membership. Its public united front cracked in 1935 when a faction, refusing to condone Soviet actions, broke away.

Other organizations emerged out of the second immigration. The small United Hetman Organization was a conservative monarchist movement favoring the exiled aristocrat and German-sponsored hetman of 1918, Pavlo Skoropadsky, to rule Ukraine. It received support from the Ukrainian Catholic Church. The intensely patriotic nationalist-republican veterans of the Ukrainian independence struggle, who came to Canada in significant numbers, made a greater impact. Their main organization, the Ukrainian National Federation, was sympathetic to the militant Organization of Ukrainian Nationalists, an underground terrorist movement in interwar Poland. Such Canadian groups as the Ukrainian Self-Reliance League denounced association with a political organization outside Canada, while the new immigrants criticized the Canadianism that lessened the commitment of older Ukrainian-Canadians to the Ukrainian cause in Europe. The Ukrainian National Federation had wide appeal, although the two churches disapproved of its slogan, "The Nation Above All." The ULFTA and the Ukrainian National Federation became bitter foes when the latter condemned the former for its unwavering support of Soviet policies in Ukraine and when the ULFTA tried to have the nationalist movement publicly identified with German fascism.[69]

These, then, were the major organizations to affect Ukrainian community life in the interwar years. Each tried to reach the people through its ideological press and workers sent to canvass and organize the countryside. What of their impact in Alberta? One Anglo-Canadian observer during the 1930s claimed that the Ukrainian bloc had been untouched by nationalism before the Ukrainian Revolution and that the nationalists' goals were too divorced from daily life to strike deep roots.[70] However, Ukrainian sentiment had existed in the bloc prior to 1917; it had been expressed, for instance, in the 1913 schools crisis and in the programs of the cultural-educational associations, and would continue to grow—but it is true that organizations introduced by the second immigration had limited appeal. The United Hetman Organization made inroads in Catholic communities, more because of initiative by the local Catholic Church at Mundare than because of spontaneous grassroots' enthusiasm; but the Ukrainian National Federation was relatively insignificant. The institutions of the second immigration fared better in urban centers, where the new arrivals were more closely concentrated. Former soldiers of the Ukrainian army organized an Edmonton Chapter of the Ukrainian War Veterans Association in 1928, for example; and Edmonton was the home of one of the first two branches of the Ukrainian National Federation.

Both the Ukrainian Catholic Brotherhood and Ukrainian Self-Reliance League appeared alongside their respective churches, but developed slowly among the farming population. The remaining Russian Orthodox communities east of Edmonton lay outside organized Ukrainian life. The ULFTA's support in the bloc was particularly strong around Two Hills and Smoky Lake, and branches existed in other parts of the province where Ukrainian workers congregated. To most Ukrainians, however, social and recreational needs were at least as important as politics, and the local national hall (or labor temple where the left wing dominated) continued to perform a vital social role.

Early in World War II, the Canadian government outlawed the pro-Soviet ULFTA. Reemerging after the USSR became Canada's ally, the left enjoyed brief popularity at a time when the traditionally anti-Soviet, anticommunist Ukrainian nationalist organizations had to curb their sentiments. During the 1945 federal election, for example, the Labor Progressive candidate for Vegreville, William Halina, felt free to criticize Hlynka's stand against continued Soviet rule in Ukraine and attempts to involve Canada in the "Ukrainian question" at San Francisco; he denounced Hlynka for "idiotic utterances," for meddling in the affairs of another country, and for putting Ukrainian-Canadians "in a shameful and ridiculous light."[71] The ULFTA's postwar successor, the Association of United Ukrainian Canadians—facing the full force of the cold war, the anticommunism of the third immigration, and decreasing social isolation and poverty on the part of Ukrainian-Canadians—has never recaptured the strength of its predecessor.

In 1940, to unite Ukrainian-Canadians behind the Canadian war effort, the major national noncommunist organizations temporarily buried their differences and formed the Ukrainian Canadian Committee. It was retained after the war, with branches across Canada, as a permanent coordinating superstructure, although its usefulness and effectiveness over the years were increasingly questioned by those active in organized community life.[72]

The years since World War II have produced new secular organizations. The Ukrainian Canadian University Students' Union and the

Ukrainian Professional and Business Federation have enjoyed relatively high public profiles. The former has been particularly active in the areas of multiculturalism, civil rights, and defense of Soviet dissidents; during the late 1970s Ukrainian students at the University of Alberta ably edited the organization's newspaper, *Student*, and made it one of the more interesting in the Ukrainian community. The Ukrainian Professional and Business Federation was formed to rectify inadequacies thought to exist in the Ukrainian Canadian Committee, and it hoped to attract many of those (Canadian-born, professionals) alienated from traditional Ukrainian organizations.

The organizations introduced by the third immigration have had little impact on Alberta outside Edmonton and Calgary, and their support comes basically from the third immigration itself. The Canadian League for Ukraine's Liberation, associated with the radical right wing of the Organization of Ukrainian Nationalists, and the Ukrainian scouting movement, Plast, are the largest. They have urban branches, and their members play a prominent role in community life, but they are largely irrelevant to the old rural bloc. Organized Ukrainian-Canadians in the postwar years have continued to argue for what they feel are their language and cultural rights in Canada and to publicize Russification, political subjugation, and the denial of civil rights in Ukraine.

In spite of the Ukrainian community's prominence, Ukrainian organizations today are experiencing problems. An outdated immigrant leadership is being criticized, membership is low, financial problems exist and the proliferation of rival groups makes the pooling of resources difficult. The Canadian-born are increasingly detached from Ukrainian issues and find many of the organizations (with their European roots and emotional associations) less relevant to their lives than the Kinsmen Club or the local Chamber of Commerce. Many have no wish to become part of the divisiveness and infighting. The result is that Ukrainian organizations are failing to attract the younger men and women who should be their natural replacements, although some are stressing dance and choral groups and social activites to draw members.[73] In recognition of these problems, the Ukrainian Community Development Committee, operating in the three prairie provinces, undertook in the mid-1980s a comprehensive community needs study on which to base future programs and strategies. It is uncertain, however, whether the 90 percent of Ukrainian-Canadians now outside organized community life will be lured back, develop their own institutions to reflect their cultural Ukrainian-Canadianism, or remain uninvolved.[74]

Identity and Assimilation

With ever-growing numbers of Canadian-born, allegiance to the traditional Ukrainian churches has dropped, intermarriage has risen, Ukrainian as a mother tongue has slipped below 50 percent (in 1981 Ukrainian was the domestic language in only 17.9 percent of Ukrainian-Canadian homes),[75] and "ethnic" community structures have increasingly failed to satisfy the needs or represent the interests of Alberta's

The Ukrainian tradition of painting Easter eggs is still very much alive today. Canadian-born Ukrainian-Canadians are discovering many ways of expressing their Ukrainian identity in a modern setting. (Courtesy Provincial Archives of Alberta)

Ukrainians. Many identify themselves as "unhyphenated" Canadians and have lost a sense of ethnic distinctiveness.[76] At the same time, Ukrainian jokes in the popular culture of the province would seem to indicate that the old image of the "stupid Ukrainian" still persists and continues to set the group apart.[77]

Nevertheless, the picture is not entirely negative. A recent study found that Ukrainian was used more frequently on a daily basis in Edmonton than in other major Canadian cities, even though its speakers were less fluent, suggesting that conditions in Edmonton are more favorable for the maintenance and practice of the group culture.[78] There is a widespread and growing interest in things Ukrainian, particularly in the realm of the visual folk arts, as many Albertan Ukrainians are rediscovering their heritage and trying to make it meaningful to their lives. Others who have retained little from their "roots" but an anglicized Ukrainian surname still share a bond with other Ukrainians in their eating habits: *pyrohy* (dumplings) and *holubtsi* (cabbage rolls) symbolize Ukrainian cultural identity at its most basic level. Ukrainian dancing, Easter egg painting, embroidery, and cooking classes are attracting not only Ukrainians who wish to preserve the culture of their ancestors, but other Albertans as well. It is in this public recognition and absorption of Ukrainian art forms and folk culture that a distinctly Ukrainian impact is now being made on Alberta.

Conclusion

Ninety years' residence in Canada has changed the Ukrainians from immigrants into citizens active in all walks of life. From farmer to court judge and musician, Albertan Ukrainians contribute to the life of the province. Few individuals add a uniquely Ukrainian dimension to Alberta's society. As a group, however, the Ukrainians have visibly enriched the province's economic, cultural, political, social, and religious life.

CHAPTER ELEVEN

The Romanian Community in Alberta
Howard and Tamara Palmer

Introduction

The history of Romanians in Alberta is closely intertwined with the history of the Ukrainians. There are two main reasons for this close relationship. First, most of the Romanians and nearly half of the Ukrainians in Alberta came from the same province in the Austro-Hungarian Empire—Bukovina—and both left for the same economic reasons. Second, a majority of each group settled in the same east central region of the province; consequently, the processes and stages of pioneering which the Romanians faced were almost identical to those which the Ukrainians experienced. The Romanians had been used to living in peasant villages with the Ukrainians in Bukovina and, to a large extent, they re-created this pattern in Alberta. With the exception of the Romanian settlement at Boian, the small, rural communities which they established were among Ukrainians. In this way, as in others, they transplanted the peasant life they had known in Bukovina.

However, the histories of the two groups are not identical. Unlike most of the inhabitants of central and eastern Europe the Romanians are not a Slavic people; rather, they are descendants of the Dacians and the Romans, who conquered the area of what is now Romania in 106 A.D. Since their language grew out of Latin, it is related to French, Spanish, and Italian, though it has absorbed substantial Slavic elements from neighboring peoples. In addition to having different cultural and linguistic origins than the Ukrainians, the Romanians in Alberta have also developed their own unique patterns of adaptation. They have never been as nationalistic or politicized as the Ukrainians and, therefore, have not been subject to the same degree of political turmoil; nor has religion been as divisive an issue for them as it has been for their Ukrainian neighbors.[1]

Despite their distinguishing characteristics, the Romanians in Bukovina at the close of the nineteenth century had much in common with

the Ukrainians. Both were agrarian, peasant people who lived close to
the land. Their cultures—homes, food, clothing, music, dances, folklore,
art, and customs—were similar and they shared a common Orthodox
faith. Given this similar cultural background and their intermingling in
both Bukovina and Alberta, it is not surprising that the two groups have
had similar overall patterns of adjustment and that their histories in
Alberta are, in many ways, parallel.

To define a Romanian is not an easy task. The national boundaries of
Romania have been subject to frequent shifts which, along with the
population's movement in the area, led to the development of multi-ethnic settlements in the country's border regions. As one scholar has
explained

> As the frontiers changed, groups of non-Romanians were incorporated within
> the national boundaries and groups of Romanians were left out of the coun-
> try. These changes made the immigration history of Romanians in North
> America more difficult to understand: the United States and Canadian census
> bureaus as well as various demographers and historians writing about Roma-
> nians in North America had at various times different definitions of who was
> a Romanian.[2]

People of Hungarian, German, Jewish, and gypsy origin (in addition to
those of Roma. 'an ethnic origin) have at various times also come to
Alberta from Ror. ·ia.

The Pioneers: 1890-1913

The first wave of Romanian immigrants came to Canada at the turn of
the century from Bukovina, which was then within the boundaries of the
Austro-Hungarian Empire. The population of Bukovina, which in 1900
numbered around 800,000 people, included 31 percent Romanians, 41
percent Ruthenians (an early term for Ukrainians), 13 percent Jews, 9
percent Germans, with a sprinkling of other eastern Europeans. At that
time, the peoples of Bukovina faced profound economic problems. The
major difficulty was the pernicious combination of overpopulation and
limited land, complicated by the absence of any substantial industry.
Successive generations had divided and redivided their land as it was
passed from father to sons. As a result, at the close of the nineteenth
century, 90 percent of Romanian landowners possessed less than the five
hectares required for mere subsistence; indeed, 75 percent had less than
two hectares. There were many peasants who did not even own that
much land; rather, they worked on the estates of noblemen and could
survive only by going into debt. Since interest rates were mercilessly
high, varying from 50 to over 100 percent, debt bondage became a way
of life for many. It was in order to escape these dismal conditions that
sizeable numbers of Ukrainians and Romanians emigrated from Bukovina to Canada.[3]

The first people from Bukovina to settle in Alberta were Ukrainians.
They had been preceded by Ukrainians from the neighboring Austrian
province of Galicia, who had first come to Alberta in 1891 and 1892 and

were entering in substantial numbers. In 1897, Ukrainians from Bukovina became part of this massive outpouring of people, and they continued to come to Alberta, unabated, until 1913; in fact, Alberta became the main Canadian destination for Ukrainian settlers from Bukovina. They developed a solid settlement bloc north of a line running from Krakow to Kalel and, extending north to the North Saskatchewan River, including such communities as Shepenge, Andrew, Wostok, and Shandro. North of the river, the Smoky Lake district formed the core of a Bukovinian settlement, extending west to Vilna, Bellis, and Spedden. This Bukovinian bloc covered a total area of 2,997 square miles. This was the region where the first Romanians in Alberta would also make their homes.[4]

However, the first Romanians who came to Canada settled, not in Alberta, but in Saskatchewan. During the 1890s and early 1900s, they established communities in the southern part of the province, near Regina. Because of these early settlements, Saskatchewan was to become and remain the largest center of Romanian settlement in the country until the 1950s.[5]

The first Romanians to settle in Alberta chose land in the predominantly Ukrainian bloc in east central Alberta, undoubtedly having heard about it from their friends and neighbors in Bukovina. They came in 1898 from Boian in Bukovt of the Ukrainian Soviet Socialist Republic. Although the town of Boian in Bukovina was almost entirely Romanian, Ukrainians from neighboring villages had come to Alberta in 1897. The first two Romanian settlers were Iachim Yurko and Elie Ravliuk. They liked the land which was still available just four miles east of what was later to become the village of Willingdon and they named the area Boian, after their home town. The land was rich in grass, lakes, creeks, and forests; the grass could feed livestock, the lakes and creeks could provide fish and water for themselves and their animals, and the trees could provide building material for homes and fuel for fires. The new settlers were also attracted to this land because it was rolling, covered with bush and dotted with streams, like their homeland in Bukovina.[6]

In their letters home, Yurko and Ravliuk encouraged their former townsmen in Boian to join them in the new country, and soon thirty families organized themselves for the journey to Canada. In the spring of 1899, two groups of immigrants packed their belongings, travelled by cart to the railhead, then by train to Hamburg, by boat to Halifax, and finally by train again to Edmonton. The newcomers then purchased or hired teams of horses and wagons and journeyed northeastward to the land where they would make their new homes.[7]

Among the Romanians who arrived from Boian prior to 1900 and who formed the nucleus of the settlement at Boian, Alberta were the Cuciurean, Cozub, Feica, Gorda, Harasim, Hauca, Hutzcal, Iftodi, Isac, Kelba, Moscaliuc, Murariu, Mihalchan, Matei, Porozni, Petruniak, Ravliuc, Romanko, Surca, Tkachuk, Sirbu, Soprovici, Svecla, Toma, Yurko, and Zaharichuk families. They were soon joined by other settlers from Boian, Bukovina, and by January 1901 there were nearly 100 Romanian families in the Boian district. Smaller groups of Romanian settlers established themselves in the rural districts of Ispas, Shepenge, Midway, Malin, Hamlin, Desjarlais, Shalka, Borowich, Zhoda and Soda Lake—all of which were within a twenty mile radius of Boian. Several families of Romanians, most of whom were trilingual (Romanian, Ukrainian, and German), also settled in the Smoky Lake region.[8]

A fascinating glimpse of an English Canadian reporter's view of the newcomers appeared in the Calgary *Albertan* in the spring of 1909. It is worth quoting in full since it gives an impression of the newcomers who had just completed a journey of several thousand miles:

> A mixed party of Romanian and Bulgarian immigrants excited a great deal of comment, by their curious clothing and footgear, at the C.P.R. depot yesterday afternoon and evening. The party, which numbers about twenty, and is composed of men, women and children, are on their way to Edmonton. While waiting for the train this morning, they encamped in one of the old waiting rooms at the depot.
>
> In appearance they are very dark, and particularly the children possess more than their share of good looks. All wore big earrings, the women and girls excelling in this particular, and also in the matter of varicolored clothing. Bright shawls draped over one shoulder formed a part of everybody's outfit. The men all wore top-boots and even the small boys of the party had gayly colored trousers tucked into the tops of small topboots, reaching midway between the knee and ankle.
>
> None of the party can speak English, but they were apparently enjoying themselves and in the best of spirits, when visited by an *Albertan* reporter and a C.P.R. policeman last night. The new arrivals are of exceptionally fine physique, and altogether appear to be a desirable class of immigrants.[9]

The early Romanian and Ukrainian settlers were usually lumped together by government officials and journalists as "Galicians." Indeed, only events in Europe during the World War I, and the postwar arrival of a nationally conscious wave of immigrants, led to a strong sense of distinctiveness between the two groups. Prior to these events, even the immigrants themselves did not have a highly developed sense of national identity; they thought of themselves primarily in provincial terms, as Bukovinians or Moldavians.[10]

The Romanians faced all the same challenges which confronted other pioneers in Alberta: building homes, breaking land, trying to obtain capital to purchase livestock and needed supplies. Once the men had built a temporary shelter and dug a well, many left in search of work, having to walk the eighty miles to Edmonton before they could learn of job opportunities. While they worked outside the settlement, their wives not only took care of the children and the aged, but also tackled the chores of pioneering alone. Many began to enlarge their clearings, to start gardens, to gather roots and berries; some were skilled and strong enough to build their own log homes.[11]

Whether built by women or men or, most commonly, by a group of people, the Romanian homes were generally very similar to those constructed by the Ukrainian pioneers from Bukovina; they were generally rectangular, two-roomed, mud-plastered log buildings with thatched roofs, and they always faced south. Although the homes of all the Ukrainians and Romanians were very similar, the dwellings which were built by pioneers from Bukovina, whether Ukrainian or Romanian, had characteristic wide overhanging eaves which formed a porch. In contrast to the more stark Ukrainian structures, the Romanian homes also had carved detail on the projecting exposed ends of the wooden beams. Many of these homes are still standing, attesting to the craftsmanship of their builders and the durability of their design.[12]

Like all pioneers, the early Romanian settlers had to be resourceful to cope with their isolation and poverty. Although lack of food was a serious problem for them, they were eventually able to raise enough crops and livestock to survive the year, with the help of their large gardens, wild mushrooms, roots, and berries. They grew sunflowers and poppy seeds which they pressed for oil to use in cooking; they ground their own grain which they made into bread and baked in large outdoor ovens; they caught fish which they pickled, salted, or dried for later use. From the hemp plant they obtained vegetable oil and processed a coarse fibre which they wove into horse blankets or made into rope. They made their own soap using waste fat and lye made from ashes. In the early period, weaving was done by hand, first with drop spindles and later with spinning wheels; their clothing, tablecloths, bedspreads, and other textiles were usually homemade in the old country style. The early settlers also had to be self-sufficient with regard to medical services. There were no doctors; consequently when illness struck, they depended on home remedies concocted from herbs and roots. At childbirth, they were attended by their own midwives.[13]

Motivated by a desire to retain the life they had known as well as by necessity, the Romanians maintained many elements of their eastern European folk culture. Because they were concentrated in a bloc, they had the support of a congenial community. This enabled them to cooperate with and assist one another and to build familiar institutions which lessened the shock of their transition to a new land. By 1921, the first census year in which there is a detailed breakdown of people of Romanian origin in the province, of the 2,017 people of Romanian descent in Alberta, 818 lived in the Victoria electoral district, which included all the Romanian settlements near the North Saskatchewan River.[14]

Origins of Community Institutions

The Romanians at Boian were devout followers of the Orthodox religion and soon after their arrival in Alberta, they made plans to establish a church. In 1901 a group met to select a site for the church building and a cemetery; two years later, work began on the first Romanian church in Alberta. The site chosen was on a hill surrounded by trees and bushes. Built entirely by volunteer labor, the church, named St. Mary's, was constructed in the style of the church in Boian, Bukovina. Work was completed in the summer of 1905, thus making it the second oldest Romanian Orthodox church in North America, the first having been built in Regina in 1902. Since there was no Romanian priest in Alberta, a

Russian Orthodox priest, who was located in nearby Wostok, was invited to consecrate the new edifice. This was done on 2 August 1905. Although few of those assembled could understand the priest's words, the adults felt comfortable with the familiar ritual and with the sense of permanency which the church gave them.[15]

The Romanian Orthodox church at Boian and those that were built shortly thereafter in the nearby districts of Romanian settlement in east central Alberta were visible symbols of the degree to which the Romanian settlers had begun to feel at home in Alberta. They had built next to the Ukrainians, their Old World neighbors, in a place bearing the name of their former home town. They lived in houses similar to the ones that had sheltered them in Bukovina. Now they also had an Orthodox church which was a profound expression of their feelings about who they were and what made life meaningful. In the community of Boian, as well as in other Romanian communities in Alberta, the Romanian Orthodox church would be the focus of community life from the days of earliest settlement to the present.

Despite this idyllic beginning, the history of the Boian church was troubled. The lack of Romanian Orthodox priests in the area and the availability of Russian Orthodox priests created conflict. The only Orthodox priests available to the Romanian settlers were either Russian or Ukrainian. However, the Romanians were not entirely satisfied with this arrangement since they wanted to hear their own language in church. In 1908, the temporary presence of a Romanian priest from Saskatchewan precipitated an internal conflict between the Romanians and the Ukrainians, who had begun attending the same church. Ultimately, the courts decided the case in favor of the Russian Orthodox faction, thus forcing the Romanians to build another church. It was built at Hairy Hill, three miles from the first building. The settlers immediately secured a Romanian priest to preside over it. Ultimately, however, the Romanians were able to regain control of the Boian church through the presence of Vasili Cohan, a Romanian-speaking priest sent to the parish by the Russian Orthodox Church in 1924.[16]

Cohan, who was born in Bukovina in 1897 and had spent some time in Manitoba, served the Boian church for a total of ten years (1924-29, 1932-37) and gained the affection of his parishioners. The length of his stay and his rapport with the people were unusual in an area where the turnover rate for priests was generally very high. From 1907 to 1940 there were at least sixteen priests—some Russian, some Ukrainian, and some Romanian—who served the parish at Boian, which did not always have a resident priest. Most priests considered Boian a remote, unattractive posting without much financial support for the priest. Cohan's cultural background, however, was similar to that of his pioneer parishioners. He was not as highly educated as some of the other priests who came to Boian; consequently, he had more in common with his parishioners.[17]

While the Romanians were establishing churches to reaffirm their ties with the past, they were also becoming concerned about the place their

Rev. and Mrs. Vasili Cohan, Boian, 1926. Rev. Cohan served as priest for ten years in the Romanian Orthodox Church in the main Romanian settlement in the province. (Courtesy Provincial Museum of Alberta)

children would have in Canada. Many of the settlers were anxious for their children to attend school. Consequently, in 1908, they organized the Boian Marea School District, and the school opened for its first session in the spring of 1909. Another school, Bojan, was located just four miles east of the Boian Marea, and the majority of children who attended were also of Romanian background. However, most of the Romanian pioneers did not have high educational aspirations for their offspring. Their large families were difficult to support and subsequently many of the second generation in the period prior to 1930 received only a few years of elementary education before they went to work or were married.

At first, communication with the English-speaking teacher in the new one-room school at Boian was difficult: none of the fifty-six pupils in the first class knew any English. But gradually the children began to learn. In the early years, classes were held only from 1 May to 1 October. In winter, road conditions and the lack of proper winter clothing made attendance virtually impossible. However, with the passing of pioneering conditions and with the increase in the number of students, the school year was eventually changed to the winter months and new rooms were added. In 1927, the Boian school became one of the first three-room rural schools in Alberta.[18]

The school helped prepare the Canadian-born generation for life in Canada through a curriculum which stressed patriotism, loyalty to British institutions, and the three Rs. The priests and the parents helped preserve the Romanian language by establishing Romanian language classes and by continuing to use Romanian at home. In the Boian school, nearly all of the students were of Romanian background and, though at times the school's teachers officially forbade its use, Romanian was the language of the school yard. Indeed, the few Ukrainian children attending the school had to learn Romanian out of necessity. On the other hand, in neighboring rural areas, Romanian children were outnumbered by Ukrainians; consequently, they became fluent in Ukrainian as well.[19]

Mining Camps and World War I: Romania

Boian and the area surrounding it was the only part of the province where Romanians were able to settle together as a sizeable group and establish their own institutions. But Romanians did settle in other parts of the province. The largest concentrations outside of the Boian district were in the urban areas and mining camps. The only other rural concentration of Romanians in the province was at Taber in southern Alberta, and even here there were just a few families. Romanians formed one of the smallest eastern European groups in the Crowsnest Pass, Canmore, Drumheller, Edmonton, and Coal Branch mining camps, but a sizeable number (350 people by 1921) lived in and around Lethbridge and worked in the mines.

The origins of the Romanian community in the Lethbridge area are somewhat obscure. Near the turn of the century, a number of Romanians, mostly young single men, came to work in the nearby mines, joining existing groups of Slovak, Hungarian, and Ukrainian miners from neighboring regions of the Austro-Hungarian Empire. Few of the Romanians had previous mining experience; they began working in the mines hoping to earn money which would enable them either to homestead successfully, or to return to Bukovina to buy land. Ultimately, however, many of them never did homestead. Instead, they remained in coal mining, despite the unfavorable working and living conditions, because it provided them with relatively good and steady wages. Some were forced to abandon their dreams of becoming farmers because the harsh conditions of mining camps and the difficulties of adjusting to a new society prompted them to resort to the solace of drink and gambling, and they became caught in a hopeless trap of debt and alcoholism.[20]

The Romanian miners who settled in the Lethbridge area developed a lifestyle similar to that of the other central and eastern European miners who formed such a sizeable part (30-40 percent in most places) of the workforce in Alberta's mining camps. The miners and their families lived in constant fear of death or injury, since fatal accidents were an all-too-common occurrence in the coal mines. Mobility was also a constant fact of life because of the seasonal nature of the work; the mines operated during the winter, but in spring and summer, miners were obliged to look for other employment. There was also a good deal of movement between mining camps.

The mining towns were built upon a definite system of social stratification, with the Anglo-Saxon miners occupying the best jobs. For the eastern European miners who occupied the lower rungs of the social ladder, living conditions were often primitive. Their houses were jerry-built and cramped, and their wives had to be resourceful managers. Almost all of them had gardens and kept animals, and the miners hunted and fished to supplement food supplies. Their wives also made clothing and soap. They collected grain from between the cracks in empty grain cars to feed their chickens and they salvaged wooden slabs from the railway to build additions on their homes or chicken coops. Being able to grow their own food was important at all times. It became crucial when the miners went on strike.[21]

Single males predominated among the Romanian miners: in 1921, for example, Romanian males outnumbered the females in the Lethbridge area by almost two to one. Hence, a boardinghouse tradition developed in which several young men would live with a family. This arrangement often made for overcrowded conditions, but it enabled young men to live cheaply in a milieu in which they could use their own language and be understood; it also enabled struggling families to supplement their incomes. With the Romanians, as with all eastern European groups in the province, large families and meagre resources also led to the encouragement of early marriages for girls.[22]

The Romanians living in the mining camps gradually became an almost indistinguishable part of the larger Slavic immigrant working class, with its hard-working, hard-drinking, mutually supportive, and sometimes violent lifestyle. Some of the Romanians and Ukrainians had intermarried in the old country; in Alberta, they and their families were gradually absorbed into the larger and more active Ukrainian community. Many of the central and eastern European groups in the various mining areas attended each other's social and cultural events; they were too few to establish their own churches or cultural institutions. Those who were religiously inclined moved in several different directions, but the Roman Catholic church and other Orthodox churches appear to have been the most common destination. Nearly all of the mining camps had a Ukrainian Labor Temple, which became the social center for many Romanians, since it provided a varied program of dances, cultural activities, and left wing politics as well as a membership largely from Bukovina. Lacking the support of a cohesive and organized ethnic community, the Romanians were more prone than other central and eastern European groups to assimilation.[23]

Since the Romanians came from the Austro-Hungarian Empire, the outbreak of World War I put them, along with all other minorities whose origins were the same—Slovaks, Czechs, Hungarians, Poles, and Ukrainians—on a difficult footing in Canada. Although they had little or no personal investment in the outcome of the war or, indeed, very little awareness of its causes, they suddenly found themselves under government and police suspicion and subject to a number of restrictions. Across Canada, 5,954 "Austro-Hungarian" immigrants were placed in internment camps, most of which were located in western Canada. The majority of internees were either miners who had been discharged from their jobs because of pressure exerted on mine management by other workers, or urban workers who had been discharged by their employers, often in response to hostile public opinion regarding "enemy aliens."[24]

For most Romanians in Alberta, the war did not mean internment.

Most of the Romanians were farmers and the authorities had no intention of interning them during wartime when food production was so important. Consequently they were subjected to the more simple inconveniences of being required to register with police and be fingerprinted, of having to surrender their firearms (a hardship to those who needed their guns for hunting), and of losing their right to vote under the Wartime Elections Act of 1918, which disfranchized "enemy aliens." However, a few Romanians, mostly miners, were interned in camps in the Rockies as prisoners of war. They were freed in May 1917 only after the Romanian government, then an allied power, intervened on their behalf. An example of the absurdity of this internment policy appears in the September 1916 official report from the internment camp at Field, British Columbia. Among the list of sixteen Romanian internees giving their occupations, regions of origin, and ports of embarkation and arrival, was Nestor Hulunga from Bukovina, whom the report listed as having been in Canada for seventeen years and having come at such a tender age that he was "too young to know" what port he had sailed from or where he had arrived in this country. However, for government purposes, since he had been born in Austro-Hungary, he was indeed an "enemy alien" and had to be interned.[25]

The Arrival of a New Wave of Immigration and the Coming of Age of the Canadian Born: 1920-1940

The 1920s brought a new wave of Romanian immigration to Alberta. This new group was less than half the size of the first wave and was, for the most part, simply absorbed by the existing community. The newcomers settled in Romanian districts, began farming, joined Romanian Orthodox parishes, and—in the case of young single men—often married the daughters of the pioneers. Although the immigrants of the 1920s faced many difficulties in their adjustment to Canada, particularly the problem of arriving on the eve of the Great Depression, their path was eased somewhat by the existence of an already established Romanian community, developed beyond the pioneering stage. Communication and transportation had improved, and the life of the new immigrant was not as isolated as the pioneers' existence had been. Also, the newcomers were generally better educated than their predecessors, enabling them to adapt more easily to the Canadian environment. Far more important, however, to the community's development was not the new immigrants, but a Canadian-born generation.

In the aftermath of World War I, Romania had acquired Bukovina. Thus, the second wave of immigrants came from an independent Romania. Most of the approximately 600 newcomers were classic examples of chain migration. As members of the families of Romanian settlers who had already established themselves, they were sponsored by their relatives or friends in Canada. Economic conditions in Bukovina were not as desperate as they had been at the turn of the century. Land reforms had been put into effect which were improving the lot of the Romanian peasant; nevertheless, some were still anxious to emigrate. In Canada, the railway companies were predictably eager to have people to settle their unsold land and to provide freight and traffic for their steamship and railway lines. The needs of these two groups—restless prospective emigrants and Canadian railway companies—were ultimately served by the Railways Agreement, whereby farm laborers and domestics were recruited by railway steamship agents and encouraged to emigrate to Canada.[26]

Some of the people belonging to this second wave of Romanian immigration to Canada came from the middle class. Those able to speak French as a second language preferred to settle in Montreal where a Romanian community had been established before World War I. Those who came to Alberta were generally from a farm background. They usually worked as farm laborers or on railway building and section gangs before they were able to save enough money to establish their own farms. Because they were often sponsored by Romanian families and naturally wanted to be near people with whom they shared a common language, religion, and often family ties, most of the new immigrants settled in the existing Romanian settlements of east central Alberta. However, the period of Romanian immigration was short-lived. The impact of the Great Depression forced the government to change immigration regulations reducing the flow of all immigrants to a mere trickle. Romanian immigration virtually ceased.[27]

The 1920s and 1930s marked the peak of Romanian cultural activity in and around Boian. With the pioneering stage at an end, with gradually improving transportation, and with the presence of newcomers and a Canadian-born generation, there was sufficient time, energy, and talent for the emergence of significant cultural expression. The settlers organized Romanian concerts and plays, revitalized a number of customs, and celebrated Romanian holidays. One important tradition of the year was the staging of a "King Herod" play during the Christmas season. The men dressed in costumes reminiscent of biblical days and went from house to house to present a short play about Christmas and to collect money for the church. The church continued to play its central role in cultural and social events. The ladies' auxiliaries to the Romanian churches sewed and embroidered folk costumes for various religious and festive occasions. Weddings remained very important social events in the community. The elaborate festivities continued for as long as three days and often attracted as many as 500 people who came to join in the eating, drinking, and general celebration.

Social activities in Boian and similar settlements were not, however, confined to events which were church-related or were expressions of Romanian folk culture. Like people in so many other small, relatively isolated communities across the province, the Romanians made their own fun. Skating parties, picnics, baseball and basketball games, and other social activities provided a warm, secure atmosphere in which young Romanian-Canadians could grow up, socialize and establish life-long relationships.[28] Michael Toma, who was born in Boian and attended school there during the 1920s, remembers:

Romanian wedding at Boian, 1926. Weddings were a major social event in the Romanian community, with festivities lasting from two to three days. Note the Romanian-style architecture of the home. (Courtesy Provincial Museum of Alberta)

In retrospect, the hungry thirties were possibly the most active years in Boian despite the lack of money. There were many people in the district, many young people. Children attended the local school and their voices could be heard at recess and at noon and on their way to and from school . . . On Sunday a goodly number of parishioners attended the church services, to listen to the gospel, to hear the choir or to exchange a bit of gossip. Should there be a wedding ceremony, and nearly all weddings were held on Sunday,

The Boian baseball team in the 1930s. The popularity of baseball indicated the degree of assimilation of the Canadian-born into Canadian society. At the same time, sports competition provided a focus for Romanian-Canadian community pride and solidarity. (Courtesy Mike Toma)

the church was sure to be packed. Dances were held regularly in the community hall. But to me as a youngster Christmas was the most joyous occasion. The school children always put on a two or three hour Christmas concert on the last school day. The adults put on a two or three hour Romanian concert on the eve of Jan. 6th. And then the following day there were the carollers who went from door to door.[29]

While these social and cultural activities were flourishing in and around Boian, important economic, political, and social changes were occurring which would profoundly affect the area. During the 1920s, Boian had developed as an active rural community which boasted a full range of institutions, including a school, a church, a community hall, a post office, and some commercial services. But in 1928, a CPR branch line was built from Edmonton to Lloydminster, bypassing Boian. This led to the permanent commercial decline of the community and the subsequent growth of the villages of Hairy Hill and Willingdon, which were situated on the rail line, just a few miles south of Boian. While the growth of Hairy Hill was short-lived and its population never surpassed 100 people, Willingdon emerged as a sizeable village and gradually became the main marketing center for the Romanians of the Boian area. By 1941, Willingdon had a population of 420. This shift in commercial patterns had a social consequence: since 75 percent of the populations in both Hairy Hill and Willingdon were of Ukrainian origin, when the Romanians increasingly shifted their focus to these communities, they became further linked to the Ukrainian majority.[30]

A Ukrainian group performing for Romanians at Boian, ca. 1930. The Ukrainians and Romanians had been neighbors in Bukovina in Europe, and were also closely linked together in Alberta through social activities. (Courtesy Provincial Museum of Alberta)

Being a minority in the area, Romanian young people were much more likely to learn Ukrainian than for the reverse to occur. Many of the Canadian born of Romanian origin grew up being trilingual, speaking Romanian, English, and Ukrainian. With the coming of age of this new generation and the growth of the new towns, interaction between Romanians and Ukrainians increased. Commerce, schools, and community dances led to greater interaction between the two groups. Intermarriage between the Canadian born of Ukrainian and Romanian origin became relatively common. Their sharing of a common religion usually enabled the young people to overcome most of their elders' objections.

Yet, despite increased mingling between Romanians and Ukrainians, at the institutional level, the two groups were diverging. A second wave of Ukrainian immigration during the 1920s, which included a number of more highly educated and nationally conscious people, contributed to a growing sense of Ukrainian identity among the earlier Ukrainian settlers from Bukovina and helped lead to the establishment of a new set of secular Ukrainian organizations. The Romanians, on the other hand, who had an ancestral country of their own, could never quite understand the intensity of Ukrainian national consciousness—an intensity nourished by deprivation since, in the modern period, an independent Ukrainian nation existed for a mere two years, from 1918 to 1920.

Social ties between Ukrainians and Romanians in east central Alberta were strong, but the Romanians—though in the minority—were able to maintain their own sense of identity. Even in the districts where the Ukrainians formed the majority, the Romanian families remained active in community life. In many cases, a Romanian chaired the school board or operated a post office and store. At Desjarlais, Andrei Fedoreak was a long-time member of the school board and operated the post office. Vasile Basaraba at Ispas and Grigori Toma at Malin were long-term school board members. In Willingdon, Nick Fedorak operated a store, M. Toma and Nick Svekla were among the community's first teachers and John Porozni served as the first president of the locally influential Willingdon Agricultural Society which was started in 1941. Many Romanians were able to play important community roles not only because they were capable people, but also because of their trilingual communication skills.[31]

The Canadian-born generation, all educated in English, had naturally been more influenced by the larger Canadian society than had their parents. In addition, they had acquired skills which enabled them to integrate with the dominant society. They brought the Romanian community closer to the mainstream of Alberta's rural society.

During the 1920s and 1930s, many young Romanians moved into occupations other than farming and mining by entering teaching or establishing small businesses. During the 1920s and 1930s Romanians became significantly involved in politics for the first time. Many became supporters of the UFA. The career of George Mihalcheon, an important leader in the Romanian community and the first MLA of Romanian origin in Alberta, illustrates both of these trends.

Born in Boian, Bukovina in 1893, George Mihalcheon came with his father to the Hairy Hill area in 1901. George's father, a widower, had little money to provide for his young children and his married daughter and her family. In 1908, at the age of sixteen, George decided that the only way to avoid the inevitable necessity of always wearing hand-me-down clothing was to make some money of his own; consequently, he worked as a hired hand for a nearby rancher. After nearly three years of this, he decided that he wanted more education. Since he had only grade one from a Romanian school in Bukovina and knew very little English, he had to start at the beginning. At the age of eighteen, the dedicated young man, determined to learn English, went to school in Vegreville. He completed grades one through six in one year. By 1917 he was able to graduate from high school and enroll in the Camrose Normal School in order to become a teacher. Throughout his schooling he supported himself by doing odd jobs.[32]

Mihalcheon was the first of several young Romanians who became teachers. Teaching was perhaps the most obvious means of social advancement for farm children. It was a familiar role and respected by rural people. In addition, there was a shortage of teachers in Alberta and only one year of study beyond high school was required. After completing the Normal School course in 1918, George was hired as the teacher for the Boian school, where he remained for seven years.

During his early years as Boian's teacher, Mihalcheon married Mary Lutzak, a girl of Ukrainian origin, whose family had settled near neighboring Shepenge at the turn of the century. The young teacher, who had a surplus of energy, became a driving force in the community, helping to institute a coop store and a community hall and organizing sports events. In addition, he became involved in the Boian local of the UFA and the United Farm Women of Alberta.

In 1926 Mihalcheon resigned as a teacher and ran as the UFA candidate in the Whitford riding. He was successful and served as the area's MLA for one term, until 1930. Since the Whitford constituency was predominantly Ukrainian, Mihalcheon's being able to speak Ukrainian and English, as well as Romanian, was essential to his being elected. But eventually his Romanian background became a political disadvantage. By 1930 there was a growing feeling among Ukrainians that they should have their own representative, and many UFA supporters feared that unless they had a Ukrainian candidate in the riding a Liberal candidate of Ukrainian background would be elected. Consequently, though he had received the UFA nomination, Mihalcheon was asked to step aside in the provincial election of 1930. Mihalcheon continued to farm and run a store in the Hairy Hill area and, throughout his career, to interpret the dominant society to the Romanian community.[33]

George Mihalcheon's strong support for the UFA was typical of the generation of Romanians who grew up in Canada. The organization articulated their grievances about the role western farmers played in the country's economic policies. In the 1921 federal election—the first which the UFA contested—114 of the 115 votes cast at Boian went to the UFA candidate. While the UFA did extremely well in rural areas across the province, the level of support in Boian was exceptional: it reflected the success of the UFA drive to bring central and eastern European immigrants and their children into the movement. This overwhelming support for the movement was gradually eroded in subsequent elections, but the UFA did play an important part in the life of the community, introducing it to the importance of provincial politics.[34]

By 1931, there were 1,366 people of Romanian origin in census district #10, which included the major areas of settlement near Boian and Hairy Hill. The Ukrainians outnumbered the Romanians nearly three to one. The second wave of Romanian immigration and the emergence of the Canadian-born generation was, by this time, creating land pressures in the Boian area, which prompted the establishment of secondary Romanian settlements. In the late 1920s and early 1930s several Romanian families from the Boian area settled in the Peace River country north of Manning, at Notikewin and Hotchkiss, and built a small church. Others settled closer by on land north of the North Saskatchewan River, and some went north to Lac La Biche. A few Romanians also moved to the Cold Lake-Grand Centre area on the Alberta-Saskatchewan border and became part of the Romanian-Orthodox parish at Pierceland, just five miles inside the Saskatchewan border.[35]

Dispersion from the original area of settlement occurred in response to an urgent need for new land created by large families and by the tendency of the second generation to remain in farming. Both trends are reflected in the lives of Nicolae Hauca and his wife Domnica who came to Canada at the turn of the century. They established a farm in the Boian area and raised sixteen children, including twelve sons, eight of whom decided to remain in farming. This was not an isolated example. Large families were the rule, obviously posing an enormous challenge for parents to provide them with support and care, as attested by Mrs. Hauca's busy weekly schedule, which included the ironing of at least thirty-six shirts. When the children of such families came of age and

The women of St. Mary's Church, Boian, in 1938 with Rev. Vasili Cohan. (Courtesy Provincial Museum of Alberta)

Nicolae and Domnica Hauca and their sixteen children in Boian in the 1930s. (Courtesy Mike Toma)

began looking for land on which to establish themselves, the need to expand into new areas became increasingly urgent.[36]

Farm life during the 1930s was not easy. All of the domestic work had to be done by hand. During the depression, pioneering patterns of self-sufficiency reemerged. While families had comfortable homes and plenty of food, they had no money to buy luxuries of any kind, such as new clothes or furniture, and they had to delay purchases of tractors and other farm equipment.[37]

The impact of the depression undermined UFA support in the Romanian community. Many Romanians like other rural Albertans, were attracted to the Social Credit movement, despite its alien religious fundamentalism. Like so many other Albertans facing the depression, they found the Social Credit promise of $25 per month irresistible. Romanians were stronger Social Credit supporters than most Ukrainians in the surrounding area. The latter were more inclined during the 1930s to support the CCF or Communist parties.[38]

Romanian support for Social Credit continued through the 1940s and 1950s. However, under the leadership of John Diefenbaker, the Conservatives presented themselves as the party of western and ethnic interests; Romanian loyalty began to shift to the party which in the 1935 and 1940 federal elections combined had received only one vote in Boian. This new Romanian allegiance has continued to the present day and most are proud that a fellow Romanian-Canadian, Bill Yurko, has served in Conservative Premier Lougheed's provincial cabinet in several portfolios and represented an Edmonton riding in Parliament. Yurko, born and raised in Hairy Hill, is a chemical engineer who managed several chemical plants in the United States before returning to Edmonton in the 1960s. At both the federal and provincial levels, Yurko has developed a reputation for independent thought and action.

Southern Settlements

While the 1930s marked the peak of Romanian activities in the Boian area, for Romanians in the Lethbridge vicinity, the interwar years were marked by numerical decline and assimilation. The mining camps were badly scathed by the depression. Even during the peak winter season, miners were laid off or forced to accept one or two days' work per week. Many had no alternative but to go on relief. Many of the miners moved to other parts of the country in search of work or turned to farming in hope of sustaining themselves and their families. As a result, the number of people of Romanian origin in the Lethbridge area declined steadily between 1931 and 1941, from 637 to 179. The miners and their wives who remained in the area often turned to small-scale market gardening and poultry raising to feed their families and help provide some income during these difficult years.[39]

The Paulencu family, who lived in Lethbridge during the years of the depression and World War II, illustrate many typical patterns of Romanian immigrant life in southern Alberta, including early roots in mining, a strong desire to escape the social environment and the dangers of mining camp life, and a general trend toward assimilation. Nicholas Paulencu grew up on Bukovina and in 1910, at the age of sixteen, came to Canada alone. Though his original dream was to return to Romania, he would live his life and raise his family in Alberta and become respected as one of the best CPR engineers in the southern part of the province.

At first, Paulencu lived in a Staffordville (north Lethbridge) boarding-house, run by a Romanian family, while he worked in the mine. He saved as much money as he could in order to repay his father the $200 he had borrowed for his passage to Canada. But he did not like mining, so soon hired on with a CPR section gang and gradually worked his way up to the position of fireman. In 1929, he married Veronica Pintiliciuc, a Canadian-born girl whose Romanian parents, along with many other Romanians, homesteaded in Manitoba at the turn of the century. The two met because their mothers had grown up together in Romania. After living for a year in Frank, Alberta and another year in Shaunavon, Saskatchewan, Nicholas and Veronica decided to settle in Lethbridge, where they moved in 1931, just as the full force of the depression was beginning to be felt.

Work on the railroad was scarce. Nicholas had to be content with working on the "spare board," substituting for other engineers or simply cleaning engines. But Paulencu was committed to "making good" in his new homeland. He changed his name to Paulence, learned English at night school, and included among his friends people from many different cultural backgrounds. Wanting to escape the working class environment of north Lethbridge, Paulence established his growing family in a small home in an English-speaking, middle class neighborhood in south Lethbridge. His three daughters took music lessons and attended the United Church. At home Veronica continued to cook Romanian food on occasion and Nick maintained many Romanian friends, but overall they identified with the dominant society.

A shock hit the family shortly after the German invasion of central and eastern Europe in 1941. While the Paulence daughters, absorbed in the activities surrounding church, school, and music, grew up with little awareness of or interest in their Romanian cultural background and numbered among their friends of some of the most respected middle class families in the city, they and their family were suddenly and forcibly reminded of their roots when Romania became involved on the Axis side of the struggle. As a result, all people of enemy alien descent in Canada, including Nick (who had left Bukovina before it was even a part of Romania) had to report to the RCMP for fingerprinting. The Paulence girls had their first taste of prejudice in some classmates' taunting questions about their loyalty to Canada.

After the war, however, the bitterness of those years quickly subsided. The Paulence family continued on its chosen course of assimilation, with each of the girls ultimately marrying outside of the Romanian community. While no story of a Romanian family is entirely typical, the Paulence story illustrates the ambition, mobility, and the tendency to assimilate which characterize many Romanian families in Alberta.[40]

Census figures help us to understand the changing settlement patterns and demographic base of the Romanian community during the interwar years. The number of people who declared "Romanian" as their ethnic origin increased from 2,017 in 1921 to 4,712 in 1931, and subsequently decreased to 4,206 in 1941. The substantial increase between 1921 and 1931 reflects the growth of the Romanian community during the 1920s, which resulted from a high rate of natural increase combined with a new wave of immigration. The largest concentrations of Romanians in the province in 1931 continued to be in the Lethbridge area, in the two largest cities and in the predominantly Ukrainian bloc in east central Alberta.

How does one explain the slight decline in the number of Romanians in the province in 1941? Some had willingly returned to their homeland during the depression or had been deported, since circumstances had forced them to go on relief. Yet, more likely the decline was more a shift in the way people reported themselves to the census takers than a significant decline in actual numbers. The decline can be largely accounted for by Germans or Ukrainians from Romania declaring themselves to be of German or Ukrainian origin at the time of the 1941 census.[41]

In 1941, three-quarters of the province's people of Romanian origin still lived in rural areas and there was no organized Romanian communal life in the cities. But this changed dramatically during the war and postwar years, and Romanians gradually became an overwhelmingly urban group. Edmonton gradually assumed the dominant role in the communal life of Alberta's Romanians and both Edmonton and Calgary attracted people of Romanian origin from rural Alberta and rural Saskatchewan as well as new groups of Romanian refugees in the late 1940s and 1950s and later in the 1970s.[42]

Wartime, Urbanization, and the Development of Romanian Organizations: 1940-1980

The wartime hysteria against Canada's aliens had only touched the Romanian community lightly. Although Romania had joined the Axis side under the leadership of fascist dictator Ion Antonescu, it was extremely difficult to implicate Romanians in Alberta or accuse them of disloyalty. Seventy percent of Alberta's Romanians were Canadian born. They were such a small group that they were almost inconspicuous and, in any case, most Canadians were ignorant of Romania or Romanian politics. Romanians were subject to all of the "enemy alien" regulations, including the stipulations that they surrender all firearms and report regularly to the police, but the larger public in Alberta was too preoccupied with the loyalty issue in regard to the Italians, Germans, Japanese, and Hutterites to turn their attention to such a small and previously noncontroversial group as the Romanians. The absence of any political organizations among them also prevented the paranoia which erupted in the spring of 1940 over the Germans and Italians (and in late 1941 over the Japanese) from affecting attitudes toward Romanians. Consequently, for most Romanian-origin people in Alberta, the war period was a time of increased assimilation as their young men left to join the armed forces, and of relative prosperity as prices for farm produce soared and steady work returned in the coal mines.[43]

The immediate postwar years brought many changes for Alberta's Romanian community: continued urbanization among the Canadian-born second and third generations and the arrival of a new group of immigrants whose region of origin, social background, and motivation for emigrating were all completely different from those of the two earlier groups of immigrants.

This new wave of immigrants was composed of political refugees from displaced persons' camps in Germany, Austria and Italy. In general, compared with a number of other European nationalities, few Romanians had been able to escape as there had been relatively little opportunity to flee before the arrival of Soviet troops in the summer of 1944. The Red Army quickly set out to implant the Romanian Communist Party in effective power.

Although elections were held in Romania in 1946, the country's communists instigated a reign of terror in which the leaders of the other political parties were arrested and either executed or sentenced to prison. Only a few were able to escape. In December 1947, the King was forced to abdicate and Romania was declared a "People's Republic." Those who did manage to escape included many professionals and some aristocrats, all of whom were sophisticated, well-educated people, often fluent in at least two, if not several, languages. Thus, unlike the earlier immigrants, who had been farmers and laborers, this new wave included people from the middle and upper classes of Romanian society.[44]

Most of the Romanian refugees settled in Montreal, Toronto, and other urban centers in Ontario, where they established refugee organizations and their own periodicals. Montreal was a particularly popular choice for them, since close ties had long existed between France and Romania, and most educated Romanians had learned French as their second language. However, some did come to Alberta. Though their numbers were few (229 Romanian immigrants came to Alberta between 1948 and 1955), they had some impact on the province's Romanian community.

For all of those who came to Canada and to Alberta, the experience of their escape had been a traumatic one, the details of which remain vividly etched in their memories to the present day. Among those who came to the province were some leading Romanian politicians and some members of the Romanian aristocracy. Lucien Greciano, an engineer, and Georges Cretzianu, a finance minister in the Antonescu's Fascist government, both worked in Calgary before accepting major business and finance positions in Montreal. Prince Constantin Soutzo and his family also immigrated to Alberta. Three years after the major part of their extensive properties had been confiscated by the communist government, they managed to escape by Soutzo posing as a Russian officer. Despite this trying experience, Soutzo, his wife, Ioana, their son, and two stepdaughters were able to establish themselves in a new country. They had salvaged enough money to purchase in 1948 the "Ricardo Ranch," 3,400 acres situated along the banks of the Bow River east of Calgary and formerly owned by Senator Patrick Burns. Princess Elizabeth Soutzo, Prince Constantin's mother, also came to Alberta during the 1940s. She worked as the Director of Nursing Services at Taber General Hospital for eight years and became an active participant in professional and service organizations and in the Anglican church in Taber until her death in 1963.[45]

Another Romanian refugee family which established itself successfully in Alberta was that of Trajan and Florica Nitescu. The son of a civil servant from Oltenia, Trajan Nitescu had been educated as a mining engineer and had advanced to the top of his profession. He had served as managing director of Petrofina and Standard Oil of New Jersey in the oil fields of Romania. He had been president of the Association of Engineers and Technicians of the Romanian Mining and Petroleum Industry and, for a brief period in 1941, had served as deputy minister for mining in the wartime government. Nitescu had travelled in the United States during the 1930s and so was familiar with the North American oil industry.

At the end of the war, he became active in a political organization which hoped to deliver Romania from communist domination but when members of the group began to be arrested in early 1948, Mr. and Mrs. Nitescu went into hiding for six months before escaping by swimming across the Danube River into Yugoslavia. They were immediately arrested by Yugoslav officials and spent a painfully trying 1½ years in Yugoslav jails. Finally, through the intervention of Mr. Nitescu's former employers, Petrofina, and the Belgian legation in Belgrade, they were able to leave Yugoslavia and go to Belgium. At that time, Petrofina was deciding to open operations in North America; consequently, Nitescu was sent to Canada and to Calgary, as managing director of the company's Canadian operation. He remained in this position until his retirement in 1967, helping to build the company into a major competitor in the oil fields. Well educated and cosmopolitan, the Nitescus fit easily into the inner circles of the oil industry. He became a member of the most exclusive clubs in Calgary, where he found his staunch anticommunism highly compatible with the prevailing political philosophy of Calgary's oilmen.[46]

The Soutzos and the Nitescus were just two families among a number of former aristocrats and professional people who fled Romania and ultimately came to Alberta. Urban, educated, politicized, and bearing a strong, upper class Romanian consciousness, these newcomers found they were separated from earlier Romanian immigrants both by their urban location and by strong cultural barriers. While those who went to Edmonton could participate in a small, but growing, Romanian community, those who went to Calgary simply formed informal groups with Romanian friends, since the number of refugees was too small to permit the development of Romanian organizations.

The movement of displaced persons to urban centers in Alberta coincided with a major trend toward urbanization among the Canadian-born Romanian-Canadians. With the discovery of the Leduc oilfields, many new economic opportunities developed in Edmonton. Young men who would previously have become farmers suddenly found a wealth of other possibilities in various trades, real estate, and small business, all of which primarily required skill and ambition and only minimal formal education. Of course not all of these young people were content to stay in Alberta; some moved to the United States.

The transition to city life was not too difficult for farm boys since they could easily put their manual skills to work in the construction industry. In Edmonton's booming economy, real estate and other businesses, such as hotels, were lucrative and had the added advantage of freeing those who were able to establish themselves from dependence on the good will of employers at a time when having an eastern European name was still often an economic handicap. Young people who moved to the cities shared a depression-born determination to achieve social and economic security. They wanted to provide a better life for their children than they had experienced; this determination, combined with hard work and economic opportunity, resulted in significant success for many, including a number of farm boys who became near-millionaires.[47]

The move by Canadian-born Romanians from east central Alberta into Edmonton was certainly not unique during the late 1940s and 1950s. Many Ukrainians from that area were making the same move; their patterns of mobility and social adjustment were similar to those of Romanians. Young people from both groups took advantage of many of the same opportunities for economic advancement (Ukrainians also concentrated in the trades, small businesses, and real estate); growing numbers chose higher education, where they specialized in the professions, including dentistry, engineering, and medicine.[48]

As a result of these changing economic patterns among the Canadian born, the number of farmers and unskilled workers among both the Romanians and Ukrainians declined during the 1950s. Also during this time the Romanians, like the Ukrainians, experienced a slow but steady eclipse of their culture. Marriage outside of the groups became increasingly common. Pressures for middle class conformity were strong and difficult to resist.[49]

Although assimilation was the prevailing pattern among Romanians during the 1950s and 1960s, some organized Romanian activities emerged in Edmonton. In 1948, people who had originally come from the rural areas near Boian and who missed their familiar church and community organizations, met to form a Romanian Orthodox church organization. This group provided a social setting which helped to ease the transition to urban life. However, the group remained small, meeting periodically in members' homes with visiting priests until 1964, when they built a parish hall and began making plans for a church building.[50]

In 1972, on the twenty-fourth anniversary of the founding of the Romanian Orthodox congregation, the group consecrated the Saints Constantine and Elena Romanian Orthodox Church in north Edmonton. The church's architectural style was based on that of a famous church in Vorontez, Romania, built in 1488. Its handmade altar was a gift from the Orthodox church in Romania.[51]

The Saints Constantine and Elena Church forms the core of Edmonton's Romanian community—one-quarter of the Romanian-Canadian families in the city (80 out of the approximately 300) are associated with it. The church provides cultural and social activities for various age groups, as well as religious services. Romanian language classes, the Balada Folk Dance Ensemble (founded in 1972) and the Canadian Romanian Society of Alberta have all been closely connected with the church. The society, whose goals include the preservation and development of the Romanian culture in Alberta, was founded in 1978.[52]

The Edmonton parish belongs to the Romanian Orthodox Missionary Episcopate, whose North American headquarters are in Detroit. This church, unlike the other major Romanian Orthodox church in North America (the Romanian Orthodox Episcopate of America), maintains close ties with the Orthodox church in Romania. A few people of Romanian background object to this close relationship, since the Romanian church must, in order to survive, be subservient to Romanian political authorities. On the other hand, this link has worked to stimulate cultural activity. The ties which the parish maintains with the Romanian embassy in Ottawa and with the church in Romania have facilitated a number of cultural exchanges, including visits to Romania by the Balada dance group from Edmonton.

The growth of activities in the Edmonton community during the 1970s resulted from a number of factors. The Romanian community in Alberta has been affected by broad North American social trends during the 1970s which have encouraged the declaration and maintenance of ethnic identity. The assertion of their group rights by French Canadians and Ukrainians has encouraged others to think in ethnic terms; at the same time the growing anonymity of urban life has stimulated the desire to maintain ethno-cultural connections. The search for one's roots became widely fashionable and government multi-cultural policies have encouraged cultural retention. In addition, Alberta's affluence during

Saints Constantine and Elena Romanian Orthodox Church in Edmonton, 1974. (Courtesy Provincial Museum of Alberta)

the 1970s provided more time and money for cultural matters and the concurrent arrival of a new group of Romanian political refugees enlivened communal life in both Edmonton and Calgary.

In Calgary, the Romanian community became organized for the first time in 1969; its activities centered around a small Romanian Orthodox parish. Although Calgary's Romanian community is smaller and less active than the Edmonton group, its origins and character are similar. The community's major growth occurred during the 1950s, 1960s, and 1970s as a result of fading opportunity in agriculture which sent many young people from the farms to the city. The majority of the approximately 100 families of Romanian background in Calgary did not, however, come from rural Alberta, but from rural Saskatchewan. Like Dan and Sophie Boghean, two of the main organizers of the Calgary group, they chose Calgary rather than Edmonton simply because it was nearer to their original homes in southern Saskatchewan. Despite their predominantly farm backgrounds and little or no postsecondary education, many Romanian rural migrants have achieved financial success through their entrepreneurial skills and hard work.[53]

There are fewer organized Romanian activities in Calgary than in Edmonton and the Calgary group has had difficulty retaining a full-time priest. These organizational difficulties are primarily due to the group's being small and relatively young, with many working wives. The Calgary group belongs to a different Romanian Episcopate than the Edmonton group, and there is considerable rivalry between the two episcopates. Because the majority of the Romanian Orthodox churches in Saskatchewan belong to the Romanian Orthodox Episcopate of America with headquarters in Grass Lake, Michigan, the Calgary group naturally developed the same tie. In 1952, this Episcopate broke away from the patriarchy in Bucharest, which it saw as being too subservient to Romanian authorities.[54]

The range of Romanian activities in Calgary has been limited by the assimilation of the Canadian born and the small number of immigrants. Among people of Romanian background in Calgary, only 20-30 percent are involved in the Romanian community; many of the Canadian born who grew up in rural Saskatchewan communities intermarried and generally did not transmit the Romanian language or Orthodox religion to their children. Third and fourth generation Canadians of Romanian origin may know a smattering of their ancestral language and be aware of their Romanian names, but they have inherited relatively little of the Romanian culture; consequently, they do not at present and probably will not in the future form part of an ethnic community.[55]

The Fourth Wave of Immigrants

The most recent addition to the province's Romanian community has been the arrival during the 1970s of a small number of political refugees. According to immigration statistics from 1970-77, there were a total of 105 immigrants from Romania who gave Alberta as their destination; the majority of these people have come during the most recent years of that time period. As a group, these immigrants are young, urban, educated, and middle class. At present, they are attempting to reestablish themselves in the professions they pursued in Romania.[56]

As political refugees, these new Romanian immigrants braved considerable personal danger in order to come to Canada; indeed, since it is virtually impossible to emigrate from Romania legally, those who left had to be daring. However, disaffection with restrictions on personal freedom in Romania and a desire for improved economic opportunity have motivated a number of people to face the risks involved in leaving. The most common method of escape is to go abroad for professional conferences, congresses, or sporting events and then defect. Some tourist travel from Romania to noncommunist countries is allowed under close government supervision, and defection is also common on these trips. When such means of escape are not possible, some people cross the border into Yugoslavia by swimming the Danube River. From there, they illegally cross the border into Italy, where they ask for political asylum. At this point the Romanian refugees, along with others from eastern Europe, are sent to United Nations' supervised refugee camps and if accepted by the Canadian immigrant authorities, from there they come to Canada. Most of the refugees have technical or professional educations; those who have come to Canada include engineers, artists, veterinarians, and other professionals. There are also some tradesmen and people with service industry experience, such as hairdressers and barbers. There are also a number of athletes among the new Romanian immigrants in Alberta, since international competitions afford an opportunity for escape. These recent refugees are already contributing their special skills to Alberta's society; some have opened modern gymnastic studios in Edmonton. Most of the newcomers are bilingual, though their second language is more often French than English.[57]

Like many other recent immigrants to Canada, the Romanian refugees face two major, interrelated problems—difficulties with language and difficulties with recognition of their professional qualifications. Soon after they arrive, they find themselves caught in the perennial immigrant snare: employers require Canadian experience, which they cannot get until someone will hire them. Besides, since they have left Romania illegally, it is often difficult for them to obtain proof of their professional qualifications. Further, the language barrier makes it difficult for them to pass Canadian professional exams as soon as they would like. This impasse forces most newcomers to find menial jobs for a few years until they can begin to reestablish themselves in their former professions. However, almost invariably, they find that they are unable to ascend the occupational ladder to the same position they had held before leaving Romania; consequently, many feel frustrated, though they are hopeful of future change. As recent refugee and economist, Vasile Matache expressed it:

> Since few Romanian university graduates and technicians came to Alberta until (recently), it appears that we will have to be "pioneers" and through our behavior and achievements to prove our professional qualifications. It will be

a difficult job under the present economic circumstances in Canada, however we have no choice, but the rewards will accrue to those that follow.[58]

The recent immigrants have a somewhat ambivalent relationship with the existing Romanian community. While their educational qualifications are generally better than those of Romanian-Canadians, they are much further down the ladder of economic success. The newcomers grew up in an atmosphere hostile to organized religion and most have absorbed the prevailing agnosticism, or atheism, of contemporary Romanian society. In contrast, the organized Romanian community in Alberta is almost inseparable from the church. Recent arrivals in Edmonton want their children to learn the Romanian language and culture, yet many are opposed to the links which the organized Romanian community has with the Romanian embassy and with the Patriarch in Romania. Although these most recent immigrants are political refugees as were their postwar counterparts, they come from a Romania completely different than the one left by the earlier waves of immigrants. Consequently, a barrier both of age and political and cultural experience separates the groups.

Thus, while the new arrivals appreciate the help they have received from the organized Romanian community in establishing themselves in Alberta, there are many cultural barriers to their participation in that community. Second and third generation Romanian-Canadians, raised in rural western Canada have little, besides language, in common with new immigrants from Romania; even that bond is not always certain since the provincial origins and hence dialect of the recent immigrants differs somewhat from those who came earlier. The relationship is further complicated by the mild paranoia which almost inevitably characterizes the outlook of the new arrivals, as is often true of other recent arrivals from the Soviet bloc; there is always the suspicion that there may be government spies among the refugees. Some recent refugees are reluctant to discuss the details of their departure from Romania, or to have their names used in any public reporting on Romanian immigrants in Alberta since they fear this information might adversely affect friends and relatives at home.

Given these cultural barriers, it would seem unavoidable that at present the new immigrants are more comfortable socially with other recent immigrants than with members of the established Romanian community. Nevertheless, a fruitful symbiosis between the two groups has already developed: the oldtimers are able to introduce the newcomers to Canadian life and help them find jobs, while the newcomers are able to provide the community with an injection of youthful vitality and an awareness of and familiarity with modern Romanian culture. For example, the Balada Folk Dance Ensemble in Edmonton has been guided by a succession of highly talented recent arrivals from Romania.

Rural Decline and Romanian-Ukrainian Relations

Postwar growth of the Romanian communities in urban centers has been accompanied by declining Romanian community life in rural areas. The number of people living in and near Boian has shrunk significantly. Increased farm mechanization has meant that land previously occupied by five or six farm families is now farmed by one, and improved transportation has made it possible for farmers to commute to their farms from nearby towns, such as Willingdon. As in all parts of rural Alberta, young people have consistently been moving out of the area since World War II, leaving an aging population. Several of the Romanian Orthodox churches in small, rural areas have been abandoned, though the Boian church, which in 1974 was declared a provincial historical site, is still in regular use. Although the Romanian-origin population in the Boian district has declined considerably, the community remains a spiritual home for many people of Romanian origin who grew up there and are now dispersed not only throughout Alberta but into many parts of North America.[59]

In the rural areas, the processes of fusion with the Ukrainian community and integration into western Canadian society have continued. Since the days of pioneer settlement, Romanians and Ukrainians have maintained a congenial relationship. In the villages of Willingdon and Hairy Hill, whose populations are still 75 percent Ukrainian-Canadian, people of Romanian origin remain active in community life. In these communities, there is an amalgamation of ethnic consciousness, community pride, and provincial and Canadian identity.[60]

Conclusion

The Romanian community in Alberta is currently facing a number of complex issues and challenges. Although they have prospered economically, they are confronted with a gradual erosion of cultural ties and an increasingly complete assimilation of the third and fourth generations. While members of the second generation, brought up in rural Romanian communities, have strong ties to the Romanian culture and the Orthodox religion, speak Romanian fluently, and maintain many elements of Romanian folk culture in their homes (such as Christmas traditions), the third generation is considerably less fluent in the language; the fourth generation generally cannot speak Romanian at all and is usually not involved in Romanian activities. The organized Romanian community is predominantly composed of people from the second and third generation, with relatively little involvement by the youth. There are some positive factors promoting the community's continued viability: travel to Romania is becoming increasingly possible (given both Canadian affluence and Romania's desire for tourist dollars), and a changed climate of public opinion has made folk culture and ethnic roots not just acceptable, but fashionable. The youthful and dynamic Romanian dance group in Edmonton has attracted not only young people of Romanian background, but also some with other ancestral roots. However, a variety of obvious social trends causes concern to community leaders and dampens their optimism about the future of the Romanian group. Urbanization, mobility, and the passing of the pioneering generation have all led to the weakening of family ties, considerable intermarriage, and a significant decline in the use of the Romanian language. (In 1971 only 205 people or 4 percent of the 4,670 people of Romanian background in Alberta, reported that Romanian was the language most often spoken at home, while 1,225, or 26 percent, still reported Romanian as their mother tongue.) The overall decline in organized religion throughout North America during the 1960s and 1970s also affected the Romanian community adversely since the church and the ethnic community have been so closely linked.[61]

Concern about the third and fourth generations' lack of interest in their ethnic culture is a common phenomenon in nearly all central and eastern European groups in the province; but the concern has been heightened among Romanians not only because of their relatively small numbers, but also because of a widespread lack of awareness in North America about Romania and the related absence of university courses in the country's language, culture, or history. Since it is not a major world language, Romanian is not taught in the school system, and the pioneering immigrant generation who spoke Romanian either exclusively or predominantly is now gone. So, there is neither much incentive nor opportunity for young Romanian-Canadians to learn their ancestral language.

While assimilation of the Canadian born is the most difficult dilemma facing the Romanian community, the question of their relationship to present day Romania is likely to remain a contentious issue within the community. The views of the Canadian born and of recent immigrants will inevitably be different, given their variant needs and perspectives. The Canadian born feel they need cultural links with Romania while the new immigrants still want to protest the political regime from which they fled. These conflicting viewpoints are also reflected in the division between the two different Romanian Orthodox churches in the province, which represent a rift that will not be mended easily. However, it should be emphasized that the question of their relationship to their homeland is not unique to the Romanians, but is repeated in various ways among nearly all of the province's ethno-cultural groups whose roots are in central and eastern Europe.

The similarities and differences between the Romanians and Ukrainians in Alberta offer considerable insight into the significance of size and cultural background in the adjustment of immigrant groups to Alberta society. As has been suggested, the experiences of the two groups have, in many ways, been similar. Each group has had three main waves of immigration at precisely the same times (prior to World War I, during the mid-to-late 1920s, and after World War II), and each wave has been progressively smaller. For both groups, the social origins, occupational adjustment, and location in Alberta of each wave of immigrants have been strikingly parallel. The pioneering experiences and settlement patterns of both groups were nearly identical and a remarkably similar proportion of the total number of each group was scattered in different parts of the province.[62]

Patterns of adjustment for the Canadian-born of both groups have been analogous and the rural-urban shift, the avenues of mobility, and the timing of movement into new professions have also been comparable. The occupational choices made by successive generations in both groups have been very similar as have their responses to outside prejudice. For some people in both groups this response was an ardent attempt at total assimilation, including name-changing; for others, it was a withdrawal into the ethnic community and an accompanying assertion of ethnic identity. Economic and geographic trends were also practically identical in each group: Boian, Ispas, and the other rural settlements underwent the same process of rural decline as nearby Ukrainian rural communities, and after World War II, Edmonton emerged as the provincial center of group life for both Ukrainians and Romanians. The church has played a similarly pivotal role in each group: it has been closely linked with ethnic culture, the clergy has been involved in the cultural as well as the religious life of the communities, and there has been conflict between different Orthodox churches as they have vied for the loyalty of each group.

These are not, of course, unexpected parallels, since the groups shared a common immigrant experience, a similar cultural background, an analogous demographic make-up, and identical economic limitations and opportunities. Romanians and Ukrainians came together from the same areas of Europe for the same reasons, settled in the same areas of Alberta, and inevitably became intertwined through intermarriage and a myriad of social, economic, and religious bonds. The prevailing attitudes of Canadians toward both peoples have evolved simultaneously, with an initial period of prejudice giving way to indifference and finally, in the postwar period, to acceptance.[63]

The Romanian and Ukrainian communities were thus closely linked in many parts of Alberta. Because of their much greater numbers (in 1981 Ukrainians in Alberta outnumbered Romanians thirty-six to one), the Ukrainians overshadowed the Romanians, but did not absorb them; their histories have in some ways been distinct, particularly at the institutional level. Because of group size and minor differences in cultural and historical background, Romanians were not as susceptible to factionalism and internal strife as Ukrainians, their institutional life was not as highly developed, and they were more prone to assimilation. At the political level, neither communism nor rightwing nationalism, both of which had a strong support within the Ukrainian community at certain periods, was particularly successful among the Romanians.

Though their numbers have been small, the Romanians have contributed to the development of Alberta. The pioneering generation, through cooperation and determination, met the challenge of pioneering. For these early Romanians, as for other eastern European peasants, land was the most important criterion of success and that is what Canada provided in abundance. Despite their poverty and their linguistic and educational handicaps, they survived without governmental assistance and helped develop park belt country that most English-speaking settlers felt was too difficult to settle. Each group of Romanian immigrants has made use of its own special background and talents, whether in farming, coal mining, the oil industry, business, or in sports.

The visible signs of Romanian presence in Alberta are few, and the historical center of the Romanian community in the province is no longer the hub of a vital, vibrant community. In the words of Mike Toma:

> If you visit Boian today, you will see the church on the hill keeping watch on the well-kept cemetery, the school below, in the valley, the farmers well-to-do but few and far between. But gone is the laughter of the school children, the ball teams, the Christmas festivities and the Romanian dancing and singing that was heard not so long ago. However, the name Boian lives on and the farmers living there are still proud of their lineage and their heritage and do their best to look after the buildings and grounds where not so many years ago so many feet had trod.[64]

The pioneering immigrants' world has undergone vast transformations. Alberta itself has changed as well. The Romanians, once strange newcomers from a far-away land called Bukovina, have made themselves a new home and have helped to fashion a new Canadian identity in Alberta.

CHAPTER TWELVE
The Polish Experience in Alberta
Joanna Matejko

Introduction

In 1981 the 37,655 people of Polish origin were the seventh largest ethno-cultural group in Alberta, and the second largest Slavic ethnic group. Included among them were the great-grandchildren of the early pioneers who arrived on this continent at the turn of the century, as well as newcomers from the Polish People's Republic.[1] The Polish people in Alberta represent the whole spectrum of occupational, educational, and social levels. They differ profoundly internally. Their integration or assimilation into Canadian society and their attachment to the Polish culture and traditions vary according to their generation, time of arrival, social origin, and personal experience.

For many descendants of the peasant pioneers who came from the most impoverished Polish provinces, their ancestors' motherland is most often associated with Roman Catholic church ceremonies, ethnic food, and folk art. For them, assimilation to Canadian society meant social advancement and higher prestige.

For the political immigrants, who found freedom and refuge in Canada after World War II, Poland's problems are still dear and close. These people are proud of their more than ten centuries of recorded history, of their highly cultured, powerful empire in the late Middle Ages, of their position as defenders of Western civilization and as an "outpost of Christianity." They have remained a romantic people imbued with an intense Polish nationalism, at the same time they have been integrating into Canadian life.

The new immigrants, who arrived during the 1960s and 1970s are mostly well-educated, dynamic, and enterprising people who have quickly become successful in their professions and who are enjoying the privileges and opportunities afforded by an affluent and free society. Their integration into the new world occurs mostly through professional circles, and is quick and relatively easy. At the same time, they maintain

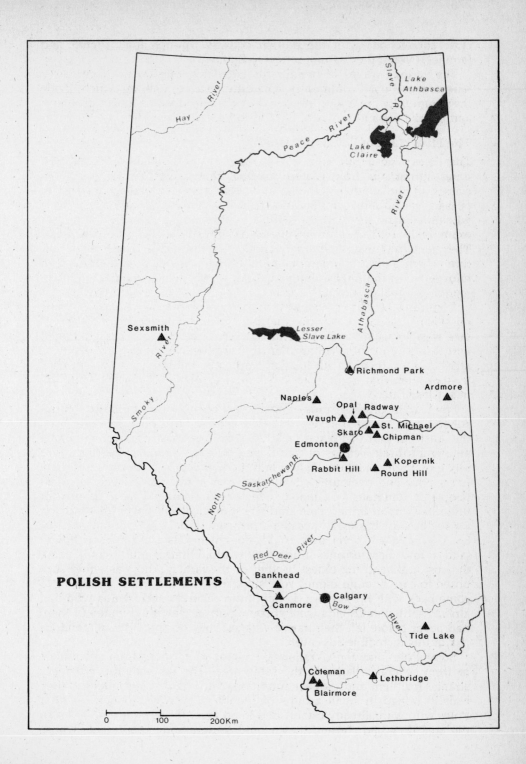

Sexsmith

Lesser
Slave Lake

Richmond Park

Ardmore

Naples

Opal Radway
Waugh St. Michael
Skaro Chipman
Edmonton
Rabbit Hill
Kopernik
Round Hill

Hay River

Peace River

Slave R.

Lake
Athbasca

Lake
Claire

Athabasca River

Smoky River

North Saskatchewan R.

Red Deer River

POLISH SETTLEMENTS

Bankhead

Canmore Calgary
Bow

Tide Lake

Coleman Lethbridge
Blairmore

River

0   100   200Km

close connections with the mother country through their friends and families, even if they cannot return to Poland.

The various waves of immigrants taken together do not comprise a harmonious Polish community. The differences of opinion which divide the community are above all rooted in attitudes toward Polish problems and toward the authorities of the Polish People's Republic.

The First Wave of Polish Settlers

The Poles who immigrated to Alberta prior to World War I resembled other immigrants from eastern Europe. They were part of the lower classes in the mother country, and were rural and village people of peasant background who had obtained little formal education. An overwhelming majority of them settled in the rural areas of Alberta. For example, in 1901, four out of five of Alberta's Poles lived in rural areas. They remained overwhelmingly rural until the 1950s. The foreign culture which Polish immigrants brought with them, and their lack of knowledge of the English language, prevented their immediate involvement in Canadian society.

According to Father Anthony Sylla, one of the first Polish-Catholic missionary priests in Alberta, the first Polish homesteader in the province was Stanislaw Banach.[2] This native of Poznan province emigrated with his parents as a young man to Tacoma, Washington. In 1895 he arrived in Strathcona with his wife and eight children. The Banach family took their first homestead and built a log cabin south of Edmonton, near Clearwater.

From 1896 onward, more and more Polish settlers came to central Alberta, and founded several Polish colonies. Most of them came from the Austrian part of Poland called Galicia, the most impoverished area among all three sections of partitioned Poland. Characterized by a rapidly growing population, Galicia had the highest rural density in Europe. In its poor and overcrowded villages, many immigration agents urged people to emigrate to Canada, which was portrayed as a country of unlimited opportunities. Free land was a magical and powerful attraction for the eastern European peasants. It meant social and economic status. So, they sold whatever they could, bought tickets and left their homeland to find their fortunes in the new world. Often families would share the cost and send the oldest brother or the father, who was either supposed to earn enough money for "shipcards" for the whole family, or to come back with his savings. Letters from relatives and friends who had already settled in Canada were encouraging, and although many of them had never before left their native villages, they accepted the tremendous risk of this incredible adventure.

Some Poles, like the Ukrainians, emigrated in groups from one village or from several villages in the same area. The new country was very strange for them and pioneer conditions very hard. Consequently, they usually settled in small groups of friends or relatives, or joined other Poles who were already established in an area. If there were no Poles in the area they had chosen, they would settle among Ukrainians, whose language they could understand. Prior to World War I the national consciousness of the Polish and Ukrainian settlers was not very strong; many identified themselves with the region they had come from rather than with Poland or the Ukraine.

The most important difference between the Polish and Ukrainian settlers was their religion. Both groups were aware of the differences between Greek Catholic and Roman Catholic liturgy and rites, and they tried to preserve these distinctions. Nevertheless, they cooperated in many ways, even in fulfilling their religious needs. They helped each other with building churches, shared some churches, and attended church services when a Ukrainian Greek Catholic or Polish Roman Catholic priest arrived in the colony.

From the earliest stages of settlement, neighbors in the Polish settlements developed patterns of mutual aid. The settlers who had built their log cabins earlier, shared them with newcomers for weeks or even months until the latter could move to their own homesteads. Neighbors volunteered to construct houses and farm buildings or to dig wells. They borrowed agricultural equipment or horses from each other. When they were better established, they would cooperatively purchase threshing machines and other farm implements.

Almost all immigrants who settled on land prior to World War I had been involved in agriculture in Poland, but they were not a cross-section of the rural population of the mother country. The majority were small farmers or non inheriting farmers. Those who settled on the land came

The family of Stanislaw Banach, first Polish settler in Alberta, ca. 1913. The Banach family arrived in Alberta in 1895, the first of thousands of Polish immigrants who were pioneers in Alberta. (Courtesy Joanna Matejko)

mostly with their entire families or brought their families over after saving some money and selecting a homestead. Almost all practiced mixed farming; this reflected not only their desire to continue familiar farming patterns, but also their concern for security. Mixed farming guaranteed a supply of basic consumer goods needed by the farmer's family. Only after many years of traditional mixed farming did some Polish settlers start to specialize, but the majority practiced diversified cropping to the end of their lives; it was only the second generation that moved toward single crops and commercialization.

To supplement the family savings badly needed for farm improvement, all members of the family contributed their share. The economic role of a woman was even more important in the Slavic than in the Anglo-Saxon farm family. As a farmer's wife, she had to do much more than run the house and bring up the children. The Polish women worked in the fields together with the men, and quite often instead of the men, because many men had to look for work outside their farms: in sawmills, on road and railway construction, in the mines, or as farm hands at better established farms. By working outside they brought some money home, learned farming techniques better suited to the new conditions, and improved their command of the English language; but the women then had the burden of doing all the work on the farm, often with a baby on their backs.

The importance and the centralizing power of the Roman Catholic church and clergy in the history of the Polish community can hardly be overemphasized. The first Polish social institution to be established in the new country, and often the only one, was the church. As soon as a sufficient number of Polish immigrants settled in an area, they built a chapel or a church in which they could worship in their mother tongue according to the customs of their ancestors. Almost all of the Polish pioneers were Catholics, deeply devoted to the Church, the only unchanging element in their lives.

At first, Masses were said in the shacks and log cabins of the pioneers, but three or four years after their arrival the immigrants would build a chapel. Their own church building expressed the immigrants' religious devotion and aspirations, but it was also a symbol of achievement in the new country. For centuries, the founding of churches in Poland had been sponsored by local landlords; consequently, to be a patron or a founder of a church was something extremely honorable in the peasants' eyes.

During the pioneer period, Polish missionary priests were in great demand, and there were never enough to provide services for the scattered homesteaders. The priest was revered as the guardian and guide of his flock, and was treated with utmost respect. In Canada the role of a missionary priest was even more important than in the old country. His functions were not limited to the performance of his religious duties. He also gave advice on family and agricultural problems, mediated between the immigrants and the Canadian authorities, helped with correspondence, acted as an interpreter, brought medicine from the city for the sick, and sometimes served as a doctor. Missionary priests were also active in

Father Anthony Sylla, one of the first Polish priests in Alberta, en route from Exshaw to Canmore, ca. 1913. His diaries are an invaluable source of information about the lives of the early Polish settlers in Alberta. (Courtesy Joanna Matejko)

the field of education, setting up schools and encouraging the Polish settlers to subscribe to Polish Catholic newspapers.

The high regard for priests manifested itself in the great hopes of immigrant parents that one of their sons would become a priest, and the missionaries helped to send several farmers' sons to St. John's College in Edmonton. The teaching at this College was in French, and it was not easy for farm boys to master one more foreign language. It was at this College that an Oblate Brother, Antoni Kowalczyk (1866-1947), spent thirty-six years as a janitor, being a model in religious life for his brethren. There he died in an aura of sanctity, and in 1952 the first steps in the process of his canonization were taken.[3] The first Canadian-born Polish priest in Alberta was Father Stanley Wachowicz of Skaro. Several Polish young men became Oblate priests, and several young women entered convents.

The Early Rural Settlements

Though the majority of Polish settlers were scattered individually and in small groups throughout Alberta, some twenty-two distinctly Polish settlements were developed from the late 1890s to the late 1920s, mostly in the central part of the province. All but two were established prior to World War I.[4]

The first group of Polish settlers came in 1898 from the Czortkow district in Galicia and settled among Ukrainians in the Wostok area northeast of Edmonton. They built a Roman Catholic chapel in 1905 and called the mission St. Michael. They were culturally similar to their Ukrainian neighbors, both in the old and new countries.

The Polish settlement of Rabbit Hill in the Nisku area south of Edmonton stemmed from the 1897 arrival of Sarnekis family, who were joined by sixteen farm families from the same Galician village a year later. Some of these settlers could afford to buy better pieces of land from the CPR or from previous owners and were considered the most progressive among the Polish settlers in Alberta.

The social life of the Rabbit Hill community centered around the church which was built of logs in 1905; a new, larger church was completed in 1917. Twenty-six families of Polish origin have remained in the area. Since the 1950s, the English language has been used in the church because of many mixed marriages; spouses are of Ukrainian, French, Irish, and German origin. Nonetheless, the third generation of Poles in Rabbit Hill has retained their mother tongue.[5]

Skaro (formerly Edna) is one of the best known Polish settlements in Alberta due to the annual pilgrimages to a religious grotto which was erected there in 1919. The community began in 1897 with the arrival of Wawrzyniec Mreczak from Galicia and Jerzy Turczanski, who emigrated by way of Brazil. They were joined by several families of relatives and friends and developed their social life around the church.[6] Intermarriage between the children of Polish and Ukrainian settlers in the Skaro area was fairly common. With the passage of time, the second generation took up homesteads of their own or opened small businesses in the nearby towns, mainly in Opal, where a small Polish community developed.

The Round Hill Polish community in the Lake Demay area was started in 1899 by two Banach brothers. Four years later, when Father Francis Olszewski initiated the Polish mission there, he listed thirty-nine adult men ready to help construct a church. On 17 March 1907, Father Paul Kulawy, OMI, took permanent residence in the newly constructed rectory. For several years the Round Hill mission was his headquarters, from where he visited all Polish settlements in central Alberta.[7]

The Polish mission of Krakow (east of Lamont) was a creation of the first Polish resident priest in Alberta, Father Francis Olszewski. He took a homestead there, and planning to develop a Polish cultural center, he enlisted the help of Polish farmers in Skaro to build a chapel, a small convent for pioneers' daughters, and a boarding school. He also named the newly opened post office in 1904. Unfortunately, a fire destroyed his mission, and Father Olszewski moved to the United States in 1911.[8]

The Polish colony of Kopernik, near Holden, began to develop in 1903 with the arrival of immigrants from two ethnically Polish villages in Galicia's Mosciska district. They came in two groups of several families with enough money to buy horses, wagons, and some agricultural implements immediately after their arrival. The Kopernik farmers constructed a church, a community hall, and opened the Polska school.[9] Three other colonies of Polish origin continued the patterns of pioneer

Religious grotto to the Virgin Mary being built at Skaro by Polish immigrants, 1910. Almost all of the Polish pioneer immigrants were Catholics, and the church played an important part in their lives. Many of those who lived in north central Alberta made annual pilgrimages to the grotto. (Courtesy Provincial Archives of Alberta)

settlement. Polish settlers arrived in Mundare in 1906, Waugh in 1908, and Flat Lake (west of Bonnyville) between 1912 and 1915.

The Richmond Park settlement northwest of Athabasca was small, but significant as the only Polish Protestant community in Alberta. The first settlers, descendants of Poles who had become Protestants during the Reformation, joined the Anglican Church in Athabasca. In the 1920s the settlement was augmented by the arrival of several families of miners who moved there from Canmore. The farms in the Richmond area were quite large and well organized; in addition to farming, some farmers operated sawmills during the winter.[10]

The Chipman settlers built and shared a church with German Catholics; those in Naples did the same with local Italians in the early 1930s. Other small groups of Polish farmers settled at Warwick, Stry, Derwent, Tawatinaw, and Ardmore.

Poles in the Peace River country were dispersed throughout the region, except for the concentration in the Clairmont area, where Joseph Tomczak started homesteading in 1912. His family became famous in the region because of their trio of pet Trumpeter Swan cygnets, which was credited with providing Grande Prairie with its symbol after it reached city status. The birds acted as watchdogs, and followed their

Polish settlers with their harvest at Tide Lake, ca. 1916. Located in one of the driest regions of the province, the settlement at Tide Lake did not survive past the depression of the 1930s. (Courtesy Joanna Matejko)

host's car to nearby Grande Prairie where they became a prime tourist attraction.[11]

In southern Alberta only a few Polish immigrants settled on the land. The largest rural Polish community was established between 1908 and 1912 at Tide Lake, east of Brooks. The majority of settlers were first brought by the CPR's agents from Pennsylvania and Buffalo, New York. By 1911 there were ten Polish families with thirty-one children and six single persons who had taken homesteads at Tide Lake. The community built both a school, called Polonia, and a small chapel. After World War I relatives and friends joined the first colonists. Gradually the Polish farms in the Tide Lake area became larger and larger as the population dwindled. During the dry years of the Great Depression, many of the children of the early settlers moved to the cities.[12]

Other Poles, also from the United States, established themselves in Acadia Valley around 1909, growing into a community of some twenty families by the 1920s. They built a church and preserved the Polish language and traditions.[13] Further south, at Fourways, Pakowki, and Empress, there were small settlements of Polish farmers, also from the United States. These settlements in southeastern Alberta, all located in the driest region of the province, were short-lived.

Miners' Communities

Mining is a centuries old occupation in Poland. It is not surprising that, in addition to establishing rural settlements, Polish settlers also established several mining communities. There were several Polish miners, mostly single men from southern Poland, who lived and worked in the Crow's Nest Pass area at the turn of the century. Only a few had Polish mining experience, but some had been employed as miners and workers in the United States. The majority were farmers and farm laborers who were attracted by relatively good wages. Another group of Polish miners settled near Banff, in Canmore, Bankhead, and Exshaw. There were six Polish families and thirty single men in Bankhead in 1910. The miners were the very first to organize Polish cultural societies in Alberta. A cultural society named *Zgoda* (Harmony) was established in November 1911 in Canmore and the Athletic club, *"Sokol"* (Falcon), was organized for young men in January 1912 in Bankhead. Both organizations included some other Slavic miners, notably Slovaks.[14] Polish miners also worked in the Drumheller, Coal Branch, and Edmonton areas.

The most active Polish mining community was in Coleman. In December 1916, the miners there established the Polish Society of Brotherly Aid to help its members in distress and to protect Polish miners against the discrimination they experienced as "enemy aliens" during World War I. The society issued each member an identity card stating that he was Polish. These documents spared their bearers much grief since they were thus saved from being regarded as Austrians or Germans. One of the main organizers, Jan Liss-Pozarzycki, was not a miner himself, but would eventually become one of the best known community leaders in

Polish miners in front of the Polish hall in Coleman in 1927. The Crowsnest Pass was a multiethnic area with many active ethnic organizations that served many different needs. The Poles were one of the largest and best-organized Slavic groups in the area. (Courtesy Walter Chuchla)

Alberta. Taking the statutes of the National Union of Poles in the United States as a model, he prepared a constitution for the newly established organization.

The society flourished in the 1920s when a new wave of Poles joined their compatriots; in 1927 it had 118 members in Coleman, 36 in Blairmore, approximately 40 in Bellevue, and 48 in Rosedale (near Drumheller). The most active branch was in Coleman which boasted a cooperative store, a Polish language school, a library of 3,000 books, a drama group, choir, orchestra, and a hockey team. The majority of Polish miners were bachelors, or men whose wives were still in Poland. For them the Polish organization was a substitute for family and homeland.

The collective and national consciousness of Polish miners was much higher than that of their fellow countrymen in the rural settlements. Many subscribed to Polish-Canadian and Polish-American newspapers, read books, were interested in political and social problems both in the old country and in the new one, and were more politicized in Canadian terms. Their command of the English language was better because they were exposed to it daily. At the same time, their involvement in the religious life of Roman Catholic parishes was less intensive than that of the rural settlers. The priest had less authority and some Polish miners were strongly anticlerical, a view that was unthinkable among the Polish farmers at that time.[15]

The Second Wave of Immigration

After World War I, immigration from Poland resumed. Many Polish immigrants brought their families to Canada after several years of separation. The men had come intending to earn money and only then to send for their wives and children, or to return home. The outbreak of the war had separated them from their families.

Being an arena of war, the Polish territories were devastated economically. Poles themselves had to fight for their independence. In December 1918, an insurrection broke out in Poznan and spread throughout Prussian Poland. After several weeks of heavy fighting conducted by improvised Polish units, a large part of the Prussian zone was liberated. Between 1919 and 1921, on three occasions Poles in Silesia rose in armed rebellion against the Germans; this resulted in Silesia being placed under Polish administration. In 1919 the Soviet army attacked Poland. The whole nation arose and threw itself into a desperate struggle for national survival. Volunteers from the United States, Canada, and France rushed to help. The commander in chief, Jozef Pilsudski, launched a counteroffensive on 16 August 1920. It resulted in a decisive victory, which determined the fate of Poland. Many Poles who came to Canada in the 1920s had participated in these national struggles, which affected their attitude towards both Poland and Canada.

The introduction of a quota system in the United States in 1921 and 1924 restricting immigration directed the stream of new Polish immigrants to Canada where immigration regulations, though discriminatory, were not as strict. Canadian immigration officials placed Poland among the "nonpreferred" countries from which only farmers, farm laborers and domestics were accepted. Many Polish immigrants came under the Railways Agreement which authorized the CPR and the CNR to procure, select, and settle immigrants from several eastern and southern European countries. Many Poles could not secure jobs in their overpopulated country. Despite agricultural reform, there was not enough land for all the peasants. Thus, the government, while not actively encouraging people to leave, tried to organize emigration the best it could, providing information for prospective migrants.[16]

The influx of Polish immigrants, mostly relatives of Canadian residents, started in 1920. The greatest number during the interwar period arrived between 1927 and 1929, and many were directed to the prairie provinces. Primarily as a result of this immigration, the Polish ethnic group in Alberta grew dramatically from 7,172 people in 1921 to 21,157 in 1931. In 1930 immigration from Poland dropped, and during the next ten years only 4,078 were admitted.

The new group of immigrants differed from the previous wave in many respects: although they had been recruited predominantly from the peasant element, there were also some workmen, policemen, ex-servicemen, small artisans, and merchants who passed themselves off as farm workers. Several frontier guardsmen, for example, came to Edmonton after being dismissed from the service in Poland. A number of these young men had received some occupational training and education in the Polish army. Many new immigrants had acquired some experience in political and social organizations. Their awareness of political and social problems and their national conciousness were much higher than those of the earlier Galician peasants. The new immigrants shared the national enthusiasm for the newly established Polish state. Their level of education was higher than the level of those who had come earlier because independent Poland had made education compulsory. The new immigrants continued to come primarily from southern Poland, but there were also many newcomers from other regions. Many young, mostly single, men found jobs in the packing plants of Edmonton, in construction and in the mines; some were able to buy trucks cooperatively and hauled coal and lumber in Edmonton and the surrounding area. Some small mines in the vicinity of Edmonton were owned by the previous Polish immigrants, and some of the newcomers found employment there.

Edmonton attracted many newcomers who were supposed to settle on the land or to work on farms. The earlier immigrants who had come to Edmonton at the turn of the century had already developed a well-established community centered around the Holy Rosary Roman Catholic parish. The church had been erected in 1912 by a group of about 100 Polish immigrants. The oldtimers welcomed the newcomers from Poland with great hopes and showed appreciation for the role the latter played in rejuvenating the Polish community.

The vigorous young men transplanted their organizational experiences to Canada. As soon as they found places to live and jobs, they tried to find a forum for exchanging experiences, for providing moral support in a strange social environment, for alleviating loneliness, and for preserving Polish customs, culture, and language. In 1927, a meeting of old and new immigrants decided to establish the Polish Canadian Society. This was the first Polish lay organization in Edmonton and it became a leading force in the cultural and social life of the Polish community for over two decades. Many oldtimers joined the organization and gave their full moral and financial support.

During the summer, many single men worked on farms, on road construction, and in sawmills; but in the winter they flocked into the city looking for the companionship of their fellow countrymen, for social and cultural entertainment, and for Polish girls to marry. As a result of this winter influx, the membership of the Polish Canadian Society soon grew to over 100 people. An amateur theater was formed which travelled to many Polish rural colonies, providing rare enjoyment to the isolated communities. Walter Rice, a musician by profession, organized and directed an orchestra. By 1932, the society was sufficiently large and active to build the first Polish Hall in Edmonton.[17] However, as the "roaring twenties" were replaced by the harsher realities of the "dirty thirties," the Polish community of Edmonton diminished considerably. Many single men left for Toronto and other cities in search of jobs. Others took homesteads and dispersed throughout the province. Some joined their relatives on farms when they heard rumors about possible deportations of unemployed workers.

During the 1920s, the Polish government established consulates in Canada and their officials paid considerable attention to perserving the "Polishness" of immigrants. They visited the largest concentrations of Poles, attended celebrations of national anniversaries, donated books and educational aids to schools and libraries, and served Polish communities with organizational expertise. The representatives of the Polish government were well received by the Polish pioneers who rejoiced in the creation of the Polish state.

In 1938, a group of Veterans' of both World War I and of the Soviet-Polish War of 1919-20, broke off from the Polish Canadian Association and established the Polish Veterans' Association. The new organization joined the Federation of Polish Societies in Canada, which was established in 1931 under the guidance of the Polish consuls as the first Polish umbrella organization in Canada. The Federation urged the Polish immigrants to maintain very close relations with the mother country and remain Poles. The Polish Veterans' Association created its own drama group, a brass band, and was very active during World War II raising funds for the war effort. It cooperated with the Canadian Red Cross and helped hunger-stricken Polish refugees in the Soviet Union.

The Calgary Polish community also increased steadily after World War I. In 1921 it numbered 287 people. Ten years later it had 807 people, and by 1941 the number had grown to 1,370. Polish immigrants were attracted to Calgary by job opportunities in the packing plants and in construction. The Polish people in Calgary tried to organize themselves during World War I and build a church, but the community was too small to afford it. The first durable organization in Calgary was a Polish club called "Polonia," which was established in November 1931 with a membership of 25 people. This number tripled within a year. In 1934 it joined the Federation of Polish Societies of Canada. As in Edmonton, the group was created by the new immigrants with the support of the old-timers. Soon, evening classes in English for adults and a Polish Saturday school for children were organized. The first teacher, Karolina Dziuzynska, had only an elementary education herself and, in Canada, had worked for several years as a domestic; but she was full of good will and worked hard. There was no remuneration for teaching and no textbooks when the school was started in 1934. In addition to the English class and Saturday school, the Polish immigrants organized a drama group and choir, and maintained contact with the Polish group in Coleman.

Lethbridge's Polish community numbered only 225 people in 1931 and 412 in 1941. Most were immigrants who arrived in the 1920s as sugar beet workers and gradually settled in the city. They created the Polish Educational Association in 1933. A group of communists created friction in the organization and the group dissolved, since communism was very unpopular among the overwhelming majority of Poles. Polish immigrants were under the strong influence of the Roman Catholic clergy which vigorously opposed communist ideology; in addition some new immigrants had participated in the Soviet-Polish War of 1919-20 and recalled that the Bolsheviks had tried to destroy the newly emerged Polish state. Some of the new immigrants were also strongly nationalistic and brought with them anti-Ukrainian attitudes. Consequently, since in Alberta communist ideology was advocated primarily by Ukrainian immigrants, many of the Polish immigrants were particularly strong in their opposition to it.

The post-World War I immigrants who settled in the rural areas were scattered throughout central and northern Alberta. They rarely joined the prewar Polish communities since there were no homesteads available in those areas. Even the children of pioneers had to look for new homesteads far away from the parental farms. The interwar immigrants established only two new Polish communities—one in the Webster and Sexsmith areas in the Peace River Country where they built a church and Polish hall and one at Ardmore, west of Grand Centre.

The Great Depression struck Polish immigrants with severity. The farmers survived because they practiced mixed farming, but laborers experienced extremely hard times. With their Slavic names and poor knowledge of English, they were often excluded from many jobs. They were afraid to ask for relief because of possible deportation. So they rode freight trains and crossed Canada in search of work. In desperation some tried moonshining in the vicinity of large sawmills and lumber camps. Some individuals who wanted to return home, but who had no money to buy a ticket, asked the authorities to deport them.[18] Others were able to get jobs by bribing the personnel in businesses.[19] Polish workers and laborers felt that they were in a worse position than the Germans or

Jews who were helped during the depression by their compatriots who owned businesses. But there were no Polish businessmen or factory owners in Alberta. A few Polish owners of small coal mines in the Edmonton area did employ Poles, but there was not enough work for all. One interesting description of Polish immigrant experiences in the 1930s is that of a man who had been a village furrier in his homeland. He arrived in Canada in 1928 and wandered across the prairies as a farm laborer. Writing in 1936, he said

> For almost five years I could not earn enough for my clothes. I had to patch old pants and shirts until patches over patches were sewn. Now I stand in the middle of the sea, neither one shore nor the other appears. Nothing to take with me to my country, nothing to do here! Who will know what I await here but my death, the only thing I can expect? If anybody paid my shipcard I would leave at once. I can't earn anything here, as I believed when I was still in my country. . . . Not everybody had as hard life as I described here. Some are successful and have enough money. But all I am experiencing here is sorrow, and in no way can I part with it. It followed me as soon as I left my country to look for success. I tried to hold on to many businesses that always began well but had bad endings.[20]

Mutual help among the Polish immigrants was quite common. Some farmers occasionally gave accommodation to unemployed Polish laborers, and some hid Polish immigrants designated for deportation. Wandering Polish laborers were occasionally the recipients of acts of kindness from Polish Jews, owners of drugstores or grocery stores. As a result of the depression many single Polish men moved from Alberta to the East.

World War II

On 1 September 1939, the German army attacked Poland. The Germans had enormous superiority in weapons and equipment, and within eight days they were at the outskirts of Warsaw. The Polish forces attempted to open a front line when another blow fell: on 17 September 1939, Soviet forces entered Poland from the east. The next day the Polish government and the high command crossed the Romanian border on their way to exile. Several thousands of soldiers made their way by way of Hungary and Romania to France and joined the Polish forces of General Wladyslaw Sikorski. A number of the Polish navy units crossed the Baltic sea and joined the British fleet. The Warsaw garrison capitulated on 28 September and dispersed fragments of the Polish forces fought until 5 October. Germany and the Soviet Union partitioned the Polish territories.

The Nazi occupation policy was designed to completely eradicate Polish culture. It started with the extermination of eminent politicians and intellectuals. All the universities, colleges, and high schools were closed immediately. Many university professors were deported to concentration camps where many of them died. About 3 million people, mostly taken in mass round-ups, were deported to Germany as slave laborers. One million Poles and 3.3 million Polish Jews were exterminated.

From the eastern Polish provinces incorporated into the Soviet Union, approximately 1.6 million Poles, including more than 200 thousand prisoners of war who had been taken by the Russians in September 1939, were deported to Siberia and other Soviet provinces. Many died of starvation, exhaustion, and hard work in the "Gulag archipelago" of the Soviet Union; some 10,000 Polish military officers were executed at Katyn in 1940. After Hitler attacked the Soviet Union in June 1941, the Polish Government in Exile made a pact with Stalin enabling General Wladyslaw Anders to establish the Polish army in the USSR. In 1942 this army was evacuated to the Middle East together with many civilians, mostly the wives and children of the Polish soldiers. The Polish units later fought in the Near East, North Africa, and Italy, while the civilians were sent to India and British Africa at the expense of the Polish Government in Exile.

The outbreak of World War II shocked all Polish communities throughout North America. Polish-Canadians responded to the tragic developments in their old country with great concern. All Polish organizations started raising money for the National Defence Fund which aided war victims, prisoners of war, refugees, and orphans.[21] In 1944 a new organization was formed, the Canadian Polish United Relief Fund, which unified all Polish organizations in a common war-relief effort. The Polish community of Alberta responded with unusual generosity, and organized frequent meetings and special drives to collect money. Many young, and sometimes even middle aged men rushed to the recruiting centers to join the Canadian Forces.

The Refugees and Their Adjustment

The fate of the Poles was decided at the Yalta Conference in February 1945, by the Big Three—the United States, Great Britain, and the Soviet Union. The eastern provinces of Poland, home for many Polish soldiers fighting together with the Allies on the Western front, were incorporated into the Soviet Union and Poland was placed under Soviet domination. There was no "Victory Day" for Poles. The recognition by the United States and Great Britain of the Polish Government in Exile was withdrawn on 5 July 1945. Embittered Polish soldiers in Italy and Great Britain, participants of the Warsaw uprising who had been deported to the German concentration camps in the fall of 1944, political prisoners who survived several years of the Nazi concentration camps, and thousands of the Polish slave-laborers in Germany felt betrayed by the Western Allies. They refused to return to the Polish People's Republic for fear of persecution. General Anders' soldiers dreaded deportation to the Soviet Union for the second time.

Many war veterans decided to come to Canada, passing as farmers (in spite of the fact that they had little knowledge of agriculture) because Canada accepted only farmers and farm laborers. Some officers thought the Canadian medical examination and interviews conducted by the members of the recruiting commission were humiliating. The mother of Marek Jablonski, now a well-known Polish-Canadian pianist, described her husband's experience with the Canadian immigration authorities in 1949 in Great Britain:

> Before the last formalities, we had to present ourselves for a medical check up in Canada House, in London. After the examination, the Canadian doctor finished by feeling Michael's muscles as he would do with cattle, then batted him on the back and said, "For pick and shovel, you will do." Michael almost had a stroke, he felt like hitting this uncouth yokel. He never was so humiliated before. But he only clenched his fists and held his temper. We could not antagonize anybody at that point. I was thinking with foreboding, "What awaits us there? If an educated person like a doctor, can be so insensitive and coarse, what about the rest?[22]

The war veterans started to arrive in Canada in 1948. The first party came to Alberta in November 1946 in a group of over 300 men, most of whom were single. The next large group of about 500 ex-servicemen arrived on 1 June 1947. All were dispatched by the Labor Department from Lethbridge to farms all over Alberta. The heroes of famous battles who broke through the Gothic and the Gustav lines in Italy, captured the seemingly impregnable fortress of Monte Cassino, opened the road to Rome for the Allied forces, and landed in Normandy were placed in Alberta as sugar beet workers and farm laborers on two-year contracts. Canadian immigration regulations prohibited the admission to Canada of all immigrants of all classes and occupations except British subjects, citizens of the United States, wives and unmarried children of Canadian residents, and agriculturalists. All 4,527 Polish ex-soldiers admitted to Canada came under a special assignment, and they had to agree to remain in agricultural employment for at least two years. The homeless and desperate Polish immigrants would accept any conditions to find refuge somewhere beyond the reach of the Soviet Union and the Polish communist government. Most moved to the cities as soon as their contracts expired.

The veterans were followed by Polish displaced persons from Germany and the veterans' families from Great Britain who had spent several years in British Africa or who had escaped from the Polish People's Republic. Several small groups of young women were brought over from the displaced persons camps in Germany to work in hospitals and sanatoriums, or as domestics. Between 1947 and 1951, over 48,000 Polish immigrants arrived in Canada and of these about 3,200 came to Alberta. In the next few years immigration diminished considerably.

The refugees differed from the previous waves of Polish immigrants. Various occupations and social strata were represented among them, from privates to generals, from peasants to aristocrats, from graduates of elementary schools to university professors. For example, among the refugees who settled in Alberta were the families of General R. Wolikowski, a military attache of General Sikorski's government who had been assigned to the Soviet Union; Peter Czartoryski, a member of the most distinguished Polish aristocratic family, and Julian Suski, a high-ranking civil servant and author of several publications in the field of public administration. These refugees settled mainly in urban areas.

In contrast to the contributions of the previous waves of Polish immigrants who were almost all farmers or laborers, those of many of these newcomers were no longer anonymous.[23] However, for the inmates of the Nazi concentration camps and ex-servicemen, it took several years to adjust, to reeducate themselves, and to become established in new professions. The third wave of Polish immigrants to Alberta was for several years underrepresented, as were the previous waves, in business and industry. Poles were unable to bring substantial financial resources with them: all started from virtually nothing. Although there were some exceptions, few of the refugees and veterans established businesses in Edmonton. Most entered the professions or clerical jobs. In Calgary, however, by the late 1970s, there were twenty-two Polish-owned small businesses. The Calgary community also included several building and office-cleaning contractors and over forty professionals of Polish origin, the vast majority of whom were immigrants.[24] In Lethbridge, several veterans established themselves as contractors, carpenters, and plumbers, becoming successful in their businesses and well integrated into the local community.

The overwhelming majority of the Polish refugees and veterans experienced the shock of resettling. A downgrading of occupational status in their first jobs was a common phenomenon. Most of them later improved their situation but many were not able to reach the position they had held in Poland. The culture-bound professions, such as law and teaching, could not be practiced without a perfect command of the English language and without meeting local requirements. Some teachers enrolled in Canadian universities and passed the necessary exams, but lawyers and professional army officers had to change their professions. As they brought with them already well-established views about the social hierarchy of more and less prestigious occupations, it was necessary for them to adjust themselves psychologically and socially to new conditions. Some became bitter and divorced themselves from Canadian realities, living in the past and remembering days of glory on the battlefields. Some found compensation in honors and positions within their own ethnic group where their status was still recognized. Others, on the contrary, cut their ties with the Polish community, especially when they married non-Polish women. Many experienced psychological and emotional difficulties.

For several years, the refugees treated Canada as a temporary asylum and hoped to return to a free Poland. Some were reluctant to apply for Canadian citizenship. The majority never ceased to recognize the emigrant Polish government in Great Britain. In this regard, they exemplify steadfast adherence to principles, even if these principles have lost their significance for outsiders.

The new wave of immigrants joined the existing Polish parishes and exerted a very strong influence on the older Polish community. They rejuvenated some of the existing organizations and created new ones. For more than three decades, the presidents of the Edmonton-based Polish-Canadian Congress in Alberta (an umbrella organization which acts as a spokesman for many different Polish organizations) were former refugees or ex-servicemen. Some of them became also eminent in their professions in Canada including: Dr. C. Rodkiewicz, an outstanding scholar in mechanical engineering; Dr. Henry Wojcicki, a renowned psychiatrist; and M. Domecki, a businessman.

The first organizations were created soon after the ex-servicemen arrived in Canada. The Polish Combatants' Association in Edmonton (SPK) was established in May 1947 as a part of a worldwide association. The first president of the Edmonton branch, Joseph Kaczmarek, was a teacher by profession and an officer in the Polish resistance movement during World War II. He served as a channel of communication for fellow veterans dispersed throughout Alberta, and he acted as a liaison between the Polish ex-soldiers and the Canadian authorities. In 1947 veterans established branches of the Polish Combatants' Association in Calgary, Lethbridge, and Coleman.

The Association was first concerned with providing help for immigrants exploited by unscrupulous employers. Later, after the completion of the veterans' contracts, it provided aid and advice to members seeking employment and accommodation. With the passage of time, political and cultural matters started to play a more important role. The social and cultural life of the Polish communities in Edmonton, Calgary, and Lethbridge became very lively. Weddings were frequent social events. The older immigrants opened their Polish halls and private homes for the newcomers and their activities.[25]

During the 1960s, the postwar immigrants started to build their own halls, often with the support of the older generation of immigrants. They also set up their own Polish language schools, libraries and credit unions. The Polish Alliance Credit Union in Edmonton was organized in 1956 by a veteran, Kassjan Koskowski, with the intention of helping Polish immigrants who did not use banking services to full capacity because of their language difficulties.

Children of the war veterans and refugees as a rule have retained the language except in those families where the mother was not of Polish origin. In addition to their involvement in the Polish language schools, many Polish-Canadian youth were involved in Polish Girl Guides and Boy Scouts.[26] They participated occasionally in dance groups, sport clubs, and short-lived students' clubs at the universities. However, the overwhelming majority of the second generation have not joined Polish organizations.

Several women's organizations have also been very active in the Polish community. The most dynamic has been the Edmonton branch of the Polish-Canadian Women's Federation established in 1958. This nationwide organization strives to preserve Polish cultural traditions, while at the same time developing ties with Canada, and establishes charitable programs. The Federation took part in United Nations festivals, organized food stands and art exhibitions during Heritage Days, prepared welcoming parties for immigrants who were granted Canadian Citizenship, and initiated many social and cultural activities.[27]

Despite their important contributions, the veterans and refugees also generated conflict within the Polish communities. They brought with them the stratification system of prewar Poland and tried to preserve their values and ideas. For example, the Polish intelligentsia were ashamed of physical labor. The older immigrants were already used to the new, more elastic social environment in Canada. They were proud of their economic advancement and could hardly accept the superiority of refugees who had arrived penniless. Differences between new and old immigrants in educational and occupational levels aggravated tensions. In Edmonton, the controversies between the prewar and postwar immigrants were so intense that they eventually culminated in a legal battle over the ownership of the Polish Hall.

Immigrants from the Polish People's Republic

After 1956, due to relaxed regulations in Poland, a number of relatives of Canadian residents were allowed to emigrate. Young people, and even some small families, left Poland for vacations or professional trips to Western Europe and from there applied for permission to immigrate to Canada. In some cases they had previously secured jobs. There were also some highly qualified specialists who left Poland to work in developing countries of Africa, and, after their contracts expired, did not return home.[28]

The motives for emigration were varied. Economic considerations played a fundamental role in many cases, but moral and political factors should not be underestimated. Some new immigrants were tormented in their mother country by a lack of self-fulfillment. Working under what they viewed as an overbureaucratized system, they felt limited. Some specialists were weary of the party policy of promoting its own members regardless of their professional qualifications, and they had no prospects for improving their professional status and material well-being. Settling in Canada opened up many new possibilities. Canada's democratic institutions appealed very strongly to some adversaries of the communist regime.

The new immigrants settled exclusively in the cities, predominantly Edmonton and Calgary, which offered better work opportunities in their professions and a more developed cultural and intellectual life than the smaller cities and towns. Most were well-educated people with university or college degrees. There was a high percentage of technicians and engineers among them, working in various fields of technology and industry. Some found employment at the universities; for example, out of twenty academics of Polish origin at the University of Alberta in the early 1980s, half had immigrated from the Polish People's Republic in the 1960s and 1970s. Among them are professors prominent in their respective fields of research: including Dr. Leszek A. Kosinski, a geographer; Dr. Edward Mozejko, a specialist in Slavic literature; and Dr. Aleksander Matejko, a sociologist. In Calgary and Edmonton several medical doctors also reestablished themselves. Some new arrivals tried their luck in private business, in spite of its being an entirely new experience for them, since private business plays a marginal role in the Polish socialist economy.

Among the last wave of immigrants, the majority of women have had the same educational and professional status as their husbands; they have tried to pursue their own careers in Canada. In Poland, women pursue professions in many areas, such as medicine, pharmacy, and education; consequently, the women were surprised to discover in Canada some sex-related disadvantages in their professional lives.

Recently, the new immigrants' involvement in the social and cultural activities of the Polish community in Edmonton has become more apparent. In 1980, about forty-five of the sixty members of the Polish-Canadian Academic and Businessmen's Club were new immigrants.[29] The Polish Culture Society, with its lecture program, initially attracted academics and professionals, but in the 1980s its membership doubled reaching some 200 people by 1984. The majority were new immigrants of various occupational backgrounds. New immigrants have also helped to establish Polish television and radio programs.[30]

In 1980 and 1981 Poland experienced a major exodus of young people. Thousands of them took advantage of the relaxation of formalities in obtaining passports and left for western European countries to improve their economic situation. Some intended to return home with savings, but after the introduction of martial law in Poland on 13 December 1981, they decided to stay abroad. From the refugee camps in Austria, West Germany, and Italy they applied for immigration to many countries including Canada. The Polish-Canadian organizations sponsored many of them; others came under the government's sponsorship program. In the years 1980-1982, Canada accepted 13,313 immigrants whose last country of permanent residence was Poland, including 2,447 (close to 18 percent) who came to Alberta.

Even though the most recent immigrants were provided with some financial support and with subsidized English language courses, they found their situation difficult due to widespread unemployment in Canada. Economic survival has occupied their effort and attention, and comparatively few have joined existing Polish-Canadian organizations. Nonetheless, a group of dedicated former *Solidarity* activists, who settled in Edmonton, succeeded in organizing a group to promote the *Solidarity* cause outside Poland and to help the Polish people in their struggle for civil rights. The organizers of this association had been released from internment camps in Poland on condition that they leave Poland for good. The communist government tried to get rid of as many *Solidarity* leaders as possible.

The immigrants from the Polish People's Republic are unequivocally bitter in their feelings towards the Soviet Union and the communist system which they recently abandoned, probably with little hope of being able to return, even to visit for many years. However, despite their anticommunist attitudes, the new immigrants have been met by the older political immigrants with some distrust. They were suspected of being indoctrinated with communist ideology in Poland and in some cases have even been publicly accused of being communist agents. Reflecting their experience in a communist country, some of the newest immigrants have demanded numerous services from both the Canadian authorities and the Polish community. Even though the cases of abuse of social assistance by the new immigrants are sporadic, they have nevertheless created an undeserved negative opinion of the new immigrant group as a whole.

Conclusion

Polish pioneers, through decades of persistent work and attachment to the land helped to build the prosperity of Alberta. The first pioneer generation of immigrants passed away with a feeling of accomplishment for having created a better future for their children and grandchildren. Many of the second and third generation remained, on consolidated larger farm units, and introduced progressive, scientific agricultural methods to farm the land that their parents originally cleared.

Nevertheless, the Polish rural settlements throughout the province have experienced steady depopulation since World War II due to technological change and urbanization. Many second generation farmers have retired to the cities. The third generation obtained a much better education than its parents and usually moved from parental farms to diversified urban occupations and professions. Carefully built and beautified chapels and churches, where Polish pioneers used to pray in their mother tongue, now serve English-speaking congregations of various ethnic backgrounds. Remote cemeteries with frequently misspelled Polish inscriptions on gravestones, grottos dedicated to the Virgin Mary, and commemorative plaques, are all reminders that at one time Polish pioneers inhabited this land.

Like that of the early pioneers, the contribution of Polish farmers, farm laborers, miners, road construction workers, and craftsmen who came in the 1920s has remained anonymous. However, the children of these immigrants have been able to achieve a higher social status.

The first two waves of immigrants, whose reasons for emigration were primarily economic, brought to Alberta the lower strata of Polish society, mostly of peasant background. The situation changed considerably after World War II when Alberta received Polish political emigrants including many professionals, scholars, and intellectuals whose names were recognized not only at local but also at national and international levels.

Geographical isolation, lack of language skills and familiarity with Canadian culture, a low level of education, differences in customs and religion, and prejudice on the part of the host society all contributed to the isolation of pre-World War I Poles from the Canadian mainstream. The pioneers established several Roman Catholic missions, and their churches were religious, cultural, and social centers. The better educated wave of Polish immigrants, who arrived in the 1920s established several lay organizations in the cities. The arrival of the refugees and veterans after World War II resulted in the rejuvenation of existing associations and in the growth of new organizations.

The current organizational life of the Polish community in Alberta is dominated by the post-World War II political emigrants. There are now over thirty Polish organizations active in the province including cultural, social, political, educational, ladies-auxiliary, and sports clubs. Some of these organizations are branches of world wide Polish organizations, such as the Polish Combatants' Association, or the Polish Scouts' Association. All these activities suggest the vitality of the Polish community, despite the fact that the children of the political emigrants have rarely joined Polish organizations, that they marry outside their ethnic group and are fully integrated into Anglo-Canadian society. However, the young Canadian-born generation has shown some interest in Polish culture.

There have been several factors unifying the Polish communities abroad in the last few years: the first Polish Pope in the history of the Roman Catholic church, the *Solidarity* movement which received full moral and even financial support in 1980-1981, and empathy for Polish society after the suppression of this movement. This empathy has been revealed in thousands of food parcels and considerable financial help for relatives, friends, and church institutions in Poland.

The new immigrants from Poland have also contributed to the persistence of the Polish community, even if they have not in large numbers joined the existing ethnic organizational structure. The older immigrants have found in the newcomers a new reference group and a new focus of attention. It would seem that the future of Polish ethnic organizations will depend not on the children of the postwar refugees, who have integrated quickly and fully into Canadian society, but rather on immigrants who were educated in the Polish People's Republic and who arrived in Canada during the last two decades.

CHAPTER THIRTEEN

The Hungarian Experience in Alberta
Howard and Tamara Palmer

Introduction

The Hungarians' presence in Alberta extends back to the earliest establishment of coal mining in the southern parts of the province. Hungarian coal miners came to southern Alberta from Saskatchewan and Pennsylvania in 1886; since then, four successive waves of immigration—prior to World War I, during the late 1920s, following World War II, and after the 1956 Hungarian revolution—have arrived. From the 1930s to the 1970s, Hungarians comprised about 1 percent of Alberta's population. In 1981, there were 15,170 people of Hungarian origin in the province. In addition, they have been sufficiently dispersed to have had an impact on almost every region of the province.

The settlement pattern of Hungarians differs from that of other central and eastern European groups. While nearly all other central and eastern European groups formed rural clusters in the central and northern areas of the province, with their city dwellers concentrating in Edmonton, Hungarians formed pockets of settlement throughout the province and settled in large numbers in southern Alberta, with their urban people coming largely to Calgary. Unlike the Ukrainians, Poles, or Romanians, whose largest wave of immigrants came to Alberta prior to World War I, the largest wave of Hungarian immigrants came during the 1920s.

Hungarians in Alberta were particularly affected by the Great Depression of the 1930s. The depression years were difficult for almost everyone in Alberta, but especially for newly arrived immigrants who did not speak English, had few possessions, had little time to establish themselves economically, and had few fellow countrymen to depend on for aid and support. The depression irrevocably altered their lives and exacted an enormous and tragic personal toll in broken dreams and broken families. The newcomers from Hungary were usually among those who were the last hired and the first fired; consequently they faced unemployment and poverty as well as social discrimination based on

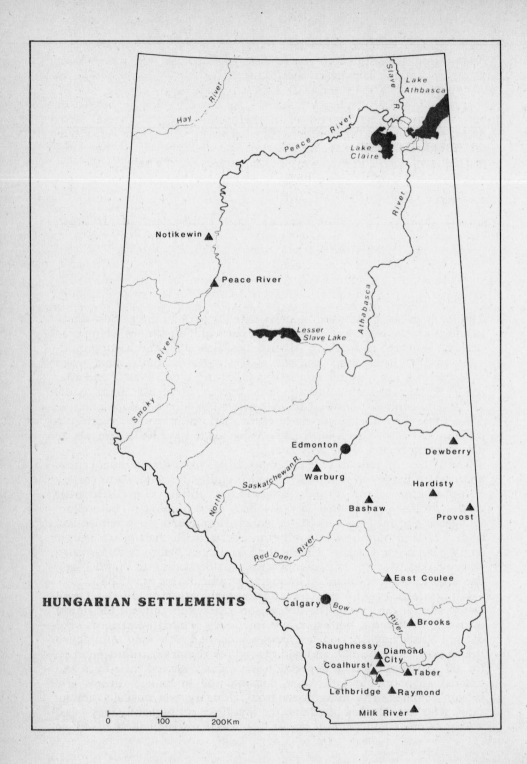

HUNGARIAN SETTLEMENTS

Hay River

Peace River

Slave R.

Lake Athbasca

Lake Claire

River

Athabasca

Notikewin ▲

Peace River ▲

Lesser Slave Lake

Smoky River

North

Saskatchewan R.

Edmonton ●

Warburg ▲

Bashaw ▲

Dewberry ▲

Hardisty ▲

Provost ▲

Red Deer River

East Coulee ▲

Calgary ● Bow

River

Brooks ▲

Shaughnessy ▲

Diamond City ▲

Coalhurst ▲

Taber ▲

Lethbridge ▲

Raymond ▲

Milk River ▲

0   100   200Km

their uncertain status as foreigners. In an attempt to extricate themselves from this hopeless situation, many of these late 1920s immigrants turned to radical politics. However, they found that their political beliefs and activities further jeopardized their already precarious position.

Throughout the chapter, we attempt to show the major differences between the different waves of immigration—important social, economic, and political differences which led to strain and conflict within the Hungarian community. Each wave of immigrants viewed the world in a different way, and each wave of immigrants faced a new set of social and economic conditions in Alberta to which they had to adjust.

The Vanguard

Large-scale emigration from Hungary began in the late 1870s. This first wave, which continued until World War I, represented the largest Hungarian migration to North America; but, of the 640,000 Hungarians who left Europe during this time, only about 5,000 came to Canada and many of this number came indirectly by way of the United States. The Hungarian settlements which these first immigrants established, including several tiny colonies in Alberta, would serve as nuclei for later waves of immigration during the 1920s.[1]

The first wave of immigrants was comprised overwhelmingly of peasants seeking escape from an oppressive social and economic system. Peasant landholdings in Hungary had been subdivided so minutely over the generations that they could no longer support a family; in addition, the mechanization of agriculture had reduced seasonal employment on large estates. Hungary's limited industrial development could not provide enough jobs to absorb the growing number of unemployed peasants and required skilled workers rather than laborers. Many of the displaced and discontented farm workers began to dream of going to North America, and of saving enough money to return to Hungary to invest in land and property. Many of the immigrants who went to the United States worked in that country's eastern coal mines; it was from these communities that the first Hungarians came to western Canada.[2]

The first Hungarians to settle in western Canada did so through the promotional efforts of Count Paul O. Esterhazy (otherwise known as John B. Pach). Esterhazy wanted to remove Hungarian immigrants from the exploitive environment of Pennsylvania's coal mines and help establish them in what he considered the healthier environment of farming. Through the settlements Esterhazy helped to establish in 1885 and 1886 at "Hun's Valley" in Manitoba and at Esterhaz, in what was then the Northwest Territories, Hungarians in the United States and in Europe became aware of the opportunities in western Canada.[3]

The first Hungarians to come to what is now Alberta, originally arrived as part of Esterhazy's plan to build up the Esterhaz settlement. In October 1886, 130 men arrived to help develop the settlement. The Count had planned to quarter the new group in Esterhaz for the winter, but was unable to because of a prairie fire which completely destroyed the new settlement. Esterhazy then arranged for the newly arrived men to spend the winter working in a coal mine near Medicine Hat, which theoretically would have enabled them to support themselves until they could take up homesteads in the spring. However, this plan also fell through. After a short period, the men left the mine claiming that they had been mistreated and "returned to the immigrant shed at Medicine Hat in a half-starved condition with no hope of getting work or food." The government provided them with food during the winter, after which a few took up homesteads in southern Alberta or went to work in the coal mines at Lethbridge (although most of them went to Winnipeg).[4]

Despite these reverses, immigration from the United States and Hungary continued, and new settlements were begun in several other areas of Saskatchewan and Manitoba. The settlers in Saskatchewan gradually expanded their operations. Their numbers continued to increase: by 1911 there were 11,648 Hungarians in Canada, more than half of whom were living in Saskatchewan. Throughout the history of Hungarian settlement on the prairies, the smaller communities which developed in Alberta maintained numerous points of contact with those in Saskatchewan, many of which were predominantly Hungarian and could therefore maintain the Hungarian language and customs and serve as cultural bases for Alberta's smaller and less homogeneous settlements.[5]

While the Medicine Hat experience was brief, the Hungarian coal miners who came to Lethbridge in 1886 formed a more permanent population. Lethbridge offered a combination of opportunities in coal mining and farming which established it as the major center for Hungarians in the province until the late 1920s. Most of the earliest Hungarian settlers to establish farms in southern Alberta had originally come to the area to work in Lethbridge's mines.

Lethbridge's first Hungarian residents were brought from Pennsylvania in 1886 by Sir Alexander Galt, to serve as a source of cheap labor for Galt's coal mines, which had been developed to supply the CPR. The immigrant miners were anxious to leave behind the frequent strikes in Pennsylvania's mines. That winter they were joined by ten settlers from Esterhaz who also wanted to work in Lethbridge's coal mines. All of these newcomers lived in a miniature ghetto of shacks, separated from the main settlement by the railway tracks.

The miners' leisure-time activities did little to endear them to either the local NWMP or the established, primarily Anglo-Celtic, business and professional elite of the growing town. For example, in June 1888 the *Lethbridge News* commented bitterly on the "uncivilized citizens" who had gotten into a fight with the police: "the existence of such a degraded class cannot be tolerated in a civilized community. If they cannot conform to our institutions, the Hungarians and Slavs must go." The Lethbridge community also criticized the miners and their families for Sabbath-breaking, intemperance, and allegedly pushing young girls into early marriages.[6]

For the business and social establishment of Lethbridge, the Hungarian presence provided them with their first experience with non-Anglo-Celtic immigrants. Even if mine management did not expect to pay

eastern European miners the same wages they paid Anglo-Celtic workers, they and the rest of the community did expect the newcomers to
exhibit the accepted British style of deportment. Thus the conflicts
between the two groups were an indication not only of linguistic and
residential barriers, but also of cultural and social barriers which would
persist in Lethbridge until after World War II.

Despite the initial negative reaction to them, Hungarian miners continued to come to the Lethbridge area and by 1901 their numbers were
sufficient for them to organize the first Hungarian Sick Benefit Association in Canada. The organization, which had twenty founding members,
would provide insurance to miners in case of sickness, accident or death,
a much needed service at a time when mining accidents were frequent
and there were no supportive governmental schemes. In addition to its
economic function, the association also played an important social role,
facilitating the maintenance of Hungarian traditions and unifying the
Hungarian working class community. By the 1920s, the club had 240
members, and with volunteer labor they were eventually able to build a
large clubhouse, which served as the focal point for organized Hungarian activity in Lethbridge until after World War II.[7]

As in many areas of immigrant settlement across North America, the
boardinghouse served as a major institution of immigrant life in the
Lethbridge area. Since there were not many families among Hungarian
immigrants, the few married women found work in partnerships with
their husbands as boardinghouse keepers. The boardinghouse provided

*The Hungarian Sick Benefit Society, founded in 1901, in Lethbridge. The sign
reads Lethbridge Club Gathering Place. The hats, badges, and other regalia
were part of the uniform for members of the mutual benefit society.*

a familiar cultural setting where immigrants could use their own language, eat familiar food, and socialize.[8]

By the early years of the twentieth century the Lethbridge coal mines had become a way station for Hungarians saving money to establish themselves in farming. Many of the Hungarians who took up homesteads and began dryland farming in the Stavely, Retlaw, Taber, Wrentham, and Milk River areas during the settlement boom of the mid-1890s to World War I, had first worked in the mines in Lethbridge. Even after they had enough money to finance their own farms, many worked in the mines during the winter and farmed during the summer.[9]

By 1916, almost half of the 1,435 people of Hungarian origin in Alberta lived in the Lethbridge area. Although at this time Hungarians comprised only a small minority in the rural communities of southern Alberta, the pioneer settlements near Taber and Milk River would become increasingly visible during the 1920s with the arrival of larger numbers of Hungarian immigrants who would be attracted to these areas.

The first wave of Hungarian immigration resulted in only one other Hungarian settlement in Alberta; this was in the central part of the province in an area known as Manfred (near present day Bashaw) southeast of Wetaskiwin, which had been opened up for settlement when the Calgary-Edmonton railway was completed in 1891. This settlement, which predated the farming settlements in the Lethbridge area, was the first Hungarian farm settlement in Alberta. Three men who had been neighbors in the Dunafoldvár region of central Hungary—John Kerik, John Meister, and John Mraz—left their homeland in 1895 and established adjacent homesteads in this newly opened section of the province. The men fashioned their first dwellings out of logs jutting into a hillside; these had thatched roofs and sod floors. The men were soon able to replace these temporary shelters with log cabins. The next job was the back breaking task of clearing the land. Many years later, one of John Mraz's daughters described their pioneering efforts:

> They brought spades, hoes, sickles and scythes, good intentions and a desire to exist as best they could ... father cleared land with oxen and a one-shared plough. Wheat was broadcast by hand, cut with scythe and sickle, threshed with a maul, and hauled by ox cart to the nearest mill (Wetaskiwin) [35 miles distant] to be turned into flour.[10]

In 1900 the settlement which the three friends had established was augmented by the arrival of several more families from Hungary, as well as a few from the Hungarian settlements in Saskatchewan. Once they had completed some of the rudimentary tasks of pioneering, the newcomers could begin to direct some of their efforts toward reestablishing familiar institutions. In 1910, nineteen Catholic families, most of them Hungarian, established a Catholic church, known as the Manfred Church. The group was unable to obtain a Hungarian priest, but the area was in a mission served by travelling Irish or German Catholic priests. On those Sundays when the travelling priest could not visit them, the parishioners gathered to read the Bible in Hungarian and sing Hungarian

The John Dubitz family and home in Manfred in 1906. This pioneer log home belonged to one of the early families in the first rural Hungarian settlement in the province. (Courtesy Dubitz family)

hymns. The group was isolated by the fact that the adults, some of whom were illiterate in their own language, did not speak English.[11]

Some of the homesteaders in the Bashaw area returned to Hungary prior to World War I, either because they could no longer endure the hardships of pioneering or because their plan had always been simply to earn money and then return home to their relatives. However, the majority of settlers stayed and, despite the difficulties and personal tragedies which they experienced, gradually established themselves on the land, developing herds of animals and acquiring machinery to ease the arduous work of farming.[12]

The Manfred settlement did not grow after 1910, nor did the Hungarian influence in the area endure. Although children of the pioneering settlers generally married within the group, the Hungarian identity in the area did not survive past the Great Depression. The surrounding community had a mixed population; it had been largely settled by Scandinavian-Americans and Germans from Russia. The small number of Hungarians were isolated from their countrymen, and the immigration wave of the 1920s brought no new Hungarian settlers to the region; consequently the Hungarian population remained at less than 100. Gradually during the 1920s, this small group integrated almost completely into the larger rural community. During the depression years and the 1940s, many people left the area for British Columbia or for other parts of Alberta. Today, with the original homes and Catholic Church gone and only a handful of people of Hungarian origin remaining, there are no visible reminders of the settlement.

The Impact of World War I

Although their economic position was still insecure, by 1914 many Hungarians in Alberta were thinking of their stay in Canada as permanent and were beginning to put down roots. But when war broke out, making an enemy of the Austro-Hungarian Empire, they found that their situation was precarious. The Canadian government treated them as enemy aliens: they were either interned or required to register with police, and those who had been naturalized after 1902 were deprived of their vote. Prevailing attitudes toward them were embodied in that hurtful and ubiquitous slur, "bohunk." Few in number, leaderless, dispersed across the province and without any effective provincial or national organization, Alberta's Hungarian community was ill-equipped to defend itself.

However, some Hungarians in Alberta attempted to change prevailing attitudes by pointing out that Hungarian-Canadians were largely opposed to the Austrian Empire and therefore should not be regarded as enemies. But such attempts were not successful; Albertans continued to regard the Hungarians in their midst as enemy aliens. Given that their status as outsiders was thus emphasized by the wartime situation, it is ironic that, as a consequence of the war, the Hungarian-Canadian settlements became more permanent than before, since Hungarians could no longer return to their homeland.[13]

Post-World War I Immigration

The second wave of Hungarian immigration, which occurred between 1925 and 1930, was to be the century's largest movement of Hungarians to Alberta. Economic and political conditions had combined to precipitate this migration which would reshape the entire structure of the Hungarian-Canadian community. Although this second wave, like the one which had preceded it, was composed primarily of farmers and workers, it also included a small contingent of middle class people and a few displaced aristocrats. Some of the newcomers left behind families, social status, and property in their quest for a better life in Canada.[14]

Virtually all of the immigrants were young men, both single and married, who hoped to make enough money to repay their passage and either return to Hungary with an accumulation of funds, move on to the United States, or eventually bring their wives and families to the new land. However, since they arrived just on the eve of the Great Depression, most were to have their dreams crushed. Many of the immigrants would find that not only could they not afford to bring their families to Canada, but that they themselves could not afford to return to Hungary. Indeed, many would not be able to be reunited with their wives and children until after World War II; for some there was to be permanent separation from the families they had left in the late 1920s— either through death or through one of the partners becoming involved in another relationship after many years of enforced separation. During the depression they could not afford to bring out their families, during the war their families could not come, and in the postwar era the communist regime prevented their families from leaving.[15]

The majority of the second wave of immigrants settled in Ontario, which soon eclipsed Saskatchewan as the center of Hungarian-Canadian life in Canada. However, the Prairies, particularly Alberta, received a substantial number of the new immigrants. Approximately 4,000 of the 34,000 Hungarians who came to Canada at this time settled in Alberta, increasing the number of Hungarians in the province from 1,045 in 1921 to 5,502 in 1931. In the background, orchestrating and directing this entire movement was the CPR which, under an agreement with the federal government, recruited, screened, transported, and placed the immigrants. The province's major coal deposits, sugar beet fields, unsettled CPR land and areas of urban growth were economic magnets which attracted the second wave of Hungarian immigrants to Alberta.[16]

To determine the forces which had propelled this sizeable migration, one must, of course, look at conditions in postwar Hungary. Military defeat led to the breakup of the Austro-Hungarian Empire, with Hungary losing control over vast sections of land to Romania, Yugoslavia, and Czechoslovakia. This contributed to economic depression and political turmoil, thus creating a climate conducive to massive emigration. In 1918, when Hungary's defeat was imminent, a bloodless revolution catapulted a liberal pacifist, Count Mihaly Karolyi, to power. In March 1919, political and economic chaos forced Karolyi to resign in favor of a left wing regime led by Bela Kun. Kun had a strong following in the country's coal mining regions; many of his supporters had been prisoners of war in Russia who had rallied to Lenin's Bolsheviks. Kun's attempts to Bolshevize the economy and to suppress opposition led to economic chaos, profound political unrest, and the collapse of his regime in July 1919. Kun was replaced by the conservative Milkol Horthy, who restored order, but suppressed movements of the extreme left. (Some of the displaced followers of both Karolyi and Kun would later come to Canada.)[17] As a result of the defeat of both revolutions, the Hungarian peasant population lost confidence in social improvements and began looking to emigration as a solution to their problems.[18]

The wave of immigration which had been set in motion by these factors in Hungary was both like and unlike that of the prewar period. Like the first wave of immigrants, the Hungarians who arrived in Canada during the 1920s were primarily agricultural workers and peasants (75-80 percent), chiefly from the northwestern part of Hungary, the country's most underdeveloped and isolated region. Their educational level was often limited; consequently their understanding of Hungarian culture consisted primarily of an awareness of traditional customs and basic religious concepts.

However, since many of the newcomers had left Hungary for political reasons, their level of political and ethnic consciousness was higher than that of their predecessors. As a result, when they began to establish themselves in Alberta, they initiated more cultural and political activities than earlier immigrants had done. Another difference between the two groups was that while the first wave had been directed primarily to the United States, the second was directed largely to Canada. During the early 1920s, the United States had set quotas which restricted the number of immigrants from central and eastern Europe. Consequently, many Hungarians looked to Canada as a new homeland.[19]

Hungarian immigrants came to Canada under the "Railways Agreement," which had been negotiated between the CPR, the CNR, and the federal government to facilitate farm immigration from central and eastern Europe. CPR officials were pleased with the agreement since many of them believed that central and eastern Europeans were much more likely than Anglo-Saxons to be able to clear the marginal, heavily timbered brush land which constituted much of the company's remaining holdings in the West.[20]

Settlement during the 1920s and 1930s

In examining the settlement of Hungarians in Alberta during the interwar decades, it is impossible to isolate examples of communities which could be considered as representative of the group's experience. The Hungarians who came did not settle together in large contiguous blocs where a standard colonization process emerged; rather they established pockets of settlement throughout the province.

The group had some common characteristics. The majority of them went to rural areas. (In 1931, 69 percent of Hungarians in the province were living in farming areas; by 1941, this figure had risen to 75 percent.) In addition, the Hungarian settlers shared a common immigrant and working class struggle and had to cope, from a very vulnerable position, with the harsh realities of the "dirty thirties"; consequently, all of the major groups of Hungarian immigrants established similar organizations in response to common difficulties. But apart from these general similarities, conditions varied widely from settlement to settlement.

The agricultural communities which the Hungarians entered varied from long-established farming settlements on irrigated prairie land, where they worked as agricultural laborers to newly opened bush areas where the newcomer from Hungary was cast in the role of a pioneer. These scattered agricultural districts differed widely in terrain and climate and, therefore, in the kind of agriculture for which they were suited. Hungarian urban settlement was equally diverse; the various urban areas and mining camps developed their own styles of life which were quite different from those in the rural areas and from each other.

In southern Alberta the immigrants were placed by the CPR through local colonization boards. Several communities in southern Alberta had branches of the Hungarian Colonization Board, which functioned as an extension of the CPR's colonization efforts. Those who sponsored the immigrants had to guarantee their employment for a year and vouch that they would not become public charges.[21]

This sponsorship system facilitated chain migration; earlier immigrants who had begun to establish themselves brought relatives and fellow villagers to existing settlements. For example, Hungarian-Germans from Polany, Hungary, first arrived in Magrath to work in the sugar beet industry in 1925; by 1931 there were thirty-one families from the same village living in the Magrath and nearby Raymond areas.[22]

With the reestablishment of the sugar beet industry in 1925, there was a heavy demand for sugar beet laborers in southern Alberta. Consequently, many of the Hungarians who came to the province in the late 1920s went first to this region. The towns and villages of Raymond, Magrath, Picture Butte, Iron Springs, Readymade, Coaldale, and Taber, all situated in sugar beet growing areas, attracted sizeable numbers of Hungarian farmers during the 1920s.[23]

Hungarian immigrants who settled in southern Alberta to work in the sugar beet industry faced numerous difficulties since the work was so arduous; however, most of them were able to adjust successfully and use their experience as a rung in the ladder of upward social and economic mobility. Many of the newcomers already had extensive experience with sugar beet farming in Hungary, and all were very familiar with the demands of hard work. Although a number soon left the area to try their luck elsewhere, a significant proportion remained. At first they rented small acreages where they lived in crude shacks. Soon they were able to send for their families. Through the work of all family members in thinning, weeding, and harvesting the beets, they were eventually able to purchase the land they cultivated, ultimately to purchase additional land and expand their operations. Like earlier pioneer settlers, the Hungarians who came to southern Alberta during the late 1920s knew the value of self-sufficiency. They planted large gardens and kept enough livestock and poultry to supply their own needs.[24] The Hungarians were separated from the existing farm community by culture, language, and religion and by social prejudices embodied in the concept of the "non-preferred" immigrant; but they began to feel at home in southern Alberta as they learned English from their employers and as their families arrived.[25]

Since sugar beet work and other farm labor was seasonal, most of the immigrants looked for other types of work in the off-season. During the winter, many found jobs in construction, in the coal mines, or in other laboring jobs. Some settled permanently in the mining camps. During the late 1920s, the number of Hungarians living and working in the Lethbridge area's mining camps, such as Coalhurst, Diamond City, Shaughnessy, and Hardieville, increased substantially. In Lethbridge, the principal concentration of Hungarians—most of them manual laborers—continued to be on the north side, where an area of four square blocks was predominantly Hungarian.[26]

Thus the Railways Agreement of 1925 had effected a dramatic change in Alberta's Hungarian community. By 1931, there were 5,502 people of Hungarian origin in the province, nearly half of them living in the region south of Calgary.[27] With this influx of new immigrants, Hungarian cultural and religious activities in southern Alberta flourished. Both the Presbyterian and Catholic churches began Hungarian-language services in several centers. Immigrants in Raymond established a sick benefit society and a youth organization; those in Taber organized a Hungarian society which built a hall where they held harvest dances and national festivals. In Lethbridge, Hungarian Presbyterian services were begun in 1926, the Hungarian Sick Benefit Society was expanded, and a Hungarian-language school and a dramatic society for Hungarian youth were established.[28]

Additional Rural Settlements

Besides the settlements in the beet-growing areas, the CPR helped to develop several other major rural colonies of Hungarians during the late 1920s in widely separated areas. One sizeable settlement emerged on CPR land at Brooks (which formed part of the Eastern Irrigation District). The area had been put under irrigation just prior to World War I. However, the war had inevitably slowed settlement: although there had been a proposal after the war to settle a group of returned soldiers, in the area, this plan had not succeeded. Consequently, between 1928 and 1930, the CPR, anxious to settle its irrigated land between Brooks and Tilley, turned to Slovak and Hungarian immigrants.[29]

Despite initial economic hardships which made it difficult for some of them to even bring out their wives and children, the seventy Hungarian households at Brooks persisted.[30] As rural people accustomed to self-sufficiency and hard work, they knew how to survive. Indeed, the community even grew during the 1930s as the CPR encouraged unemployed immigrants in Calgary to relocate on the land. Irrigation enabled the farmers to grow grain and fodder, and many raised paprika and corn—traditional Hungarian products—in their gardens. The settlers did not organize many Hungarian activities; community-wide events were largely restricted to the occasional visits of Hungarian-speaking Catholic priests and Presbyterian ministers. However, after surviving the privations of the depression decade, the Hungarian farmers were able to achieve prosperity during the 1940s and 1950s, and many of their children remained in the Brooks area to continue successful farming operations.[31]

Another group of over 100 Hungarian farm families settled in the Warburg district east of Leduc in the late 1920s and early 1930s. They came to this area under a plan devised by the CPR to settle its brush-covered land. Hungarians settled throughout the area from Genesee to Breton, but the largest concentration was at Warburg.[32] Most of the families who came to this area followed a common immigration and settlement pattern. While the settlers were from several different regions of Hungary (as well as a few who were ethnic Hungarians from Romania and Czechoslovakia), they all came to Alberta in groups of families. In several cases, groups of two or three brothers immigrated together, or one brother helped bring over the others. The settlers included many who had first tried their luck elsewhere, either on Saskatchewan's farms, in Drumheller's coal mines, or in southern Alberta's beet fields. The men came first and worked for a couple of years to establish themselves before bringing their families to join them. Almost all were young people in their twenties or thirties and most were married.[33]

The Warburg settlers had to perform the same backbreaking tasks of pioneering as the pre-World War I immigrants, but they were faced with the additional burden of having to accomplish these tasks during a time of severe economic depression. The newly arrived immigrants knew virtually no English and often possessed little more than the clothes they were wearing. They had no cash reserves to see them through difficult times, yet they still had to make payments on their CPR-owned land. While the railway had offered easy terms and reasonable repayment terms, payment had to be made nonetheless and cash was not easy for the newcomers to acquire. A few eventually lost their land. However, by the late 1930s, the settlers' economic prospects were improving. Clover and honey were becoming important cash crops, and agricultural prices were beginning to rise.[34] By the end of the decade, most of the Hungarian newcomers had established themselves successfully.[35]

Despite the hardships of pioneering and survival of the depression, the settlers helped each other to cope with the demands of pioneering and the problems of isolation.[36] In so doing, they developed an active social and cultural life. In the winter of 1931-32, a group of the settlers formed the Petofi Club, named after a famous Hungarian poet. During the winter, the club held frequent dances and plays in the community hall and established a Hungarian library. The club's activities were open to the entire community, and some of the older Anglo-Saxon pioneers and other newly arrived immigrants (most of them of Polish, Czech, or German background) participated. One of the area's pioneers remembers that:

> Around that time there was a great influx of emigrants from all parts of Europe and other parts of the world. When newcomers joined the earlier pioneers in the area, the dances took on the atmosphere of a small United Nations party. Some people came to dance; others came to watch, but everybody came to visit. It was the place where you could meet most of your friends and neighbors and make new friends and find out how everybody was doing.[37]

While the Hungarians in the Warburg settlement were becoming a cohesive community during the 1930s, forces were at work which inexorably moved the newcomers toward acceptance and, ultimately, assimilation into the larger society of north central Alberta. The settlers in the area had much in common. Even as late as the last years of the 1920s and the early years of the 1930s, the region was still in the midst of pioneering, and all of the various peoples who came there were involved in the early stages of community building. Many of the area's settlers shared a common religion since most were Catholic; they also shared the experiences of being immigrants and of having to struggle to survive the depression. While the Hungarians were one of the area's largest groups —the 1941 census reported about 300 people of Hungarian origin, or roughly 10 percent of the population in the municipality—they were nevertheless a minority and they began to blend in with the other settlers. This pattern was in sharp contrast to the situation in southern Alberta, where most Hungarian settlers came to previously established, predominantly Anglo-Saxon communities and for many years remained on the margins of these communities.[38]

In addition to Warburg, the north central region of the province attracted two smaller Hungarian settlements—one in the area of Heatherdown, a post office northwest of Stony Plain, and the other at Cosmo, near Sangudo. The Hungarian experience in both of these settlements was similar to that in Warburg: the remote and bush-covered terrain bred a pioneer culture of survival which dispelled ethnic boundaries.[39] The Cosmo settlers developed some Hungarian group life; there was a concentration of Hungarian Presbyterians in the area and they were visited periodically by the Hungarian minister from Calgary. However, since the number of Hungarians was smaller than in Warburg, Hungarian institutions did not emerge as fully.[40]

There were several other concentrations of Hungarian immigrants in east central Alberta. During the late 1920s, a few Hungarian farm families settled on CPR land at Hardisty, Provost, Mannville, Dewberry, and Vermilion.[41]

The most remote of the province's Hungarian settlements was in the Peace River district. During the late 1920s, this northern region of Alberta was experiencing its major settlement boom. Several hundred Hungarians were attracted by this northward rush, and they established two major settlements—one at Warrensville a few miles northeast of the town of Peace River, the other at Notikewin, just north of what would become the town of Manning. Some of these Hungarian immigrants had previously lived in Saskatchewan or the United States. Like all new Peace River country settlers in those years, they were faced with difficult conditions. During the 1930s, the region's isolation, harsh weather, and primitive stage of development motivated many to migrate yet another time, to other parts of Alberta or to British Columbia, where a number of Hungarians began fruit-growing in the Okanagan Valley. Nevertheless, by 1941, there were still 280 people of Hungarian background in the Peace River district, with about eighteen families in each of the two major settlements; however, farming was so marginal that even as late as 1949, a Hungarian-speaking priest visiting Warrensville found only three families who could afford cars. The rest came to church services in horse-drawn buggies.[42]

The Mining Experience

Many of the Hungarian immigrants who came to Alberta during the 1920s found work in the province's coal mines, particularly in Lethbridge and Drumheller, but also in the Crow's Nest Pass and Edmonton. Most who did so were from the northern regions of Hungary, where there are numerous coal deposits; consequently, they had previous mining experience. Others moved from farm labor into mining as part of a seasonal work cycle and then remained in mining during the depression when jobs in other industries became scarce. They were attracted by the relatively high wages in mining; however, work in the industry was always sporadic.

In addition to the large group of Hungarian miners who had settled in the Lethbridge area, another major concentration of Hungarians developed in the Drumheller Valley, which was one of the province's foremost coal-producing regions in the late 1920s and early 1930s. In 1928 a railway line was completed between Drumheller and Rosemary, which made way for the opening of a series of coal mines from Rosedale east. Four of the biggest mines were opened at East Coulee, and the mining camp boomed from virtually nothing in 1927 to a town of 1,200 by 1933, approximately two-thirds to three-fourths of the population being of Hungarian origin. In the Drumheller Valley as a whole during the late 1920s, there was a population of 10,000. This number included approximately 2,000 miners working in twenty-nine different mines which were producing over 1.5 million tons of coal annually, primarily for domestic use. Hungarian miners were scattered throughout the twelve Drumheller Valley towns and worked in all of these mines, but their greatest impact was in East Coulee.[43]

East Coulee was a typical Albertan mining camp, composed overwhelmingly of young men whose work was difficult, dangerous, and seasonal. In light of their strained economic circumstances and the sporadic nature of coal mining, most of them felt no permanent attachment to the community; thus, the town's physical and social milieu reflected both their dominance and their transience. Most of the houses were one-room shacks for bachelors, though there were also some two and three-room houses for married men. That the community grew almost overnight, unconstrained by municipal bylaws, gave it a jerry-built character, with helter-skelter streets, and an absence of paint and other aesthetic amenities.[44]

The mines operated on a seasonal basis and people would come and go accordingly. The mines worked steadily throughout August and September. Then, they remained open for one or two days a week, until February or March, when they closed for the year. Thus, beginning in October, the miners would find out if they would work on a day-to-day basis. When the mines were closed, many of the miners quickly used up their meagre savings and were forced into debt to the town storekeeper. Consequently, they looked for work elsewhere: on the railroads, on farms, or in the cities as laborers.[45]

Social life in the mining camps, such as East Coulee, provided a marked contrast to the quiet, conservative nature of life in the province's agriculturally-based small towns. Transience, the predominance of single males, most of whom were recently arrived immigrants, and economic insecurity led to a lifestyle characterized by poverty, heavy drinking, explosive political discussion, occasional violence, mental depression, and family instability. Unlike their counterparts in most other small Albertan towns, the Catholic priest and RCMP officer in East Coulee were two of the community's most unpopular figures. Women and children sometimes went to Mass, but in general organized religion played very little role in the community. When an Hungarian-speaking Catholic priest arrived in the Drumheller Valley in 1946, he found only three adult Hungarian males attending Mass. The major social center was not the church, but the Hungarian hall. The left wing Hungarian Sick Benefit Society, which the Hungarian miners established, held twice-monthly activities in the union hall, including concerts, plays and dances, complete with Hungarian music. These events attracted both Hungarians and non-Hungarians from throughout the valley.[46]

In the mining towns, as in the rural areas, self-sufficiency was crucial to economic survival. Families took in boarders to help make ends meet.[47] Miners and their families kept large gardens, and from nearby farmers, they bought pigs and cattle which they butchered, smoked, and cured. However, the relationship between family size and self-sufficiency was markedly different for the miners than for the farmers. The latter had large families, but the miners usually limited their families to two children. This difference was a reflection partly of religious outlook, since the farmers tended to be more religious than the miners, but primarily of the differing economic implications of family size for the two groups.[48]

Urban Communities

In addition to its impact on the province's mining communities, the immigration of the 1920s led to small concentrations of Hungarians in Calgary and Edmonton. These formed the beginnings of the communities which, in the postwar era, would overshadow the rural settlements. The Hungarians who settled in both cities were poor; they were members of the working class, and they faced immense difficulties because of depression conditions.

Calgary had six times as many Hungarians as Edmonton in 1931 and three times as many in 1941. Hence a more vigorous Hungarian community developed in Calgary, with a variety of religious, social, and political organizations and activities. There had been almost no Hungarian residents of Calgary prior to 1921; in that year there were only 21 people of Hungarian origin in the city and its vicinity. But by 1931, the number of Hungarians had increased to nearly 700 in a population of 84,000. Most of the newcomers arrived in the latter half of the decade. Although many Hungarian immigrants established permanent residences in Calgary and acquired industrial jobs—in the sawmills and wood-preserving companies, in meat-packing plants, iron works and foundries—many others only came to Calgary for casual employment during the off-season, when work in the coal mines, sugar beet fields, and on the railways in other parts of southern Alberta was at a standstill. That Calgary emerged as the largest center of Hungarian population in the province was partly due to its being a major CPR divisional point. Immigrants arriving in the city by train could quickly find jobs on railway gangs through Calgary's CPR offices. In addition, Calgary was centrally located in relationship to the labor-intensive coal mines and sugar beet fields of southern Alberta.[49]

Some of the Hungarian immigrants, unable to get jobs in industry or on the railways, but too proud to go on relief, found work in the Chinese-owned greenhouses. In the days before refrigerated trucks brought in produce from California, these enterprises conducted a bustling trade. But the work was hard, the hours were long, and the wages were low. The greenhouse worker's day, for which he or she was paid $.10 an hour, began at 4:00 A.M. Many of the women employees remember that in winter, they worked with gunny sacks tied around their legs to help them withstand the cold. In summer, many of the immigrant men cut the lawns of wealthy homeowners in Mount Royal. Their wives worked as domestics or in restaurant kitchens. Since they had so little capital and no business experience, very few Hungarians were able to establish their own small businesses during these years.[50]

During the late 1920s and the 1930s, Calgary's Hungarian community was transient, male-dominated, and residentially segregated. As with many other immigrant groups, residential segregation developed because of economic circumstances and a tendency to congregate for mutual support. The area of Hungarian concentration was in the east end of town, between Ninth Avenue South and the Bow river, between First and Sixth Streets East. Four grocery stores were established which catered to the district's residents by selling Hungarian garlic sausage, liver sausage, pickled herring sauerkraut, paprika, rye bread, and other Hungarian specialties. Within this community, Hungarian bachelors could board with Hungarian families who often became their surrogate families.[51]

Facing poverty, prejudice, problems of cultural adjustment, and living in close proximity, Calgary's Hungarian immigrants developed a closely knit community. In 1932, several of the community's leaders organized the Hungarian Canadian Club of Calgary to provide a social focus for the group and to keep alive Hungarian traditions. It sponsored a wide range of activities, including a youth organization, a women's group, a summer school, a library, and a burial society; it also organized plays and dances. Maintaining the Hungarian language was not a major concern, since the Canadian born spoke Hungarian as their mother tongue. The club crossed religious lines by uniting both the Catholic majority and the Presbyterian minority in a common effort. An Hungarian-speaking

Bishop Carrol, the Catholic bishop of Calgary, with the Hungarian Catholic community in the late 1930s on the occasion of the blessing of the Hungarian flag. (Courtesy Ann Lazlock)

Catholic parish and an Hungarian Presbyterian church were also established in Calgary during the 1930s. Relations between Catholics and
Protestants were generally cordial, and they cooperated in many community activities.[52]

Although Edmonton emerged as the unofficial capital of organized
ethnic life for several central and eastern European groups in Alberta
during the interwar era, Hungarians comprised only a tiny proportion of
that city's population, and they had virtually no organizations in the city
until World War II. During the late 1920s, immigrants from the mining
regions of northern Hungary began arriving in Edmonton in the hope of
finding work in the nearby coal mines. But mining was seasonal work, so
the number of Hungarians in the city fluctuated erratically. During the
1920s and 1930s, the factors of size and transiency made it impossible
for the Hungarians in Edmonton to establish either religious or social
organizations.[53]

Surviving the Great Depression

The Great Depression was particularly difficult for the newly arrived
Hungarians. Except in the Lethbridge area, there were no existing Hungarian communities which could help the newcomers in establishing
themselves. Nor could they turn to the government for help; its concern
was to design strategies (including deportation) for keeping immigrants
off relief rolls. Immigrants in urban areas and mining camps were faced
with unemployment, underemployment, and low wages. Farm workers
in southern Alberta faced backbreaking work in the sugar beet fields and
those who went to northern Alberta found harsh pioneering conditions
on isolated, bush-covered terrain. All of the immigrants had to cope with
the simultaneous impact of economic crisis, family separation, and culture shock. Many found the spiritual strength they needed from religious
and cultural activities. Another sizeable group advocated radical political
solutions to world-wide economic crisis. In the mining towns and in
some of the rural areas, Hungarian immigrants were attracted to socialism and communism. They established and supported Hungarian-language organizations which were linked to the Communist Party of Canada and subscribed to left wing Hungarian newspapers; some became
actively involved in political issues at both national and international
levels. The support of a number of the new immigrants for communist
ideas split the group. In several Hungarian communities tension developed between the conservative church and nationally oriented faction
and those who supported the left.

Strong leftist support in several of the province's Hungarian settlements resulted from a combination of local economic conditions, Old
World political beliefs and outside organization and support. In 1927,
Hungarian leftists in Hamilton organized the Canadian-Hungarian
Mutual Benefit Federation to provide both health insurance and political
education for Hungarians across Canada. The group organized branches
among Hungarians throughout the country, including branches at Calgary, Lethbridge, Picture Butte, Taber, Shaughnessy, Hillcrest (in the

Crow's Nest Pass), and in the Drumheller Valley at East Coulee, Midlandvale, Nacmine, Newcastle, and Rosedale. Most members of the organization also subscribed to the left wing newspaper, *Kanadai Magyar Munkas* (Canadian Hungarian Worker), which began publication in 1929.

Support for the left among Hungarians varied in each community, depending on economic conditions, leadership and political experience in the Old World. The left's strongest support came from the mining camps, particularly those in the Drumheller Valley. Many participated in the cultural activities of the Sick Benefit Federation, including a number of dramatic productions which were strongly proletarian and anticlerical.[54]

The growing class consciousness among many Hungarians found expression in their support for mine strikes and sugar beet strikes and for the Republican side in the Spanish Civil War. A portion of the Hungarian miners supported the attempt of the Mine Workers Union of Canada, which was linked to the communist-dominated Workers Unity League, to displace the more conservative United Mine Workers of America in the coal fields, and participated in strikes in several coal towns in 1932. However, the Great Depression was not a propitious time for the formation of a new union, and the Mine Workers Union of Canada was ultimately crushed by the existing union, the coal operators, and the police.[55]

Hungarian support for the communists in the mining camps, along with intensified job competition during the depression, precipitated a wave of discrimination, which in turn merely served to confirm the miners in their communist beliefs. Hungarians thus became part of the larger pattern of conflict between conservative Anglo-Celts and radical non-Anglo-Celts in the Drumheller Valley. Like other foreign-born people in the Valley, the Hungarians found themselves subject to discrimination in the allocation of jobs and in the distribution of relief money. Discrimination also extended to acquiring Canadian citizenship. The RCMP searched the homes of any Hungarians who applied for citizenship. If the police found copies of *Kanadai Magyar Munkas*, or if the applicant was known to be a communist supporter, it was almost certain that he or she would be denied citizenship papers. Thus, by keeping the major source of leftist support—immigrant workers from eastern Europe —off the electors' lists, the more conservative and more powerful factions in the community were able to curtail dramatically the electoral influence of Communists in the Drumheller Valley.[56]

The class consciousness of Hungarian sugar beet workers in southern Alberta and the deterioration in relations between the newcomers and the host society is reflected in the strikes of 1935 and 1936, in which workers refused to sign contracts with beet growers until their demands were met. Among the beet workers, Hungarians were the largest single immigrant group; the Beet Workers Industrial Union, which was affiliated with the communist-dominated Worker's Unity League, tried to organize them, along with other immigrant beet workers. The beet growers condemned the strikes on the ground that they were conducted by a communist union; in May 1935, striking workers were given notice that unless they signed their contracts immediately, they would be evicted from their shacks on the growers' properties. A few workers were evicted before the two sides came to terms. In 1936, the Beet Workers Industrial Union again tried to gain recognition as a bargaining agent and attempted to negotiate a better contract for the beet workers, but the growers remained obdurate in their refusal to recognize the union. When the growers' association began bringing in strikebreakers and evicting workers from their homes, the workers called off their strike and signed their contracts. The union remained impotent; however, because of the strikes the image of Hungarians and other central European beet workers shifted during the mid-1930s from that of hard workers to potentially dangerous communists, a stereotype which embodied both class and ethnic conflict. However, the labor conflict was not sufficiently long-lived to effect a permanent worsening of grower-worker relations.[57]

In addition to unionism, one cause which captured the loyalty of many who supported the left during the 1930s was the Spanish Civil War. Tired of being unemployed, weary of crisscrossing the country looking for work, and anxious to become involved in the struggle against the fascist threat in Europe, about fifty Hungarians from Alberta joined the contingent of Canadian volunteers who went to Spain to fight General Franco's forces. Among the casualties in Spain were a Hungarian from Taber, three from Lethbridge, and four from the Drumheller Valley.[58]

The decade of the 1930s was a trying time for the Hungarians in Alberta. The group was economically insecure and linguistically and residentially isolated from the larger society; and it experienced sharp internal conflict based on political differences. Ironically, however, one factor in the group's ability to survive the depression was its isolation since it spurred the growth of economic, social, and cultural institutions which helped the immigrants to cope with their situation. The decade of the 1930s marked the golden age of Hungarian cultural activities in the province.

The Exception to the Rule: Barons on the Prairies

Unlike most Hungarians who emigrated to Alberta during the 1920s, Barons Josef and Endre Csávossy did not flee a life of toil and poverty. The young barons were descendants of a wealthy and influential family. Josef, born in 1894, and Endre, born in 1897, had spent their boyhoods in Austria-Hungary where their father owned five estates, the largest of which encompassed 5,000 acres and employed 300 men. The Csávossy property had been passed down through the family for four generations and the family had earned a place in the Hungarian House of Magnates (similar to Britain's House of Lords). After attending private schools and university, the young men assumed they would take their places managing the family's estates; but the aftermath of the war interfered with their plans. When the Romanian government took over their property with minimal compensation, they were immediately faced with the decision of where to emigrate. After unsuccessful attempts to purchase land in India and South Africa, they were eventually convinced by a CPR agent in London to settle in Canada.[59]

Although the Csávossy brothers knew very little about Canada, they had little trouble choosing their Canadian destination. They had heard about the Cochrane area from a farmer they had met at an agricultural exhibition in London. They remembered his descriptions of the nearby Rockies and thought such a setting would remind them of the Alps. CPR officials made a special effort to facilitate their emigration and introduced them to a number of influential Canadians, including the company president. The Csávossys arrived in Calgary in March 1925 and soon purchased the Bow River Ranch at Springbank, southeast of Cochrane. Later that year they assisted in the emigration of four Hungarian families from their estate to help them with the work on their new land. They wished to re-create something of their previous lifestyle and were anxious to remain on the land.

The young aristocrats had virtually no practical experience in farming, but they made the most of their adventurous life in Alberta. Their new home, an abandoned ranch house, provided a marked contrast to the commodious manor house they had left in Hungary. They converted the ranch into a mixed farm and were among the area's first large grain growers. By the late 1920s, a time of high grain prices, they had a prosperous operation. Riding a crest of prosperity, Baron Joseph purchased a Gypsy Moth airplane and was soon exploring southern Alberta as a barnstormer.

But when the Great Depression hit, its impact was felt by those who had been flying high, as well as by the recently arrived Hungarian who had not yet gotten his feet firmly planted on Canadian soil. Limited markets for grain soon shriveled the Csávossy's income, which reduced the scope of their operations. In 1936 the brothers' fortunes hit their lowest point when a prairie fire devastated their crops and machinery.

Andrew and Josef were well educated, were fluent in English, and were readily accepted as colorful additions to the class-conscious, elite social circles of Calgary and Cochrane. Despite their few contacts with Calgary's working class Hungarians, they did not sever their Hungarian connections. They hired Hungarian cooks, maintained frequent contact with their homeland and kept a multi-lingual library of over 2,000 volumes. Living as they did within the charmed circle of Calgary's ranch-based elite, the Csávossys were able to maintain something of their Old World life. But like other Hungarian immigrants, they also had to change considerably in order to adjust to their new home; and, despite experiencing their share of hardships, like many other Hungarians, they did not regret coming to Canada.[60]

The Impact of War: The Turbulent 1940s

The 1940s brought new opportunities and new challenges for Hungarians in Alberta. The war, with its accompanying mobilization and renewed economic activity in the province's mines, factories, and farms, solved the problems of unemployment and poverty. It also enabled farmers to expand their holdings and, often for the first time, to purchase tractors, trucks, and cars. The 1940s also brought a strong urban trend since some of the immigrants and many of the second generation responded to economic opportunities in the cities. Relative prosperity during wartime enabled many immigrants to begin to feel established and settled in Alberta; many in the cities were able to purchase their own homes.

But circumstances for the Hungarians were not all sanguine. Between 1939 and 1941, Hungary had been neutral, but in 1941, in response to German pressure, a desire to regain territory lost after World War I, and to a fear of Russia and communism, Hungary joined the Axis' cause and declared war on Russia. This immediately placed Hungarian immigrants who had not taken out Canadian citizenship in a difficult position. The Canadian government treated them as "enemy aliens"; they were finger-printed and subjected to police surveillance. However, unlike such groups as the Japanese, the Germans, and the Hutterites, most Hungarians passed through the war years unscathed. Indeed, the war offered the opportunity for second generation Hungarian-Canadian men to prove their loyalty in the armed forces: many did so.[61]

With depression and war having virtually stopped new immigration, the second generation assumed a growing importance during the 1940s. One member of this new force recalls that "there was a great difference between the first and second generations." The views and concerns of the children were inevitably different from those of their parents, and their experiences during the 1930s and 1940s pushed them overwhelmingly in the direction of assimilation into Canadian society. The older immigrant generation had remained segregated in closely knit Hungarian communities during the 1930s; many of the younger generation felt constrained by this kind of existence and wanted to leave it behind. The 1940s presented them with the opportunities to do so.[62]

A variety of social and economic factors facilitated the assimilation of the second generation—those who were born in Canada or had immigrated as children. English was their first language and sports their passion. Their parents continually stressed the importance of education as a means of getting ahead. A sizeable number of the second generation went on to become professionals—doctors, lawyers, social workers, nurses. The prejudice that many of them encountered had convinced them that assimilation (in order to meet an English-Canadian norm) was the only way to find acceptance and economic success in Canada. John Marlyn's novel, *Under the Ribs of Death*, the story of a young Hungarian-Canadian boy growing up in Winnipeg during the interwar years, portrays graphically the dilemma of the second generation. The protagonist assures his father fervently that:

> the only people who count are the English. Their fathers got all the best jobs. They're the only ones nobody ever calls foreigners. Nobody ever makes fun of their names or calls them bologna eaters or laughs at the way they dress or talk. Nobody, cause when you're English it's the same as being Canadian.[63]

A change of name was one way of escaping limitations on mobility and some young Hungarian-Canadians in Alberta did this to improve their chances for economic success and social acceptability. But the war provided opportunites for many to establish a new life without concealing their identities. Joining the armed forces not only provided a job, but also helped to dispel the taint of disloyalty which left wing political activities during the depression and Hungary's wartime alliance with the Axis powers had given to the image of Hungarians in Canada. The war brought together Canadians from a variety of ethnic backgrounds and removed social barriers.

Thus, a number of factors, including patriotism, prejudice, mobility, urbanization, and intermarriage, combined to foster assimilation of the second generation. Given existing negative attitudes toward ethnic diversity in the province and the dispersion of Hungarians in widely scattered settlements, the 1940s would have been in any case a period of growing assimilation among young Hungarian-Canadians; the war just hastened the process. These striking demographic trends are reflected in the 1951 census. By that year, the urban ratio of Hungarians had increased from one-quarter in 1941 to nearly one-half. Because of wartime mobility, the number of people of Hungarian origin in the province actually declined slightly, from 7,892 in 1941 to 7,794 in 1951.[64]

The war and postwar years saw a decline in Hungarian cultural and political activities in Alberta. This was not merely the result of generational differences; rather, it was a reflection of a complex web of economic, social, and demographic developments. In Lethbridge and Calgary, growing economic prosperity and consequent mobility precipitated the breakup of the urban Hungarian neighborhoods. Support for the war effort temporarily united both religious and communist factions within the Hungarian community, thereby reducing internal political conflict. The war precipitated a decline in the numbers of Hungarians involved in specifically Hungarian churches, since war made it more difficult to get Hungarian clergy to serve the various Hungarian communities scattered throughout the province. And, by the end of the war, Hungarian left wing political activity and commitment had ebbed. A number of the leftist leaders had returned to Hungary hoping to participate in building an Hungarian socialist state; war and postwar prosperity blunted the radicalism of those who remained. The cold war atmosphere of the late 1940s and the 1950s also undermined support for the left.[65]

In the province's farming areas and mining towns, the decline in Hungarian group activities was irreversible due both to outward migration and to increased integration of individual Hungarians into rural Albertan society. With the postwar influx of two new waves of immigrants, the Hungarian ethnic community of the postwar era would be dominated by new people and new issues, and would be almost exclusively urban.

A New Era: The Impact of Post-World War II Immigration

The third wave of immigration from Hungary—the movement of displaced persons—was very different from the two previous waves. It was composed of urban, educated, middle class people fleeing the threat of Soviet occupation and communist domination. There were three different groups: those who had been removed as forced labor to Germany during the war, those who left with the retreating German armies in early 1945 in the face of Soviet invasion, and those who escaped the communist reign of terror in 1948 and 1949. Included in all three categories were former government bureaucrats, members of the army's officer corps, and middle class professionals.[66]

Through the International Refugee Organization, the immigrants were admitted to Canada under sponsorship in quotas set by the Canadian government. The Hungarian clergy in Canada, both Catholic and Presbyterian, played a central role arranging for the sponsorship of the displaced persons by members of the Hungarian-Canadian community. Between January 1946 and June 1956, the number of Hungarian refugees in Canada reached a total of 12,332; approximately 800 of these came to Alberta. Because they were mobile and would not make severe demands on the Canadian housing market, the federal government gave priority to single immigrants. Before their families could join them, married men "had to accumulate enough capital to satisfy the investigating officials that all dependents would be adequately maintained on their arrival." As a consequence of these regulations, most of the Hungarian immigrants to Canada were young, and men outnumbered women by a ratio of 9 to 6.[67]

While the adjustment faced by the postwar immigrants was much less traumatic than that of the immigrants of the 1920s, nevertheless, the process was not easy. The displaced persons who went into farm work or mining when they first arrived seldom remained after their contracts were over, but left for the cities, either in Alberta or elsewhere in the country.

That the newcomers stayed only temporarily in rural areas is not surprising, since most were educated people with urban backgrounds. Nor were they alone in their decision to move to the cities; during this period, some of the 1920s immigrants and most of their children were also leaving the farming and mining communities for expanding urban centers. However, once they arrived in the cities, they encountered barriers to mobility. In postwar Alberta, immigrants did not find universal acceptance. They discovered that employers expected them to speak English and to have Canadian work experience, that use of their native tongue with fellow countrymen on the job was resented, and that they were constantly stigmatized by the pejorative label, "D.P." They were often isolated from the mainstream of English-speaking society, and there was little intermarriage with non-Hungarians. While many were able to find work as laborers, particularly with the railways, they often found that they were locked into these jobs because their previous education was unrecognized. The most adaptable among them were eventually able to improve their positions and some ultimately met the exacting standards of Canadian professional associations, thereby requalifying to enter their former professions. But such advancement required tremendous effort.[68]

The postwar immigrants had grown up during a period of strong nationalism in Hungary and tended to be intensely nationalistic; consequently they usually joined the existing Hungarian institutions in the cities. Their interest and participation revitalized these organizations, and a number of the newcomers soon found themselves in leadership positions. In addition, despite their small numbers, they established several new Hungarian organizations. Those who went to Edmonton helped to energize the Hungarian Cultural Society, which working class immigrants from the earlier wave of immigration had established in 1945.

In both Calgary and Edmonton, the postwar immigrants established branches of the Hungarian Veterans Association, an international organization founded to provide comradeship among former members of the royal Hungarian Army and "to promote, preserve, and protect Hungarian culture and social life." Branches of the Hungarian-Canadian Scout movement also emerged in Alberta during the 1950s. Many of the new immigrants were particularly dedicated to scouting since it had been suppressed in postwar Hungary.

In contrast to the antireligious views or religious indifference of the left wing immigrants who came to Alberta during the 1920s, the postwar immigrants tended to place a high priority on religion. They had come from a society in which religion had been very important and where there had been an active social life associated with the churches. This background, coupled with staunch anticommunism, predisposed the postwar immigrants to active church involvement. In addition, there were a number of clergymen, both Catholic and Presbyterian, among the displaced persons, who were able to provide leadership for the province's Hungarian churches. Consequently, one effect of the postwar immigration was a revitalization of religious institutions and activities. A new Catholic parish was established in Edmonton, and the old Hungarian parish in Calgary, St. Elizabeth of Hungary, was reactivated in 1952. Hungarian Presbyterian churches were also established in Lethbridge in 1949 and in Edmonton in 1950.[69]

The Refugees

Just as the displaced persons were beginning to feel established in Alberta, a new and much larger wave of political refugees from the 1956 revolution in Hungary arrived in the province. On 23 October 1956, the demand by Hungarians for sweeping reforms in the communist regime led to an armed clash. The first battles in the streets of Budapest caused the collapse of the communist government, but the massive entry of Soviet troops on 4 November sealed the revolution's fate. Soon, over 200,000 refugees poured over the border into Austria. By the end of the year, thousands of the refugees had come to North America; between 1 July 1956, and 30 June 1959, 37,000 Hungarians were admitted to Canada. The Canadian government took unprecedented steps to facilitate the entry of these refugees, removing almost all the usual restrictions.

The classes of persons in Canada eligible to sponsor refugees were broadened, normal medical examination procedures were reduced, and free transportation by sea or air was provided.[70]

This new wave of immigration brought approximately 3,000 refugees to Alberta. Like those who settled elsewhere in Canada, those who came to Alberta were primarily young people; half of them were under twenty-nine, and many were students. Nearly half were single and men outnumbered women by a ratio of 3 to 2. Of those who had been in the work force prior to fleeing Hungary, the majority were either skilled workers or professionals. Their youth, education, and motivation to succeed proved to be major assets. A more receptive social climate, better economic opportunities, the presence of an already well-established Hungarian-Canadian community, and their own values and skills combined to produce a striking success story.[71]

Some of the 1956 refugees were placed as farm workers throughout the province, but the majority were placed as laborers in the major cities. Given the shortage of industry in Alberta, technical workers had difficulty finding positions related to their backgrounds, but there were many jobs available in the construction industry. Because Calgary's Hungarian community was the largest in the province, it received the largest number of refugees. The government established temporary reception centers to accommodate the influx of newcomers, and members of the Hungarian community supported the effort by providing additional accommodation, finding jobs, and working as translators. Much of the task of helping the refugees was organized through the Hungarian churches, but other groups, such as the Knights of Columbus and the Citizenship Councils, were also involved in the effort. In total, nearly seventy civic groups in the province participated in the resettlement programs.[72]

In spite of the Canadian government's response to the Hungarian refugees of 1956, the refugees experienced problems and dissatisfaction during the first year after their arrival. Accustomed to a welfare state in Hungary and cherishing the exaggerated promises made to them by some Canadian immigration officials in Europe, many were discontent with the primitive accommodation in the hurriedly arranged reception centers; they resented being expected to take whatever job was offered regardless of their background. Most were members of Hungary's educated middle class, but they found that in Canada they were being welcomed as unskilled laborers and domestics.[73]

A few of the newcomers, overwhelmed by the process of adjustment, either returned to Hungary, or became locked into low-paying jobs, underemployment, and welfare. The degree to which a refugee was able to adapt to his changed circumstances depended on a number of factors, including his age, occupational background, and personality. The transition was particularly difficult for people whose professions were not easily transferable, such as teachers and lawyers. Tradesmen and engineers had less difficulty. Some of the discontented left for what they hoped would be better conditions in the United States. But most made the adjustment to Canadian society, completed their educations, and established themselves in the new milieu. Being married was often an asset for male immigrants, not only because of the personal security it provided, but also because the income of working wives was often crucial to a family's economic mobility.[74]

Beginning in the early years of the Great Depression, Hungarians had been changing from one of the most rural groups in the province to one of the most urban. Like the displaced persons, the 1956 refugees contributed to this trend toward urbanization. Most of those who at first went to rural areas moved to the cities as soon as possible. By 1961, the refugees had helped to swell the number of people of Hungarian origin in Lethbridge to 1,497, in Calgary to 4,168, and in Edmonton to 2,225. Between 1951 and 1961, the total number of Hungarians in Alberta had almost doubled, to over 15,000 and the percentage of urban dwellers among this number had climbed to two-thirds. Edmonton acquired a sizeable concentration of the Hungarian intelligentsia and professional class since the University of Alberta made special arrangements to help some of the refugees complete their educations.[75]

The 1956 refugees helped to effect a striking change in the class composition of the Hungarian community in Alberta. Prior to 1950, Hungarian communities in the urban centers were working class; they are now overwhelmingly middle class. This is partly because of the mobility of second generation Hungarian-Canadians, but primarily because of the impact of postwar immigration. Calgary attracted many refugees who had training as geologists and geophysicists. The Calgary community now includes a number of businessmen and engineers who work in the oil industry and some who have established private engineering firms. Arpi's Industries and C.K. Steel are among the large businesses in Calgary established by Hungarian refugees.[76]

Like the earlier Hungarian immigrants, the 1956 refugees initially encountered a number of difficulties in Canada; however, several factors promoted their predominantly successful adjustment. Their image as "freedom fighters" during the cold war era tended to minimize prejudice against them. Their education and skills were welcome in a booming economy. They did not have to hide their origins in order to succeed. Upon arrival, the refugees found a well-established Hungarian-Canadian community which was able to offer them considerable help. Unlike the post-World War II displaced persons, they were not haunted by the long trauma of war.

Some of the 1956 refugees joined into the activities of the Hungarian community, but many did not; rather, they made a conscious decision to become assimilated into the larger Canadian society as quickly as possible. Many who came singly often intermarried with Canadian women, and their children seldom developed strong bonds with the Hungarian community. Historian Paul Body has attempted to explain the relative lack of attachment of the 1956 refugees across Canada to the established Hungarian communities:

> experiences of these people in Hungary predisposed them to question established social and moral ideals. This does not mean that they abandoned moral

and social commitments, but it suggests that as emigrants they reconsidered such commitments in the light of their painful disillusionment with ideological systems. When they settled in western societies, they sustained deep skepticism toward traditional values. In many cases, their search for new values did lead to the rejection of ethnic, community and religious relationships and to the pursuit of predominantly individual career goals.[77]

Nevertheless, this new and large wave of immigrants did give impetus to existing Hungarian social and cultural organizations, language schools, and churches; and some were involved in establishing new dance groups and choirs. The refugees founded only one of their own organizations, the Hungarian Freedom Fighters, a branch of an international association. Like branches of the organization elsewhere, it is strongly anticommunist in its orientation and is dedicated to bringing freedom to all countries, but particularly to Hungary and other nations presently under Soviet domination.

Conclusion

While members of the pioneer wave of Hungarians have now passed into history, people from the three later movements—the 1920s' immigrants, the postwar displaced persons, and the 1956 refugees—are very much a part of present day Alberta. Almost 40 percent of those of Hungarian origin in Alberta are immigrants, the highest percentage of any central and eastern European group in the province. Because of significant differences in their class backgrounds, the conditions they left behind, and Canadian circumstances when they arrived, the character of each of these last three waves of immigrants has been distinct. In the words of two Hungarian Presbyterian ministers in Alberta, "differences in attitudes in these three groupings [is] enough to make them appear as three ethnic groups with a language link."[78]

Relationships among the different waves of immigrants have been marked by both cooperation and conflict. The oldtimers did as much as they could to help the refugees when they arrived; however, a feeling of mistrust developed between some members of the two groups. There was a tendency among some of the postwar refugees, who were educated and middle class, to look down upon the earlier wave of immigrants as "peasants". The newcomers were disdainful of the limited financial position of the "oldtimers" and were baffled and irritated by the leftist political orientation of some of them. For their part, the earlier immigrants felt that their struggles were misunderstood and unappreciated by the recent immigrants, who arrived during a time of economic prosperity and who also received aid from the government and the Hungarian community. This inevitable conflict, however, has been blunted with the passage of time.

In addition to class differences among the different waves of immigrants, the Hungarian community has also been split along political and religious lines; however, despite these differences, the community has developed a wide range of common activities. The churches acted as equalizers, keeping dissension within church-related activities to a minimum. Cultural and social organizations in Calgary and Edmonton have multi-purpose facilities and a wide range of activities for all age groups, thereby embracing all the waves of immigrants. The Hungarian Cultural Society in Edmonton and the Hungarian Cultural Center in Calgary, established in 1978 as an "umbrella organization for all Hungarian organizations in the city," provide a year-round calendar of events, including dances, bingos, bazaars, fashion shows, arts and crafts classes, and other activities. Two of the most active Hungarian organizations in the province are the Hungarian Senior Citizen clubs in Calgary and Lethbridge which are recapturing some of that vitality and sense of community which was so important to many of the immigrants who arrived in Canada in the late 1920s.[79]

Many of the dilemmas, concerns, and opportunities currently facing Hungarians in Alberta are common to all of the central and European minorities in the province. For all of these groups, the church occupies an important part in their institutional life; and conservative, anticommunist sentiments form the basis for political attitudes and activities. For all, the question of relations with the homeland government and their Canadian embassy representatives is a difficult one that strongly divides the community. The Hungarian government is anxious to promote Hungarian cultural activities abroad and to support cultural exchanges; but some Hungarian political refugees have built their lives around opposition to the communist regime in Hungary and adamantly oppose any cultural links with the Hungarian government. Other leaders in the community feel that it is impossible to keep Hungarian culture alive in Canada without ongoing and creative contact between the two countries, particularly in such areas as folk music and folk arts.

A more crucial dilemma, which is also shared by other central and eastern European groups, is posed to the very future of organzied Hungarian life in Alberta by the paucity of new immigrants and the assimilation of the Canadian born. Some Hungarian refugees are still arriving; immigration statistics during the 1970s and 1980s show about thirty Hungarians per year coming to Alberta. But they are too few in number to have any significant impact on the community. For most Hungarians, those who are anxious to have their children maintain a sense of Hungarian identity and a knowledge of Hungarian folk culture face an uphill struggle. Saturday morning language schools are seldom popular with ethnic youth, and Hungarians are both too few in number and too indifferent to the question for the Hungarian language to be introduced into the school system. Nor is the group's demographic structure conducive to vibrant youth activities: the 1971 census showed the Hungarians to be one of the groups in the province with the smallest percentage of its total numbers in the under-fifteen category.[80]

However, the prognosis for the youth involvement and continued group vitality is by no means altogether bleak. The Hungarian community has considerable leadership talent which has promoted the continued development of several dance groups, as well as other folk arts such as embroidery and cooking. This, along with several other factors, including travel to Hungary and the federal government's multi-cultural policy, has promoted a continuing interest in ethnic heritage among Hungarian-Canadians and their children. Canadian born leaders of the Hungarian community, see the need to adapt folk traditions to modern circumstances and to share their culture with other Canadians if it is to be kept vibrant and meaningful. Many second and third generation Hungarian-Canadian youth find value and meaning in the social and cultural activities which keep them in touch with their roots.

Hungarian organizations in the large cities have been among the most responsive in the province to the new opportunities provided by the growing public acceptance of multi-culturalism. For example, the annual Hungarian fashion show in Edmonton expresses this new philosophy of cultural sharing: the culture which is shared is not a static gift from another time and place, but rather, one which is alive and reflects the influence of both modern needs and Canadian conditions. The show has recently expanded to include the participation of additional ethno-cultural groups. Edmonton's Hungarian community also sponsors an annual Csardas Ball, which has become an important social occasion not only for Hungarians, but for many others.

A number of factors, including the increased educational levels of Albertans, the improved social and economic status of Hungarians, and the heightened awareness of Hungarian culture promoted by greater efforts at cultural sharing, have combined to change drastically the image of Hungarians in Alberta. The negative stereotype embodied in the epithet, "bohunk" has given way to a positive stereotype reflecting an appreciation of their contributions to *haute cuisine*, and high culture, particularly through such musicians as Bartok and Kodaly, and a respect for their courageous stand as "freedom fighters." Arpad Joo, a former conductor of Calgary's philharmonic orchestra, has contributed to this appreciation of Hungary's rich cultural tradition.

Like the larger history of Alberta, the Hungarian experience in the province is one of pioneer struggle, mobility, social and political conflict during the Great Depression, and urbanization and growing prosperity in the years following World War II. While geographic mobility has been a dominant theme in Alberta's history generally, it has been accentuated in the Hungarian experience. Their particular vulnerability as seasonal workers contributed to the substantial movement of Hungarians between mining camps and farms at the turn of the century, and later, during the 1920s. That a number of Hungarian immigrants arrived in the late 1920s, on the eve of global economic disaster, meant that a particularly high percentage of them would be caught up in the search for scarce jobs—a restless quest which came to symbolize a decade of despair.

The war effected a dramatic change on the economy, but in so doing, uprooted many people once again. The decline of coal mining after the war led to a wholesale departure from the mining camps and into the cities. Farm workers too, including the postwar refugees who had been placed in rural areas, decided to seek better opportunities in the cities, thus becoming part of the widespread urbanization which was changing irrevocably the profile of Alberta.

Although they established a number of organizations, the Hungarians in Alberta have not been highly visible. One reason for this has been that they were scattered in small pockets throughout the province and there were few communities which were predominantly Hungarian. Today, rural settlements provide little evidence of the Hungarian presence.

Despite their relative invisibility, the Hungarians have had a significant impact on Alberta's development. The first two waves of immigrants played important roles in the coal mining camps, the sugar beet fields, and the pioneer agricultural settlements. Postwar Hungarian immigrants have contributed to the building of the urban centers, and many immigrants and second-generation Hungarian-Canadians are currently involved in various facets of the province's professional, business, and economic life. Hungarian-Canadians are proud of the achievements of the postwar refugees and the children of the immigrants who arrived in such trying circumstances during the 1920s. In the apt phraseology of historian N. F. Dreisziger, the Hungarian-Canadian experience has been one of "struggle and hope." Each wave of immigrants has struggled and overcome major obstacles in their new homeland.

CHAPTER FOURTEEN
Alberta's Jews: The Long Journey
Max Rubin

Alberta's Jews have contributed much to the province's society, economy, arts, and education. However, despite the nearly 100 years that they have been a part of the Albertan scene, little is known about them.

The world of the Jew in Europe before the twentieth century was a harsh one. The "shtetl," small town or village, where most Jews lived in Eastern Europe was a dreary place. The "shtetl" had emerged as a result of forced segregation by successive Russian Tzars and periodic violent persecution of Jews in Eastern Europe. In order to protect themselves from the outside world, the Jewish community established a strong social code. The many rules governing Jewish life were rigorously fulfilled to the point where Jewish society became introverted and almost homogeneous. At the same time, the creation of such a structure prevented, except on an economic level, social contact between Jews and non-Jews. One the most significant deterrents to social interaction was the strong observance of dietary laws:

> Not only were Jews forbidden to eat certain categories of land animals, fish, fowl, and plant foods, but also they were required to slaughter animals and prepare foods in special, ritually prescribed ways. This observance of dietary laws meant that Jews could not share food and drink with non-Jews outside the confines of the Jewish community, for they could never be sure that every minute detail of each ritual dietary requirement had been met.[1]

The strong adherence to Jewish law developed an ingrained consciousness that determined the lifestyle of the eastern European Jew. It was a consciousness that was not easily changed and the Jews coming to America and Canada initially tried to conform to the Jewish practices taught to them in the "shtetl." Yet once settled in a new country, free from the restraints of the "shtetl" and free from the overt persecution of his non-Jewish neighbors, the Jew relaxed his natural defenses.[2]

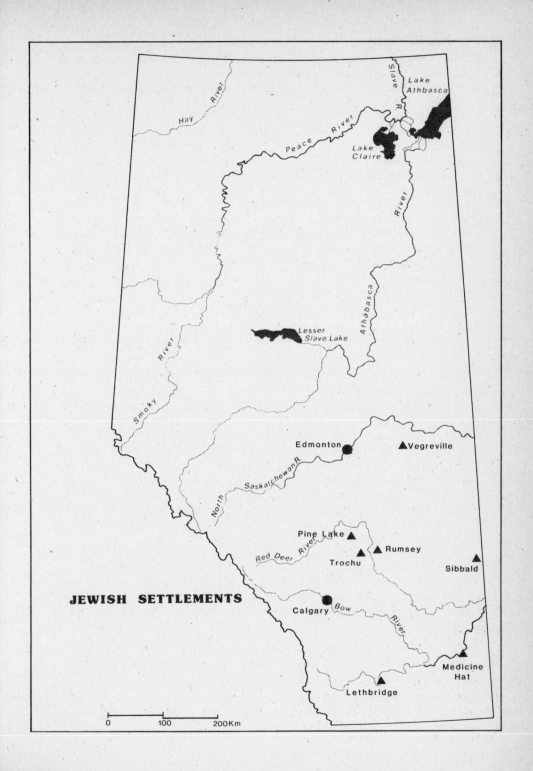

JEWISH SETTLEMENTS

Edmonton ●   ▲ Vegreville

Pine Lake ▲
Trochu ▲   ▲ Rumsey
                            ▲ Sibbald

Calgary ●   Bow

                        ▲ Medicine
                            Hat

Lethbridge ▲

Hay River
Peace River
Slave R.
Lake Athbasca
Lake Claire
River
Lesser Slave Lake
Athabasca
River
Smoky
North Saskatchewan R.
Red Deer River
River

0   100   200Km

The First Pioneers

The first record of Jews in the Canadian West can be traced back to the 1860s when several Jewish fur merchants from Minnesota began buying furs at Fort Garry (now Winnipeg).[3] It was not until 1882, however, that Jews came to settle permanently in large numbers in the West when the Canadian government decided to promote Jewish settlement in the West. The federal government's action was coincidental with events in eastern Europe. The assassination of Tzar Alexander II of Russia in 1881 triggered an intense wave of anti-Semitic pogroms in the Ukraine. Thousands of Jewish families were left destitute and homeless.[4] Protests by Jews in western Europe encouraged the formation of Jewish relief organizations. One of these was the Mansion House Committee in London, England. This group, under the auspices of the Baron de Hirsch, a French Jewish philanthropist, saw emigration of the victims as a partial solution to the Jews' plight. Canada seemed an attractive site for Jewish settlement. This enthusiasm was initially matched by that of Canada's High Commissioner in London, Sir Alexander Tilloch Galt. Galt wrote the Prime Minister, Sir John A. Macdonald:

> From what I learn these Russian Jews are a superior class of people, partly farmers, but generally trade people. . . . I found American Jews were actively promoting emigration to the United States and I thought what was good for them, could not be bad for us.[5]

Macdonald, though, was hesitant in giving his support to the project. Only after a year of debate on the topic with Galt did he reluctantly accept the idea of allowing more Jews into Canada. It would be another eight years before Jews decided to settle permanently in Alberta.

Jacob Diamond and his brother, William, were eastern European Jews who went to the United States before coming to Canada. In search of better economic opportunities, which were lacking in their native Lithuania, the brothers travelled to the New World. Jacob Diamond arrived in Alberta in 1888 and became involved in the liquor trade, while William Diamond joined his brother in 1892 and opened a tailoring shop in Calgary.[6] Prior to the Diamond brothers, only a few adventurers and itinerant Jewish pedlars had visited the province.[7]

The Jews were not immune to the wave of antiforeign sentiment that began to build in western Canada in the 1890s. Even though their numbers remained relatively small, local newspapers evoked the image of Shylock in opposing Jewish settlement. In June 1893, *The Macleod Gazette* editorialized against the arrival of sixteen Jewish settlers in southern Alberta:

> They are apparently of German extraction, and from casual view we should take them to be Jews. They have all the familiar characteristics of that race, even down to the heavy watch chains and massive rings.[8]

The editorial claimed that they were not suited to be farmers. Further mention of the supposedly undesirable nature of the new settlers was made by *The Calgary Herald:*

If these people are the only settlers that can be obtained for the Northwest, there would even then be no reason to spend money in bringing them here to let them loose on the public, while practical men who can turn the prairies into fruitful fields are being forced away by the petty annoyances to which they are subjected on attempting to come into the country.[9]

This group of Jews was part of a larger group who settled in 1893 in central Alberta near Pine Lake where they attempted to farm. They ran into immediate difficulties with pioneer conditions. The Agent for Dominion Lands had to distribute some $400 to seventy destitute Jews in the Pine Lake area in March 1894. This money came not from the federal government, but from a Jewish relief agency in London, England.[10] The federal government took no further steps in aiding the colony, except to send the Russo-Jewish Committee statements and letters urging it to help the settlers.[11] Because of their inexperience at farming and because aid was not readily available, most of the people soon left Alberta, many of them moving to the United States.[12]

Despite the failure of the first Jewish agricultural settlement in Alberta, the Diamond brothers provided the scattered and relatively small Jewish community with two determined settlers. The Diamond brothers were here to stay, and in 1894, rented the Calgary Masonic Hall for the Jewish High Holy Day services. These services were a success: those in attendance included the two Diamond brothers; five commercial travellers; a Jewish farmer, Podersky, from Lacombe; and two Edmonton Jews, including Abe Cristall, one of the first Jews to settle in the area.[13]

The early Jewish pioneers were willing to accept challenges. A case in point is Edmonton's Abe Cristall. In 1893 he came to Edmonton, after a series of failed business ventures elsewhere. A Ukrainian Jew, Abe Cristall was twenty-five years old when he disembarked at Montreal. Two years as a farmer in the Brandon area did not prove financially rewarding. In 1893, after spending some time at a Jewish farm colony at Wapella (in what was later to become Saskatchewan), he moved to Edmonton where he worked as a pedlar and established a cartage-drayman operation. A year later he went into the liquor business, and in 1895 he opened the first general store in Alberta to be run by a Jew. From this beginning he was able to launch a highly successful business career that would include ownership of several Edmonton hotels and land along Edmonton's main street.[14]

Nurturing the Jewish Identity

By 1906, Calgary had a small, thriving Jewish community. Most of its Jewish population came to Canada by way of urban centers in the United States.[15] In pioneer Calgary, the Jews lived primarily in the east end of the city on either side of the railway tracks where housing was inexpensive and where most of the city's businesses were located: Jacob Diamond's liquor business was located here, and Herman Bercuson, J. A. Guttman, and Phineas Waterman operated dry goods stores.[16]

In 1906 a number of Jews in Edmonton took concrete steps to set up a Jewish religious council, the first in the province. Lead by William Diamond, who had moved to Edmonton from Calgary in 1905, the council was able to procure the services of a lay preacher, Hyman Goldstick, to officiate at various Jewish religious functions, such as circumcisions, bar mitzvahs, weddings, and funerals. Goldstick became the first permanent spiritual leader of Alberta's Jewish community.[17]

The Edmonton Jewish community in 1906 had no kosher butchers, no religious schools, or cheders; it even lacked a synagogue where religious services and social functions could be held. Nonetheless, as a result of Goldstick's work, many Jews came to the High Holy Day services in September 1906. Still, many of those in Alberta's small Jewish community kept a low profile among members of the general public. On occasion, the general public's lack of knowledge about Jews provided some trying moments for the Jewish community, on issues such as working on Sunday.[18]

The Farm Colonies

The establishment of Jewish farm colonies in Alberta bolstered the tiny pioneer Jewish population already in the province. As early as the early 1800s in Russia, Jews were desirous of becoming farmers and the Tzarist government at the time was considering settling Jews on the land.[19] Many Jews wanted to get out of the ghetto, and they saw in America freedom from religious, social, and economic oppression.[20] In 1882, when the Jewish Colonization Association (JCA) was established as a vehicle to remove Jews to farms outside Europe, Canada became a likely place for Jewish farm enterprises. While the first Jewish farm colony at Moosomin, Saskatchewan in 1882 was a failure, other Jewish farm colonies soon followed at Wapella, Saskatchewan, 1888; Hirsch, Saskatchewan, 1892; Lipton, Saskatchewan, 1901; and Bender, Manitoba, 1903. The JCA-sponsored farm colony at Rumsey-Trochu represented the first major attempt at a Jewish farm settlement in Alberta besides the short-lived and abortive colony near Pine Lake.

The JCA first sent out a group of young Jewish men from Montreal who found fertile land along the Red Deer River. They chose land near Trochu, Alberta. At first there were seventeen settlers, representing several Jewish families: the Watermans, Guttmans, Nelsons, Braunbergs, and the Kramers.[21] With good land, a water supply, and the determination of the new settlers to be successful at farming, the beginnings looked promising. It was soon apparent to the Trochu farmers that there was more to farming than owning land and tilling the soil. A letter to the JCA in 1908 appealing for aid gives a clear picture of the difficulties they faced:

> We the undersigned have settled here, and have take up homesteads, about two years ago. Each of us has made considerable improvements on his homestead such as building, fencing and brought some land under cultivation nearly every one of us has more or less cattle. But owing the recent hard times, and the scarcity of work in the west, we find ourselfs in very bad positions, and practically unable to proceed with our undertakings, although some employment could be found in the summertime but to leave the farm in

the summer time means to neglect the farm work, and by not making any progress, some of us will be compelled, sooner or later, to abandon theire homesteads, on which we have spend so much work and money. Some of us need horses, some need some implements, and other need some dairy cows to be able to support themselves untill they start to get results from the land; We need aid and if we do not get it in time a large amount of labor, energie and money will be lost [sic].[22]

The JCA was slow to act. Only after two years did the JCA send its Winnipeg agent to Trochu to distribute money for seed to needy farmers.[23]

The Trochu group had been homesteading less than a year when the JCA established another group of settlers just east at Rumsey. Although the colonies lacked a "shochet" (ritual slaughterer) or rabbi, they were able to enlist the aid of a Jewish homesteader, Judah Shumiatcher to serve as a Hebrew teacher. Without being able to read Hebrew one could not actively participate in Sabbath services.[24]

Rumsey-Trochu became one of the largest and most prosperous of the prairie's Jewish farm settlements. In 1906, there were only eleven Jewish homesteaders holding title to 4,000 acres. Three years later there was more than double this number of settlers in the colony. As most of the original settlers came from the Gomel area of Russia, the colony was basically homogeneous.[25]

The Charles Waterman family on their Trochu farm in 1917. The Watermans were one of the first Jewish families in the farm colony at Trochu. (Courtesy Glenbow Archives)

A Jewish group at Rumsey, ca. 1910. This Jewish farm colony was one of the more successful Jewish farm communities in western Canada. (Courtesy Glenbow Archives)

Because the Jewish colony formed a major segment of the population in the Rumsey area, the Jews took an active part in the community's affairs. Both J. A. Guttman and Max Waterman were appointed as Justices of the Peace and as trustees of the Tolman School District. They became the first Jews in Alberta to hold such positions. Such positions in Russia would have been beyond the reach of any Jew.[26] Another first for the Jews of Rumsey-Trochu was the establishment of the Jewish Farmer's Cooperative Credit Union which provided the colony with a financial base. The JCA also provided support, and in 1916 lent the colony money to build a synagogue and school.[27] The colony failed to attract a permanent rabbi, but the synagogue still served as a religious and social meeting place for the farmers.

Following World War I, the Rumsey-Trochu colony absorbed a large group of Polish Jews. The new immigrants lacked the necessary means to start farming. Bad crops due to drought from 1921 to 1923 ruled out any possibility of the new arrivals succeeding. As a result, most of the newcomers moved on to Calgary and other Albertan towns.[28]

The following years of drought in the Rumsey-Trochu area brought major hardships. Many of the colony's farmers had over-extended their credit as a result of a land boom just after World War I. As the JCA's colony inspector ruefully remarked in 1922, the farmers were their own worst enemies:

> There is not even a single farmer in the Rumsey district who has funds available to cover his current expenses or to provide himself with seed and feed .... A number of farmers, however, are too badly involved for us to assist

them. (A.R), for instance, who bought a half section of land for $20,000, paid in $10,000 in cash and still owes $10,000 on the land, cannot be assisted by us because the market value of his land right now is not more than $6,000 or $7,000. His loss is therefore entirely due to buying lands when prices were very high and inflated. Several of the farmers are applying to us for loans of about $200 for the purchase of seed and feed, and offering us sub-standard security as their lands and chattels are already mortgaged to Companies and to the Bank. Those farmers cannot obtain assistance elsewhere and our advancing loans to them should be looked upon entirely from a semi-philanthropic viewpoint as a means of maintaining the Rumsey Colony.[29]

With debts piling up, many Jews gave up the land and moved to Calgary, which had a sizeable Jewish community. The colony lost more than half of its seventy families during the 1920s. The Depression of the 1930s all but wiped out the remaining colonists who once dreamed of a new beginning in the New World. The bleak years after 1933 took their toll. By World War II only two Jewish families were still actively farming at Rumsey.[30]

Sibbald

Sibbald in east central Alberta was the only other Jewish farm colony in Alberta. Also a JCA enterprise, it was settled by North Dakotan Jewish farmers in 1911. These farmers were once transplanted Europeans who were not doing well in North Dakota, and saw a golden opportunity to better themselves on the Canadian prairie. But the community was located in one of the driest parts of the Palliser Triangle. Drought years were common in the area long before the disastrous drought of the 1930s. For the settlers, Sibbald proved another North Dakota, with poor natural vegetation, soils, and rainfall.[31] Unlike Rumsey-Trochu, where communal organizations took a number of years to get formally established, the Sibbald farmers, soon after their arrival, constructed a community hall to serve the Jews in the district as a meeting place for social, religious, and educational functions. They built a house for a rabbi and attracted at least three rabbis to the colony during its short existence.[32]

The Sibbald Jewish colony was active in the general community's affairs. Many colonists belonged to the Sibbald Agricultural Society.[33] However, because of drought and depression, by 1934 only five Jewish farmers remained in the area.[34] For all practical purposes the dream of Jews as farmers in Alberta ended with the coming of the Depression.

Vegreville: A Unique Community

One of the small towns where Jews established themselves was in Vegreville, just east of Edmonton. Vegreville represents something of a unique community in Alberta in that its Jewish population lived side by side with larger numbers of Ukrainians and French Canadians. In 1911, Vegreville and district had eleven Jews, and by 1921 it had fifty-nine. Most of the families were involved in the retail and wholesale trade. Their own eastern European background and language skills made it possible for them to relate easily to the Ukrainian majority in the surrounding area. Two prominent Jewish businessmen in Vegreville were members of the town's Board of Trade and, one, Harvey Bloomfield, was a member of the local branch of the Temperance League, a Mason, and a member of the local hospital board.[35] On a communal level, Vegreville's Jews established several branches of Jewish fraternal organizations. Hadassah, a Jewish women's fraternal organization, and the Hebrew Association were Zionist groups founded in order to raise funds for Jewish settlement in Palestine.

However, the Jewish community failed to grow appreciably because of the small size of the town. Larger centers, such as Calgary and Edmonton, had greater economic opportunities and much larger Jewish communities. The attraction of the religious, cultural, and social life of larger Jewish centers doomed small Jewish communities such as the one at Vegreville.[36]

Urban Alberta and Religion

One of the main goals of Jews in Alberta was to maintain their religion. Without a spiritual leader or a synagogue, Jews found it difficult to practice their religious beliefs; without these services few other Jews would be attracted to live in the community. The building of synagogues in both Edmonton and Calgary in 1911, provided a young Alberta Jewish community with focal points on a religious and social level.

Rabbis perform many communal tasks. These include such services as "mohel," where the rabbi performs circumcisions, "shochet," where the rabbi acts as ritual slaughterer of animals, and "chazzan," where the rabbi leads the congregation in prayer.

A more time-consuming role for the rabbis in Alberta was that of community conciliator, since there was no rabbinical council in Alberta to look after social problems and religious disputes. At first, the role was undertaken by the Chief Rabbi of western Canada who was located in Winnipeg. As the community grew larger, the Chief Rabbi was less frequently called upon.

Lethbridge

The third largest concentration of Jews in Alberta, after Calgary and Edmonton, is in Lethbridge. The first Jewish family, the Moscovichs, arrived in 1908, and they were soon joined by a number of Jewish families from eastern Canada. By 1911, Lethbridge had some fifty-four Jewish citizens. Most of these were small businessmen, working in the dry goods businesses or as cattle buyers. Most of their children, however, chose not to follow in their fathers' footsteps because of the attraction of more prestigious and secure occupations in law, dentistry, and medicine.[37] Lethbridge's Jewish families built a synagogue and organized branches of the Canadian Zionist Organization and Hadassah. The smaller Jewish community of Medicine Hat, often cooperated with the Lethbridge group in Zionist activities. Many members of the Medicine Hat community, though they had their own synagogue, also maintained religious affiliation with the synagogue in Lethbridge.[38]

Jewish community at the Purim Ball in Lethbridge, February 1910. This ball, held in commemoration of Queen Esther in the Old Testament, brought together Jews from across southern Alberta, including some from as far away as Medicine Hat. (Courtesy Leo Goodman)

The Great War: 1914

The coming of World War I saw a concerted effort by Alberta's Jews on behalf of war relief.[39] The closing of immigration from Europe due to war did not prevent national Jewish organizations from planning for future immigration. Both the Canadian Jewish Alliance and the Canadian Jewish Congress, founded in 1919, made plans to patriate Jewish war victims from Poland and Russia. In Alberta, the Edmonton B'nai B'rith also made plans to aid Jewish immigration, and in 1923 it assisted thirty-five homeless Ukrainian Jewish families to immigrate to Canada.[40]

Boom and Bust: 1920s

The situation in eastern Europe after World War I was chaotic for Jews. The old order personified by the Tzar and an aristocracy was replaced during the 1920s by a new order characterized by parochial nationalistic regimes. For the Jews of Russia, the physical pogroms may have ended with the triumph of the Red armies in 1921, yet "in the successor states, systematic pogroms, in the form of economic discrimination, laid the groundwork for the dehumanization of the Nazi period."[41] In Poland, Jews were commonly blamed for the poor state of the Polish economy. The situation became so bad for Poland's Jews that during the Polish election of 1922 Warsaw's Jews could not venture into the streets for fear of their lives.[42] In a political and social climate such as this, many eastern European Jews looked for ways to escape. The condition of the Jewish community in Poland and Russia significantly affected the Calgary Jewish community.

The coming of the Switzer and Shumiachter families to Calgary changed the Jewish community's social makeup. While the Shumiachter family had been in Canada since before World War I, their extended family was still in Russia. The Switzer family had already begun the process of emigrating from Poland before 1918. The large size of both families, coupled with the fact that most of the family members who

Abraham and Bella Singer and family, Calgary, ca. 1919. The Singers were one of the prominent Jewish families in Calgary. Bella Singer played an important role in sponsoring Jewish immigrants in the post-World War I era. (Courtesy Glenbow Archives)

came to Canada went to Calgary, made these two families dominant in the social and economic life of the Jewish community.

The Switzer and Singer families came from Radom in southern Poland. In 1906, Radom had a population of over 800 thousand people, of whom 113 thousand were Jews.[43] Poverty, anti-Semitism, and the fear of being conscripted into the Polish army made Abraham Singer cross the Polish border into Germany. Singer picked Alberta, Canada for his new home, and, after living in the Rumsey-Trochu colony for a short while, finally settled in Calgary. After bringing his wife, Bella, from Poland by way of Toronto, both of them started a number of boarding houses for fellow Jewish immigrants. At the same time, Mrs. Singer worked at Calgary's Palliser Hotel as a housekeeper. By saving money, she was able to bring most of her family to Canada, including a larger number of Belzberg relations. From 1919 to 1947, Mrs. Singer managed to resettle more than a hundred Jewish families in Alberta, many of them her relatives. She later went into the hotel business in Banff and used this enterprise to buy land in east Calgary and Bridgeland.[44] For years her land acquisitions would form the basis for a major land development company, United Management.

Before the depression of the 1930s, most of Calgary's Jews lived in an area east of Centre Street South between the Bow River and Twelfth

Young Men's Hebrew Association baseball team, Calgary, ca. 1912–1914. Sports activities like baseball both furthered the integration of young Jews into Canadian society, and yet at the same time helped them to maintain their Jewish identity. (Courtesy Glenbow Archives)

The interior of Mendel Pepper's clothing store in Calgary, ca. 1914. Jews have played a prominent role in clothing merchandizing in Alberta since the turn of the century. (Courtesy Glenbow Archives)

Avenue. The Jewish community re-created in Calgary in a small way the community atmosphere of eastern Europe. Here along Sixth and Seventh Avenues South East were kosher butcher shops, Jewish groceries, and Jewish secondhand dry goods stores. Many Jews also lived in the Bridgeland area north of the Bow River with German, Italian, and Ukrainian neighbors, where they established Jewish bakeries and grocery stores. After World War II, the center of the Jewish community moved significantly as the complete community made a gradual move out of these two areas, and into more prosperous neighborhoods.

The Jewish Character: The Bundists

By 1931 Alberta had just over 3,700 Jews, of whom only 8 percent were rural. Most of Alberta's Jews lived in Calgary, Edmonton, and Lethbridge. They owned their own businesses and usually kept to themselves. Most were still not that far removed from the pogroms of Europe and the anti-Semitism and economic barriers they had once confronted in their everyday lives. But if the Jewish community seemed homogeneous to Alberta's non-Jews, it was a false impression. In reality, there existed in Alberta, as in other parts of North America, two major Jewish groups: the religiously conservative Hebraist group and the smaller predominantly left-wing Yiddishist group.

The two groups were quite dissimilar and often met in head-to-head confrontation. The Hebraist group in Alberta was represented in most

Jewish families. There were fewer Yiddishists, but nevertheless they were strongly active in community affairs. A misconception often harbored by many Hebraists about the Yiddishists was that a Yiddishist and Bundist were the same thing. This was not really so. The Yiddishist could point proudly to a heritage far beyond the scope of the Bundist movement, which was a socialist political movement. Yiddish is a centuries old vernacular used in the Russian Pale. It was a hybrid language, a mixture of many other languages, such as German, Hebrew, Polish, and Russian. It had a literary past, mainly based on Hasidic religious fables, folk songs, and plays.

Yiddish as a modern language had its beginning in Russia in the 1870s. It was at this time that Sholom Abramovich began to write social criticism based on the squalor found in the Jewish community.[45] About the same time, a group of Russian Jewish socialists, known as Bunists, adopted Yiddish as their primary means of communication. Thus Yiddishists and Bundists came to be regarded as synonymous, although they often diverged on issues relating to social habits and religion.

In Alberta, as elsewhere in Canada, those Jews who supported Yiddishist schools, such as Calgary's I.L. Peretz School and Edmonton's Shalom Alechem School were not all leftists. However, a significant number of Yiddishists in both communities were Bundists.[46]

The "Arbiter Ring" or Workman's Circle, a fraternal Jewish Bund

The first graduating class, 1934–35, of the I. L. Peretz school in Calgary. (Courtesy Glenbow Archives)

Founders of the Arbiter Ring School in Edmonton, ca. 1938. (Courtesy Provincial Archives of Alberta)

organization first appeared in Alberta in 1912 in Calgary.[47] The "Arbiter Ring" in Edmonton was founded in 1921 as a branch of the American Workman's Circle. The founders of the bunds were not really that much different in background from Alberta's other Jews. They came from the same shtetls in Poland, Russia and Romania, and believed in the need for a homeland for the Jews. However, on social issues they were worlds apart from the conservative Jews.[48]

The Edmonton "Arbiter Ring" was very active in establishing a Yiddish day school, theater, and an interest-free loan society. The "Arbiter Ring" found itself unable to compete with the conservative Jews of Edmonton for financial support, however. The school declined in the 1930s, but Yiddish theater is still popular in Edmonton.[49]

The Depression and the 1930s

Canada's Jews were significantly affected by the Depression. With the Conservative federal government of R.B. Bennett passing legislation halting immigration to Canada, Jewish immigration decreased to almost nothing. Despite the terrible conditions facing Jews in many parts of Europe during the 1930s, very few Jews entered Canada. Canada's restrictive immigration policy was particularly strict about Jewish refugees because of widespread anti-Semitism in Canada during the 1930s.[50] Alberta's Jewish community, which increased from 3,242 to 3,722 between 1921 and 1931, did not grow appreciably during the next ten years. Much of the population increase in Alberta's Jewish community came as a result of migration of Jewish farmers from Saskatchewan and

Manitoba. A small group of Saskatchewan Jews established a colony near Hythe in the Peace River District in the 1930s. In 1937, the CNR thought of settling German Jewish refugees in the Peace River District, but eventually abandoned the plan.[51]

The lack of Jewish immigration in the 1930s had a negative effect on the small Albertan Jewish community. Some Albertan Jews gave up their Jewish identity altogether. Others in the Jewish community, not ready to part with their Jewish past, sought a middle ground between Jewish orthodoxy and complete assimilation. Alberta's Jews found themselves in the 1930s receptive to change.

The most significant change in Alberta's Jewish community was the move from orthodox to conservative Judaism. The latter offered a more contemporary religious service, mixed male-female seating and a choir:

> Conservatism offered no new religious dogmas, but held out instead the prospect of religious continuity with a modification of the existing requirements of Halakha, those numerous regulations which encompassed the life of the Orthodox Jew. It sought acculturation within a new Jewish context which could happily harmonize tradition and change.[52]

In Edmonton, a group of young Jewish businessmen and professionals started Alberta's first Conservative synagogue, Beth Shalom, in 1934. In Calgary, a group of second generation Canadian Jews formed the House of Israel Association, which in time became the Conservative Beth Israel Synagogue.[53]

After World War II, many Jews who had not joined the Conservative synagogues, but still wished to be practicing Jews, turned to "modern" Orthodoxy. Modern Orthodoxy is a post-World War II phenomenon. It combines a mixed male-female seating arrangement with the basic Orthodox ritual. Both Edmonton and Calgary have Conservative and Modern Orthodox synagogues, each supported by wealthy Jewish families. In Calgary's case, the present difference between Conservative and Modern Orthodox is almost nonexistent. The once predominantly Orthodox Jewish community in Alberta is now basically Conservative in its religious practices.[54]

This change in the Jewish community's practice of Judaism occurred during the 1930s. The change was not peculiar to Alberta's Jewish community, but also occurred in the larger Canadian Jewish community. The face of Canadian Judaism was changing, something that was frightening to some leaders of the Canadian Jewish community.

Much more frightening however was the ever present spectre of anti-Semitism. During the late 1920s and 1930s Alberta and the other prairie provinces experienced an upsurge of nativism or anti-immigrant sentiment. While certainly not as virulent as European anti-Semitism, the North American version had some impact on western Canada's population. While Jews were not the only minority to experience prejudice, it has left a bad taste in the mouths of many Albertan Jews even though they feel that relations between Jews and non-Jews have generally been good in Alberta.[55]

World War II and Its Aftermath

World War II ended the Depression of the 1930s and brought with it the Holocaust, the genocide of six million Jews. While Alberta and its Jewish community were far away from the scene of the Holocaust, it had a major psychological impact on the Jewish community. The Holocaust awakened in the Jewish community a long dormant need to be recognized as Jews. Some Jews had thought of themselves as Canadians or Albertans first, Jews second; events in Europe changed that.

As in World War I, Alberta's Jewish community participated actively in helping the Canadian war effort on the home front. Under the auspices of the Canadian Jewish Congress's local branches, the community collected thousands of dollars in the form of food, clothing, and money. Many Jewish young men served in the Canadian Armed Forces, members of Alberta's Jewish community bought War Bonds, while a number of Jewish families tried to adopt Jewish refugee children, then living in Europe.[56]

The late 1940s saw a small influx to Alberta of Jewish refugees, many of whom were survivors of Nazi concentration camps. Most of these new immigrants were the sole survivors of their families and were sponsored by Jewish families who had kinship ties with them. With the help of the Jewish community they built new lives for themselves. Yet, they never forgot the concentration camps, which are still a vivid memory.[57]

Ever mobile and striving for greater economic and social status, Alberta's Jews continued their movement from the urban core to the suburbs. In many instances, the removal of a Jewish family from Bridgeland in Calgary, for example, to more fashionable addresses in the Mount Royal or Britannia districts was psychological as well. For these upwardly mobile Jews, a better address meant possible access to Jewish community leadership and told non-Jews that they had arrived.[58] In Edmonton, the Jews moved west towards the Glenora district which was predominantly made up of people of British origin. In Calgary, the same trend occurred: the Jewish community moved from the downtown area to one with predominantly British-origin residents.[59]

The war did not heal the rift between the Hebraists and Yiddishists. In Calgary, the I.L. Peretz School remained the focal point for Calgary's Yiddishists. Discussion of the possibility of the union of the Hebrew and the I.L. Peretz School caused both groups to grow even further apart. The Hebraists and Yiddishists refused to yield in the area of language priorities.[60] In recent years, the Hebraist-Yiddishist conflict has had little effect on parents choosing one school over the other for their children. Most Jewish parents prefer to send their children to the school closest to them, which, given Jewish residential patterns in the city, is generally the Calgary Hebrew School.

Jews in a Larger Community

The knowledge of centuries of persecution and being singled out as different has not made Alberta's Jews totally removed from the rest of society. Despite the small size of the Jewish community, less than 0.5

percent (9,460) of the total provincial population in 1981, Alberta's Jews could be found as judges, university presidents and chancellors, and as major contributors to the arts. A small number of Jews have also been active in politics in the province, including Harry Veiner, a long time mayor of Medicine Hat. In other fields, Abe Fratkin, a professional musician, founded the Edmonton Symphony during World War II, while S. Leiberman, Joe Shoctor, and Henry Singer brought their managerial and entrepreneurial talents to the founding of the Edmonton Eskimos. Joe Shoctor, a lawyer, founded Edmonton's Citadel Theatre and Henry Singer, a merchant, helped start Edmonton's Klondike Days. Calgary's Jews have also taken an active interest in cultural activities. Several members of Calgary's Jewish community, including Martha Cohen and Jack Singer, played a key role in the development of Calgary's Center for Performing Arts.

The Present

Since World War II Alberta's Jews have enjoyed prosperous years. The number of Jews in the managerial and professional classes in the province is well above the provincial norm. The 1971 census noted that on a national average, "Nearly one-third of Jewish males are engaged in professional and higher managerial occupations, compared to less than one-seventh of males in all other ethnic groups."[61] Jews in Alberta have always been strongly represented in commerce, whether at the retail or wholesale levels. By being self-employed, they did not have to depend on the good will of Gentile employers. However, by the 1970s, Alberta's Jews had graduated from retail and wholesale store ownership to the legal and medical professions. They had also moved into high risk management or ownership of multinational distributing and financial corporations such as General Distributors (Sony) and First City Trust.[62]

The New Community

The Jews who are second and third generation Albertans are proud of their economic accomplishments. However, many in the Jewish community, whose fathers and grandfathers were born in Europe, take a modern view of Judaism. True, they want their children to receive a Jewish education, but to keep kosher or to go to a synagogue more often than on special religious holidays is not as important as it was to their fathers and forefathers.

At the same time, the Alberta Jewish community is still suspicious of outsiders, even fellow Jews. For example, two groups of Jews from quite dissimilar backgrounds came to Alberta during the 1970s and found acceptance within the more established Jewish community somewhat problematic. The first group, of Israeli origin, settled in Calgary because of the city's position as the petroleum capital of Canada. Many had been associated with the petroleum industry in Israel. Largely from the professional classes, most of their friends are fellow Israelis, since they feel uncomfortable with Canadian Jews and vice versa. Many Canadian Jews think the Israelis should still be in Israel. The Israelis, for their part, come to Alberta because of job opportunities and the freedom from bureaucracy and fear of war. Still, the Israelis represent to Canada's Jews a sad reminder that Israel is not a utopia. In many Jewish homes in Alberta, the constant state of war in the countries around Israel and the precarious state of the Israeli economy rules out any fleeting desires to move to Israel.

The other group to come to Calgary and Edmonton, Soviet Jews, consists of about 300 hundred families in each city. Like the Israelis, the Soviet Jews have quite dissimilar backgrounds from Albertan Jews. Few are fluent in English, and they lack managerial skills, although many have technical skills or strong academic backgrounds in science. But they lack a knowledge of Judaism and its practices because of official Soviet contempt for religion. The Soviet Jews feel more comfortable with Russian values and customs and sometimes find themselves lost in an alien democratic capitalist society. There will have to be adjustment on both sides before they are accepted by fellow Jews.

Conclusion

During the 1970s, Alberta's Jewish communities, like the rest of the province, experienced tremendous growth. The number of Jews in the province increased from 7,000 to 10,000 with almost all the growth in Calgary and Edmonton. The influx of new residents was motivated by economic opportunities in Alberta. Sizeable numbers of newcomers came from Winnipeg, Toronto, Israel, the United States, South Africa, and the Soviet Union.

With this sudden growth came an increased demand for the expansion of existing facilities and services, and the creation of new ones. Almost simultaneously, major Jewish community centers combining social, cultural, and recreational facilities were opened in Calgary (1979) and Edmonton (1980). For the first time in the province's history, Reform temples were begun in both cities; and a private elementary school with a traditional (Orthodox) philosophy started in Calgary. A private enterprise newspaper, *The Jewish Star*, was founded in 1980, serving both Calgary and Edmonton.

These major changes in the size and composition of Alberta Jewry have placed palpable strains on the community's finances, manpower, leadership, and unity. Funds must be found to support new and expanded services, and volunteers must be enlisted and cultivated to guide their development. While organized community councils have existed for some years in Calgary (1952) and Edmonton (1953), the latter has been reorganized as a federation, and both are witnessing spirited discussions between young and old, "establishment" and newcomer, traditional and "modern" Jew, about the nature and direction of the future of Jewish life in the province. In addition, the world-wide Jewish problem of integrating Russian and Israeli newcomers into a society so foreign to them remains to be solved. Although anti-Semitic sentiment is not pronounced in the province, the anti-Semitism which came to light in 1983 with the firing of an Eckville school teacher for his anti-Semitic views gives cause for concern.

Because of growth and diversity in the Jewish community, and lingering anti-Semitism, a major challenge to the resourcefulness and imagination of Alberta's Jews lies ahead. They must forge their future and, like all Albertans, define a new identity.

CHAPTER FIFTEEN
The Hutterites in Alberta
Robert Macdonald

Life on the Colony

Visitors to larger towns and cities in southern Alberta might notice a family whose dress distinguishes them from most of the population. The man with a close-clipped beard wears black denim pants and jacket, a colored shirt, and broad-brimmed black hat, while his wife is dressed in a long plaid or flowered skirt, an apron, and a polka-dotted kerchief. The children are miniatures of their parents, though the smaller girls are dressed in bright yellow, pink or blue plaid dresses and similar bonnets, and the boys have a pill-shaped cap with a peak. These people are Hutterian Brethren or Hutterites, whose communal, agricultural way of life and stubborn resistance to assimilation have made them a source of controversy on the Prairies and an object of several government enquiries and academic studies. There are about 23,000 Hutterites located in the three prairie provinces and in North and South Dakota, Minnesota, Montana and Washington; however the largest concentration —about 7,400 in 116 colonies—is in Alberta.[1]

To understand the Hutterites, their place in Alberta, and the controversy which has accompanied them, it is important to understand their origin, history, and beliefs. They are a product of the Protestant Reformation of the sixteenth century, when the questioning of Catholic dogma and practices led to a proliferation of groups seeking to retrieve the "true" meaning of the Christian Gospel. From lay Bible-study groups that were expelled from Zurich, Switzerland in 1525 emerged a movement known as the Anabaptists which took root in the Netherlands, northern Germany, southern Germany, and the Austrian Tyrol. The movement shared several beliefs, including:

> reconstruction of the church according to the New Testament pattern and entirely separate from the state; adult baptism following repentance and confession of faith; the priesthood of all believers stressing man's relation to God

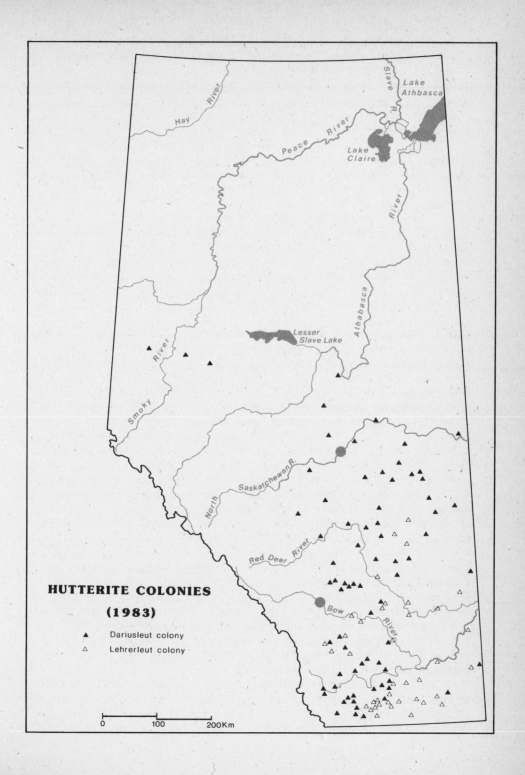

HUTTERITE COLONIES

(1983)

▲ Dariusleut colony
△ Lehrerleut colony

0   100   200Km

and equality between men; internal discipline based on free decision and exclusion of those who become apostate; pacifism and refusal to swear oaths; and non-conformity with the outside world.[2]

Descendants of these Anabaptists, or adult baptizers, include the Mennonites, who are found throughout the American and Canadian Prairies, and the Amish, who are chiefly located in southwestern Ontario, Iowa, Ohio, and Pennsylvania. Though there were more radical Anabaptists in the sixteenth century, notably at Muenster, the most radical (in terms of the sixteenth century) of the Anabaptists still in existence are the Hutterites. The group takes its name from Jakob Huter, who organized disparate groups in 1528 in Moravia. The Hutterites base their communal lifestyle on the primitive church described in Acts 2:44: "And all that believed were together, and had all things in common."[3]

The fundamental characteristics of Hutterian society rest on this essential religious base. Thus for the Hutterites, daily life cannot be separated from religious convictions and a specific world view. For them, absolute authority comes from God, who has created everything in a divine order and hierarchy. This order, which reflects God, is spiritual, unchanging, and eternal, while that made by man is changing and transitory. The communal lifestyle is hence permanent, ordained by God in the early church. Because man was created by God, man's chief end in life is to obey God's orders; thus, throughout a Hutterite's life, from early education to baptism, marriage, and responsibility in the colony, he is taught to worship God and obey the divine order and law as revealed in Scripture. Hutterites believe there is a conflict between the spiritual world of God's order and hierarchy, and the carnal world of man's creation. The original sin of Adam and Eve was their disobedience of God's laws. And this rebelliousness in man must be broken: the individual must become submissive to the will of God, for only through obedience and repentance of sin can one receive the grace of God and hence eternal life.

For the Hutterites, man's rebelliousness is reflected in the carnal world. A glance at the myriad of social problems affecting contemporary society illustrates to them man's rebelliousness and covetness, and the consequent danger for the Hutterites of submitting to this secular world. Consequently, remembering that man's higher purpose is to obey God, Hutterites take seriously the injunction "Be not conformed to this world." (Romans 12:2) Thus Hutterites have kept their Tyrolese and Carinthian dialect, have continued to use High German in religious services, and have clung to their historic patterns of dress and organization. As indicated above, the Acts of the Apostles is interpreted to mean that God's law requires communal living. Every member contributes his time, labour, and talents for the good of the community; those unwilling to accept the discipline and complete sharing of material goods are excluded from community membership.[4]

Divine order is reflected in the hierarchy of Hutterite society. As God is lord over man, man is lord over woman, parent over child, older person over younger. This sense of hierarchy is also reflected in the socio-economic positions of Hutterites, since heads of operations are elected by adult men of the colony. The preacher, also elected, is the moral guardian of the colony and thus commands the greatest respect in the colony hierarchy. The process of election is interpreted as a visible sign of God's will for the individual. For Hutterites marriage also reflects the divine hierarchy and is the preferred state for some 99 percent of the adults since it is believed to lead men and women closer to God. But in the colony and in marriage, women are submissive to men.[5]

The word of God as revealed in the conservative, unchanging Hutterite interpretation of the Bible, especially the New Testament, dictates that the law of God is superior to the law of men. Governments made by men are necessarily reflective of man's rebellious character. Hutterites are aware of the persecution that Christ suffered at the hands of government and aware of Christ's warnings to his disciples that they would be persecuted. (Matthew 10:16-19) They refuse to take an oath of allegiance for that would imply submission to the laws of men. This suspicion of government is reinforced by Christ's injunction to turn the other cheek and the sixth commandment "Thou shalt not kill." Consequently Hutterites refuse to participate in wars.[6] Through sermons essentially unchanged since the sixteenth and seventeenth centuries and passed on from preacher to preacher, the conservative attitude to the world is maintained. For Hutterites, to live surrounded by unbelievers implies suffering and martyrdom, which is reflected in their own history, something learned as they grow up.

The structure of colony life—its hierarchy and routine observances—is anchored in the ultimate purpose of obeying God's will as revealed in Scripture. The basic beliefs derived from this premise are ever present in the daily lives of colony members, and this belief system is imprinted upon them from birth to death by a comprehensive process of socialization and education.

In the period following a child's birth (after the mother has returned to the work force), he or she is cared for by an adult woman or older girl. As the child grows older, he becomes less dependent on his family and more integrated with his peers. By age two or two and a half, his formal education begins in the kindergarten or *kleinschule*: games often imitate the adult roles in the colony, under the strict supervision of the kindergarten mother who demands and gets respect and obedience. At meals, children learn to recite prayers as well as sing some Hutterite hymns dating from the early history.

At age six or seven, children graduate to the German school which runs before and after the English or public school. Both schools are generally held in the dual purpose, one-roomed church, though increasingly colonies are using separate facilities for church and school. Disciplining the children is the responsibility of the German teacher who has been especially elected by the elders of the colony. His self-taught expertise rests on traditional methods and theory laid down by early leaders in the sixteenth and seventeenth centuries. The method stresses learning in small pieces, learning at one's own rate, and memorization of rules. Children are taught to speak only when spoken to, to obey adults, and to

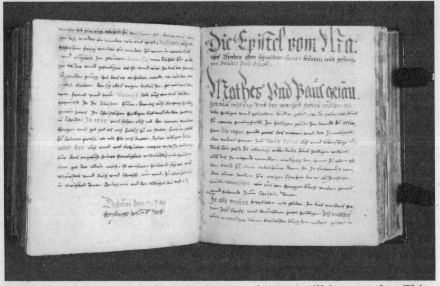

Book of Hutterite writings from the 1560s and 1570s, still in use today. This old German writing style continues to be taught as authoritative manuscripts (or texts) are copied by members for use in church and education. (Courtesy Glenbow Archives)

learn how to behave at the table. There is a minimal use of corporal punishment: punishment is meted out by standing in front of other children.

The academic lessons include practising writing German script, reading German, reciting verses from the hymn book, the Book of Psalms, the New Testament, or a biblical history book. The catechism, episodes of Hutterite history, and fundamentals of mathematics are also on the curriculum. In addition the children learn the fundamentals through rituals or meals eaten in the common dining room of the colony. As well as their lessons, the children are assigned work around the colony—whether helping women cleaning up the dining hall or helping men with livestock.

Besides the German school and work, the children attend the English or public school. There they learn from a series of outside teachers who teach the basic provincial curriculum, with modifications such as absence of audio-visual equipment and no teaching of music or evolution. Older children help younger ones learn.

At age thirteen or fourteen, children begin to look forward to the day when they become adults and leave school. Activities center around colony roles. By custom, at age fifteen, children become adults and leave school, taking their place with other adults in the dining room. Tools, clothing material, and a locked chest are given them at this time.

Subsequently young people are assigned apprenticeship roles in the colony—emphasizing their contribution to the community. For young men the seeding and harvest seasons or construction of buildings stress the hard work. During this period as adults, the young persons test their identity among their peer group and within the colony. While some may leave the colony, as a rule the social, psychological, and economic security draws them back. On Sunday afternoons they attend Sunday School, where the morning's sermons are reinforced. In evenings they might gather to sing traditional songs.

Around twenty-one or twenty-two, young Hutterites are usually baptized into the community. In the preceding weeks, usually at Pentecost, they study the catechism and undergo an examination of their understanding of the Hutterite faith. Upon baptism, by the laying on of hands and the pouring of water, the youth signify voluntary acceptance of the tenets, a submission to God's will and law. Defection or breaches of the faith after baptism become serious matters.

Upon baptism, men are further socialized by being given voting privileges and specific economic responsibilities. In subsequent years, they may be elected to manage one of the specific units, such as the poultry, sheep, hogs, or cattle. Finally, a man could be elected farm manager. With each involvement as a manager or member of the governing Council, the interests of the community become uppermost in the mind of a Hutterite.

Marriage also leads to increased acculturation. The marriage usually is between members of different colonies within the *Leut* or group, especially as Hutterites become more mobile and visit more frequently. Formal permission is sought from parents and respective preachers. For the wife, it means adjusting to her husband's colony. As children come along, the couple becomes more aware of its duty to bring the children up in the faith. Often, increased colony responsibilities come at this time, whether related to an enterprise or in the women's sphere.

The highest level in the Hutterite socialization process is reached when the man is elected to the Council. There, the preacher, the *Wirt* or colony manager, the Field Manager (in charge of work schedules), the German teacher, and one or two unit bosses decide on directions for the colony such as modernization of equipment or housing, labor-saving devices, and future expansion or establishment of daughter colonies. Clearly responsibility for others is implicit.

A major decision occurs when the population of the colony becomes too great for the number of people or "souls" on available land: there is a manpower surplus which, coupled with a limited number of managerial positions in the colony, means the younger men become frustrated. Ordinarily this may happen when the number of "souls" reaches 100 to 110. In the past the high birth rate of Hutterites, with an average family of nine children, had led to the establishment of daughter colonies every fourteen to seventeen years.[7] However, recent data suggests that the birth rate has been declining: partly because of later marriages, partly because of growing material comfort.[8] The rate of population increase, as well as the increasing cost and decreasing availability of large blocs of land, has slowed down the rate of colony formation.

When a daughter colony is formed, depending on the group or *Leut*, the two colonies may act together until such time as it is seen that the new one can stand on its own. In any case, assets are divided and members move to the new colony according to lot. The division creates the pressure of additional work on the younger colony members.

Historical Background

Throughout the process of socialization, including the daily church services, Hutterites are acutely aware of their history. In the early years of the Anabaptist movement in the 1520s, its leaders were jailed and executed by imperial authorities trying to suppress the religious revolt and the simultaneous peasant revolts of the period. The communal Anabaptists, especially in Tyrol and Moravia, were organized by Jakob Huter during the 1530s. Their opposition to war and war taxes were soon seen as a direct threat to imperial authorities, and in 1536 Huter was arrested and burnt at the stake. One of his successors, Peter Riedemann, had been jailed at Marburg, and his *Confessions* written at this time, remain the standard doctrinal interpretation for Hutterites.

Throughout the sixteenth century, the Hutterites took refuge protected by Moravian nobles. But the power of these nobles waned; and in response to a new Turkish invasion, imperial authorities harrassed the Brethren, causing many to flee to caves and cellars. This harassment reached a peak in the 1620s when the Protestant nobles were crushed during the Thirty Years' War. With the forces of Catholicism and imperial authority in control, Hutterites fled from Moravia to Hungary where Protestant nobles, who needed the Hutterite skills as artisans and agriculturalists, protected them. Nonetheless there was a concerted effort by imperial authorities to persecute and convert the Brethren. Pressure was such that the practise of community of goods, always in tension with family responsibilities, was abandoned from 1683 to 1761.[9]

During the reign of Maria Theresa from 1740, the persecution intensified. Remnants fled to Transylvania and Wallachia, where they made converts from among other Protestants. The significance of this persecution can been seen in that many of the Hutterite folk songs sung today date from this period and draw a parallel between the persecution of the Hutterites and the suffering of the Hebrews under the pharoahs.

Finally, in 1770, a remnant of approximately seventy, which had reestablished the community of goods, accepted an invitation from Catherine the Great of Russia to settle in the newly conquered territories of the southern Ukraine. There, along with other German settlers, including the Mennonites, the Hutterites demonstrated the value of their hard work and of their skill in cultivating the land. Their stay in Russia was relatively peaceful. Prosperity, population pressures, and peace—as well as contact with noncommunal Mennonite villagers—led to another move and a second abandonment of the community of goods after 1818. However, by this time the artisan skills of manufacturing had deteriorated, and increasingly the Brethren concentrated on agricultural pursuits. Though they lived in villages and accepted mutual aid, the lifestyle was essentially one of individual, self-sufficient families. Beginning in the 1850s a remnant felt this lifestyle was not in keeping with the communal pattern of their forefathers. As a result of this revival, in 1859 a group under Michael Waldner, a blacksmith (schmiede) who had been elected preacher, reestablished a communal lifestyle. He was followed in 1860 by the preacher Darius Walter who organized a second group.

At the point of reorganization, however, the Brethren were confronted by a new situation. During the decade of the 1860s, Russification policies of the Tsarist government threatened minorities such as the Mennonites and Hutterites. This pressure to assimilate culminated in 1871, when military exemption was withdrawn. Consequently in 1873 two Hutterites accompanied a Mennonite delegation to the United States in search of new lands and respect for their way of life. The result was a decision to locate in what is now South Dakota. The Schmiedeleut and Dariusleut, named after their founders, set sail for the United States in the summer of 1874. A third group reorganizing under Jacob Wipf, a teacher (lehrer), left in 1877 to settle near the other two groups.[10]

The reorganization into three distinct groups was to have a significant and long-term effect on Hutterian development. Although there was interaction and intermarriage at first, they each developed slightly different customs in clothing, schooling, marriage, election of preachers or managers, creation of new colonies, farming practises, and attitudes towards the outside society. These differences have created difficulties in cooperation. Marriage is now within each group or leut, further limiting cooperation.

In the Dakotas, the approximately 400 Hutterites experienced the same challenges as most pioneering families. But they soon adapted to agricultural production and established small home or agriculturally based industries such as flour mills. They also adjusted to the American public school system, by accepting English-language schooling supplemented by their own German-language schooling. Prosperity and growth enabled them to establish new colonies.

However the outbreak of the Spanish-American War in 1898 threatened the continuance of their pacifist lifestyle. As a result, some looked to Canada and in 1899 received assurances from the Canadian authorities (desirous of enticing settlers to the West) that their pacifism would be respected, that they would be accorded full religious freedom including the right to set up independent schools, that they would not be required to take oaths or hold public offices, and that they would be allowed to continue their communal lifestyle.[11] The Canadian government could offer these guarantees because it controlled lands and settlement in much of western Canada, and existing legislation already permitted farm groups to live in hamlets and to enjoy military exemption. This 1899 agreement is significant since it was the basis on which Hutterites later came to Canada, but its terms have caused confusion and controversy throughout their stay. Some of the clauses referred to provincial responsibilities which were outside the authority of the federal government, especially after provincial status and land control were ceded to Alberta and Saskatchewan in 1905 and 1930.

The entry of the United States into World War I in 1917 brought persecution for the 2,000 Hutterites. Their German language and their pacifism, as well as their wealth, made them targets. Property was destroyed, livestock stolen, and a number of Hutterite men were drafted, subjected to the humiliation of the military induction process, and put into conscientious objector camps where they were given poor food and living conditions. Four men were imprisoned first at Alcatraz then at Fort Leavenworth, Kansas, were separated from their families, and were subjected to brutal treatment which resulted in the death of two. Since this martyrdom and persecution experience confirmed the dangers of the outside world, the Hutterites decided to look for a new home.

They decided to take advantage of the 1899 agreement with Canada. Between 1918 and 1920, most of the colonies moved north at considerable loss. Six *Schmiedeleut* colonies purchased land near Portage la Prairie in Manitoba, while five *Dariusleut* and four *Lehrerleut* settled in southern Alberta. The *Lehrerleut* purchased land between Magrath and Cardston, while some *Dariusleut* bought CPR lands northeast of Calgary near Beiseker. The land and farming practises were similar to those they had been used to in South Dakota. However the specific decision to locate in southern Alberta was taken because land agents had assembled land in that area.

The first years in Alberta were not easy. Buildings had to be erected in the familiar pattern (houses and dining hall in the center, operational buildings on the outside), wells dug or creeks dammed, livestock

View of a Hutterite colony in 1963. The Hutterite colonies are a feature of the prairie landscape. Note the typical colony located near water with the farm operations around the edge and the living quarters in the center. (Courtesy Glenbow Archives)

and machinery purchased. In addition, agricultural prices fell at the end of the war. Consequently the establishment of their communal living patterns entailed considerable hard work and sacrifice.

No Strangers to Controversy: Attitudes towards Hutterites in Alberta

The normal challenges of establishing colonies in a new land were not the only things confronting the Hutterites. In the beginning they encountered hostility from veterans' groups, newspapers, and some politicians. It was not just their pacifism and their use of the German language which was attacked, but also their communal living style and resistance to assimilation. In response, the Canadian government in 1919 restricted the immigration of Mennonites, Hutterites, and Doukhobors. But this was relaxed in 1922, and during the next decade the remaining colonies moved north. Because of the high birth rate and initial lack of capital to purchase adequate acreages, many of the original Hutterite colonies established daughter colonies within five or six years of settling in Canada.

As new colonies were established, controversies arose over the desirability of the Hutterites as neighbors. Some Hutterites wondered if these attitudes foretold of new persecutions. Although school inspectors reported cooperation by the colonies, schools became an issue.[12] The one-room colony schools were not much different from most rural schools in the province in that they drew students from a small area and were run by local trustees. However, the colony schools were held in the church, and the influence of the outside teacher was restricted by the Hutterite philosophy, by the German school before and after school, as well as by the daily church service. The distinctiveness of the Hutterite schools was a source of irritation to residents who viewed the schools as a potential means of assimilation.

During the depression, attitudes towards Hutterites changed. In areas of Alberta buffeted by drought and soil drifting, crop failures, and consequent tax arrears, the presence of the Brethren began to be seen as an advantage.[13] Their diverse agriculture, relative self-sufficiency, and austere living style enabled them to survive price declines or poor crops. Because of the depression and growing unemployment, the Bennett government had severely restricted immigration to protect native Canadians. Nonetheless, around Raymond, when the last American Hutterite colonies were in the process of moving to Canada, local businessmen were anxious for them to locate there.[14] This is not to say Hutterites were regarded favorably by everyone, nor that attempts to assimilate them were not made. Indeed even by the late 1920s there were concerns expressed by rural and farm organizations about the impact of Hutterites in a changing rural society. Nonetheless, the depression era was a period of generally positive attitudes toward Hutterites. Despite this favorable record, Hutterites shared equally with their neighbors the problems of low yields and low grain prices. Their position was difficult: while they had substantial livestock operations, these were based on grain production and they had not adapted to irrigation

as had some of their neighbors. Shortage of capital delayed their purchase of machines and hence their ability to expand holdings.

With the outbreak of World War II, attitudes changed once again. The
basis of the controversy remained the differences between Hutterite life
and that of the surrounding rural society. Fundamental to the conflict
was their communal lifestyle, their pacifism, and the use of the German
language. The rise in agricultural prices during the war enabled Hutterites, along with other farmers, to expand their acreage. Although Hutterite purchases were small, their potential for expansion frightened
other farmers. These latter saw their own sons fighting for Canada while
Hutterites remaining at home were "profiting" from the war. Salient
facts about the Hutterites were usually ignored, such as the fact that
many Hutterites served in alternative service, especially in forestry
projects, and contributed to the Red Cross. Some colonies bought Victory
loans, but refused interest on them for some years after the war.

Agitation during the war against the Hutterites was strongest in the
area south of Lethbridge where they were concentrated. In response to
demands, in 1942 the Social Credit government introduced restrictive
legislation. The cabinet spokesman was Solon Low who represented
Raymond. After praising the Hutterite contributions, Low indicated
that the measure was introduced to "allay public feeling which has been
aroused to the point of violence." But he claimed that it was "not a
persecuting measure."[15] The 1942 Land Sales Prohibition Act prevented
land purchases and leases by Hutterites, Doukhobors, and other aliens
until after the war. Constitutional challenges led to an amendment.

Though anti-Hutterite opinion focussed on the divergent Hutterite
lifestyle, it also resulted from changes taking place in rural society.
Though these changes had been occurring since the 1920s, a number of
forces at work during the post-World War II period accelerated the
process. Increasing mechanization of agriculture meant a decrease in the
need for labor. Mechanization also led to larger farm holdings. As a
consequence there was rural depopulation, which was hastened by
school consolidation and improved highways. This major shift in rural
Alberta's society inevitably created anxieties, and the Hutterites became
an obvious target of attention and a perceived cause of the problems
associated with it.

In 1947 an all-party committee of the legislature was empowered to
investigate the Land Sales Prohibition Act and the impact of Hutterites.
Most of the briefs opposed the Hutterite way of life and perceived
their lifestyle as detrimental to rural society. Schools were seen as a
means to integrate them into the larger society. Despite evidence of
cooperation with school teachers and prompt payment of bills on goods
purchased locally, the Committee felt that land restrictions should be
maintained and a procedure established to regulate land purchases. In
the Act which followed, Hutterites were restricted from establishing new
colonies less than forty miles from an existing colony. Moreover, the
amount of land a colony could obtain was limited to what the colony
had in 1944, or to 6,400 acres.[16] Further, there was to be a ninety-day

period in which the land was for sale to the public before the Hutterites could buy it. The agitation and the resulting land restrictions meant that colonies could no longer expand nearby.

The significance of the Act, which limited colonies from purchasing or leasing land, was that for the first time Hutterites in Alberta were faced with overt legislation aimed at restricting their way of life. Despite pressure in other jurisdictions, Alberta was the only province or state where they lived which had discriminatory legislation. Consequently Alberta's Hutterites felt they were singled out for discrimination, just as their ancestors had been. They had few defenders outside of some clergymen, a few lawyers, and the small CCF party.[17]

Because of their high birth rate, resulting in average families of nine children, Hutterites continually had to find more land for existing colonies or had to establish new colonies when they no longer had responsible positions for all the men.[18] Rural groups felt strongly that Hutterites were circumventing the Act through leases or individual purchases. In 1958 the government appointed another committee to investigate the problem. The by now familiar objections to their lifestyle, purchasing habits, and their impact on land prices dominated the hearings. The extent to which the letter of the law was adhered to was a focus of the enquiry. As a result this non-legislative committee recommended retention of the restrictions. Hutterites objected to being singled out for special treatment.[19]

In 1960 the Act was changed to establish the Communal Property Control Board. Until dropped, public hearings became forums for the anti-Hutterites; the Board's recommendations after analysis were subject to cabinet approval. Political decisions at this level were subject to controversy, and in 1967 Hutterites near High River and their lawyers challenged the constitutionality of the Act. In the end the Supreme Court ruled that it was predicated on land planning not religious persecution. In addition, in 1969 and 1971, the Hutterites unsuccessfully challenged the school-leaving age of sixteen.

In 1971 a controversy in Starland, near Drumheller, erupted when the Board allowed a new colony, contrary to earlier promises. Public outcry led the new Progressive Conservative government to establish a new legislative committee to investigate the issue. Not only did the committee hear briefs and visit colonies, but it systematically investigated long-standing complaints of purchasing practices, land prices, poor citizenship, nonpayment of taxes, poor education, and disobedience of the law. Partly as a result of the enquiry and fears the restrictions would be contrary to the new human rights legislation, the Communal Property Act was repealed. The Premier resisted a demonstration and letter campaign. The change in governmental attitude reflected the increasing urban base of Alberta's population.[20]

The Hutterite Response in Alberta

The Hutterites' historic experience with the outside world, especially Alberta, has tended to confirm for them their world view that the faithful colonies were surrounded by a Godless, hostile society bent on breaking down the colony and assimilating them by schools and discriminatory legislation. In addition, given the nature of Alberta's society with its urbanization and accompanying social problems, this outside society had little attraction for the Brethren compared to the security of the colony. They could not allow their children to be exposed to such external temptations. [21]

Throughout their history, Hutterites have resisted change. Nevertheless, the Brethren have changed since they came to Alberta. For the past twenty-five years, but particularly in the 1970s and early 1980s, they and other farmers have been caught in the cost-price squeeze, created by slowly increasing prices for grain and livestock and rapidly increasing costs for land, fuel, and machinery. During the 1940s, after considerable debate, especially among the younger men, they opted for labor-saving machines such as tractors, combines, and trucks. Today Hutterites do not regret the passing of the horse and accompanying slow transportation. Their facilities tend to contain very up-to-date equipment, though they are early adapters rather than innovators. The large-scale operations and consequent lower overheads mean they adopt new machinery more quickly than the ordinary farmer.

As anthropologist John Bennett has indicated, since World War II and especially since the 1960s, Hutterite lifestyle has changed perceptibly. Even in the older colonies, Hutterites, like other rural residents, have modernized their homes by installing facilities such as indoor plumbing and by providing a few amenities for families such as summer playsheds, all within the communal framework. While some older colonies retain the two-storey wood or stucco style, a few older colonies and especially newer colonies have adopted one-storey multi-units with spacious basements. The homes are more highly decorated with flowers and plants than they were in the past, and some even have fences. Many of the modern conveniences for residences, such as electric sewing machines, covered floors, electric polishers, or hot plates, have been accepted partly at the insistence of women, despite their being unable to vote in colony affairs. Adopting home conveniences has made women's work easier and hence considerably enhanced their position: but women are still below men in the hierarchy. Historically it was the younger men who pressed for the adoption of modern and efficient machinery for farm operations, but more recently it is often the women who successfully request the purchase of household conveniences. When the newer colonies easily incorporate conveniences, they put pressure on older parent colonies to modernize.

Just as there have been significant internal changes in colony life, the physical location of the colonies has evolved over time. The government policy of no colonies within forty miles of each other, which was later reduced to twenty-five miles, and the policy of only two colonies per county and municipal district or 5 percent of the land, changed the spacing of colonies. Beginning in the 1940s and 1950s, but accelerating in the 1960s and 1970s, Hutterites (especially the *Dariusleut*) have

moved out of the original settlement areas around Lethbridge and Beiseker and are now spread across the province. By the early 1970s
colonies were established in the Peace River region.[22]

Moving into new areas has created a need to adapt agricultural
practises to new climatic and soil conditions, often adding further costs.
The moves have also meant that colonies have become differentiated
through emphasis on different types of production. In the north, for
example, better rainfall means larger pastures for dairy herds; consequently northern colonies have specialized more in dairying. Others
have invested heavily in large sanitary hog barns, while some have a
flour mill or tannery. Around Edmonton and in the Peace River area,
there are greater opportunities for honey production.

As the colonies have evolved and dispersed across Alberta, they have
become less isolated from outside influences. Today travelling is much
more commonplace than it was in the past, partly because colony dispersion has made it necessary to go considerable distances to visit relatives.
Mechanization and improved transportation have created more leisure
time and enabled people to visit more easily, often in vans or station
wagons. As well, certain skills such as broommaking or medical skills
have been replaced by a greater reliance on outside services. A more
frequent sight today is that of Hutterites in town.

*Hutterites at a blood donors' clinic in Lethbridge. This scene reflects
Hutterite interaction with the outside community, especially their
participation in those philanthropic activities that are in harmony with their
Christian beliefs. (Courtesy The Archives, Sir Alexander Galt Museum, City
of Lethbridge)*

This increased travel has heightened the Hutterite's awareness of the outside world, though this increased awareness is by no means accompanied by envy. Contact with the outside world has also become more frequent as a result of the increased visits to the colony by outsiders such as tourists or students. Hutterites have also become more involved than previously in adjoining communities. Some Hutterites have participated in blood donor clinics, have joined seed cleaning cooperatives, and in one community have joined a local Chamber of Commerce. Dependence on outside markets for their cattle, sheep, poultry, or swine has forced enterprise managers to read farm journals and newspapers and to visit agricultural research stations in order to keep abreast of the latest agricultural developments. Finally, the profitability of their enterprise in a complex world has made it necessary for the Brethren to rely on advice from lawyers and chartered accountants.

Given the pressures inevitably inherent in trying to maintain an ascetic communal way of life amidst an affluent society and given the problems of finding large blocs of land in areas where land prices have escalated, it is not surprising that some colonies have had internal conflicts and even wholesale defections. Most of those who leave the colony are young men who have not yet been baptized. The majority return to the colonies, partly because of the security which colony life offers and partly because of their upbringing, which does not equip them with the intellectual and social skills necessary to cope with a predominantly urban society. Often when both men and women have defected it has been in reaction to either a particularly rigid leadership or a weak leadership unable to discipline members. In some colonies in southern Alberta, the pressures have been strong enough that the communal farm has disintegrated and children are sent to school off the colony. Other colonies are aware of these developments and consequently, through elders' and preachers' meetings, try to prevent large-scale defection.

While these defections are significant, they are not typical. Modifications in lifestyle and experience have for the most part taken place within the limitations of communal life. Colony leaders attempt to control changes so that they do not have a negative impact on the colony. Decisions to introduce modern changes are made on the basis of their effect on the colony's productivity as an agricultural enterprise.[23] Often discussions take place within the whole *leut* or group. The annual meeting of ministers permits full discussion of problems, enables planning of new colonies in an orderly fashion, and controls directions individual colonies or several colonies may be heading.

Like modern technology, the provincial school system is a potentially disruptive force, so the colony attempts to minimize its impact. Colony leaders inform the English teacher about the Hutterite philosophy and way of life and though they do not interfere with the teacher's lifestyle they admonish their children to avoid it. Historically Canadian society has seen the assimilation of immigrant or minority groups as one of the functions of the school, and certainly this has been the concept advocated by Hutterite opponents. The Hutterites' awareness of this assimilative threat, as well as their memory of earlier experiences in South Dakota or in Canada during the 1920s (when Hutterites sent outside for schooling left permanently), has heightened the Hutterite desire to control the effects of schools. The "lessons" of the renegade colonies in this regard have also shaped their views. It was with this in mind that, when the Athabasca Colony in 1962 temporarily sent children off the colony to school, the elders of the other colonies persuaded them to abandon the practise.

More significantly the school programme itself is seen as a threat, if not controlled. This control involves several aspects. Technological aids such as film, television, radio, or phonographs are not allowed. Music and competitive sports are discouraged, and theologically suspect themes such as Darwinian evolution are vigorously resisted. Emphasis is on the practical applications of the traditional three Rs. A further control reflects the fact that traditionally the one-room colony school takes place in the building which also serves as the church, making it difficult for the teacher to put up pictures or posters. Recently some of the colonies have constructed a building with a separate room for the school or built a workroom for the teacher with portable bulletins or blackboards. Nonetheless compared to noncolony schools, the teacher in a colony operates in a circumscribed fashion.

Conclusion

Despite their relatively small and scattered population, making up about 0.3 percent of that of Alberta, the Hutterites have made an important contribution to the province's mosaic.[24] Hutterites have not made contributions in the search for medical or scientific knowledge, in the creation of literary or dramatic works or visual arts, or in the development of business or politics. Their musical contributions have been limited to their traditional folk and religious songs, and their handicrafts have been circulated only among their own members. But the Hutterites have played an important economic role in Alberta.

As the 1972 Alberta legislative report indicated, Hutterites have made contributions to local and provincial economies. Some of these contributions reflect the practical application of their Christian beliefs through assistance to their neighbors, while others reveal their business and agricultural acumen. In 1971, Hutterites received 3 percent of all total receipts earned by Albertan farmers on less than 2 percent of the arable land in the province. Moreover, they received a higher proportion of their income from livestock operations than did ordinary farmers, and in doing so almost half their expenses were purchases from other farmers. Though their grain production is proportionate to their land holdings, in other enterprises such as dairying or hog raising, it is estimated that Hutterites produce approximately 10 percent of the provincial total. Similarly, in the area of poultry production, the Hutterites have perhaps 10 percent of the laying hens and from 70 to 90 percent of the ducks and geese in the province. Clearly Hutterites have contributed to the diversification of Alberta's agriculture. Thus for agriculture—the backbone of Alberta's economy and a resource renewable long after petroleum resources have declined—the efficient production of the 116 colonies is significant; and since Alberta continues to be called upon to provide food for the world, the Hutterites will continue to play a significant role.

While Alberta's population has become increasingly urban, the Brethren have remained on the land. In fact their population density per acre is considerably greater than the rural average, particularly in the more open and drier southern portions of the province. Geographers note the continued existence of colonies at a time when other hamlets are disappearing.

Hutterites have also been involved in the evolution of the self-image of Alberta's society. Their presence has provoked controversy and conflicts since their arrival over six decades ago; this controversy has had profound effects on provincial policy, especially in the three decades after the beginning of World War II. The "Hutterite question" provided tests for Alberta's human rights legislation, including the initial test for the present Bill of Rights. The conflicts between the Hutterian way of life and that of mainstream Alberta have thrown into relief debates concerning assimilation and tolerance of minority groups. The colonies, which are widely visited by Alberta's school children, seem destined to continue to perform an educational function. Most of all, the extent to which the Hutterites can retain their cultural uniqueness in turn helps to sustain the viability of Alberta's cultural mosaic.

CHAPTER SIXTEEN

The Black Experience in Alberta
Howard and Tamara Palmer

Introduction

Although they may have heard of the famous black cowboy, John Ware, few Albertans realize that blacks in the province have a unique and fascinating history that spans the twentieth century. Fur traders preceded John Ware, other black cowboys were his contemporaries, and many more black American farmers, independent businessmen, and porters and their families followed him north from their native United States in search of freedom and prosperity. Just after the turn of the century and the immediate years that followed, approximately 1,000 black Americans fleeing persecution in the United States immigrated to Alberta and established several small farming communities. Some also settled in urban areas, particularly Calgary and Edmonton, where they recreated in miniature the institutional life that was associated with blacks in American cities.

The white response to the new black presence also followed the American pattern. Albertans were the major force behind the federal government's restrictions on black immigration to Canada (introduced in 1911), and white residents of Calgary and Edmonton erected a wide range of discriminatory barriers against blacks. The white response to blacks in Alberta included petitions opposing black immigration, petitions in the major urban centers advocating segregation, and even one minor antiblack riot during World War II. Legalized segregation and patterns of violence were absent, but the blacks did not find a haven of tolerance in Alberta.

The number of blacks in the province remained almost constant from 1911 to the 1960s, but the proportion of blacks in the province declined consistently during the same time period. This decline must be viewed against the backdrop of early black experience in Alberta, taking into account the internal life of the black community, black settlement patterns in the province, and patterns of black-white relations. The history

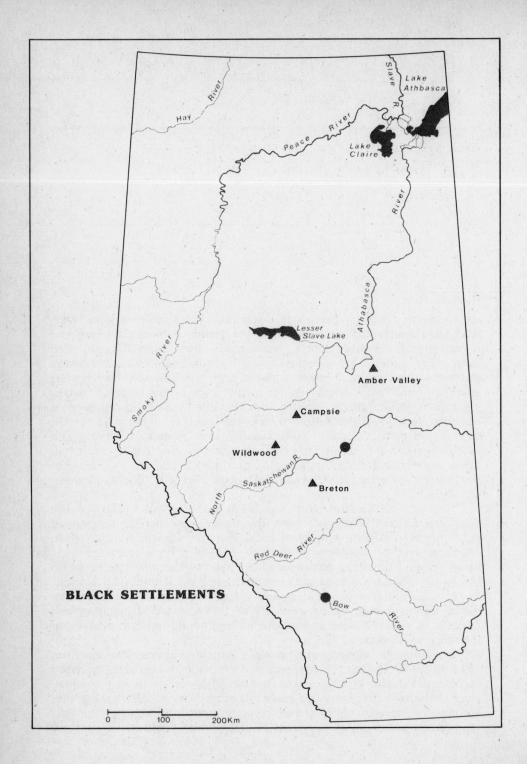

BLACK SETTLEMENTS

Hay River

Peace River

Slave R.

Lake Athbasca

Lake Claire

River

Athabasca

Lesser Slave Lake

Amber Valley

Campsie

Wildwood

Smoky River

North Saskatchewan R.

Breton

Red Deer River

Bow River

0   100   200Km

of the black community in Alberta was determined by the interplay of black American culture, national immigration policy, localized factors of the province's rural life, and dominant North American patterns of race relations.

Traders and Ranchers

Most of the blacks who first came to Alberta were men. They came as individuals and were widely scattered across the province. The earliest blacks came as HBC employees, but little is known about their backgrounds or their lives in Alberta.[1] Two independent traders who gained considerable notoriety during the 1870s and 1880s were Dan Williams, a fur trader in the Peace River district, and William Bond, a black whisky trader in southern Alberta. Williams trekked to the Peace River area in 1869 in search of gold. The mini-gold rush in the Peace district was short-lived so Williams decided to become a fur trader. Staunchly independent, he clashed with the HBC, and his readiness to use his rifle soon got him into trouble with the police. Although the many legends surrounding the life of Williams in the Peace River country make it difficult to separate fact from fiction, we do know that he made a vivid impression which had a lasting impact on the whites' perceptions of blacks in parts of northern Alberta.[2]

During the 1880s and 1890s approximately one-fourth of the American trail drivers from Texas to the northern ranges were black. Having reached Montana some of these cowboys, both black and white, decided to push further north across the Canadian border. One of these men was John Ware. His life and career provide an example of both the opportunities and the limitations which existed for blacks in Canada's Northwest.[3]

Born a slave on a plantation in South Carolina, John Ware was just nineteen when the American Civil War (and legalized slavery) ended in 1865. Rather than work for his former owners, the adventuresome John chose to seek a new life in distant Texas. There his youth, physical strength, and newly acquired skills with horse and lariat, qualified him to join a cattle drive north to Montana. After reaching Montana, Ware was hired to herd cattle further north. The now experienced cowhand crossed the Canadian border in 1882.[4]

John's willingness to endure long hours in the saddle under severe conditions impressed the local cattlemen. For ranch work his illiteracy posed no handicap. His warm personality, sense of humour, and willingness to help soon made him popular. The *Macleod Gazette*, for example, referred to him as "not only one of the best natured and most obliging fellows in the country, but he is one of the shrewdest cow men."[5] Even the antagonistic or indifferent white cowboys developed a grudging admiration for Ware after witnessing his impressive rides on unbroken horses.

John's own adjustment to his new country came relatively easily. Certainly there was some discrimination, but it did not deter him. When he visited Calgary for the first time in 1884, John soon found that he was an unwelcome visitor in the frontier town. A black man had been arrested for murder. Nevertheless, the tough cowboy stayed when offered work unloading freight wagons for the I. G. Baker Company. It did disturb Ware, though, that while working as a freight handler, he was questioned by the NWMP in connection with a horse theft. Because of the white racism at that time, the color of his skin made him immediately suspect. This experience prompted him to leave Calgary, and never again did he seek work there.

During the next five years, Ware worked on the Quorn ranch near Calgary, handling its herd of thoroughbred stallions. Gradually he acquired his own land on Sheep Creek near Millarville, bought a small herd of cattle and registered his brand (9999). Through his ranch friends he met Mildred Lewis, the nineteen year old daughter of a black farmer from Ontario, whom he married in 1892. John and Mildred lived on Sheep Creek until the turn of the century.

Ware in 1902 decided to become a horse rancher and moved his wife and five children to the Brooks district. Here in this relatively isolated area his luck turned. His family's hopes were broken when his wife became seriously ill in the spring of 1905 and died. With the help of his mother-in-law and friends, John Ware cared for his five children and his ranch all that summer. That fall Ware, on the eve of his fiftieth birthday was fatally injured by a fall from his horse. The Lewis family subsequently raised the Ware children.

John Ware's life story, despite its tragic ending, is an inspiring one. Born a slave, he had proven himself as a freed man. While not finding complete racial equality in Canada's Northwest, he had been given an opportunity to advance well beyond the possibilities offered his relatives and boyhood friends in South Carolina. Despite the odds against him, he had gained respectability in Canada, as a landowner and widely known rancher.

The blacks who, like John Ware, came to Alberta prior to 1910 were few but highly visible. Blacks were thought to be different and exceptional, and were automatically expected to play certain roles. Although individual blacks did not encounter any overall pattern of rejection, stereotypes abounded and prejudice was undeniable. Despite the 1901 census noting only twenty-seven widely scattered blacks in all of the territory which was soon to become Alberta, a complex folklore among the whites concerning blacks had already begun to develop. This folklore, combined with prejudices which white settlers brought with them from elsewhere and frequent newspaper articles on race relations in the United States, predetermined the reaction of Albertans to the first major influx of black settlers between 1908 and 1911.

While the whites clearly distinguished themselves from blacks, it is interesting to note the Indians' reaction to them—blacks and whites were the same people. The first blacks in the Northwest had come as employees of the HBC. According to George Simpson, the Governor of the HBC, Pierre Bungo, a black fur trader had caused great curiosity among the Indians. Writing in 1841, Simpson recalled: "This man they inspected in every possible way, twisting him about and pulling his hair, which was so different from their own flowing locks; and at length they came to the conclusion that Pierre Bungo was the oddest specimen of a white man that they had ever seen." Henry Mills, a black trader in southern Alberta in the 1860s and 1870s married a Blood Indian woman and gained acceptance by the tribe. David, Henry's son, was known by the Bloods as "black white man." The descendants of this well-known bullwhacker, scout, and government interpreter are today members of the Blood tribe. To the Indians, the first blacks in Alberta were culturally the same as whites.[6]

The Coming of Black American Refugees

The nature of the black community in Alberta changed dramatically between 1908 and 1911 with the arrival of approximately 1,000 blacks fleeing a rising tide of racial discrimination in Oklahoma and adjoining states. This wave of immigration profoundly shaped the black experience in Alberta for much of the twentieth century. It led to the founding of one all-black community, Amber Valley, of several other black rural settlements in the Edmonton area, and to the first significant numbers of blacks in Edmonton and Calgary.

The early years of the twentieth century saw a combination of circumstances in both Canada and the United States which generated a movement of blacks to Alberta. The Civil War and the end of slavery had not fulfilled black Americans' hopes for freedom. In the years following the Civil War, southern whites had constructed a new set of legally sanctioned social arrangements designed to segregate and control blacks. Attempts to "keep blacks in their place" began with groups such as the Ku Klux Klan, which specialized in terrorizing individual blacks. These informal efforts were soon followed by legally sanctioned segregation. In 1890, Louisiana passed a law providing for racially "separate but equal" accommodations on public transit and this approach was soon adopted by other southern states. Also in 1890, Mississippi disenfranchised blacks; all of the southern states were quick to follow suit.[7]

Black response to this new wave of repression was diverse. Some blacks preferred to adopt Booker T. Washington's philosophy of staying where they were and working hard. Others began moving to the industrial cities of the northern states in search of economic opportunity. Still others responded to the call of cheap land and the hope of freer social conditions in Kansas and Oklahoma. Several black leaders even hoped that an all-black state could be created in the former Indian territory of Oklahoma. Though this dream was never realized, blacks were able to establish at least two dozen all-black towns in the state, and by 1910 its population included nearly 150,000 blacks.[8]

Many of the blacks who eventually settled in northern Alberta were among those who had gone to Oklahoma seeking refuge. For example, Jeff Edwards, one of the founding fathers of Amber Valley, was originally from Arkansas. Hearing that there was no segregation in Oklahoma, his family had moved west. They were sadly disappointed.[9]

The blacks in Oklahoma had never been fully accepted as social equals by either the whites or the Indians. The first blacks in Oklahoma had been forcibly removed from their homes in the southeastern states during the 1820s and brought to the area as slaves to the Indians. At the end of the Civil War, each of the five Indian tribes had responded differently to the abolition of slavery. Each developed its own unique relationship with its former slaves. Two tribes—the Seminoles and the Creeks—assimilated the blacks and intermarried with them, whereas the Cherokees, Chickasaws, and Choctaws did not. Approximately one-third of the blacks who would eventually come to Alberta were people of mixed black-Creek and Seminole ancestry who had been educated in Indian schools.

Despite hopes that Oklahoma would become a haven for blacks, their condition deteriorated with the large-scale influx of whites during the 1890s and further degenerated once Oklahoma obtained statehood in 1907. Oklahoma repeated the pattern which had become familiar in the southern states: whites used violence to intimidate blacks and prevent them from exercising their vote; blacks were given access to few occupations besides menial labor; and schools were segregated. In the debate over Oklahoma's statehood, blacks were systematically prevented from participating. Southern Democrats dominated the area's politics and, once statehood was achieved, they quickly introduced legislation requiring separate schools. They also passed the infamous "Jim Crow" laws which required segregated facilities on trains, in waiting rooms, and in other public accommodations.

Bolstering these legal barriers was the spectre of violence ever-ready to erupt in small town Oklahoma, where burnings, lynchings, riots, and expulsions kept blacks in a perpetual state of uneasiness. Further impetus to emigration came in 1910 when the powerful southern Democrats spearheaded an amendment to the state constitution. The "Grandfather Clause," provided that only those who could vote prior to 1 January 1866 or who were direct descendants of those who could vote on that date, were eligible voters. Since almost no blacks were eligible to vote in 1866, they were thus effectively disfranchised. Many blacks in Oklahoma were ready to look for a new home.[10]

At the turn of the century, the Canadian government began advertising in the American Midwest and Southwest in hopes of attracting American farmers to the Canadian prairies. Their campaign was ultimately successful in attracting over one-half million American farmers; however, Canadian officials had not planned on attracting black American farmers. When a number of Oklahoma blacks looking for a better life for themselves and their children responded to the Canadian call for settlers, Canadian government officials were faced with a dilemma. They did not want blacks. Now the agents must convince white American farmers that the Canadian climate was certainly not too cold to live in while simultaneously convincing American blacks that the Canadian climate was indeed totally unsuitable for them.

Although immigration officials and the Liberal politicians who were in power federally were not anxious to have blacks come to Canada because of prevailing racist sentiments (either their own or those of their constituents), they were nevertheless reluctant to introduce legislation which specifically excluded American blacks, since they did not want to offend either the American government or black voters in eastern Canada. Consequently, several subterfuges were devised which effectively blockaded black immigration. Although approximately 1,000 blacks did make their way to Alberta at this time, their numbers would have been much more substantial had the Canadian government not quickly erected invisible, but nevertheless effective, barriers.[11]

By the spring of 1911, the issue of black immigration had been kindled sufficiently to assume both national and international proportions. There had been a localized controversy surrounding the possible settlement of a few hundred black farmers in the Edmonton and Calgary areas in 1908 and 1909.[12] The question of American Negroes immigrating to Alberta, however, only became a major provincial issue in 1910 and 1911 with the proposed immigration of a new group of Oklahoma blacks and people of mixed black-Indian ancestry.[13]

Frank Oliver, Minister of the Interior and the man responsible for Canada's immigration policy, was particularly susceptible to public pressure on this question since many of the blacks had taken or intended to take up farms in his home riding of Edmonton. The most vociferous expression of antiblack sentiment had come from groups in the Edmonton area: the Boards of Trade in the area, the Edmonton Trades and Labour Council, women's organizations (particularly the IODE), and newspaper editors importuned the federal government with resolutions, petitions and editorials opposing an influx of blacks. They warned that western Canada would be importing the racial problems of the American South.

Drawing on existing American myths and stereotypes, some of the petitions also gave vent to fears about blacks being a potential economic and sexual threat. The Edmonton Board of Trade led the opposition to black immigration. At a time when Edmonton's total population was only 25,000, the board's petition opposing the entry of blacks attracted over 3,000 signatures. Boards of Trade at Strathcona, Fort Saskatchewan, Calgary, and even the French-speaking village of Morinville also endorsed the petition to the Prime Minister, which read as follows:

> We, the undersigned residents of the city of Edmonton, respectfully urge upon your attention and upon that of the Government of which you are the head, the serious menace to the future welfare of a large portion of Western Canada, by reason of the alarming influx of negro settlers. This influx commenced about four years ago in a very small way, only four or five families coming in the first season, followed by thirty or forty families the next year. Last year several hundred negroes arrived in Edmonton and settled in surrounding territory. Already this season nearly three hundred have arrived; and the statement is made, both by these arrivals and by press dispatches, that these are but the advance guard of hosts to follow. We submit that the advent of such negroes as are now here was most unfortunate for the country,

and that further arrivals in large numbers would be disastrous. We cannot admit as any factors the argument that these people may be good farmers or good citizens. It is a matter of common knowledge that it has been proved in the United States that negroes and whites cannot live in proximity without the occurrence of revolting lawlessness and the development of bitter race hatred, and that the most serious question facing the United States today is the negro problem . . .There is not reason to believe that we have here a higher order of civilization, or that the introduction of a negro problem here would have different results. We therefore respectfully urge that such steps immediately be taken by the Government of Canada as will prevent any further immigration of negroes into Western Canada.[14]

Oliver and his officials considered several responses to this public outcry from newspapers and politicians across Canada. Although officials within Oliver's department were already convinced that Negro immigration should be discouraged, in 1910 the minister sent W.J. White to report on the situation in Oklahoma. In September of that year White, living up to his name, recommended that blacks should be prevented from coming to Canada. The minister agreed. Immediately Oliver's department commenced discouraging blacks who requested information. It also began to apply rigorous financial and medical examinations at the border for those who did come. The latter measure was largely ineffective since most of those who arrived at the border had money, equipment and livestock for farming, and were in good health.[15]

In the spring of 1911, when the public outcry became most intense, Oliver drafted an Order in Council to bar black immigration. But concern about Canadian-American relations and about Canada's public image eventually led the government to continue its reliance on informal exclusionary policies. The Canadian government hired agents to go to Oklahoma for the purpose of discouraging black immigration, and it requested that Canadian railways ask American railways to discourage black migration to Canada. One agent the government hired was a black medical doctor from Chicago who enlisted the support of black clergymen in Oklahoma. He spoke in several churches, telling prospective emigrants that in Canada they would either starve or freeze to death, that the soil was poor and that, in any case, they would have trouble getting across the border. This time the informal policy was effective; black immigration to Canada virtually ceased. By 1912 Oklahoma blacks seeking a new home turned their attention to back-to-Africa movements.[16]

The Rural Black Experience

By the time the government began to discourage black immigration, there were already approximately 1,000 blacks in Alberta. Most of them were located in several small farming communities which had been established between 1908 and 1911 within a 100-mile radius of Edmonton. The four largest settlements, all of which contained blacks from Oklahoma and surrounding states, were at Junkins (now Wildwood) near Chip Lake; Keystone (now Breton) southwest of Edmonton; Campsie, a small hamlet near Barrhead; and Amber Valley, twenty miles east of Athabasca. All were isolated, bush-covered areas where the farm land was marginal and the climate was cool and moist. Although it is not entirely certain why the blacks chose these particular areas, given their comparatively late time of arrival, it was almost inevitable that they would settle in more isolated areas with poorer soil. However, they did not simply choose the land which was most readily available at the time; they overlooked more suitable and less heavily wooded land in favor of isolation. The black pioneers apparently deliberately picked isolated areas because they wanted to be independent of white racism, and wanted to have large enough tracts of land to establish predominantly black settlements. Although there is no firm evidence on the subject, they may also have been directed to these fringe areas by immigration officials who were aware of the apprehensions that their arrival had aroused among whites.[17]

The land the black homesteaders chose did have a number of favorable features: ample water, grass, and timber. Although wooded land was unfamiliar to the settlers who came from Kansas, many of those from Oklahoma had lived in wooded areas and had experience with clearing trees. The Kansas people were plains farmers experienced in grain farming, but they had to adjust to the new terrain. The Oklahoma farmers, on the other hand, had experience with clearing bush; but the crops they knew best, cotton and corn, could not be grown in this new land.[18]

Georgia and Grandma Payne on the Payne farm at Wildwood, ca. 1912.
Wildwood was the second largest of the four black, rural settlements in
northern Alberta that were established by blacks fleeing persecution in the
southern United States.

The black pioneers' choice of isolated and marginal land decisively shaped the eventual development of the communities they established; it was a decisive factor in their eventual stagnation and decline. Economic opportunity was always very limited in these settlements, as was good available farm land on which to expand. However, isolation helped to protect the blacks from discrimination and worked to promote a strong sense of community among them.

The first black settlers came from Oklahoma in 1908. They settled in the Wildwood area, about eighty-five miles west of Edmonton. Wildwood eventually became the second largest rural black settlement in the province. When they first arrived, the immigrants encountered heavy timber, swamps, bullflies, and isolation. There were no roads, so the trip to Edmonton for supplies took three or four days in dry weather and up to a month in poor weather. At first, the new settlers tried to grow wheat, barley and oats. They were unsuccessful because of the difficulties of clearing the land and early frosts; so, in order to survive, the men began to look for work outside of the settlement. They were fortunate that in 1910 and 1911 two transcontinental railroads were being built through the region, and they found construction jobs on the lines that were passing near Wildwood.[19]

The black community at Wildwood developed many of the patterns of economic and social self-sufficiency which characterized all the rural black settlements in the province. Local game, fish, berries, and vegetable gardens provided a sizeable part of their food supply. Absence of professional medical help and difficulties in transportation meant they had to rely on midwives at times of birth and home remedies in times of illness. The community also developed an active social and religious life. They established their own Baptist church, began an annual picnic on 1 July which included sporting events, songs, recitations, plays, and a dance, and generally formed a cohesive community. Agnes Leffler Perry recalls: "We organized singing groups, practiced plays, and enjoyed ourselves winter and summer. We were like one big family."[20]

While some of the settlers were eventually able to farm successfully, the economic marginality of the community meant that, like many other small Alberta settlements, their main export was people. Some returned to the United States because of the weather or primitive pioneering conditions. During World War I, younger blacks went to Edmonton to find work or join the army and more left during the depression of the early 1920s. At the time of the 1921 census, when the number of blacks in the area was already declining, just under 150 lived in the Wildwood area. Ultimately, the common pattern was for the community's young people automatically to go elsewhere; consequently the descendants of Wildwood's original pioneers have made a contribution as teachers, ministers, musicians, businessmen, and other professionals not only in nearby Edmonton, but also in other communities across North America. There are now only a few black families still farming in the Wildwood area, most of them descendants of the original settlers. In Wildwood, as in other rural black settlements in the province, there has been considerable intermarriage with whites, a strong indication of the degree to which the blacks ultimately gained acceptance as good farmers, good neighbors and law-abiding citizens.[21]

The second predominantly black settlement in Alberta—Breton—began in 1909. The community was founded through the efforts of Bill Allen and Charlie King, Sr. The story of Bill Allen is typical of many of the blacks who immigrated to Alberta at this time. He had been born in Georgia before the Civil War. After the war, he moved west, living in Kansas, Oklahoma, and Utah, but he found that he was always coming into conflict with his white neighbors. He would settle in an area only to find that conflict developed with the whites and forced him to move on. After a violent encounter with eight Ku Klux Klansmen in Oklahoma, Allen left Oklahoma because he recognized that it would only be a matter of time before he would either have to kill someone or be killed himself. He moved to Kansas, then to Utah, and finally to Canada to keep from constantly being embroiled in fights.[22]

Bill Allen was instrumental in recruiting other settlers to come to the Breton area. Approximately thirty-five families, including several who arrived from Okmulgee, Oklahoma in 1911, settled in the area. According to one account, the blacks picked this isolated area, fifty miles from the nearest railhead, because it made possible the development of a predominantly black settlement. Several of the families had several sons and were looking for land for them. Since there were only two or three white families in the entire area when they arrived, the black settlers dominated the community. They built their own church, the Good Hope Baptist Church, and established the Funnell School. Their social activities included dances, concerts, ball games, and picnics.[23]

The isolation of Breton made possible a cohesive black community, relatively free from conflict with whites. But it also imposed almost insuperable economic difficulties. The trip from Breton to the nearest railhead at Leduc, fifty miles distant, which had to be done between harvest and snowfall, was a difficult one and could take several weeks.

The Breton settlement began to disperse as early as World War I, when a number of the settlers' children returned to the United States or enlisted in the Canadian army. The community's cohesion was further weakened by the coming of the railway in the late 1920s, which brought an influx of white settlers, and then by the Great Depression. Nevertheless, a few black families have remained to the present day. Charlie King, Jr. played an important role not only in the Baptist church and Funnell School, but also was a leading community leader in the UFA and later the CCF.

The black settlement at Campsie followed a pattern similar to that of Wildwood and Breton. A group of about ten black families came to the hamlet of Campsie, just south of Barrhead, in 1910. Some of the families came from Oklahoma, but some were from other southern and midwestern states. Campsie was just in the process of being settled, and there were already a number of people from the United States, Great Britain, and Ontario living there when the blacks arrived.[24]

The black settlers, who eventually comprised nearly one-third of the district's people, tended to concentrate in an area just north of the post office which, besides the school, was the only community institution. During the next few years the original families were joined by others, but the influx was offset by the outflow of those who found the climate too severe and consequently did not remain long. At the time of the 1921 census there were fifty blacks in the Campsie area.[25]

The blacks of the community socialized extensively with each other, often organizing dances or debates which they held in a private home. They also built a church. They had to rely on their own resources for entertainment because Amber Valley, the largest black settlement in the province, was 100 miles away and thus too far for much contact to be established. Black people who grew up in the community of Campsie remember encountering prejudice from teachers and from the white settlers who tried to keep them out of the local school. In 1924, feelings were running very high, as indicated by a charge laid against a local black for assaulting a teacher who refused to allow black children to attend the local school. English and Scottish immigrants in the area were as likely to be sources of prejudice as American immigrants.[26]

With all the land in the area being taken up and with immigration being closed to additional black farmers, the black community at Campsie was fated to decline. Its numbers dwindled during the depression and World War II. The pioneer generation passed away and the second generation moved elsewhere in search of better opportunities and steady incomes. Presently, only one black family remains.

While social and economic patterns in Campsie were generally similar to those in the other black settlements, religious developments took a unique turn. An Ontario-based religious sect, the Standard Church of America, made a strong impact on the black community at Campsie during the mid-1930s; subsequently black preachers from Campsie carried the message to other blacks in both rural and urban Alberta. From this beginning, the Standard Church of America would become the main church for blacks in Calgary.

The Standard Church of America had originally been established in 1916 by Reverend Ralph Horner, a former Methodist evangelist in Ontario. It was part of the larger Holiness movement which had developed in the United States following the Civil War as a reaction to Methodism's becoming associated with middle class status and conventional religion. Like other Holiness sects, the Standard Church of America emphasizes the need for an emotional experience at conversion, the need for the experience of a second blessing or sanctification (which is attributed to the direct operation of the Holy Spirit in the heart of the believer), the need to strive for perfection, and the need for the Holy Spirit's guidance in all events of life.[27]

That an Ontario-based sect would have such an impact on the blacks of Alberta may, on the surface, seem surprising; but there are many parallels in black urban America where the Holiness movement also gained a substantial number of adherents. The Standard Church of

America first made an impact on the Campsie community in 1935 when a white preacher conducted a week-long revival which made a powerful impression on all of the black families in the area. At least one member of each family became attached to the Standard Church of America as a result of this experience. Finally, over one-half of the blacks in Campsie joined, and five young Canadian-born blacks decided to devote their lives to preaching.

Andrew Risby was one of these young people. Born in Campsie in 1918, he grew up on the family's farm. The revival meetings in 1935 impressed him so strongly that the next year, at the age of eighteen, he decided to devote his life to the ministry. After taking correspondence courses from the Standard Church of America, he began preaching in the larger black settlement at Amber Valley, then in 1945 moved to Calgary. He became the minister of the Standard Church of America, and helped make it the main church for blacks in Calgary and one of the primary focal points for the local black community.[28]

The largest rural settlement of blacks and the only one that remained virtually all-black was Amber Valley (originally known as Pine Creek). Unlike the other black rural settlements, Amber Valley has survived both depression and war. But the most striking aspect of Amber Valley is the degree to which its history mirrors the history of nearly all small northern Albertan hamlets removed from major transportation routes. The black pioneers of Amber Valley faced all of the same problems that were faced by other Albertan pioneers on the northern fringe of the park belt and they met these challenges in much the same way.

The first settlers began arriving in Amber Valley in 1910. This first group was joined in the spring of 1911 by other family members and friends, some of whom came together in a group of ninety-three adults and fifty-six children brought from Oklahoma by a black clergyman, Parson H. Sneed. Sneed was a Baptist minister, a farmer, and a Mason; he had organized the group of settlers through his Masonic ties.[29]

Even prior to their settling in the area, a sense of community existed among many of the blacks who came to Alberta since most came as families who had been neighbors in Oklahoma or who had belonged to the same fraternal organizations. Both the Masons and the Oddfellows had gained popularity among American blacks in the late nineteenth century as vehicles for combining social and cultural expression with economic advancement and mutual relief. Black lodges of both of these organizations had disseminated information about Canada and had organized groups of potential emigrants.[30]

The first tasks awaiting the Amber Valley settlers were building homes and preparing the land for crops. The land they had chosen was covered with heavy brush and had to be cleared by hand with axes and grub hoes. The spruce stumps were often as large as 3' in diameter, making the work difficult and exhausting. On a good day, a strong man could clear several square yards; but other times it was impossible to clear even one large tree in a day.[31] Given these difficulties, only relatively small amounts of land could be cultivated; by 1920 the average amount of cropped land in Amber Valley consisted of only thirty-three acres.[32]

The Amber Valley settlers were beset with other difficulties: they were invaded by hordes of insects, their land had poor drainage, and they soon learned that early frosts made harvests uncertain. Like other settlers on the pioneer fringe, the Amber Valley blacks had to supplement their meagre farm incomes by working out of their settlement. A number of the men ventured to Edmonton to work in meat-packing plants or on construction; others hired themselves out as loggers, or worked as freighters to northern trading posts at Wabasca, Forts McMurray and Chipewyan, or worked with construction crews building the railroads. This left their wives to face alone the challenges of surviving with their families on the new and inevitably primitive homesteads.[33]

Like many other immigrants to Alberta, both before and after them, the Amber Valley settlers found it difficult to adjust to the extremes of a northern climate. Being used to the relative mildness of Oklahoma, they had to learn to dress for the bitter winters and to build houses that would keep out the severe cold. Nor did they have much time to learn these things since the winter of 1910-11—their first in Canada—was a severe one with the temperature dropping to -66°F in January. One of the early settlers reacted with the comment that "any country where a man's got to wear two pairs of pants ain't fit to live in."[34]

Like so many pioneering communities, Amber Valley was isolated. In the early years, there were no roads and the only trails were those that had been slashed out by hand. Because of the difficulty and distance involved in travelling, the women were seldom able to leave the settlement. It took two days for settlers to make the return trip to Athabasca for supplies if the trails were reasonably dry; if the trails were wet, the trip might take three or four days. Self-sufficiency was essential to survival especially since a series of crop failures postponed their first successful harvest for ten years. Many relied on eating rabbits, prairie chicken, moose, and fish. All the settlers had gardens, canned wild fruit, and kept cattle and chickens for home use. They also had to become self-sufficient in medical matters since there was no doctor in the isolated settlement. The women had to rely on each other to act as midwives at births, and home remedies were all they had to deal with sickness.[35]

Despite the difficulties they faced, the newcomers were determined to succeed. Seventy-five of the original ninety-five black homesteaders in the Amber Valley area remained on their land long enough and cleared enough land to receive their homestead patents. This was a much higher success rate than among prairie homesteaders generally, where just over half those who began homesteading remained to take title to the land.[36]

Although they were isolated from the outside world by a lack of transportation and communication, Amber Valley residents were not isolated from each other; they had a strong sense of community and soon established social institutions. A school was begun in 1913 and a nondenominational church in 1914. In the United States, the church had been an important institution for blacks, providing them with comfort, an anchor for their community and a source of careers for the ambitious; so naturally they brought the church with them. As in the American South, most of the Amber Valley settlers were either Baptists or Methodists. Social activities in the community included parties, dances, and (after 1915) the famous Amber Valley picnic, a two or three day event which drew people from a fifty-mile radius. The picnic provided foot races, horse races, games, greased pig chases, greased pole climbs, pulling contests, good food, and dancing. Sports were important in the community from the beginning and the valley would eventually become known throughout the north for its baseball team. Boxing also became a favorite sport, and a number of young men from Amber Valley earned provincial and national honors. The strong sense of community solidarity that existed in Amber Valley was further reinforced by intermarriage among the Canadian-raised generation. The original families, such as the

The Thomas Mapp family and relatives, Amber Valley, ca. 1925. The Mapps were among the earliest arrivals in Amber Valley, which was the center of the black community in Alberta for decades. (Courtesy Glenbow Archives)

The Amber Valley baseball team, ca. 1930s. The team was known throughout north central Alberta and promoted community solidarity and pride. (Courtesy Glenbow Archives)

Edwards, Mapps, and Bowens eventually became united not only by a common immigration and pioneering experience, but also by family ties.

Ethnic relations were not a serious problem in the Amber Valley area. They experienced initial difficulties in getting bank credit, attending dances or other social functions, or obtaining employment or accommodation at nearby Athabasca.[37] Once World War I broke out, the young men at first found it difficult to be accepted into the army (though five young men from the community were recruited for a labor battalion). Indians and Metis were two of the largest groups of people living nearby, and the blacks got along well with them. The Indians taught the blacks basic skills of northern survival, such as woodscraft and tanning, while the blacks provided hospitality and taught the Indians how to play baseball. There were several cases of Indian-black intermarriages in the Amber Valley area, which was not surprising considering the fact that many of the settlers who came from Oklahoma were themselves of mixed Indian-black ancestry.[38]

Despite a vigorous community life and the relative absence of prejudice as a long-term community problem, Amber Valley had a limited future because of its location. The settlement continued to grow from its establishment in 1910 until it reached its peak in the 1930s. At its apex it covered approximately fifteen miles east and west and five miles north and south and contained about 350 black residents, which was 95 percent of the area's population. The town center consisted of a small store, a two-room school, and a post office. But even before the depression of the 1930s, which destroyed so many rural communities in Alberta, blacks were leaving Amber Valley. Some could not tolerate the climate, the isolation or the primitive conditions and grew disillusioned with farming. They returned to the United States or moved to Edmonton. Older children were forced to go to Athabasca or Edmonton if they wanted to complete high school. Since many of the settlers had large families, some with as many as ten and even fifteen offspring, children often left home at an early age not only for education, but to become domestics in Edmonton or to work on the railroad. During the 1920s, black farmers got beyond the subsistence farming stage and began raising cattle and exporting grain. When the price of wheat was high in the late 1920s, they also bought mechanized farming equipment; however, this mechanization meant that bigger farms were necessary to make economical use of expensive equipment so many marginal farmers sold out.[39]

Amber Valley survived the Great Depression, but World War II proved too much for the already floundering community. During the war, many of its young men left to join the armed forces and others departed for better wages in the city. In the postwar years Amber Valley followed the same pattern of decline that was experienced by other rural hamlets across the prairies. Only a handful of black families still live in the area. White farmers now own most of the land originally pioneered by blacks. Nevertheless, a sense of pride still remains in the Amber Valley community. Amber Valley has remained a spiritual home for hundreds of people who grew up there and who are now scattered across western Canada and the United States. Homecomings and a community center have revived some of the spirit of the pioneering days.[40]

The Urban Black Experience

Not all blacks who immigrated to Alberta during the early part of the century went to isolated rural areas. By 1911 the census reported 208 blacks in Edmonton and 72 in Calgary. Nor were all of these from rural settlements in Oklahoma; a number had come as individuals—not only from various parts of the American South, but also from northern American cities. For those blacks who chose the rural pioneering settlements, the main problems would be a harsh climate and marginal land. Those who chose the cities, or were forced to the cities by lack of economic opportunity in the rural areas, found their opportunities limited yet again by prejudice and discrimination.

The decline of the rural black communities led to a steady increase in the numbers of blacks in the cities after 1911. While the overall number of blacks in the province remained almost constant at approximately 1,000 from 1911 to the 1960s, the proportion of Alberta blacks in the cities shifted from 30 percent in 1911 to 80 percent by 1971. The impact of rural black settlements on the urban communities is obvious if we compare the number of blacks in Calgary and Edmonton. The black community in Edmonton has always been substantially larger than the one in Calgary; it was three times larger during the 1920s, 1930s, and

1940s, and it has remained twice as large into the 1970s due to the proximity of all the rural black settlements.[41]

Despite their small numbers, the history of blacks in Alberta's two main cities has been a microcosm of the larger North American urban black experience in the twentieth century: the economic position of blacks, the role of the church within the black community, the patterns of race relations, and the roots of changing attitudes toward blacks—in all of these aspects of Alberta's urban black experience one sees a repetition in miniature of the larger black experience.

Blacks: Their Work, Entertainment, and Sports

The life of the urban Negro in Alberta has been, until very recently, largely a working class experience. Although few of the immigrants who came to Alberta from Oklahoma and elsewhere in the United States were completely illiterate, their educational background was limited. Nor did the first Canadian-born generation have much opportunity for education. The isolated, sporadically convened rural schools, which most of the Canadian born attended did not prepare them for higher education. When they migrated to the cities, they found themselves confined to service jobs, because of their limited education and skills and because of stereotypes held by the larger white society. Most whites assumed that blacks were naturally meant to serve, and that is the role they occupied in Alberta prior to the 1950s. Calgary's community was composed primarily of porters. In Edmonton there was more variety. The blacks' community there included not only those who did the heavy work involved in building roads, sewers, and bridges, but also included a group of entrepreneurs who were not entirely dependent upon a black clientele. The emergence of this class of Negro businessmen reflected a similar trend in northern American cities.[42]

The phenomenon of the black porter exemplified ethnic occupational specialization which combined self-reinforcing racial stereotypes with concrete advantages. At a time when most long distance travel was by train, the porter's job was a steady one and, therefore, highly prized over sporadic types of employment or no employment at all; indeed, in Calgary during the 1920s and 1930s the job of porter was virtually the only one open to blacks. Although the porter played a servile role, he commanded a certain respect and received between $42 and $95 monthly, together with tips which might be as much as $35 on each round-trip. This amounted to a decent, if modest, income by the standards of the day. However, the work was not easy. A porter might be gone sixty to eighty hours at a time, and he usually worked as much as eighteen or even twenty hours a day. Many of the Alberta-born blacks who could not make a living in Amber Valley or the other rural settlements moved either to Calgary or Edmonton and became porters. Some of these people spent virtually their entire working lives as porters, retiring after forty to fifty years of service.[43]

Like those who lived in other parts of Canada or the United States, many of Alberta's urban blacks found that while most doors were closed

Railway porters in Edmonton in the 1920s. Black porters were an important part of both the Edmonton and Calgary black communities until the 1950s. (Courtesy Provincial Archives of Alberta)

to them, they could excel and find recognition in the less rigidly guarded, more fluid, informal worlds of entertainment and sports. They could not support themselves through these endeavors, but they could find some prestige and supplement their incomes. Immigrant pioneering farmers had little time to develop their musical talents; but as the Canadian-born generation began moving to the cities, they discovered that in the staid, conservative atmospheres of Calgary or Edmonton, there was a dearth of entertainers; a number of them found they could fill this void. Consequently several predominantly black bands were formed which played at dances and performed in clubs.[44] This musical tradition has continued. For example, in Edmonton, Clarence "Big" Miller's Big Band jazz sound has become extremely popular. Miller played with some of the most prominent American black musicians such as Louis Armstrong before coming to Edmonton in the early 1970s. From the 1920s to the present, touring black musicians (at the early chatauquas, the musical review groups at the Calgary Stampede, and at discos) have been an important part of Alberta's musical life.[45]

Blacks in Alberta also achieved recognition in almost every sport: including boxing, baseball, track and field, hockey, and professional football. Prior to 1950, the best known black athletes in the province were boxers. Joe "Dad" Cotton, born a slave in 1853, moved to the American west coast after the Civil War and became a heavyweight prize fighter. He fought not only in the United States, but in Australia and England before coming to Edmonton to live in 1912. He opened a boxing club in Edmonton and worked as a boxing referee, but not before he fought his last fight in Drumheller, Alberta. At the age of sixty-one, he won by a knockout. Harvey Bailey of Edmonton, who boxed during the 1930s, became Canada's flyweight champion; he was known as "Flash Bailey" because of his speed. Another Edmontonian, Bennie Geary, won the western Canadian welterweight championship, while Vern Escoe held the Canadian heavyweight championship in the 1940s.[46] Jesse Jones, an Edmonton black, became a nationally known track and field star in the 1920s.[47]

Alberta's Invisible Barriers

Blacks in Alberta faced restrictions with regard to housing and public facilities. While these were never sanctioned by law as they were in many parts of the United States, informal discrimination was widespread. Patterns of discrimination changed little throughout the 1920s and 1930s; however, it began to become more evident as the numbers of blacks in both Calgary and Edmonton increased. Some hospitals refused to admit blacks into nurses' training programmes; many landlords would not rent to blacks, and numerous businessmen would not hire them. Proprietors of a number of dance halls, beer parlors, swimming pools, and skating rinks made it clear that they did not welcome blacks. One of the most difficult parts of this discrimination was that since there was no consistent policy in these businesses, blacks never knew if they would be allowed into a particular establishment, or whether they would be excluded. On a one-to-one basis, Alberta blacks developed many close friendships with individual whites. But in impersonal public settings, blacks were continually surprised by some white Albertans' capacity for small-mindedness.[48]

The attempts that were made in Calgary and Edmonton to have discriminatory restrictions formalized failed. For example, in the spring of 1920, nearly 500 residents of the Victoria Park district of Calgary signed a petition asking that blacks be prevented from residing in their district: "We request that they be restrained from purchasing any property in the said district and any who may now be residing there will be compelled to move into some other locality." This petition was signed by three-fifths of the householders in the neighborhood. City Council responded to the petition by writing to sixteen other Canadian cities, asking whether or not they segregated blacks or prevented them from residing in their cities. After receiving negative replies from several of them, the council turned down the petitioners' request. Similarly in 1924, an Edmonton City Commissioner's request that blacks be banned from all public parks and swimming pools was overruled by City Council.[49]

In Calgary, discrimination in housing contributed to black residential segregation. The first area of black concentration was in the vicinity of

Eighth Avenue and Fourth Street East, which was within close walking distance of the CPR station and, therefore, convenient for porters. Later, blacks began moving into the working class neighborhood of Riverside and near the oil refinery at Inglewood, where there were heavy concentrations of immigrants. Blacks in these areas formed only small pockets; their numbers were not sufficient to create anything like a Negro neighborhood. That the blacks did form residential concentrations was partly due to economic circumstances; but these patterns were reinforced by discrimination. Black residential segregation seems to have been less common in Edmonton than in Calgary.[50]

The antiblack sentiment which developed in Alberta was sporadic and, with the exception of the campaign to restrict black immigration in 1911 and the occasional unsuccessful petition, was not organized. During the late 1920s and 1930s, a small Ku Klux Klan developed in Alberta with local members in approximately fifty towns and villages as well as in most of the major cities. But the Alberta Klan's venom and political activities were not directed against blacks. The Alberta Klan developed as an offshoot of a larger one in Saskatchewan and arose primarily in response to the influx of central and eastern Europeans during a period of anxiety about social change. For the Alberta Klan, anti-Catholicism was the major article of faith, and most of its literature and activities were directed against combatting the influence of Catholics and the Catholic church and stemming the influx of predominantly Catholic central and eastern European immigrants. Most of the Klansmen, like so many other Albertans, were simply unaware that there were any black settlements in the province. While some of Alberta's blacks were apprehensive about the existence of the Klan in Alberta, the rise of the Klan during the late 1920s and its demise in the early 1930s had virtually no impact on Alberta's black community.[51]

Although prejudice in the cities may have been unorganized, it was real nonetheless and hampered the potential growth of the black population in both Edmonton and Calgary. Young Alberta-born blacks arrived in the cities wondering at times why their parents had ever come to Canada, often resenting the toll that pioneering had exacted from their parents' lives. When they encountered prejudice in the cities and felt that whites were being promoted over them simply because of their color, they began to look for other options. If wages for the same work were higher in large American cities, the atmosphere surrounding race relations not much worse, potential marriage partners more plentiful, and the climate better, why not move to the United States? While the black populations of Calgary and Edmonton grew in the interwar years, the two cities certainly did not absorb all those leaving the farming areas; indeed, from 1921 to 1951, the number of blacks in the province actually declined from 1,048 to 702.

Community Organizations

The first black organizations were developed in Alberta shortly after the arrival of the initial groups of immigrants. These organizations served to

The African Methodist Episcopal Church in Edmonton, 1921. Black churches provided perennial focal points for blacks in Alberta, meeting both social and religious needs. (Courtesy Glenbow Archives)

reaffirm group culture and identity and provide an alternative social world to blacks during a period of widespread discrimination. In the period prior to the 1950s, black churches played central roles in the black community; they continue to do so for many of Alberta's older black residents. As in the United States and eastern Canada, over half of Alberta's blacks have been either Methodists or Baptists. Edmonton, for example, had both an African Methodist Episcopal church and a Baptist church. From the time of its organization in 1910 until the 1950s, the Shiloh Baptist Church was one of the main centers of the Edmonton black community and continues to be a focal point for some Edmonton blacks. The largest predominantly black church in Calgary, the Standard Church of America, has maintained the revivalism and the intensely emotional religious experience advocated by its Ontario-born founder—a tradition which was also very much a part of the black religious experience in the United States. In the absence of other effective and durable black organizations, the predominantly black churches have been the black community's most important institutions.[52]

Secular black organizations have simply not enjoyed the longevity which has characterized the predominantly black churches. The Colored Protective Association, formed in Calgary around 1910, organized social activities and fought organized discrimination such as the Victoria Park petition. In Edmonton the first secular organization, the Universal Negro Improvement Association had close ties with both the Methodist and Baptist churches. The organization was a branch of the New York-based organization of Marcus Garvey, dedicated to black self-improvement. Organizational activity reached a peak in 1921 when, under the auspices of the Universal Negro Improvement Association, two other organizations were established. The Negro Welfare Association of Alberta was established to deal with the growing problem of unemployment among Edmonton's blacks, while the Negro Political Association of Edmonton fought for black rights. While these organizations declined during the 1920s, others developed to take their place. However, they were beset with the same problems that plagued black organizations across the country: the lack of a national black organization to provide help, the absence of a sizeable middle class to give leadership to the groups, the churches' acceptance of the status quo, and the underlying feeling that organizations might hinder, rather than help, by making the group more visible. The small numbers of blacks in Alberta and the high rate of mobility and transiency of the porters (particularly in Calgary) was also a factor in the weakness and impermanence of the secular organizations which did develop. The most long-lived black secular organization in Edmonton was the Masonic Order which was closely linked to the Shiloh Baptist Church.[53]

The Impact of World War II

World War II and the early postwar period brought many changes in attitudes toward blacks and in their position in Alberta's society. While change was gradual and halting, the social and economic condition of the province's blacks began to improve. The war sounded the death knell for rural black communities, but it also helped bring greater opportunity for urban blacks. Economic advancement for Canadian-born blacks had been hindered by the Great Depression; but the war, despite its horrors, created economic opportunity.

Events in Calgary at the beginning of the war did not bode well for the acceptance of blacks into Alberta's society. In April 1940, a group of 300 servicemen attacked the home of a black bandleader. Only prompt police action prevented a more serious riot. Like many other incidents of soldier-instigated violence during the war, this riot began with a fight over a woman. According to press accounts, a member of the 49th Battalion, which was drawn primarily from northern Alberta, attended a Saturday night dance. His female companion paid too much attention to a black musician. In the fight that ensued, the soldier suffered an injured eye. The following night, to avenge this alleged assault, a mob of 300 soldiers from the 49th Battalion stormed the residence of the orchestra's black leader, smashed windows, wrecked the interior of his home, and attacked a white soldier who was married to the bandleader's sister. More serious violence was prevented by the arrival of forty policemen, both military and civil; they rescued both the band leader and the white soldier, who had by that time been stripped of his uniform by an enraged crowd. The police then took the black musician and his brother-in-law into protective custody and the mob of soldiers tramped back to the center of the city. Only additional quick action by the military police prevented a more serious assault upon the black district of the city. The police lined up across the street where most of the black population resided and ordered the mob to "fall in." After a few tense moments, the soldiers complied and were marched by their officers back to the barracks.[54]

While Calgary's antiblack riot was not momentous, it indicated that two common assumptions concerning white-black relations in North America were still part of Alberta's social landscape: the old myth about the danger of black males to white women and the idea that blacks were "fair game" for the riotous escapades of young white males.

Generally speaking, however, despite this isolated incident, the appearance of blacks in uniform was a deterrent to those who would deny blacks their rights. Many of Alberta's Canadian-born blacks enlisted in integrated regiments and, while many of them did not return to Alberta, it became increasingly difficult to discriminate against those black veterans who did. The building of the Alaska Highway during the war years also had an impact on the treatment of blacks. The three American all-black construction units which came through Alberta en route to this project did not spend much time in Calgary or Edmonton; when they did, they demanded and received equal treatment.[55]

It was also during World War II that blacks made their first breakthrough in the provincial civil service. In 1943 Ruth Heslep, an Alberta-born black, needed the help of MLA Percy Page to get a job as a stenographer, but in doing so she breached one of the past's invisible barriers. The working conditions for porters in Alberta also improved during the war through the efforts of the American-based Brotherhood of Sleeping-car Porters. During the war, membership in the union grew rapidly and by 1948, it won recognition in Canada. By the war's end, porters' wages had climbed to nearly $200 monthly plus tips and the work month had been reduced to sixteen days on the road.[56]

The War on Racism and the Emergence of Black Pride, 1945-1985

The modest advances made during the war years were followed by more substantial progress. Hitler's racist atrocities had heightened sensitivity across North America to the dangers of racism. This new awareness was reinforced by press coverage of developments in the southern United States and in South Africa and by the activities of some liberal-minded white groups. At the end of the war, white Albertans in Calgary and Edmonton became aware, many for the first time, of the existence of racism in their midst. The press began to publicize incidents of discrimination against blacks in hotels, beer parlors, dance halls, and swimming pools. Several city councillors in Calgary, attempted to organize to combat racial discrimination. The Alberta Federation of Labor also began to concern itself with the question of discrimination against Negroes in the workplace.[57]

At the same time that liberal-minded whites had begun to concern themselves with racism, more Alberta blacks organized to fight racism and discrimination publicly. In 1947, Calgary's blacks organized the Alberta Association for the Advancement of Colored People. They had the assistance of Philip Randolph, the leader of the Brotherhood of Sleepingcar Porters, and of Stanley Grizzle, a Toronto-based CPR porter who was also a veteran of the war, a union organizer, and Canada's strongest advocate of equal rights for blacks. Although the organization was limited to Calgary, for a decade it played a crucial role in the social and political life of Calgary's black community. The establishment of this organization indicated a new mood among blacks, particularly the Alberta born. Some were now willing to meet discrimination face-to-face and to fight it.[58]

Despite its name, the Alberta Association for the Advancement of Colored People was autonomous from other black organizations in Canada or in the United States. The organization's goals were to raise funds for scholarships to young blacks, to fight obvious forms of racism in jobs and in public accommodation, and to change the public's stereotyped image of blacks. Composed of a few whites as well as blacks, the organization included people of all ages, though its strongest appeal was to the younger blacks. The group encountered many of the same difficulties facing other black organizations in Canada. It did not receive much support from the church, and some of the older blacks disliked the attention which the organization's activities brought to the black community. The association eventually went into temporary decline in the late 1960s—partly because of conflicts within the black community and partly because it had achieved its major goal of outlawing discrimination in jobs and public accommodation.[59]

The path of the Alberta Association for the Advancement of Colored People during the late 1940s and 1950s was made easier by the arrival in Alberta of a number of black athletes, particularly professional football players, whose star status did much to change attitudes toward urban blacks. Woody Strode, "Sugarfoot" Anderson, Rollie Miles, and Johnny Bright were pioneer black football players in Calgary and Edmonton. These superb athletes became extremely popular with fans of both the Calgary Stampeders and the Edmonton Eskimos. Unquestionably, black athletes had a positive impact on attitudes toward blacks already in the province. Anderson, Bright, and Miles liked the province so much they eventually made their homes in Alberta, and they were followed on the football field by many more black American players.[60]

International events were equally important in effecting a change in attitudes toward blacks in Alberta. Awareness of the problems arising from racial discrimination were heightened through Canada's involvement in the Commonwealth, which eventually came to be dominated by nonwhite members. Perhaps even more important was a growing awareness of the American civil rights movement. The 1950s and 1960s were decades in which the American blacks regained their constitutional rights. In 1954 the Supreme Court ruled that segregated schools were unconstitutional. The black protests gained momentum: they included the 1955 black boycott of buses in Montgomery, Alabama, the 1957 incidents at Little Rock, Arkansas, the sit-ins and freedom rides of the early 1960s throughout the American South, and Martin Luther King's civil rights demonstrations. These events led to Canadians' increased sensitivity to the problem of racial discrimination in their own country.

The Alberta government's passage of civil rights legislation was indicative of a significant transformation in public attitudes. In 1955 Alberta became the third province to enact a Fair Employment Practices Act; in 1957 it was the sixth to legislate an Equal Pay Act; and in 1966 it was the fourth to introduce a Human Rights Code. Critics of these acts could charge with some justice that they lacked teeth and did not impose sufficiently severe penalties on individuals who violated them. Yet overall the new legislation undoubtedly helped to curb discrimination in the province.[61]

This changed climate of opinion, coupled with economic opportunity in Alberta's cities, made it possible for blacks to achieve a new stature during the decades of the 1950s, 1960s, and 1970s. The number of black porters in the province declined with transcontinental passenger traffic. But concurrently, new types of jobs were becoming available to blacks. Some still worked in traditional menial jobs as shoeshine men, taxi-drivers, laborers, domestics, and garbage collectors and specialized in small service businesses such as janitorial services and beauty shops; many, however, were moving up the ladder among city hall workers and getting more skilled jobs as heavy equipment operators, tradesmen, or truck drivers. Blacks also began moving into technical and middle level managerial positions. Black women became secretaries and teachers.

Calgary black women also made names for themselves in the professional world and in public service. Violet King, who grew up in Calgary, was admitted to the Alberta bar in 1954 and became both the first black woman to practice law in Canada and Calgary's second woman lawyer. Virnetta Anderson, who came to Calgary from Arkansas in 1952 with her husband, football player "Sugarfoot" Anderson, became widely known in the city for her civic activities. In 1974, she ran successfully for Calgary City Council, thus becoming the first Alberta black (besides those who were elected as school trustees in the black rural settlements) to be elected to a public post.[62]

The 1960s, 1970s, and 1980s have been a period of greater acceptance and increased integration for black Albertans. Although it has not disappeared completely, prejudice toward blacks has declined dramatically. Blacks now live throughout Calgary and Edmonton. The formerly predominantly black churches in both cities are completely integrated. Ties of family and friendship among the blacks are still strong, but the decline of both prejudice and community institutions is leading toward the inevitable erosion of a distinctively black Canadian community.[63]

The arrival during the late 1960s and the 1970s of several thousand blacks from the West Indies and a few from Africa, has had relatively little impact on the blacks already in Alberta. The Alberta-born blacks feel little sense of kinship with the new arrivals and little desire to identify with them. Consequently, there are few institutional links between the three groups. West Indian blacks who now greatly outnumber the native-born blacks have their own distinctive cultures, and have established several Caribbean cultural, sports and social associations. Organizations which have developed during the 1980s to serve the interests of all blacks whether immigrant or native-born include the National Black Coalition, the Congress of Black Women of Canada, and the Black Women's Association.

Paralleling the growing trend toward integration, there has been a minor resurgence of black pride among the Canadian-born generation and an identification with North American blacks. This feeling, which has been strongest in Edmonton where it was embodied during the 1970s and early 1980s in several different organizations which sponsored cultural and social activities, was to some extent prompted and encouraged by the black pride movement in the United States. It has also been given impetus by an awareness among Canadian blacks that (as expressed in *The Communicant*, an Edmonton-based newsletter for black Albertans), "as a race we are slowly losing our identity."[64]

The black pride movement has been nourished by the growing achievements of blacks in many fields across North America as well as by the continuing success of young blacks in the sports, entertainment, and business worlds in Alberta. There are now several successful black professionals and businessmen in Edmonton and Calgary. Among the few blacks remaining in the rural areas are several successful farmers.[65]

Conclusion

In order to understand fully the black experience in Alberta, one must compare it to the experience of other immigrant groups and to the experience of blacks elsewhere in North America. In some ways, the history of Alberta blacks has been similar to that of other ethnic and racial groups in the province. The rural pioneering struggles and achievements, the establishment of familiar institutions to help cope with a new life, the rural-urban transition, and the shift from a refugee consciousness to a strong identification with Canada—all are part of a pattern that has been repeatedly followed by many ethno-cultural groups now part of Alberta's population.

But Alberta's blacks have also faced problems and issues which have affected few other groups. Although stereotypes accompanied almost every group that came to the province, the stereotype about blacks has been among the most highly developed despite the small number of blacks in the province. When black families began coming after the turn of the century, Albertans already had an entire arsenal of reasons why they did not want them in the province. Some of these stereotypes were brought by immigrants from eastern Canada, the United States, Great Britain, and elsewhere; most came directly from American popular culture, which has had a strong and growing impact on Alberta throughout the twentieth century.

Until the 1960s, the blacks were regarded as good material for mind-less entertainment. Service clubs, musical groups, and school children throughout the province performed minstrel shows in which white actors blackened their faces and entertained audiences with the image of the shuffling, shiftless, and happy Negro. In his famous radio broad-casts, Premier William Aberhart occasionally used Negro jokes to enter-tain his audience and to illustrate some point about Social Credit. Ameri-can radio shows, movies, novels, and magazines all brought certain stereotyped images of American blacks into the homes of Albertans.[66]

While the experience of blacks in their own province was practically unknown to them, Albertans, because of the proximity of the United States, had many notions about blacks in general, and these notions were largely racist. According to the popularized pseudoscientific dogma about race, which prevailed until World War II and lingered for some years afterward, blacks were at the very bottom of the world-wide racial pecking order. Other groups in Alberta encountered prejudice because of cultural, linguistic, political, or religious differences, or because of partic-ular wartime alignments, but blacks encountered prejudice simply because of the color of their skin.

Did the American blacks who came to Alberta find the haven of tolerance for which they had hoped? The record reveals that they encountered considerable prejudice, but except for the province-wide reaction in 1911, it was localized, sporadic, and largely unorganized. What is more important, the prejudice that existed was never formalized into law and only once erupted into violence. Not only in the American South, but even in Alberta's neighboring western states such as Montana (which had about the same number of black residents as Alberta) dis-crimination was codified into law; for example, laws existed in several western states outlawing interracial marriage. Although some of the same patterns of discrimination in public accommodation and entertain-ment centers existed in Alberta, they did not have the force of law which they had in the United States and they were not universally applied.[67]

The absence of legal restrictions on blacks in Alberta justified the pioneering generation's decision to come to Canada. Some Alberta blacks tell stories of pioneering parents who, after returning from visits to relatives in the United States, literally kissed the Canadian soil. The Canadian born, however, often regarded the absence of legal restrictions as something of a mixed blessing. The amorphous, rather than codified and open, character of discrimination left them unsure of where they stood and never certain of when they might next encounter prejudice, or of just who to blame for their limited opportunities. The absence of legal restrictions also inhibited the development of strong black organizations; prejudice undeniably existed, but since it was so indeterminate, how could it be fought? And, in any case, were not blacks in Alberta better off than those in the United States?[68]

Undoubtedly, given prevailing attitudes toward blacks in Alberta, the key variable in explaining the better position of blacks living in the province as compared to that of black people in many other parts of

North America, has been their small numbers. Although there were far too few blacks for politicians to court their votes, they were also too few in numbers for politicians to appeal to prejudice against them as a way of attracting white votes. Blacks in Alberta were seldom a public issue; except for very brief periods, they were not perceived as an economic, political, or cultural threat to anyone. For the most part, blacks were simply ignored.

Paradoxically, however, their small numbers are the result, in part, of prejudice. Restrictive immigration policies kept out larger numbers until the late 1960s, and these tight policies were at first enacted partly in response to strong public pressure from Alberta. It is also significant that the number of blacks in Alberta did not grow; there was a steady decline in their percentage within the Alberta population from 1911 to 1961. Blacks were certainly not the only people to leave a province which, until after World War II, offered only limited economic opportunity, but they are one of the few ethnic groups whose numbers did not increase at all as Alberta's population as a whole increased. To be sure, this decline was partly a reflection of the nature of the rural black farming settlements—their economic marginality, their isolation, their harsh climate, and their dearth of potential marriage partners—but it was also a reflection of the lack of opportunities for blacks in the province's urban centers.

The history of blacks in Alberta is the story of a small and, until recently, closely knit group which having faced adversity and having successfully struggled against it, is now finally in a position to take full advantage of Canadian life. Black Albertans can look back with pride on the courage and endurance of their pioneering forebears.

CHAPTER SEVENTEEN
The Japanese in Alberta
Ann and David Sunahara

When Kumataro Inamasu stepped off the train in Calgary on New Year's Day, 1906 and headed for the Alberta Hotel, he may have been mistaken for a Chinese. A more knowledgeable observer might have recognized him to be Japanese, for small groups of Japanese railway workers had been passing through Calgary since 1901. Inamasu was not a transient railway worker. He was the Alberta Hotel's new pastry chef and the first Japanese to settle permanently in Alberta.[1]

The Pioneer Years

Kumataro Inamasu was not the only Japanese immigrant to settle in Alberta in 1906. That year also saw the arrival of Takemoni Nagatani, a recent graduate of the Ontario College of Agriculture. Between 1906 and 1910, Nagatani brought several Japanese farmers to the 10,000 acres of land he had leased at Cheadle, a small community twenty miles east of Calgary. Alberta's climate and the farmers' inexperience, however, soon killed Nagatani's hopes for a Japanese settlement. Many of his settlers moved to the Pacific coast and Calgary. Those who stayed took up jobs on area farms to learn dryland farming techniques from more experienced farmers.[2]

Many of the first Japanese to come to Alberta were brought by labor contractors. Two Japanese labor contractors, Bueimon Nakayama and Ichiro Hayakawa, supplied almost 1,000 laborers to work in the sugar beet industry and to help build irrigation systems and railroads.[3] The workers brought to Alberta by these labor contractors did not come to settle permanently. They came to earn money to buy farms on their overcrowded home islands of Kyushu, Honshu, and Okinawa in Japan. Without this stake they could not hope to own a farm, for most were younger sons and as such could not inherit the family farm. The family farm would be left to only the eldest son. These first transient workers from Japan knew little of their destination; they had little need to

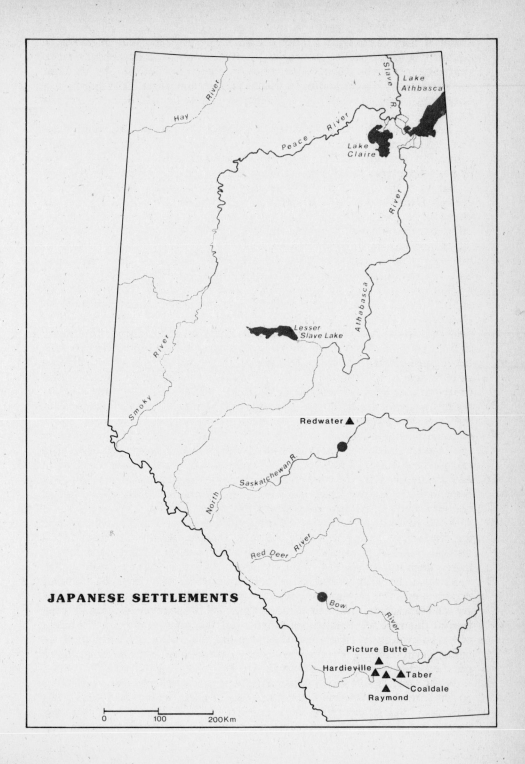

JAPANESE SETTLEMENTS

Hay River

Slave R.

Lake Athbasca

Peace River

Lake Claire

River

River

Lesser Slave Lake

Athbasca

River

Smoky

Redwater ▲

Saskatchewan R.

North

Red Deer River

Bow

River

Picture Butte ▲

Hardieville ▲ ▲ ▲ Taber

▲ Coaldale

Raymond

0   100   200Km

know. If they came with a labor contractor, everything was prepared in advance: a job, hospital insurance, mail delivery, and sometimes food, clothing, and tools. Those who came on their own found jobs through the owners of the boardinghouses where they lived. Boardinghouse operators often ran labor-contracting services in addition to renting rooms.[4]

The arrival of Japanese laborers in Alberta did not go unnoticed. Like British Columbia, Alberta had a strong racist tradition. White Albertans commonly thought of Asians as racially inferior and incapable of adopting western ways.[5] Many working men thought Asian immigrants threatened their livelihood. Nonwhite workers, the unions argued, accepted lower wages and consequently depressed the wages of all workers. In addition, many felt that working with an Asian was degrading and a threat to their own social standing.[6]

The anti-Japanese rhetoric spouted by unions and newspaper editors, however, faded quickly. When the Japanese arrived, the sugar beet industry in Alberta was in the midst of a critical labor shortage and any worker, regardless of color, was a valuable commodity. The second and perhaps more important reason for the anti-Japanese rhetoric dying out was that very few of the migrant workers stayed in Alberta. Most Japanese moved to the the Pacific coast and into the interior mountain states of the United States, where the climate was more to their liking. Most of the Japanese who remained in Alberta settled on farms in the Raymond area. Only a few moved to Edmonton and Calgary to set up small businesses or to work as cooks, bellhops, barbers, and restaurateurs. In the cities, their numbers were too small to warrant comment except from the most intransigent bigots. By 1911, only 244 Japanese immigrants remained in Alberta.[7]

The only town in which Japanese formed a significant minority was Hardieville, a mining town just north of Lethbridge. Unlike the reception Asians received in most Albertan towns, the Japanese who moved to Hardieville were not greeted by a hostile populace. Hardieville was a polyglot town where no group could claim preeminence.

While federal law prevented Japanese from working underground in the Hardieville mines, in most other respects Japanese were treated the same as all the other miners. A local union leader, Frank Sherman, in large measure was responsible for this. Sherman had engineered the acceptance of Asians into District 18 of the United Mine Workers of America in 1908. He did this to prevent the owners of the Hardieville mines from using the Asians as scabs.[8] While federal legislation prevented the Japanese miners from earning the top wages paid to underground workers, as union members the Japanese were paid the same as white workers doing similar work. They received between $2.40 to $2.85 per day, very attractive wages for the time.

By the time World War I broke out, Japanese workers no longer relied on the contract labor system which had brought many of them to the province. Their greater fluency in English enabled them to find work for themselves in Alberta's sawmills and mines. By this time too, some had even acquired their own businesses and farms. The initial farms were bought in 1912 near Raymond and in the Redwater area, north of Edmonton. The Japanese in Raymond had originally been brought in by the Knight Sugar Company to work in the sugar beet fields in the area. By 1914, in Calgary, Japanese operated eight small businesses.

As Japanese became better established in Alberta they developed their own community organizations. In February 1909, ten Calgary residents formed the "Nihonjin-kai" or Japanese Society. The goal of this organization was to provide companionship and mutual assistance. In 1913, the settlers in Raymond formed a small vegetable cooperative and one year later, a "Nihonjin Kyokai" of their own. Like the society formed in Calgary, this organization provided companionship and mutual assistance. It was also formed to promote better relations and cooperation with non-Japanese settlers in the area.[9]

World War I

The outbreak of World War I marked the movement of a very unusual group of Japanese immigrants to Alberta. When the war broke out, many Japanese in British Columbia thought that by joining the Canadian army they could demonstrate their loyalty to their adoptive country. This they felt would ensure the Japanese of a fair and equal place in Canada, and help them overcome the many aspects of legalized discrimination which they faced in British Columbia. By May 1916, 202 Japanese in British Columbia had joined the Japanese Volunteer Corps, had passed the necessary medical examinations, and had begun training while waiting to be called up. Their efforts were in vain. British Columbia's military division, under pressure from provincial politicians, said it would take the Japanese from British Columbia only as a segregated regiment knowing there were not enough Japanese to form a complete regiment. Blocked in British Columbia, many of these Japanese volunteers came to Alberta to enlist. The recruiting officers in Alberta were willing to take the Japanese volunteers, for many were veterans of the Russo-Japanese War of 1905-1906. By the end of the war, 196 Japanese Canadians, including five Japanese Albertans had served in the trenches in France and Belgium and in ten different battalions. Over a quarter of these soldiers (fifty-four) were killed in action and almost half (ninety-three) had been wounded. Two of those killed were from Raymond.[10] Beyond the deaths and injuries suffered by the Japanese Canadian soldiers, there was one further tragedy that awaited the returning veterans. Their hopes for a place in Canadian society were not to be. Despite their demonstrated loyalty to Canada, full citizenship rights would have to wait until after another world war was fought with all its tragic consequences for Japanese Canadians.

World War I signalled important changes in the community life of Japanese in Alberta. Prior to the war, the Japanese immigrants to Alberta were almost exclusively young men. The war period saw the arrival of Japanese women in Alberta. Some of these women were joining their husbands whom they had married before their husbands had left Japan

Japanese bride Tsuki Hironaka, born March 22, 1894, in Japan. The marriage between her and her husband Yoichi was arranged by their families. She came to Canada as a "picture bride," meeting Yoichi for the first time on April 9, 1913, in Vancouver. They were married there the following day. (Courtesy Provincial Museum of Alberta)

for Canada. Others had entered into arranged marriages during return visits to Japan by their husbands. For a third group of Japanese wives, the first time they met their husbands was when they stepped off the train in Alberta. These were the famous picture brides. The bride's picture would have been sent with those of other prospective brides to her future husband by his parents. From these pictures he would pick a bride. After both the prospective groom and bride had agreed to the match, there would be a proxy marriage in Japan; then the bride would make the long journey from her home in Japan to a new life in Alberta.[11]

Alberta was a rude shock for most of the new Japanese brides. Their new home was a far cry from the life they knew in Japan. What confronted them was not the golden land they had heard about, but rather a vast empty prairie landscape dotted with the rough shacks which were to be their new homes. Like the new brides from Europe, these young women from Japan had little alternative but to dry their tears and build a life for themselves and their husbands. Their lives became a never-ending round of hard work. There were always meals to be made, clothes to be sewn, mended, and washed, chickens to be fed, and cows to be milked. Produce had to be taken to market; firewood had to be chopped and water hauled. In season, these pioneer Japanese women preserved vegetables and meat to carry their families through the winter, and they worked with their husbands in the fields. In time their shacks were replaced by better houses, and their growing children began to share some of their chores. The children also helped to lessen the loneliness of these farm women who were separated by culture, language, and distance from their neighbors.[12]

The Twenties: A Time of Building

The twenties were a time of change for Japanese Albertans, a time when their very identity began to take on new hues. The prejudices brought by Japanese from Japan against one another began to fade. In Japan, the Okinawans who settled in Hardieville and Coaldale would have not been viewed by the Japanese who settled in Raymond as true Japanese. Rather, they would have been seen as cultural and social inferiors. By 1924, these groups were sharing an annual picnic, with each group hosting the other in turn. Social and class differences which were important in Japan became obscured in Canada.[13]

Central to the change in the Japanese Canadian identity was the maturing of the Nisei generation, the children born to the immigrants from Japan. These children, like the children of other immigrants, were exposed to the acculturating forces of the public school system and of non-Japanese playmates. They adopted English as their primary language with Japanese being spoken only at home. While there was some conflict between their lives at home and at school, the conflict was minimal. There was an essential similarity in the values they learned from their parents and teachers. From both they learned the work ethic, respect for authority, and a sense of "British" fair play. From their par-

The Young Buddhist Association baseball team in Raymond in 1935. Canadianization of the Nisei (the second generation) and continuing group solidarity went hand in hand. (Courtesy The Archives, Sir Alexander Galt Museum, City of Lethbridge)

ents they learned to respect their teachers and value education. The Nisei soon gained the reputation of being model students, quiet, hardworking, and eager.[14]

While the rapid Canadianization of the Nisei pleased their teachers, the loss of Japanese culture disturbed many of their parents. To combat this, in 1929 the Japanese in Raymond founded a Buddhist Church in a building used previously as a Mormon Church. Here they started a Japanese language school and began a martial arts society.[15] It was an ambitious undertaking which, while not altogether successful, did teach Albertan Nisei to appreciate some of the strengths of their parents' culture.

The Interwar Years

The 1930s brought many changes to the Japanese in Alberta. The layoffs caused by the depression forced the Japanese miners in Hardieville to take up farming full-time. To ease the transition, the miners' "Doshi-kai" or Friendship Society was turned into a "Nokai" or Agricultural Society through which they bought farm supplies and learned better farming methods. The Japanese Albertans also began to move into the newly opened irrigated farm land near Rosemary and Duchess, two small farming communities halfway between Calgary and Medicine Hat. Here they initially received a hostile reception from their white neighbors. That hostility was soon overcome, however, as the neighbors came to know one another.[16]

Float for the First of July parade in Raymond, ca. 1930. The Japanese gradually began to find acceptance in the Raymond area during the inter-war years. (Courtesy Provincial Museum of Alberta)

The interwar years saw two racially motivated incidents. The first arose following Japan's invasion of China in 1931. The Chinese in Alberta protested the invasion by agitating against Japanese Albertans. Japanese-made goods were boycotted, Japanese stores were picketed, and Japanese were refused service in Chinese businesses. The response of Japanese Albertans to the invasion of China was mixed. The immigrants from Japan realized the world condemned Japan's action but they still found it difficult to criticize the land of their birth. They found the Chinese protests embarrassing, but recognized they could do little to combat them.[17] The second anti-Japanese incident was more damaging. In the spring of 1936, the Alberta Beet Workers Union struck to protest their low wages and poor working conditions. Beet growers near Lethbridge reacted by hiring miners laid off from nearby coal mines. Some of these miners were Japanese. Protesting the use of scab workers, the union focused its anger on the Japanese among the strike breakers. While the strike was settled peacefully, the presence of Japanese among the strike breakers served to reinforce the prejudices of some of the beetworkers, prejudices which would resurface during World War II.[18]

World War II

At the outbreak of war in 1939, there were only 540 Japanese Canadians in Alberta. Most of these were farmers in southern Alberta. The war would change their lives forever. The war would transform the lives of Japanese in Alberta and in the rest of the country.

When war was declared, some of the Nisei responded in the same way their fathers had done more than twenty years earlier. They saw the war in Europe as an opportunity to demonstrate their loyalty to Canada. To many of their parents, however, the war was more threatening. They saw the barroom patriots in the spring of 1940 agitating against Italian and German Canadians. They saw the local branches of the Canadian Legion challenging the loyalty of their neighbors whose only crime was that they had left Germany and Italy many years earlier to make new lives for themselves in Canada.

The war in Europe revealed how little attitudes had changed since World War I. In British Columbia, young Nisei were refused induction into the army. British Columbia's politicians still feared that, if Japanese Canadians were allowed to enlist, they and their wives would be entitled to vote. In Alberta, however, Asians had the vote, and seven Alberta Nisei were able to enlist in 1940.[19]

The start of the war in the Pacific on 7 December 1941 raised the fears of Japanese Albertans. They feared that the hostility directed against their German and Italian neighbors in 1940 would now be directed against them. Fortunately, their fears proved groundless. *The Calgary Herald* and the *Lethbridge Herald* cautioned the public not to discriminate against Japanese Albertans. The editors of the *Calgary Herald* wrote that it was important to remember that, "the yellow peril does not necessarily crouch under every yellow skin."[20] The *Lethbridge Herald* reminded its readers of the contributions made by Japanese Albertans to the life of their community, of the hard work and long residence of Japanese Albertans, of their support for the Red Cross, and of the public declarations of loyalty by Japanese leaders. Most importantly, perhaps, the paper reminded the public that some of the young Japanese Albertans were already serving with the Canadian forces in Europe. Most Albertans took the reassurances of the press and Japanese leaders to heart. While a few allowed their bigotry to surface, most Albertans went out of their way to reassure their Japanese friends that the war made no difference to their friendship. Ironically, it was the CPR that committed one of the few hostile actions against Japanese Albertans. In early December 1944, the CPR, which had brought many of the original Japanese to Alberta, fired all its Japanese Canadian employees. Very few other employers showed so little sense and compassion.[21]

Japanese Canadians in British Columbia were not as fortunate, and their fate was to affect the lives of their Albertan cousins. Following Pearl Harbor, British Columbia's press took a conciliatory attitude. It told its audience that Canada's quarrel was "with Japan not with Japanese nationals here or people of Japanese blood."[22] The politicians from British Columbia, however, were quick to exploit the public's fear and anger. To gain political support the politicians demanded that the federal government remove the "Japanese menace" from the province. Responding to these demands—and at the same time ignoring the advice of the RCMP and the military that the Japanese in B.C. were harmless—the federal Cabinet, in February 1942, ordered the removal of every man, woman, and child of Japanese ancestry residing within 100 miles of the Pacific coast.[23] Some of the Japanese Canadians who were forced from their homes in British Columbia found their way to Alberta. They came in response to a request from Alberta's sugar beet growers to the British Columbia Security Commission, the civilian agency set up by the federal government to supervise the uprooting of the Japanese. Alberta's sugar beet growers were facing yet another labor shortage. Many of their workers had left the fields for work in the war industries or had enlisted. Those who remained were again threatening to strike. The sugar beet growers saw the displaced Japanese as a source of cheap labor which the unions would not attempt to organize. Accordingly, in early February 1942, W. F. Russell, the secretary of the Alberta Sugar Beet Growers' Association, wrote to the government about the possibility of using displaced Japanese Canadian farmers in southern Alberta.[24]

When the growers' request became known to the public and the first Japanese from British Columbia began to arrive, opposition in the province began to build. In March 1942, the Beet Workers Union, city and labor councils, local Canadian Legion branches, boards of trade, and citizens committees throughout southern Alberta demanded that Japanese from British Columbia not be admitted to the province, and if they were admitted, that they be guarded by the army and removed from the province after the war. Southern Albertans, who for years had Japanese neighbors, were not immune to the wartime hysteria. Careful to distinguish between "their" Japanese and Japanese British Columbians, residents of Raymond, Lethbridge and Taber held public meetings to protest the proposed movement of Japanese British Columbians into southern Alberta. This, they felt was just a way of exporting British Columbia's problem to Alberta.[25] The beet industry leaders who were responsible for bringing Japanese to the province contributed to the public's fears.[26] After a trip to the coast, where they were told by the RCMP that Japanese Canadians were not a security threat, the industry leaders told the public that Japanese Canadians were a threat to the security of the west coast. Moreover, they told the public that Albertans should take the displaced Japanese because by doing so they would ensure the security of Canada's west coast. In addition, the representatives of the sugar beet industry argued that sugar production was crucial to the war effort and that the Japanese from British Columbia, while undesirable, were the only experienced farm labor available to harvest the crop.[27]

Alberta was the only province to demand a written promise from the federal government to remove the displaced Japanese as soon as the war was over.[28] In addition, Alberta's Premier, William Aberhart, demanded that the federal government assume all health and education costs for these Japanese British Columbians. Imposing these conditions helped to mollify the public, but did little to make life for the displaced Japanese Canadians any easier.[29] Living under the conditions imposed by Alberta, however, was the lesser of two evils. The Japanese British Columbians who came to Alberta had been in imminent danger of having their families broken up. Had they not chosen to try their luck in Alberta the

Japanese evacuees arriving in Picture Butte from Mission, British Columbia, in April, 1942. Their only crime was that they were of Japanese origin. (Courtesy The Archives, Sir Alexander Galt Museum, City of Lethbridge)

men and older boys would have been sent to work on road gangs, and the remaining family members would have been sent to live in the shacks and slums of ghost towns in isolated mountain valleys in British Columbia.

Many of the families who came to Alberta were farm families from the Fraser Valley. They came presuming that their exile would be temporary—a year or two at most. They believed that once the hysteria on the west coast subsided they would be permitted to return to their farms. Before coming to Alberta, the Japanese Canadian exiles were assured that they would have decent housing, a reasonable standard of living, and more freedom than they would have had in British Columbia. They were also told that they would be settled close to other Japanese from British Columbia. The reality of their reception was very different. For housing, many were given granaries and chicken coops.[30] For drinking and sanitation, they were told to use the sloughs and irrigation ditches. The work waiting for them was back-breaking. Some of their employers treated them as virtual prisoners-of-war.[31] For the displaced Japanese, there was no escape from the harsh conditions forced on them by the beet growers. They could not leave the farms they were assigned to, and they could not even augment their income by taking off-season jobs in such centers as Lethbridge, Edmonton, and Calgary. Most of Alberta's city councils had passed local ordinances prohibiting Japanese from moving to their towns. A request by a Japanese Canadian to move into town, regardless of whether he was originally from British Columbia or Alberta, would automatically cause an uproar in the council chambers. Councils rejected these requests regardless of who made them. It did not matter that a prospective employer made the request, or that a Japanese Albertan wanted to move to town to go to school or to join a family member. The fact that the person was Japanese was sufficient reason to refuse the request. A few did move to the towns in defiance of the local councils. Most of these Japanese worked as domestics and were aided in their underground life by their Caucasian employers.[32]

The response of the displaced Japanese to the conditions on the sugar beet farms was typically Japanese. After lodging their protest with the British Columbia Security Commission, they worked to better their lot. With building materials given them by the Commission, they tried to repair the granaries and shacks they were living in. Even after making repairs, however, their housing remained woefully inadequate for a prairie winter. Often three generations would be crowded into an uninsulated granary. A wood stove would occupy one end of the shack and a sleeping platform the other. In this one room, grandparents, parents, and children ate, slept, and worked. One mother of ten remembers that the conditions:

> made you very angry. But the anger killed the sorrow and the hurt, and the anger itself was destroyed by making a living. I became too busy to be angry.[33]

The harsh working conditions and the crude living accommodations were only the immediate problems facing the displaced Japanese. They

Road camp life, 1942. (Courtesy Public Archives Canada)

*The Takeyasu family harvesting sugar beets in Picture Butte in 1943.
Japanese-Canadians were uprooted from their homes in British Columbia in
1942 and brought to work as laborers in the sugar beet fields of southern
Alberta. (Courtesy The Archives, Sir Alexander Galt Museum, City of
Lethbridge)*

also faced the problem of having to make a living in a hostile province.
Because of the conditions imposed on them, 90 percent of the 2,664
Japanese from British Columbia were virtually impoverished by the
spring of 1943. Only 15 percent had found work during the winter of
1942-43. Forty-two percent were on relief and many more were borrow-
ing against their next year's beet contracts to avoid the humiliation of
having to ask for relief.[34]

Faced with destitution, the displaced Japanese began to organize. They
organized secretly, for they did not have the right of free assembly.
Their secret work was helped by the fact the Japanese on neighboring
farms often came from the same village in the Fraser Valley. Thus the
old prewar organizations and leadership were still available.

Much of the work of organizing the Japanese from British Columbia
fell to Seiku Sakumoto. Before the war, Sakumoto had been the English
language secretary of the Japanese Camp and Mill Workers Union. After
coming to Alberta on his own, Sakumoto immediately tried to improve
the lot of the Japanese. He first tried to arrange for the Japanese to join a
local vegetable growers' cooperative. Many of the Japanese had been
vegetable farmers before the war. The local whites, however, objected to
land being sold or even rented to the Japanese from British Columbia.
Frustrated by this opposition, Sakumoto organized the Japanese beet
workers who lived north of the Old Man River into a Beet Workers

Association. In this, he was helped by Sadayoshi Aoki and Minoru Kudo, both respected Japanese language school principals from Vancouver and Mission City before their uprooting. The Beet Workers Union was soon followed by a second organization, the "Shinwa Kai" or Benefit Association in Raymond.

One of the first problems tackled by the organized beet workers was their poor contracts with the beet growers and an attitude on the part of these farmers that Japanese could be dictated to with impunity. By the spring of 1943, these problems had caused 175 Japanese families to request a transfer to different farms. The Growers' Association refused these requests, arguing that under the terms of the agreement with the British Columbia Security Commission the Japanese were compelled to stay on the farms assigned to them. Faced with this refusal, the Japanese adopted what must have been at the time, a desperate strategy. They negotiated their 1943 beet contracts with the growers, then refused *en masse* to sign them until the growers permitted the Japanese to transfer from one farm to another.[36] The growers discovered that the beet workers' unions they had dealt with before the war were very timid compared to the Japanese. They failed to realize that the Japanese, denied the right to leave, had no alternative but to fight for their rights.

A second major problem facing the Japanese from British Columbia concerned the question of school fees. This problem was especially critical because of the high value placed on education by Japanese. The Japanese had come to Alberta assuming the federal government's promise of a "normal family life" meant that their children would receive free public education. The Alberta and federal governments, however, could not agree on who should pay for this education. They solved their differences by leaving the entire issue of school fees to each local school board. These boards charged $70 a year for each Japanese high school student, a sum large enough to deny a high school education to some Nisei. The Japanese countered the demand for school fees by arguing that, as workers in the school district, they were already contributing to the tax base. This, they argued meant their children were entitled to free education just as any other worker's child would be given free education. Most school boards finally granted some concessions. By 1946, only the Raymond school board continued to charge full school fees.[37]

In coming to Alberta the displaced Japanese were not completely without allies. The strongest of their allies were the Japanese who were long-time residents of the province. The Japanese living near Lethbridge and in Edmonton and Calgary opened their homes, churches, and associations to the Japanese from British Columbia. They helped them to find jobs on better beet farms, to join the food cooperative in Raymond, and to establish a similar cooperative in Coaldale. They also helped the newcomers to start Buddhist churches in Picture Butte and Coaldale. The Japanese from British Columbia were welcomed into existing mutual assistance organizations and helped to form new ones. These mutual assistance organizations worked to improve the living standards of their members.[38]

By helping the Japanese from British Columbia, the Japanese Albertans placed themselves in a precarious position. They were already under suspicion themselves: on September 8, 1942, they had been placed under the same restrictions that had been applied previously to Japanese from the Pacific coast.[39] Like their British Columbia counterparts, Japanese Albertans were not permitted to travel more than twelve miles from their homes without a special permit. Their phone calls and mail were subject to censorship. The meanness of these regulations is illustrated by the case of a long-time Japanese resident of Raymond. This man, with two sons serving with the Canadian army in Europe, waited from 1944 to one year after the end of the war, 1946, for permission to buy a small field adjoining his own farm.[40]

Postwar: A Time of Rebuilding

Having moved the Japanese from the coast, the federal government was faced with the problem of what to do with them when the war ended. Politicians in British Columbia refused even to consider the possibility of Japanese Canadians returning to the coast. To discourage Japanese from doing so, the federal government ordered the sale of all personal and real property of the Japanese who had been moved from the 100-mile zone along the coast: this, it was reasoned, would insure that the displaced Japanese had nothing to return to. Many of the farms that were sold had been owned by the Japanese who had been moved to Alberta at the beginning of the war. Having sold off the property of Japanese Canadians, the federal government planned to disperse them across Canada. The federal government believed that by doing so, they would ensure the destruction of a cohesive Japanese Canadian community.[41]

Albertans were divided on what to do with the displaced British Columbia Japanese. In 1942, Alberta had extracted a promise from the federal government to remove all displaced Japanese at the end of the war. In 1945, many Albertans demanded that Premier Ernest Manning hold the federal government to its promise. Civic groups, the Union of Alberta Municipalities, and the Alberta Federation of Labor lobbied for the removal of the displaced Japanese from Alberta. These demands were in full accord with Manning's own sentiment, but for very different reasons. The Union of Alberta Municipalities and the Alberta Federation of Labor thought the Japanese would undermine labor relations in the province.[42] Manning believed that religious affiliation determined national loyalty and that because many of the Japanese Canadians were Buddhist, they could not possibly be loyal to a "Christian" Canada.[43] The views of Manning did not go unopposed. Christian church groups condemned Manning's ideas as "unjust and un-Christian." They argued that, "it is our duty as Christians to win their loyalty to Christ through Christian treatment." The press added their voice to the growing opposition to Manning. The press argued, "if we had the slightest conscience at all we would release them from bondage, restore their full civil rights and recompense them for the economic loss they have suffered."[44]

In the end material rather than moral considerations determined the fate of the displaced Japanese. The sugar beet industry was in the midst of another labor shortage. The German and Italian prisoners-of-war who had worked the beet fields in 1945 were being repatriated. Anxious not to lose their only source of labor, the southern Alberta sugar interests began to pressure Manning to keep the Japanese in Alberta. Faced with the opposition of influential groups, Manning agreed in March 1946 to permit them to remain in Alberta. His decision, however, was not made public. Manning informed the sugar interests of his decision, but withheld the news from the public. He thought that by keeping quiet on the issue public feelings would subside.[45] While his actions reassured the sugar beet interest, Manning's apparent indecisiveness caused the displaced Japanese to question whether they had a future in Alberta. Anxious to establish a permanent home, many took advantage of the federal government's resettlement program and moved east to the fruit and vegetable districts of southwestern Ontario. Few were interested in returning to the Pacific coast. As one petition urging the lifting of travel restrictions observed:

> we are not stupid enough to want to rush into a province which seems to be crammed with racial intolerance and where we would only suffer discrimination of every sort . . . We are smarter than most people give us credit for and will not rush back to B.C.[46]

It was not until 26 March 1948, almost three years after the end of the war, that Premier Manning announced that Japanese Canadian residents of Alberta were entitled to the same rights and privileges as any other Albertan.[47] With two exceptions, both of which were the result of federal regulations, this marked the end of official governmental discrimination in Alberta against Japanese.

While Manning's announcement eliminated legalized discrimination, there were still major social barriers facing Japanese Albertans. Japanese in Alberta faced continued discrimination in the workplace, in housing, and in education. Those Japanese most affected were the Canadian born Nisei, for they were just beginning to establish themselves in careers and to start their own families. For the Nisei, the 1950's were years of struggle. Faced with discrimination, their only resources were their own determination and industry. In their struggle, the Nisei were not motivated by material considerations alone. Rather, they recognized that economic and social security were necessary if their children, the Sansei, were to be protected from a hostile government and public.[48]

During the 1950s the leadership and goals of Japanese Canadian organizations changed. The immigrant generation was reaching retirement age, and the leadership of the Japanese Canadian communities passed to their Canadian-born children. The economic isolation of Japanese Canadians which necessitated purchasing and marketing cooperatives disappeared and, as a consequence, one of the main reasons for separate Japanese organizations also disappeared. The need to fight for political rights and compensation for wartime losses was lessened by the granting of full civil rights and the payment of limited compensation by the federal government for property lost during the war.[49] The only political fight in the 1950s concerned Canada's immigration laws which discriminated against nonwhites. Much of this fight, however, was taken up by the larger Japanese Canadian organizations in eastern Canada. In the 1950s the role of Japanese organizations became primarily social. Even in this role, Japanese organizations declined in importance because Japanese Canadians were beginning to have more social contacts with non-Japanese.[50]

Although the importance of Japanese organizations declined during the 1950s, one annual social event retained its place in the lives of Japanese Canadians. Every summer Japanese Albertans in each center would gather together for an annual picnic. For the picnic, the women prepared generous quantities of food. The day's menu included teriyaki chicken and bowls of vegetables cooked with fried noodles. There would be simple rice balls topped with a piece of black seaweed, small fried bean curd bags filled with rice, and rice wrapped in sheets of seaweed and rolled jelly roll fashion around pickled ginger, egg, gourd, dried mushroom, and a strip of green vegetable. In addition, small tightly sealed bottles of soy sauce, bags of oranges, and Japanese pickles would be packed for the picnic lunch. The picnic meal would be only a small part of the day's activities. There would be foot races for the children and novelty events such as an egg and spoon race and three-legged races. Contests would be held in which the blind-folded contestants would try to break a watermelon with a stick. At every picnic, the young men played baseball, and there would be the obligatory peanut scramble for the children. The picnics invariably ended in the same way. The children, lined up abreast, would pick up all the bits of paper and refuse from the day's activities. Upon consigning his refuse to one of the park's litter containers, each child would receive one final bag of candy as a reward. The picnics were more than just times for recreation: they were times to renew old friendships. They brought the community back together in a way reminiscent of the days before the war. They were an expression of the solidarity of Japanese Canadians.

In the 1950s and 1960s, the Japanese Canadian community in Alberta changed dramatically. Economically the Japanese rose into the middle class. Socially, their place in Alberta's society changed even more dramatically. After the war, many Albertans had called for the expulsion of Japanese from the province. Yet in the 1960s the city of Lethbridge, a city which during the war had banned Japanese, commissioned a Japanese garden as its Centennial project.

In many ways, the changing place of Japanese Canadians in Alberta can be seen in the history of a small Anglican church in Coaldale. In 1946, Canon Gordon G. Nakayama founded an Anglican parish among Japanese in the Coaldale area. The church was a building moved from the Tashme detention camp at Hope, British Columbia, where many Japanese Canadians had been held. In the beginning, only Japanese attended. During the 1950s, however, more and more non-Japanese joined the church, replacing many of the Japanese who had moved to Edmonton, Calgary, and Lethbridge. By the time Canon Nakayama retired, his parish was more Caucasian than Japanese. The old distinctions based on race had eroded.[51]

The mid-1960s marked the arrival of a new group of Japanese immigrants to Canada and Alberta. From the mid-1920s until the mid-1960s, because of restrictive immigration laws, there was virtually no immigration from Japan to Canada. When these laws were changed, a small trickle of Japanese migrants began to arrive. The new immigrants from Japan, called the Shin-Issei, were very different from the immigrants who arrived more than a half century earlier. Unlike those who came before them, the Shin-Issei were generally well educated and entered Canadian society directly into the middle class. Rather than settling in rural Alberta as had their predecessors, the new arrivals settled primarily in Edmonton and Calgary.

The Shin-Issei's arrival in Alberta benefitted the existing Japanese Canadian community. They brought with them some of the traditional skills which had been lost. They caused a resurgence in interest in the Japanese language. In Edmonton, the Japanese language school started by the Shin-Issei for their own children began to give language lessons to the Nisei, their children, and their grandchildren. The Shin-Issei exposed many Japanese Albertans for the first time to traditional crafts, music, and dance. Their arrival added new life to the Japanese Canadian community.

Today, the Japanese Canadian community is far less cohesive. Where thirty years ago, almost all Japanese families would attend the annual summer picnic, today only a minority attends. Thirty years ago, a Caucasian face would have been a rarity. Today, many of the children who ran in the foot races of the 1950s are accompanied by a Caucasian spouse and children who are only part Japanese. The intermarriage rates now exceeds 80 percent.[52]

The third generation of Japanese Canadians, the Sansei, have reached maturity. They differ from their parents in that they grew up without the experience of the war and in relative isolation from other Japanese Canadians. They still carry with them, however, many of the same values which enabled their grandparents to survive the war and for their parents to find a respected place in Canadian society. The Sansei still exhibit the dedication to education which took their parents into the middle classes. Today, the number of Sansei artists, scientists, and professionals far exceeds what would be expected given the size of the Japanese Canadian community in Alberta.

Although the day-to-day world of the Sansei differs enormously from the early life of their parents, a few rude reminders of those early days still persist. When Sansei delegates from across the country gathered for a Japanese Canadian centennial conference in Calgary in 1977, they told stories of lingering discrimination.[53] Perhaps because of these few reminders of harsher times, many Sansei are fighting to ensure the suffering of their parents and grandparents was not in vain. A movement has been started to urge the government of Canada to redress the wrongs committed during World War II. Several forms of redress have been proposed. At a minimum, the Sansei and others who are lobbying the government want an official parliamentary pronouncement acknowledging the wartime innocence of Japanese Canadians and the wrongfulness of the actions taken by the government against them. Demands have also arisen for financial compensation for the wartime experiences, for the repeal of the the War Measures Act, the legislation used to displace the Japanese, and for changes to the constitution to prevent governments from disregarding the Charter of Rights and Freedoms. The war that almost destroyed the Japanese Canadian community is now providing the impetus for many Japanese Canadians who were isolated from that community to reaquaint themselves with it. Many Sansei, who often had little contact with other Japanese Canadians, are now actively involved in the the redress movement. While fear of a public backlash still haunts many, the widespread support for redress is indicative of the Japanese Canadian community's social, economic, and political maturity.

The first Japanese immigrant came to Canada in 1877, and the first Japanese immigrant to Alberta arrived in 1906. Many of the original settlers came not intending to stay, but remained to raise children, grandchildren, and great-grandchildren. Others arrived in the province during World War II. The most recent arrivals came in the mid-1960s, and since that time have prospered with other Albertans. The community has gone from field hand and coal miner to urbanite and professional. Most of the traditional Japanese ways have been lost. In their place, new traditions have evolved, traditions which were forged by struggle, and which reflect the dual heritage of Japanese Canadians.

CHAPTER EIGHTEEN

South Asians in Alberta
Norman Buchignani

Introduction

For many decades, traditional Canadian stereotypes of immigrants were as straightforward as they were inaccurate. Immigrants were divided into Britishers, Americans, and "foreigners." The category of foreigners lumped together a wide assortment of non-British Europeans who were generally pictured as making up the lion's share of immigrants. Until after World War II such immigrants were actually in a minority, but Canadian sensitivity to their cultural distinctiveness made them appear to be far more numerous than they were. Since World War II, the range of immigrants has shifted considerably, and Canadian stereotypes have changed accordingly. Unfortunately, these stereotypes are no more accurate than they were before. Whereas earlier stereotypes illustrated Canadians' high sensitivity to cultural difference, more recent ones show that Canadians are equally sensitive to perceived physical difference. Today's predominant popular conception of immigrants is that most are from the Third World and are primarily people of Chinese, Carribean, and "East Indian" origin. While they hardly predominate, these people presently represent about 30 percent of the total immigrant flow. They and their children number at least three-quarters of a million, or one out of every thirty Canadians.

Because Canada's immigration regulations were racially restrictive until the 1960s, very few of these "visible minority" immigrants were here before that time. Consequently, most of these people and the ethnic communities which they represent have become established very recently. Unlike many recent immigrants from more traditional source countries, they have largely had to establish Canadian roots on their own without the benefit of knowledge accumulated by earlier immigrants. A further difficulty for these people is that because they are new to the Canadian social landscape, they often arouse suspicion. Other Canadians wonder who they are, what they want, if they will "become

Canadian," and what they can contribute to Canada. For many Canadians these questions remain unanswered.

South Asians, or people who are commonly referred to as East Indian, have only been part of the Alberta landscape in significant numbers for the past twenty-five years and in this sense telling their story is quite straightforward.[1] On the other hand, writing about people of South Asian origin is nearly as ambitious as writing about Europeans in general. Like Europeans, people of South Asian origin (hereafter South Asians) originate from many places with diverse histories, and they exhibit an enormous range of cultural, linguistic, and religious identities. One can best define South Asians as people who ultimately derive from the Indian subcontinent. South Asia includes several countries, each with its own national destiny: India, Pakistan, Bangladesh, Sri Lanka (formerly Ceylon), Afghanistan, Nepal, and Bhutan.

The cultural range in most of these countries is enormous. In India alone, there are over 600 million people. Even today, the village is the bulwark of India and 70 percent of its people live there; this ties many Indians intimately to local cultures and local identities.[2] Today there are a dozen major mutually unintelligible languages spoken in India, not to mention another 100 or so minor languages. There are equally profound differences in religion; the majority of people are Hindus, but there is a vast range of beliefs and customs practiced as Hinduism. There are also three times more Muslims in India than there are Canadians altogether, as well as millions of Sikhs, Christians, Parsis, and people subscribing to tribally-based religions. These differences are further compounded by strong regional identities, by one of the most complicated systems of class and caste in the world, and by enormous differences between life in the villages and life in the cities. In such a complex place as India, ethnicity cannot be separated easily from other identities, but by any definition there are literally hundreds of large ethnic groups. The situation is somewhat analogous in the other countries of South Asia. Moreover, not all people of South Asian origin actually live in South Asia. Some have emigrated to other continents. The relatively long time which these migrants have spent outside of South Asia has changed many of them profoundly, much like immigration to North America changed European settlers.

The great majority of South Asia was British colonial territory from the early nineteenth century until after World War II and during this time South Asians emigrated in large numbers. Most of the overseas communities which these South Asians originally founded were within the British Empire. The British turned to India for a replacement labor supply after slavery had been abolished, and by the 1850s they were indenturing Indians for overseas labor. Indenture for Indians was inevitably brutal and highly exploitative—it was a "new system of slavery" which created a whole set of new peoples.[3] In Mauritius, Uganda, Fiji, South Africa, British Guyana, Trinidad, and other places in the Caribbean, peoples arose who were culturally South Asian but who were very different from peoples in South Asia itself. Later, overseas populations developed when Indian merchants migrated to the earlier focal points of settlement as well as to South Africa, Uganda, and Kenya. Others dispersed across the empire in the British army—to Hong Kong, Singapore, Egypt, and elsewhere.

Despite the diversity among these peoples, some general commonalities can be found among them. Again, the European analogy is useful. To be sure, Europeans are separated by differences in language, culture, religion, identity, and even biology; at the same time, however, all of these diverse Europeans have participated together in the major currents of Western history dating back to pre-Christian times. In many ways the South Asian experience has been similar. Bounded by mountains to the north and the ocean to the south, South Asia has always had enough isolation and autonomy to produce cultural forms and beliefs which span the whole area. Cities in northern South Asia go back to at least 3000 B.C.[4] About 1500 B.C. what are today Pakistan and Northern India were invaded by people who called themselves Arya; these nomadic, warlike people conquered the whole region and imposed their culture upon the local inhabitants. Out of the beliefs of these conquerors arose Hinduism, the world religion which has been inextricably intertwined with South Asian culture and history.

Like all great religions, Hinduism supported a vast array of moral and intellectual precepts, which became universal aspects of South Asian culture. These included a very strong emphasis on the family, a tendency to make very fine social distinctions, coupled with an ability to live together separately, a deep interest in philosophy, and a strong sense of continuity. Of course not all South Asians are religious Hindus, but Hindu secular thought pervades the region.

Another unifying force in South Asia has been a common colonial experience. For the greater part of the continent, colonialism dates back well before the entry of the British, to the Islamic invasions of 1100-1200 A.D. Muslim, Turkish, and Iranian-speaking invaders eventually ruled most of what is today Pakistan and northern and central India until European intrigues and local uprisings destroyed their power in the 1800s. At its peak (1556-1605) the Mogul Empire was probably the most powerful in the world. Mogul rule resulted in many millions of converts to Islam and to a greater uniformity of culture within South Asia than would otherwise have been the case.

The British who superseded the Moguls were far more thorough colonizers and have forever made their mark on the whole region. They created a complete range of pseudo-British social and political institutions in India. English became a major *lingua franca* and was the language of the bureaucracy and of higher education, as it is today. British rule also created whole classes of highly-anglicized South Asians, who had to adopt British customs for the purposes of economic and social advancement. These people became the mainstay of the national middle classes in the independent countries of South Asia after World War II.

Given their highly complex history, one must use care in talking about

South Asians in order to avoid the dual pitfalls of seeing South Asian groups as somehow "all the same" or seeing them each as unique. Perhaps the most realistic way to go about this is to consider South Asians in Alberta in terms of the many *ethnic groups* of which this population is comprised—groups of people who see themselves as socially and culturally distinct. Ethnic identity and identification are dual processes which many South Asian Canadians use to form the basis for association with each other. As we shall see, South Asian criteria for ethnic similarity are finely drawn and have resulted in the proliferation of ethnic communities wherever South Asians have settled.

The Pioneers

For many years the history of South Asians in Canada was the history of their experience in British Columbia. Very few South Asians lived elsewhere in Canada until the 1960s. South Asians came to British Columbia early in the century and their experience there was to have profound effects on their settlement in the rest of the country. For this reason it must be looked at briefly, if only to set the context for Alberta.

At the turn of the century British Columbia was unique among the provinces in one important respect. It alone had developed race relations characterized by profound conflict and continual attempts to subordinate minority groups on the basis of race.[5] The focus of this animosity had been first Chinese, and then Japanese immigrants. Chinese had been coming to British Columbia since 1858 and by the 1870s they had begun to be seen as unassimilable, an economic threat to white Canadians, immoral and uncommitted to Canada. The result was a parade of anti-Chinese legislation, which attempted to subordinate the Chinese to the lowest levels of the society and the economy.[6] The Chinese were disenfranchised, were barred from a whole range of occupations, and were socially segregated. The provincial government continually pressured its federal counterpart to ban Chinese immigration. However, the federal government was more responsive to the CPR and other large businesses that claimed to need Chinese labor than it was to the British Columbia legislature; their only response to the latter was to levy a $50 entry tax on Chinese in 1885.

Japanese migrants began arriving in substantial numbers in the 1890s, and their arrival provoked the same racist response.[7] By the middle of the next decade the Japanese faced similar political, social, and economic disabilities as the Chinese. Even so, thousands of Japanese continued to come, attracted by what were extremely high wages by Japanese standards. At that point the federal government resolved to stop Asian immigration. Ottawa moved against Chinese immigration first. It did so by raising the entry tax on Chinese immigrants to $500 in 1903-04. This tax was so impossibly large that it shut off Chinese immigration for quite some time. Similar measures could not be attempted against the Japanese, because Japan was not willing to see Canada unilaterally act against its citizens. Japanese immigrants continued to come to British Columbia, and hysteria against them mounted.

South Asians first came to British Columbia at just this inopportune time; consequently, they were almost immediately subject to the full brunt of racial antipathy which had been building for fifty years. The first arrivals actually came from Hong Kong in 1903, where previously most of them had been in the British army. They had first heard of Canada from compatriots who had travelled through in the year before on route to the coronation celebrations of Edward VII.[8] The great majority were Sikhs, an ethnic and religious group which comprised a substantial proportion of the British India army. Sikhs originated in Punjab in northern India, and then numbered only a few million people altogether. Even so, they were already to be found in small numbers all around the world. Independent and self-reliant, they had flexibly adapted to social and economic conditions wherever they went. Canada presented the attraction of high wages, and they were prepared to do what they could to exploit the country's potential.

White British Columbians were equally prepared to see that they did not. In spite of this anti-Asian hostility, the Chinese entry tax had created a scarcity of cheap manual labor and Sikhs did not initially have difficulty in getting work. This prompted them to write to their friends and relatives, who began to arrive in larger and larger numbers. By 1907 as many as 700 arrived on a single ship.

Ottawa had already been negotiating with Japan to limit immigration, and it set out to find a way to terminate Sikh immigration as well.[9] However, the British were unwilling to see Canada ban Indian immigration overtly because they were afraid it would provoke nationalist unrest in India. So William Lyon Mackenzie King (the Deputy Minister of Labor) was sent to British Columbia to deal with this dilemma. His solution to the problem was as elegant as it was devious—the passage of an Order in Council which simply stated that immigrants had to come to Canada on a direct passage from their country of origin. Since there was no such way to get from India to Canada, Sikh immigration was effectively terminated. Even the wives and children of those who were already here were forbidden to come.

The Sikh community in British Columbia banded together to fight the immigration restrictions. Nevertheless, despite innumerable court battles, personal representations, and petitions to all levels of government, the ban remained in force. Even an attempt in 1914 by 376 South Asians to charter a ship in Hong Kong and sail to Canada was rebuffed; the *Komagata Maru* was quarantined in Vancouver for two months until it was finally forced by the Canadian naval cruiser HMS *Rainbow* to return to Asia.[10]

Faced with racial animosity and this ban on immigration, many South Asians left Canada bound for India or the United States. By the outbreak of World War I, there were fewer than 1,500 immigrants left in British Columbia out of the almost 6,000 who had initially arrived. Those who stayed, though, quickly achieved economic security despite the many racial restrictions under which they labored. By then, Sikhs were largely to be found where there were large saw mills—then chiefly around

Vancouver and on Vancouver Island. There they developed strong communities centered around their religious institutions, particularly the Sikh temples (Gurdwaras). Sikhs were finally allowed to bring their wives and children to Canada in 1919. The continuous passage regulation was, however, to remain in force until 1947, effectively barring all other South Asians from immigrating to Canada.

Very few of these pioneers chose to settle outside of British Columbia, despite the fact that this was the only province in which their privileges were significantly restricted by law. This settlement pattern is an historical accident; British Columbia was the place where South Asians had originally landed, and this was enough to guarantee that most would remain there. British Columbia was also the only place in the West where Sikhs could find the kind of high paying wage labor they sought. Very few were interested in agricultural work, despite being among the most sophisticated farmers in India; agricultural labor paid very poorly and without their families, it was very difficult for them to begin farming. However, a number of Sikhs were employed by the railroads up to the early 1920s in roadbed clearing and track laying, and some of these individuals were almost certainly the first South Asian immigrants to visit Alberta. Small communities of Sikhs had formed in the eastern British Columbia towns of Golden and Revelstoke, and these individuals worked the line well into Alberta. However, the ethnic division of labor on the railroads was such that Sikhs were unable to continue very far into the province. No South Asian communities were to arise in Alberta before the 1950s.

Even so, beginning just after World War I, a handful of Sikhs began farming in southern Alberta. Near Lethbridge a group of three men began farming together in 1928. Until the 1950s they were the only South Asians in the area. Another such group was farming near Medicine Hat. Still another Sikh man, Harnan Singh Hari, began a farm in the Glenmore district near Calgary, which he and his family eventually expanded to two sections. In addition to these farmers, a few other Sikhs attended the University of Alberta in the 1920s. One of these was Kernal Singh Sandhu, who subsequently obtained a Ph.D. at the University of Toronto. Another, Hazara Singh Garcha, received an M.A. in agriculture in Alberta, and subsequently returned to British Columbia, where he became an important community spokesperson.

Because the ban on South Asian immigration continued in force throughout the interwar years, the only legal new arrivals were the wives and children of those already here. This low level of immigration continued right through World War II. Late in World War II it was clear that one of the non-negotiable conditions of Indian support for the British war effort was postwar independence. Colonial India was to be divided into the new countries of India and Pakistan, and Ceylon would become independent as well. This made it difficult for the Canadian government to allow British Columbia's restrictions on South Asians; unlike its colonial predecessor, the newly independent Indian government would not quietly accept such discrimination against its nationals.

Consequently, in 1947 South Asians in British Columbia were finally granted the vote and all other legal limitations on them were removed.[11] In the same year the federal government eliminated the continuous passage regulation. In recognition of their new-found independence India, Pakistan, and Ceylon were allowed token immigrant quotas in 1951; thereafter 300, 150, and 50 people, in addition to the wives and children of legal South Asian residents who were already here, would be allowed to immigrate yearly from these respective countries.

This quota system persisted until 1962 and under it a small number of people of South Asian origin began to settle across the country. However, most went to metro Toronto, the area from metro Toronto to Windsor, and to Vancouver. Even so, a slowly increasing trickle began to come to Alberta and the other prairie provinces in the late 1950s. Virtually all of these people were school teachers and their families who typically went to small towns and rural areas where there was then a shortage of teachers.[12] According to the census, there were only 208 people of South Asian origin in Alberta in 1961.

Relatively large-scale immigration of South Asians to Alberta began in the 1960s as a direct result of further changes in the Canadian immigration regulations. Early in the decade, the last racial and national restrictions were eliminated and, from 1967 on, prospective immigrants were screened primarily on the basis of economic and social criteria. Most South Asians selected were consequently very highly skilled. In essence, this system of immigrant selection instituted an era of professional immigration into Alberta.

Because of the wide variability of ethnic and cultural backgrounds among these early South Asian immigrants to Alberta, it is difficult to summarize their situations. Whereas in 1960 there were only a few isolated families and individuals in the province, by 1970 there were a number of distinct ethnic and religious communities located primarily in Edmonton and Calgary. Perhaps a few biographical examples can serve to illustrate this variability better than anything else:

Ajit Singh Bains (a pseudonym) was born to a wealthy Sikh family in Lahore. His family was forced to move across the newly formed India-Pakistan border at the time of partition. He took a B.A. at Punjab University and subsequently received an M.A. in civil engineering from the University of California. Ajit worked for a while in Britain at a variety of unchallenging technical jobs. He heard of the prospects in Canada from a cousin, and immigrated to Calgary in 1964. After a series of marginal jobs, he secured a position with an international oil company. In 1968 he went back to India to get married; prospects for educated people like himself were so bad there that he made the commitment to stay in Canada. His wife has an M.A. in English and now works as a librarian for a local government agency.

Mr. de Silva (another pseudonym) was born to middle class Sinhalese Christian parents in Columbo, Sri Lanka. Both his parents were teachers and he received a good education, most of it in English. He studied chemistry, first in Sri Lanka and then in England. While in England he was offered a postdoctoral position at the University of Alberta. He was one of the first Sinhalese in

Edmonton. His postdoctorate turned into an offer of a regular position, which he accepted. He subsequently left Alberta for a better job in Ontario.[13]

The sequence above was to be repeated many times during the 1960s as individuals from over twenty different ethnic, religious, and national groups of South Asians began to arrive in the province. These individuals were chiefly from middle class backgrounds in their respective countries of origin. Many already had overseas experiences of one sort or another, such as university training, work in Britain or in Third World countries, or they had already emigrated to another country. Indeed, many South Asian individuals were "pre-adapted" to life in Canada.[14] Virtually all men spoke English and had received their higher education in English. Most had much in common with their professional Canadian colleagues and made an easy transition to Canadian society.

The Development of South Asian Communities in Alberta

By 1971 the number of South Asians in Alberta had grown to about 4,400. Most of them were very recent immigrants, chiefly from India and Pakistan. In addition, a small but growing number had already begun to arrive from other provinces; like many other Canadians they were attracted by the economic opportunities in Alberta. South Asian Albertans quickly formed strong social networks of association with each other, primarily on the basis of their various ethnic and religious backgrounds. Because of the early Sikh connections with Canada, a very high proportion of 1960s immigrants were Sikhs. In 1967 Sikhs in Alberta formed the first South Asian associations in the province—the Singh Society of Calgary and the Edmonton-based Sikh Society of Alberta. Almost all of the other South Asian ethnic and religious communities in Alberta have subsequently followed the Sikhs' lead and have begun associations.[15]

During the 1970s, South Asian immigration to Alberta increased dramatically. By the end of 1984 there were about 20,000 people of South Asian origin in Alberta—about 1 percent of the population. This proportion is about the national average, in that there are now about 310,000 South Asian Canadians in all. These new Albertans come from a wide range of national and regional contexts. Only about one-third to one-half of these immigrants of the past decade have come directly from India. Perhaps 10 percent come from Pakistan and another 3 percent come from Sri Lanka. The rest come primarily from places far from South Asia—East Africa, Britain, Fiji, Guyana, and Trinidad. As mentioned, most of these individuals tend to see themselves as members of subnational groups based on ethnicity or religion. In a *very* approximate sense, the following table represents the number of individuals who are presently members of these various groups:

Group	Place of Last Residence	Number
Sikhs	Punjab, East Africa, Britain	9,500
Ismailis	East Africa, Britain	3,000
Pakistanis	Pakistan	2,500

Gujarati Hindus	East Africa, Gujarat (India)	2,100
"Northern" Hindus	Hindi-speaking India	2,100
Fijian Indians	Fiji	2,000
Guyana Indians	Guyana	1,700
Punjabi Indians	Punjab (India)	1,200
Bengalis	Bengal (India)	800
Trinidadian Indians	Trinidad	800
Indian Tamils	Madras (India)	600
Malayalam-speakers	Kerala (India)	600
Sinhalese	Sri Lanka	600
Gujarati Muslims	East Africa	500
Goans	Goa (India)	500
Bangladeshis	Bangladesh	500
Others		1,000
Total		30,000

Table 1. An Estimate of South Asian Groups in Alberta, 1984.[16]

The above-mentioned groups are so diverse that it is useful to discuss each one separately. South Asian ethnic identifications are very complex, for they are almost always created out of a synthesis of cultural, religious, national, and linguistic criteria. Therefore, they cannot be separated clearly by any single factor whether it be religion, language, culture, or nationality.

Sikhs

Sikhism began as a religious movement. It is a monotheistic, democratic religion based on the teachings of ten Gurus or teachers.[17] The first of these was Guru Nanak (1469-1539). The tenth and last Guru was Gobind Singh (1666-1708), who added the final elements to the religion. Guru Nanak had been a universalist who decried sterile religious rituals, idols, and social distinctions such as caste. Guru Gobind Singh reconciled this philosophy with defense of the faith, creating the *Khalsa* or community of believers and providing them with the intellectual means to defend Sikhism from external oppression. It was he who gave male Sikhs the five markers *(Kakas)* of their faith—to wear their hair uncut *(Kesh)*, to carry a comb in the hair *(Kangha)*, and to wear a pair of shorts *(k-Kachha)*, a steel bangle *(Kara)*, and a short sword *(Kirpan)*. The practice of covering a man's uncut hair with a turban led to the turban becoming an informal marker of Sikhism which is perhaps the most evident to non-Sikhs in Canada. Guru Gobind Singh also renamed all male Sikhs Singh (Lion) and all women Kaur (Princess). As practised, Sikhism has no priests, no intermediaries between the individual and God, no idols and few rituals. Public worship primarily involves people assembling in the *gurdwara* to recite teachings of the Gurus and to eat *langar*, the communal meal that is always available to anyone after a Sikh service; its origins were in Guru Nanak's desire to abolish caste barriers between converts to Sikhism.

Sikh religion began among the people of Punjab in northern India and has ever afterwards been intimately associated with Punjabi language and culture. For example, the collected teachings of the ten Gurus were assembled into the *Guru Granth Sahib,* which is written in Punjabi. Today virtually all Sikhs are Punjabis, yet both religion and many cultural practices differentiate them from other Punjabis.

The Sikh population of Alberta is probably the most diverse of the different South Asian communities, a fact which reflects its relatively large size. Sikhs are among the most mobile of South Asian peoples. Many Albertan Sikhs have not come from the Punjabi heartland; indeed, many have never been in India. Most of these overseas Sikhs have come to Canada from East Africa, either directly or by way of a stay in Britain. They were part of the large South Asian population which had established itself in Uganda, Kenya, and Tanzania during the time of the British rule. Many were engaged in retail trade, transportation, manufacturing, and government service. Sikhs comprised 6 percent of South Asians in these countries. Gujarati-speaking Hindus and Muslims together comprised 70 percent and Hindu Punjabis 10 percent. They were all affected by the change in political relations at independence. This was most marked in the case of Uganda, where Idi Amin eventually demanded that all South Asians leave the country. Some Albertan Sikhs were among the 6,000 South Asian political refugees from East Africa that Canada accepted in 1972-73. Most East African Sikhs have come subsequently either from adjacent Tanzania and Kenya, or from Britain.

As the Sikh communities in Alberta grew, the range of individuals increased accordingly. Sikhs who arrived in the 1960s came at a time when skilled people were in very high demand in the province, and they have succeeded in finding a secure place for themselves in the province's economy. Those who came in the 1970s are much more varied occupationally, and Sikhs now can be found working in virtually every kind of job. Sikhs have had an independent entrepreneurial tradition and many prefer to work for themselves. This has led to the emergence of hundreds of Sikh-run businesses in Alberta. Because of a lack of capital, most of these are relatively small, the self-owned taxi being the most common. Sikhs have established a number of small stores, travel agencies, and other small businesses in Edmonton and Calgary, and a few Sikhs are important in real estate and development. Several hundred Sikhs currently reside in Red Deer, Lethbridge, and Medicine Hat, and a handful live in smaller centers in central and southern Alberta. Several hundred single men are now employed in railway work and resource development in the north.

With this increase in the number of Sikhs in Alberta has come an increase in the range of community institutions in Calgary and Edmonton. In Calgary, the Singh Society, which now has over 1,000 members, finished the impressive Guru Nanak Centre in 1979 at a cost of $850,000. The Centre operates as a meeting place for Sikhs and a place where Punjabi language classes can be taught. In Edmonton there are presently three Sikh associations, each of which organizes religious and social functions. The oldest of these is the Sikh Society of Alberta, which has now been in existence for almost fifteen years. It presently has over 500 active members. Its members are perhaps the least traditional of these three associations. In late 1981 the Sikh Society moved into new quarters in the Sikh Centre. The Siri Guru Singh Sabha was founded in 1977 by Sikhs who wished to maintain more traditional Khalsa Sikh practices. It also has about 500 members and maintains a small *gurdwara* in southwest Edmonton. The third association is called Nanksar, whose members hold closely to the teachings of Sant Nihan Singh, a living Sikh teacher.

In addition to the religious activities of these associations, they are active in representing Sikhs to government and to the public. This has been a particularly important function, for Sikh men who continue to wear the five *kakas* are very visible and consequently are more frequently the objects of racial discrimination than other South Asians.

Muslim South Asian Groups

The complexity of Alberta's South Asian population cannot be better illustrated than by a comparison between Sikhs and Pakistanis, who are also one of the largest South Asian groups in the province.[18] In contrast to Sikhs, Pakistanis are a *national* rather than an ethnic group—they are former citizens of Pakistan. Inasmuch as Pakistan was created in 1947, its population continues to have a very mixed ethnic and linguistic background. Many of its citizens were Muslim Indians who moved to Pakistan at the time of partition. At the same time, what is now Pakistan already contained a number of distinct peoples, defined primarily by region and language—Punjabis, Sindhis, Baluchis, and others. In Pakistan these divisions continue to run very deep. Even so, the great majority of Pakistanis participate in one greater unifier—Islam. Most Pakistanis are Sunni Muslims, and this is also true of immigrant Pakistanis in Alberta. Their national and religious identifications are so strong that Pakistanis do not feel that they have much in common with other South Asians in Alberta. Thus, the Pakistani communities of Calgary and Edmonton are almost entirely distinct from those of the Sikhs and others.

The fact that most Pakistanis are Muslims has resulted in considerable interethnic contact between them and other Muslims. In Edmonton, Pakistanis jointly use the Al-Rashid mosque. This mosque and Islamic cultural center was founded by Lebanese immigrants in 1938, making it one of the oldest extant mosques in North America.[19] Today Pakistanis share its facilities with Muslims of many other nationalities—Egyptian, Lebanese, Palestinian, Indian, and others. For large religious observances, Pakistanis in Edmonton meet separately. Pakistanis in Edmonton have their own associations and are active in the local Urdu-Muslim Cultural Association. The Pakistani community in Calgary is somewhat smaller than it is in Edmonton, but it is equally active; community activities center around the Pakistan-Canada Association of Calgary.

Pakistani Albertans are now quite varied in occupational and class backgrounds. The first Pakistanis arrived in Alberta under the old quota system around 1960. From then until the mid-1970s almost all immigrant men were professionals. Subsequently, many Pakistani immigrants have been skilled blue- and white-collar workers.

Pakistanis are one of many ethnic or national groups in Alberta which subscribe to the Sunni branch of Islam. They share their faith with a wide variety of Arabs, Indonesians, and Turks, as well as with other South Asians whose ethnic origins are diverse. In Alberta today, there are a number of Sunni Muslims from Gujarat and other areas of North India. Perhaps one-fourth of all Fijian Indian immigrants and some South Asians from the Caribbean are also Sunnis. One of the most important of these smaller Sunni groups in Alberta are people from Bangladesh. At the time of partition, the eastern portion of Bengal became East Pakistan. East Pakistan was separated from West Pakistan by language, culture, and 1,000 miles. Its inhabitants were soon dissatisfied with being governed by the wishes of numerically larger West Pakistan, and this culminated in civil war in 1972. The outcome was the new state of Bangladesh. Bangladeshis have never come to Canada in large numbers, but their presence here is growing steadily. Like Pakistanis, Bangladeshis are Sunnis, but in culture and language they share much with Bengali Hindus from across the border in India. Bangladeshis in Alberta are relatively few, but they participate in an active round of cultural and social events. There is presently a Bangladesh-Canada Association in Calgary.

Bangladeshis and Pakistanis illustrate how unclear the line is between ethnic and religious identity for many South Asians. For example, Pakistan itself was created as a result of political conflict between Hindus and Muslims in colonial India and most Pakistanis identify so strongly with their religion that it is really part of their ethnicity. At the same time, they have little to do with their coreligionists from Bangladesh, for whom the same religion is also a strong component of group identity.

One of the largest Muslim communities in Alberta at present are the Ismailis.[20] The Ismailis are an entirely separate sect of Islam whose origins are in the era of the Prophet Muhammad. At the death of the Prophet, many of his followers believed that strong religious leadership would continue in his line in a series of successors (*Imams*). These Muslims are called Shia. They include most Iranians as well as sizeable populations in almost all other Islamic countries. Nizari Ismailis are one of many separate Shia traditions. They differ from other Shia Muslims in that they trace descent from Muhammad through his nephew Ali and then through a specific hereditary line of *Imam*(s). The Nizari Ismailis acknowledge H. H. Aga Khan IV as the forty-ninth *Imam*, and he is the preeminent leader of their religion. Ismailis have a centralized religious structure which ties all the world's Nizari Ismaili communities together.

Most of today's Ismailis are South Asians whose ancestors were converted to the faith during the long period of Muslim rule in northern India. Most South Asian Ismaili converts were Gujaratis. In the mid-1800s, when Hasan Ali Shah, Aga Khan I arrived from Iran, India became the most important Ismaili center in the world. Many Ismaili Gujaratis subsequently went to East Africa at the turn of the century. By the 1960s continual migration had increased their number there to between 50,000 and 60,000. Under the guidance of Sultan Muhammad Shah, Aga Khan III, these communities modernized rapidly. Ismailis in East Africa did well for themselves economically, which made their businesses obvious targets for Africanization as Independence approached. This culminated in Idi Amin's expulsion of all South Asians from Uganda in 1972.[21] Thousands of refugee Ismailis came to Canada in 1972-73 and thereafter. There are about 30,000 Ismailis in Canada today.

Edmonton and Calgary are important Ismaili centers, and Ismailis in both cities are very well organized. In each city there are several centers which serve as meeting places for worship and instruction (*jamat-khana*(s)). Most Ismailis have only been in Canada for a very short while and consequently most of these centers are not yet permanent facilities. Even so, they are actively used for devotional prayers and group observances. They are also used as schools in order to instruct children in the religion and in Ismaili history and culture.

Like other South Asian Canadians who come from East Africa, Ismailis' lives were severely disrupted only a few years ago. Many people lost everything they had in the exodus. Even so, Ismailis in Alberta have quickly rebounded. Although there is still underemployment in the community, the initial phase of social disorientation is largely past for most Ismailis and they are rapidly adapting to their new country. Their strong entrepreneural tradition is already reflected in the emergence of a wide range of Ismaili-run businesses in Alberta.

Hindu South Asian Groups

Hinduism is a religion, not an ethnicity. Its practise is so variable that it more often supports, rather than creates, already extant ethnic differences. Hindu religion and culture are, nevertheless, important facets of the lives of many people throughout Alberta and they bring people into association with each other.

If all Hindus in Alberta were grouped together, they would probably constitute the largest religious block among South Asians. Lacking any centralized authority, Hinduism has always adapted to the social environment in which it has existed, and therefore has never been easy to analyze. Practise and belief differ widely among the world's several hundred million Hindus. Alberta's Hindus have had to reconcile this and have done so in an imaginative fashion. Both Calgary and Edmonton have maintained strong Hindu associations—the Hindu Society of Calgary and the Hindu Society of Alberta. Indeed, these organizations were among the first South Asian associations created in Alberta. Both were started a decade ago by professionals from widely varying backgrounds, who had to resolve the problem of differing Hindu practise. This was done by limiting joint services to devotional practises and to the celebration of major calendrical events such as *Holi* and *Diwali*.

A traditional South Indian Hindu wedding in Calgary, 1984. (Courtesy S. Padmanabhan)

As the Hindu populations of these two cities grew, so did the range of Hindu Society activities. In Edmonton, the Hindu Society presently sponsors services in Hindi, English, and Sanskrit. Since mid-1981 these services have been held in the new Hindu Cultural Centre. The Hindu Society of Alberta also supports a variety of music and dance activities as well as Hindi language classes for children. The Calgary-based society began in 1973 and now has perhaps 100 families involved on a regular basis. Monthly services are held in English. The association is also planning to establish a Hindu cultural center as soon as the required funds can be collected. The Calgary association has been involved only in religious activities.

As mentioned, Alberta's Hindu population consists of people from a number of distinct groups. Let us briefly consider some of these.

Punjabi Hindus are religious Hindus whose culture and first language is Punjabi—the language of Sikhs and the predominant language of the whole Punjab region of India and Pakistan. Punjab is a continuous culture area, so its residents have always shared a good deal in terms of culture and history. Partition left most Punjabi Hindus and Sikhs on the Indian side of the border and most Muslims in Pakistan and their subsequent experiences have been quite different.

A considerable number of Punjabi Hindus come from East Africa, where their parents and grandparents had established themselves along with many of the other groups mentioned previously. Others have come by way of sojourns in Britain. Today they are one of the largest regional groups of Hindus in Alberta. Most are professionals and businessmen and as such share much with their compatriots from other South Asian groups. At the same time these links are crosscut by their cultural commonalities with other Punjabis and by their association with other Hindus. Punjabi Hindus have been very active in the Hindu societies in Calgary and Edmonton.

Hindi is the major language of north central India, and it is spoken by more people than any other South Asian language. Hindi is the predominant language in a number of Indian States and therefore crosscuts many ethnic and regional differences. Consequently the term "Hindi-speaking Hindus" is simply a shorthand phrase to refer primarily to people originally from Uttar Pradesh, Madhya Pradesh, Bihar, and Rajisthan. Immigrants from this part of India have many class, occupational, and cultural parallels with their Punjabi counterparts.

Gujaratis in India have a long tradition of regional and ethnic distinctiveness. Although most of them are religious Hindus, they speak Gujarati, which is distinct from Hindi and Punjabi. They share this language with Ismailis and Sunni Muslims from Gujarat. Like Sikhs, Gujaratis have been noted for their strong ethnic solidarity and for their tradition of overseas migration. The majority of South Asians in East Africa were Gujaratis. In addition to those in East Africa, small communities of Gujaratis can be found wherever there are other South Asians. Many have made a specialty of entrepreneurial activities.

In Alberta Gujarati Hindus have expressed their cultural and linguistic distinctiveness by creating separate societies. These two associations are the Alberta Gujarati Association (Edmonton) and the Gujarati Mandal (Calgary). Calgary's community is substantially larger than Edmonton's. Perhaps as many as 65 percent of Gujarati Hindus in Alberta have come from East Africa, where they left "courtesy of Idi Amin." There was always close communication between Gujaratis in East Africa and those in India and these two peoples have not therefore become very culturally distinct; consequently East African and Indian Gujaratis in Alberta form essentially one community.

Like present day Punjabis, Bengalis are partially an artifact of the partition of India and Pakistan. Prior to the partition, Bengal was a unified cultural and linguistic area whose many people had a long and distinct historical tradition. Hinduism and Islam were the predominant religions of the region. At the time of partition, Bengal was divided in two, roughly according to the distribution of Hindus and Muslims. Hindu West Bengal became part of India, while Islamic Bengal became the core of East Pakistan. As in Punjab, this religious and political division was hardly a clean one, and many Bengali Hindu immigrants to Alberta were actually born in what today is Bangladesh.

Bengalis share much of Hindu tradition with other North Indians, but speak a language which is distinct from that of their neighbors to the west. As with so many of the other groups considered herein, the majority of Bengali adults in Alberta are highly skilled. Like the Gujaratis, they have formed associations in Calgary and Edmonton—the Bengali Cultural Association of Calgary and the Edmonton Bengali Association. Bengali language classes for children have been developed in both

Edmonton and Calgary. In addition, Bengalis have maintained their well-known creative tradition by hosting far more cultural events than one would expect from such a small population.

Although the Aryan invasion occurred over 2,000 years ago, it still has consequences for South Asians. When the Aryans conquered north and central India, they were powerful enough to impose many of their cultural traditions on the local peoples of the region. Perhaps the most important of these were Sanskrit-based languages which now predominate throughout that part of South Asia. The Aryans were not able to subdue southern India, and as a consequence this part of the subcontinent has always had a distinct cultural tradition. Most of the languages of the area belong to the large Dravidian class of languages. The largest of these southern language groups are Telugu, Tamil, Malayalam, and Kannanda. Each of these languages roughly reflects regional culture and identity.

In Alberta, people from south India can be divided according to their regional identification. Most southerners are Hindus and as a consequence, some of them have close ties with their northern and overseas coreligionists. Immigrants have not come to Canada from all parts of south India equally. Basically, more have come from Kerala (Malayalam-speaking) and Madras (Tamil-speaking) than from elsewhere in the region. Unlike most other people from the south, those from Kerala are quite mixed religiously and many middle class people are Christian. People from Kerala have also had a significant tradition of migration, both in South Asia and elsewhere, so many of those in Alberta have extremely varied histories. A number of Kerala people came to Alberta in the 1960s as teachers and nurses and settled across the province. Small numbers are still to be found in Lloydminster, Red Deer, and Peace River.

Tamil speakers from India, most of them religious Hindus, are also quite numerous in Alberta, and have formed the Tamil Cultural Association in Edmonton. They share language and a number of cultural traditions with Tamils from Sri Lanka (see below); consequently, members of these groups do get together for cultural events. In the past five years a few people have also come to Alberta from Mysore (Kannanda-speaking) and Andra Pradesh (Telugu-speaking), and a small Kannanda association has been founded in Edmonton.

Other South Asian Groups

The approximately 1,500 to 2,000 Fijian Indians in the province are entirely distinct from previously mentioned groups.[22] Most of the ancestors of today's Fijian immigrants went to Fiji as indentured laborers between 1865 and 1920. They came from throughout India, well representing the north and the south, the Hindus, and the Muslims. The severe conditions of indenture and several subsequent generations of struggle have welded these people into a distinct group whose identity is strongly tied to Fiji. They do not consider themselves to be Indians, but rather Fiji Indians.

After the period of indenture, most Indians in Fiji moved into cash crop farming; Indians are still primarily responsible for the growing of the sugar crop which is still the economic mainstay of these 400 South Pacific islands. In addition, they quickly moved into other areas of the economy, particularly into retail trade, transportation, and skilled blue collar jobs. When Fiji received its independence in 1970-71 the situation of Indians living there changed considerably. Although Indians are presently about 51 percent of the population (at 256,000), a coalition of native people and Europeans has formed the government ever since independence. As a consequence, Indians are rather insecure about the future. Unemployment and underemployment in Fiji are already severe problems and many have therefore decided to leave. Fijian immigration to Canada began in the early 1960s and to date has numbered about 12-14,000 people. While this may seem to be a small figure, by Fijian terms it is substantial. Almost 5 percent of all Fijian Indians are presently in Canada.

The largest flow of Fijian immigrants to Canada came in the mid-1970s when the Canadian government was looking for skilled blue collar and white collar workers and these are primarily the types of Fijians who have come to Alberta. Common occupations among Alberta's Fijian Indians include automotive repair, carpentry, welding, accountancy, and office work. Fijians are more westernized than any other South Asian group, with the possible exception of their counterparts from the Caribbean. All of them know some English when they arrive here and most have been very heavily influenced by British culture and education. In Alberta they have formed distinct social communities and most have very little to do with South Asians of other backgrounds. Fijians have their own association in Calgary, the Fiji Multicultural Society. Edmonton's Fijian Indian population is somewhat larger than Calgary's, but it is more loosely organized. There is a Fijian-run store in Edmonton specializing in South Pacific foods. Fijians in Edmonton have been quite active in soccer and cricket, and occasionally play soccer matches with Fijians from Calgary.

Fijians have many parallels with South Asian peoples who come from Guyana, Trinidad, Jamaica, and the other countries of the Caribbean. The largest populations of Indians in the Caribbean arose in British Guiana and Trinidad. Like Fijians, the ancestors of today's Caribbean Indians were primarily indentured laborers. After indenture, most Caribbean Indians went into farming or farm labor. Some moved into retail trade and transportation. By the time of independence, Trinidad and Guyana were profoundly divided on the basis of ethnicity. While in Fiji the main division was Native Fijian-Indian, in the Caribbean it was primarily Indian-Black. Post independence domination of Guyanese politics by Blacks has led to a large movement of Indians out of the country. Many have come to Canada. So also have Indians from Trinidad and Tobago.

Caribbean Indians generally follow the occupational pattern of Fijians. Also like Fijians, Guyanese, and Trinidadian Indians have developed a distinct group identity to the extent that in Alberta they have relatively little interaction with South Asians of other backgrounds. Caribbean Indians follow their Fijian counterparts in one other important respect—they have been highly influenced by British culture and British-oriented education. Consequently, they find it easy to adapt to Canadian social and cultural patterns.

This inventory does not exhaust the variety of South Asian groups in Alberta. There are several others, each with at least several hundred members. Mention should be made in particular of people from Sri Lanka.[23] At independence, power essentially devolved onto the largest ethnic group in Ceylon, the Sinhalese. The Sinhalese have traditionally predominated in Ceylon, forming the state and society in their image. Isolated from the Indian mainland, they have been the only major group in South Asia to maintain a Buddhist religious tradition. During the colonial rule, the people of Ceylon were successively influenced by the Portuguese, the Dutch, and the British; these influences were somewhat countered by a rise in Sinhalese nationalism after independence, when the country was renamed Sri Lanka.

Today 28 percent of the citizens of Sri Lanka are not Sinhalese. Most of these are what are locally termed Ceylon Tamils—people who speak Tamil though they have been resident in Sri Lanka for many hundreds of years. Most Tamils are Hindus, which adds another dimension to the cultural separation between the Sinhalese and the Ceylon Tamils. A limited number of both have immigrated to Canada. While these two groups feel their own particular ethnic origins quite strongly, they never-

South Asian music producers at Edmonton's multicultural radio station CKER, 1983. (Courtesy S. Padmanabhan)

Malini Moorthy in a Bhavath Analyam pose, Heritage Day, Edmonton, 1984.
(Courtesy S. Padmanabhan)

theless have considerable interaction with each other in Alberta. This is reflected in the establishment of a Sri Lankan Association in Calgary which has tried to bring both groups together. The Sinhalese feel very distinct from people from India and have had relatively little to do with them. This is less the case for Ceylon Tamils, who share a language and some cultural conventions with Tamils from India.

Mention should also be made of people from Goa, or Goans. Goa is a coastal part of India which was a colonial possession of Portugal until well after independence. Goa is small and the Portuguese cultural presence there was very strong. As a consequence, many Goans speak Portuguese, have Portuguese names, and are Catholic. In addition to Goans from Goa, a considerable number of Goans in Alberta are from East Africa. Goans in Calgary have an association which organizes a wide variety of social activities.

In addition to organizations based on ethnicity, there are a number of organizations presently in existence which either act as umbrella organizations or are involved in musical or artistic expression. The already mentioned India Canada Association of Calgary and the Council of India Societies of Edmonton are of the former type. Much of their work has involved important human rights issues; they have been particularly active in combatting discrimination. In Calgary a specific organization—the Committee of South Asians—has been created to deal with discrimination. Umbrella organizations have also been established in those areas of the province where individuals of particular South Asian ethnic groups are too few to merit the creation of ethnic organizations. These include the Central Alberta Indo-Canadian Association (Red Deer), the Eastern Cultural Society (Fort McMurray), and the Indian Community (Medicine Hat).

South Asian Albertans have also been very active in maintaining and propagating their many artistic and musical traditions. This is well illustrated by the Raga-Mala Music Society of Calgary, which has held many concerts of Indian music in that city. They have also brought to Alberta some of the most famous interpreters of Indian music, including Ravi Shankar, Chitti Babu, and Ali Akbar Khan. Virtually all of the larger community organizations also offer instruction in traditional dancing, and South Asian entrepreneurs have been bringing a steady stream of classical and popular performers to Alberta for many years.

South Asians have also been active in a wide range of sports. Fijians, Guyanese, Trinidadians, Ismailis, and Pakistanis all either have their own cricket clubs or participate in such clubs. These cricket players play in leagues in Calgary and Edmonton and occasionally participate in intercity and interprovincial contests. Informal soccer teams abound, and badminton and ping pong games also bring South Asian people together.

Adaptation, Accommodation, and South Asian Albertans

South Asians are easily the most diverse of ethnic "groups" in Alberta, but it is appropriate to consider also the commonalities of their experience in Alberta. The great majority of South Asian adults in Alberta are immigrants. In this respect they are people of two worlds—Alberta and the one into which they were socialized. A great many South Asian immigrants have had certain class advantages in reconciling these two worlds, largely because they were already familiar with the English language, as well as with a wide range of Western institutions.

This is not to say that South Asians have had no settlement problems. Many South Asian cultural traditions are quite different from parallel beliefs and behaviors in Canada. When these cultural values clash with Canadian customs, substantial moral and practical dilemmas often result. For example, South Asians typically see the family as an extremely important social and economic unit. This is partially a result of tradition, partially an expression of practical economic and social reality: whether in Fiji, Pakistan, or East Africa it is the family which provides the basis for security. South Asian Albertans are therefore very concerned about a shift towards North American forms of family life, for they see this as signalling the imminent destruction of the family unit.

This concern about the family is typically focussed on the two major familial relations—the relationship between spouses and the relationship between parents and children. Although a good many South Asian Albertans lived in extended families before they immigrated, this is rather rare here. Most families are either nuclear or nuclear families with one additional family member. Immigration has produced many stresses between husbands and wives. Women frequently go out to work for the first time, where they are exposed to a wide range of new experiences; however, they continue to do most work relating to home and children. Men find it unrealistic to maintain a traditional South Asian role as the head of the household. Marital conflict frequently ensues.

Similar forces bring stress to relationships between parents and children. Parents in these many ethnic groups take different positions on the degree to which they would like their children to maintain the traditions of their ancestral culture. Even so, North American society undermines such cultural traditions by socializing children to North American ways. South Asian children quickly identify with their Canadian friends and take on their values. As a result of this pervasive socialization, South Asian Albertans of the second generation will be culturally very similar to their non-South Asian peers. However, their degree of assimilation will vary among these many groups, for they do not all have the same orientation towards assimilation. Fijians, Trinidadians, Guyanese, and those from most numerically small ethnic groups are likely to be almost completely assimilated in the second generation. Others, such as Ismailis and Muslim Pakistanis, will probably retain their religious distinctiveness but will lose much of the rest of their cultural heritage. Groups such as the Sikhs, with a very strong ethnic consciousness will teach most of their children Punjabi and the dictates of Sikh religion; most will probably marry other Sikhs. No South Asians have experienced this rate of intergenerational cultural change before and it comes as something of a shock to many parents.

In addition to the social forces which create conflict within the South Asian family, there are several other ongoing processes which create further difficulties for South Asians. One of these difficulties, which they share with many other immigrants, is the problem of securing adequate employment. Like many other immigrant groups whose pioneers came in the 1960s, the occupational life chances of South Asians vary according to when they arrived in Alberta. The immigrants of the 1960s came at a time of high demand for their skills. In contrast, immigrants arriving in the early 1980s share in the disturbing malaise which has affected the whole of the Canadian economy—underemployment. Until 1981, very few South Asians in Alberta were unemployed, but a great many were underemployed, working at jobs well below their capabilities. This was particularly true of professionals and other highly skilled South Asians. Other Canadians share this problem, but it is somewhat exacerbated among South Asians because of two factors: the difficulty of adequately demonstrating their training and skills because they were acquired overseas, and the problem of racial discrimination. One of the primary impediments which South Asians and other immigrants face is that the onus is on them to show that they have adequate job qualifications, yet to do so is often very difficult. A Fijian may have been a welder for twenty years, but if he cannot show a record of formal apprenticeship and journeyman status he may never become a welder in Canada. Today's economic hard times have exacerbated these problems.

Another process of adjustment which all South Asians must go through is establishing relations with other Canadians. On the whole, this process has proceeded very smoothly in Alberta. Such things are difficult to quantify, but it is certain that few South Asians in Alberta today are socially isolated from other Albertans. Most have a number of Canadian friends and social acquaintances, and a substantial number do not participate in specifically ethnic social relations at all. Indeed, one of the dangers of dealing with South Asian Albertans in terms of their ethnic group origins is that it conveys the inaccurate impression that their behavior and social relations are far more ethnically oriented than they actually are. Few work for each other, none shop exclusively at South Asian stores, and there is nothing remotely approaching a South Asian neighborhood anywhere in the province. If only for practical reasons, virtually all South Asians have quickly integrated into Alberta society. This smooth socioeconomic integration has been assisted by several historical facts. First of all, there was originally little anti-Asian feeling in the province. Many South Asian immigrants of the 1960s comment on how Albertans were frequently surprised and interested in the fact that they came from India or Pakistan. This easy association was also facilitated by the small numbers of South Asians who came in the initial wave and by the fact that so many were highly westernized.

Unfortunately, this generally positive relationship between Albertans of South Asian origin and others has been marred by the rise of anti-South Asian prejudices among some elements of the population. These arose chiefly in the mid-1970s and seemed to have reached a peak in 1977, a year when they were forcibly expressed in a number of racial incidents. The content of these prejudices centers on a stereotype of "the" South Asian that is an antithesis of what has been presented here. It is a stereotype which recognizes no differences between people of South Asian origin—they are all "Pakis," "Hindus," "Ragheads," or worse. Beyond this, the stereotype totally repudiated the rich cultural and historical heritage of these many peoples and replaced it by a British colonial image of "the Indian," as racially distinct, crafty and devious, unfriendly, lazy, morally corrupt, argumentative, socially irresponsible, and self-centered.

What accounts for some Albertans harboring such an unrealistic and negative image of South Asians? Are South Asians themselves responsible for it? Basically not. Rather, the problem is primarily with the prejudiced individuals, whose stereotypical thinking reveals more about them than it does about those who are its focus. Part of this negative stereotype of South Asians is rooted in Canada's British heritage—particularly a sensitivity towards biological differences. South Asians vary tremendously and exhibit no biological type. Without cultural or contextual markers, many South Asians could not be distinguished from other Caucasians. Nevertheless, many people believe that South Asians are biologically distinct and think that this distinctiveness correlates with certain behaviors and beliefs. Most South Asians are indeed physically darker than the Alberta norm and consequently can properly be called "visible minorities." Racist thinking is such that this visibility can have substantial consequences. To the racist it inevitably implies that whatever things he or she believes that South Asians do which he or she dislikes are permanent—"they're just that way." Second, it tends to reinforce a tendency to stereotype individual South Asians—"here comes another one." Third, physical difference is a stigma—a mark of variance that can prestructure interaction before a South Asian even speaks.

It would be naive to suggest that this stereotype was constructed out of thin air. Some Canadians may still have a tendency to think in racial terms, some may be influenced by images of poverty and political instability in South Asia, and others may have individual needs which are fulfilled by racist beliefs. Even so, there were some aspects of cultural difference between some South Asians and Canadians which led to misunderstanding on both sides. However, these were far more commonly justifications for racist belief rather than their cause.

Today discrimination remains a serious concern to many South Asians in Alberta. They worry about whether or not they will be able to have access to a full range of rights, as well as to privileges commensurate with their abilities and labor. In these things, no one can honestly say that ethnicity does not matter. Name calling, vandalism, acts of physical violence, and obvious incidents of job and housing discrimination against South Asians continue to be frequent enough to make such a claim naive. Common assurances by Alberta Human Rights officers about the relatively few complaints of racial discrimination they receive are similarly naive. Even so, no one can tell a South Asian Albertan how much his or her life chances are going to be affected by discrimination; the information is just not available. This uncertainty makes it hard for South Asians to feel secure about their place in Alberta society. Even when they do not come face-to-face with discrimination, their awareness that it exists makes them feel self-consciously visible and vulnerable. In this respect, the spectre of discrimination lowers their psychological standard of living.

The Future

The period of high growth and radical change is now over for most South Asian groups in Alberta. The lingering downturn in the Canadian economy is primarily responsible for this, in that economic factors strongly affect the number of immigrants Canada accepts. Future newcomers will be able to follow trails blazed by pioneering South Asian immigrants over the past twenty years. Their incorporation into Canadian society should, therefore, be fairly smooth.

Because immigration is likely to remain low for a long time, the character of all South Asian communities in Alberta will continue to change. Every year a higher proportion of South Asian Albertans will be long term, well-settled residents. This will certainly reduce the potential for cultural misunderstanding between South Asians and others. It will also lead to more Albertans getting to know people of South Asian origin on a personal basis. Low rates of increase will also inevitably help to reduce the prevalence of anti-South Asian prejudice.

The 1980s will see the rise of the second generation among most South Asian groups in Alberta. This has already brought the intergenerational stresses that are so common among other immigrant communities. When the second generation comes into adulthood they will increasingly set the tone for what it will mean to be South Asians in Alberta. It is presently an open question as to how the younger generation will approach the heritage of their parents. What is certain is that their identification and culture will be fundamentally Canadian. Hopefully, the social and intellectual climate of Alberta will then be such that they will not entirely forsake their roots. Through the creation of associations, language schools, religious institutions, and cultural centers, their parents are presently trying to provide them with cultural insurance so that the second generation will have links to their ethnic heritages if they want to use them.

One hopes that the future will also see Albertans coming to understand more about South Asia and South Asians than they do at present. Ever-increasing interaction between South Asians and others will contribute to this goal, but South Asian Albertans are so few that this alone cannot effect a radical change. Already, South Asian associations are making a conscious effort to introduce other Albertans to their cultures. Community centers are being built with this function expressly in mind. If this attempt is successful, Alberta can only benefit, for South Asians bring with them a rich heritage that will be a valuable addition to the province's cultural life.

CHAPTER NINETEEN
Khmer, Lao, Vietnamese, and Vietnamese-Chinese in Alberta
Doreen Indra[1]

Historical Background

To many Canadians the term Southeast Asia refers primarily to the war-torn countries of Kampuchea, Laos and Vietnam and conjures up images of fleeing refugees and great strife. Indeed, this view is not altogether inaccurate. Hundreds of thousands of people have left these three countries in the past decade, often under desperate and dangerous conditions. Some have come to Alberta, where today they are just now in the process of settling down and beginning life anew. At the same time, that they are now in Alberta is an outcome of historical forces which have been developing in Southeast Asia for several centuries; we must look in some detail at these developments in order to provide a context for these people's short experience in Alberta. The saga of these new Albertans is the topic of this chapter.

To begin with, Vietnam, Kampuchea and Laos are geographically adjacent, yet very different culturally and socially. Together with Burma, Malaysia, and Thailand they make up a larger geopolitical area which Europeans initially called Indochina. The term is apt because there the cultural spheres of India and China meet.[2] Indeed, this cultural divide separates Indian-influenced Laos and Kampuchea from Chinese-influenced Vietnam.

From an even broader perspective, Indochina is part of Southeast Asia, which also includes Indonesia, Brunei, Singapore and the Philippines. This vast geographical area has several features which unite it: tropical ecology, intensive agriculture, ancient civilizations, a history of reciprocal conquest and colonization, and a large amount of political uncertainty and instability. Today, this is an area where countries are sharply divided along political lines—lines which are aligned with the super-powers: China, the Soviet Union, and the United States. Kampuchea,

Laos and Vietnam are now under the influence of the Soviet Union. In contrast the anticommunist governments of the Association of Southeast Asian Nations—Thailand, Malaysia, Singapore, Indonesia, and the Philippines—are in the American sphere of influence. This balance has only recently been struck and for the past thirty years Southeast Asia has been a battleground of the great powers. A glance backward into the region's history makes it clear that this kind of conflict has shaped life in the area for a very long time.

Vietnam

Vietnam has been in the news for the last three decades and has appropriately been called a Culture of War.[3] Conflict is a function of Vietnam's geography. Like Canada, Vietnam borders on a giant, militarily powerful state. Vietnamese have had to fight constantly against Chinese incursions into their territory. In fact, for 1,000 years (111 B.C. to 939 A.D.) China controlled Vietnam. After many centuries of domination, some Vietnamese adopted Chinese customs, and Vietnam had a social and political structure superimposed upon it similar to that of China. Still, the vast majority of Vietnamese peasants remained isolated from this process and hostile to the Chinese.

The Vietnamese finally expelled the Chinese, but this did not end conflict in the area. After ten centuries of war, Vietnam had a highly organized military and an expanding population which needed more land. It acquired this new territory including half of the adjacent Khmer (Cambodian) Empire through military conquest. Central Vietnam was part of the Khmer Empire in the thirteenth century; most of southern Vietnam was Khmer territory until the eighteenth century. Khmer distrust of the Vietnamese today is deeply rooted in this historical conflict, just as is Vietnamese distrust of the Chinese.

Vietnamese independence from the Chinese and Cambodians came earliest to the North and spread South over the centuries. When Vietnam was unified in 1786 the peoples of North, Central, and South Vietnam were, therefore, culturally distinct. Predictably, North-South conflict soon arose and lasted until the late 1800s.

Beginning in the 1500s, Vietnam slowly came under the influence of European colonizers. Portuguese traders first came to southern Vietnam in 1536. The Dutch arrived in the North soon after.[4] The French began to set up Catholic missions in 1664. They also created the French East India Company to trade in the area. By the 1800s French missionaries and businessmen involved themselves more and more in local politics, for which they were frequently chastised by the local Vietnamese government. The French government responded with military retaliation against the Vietnamese. Once in the area, French military forces did not leave; rather, a slow process of French conquest of Indochina began in 1858. Since Vietnam's expansion had been at the expense of Khmer and Lao territories, both of the latter saw an advantage to their own national survival in having the French in the area. They eventually became

French Protectorates at their own request. Despite a vigorous resistance, the Vietnamese were finally conquered by the French in 1883.

The French quickly tried to introduce their own culture into Vietnam, much as the Chinese had done earlier. Some Vietnamese were soon being French-educated at home and abroad; these same individuals manned the colonial administration. Others were sent to administer the colonial bureaucracy in Cambodia and Laos, which had also been colonized by the French. Even so, French cultural influence on Vietnam was never so strong as to weaken Vietnamese identity, since the Vietnamese had maintained a distinctive civilization in the area for over 2,000 years. Moreover, conflict with the Chinese, Khmer, Thai, and French continuously served to support a distinctive Vietnamese identity. This separate identity was reinforced by Vietnamese culture, which though much influenced by the Chinese was distinct from all others.

During the French rule the country's ethnic balance shifted with the rapid expansion of Vietnam's second largest ethno-cultural group, the Chinese. It has been suggested that the first Chinese immigrants to Vietnam came around 1670.[5] Much later, the French opened up new economic opportunities that brought successive waves of Chinese immigrants to Vietnam. The greatest influx of Chinese occurred after 1920. While the French began to grant Chinese permanent immigrant status in Vietnam in 1862, many Chinese refused to take out citizenship. This contributed to their minority status in Vietnam.

The French in Vietnam governed the Chinese indirectly. Soon, the Chinese had created a virtually complete set of parallel institutions separated from the Vietnamese. This effectively kept Chinese in their own areas, interacting with Vietnamese primarily in business. And it was business that was the Chinese specialty in Vietnam. This, in turn, was dependent on profound changes in the Vietnamese economy brought about by French rule.

Vietnam was a traditional agricultural society when the French established control in the 1880s; consequently most people were peasant farmers. These peasants were not tied into a cash economy. They lived in modest homes, had little material wealth, but normally had an adequate amount to eat.[6] The French developed industry, built railways, and encouraged cash-crop agriculture. In other words, they provided the infrastructure for an economy tied into a world market. Soon, Vietnam became the third largest exporter of rice in the world and coffee became a major plantation crop.

These economic changes drastically altered Vietnamese society. The French made extensive use of the Chinese as middlemen between themselves and peasant producers. Retail trade also came under the control of the Chinese. This isolated the Chinese from both the French and the Vietnamese. By 1975 there were at least 1.5 million Chinese in Vietnam, more than one-half of them living in Saigon. This made the Chinese by far the largest non-Vietnamese ethnic group in Vietnam. Although there were still thirty Vietnamese for every one Chinese, the Chinese were economically important out of proportion to their numbers.

Although many elite Vietnamese became closely identified with French culture and French interests, a strong Vietnamese identity maintained Vietnamese nationalism, even though the French ruthlessly tried to suppress it. Vietnamese students in Europe soon acquired leftist political philosophies which they exported to Vietnam. There they found fertile ground among the peasantry, who were becoming more and more impoverished under colonial rule. This movement coalesced under Ho Chi Minh in the 1930s.

World War II was to lead to France's demise in Southeast Asia. France was defeated by the German army in 1940. The subsequent pro-Nazi Vichy government took over control of Indochina in the name of France. Japanese troops already occupied large parts of China and soon demanded the right to station troops in Vietnam. Vichy France had little choice but to give in to Japanese demands. Through this tactic, the Japanese took over direct control of Indochina in 1945.

After the defeat of the Japanese, the French tried to recover their colonial control over Indochina. With the assistance of the British, they resecured dominion over Southern Vietnam, and recovered Laos and Cambodia. A protracted war then began for control of northern Vietnam. By 1954 the French were decisively defeated by the Viet Minh and agreed to leave the North. With the establishment of a government in the North under the Viet Minh approximately 900,000 anticommunist Vietnamese fled to the South.[7] Many were Catholics who feared that the new government would repress religious practice.

Indochina quickly became a superpower battleground; American involvement in the Korean conflict had already led to military support of the French. This quickly evolved into similar support to the "interim" anticommunist government of South Vietnam under Ngo Dinh Diem. The Soviet Union and China gave similar support to Ho Chi Minh and the Viet Minh. The 1954 Geneva Peace Conference on Indochina had envisioned a unified Vietnam and had agreed to a temporary division of the country until elections could be held for a new national government. These elections were never held, and anti-Diem guerrilla warfare soon arose in the South. In 1962 there were 16,000 American military advisors in South Vietnam. By 1970 there were 500,000 American troops who together with another half million South Vietnamese troops were involved in an all-out war with the communist insurgents. By 1973 it was clear that this unpopular war could not be won and the United States decided to leave Vietnam. This set the stage for the first exodus of people from Vietnam.

Cambodia

The Khmer (Cambodia is a synonym of Khmer) people are considered by many to be the longest inhabitants of Indochina.[8] They established themselves in the region around 1500 B.C. Many people traditionally associate Cambodia with the great temple complex of Angor Wat. Angor aptly symbolized the past glory of the Khmer empire. By 1150 A.D. this empire included present day Kampuchea, Central and South Vietnam,

Laos, most of Thailand, lower Burma, and part of the Malay peninsula. At that time, "after China, it was the largest and most powerful country in the Far East."[9]

By the thirteenth century, Cambodia had lost the territories now known as Thailand and Laos. The great irrigation-based civilization they had built up was destroyed by invading Thai. For two centuries the Thai continued to invade Cambodian territory until the Portuguese began to assist the Cambodians in the late sixteenth century. By 1471, Vietnam had conquered Champa (central) Vietnam and had settled many Vietnamese nationals on Cambodian territory.[10] Cambodia had been caught between Thailand and Vietnam in a massive struggle for territory and power. As late as 1834, Vietnamese invaders claimed all of Cambodia to be their legitimate territory. By this time Thai power had declined and they in turn began to see the Vietnamese as a threat. Together, the Thai and the Khmer drove the Vietnamese out of all Cambodian territory, with the exception of what is now South Vietnam. It was at this time that the Cambodian king (1855) first asked the French to "protect" Cambodia; in 1863 France formally made Cambodia a Protectorate under which the institution of the monarchy was continued. Cambodia became independent in 1953 as a constitutional monarchy under the charismatic Prince Norodom Sihanouk. He was to govern until 1970.

From 1953 to 1970 Prince Sihanouk moved neutral Cambodia towards increasingly friendly terms with China. During a trip to Peking in March 1970, Sihanouk was deposed by one of his aides, Lon Nol. Fighting soon developed between Lon Nol (backed by the United States) and the communist Khmer Rouge (supported by China). This civil war ended in total victory for the Khmer Rouge in April 1975. Pol Pot became the head of the government of Democratic Kampuchea.

Subsequent events in Kampuchea under the Pol Pot regime horrified world public opinion. In 1975 Cambodia's population was not much more than 7 million—about 6,200,000 Khmer, 450,000 Chinese, 450,000 Vietnamese, and 200,000 others.[11] In the next three years virtually all educated Cambodians or those associated with previous regimes either fled or were executed. All overt or implied resistance to the new government met a similar fate. To these numbers must be added at least several hundred thousand Cambodians who perished through starvation and disease during this period. Over a million Cambodians chose to flee, primarily to refugee camps in Thailand. Many of those who survived the journey are still there. As if the disasters of the Pol Pot era were not enough, in 1979 Kampuchea was invaded by the Vietnamese who quickly deposed Pol Pot and set up a puppet regime under Colonel Heng Samrin. Pol Pot and a small force of supporters continue to wage a guerrilla war against the Vietnamese and their Kampuchean collaborators.

It should be briefly noted that the Khmer are very distinct culturally from the Vietnamese. First, they speak unrelated languages. Although both maintain a paternalistic extended form of family kinship, the Khmer have been as greatly influenced by India as have the Vietnamese by

China. Moreover, although both are primarily Buddhist, the Vietnamese (Mahayana) and the Khmer (Theravada) traditions are very different. Architecture, writing systems and political forms follow the same cleavage. These cultural differences reinforce the traditional antipathy between the Khmer and the Vietnamese.[12]

Laos

Laotian national history dates from 1353 A.D. when Laos was established as a separate kingdom. It remained independent until 1571 when it was conquered by Burma and later by Siam (Thailand).[13] Laos also became a French colony in the late nineteenth century and gained independence in 1953. Of the 3 million people who live there, approximately 50 percent are estimated to be ethnic Lao. The largest minority are a tribal group, the Ta Hmong, who the French called Meo. Smaller minority groups also exist, including the Tai Dam, the Ka (Montagnard peoples), and some Chinese. Culturally and linguistically the Lao are closely related to the Northeastern Thai, who were once part of their kingdom. They sharply separate themselves from both the Vietnamese and the Khmer on cultural, linguistic, and identity criteria.

Since independence, Laos has been in constant political turmoil with right, left and neutralist forces struggling for political control. The Pathet Lao (who were North Vietnamese-supported) refused to participate in any government that was not theirs; the right (American and Thai-oriented) was formed out of the old ruling parties and was equally inflexible. As for Vietnam and Cambodia, 1975 was also a crucial year for Laos. In 1975 South Vietnam's government collapsed. In the same year, communist forces took over Cambodia and Laos. Behind the communist Pathet Lao stands a Vietnamese occupation force which continues to dictate terms to the new government. Since 1975, refugees have fled Laos to Thailand. The Laotian economy is disorganized, and people have little food. There is still a state of low-grade war in the country as people loyal to the old "Royal Lao Government" fight to drive out the Vietnamese and the Pathet Lao.

By 1975 superpower confrontation had entirely transformed Vietnam, Laos, and Kampuchea, decimating traditional cultures and patterns of life. Destruction of property and life was immense. In Vietnam the war had produced over 2.5 million casualties; 11 million people were homeless and half the population had been displaced. Almost fourteen million tons of high explosives had been used in the area by the United States alone. Indochina was in ruins. Entirely new political alignments had been drawn and new governments were being created in all three countries. This situation created an enormous number of winners and losers, people who benefited from the changing situation and people who lost everything. One of the products of this conflict was a refugee exodus to Canada and Alberta.

Immigration to Canada

Southeast Asians came to Canada in three distinct phases. Each of these phases brought different people with distinct reasons for coming. The first Vietnamese came to Canada in the early 1950s.[14] Most came under the Columbo Plan, which gave Canadian government scholarships to Third World students. Other Vietnamese (and a handful of Lao and Cambodians) arrived from the United States, Europe, Australia, New Zealand and Japan in the 1950s and early 1960s. Many did not want to return to Vietnam while their country was at war and they remained in Canada. By 1970 it is estimated that about 1,200 Vietnamese had come to Canada. Most settled in Quebec. They often represented the most promising young men from their respective countries. As one of them claimed:

> Canadians were very impressed with us. They thought we were smart and worked hard. That is because we were a highly selected group. These people paved the way for Canadians to think well of Vietnamese.[15]

Though they were few in number, these young men made important contributions to Canada and to their home countries. Cambodian students also made their mark. Most were educated in francophone Quebec. Several stayed and are teaching in Quebec universities.

Similarly, the majority of Vietnamese who came to Canada before 1970 are now established and successful. A high proportion are engineers, professors at universities, doctors and accountants. In Montreal and Toronto these "pioneers" formed the first Vietnamese associations and newspapers in Canada. By 1970, Toronto, Montreal and Quebec City had an impressive range of Vietnamese organizations, including political associations, student organizations and several publications. Communist takeovers in Laos, Cambodia and Vietnam ended this era of student immigration in 1975.

The Second Wave

By early 1975 American troops were quickly pulling out of Vietnam. The Thieu regime in the South began to disintegrate. As the North Vietnamese army moved toward Saigon many South Vietnamese soldiers and civilians fled before them. It was a poignant sight that many North Americans watched on television.[16] South Vietnamese had heard many atrocity stories about communist treatment of people in occupied areas. In particular, those who had left the North in 1954 had seen first hand the disruptions brought about by the communist takeover at that time and were afraid of possible reprisals. Huge crowds lined up at the American Embassy in Saigon hoping to escape. Near the end, American helicopters evacuated many soldiers and civilians onto barges in the South China Sea until they could be forwarded to receiving countries. Many of these soldiers did not even know that they were being evacuated. As one officer told it:

> It was chaos. We just got orders to fly a normal mission. In fact we landed on barges in the sea and were then taken to Guam. We never had a chance to say goodbye to our families and they had no idea what had happened to us.

By mid-April 1975, the American government had agreed to provide a means of leaving Vietnam to American citizens, their dependents, Vietnamese currently employed by the United States, and to alien dependents of the United States.[17] They did not intend to accept responsibility for other Vietnamese who were at high risk because of their political support of the United States. Over 145,000 persons from Vietnam fled through American channels and arrived in the United States by mid-1975.[18]

In response to these events, in April 1975 the Canadian government declared that because of the changed political situation, Vietnamese and Cambodians already in Canada could apply for immediate immigrant status. The following month, Canada admitted 2,000 refugees from evacuation camps in the United States. Another 1,000 came from other countries.[19] Thereafter a small flow of Vietnamese political refugees continued.

Virtually all of these newcomers to Canada were ethnic Vietnamese. They can be divided into two general categories. Many were urban, professional people who had been in the South Vietnamese bureaucracy, in the military, or in business. The majority were originally people from the North who had already fled South to escape communist rule at the time of the defeat of the French army in 1954. The other broad category at this time were younger men who were primarily lower-ranking military men or students. A reason that many of these people frequently gave for having chosen to come to Canada is simply that they did not feel good about living in the United States. Virtually all had fought together with Americans so when the United States pulled out of Vietnam, they felt they had been deserted.

About 60 percent of those who arrived in Canada in 1975-76 settled in Quebec because of their facility with French language and culture. About 1,000 went to Ontario. Several hundred went to Vancouver and a smaller number took up residence in the Maritimes, Manitoba, and Saskatchewan. Less than 100 initially came to Alberta.

In Quebec and Ontario, the already-established Vietnamese quickly came forward to assist the new arrivals. In addition, Canada Employment and Immigration provided them with basic necessities—hotel accommodation, money for clothing, and food.[20] In the early days of settlement there were no other support programs available and people made their way as best they could. It was a trying, lonely, and difficult process to settle in a strange environment with very little help, just having lost family and country.

It should be noted that even at this time Canada carefully selected the individuals who were allowed entry. Although defined as political refugees, those who were able to come were highly skilled.[21]

Despite initial difficulties, these 1975 refugees began to establish communities across Canada—communities in which people came together to share and compare experiences in Canada and to affirm their Vietnamese identities. These women and men were to become important community leaders in the future. Although there were a few Vietnamese professionals already living in Alberta, the history of Indochinese in Alberta really begins with the 1975-76 exodus of Vietnamese and their subsequent settlement in the province. These few people were to set the stage for succeeding events. They were similar to Vietnamese settling elsewhere in Canada at the time. About half came in family groups, while the rest were either single men or men separated from their families. Most of them came to Alberta directly from holding camps in the United States. A few others came directly from Guam. Few of them had heard of Alberta before and they knew virtually nothing about it. A primary deciding factor was often the suggestion from immigration officers that job prospects were good in Alberta:

> Alberta? Never heard of it before. I wanted to leave the United States and I would have gone anywhere they would accept Vietnamese. In the camps in California, Canadian immigration officials said it was easy to find a job in Western Canada. When I arrived in Edmonton I felt more freedom here than in the U.S. There you had to have a sponsor before you could get out of the camp. Here we were sponsored by government. We could live like other Canadians. If we got lost, we had to find our own way. But it was a very strange country and no one to help us. I couldn't even ask people for help because I couldn't speak English. I had to have a piece of paper to communicate.

For some time, Vietnamese did not disperse across Alberta. Rather they stayed primarily in Edmonton and Calgary.

Edmonton became the center of Vietnamese activity in Alberta; by early 1976, 203 Vietnamese were living in that city.[22] Eighty-eight percent of these refugees were under the age of twenty-five. Even at this early date, secondary migration from other provinces to Edmonton was considerable as people moved to Alberta in search of jobs. This pattern of migration was to increase dramatically in the following years.

The first Vietnamese to come to Calgary in the early 1970s were Dr. Pierre Tu, an economics professor at the University of Calgary, and Mr. Truong Van, a civil engineer. They are brothers-in-law. Mrs. Van (no relation to the above) was the first Vietnamese woman to come. From June to December 1975, roughly thirty people (approximately twenty men and ten women and children) arrived in Calgary. Of the twenty men, fifteen were single. Most were naval or air force officers. A few of these men found work in northern Alberta and would travel back to Calgary for weekends. One lone Vietnamese was living in Red Deer by 1977.

In Calgary, the new arrivals were first lodged at a downtown hotel. Since many of the men understood some English, they could move rather easily around the city, look for work, buy clothes, and scout local Chinese shops for familiar food items. Practically everyone found a job within a month, and most only stayed about a week in the hotel before finding more permanent accommodation. All the single men rented apartments in the same building while most married couples lived close by in the vicinity of 15th Avenue and 11th Street S.W. This area of the city continues to be an extremely popular one with all Indochinese people because it is central, has good transportation and inexpensive, available accommodations. There being initially only 30 people in all, the

Vietnamese remained close to each other, and on weekends and other opportunities, most single men would spend time with other families. By the end of 1976 the number of Vietnamese in Calgary had expanded to about 150.

In both Edmonton and Calgary the initial jobs that men found were often in industry.[23] Rarely did anyone immediately get a job in which they could use their education and work skills to the fullest. But the newcomers were very pragmatic, having made up their minds to do what they could in order to get established, while keeping an eye on future recertification and retraining opportunities. A number of men in Calgary and Edmonton eventually went to technical institutes for this purpose. Others had their Vietnamese engineering credentials recertified. Women experienced the same problem. A high school teacher became a seamstress; a highly skilled secretary became a sheet metal worker. Many women went to work for the first time in sewing factories or in low-paying service jobs in order to support their households while their husbands were in training programs. Thus, women often maintained a home and were at the same time the sole earner in the family. The following story is typical:

> It was August when we arrived in Edmonton. The leaves were starting to turn yellow and were falling. It was the first time I had been away from home, from my mother. I was very homesick. I didn't have any thoughts at all about Edmonton. I stayed in the house and took care of the children. My husband started to work for $2.75 an hour. We kept hearing that life in Vietnam was very hard; we felt so lucky but homesick. My husband worked for a stereo store for one year after which he was given a raise to $3.00. Later another Vietnamese who worked in a hospital got my husband a job as lab technician and he stayed there for a year before going back to college. I went to work in a steel factory and later a sewing factory while my husband was in school. In the first year here, my father died. No one wanted to tell me. In the same year my husband lost his father and old grandmother in Vietnam.

People immediately recognized that English fluency was an important requisite for their successful establishment in Alberta and thus gave high priority to English as a Second Language (ESL) training. At first this was rather liberally available and both men and women were initially supported by the government while learning English. As the number of refugees increased this privilege was typically extended only to the "head of household," then only when employment counsellors thought it would lead to a job. Thereafter, few women were supported while attending ESL classes. Even so, in an overall sense, many of these early refugees feel lucky that they came to Alberta when they did. Their numbers were small and government departments responsible for responding to refugee needs could deal with them as individuals. Several government workers went out of their way to help these Vietnamese.[24]

Although they quickly achieved a degree of economic stability, the first year in Alberta was often a sad one. They worried about their families in Vietnam. Usually, individuals here were the only ones in their extended-kin networks outside of Vietnam. Communications with

Vietnam were difficult and sometimes nonexistent, and there was a massive lack of information on conditions there. Even if they knew about their relatives, they could do little for them. Moreover, their relatively secure position in Alberta contrasted so strongly with the hardships of their friends and relatives in Vietnam that this generated a good deal of guilt and anxiety. Even today, many of these pioneers have not been united with their families.

These conditions led to a variety of psychological syndromes. People often complained of insomnia, weakness, heart palpitations, stomach pains, nausea, and depression. A few individuals became severely withdrawn and unmotivated. Most suffered a profound sense of normlessness, purposelessness and powerlessness.[25] People often compensated by saving all the money they could and sending it to Vietnam. Parcels of medicine, food, and clothing were frequently sent on a monthly basis; and this frequently entailed great sacrifice and conflicts of obligation. On the one hand, no matter how much one sent back one could never send enough to make much of a difference. On the other, it placed severe financial burdens on individuals here, many of whom were forced to take on two jobs. Moreover, it meant that few could afford to stop working to retrain, learn English, or go to school. As one person put it:

> It is not unusual for people in camps to write asking for your help. They are desperate. Already we are under enormous pressure supporting our own families in Canada, then in Vietnam and we must help family in camps often too. How can a person do all this?

The first year was also one of apprehension about life in Canada. These newcomers were the first Indochinese in Alberta; there were virtually no other Vietnamese to tell them what to expect regarding anything. People had told them the winter was "cold" on the Canadian prairies. Many were afraid; they did not know how cold "cold" is. One person reported that he panicked the first time he saw snow and stayed home from work. "A little later in the day," he reported, "I went outside to see for myself and I really felt nothing. No problem at all—not anything as bad as we had thought it would be." When one woman realized that she could safely go out in the snow she took her son, ran out into it and ate some, for it looked very much like a Vietnamese dessert. Soon, the Alberta climate was no longer feared, but it would always remain alien.

Alberta's social environment was also very strange. Canadian customs were unusual. For example, it was quickly realized that it was not customary to visit a Canadian without first calling. In contrast, visiting at any time is frequent in Vietnam and always welcomed. Other social differences were substantial—differences in male-female relations, criteria for status and friendship, employer-employee relations, the place of the state and its institutions in their lives. A similar gulf existed between Canadian and Vietnamese cultural values. As a consequence, these first Vietnamese Albertans approached Canadian society very tentatively and kept most of their initial social relations within the small, but growing,

Vietnamese communities of Edmonton and Calgary. For a long time, the community acted as a support group for new arrivals, especially on weekends, when people would visit with each other. In this respect the community was also a device to integrate people's pasts with their new experiences in Canada.

Under these new conditions, traditional women's roles changed dramatically. Because so many men came here alone, those relatively few families who were here became symbols of stability and the women in them, mothers to them all. In a sense, families became social and psychological sanctuaries. Because their husbands often went to work or to college immediately after arriving in Alberta, women were often the first to find out how to do the vital things—how to take a bus, where to shop, how to enroll children in school, how to use the post office, the bank, and credit cards. Women were frequently at the vanguard of new cultural information for they were faced with a far more demanding situation than men. Men initially needed to know primarily about their occupation and how to get a bus to their job. In contrast, women were required to maintain family life, work, and at the same time be the family's main interface with Canadian social and economic institutions. This was doubly difficult because the traditional role of women in Indochina was restricted primarily to private family affairs; their role in the public sphere was secondary to that of men.

It should be noted that not all of the 1975-76 pioneers were ethnic Vietnamese. In late 1975 approximately ten ethnic Chinese from Vietnam arrived in Calgary. They had left Vietnam because they sensed the future there would not be very promising under a communist regime. They were business people and in a few years one family established the first Southeast Asian business in Calgary—the Tong Shan Food Store.

Even after the initial exodus from Vietnam, the communities of Calgary and Edmonton continued to grow quickly. In 1976 more people arrived from the United States. Others continued to come from eastern Canada. By 1978 there were about 400 Southeast Asians in Calgary and another 450 in Edmonton.[26] By 1979 a few people had ventured outside of Edmonton and Calgary, particularly young men who went north looking for work. The great majority were ethnic Vietnamese. Most of them were reasonably well settled, considering the circumstances of their flight from Vietnam and their continued separation from their culture, friends, and kin.

Third Phase: Boat and Land People

In November 1978 a ship called the *Hai Hong*, which was carrying 2,500 refugees who were fleeing South Vietnam, caught world attention.[27] The ship's captain tried to dock the *Hai Hong* in Indonesian waters and was ordered to leave; the Indonesian government knew that many others were on their way and the country did not have the financial resources to support thousands of refugees. This was true of other Southeast Asian countries, most of which are quite poor. The Singapore navy subsequently made sure the *Hai Hong* would not land there. On 9 November, the ship docked in Malaysia. Although Malaysian authorities also wanted it out of their waters the *Hai Hong* remained. Food, water, and medicine were sent to the ship, but refugees were not allowed to disembark. Some people would remain confined to the ship for months.

Although the plight of the *Hai Hong* first focussed world attention on Southeast Asian problems, people had been fleeing Vietnam and Laos continuously since the governments of each country changed in 1975. Vietnamese and ethnic Chinese had been leaving Vietnam by using small boats or by walking to Thailand. Later Cambodians and Lao had also begun to flee to Thailand. Until the *Hai Hong* incident, the press had taken very little notice. Thereafter, this was impossible, because the exodus had reached massive proportions by 1979. Literally hundreds of thousands of people were fleeing from Vietnam and Kampuchea at great risk to their lives. People leaving Vietnam by sea faced incredible odds, which included the very real possibilities of capture by government officials, traitorous behavior by intermediaries, hunger and thirst on small overcrowded boats, attacks by pirates, and possible rejection by receiving countries. Many drowned in the sea. Similarly, many people leaving Kampuchea never made it to the Thai border. Those who did were often interned in lawless camps under shocking conditions.

What made people face these odds? There were a variety of answers to this question, depending on the country involved. In South Vietnam, the communist regime which took control in 1975 did not initiate massive reprisals against their vanquished foes; nevertheless, the new government considered these people to be untrustworthy. Many were systematically removed from positions of power and privilege and some were sent to "reeducation camps" to learn the country's new political line. At the same time the government began a massive reorganization of Vietnam's economy, which had been virtually destroyed by the combined effects of the war, the American pullout, and the collapse of the Thieu regime. This left many urban and military people unemployed; many were sent to the "New Economic Zones" where they were expected to hack new farms out of the bush. Many refugees believed that people sent there lacked food, water, medicine, even tools to work the land, and that being sent to the New Economic Zones was almost certain death. Needless to say, a substantial number of ethnic Vietnamese saw little prospect in remaining in the country under these political conditions, so they fled.

At the same time the government began to reconstruct the urban economy along socialist lines. Part of this program was a process of nationalizing a variety of businesses and making other private businesses redundant. This policy hit the ethnic Chinese severely, for they largely controlled the retail trade and small-manufacturing sectors of the economy. By 1978 many Chinese families found themselves virtually shut out of their traditional businesses and occupations. To make matters worse, political relations between Vietnam and China soured and this augmented the long-standing antipathy which many Vietnamese traditionally had for Vietnamese-Chinese and vice versa. Consequently many

Chinese families collected whatever financial resources they had and began sending people out of the country by boat. In contrast to their Vietnamese counterparts, the Chinese were allowed to leave by government officials as long as they paid the appropriate people.[28] Flight for the Chinese was nevertheless dangerous:

> Our family sold much of what we owned for gold; there was only enough to pay for one of us to get out. As the oldest daughter, I was picked. The first time I tried to get out the boat was so overcrowded that it capsized. Many people drowned. The second time the boat did not arrive. On the third try I made it to Malaysia after being at sea three weeks. We were packed so tightly on the boat that many people became sick or injured. We ran out of both food and water before we got to Malaysia.

In Kampuchea the reasons for flight were even more direct. For many people the only option was death, either through starvation or at the hands of Pol Pot's henchmen. Across the border they went by the thousands, from all classes and conditions. Far more desperate and far more numerous than those who left Vietnam by sea, these land people were initially ignored by the media, government and public concern focused on the boat people.[29]

Canada's response to this Southeast Asian exodus was initially limited. From 1975 through 1978, Canada had admitted a total of 9,060 Indochinese refugees. The *Hai Hong* incident was to foreshadow the beginning of a third phase of Southeast Asian immigration that would dwarf those before it. Canadian government acceptance of second wave Vietnamese as political refugees had been a token gesture to the United States, which had tacitly accepted its responsibility in creating a situation which forced these people to leave. The Canadian government was still operating under this premise when it took in 604 people from the *Hai Hong* in November 1979, 50 of whom came to Alberta. Once they had been accepted, it was impossible for the government to ignore the fact that the thousands of people who were then afloat on the South China Sea were, if anything, in a worse plight than those who had been aboard the *Hai Hong*. Government policy had to be reformulated.

A Unique Canadian Response

The Immigration Act of 1976 provided an important provision which would greatly affect this refugee movement. It maintained that "any church, corporation or group of five or more Canadian citizens or permanent residents could sponsor a refugee."[30] This clause led to a level of public involvement in refugee settlement unique in Canadian history and in the world. In June 1979 the government agreed to take in 8,000 refugees at its own expense adding an extra 4,000 person quota for refugees coming under private sponsorship. The challenge was clearly put: those 4,000 people would only be allowed to come if churches, organizations, or groups of private citizens were willing to financially support a refugee or refugee family for up to a year (if necessary). In addition, sponsors would be responsible for a whole range of settlement tasks. It was no light burden. Even so, the Canadian response was enormous.

The lead was carried by a number of church organizations—Catholics, Anglicans, Mennonites, Baptists and others. Thereafter, the number of private sponsorship groups mushroomed. The government responded to public pressure by offering to raise the quota on *privately* sponsored refugees to 21,000. The government would then sponsor one refugee for each one sponsored privately. It was clear that the government expected that the public response would be so low that the overall number of incoming refugees would be small. In fact, public response was so great that this quota was extended in only four months. In 1979 alone, 24,573 Southeast Asian refugees arrived in Canada, with many more sponsored people on the way.

Taken unawares by this outpouring of public support, the Conservative government was unwilling to further increase its commitment, but allowed private citizens to continue to sponsor people. A few months later the newly elected Liberal government decided to support another 10,000 refugees bringing the quota up to 60,000 by the end of 1980. Indochinese refugees numbering 35,446 arrived in Canada in 1980. About 20,000 came in 1981. Since 1981, Indochinese have increasingly come through normal immigration channels. There are now about 120,000 Indochinese of all nationalities in Canada.

Alberta received a disproportionate share of people, largely because economic conditions in the province were generally far better than elsewhere in Canada. In 1979 alone 3,100-3,200 refugees arrived in Alberta directly from overseas—13 percent of the yearly total.[31] Approximately 4,700 arrived in 1980.[32] In addition to these, at least another 5,000 refugees came to Alberta from other provinces by the end of 1981 to look for jobs. The following table gives the minimum number of Vietnamese, Vietnamese-Chinese, Lao, and Khmer in Alberta at the end of 1984:

Ethnicity	Number
Vietnamese	10,000
Vietnamese-Chinese	10,000
Lao	1,500
Khmer	500
Total	22,000

Table 1. Southeast Asians in Alberta at the end of 1984.[33]

In essence, the Southeast Asian population of Alberta has increased 20 times since 1977. This alone would have presented a massive challenge in terms of settlement and adaptation—a challenge faced by so many immigrants to Canada, including those Vietnamese pioneers of a few short years before. But many of these Southeast Asian refugees had suffered desperately. Almost all of them had undergone great risks in leaving their homes. Most had lived with death, disease, violence, and uncertainty as they escaped. Consequently, these boat and land people were under much greater psychological pressure than those who came before.

Their backgrounds were also more varied. Thousands were Vietnamese-Chinese, a group entirely new to Canada. Although Vietnamese-Chinese frequently spoke the same language as other Canadians of Chinese origins, for the most part they formed their own distinct communities. Generations of life in Vietnam had made them quite different from other Chinese. Hundreds were Lao, who also had no established communities to join in Alberta. The few Khmer who arrived before 1981 were similarly isolated. This variability extended in several other directions as well. Included among the Vietnamese refugees were people from a far wider range of class, occupational, and regional backgrounds than before; as a whole they were younger, less well educated, and less Westernized than previous immigrants. Many Chinese and some Vietnamese came from North Vietnam and consequently had less familiarity with Western institutions than their compatriots from the South. Conflict between Vietnam and China had led to a deterioration in the status of ethnic Chinese in the North and as a consequence many had fled. An upper middle class Vietnamese-Chinese male from Hanoi told the following story:

> Chinese and Vietnamese mostly had had good relations for years. Our children went to Vietnamese schools. I had married a Vietnamese woman. Sometimes there would be trouble but mostly it was alright. I had a very responsible position in Hanoi. So did other Chinese but in 1978 things began to change. There was a feeling around and then Vietnamese friends began to tell us that it may be important to us to be careful. I was demoted several times in my work; my children couldn't go to school anymore. Suddenly it was suggested that we should think of leaving the country. This was happening to all the Chinese. We couldn't believe it. Finally I lost my job altogether; soldiers would come around and ask us to leave.

At the same time a few dissatisfied Vietnamese also left the North by claiming they were Chinese.

The variability among these newly arrived refugees was compounded by the profound cultural, linguistic, and identity differences between the Vietnamese, Vietnamese-Chinese, Lao, and Khmer—differences at least as sharp as between the most divergent European countries. Although each group had been reduced to refugee status by the same great military and political conflagration, each had a unique heritage, which thereby created divisions among them that were compounded by their profound historically justified suspicion of each other. Once in Canada, members of each group almost universally went their own way, formed their own separate communities, and hence experienced their own unique problems.

Because the third wave mounted so quickly and reached such a high level, existing social service facilities in Alberta were entirely inadequate to deal with it. Initially refugees were "settled" much as were those who had come previously. They arrived in Calgary or Edmonton at the end of a long series of flights from Southeast Asia, to be met at the airport by a battery of government officials, sponsors, representatives of private set-tlement agencies, and the media. They were then "processed" to confirm that they were the individuals who were expected. Thereafter, their immediate fate depended upon whether they were government-spon-sored or privately sponsored refugees. In the early days private sponsors were relatively few, so most newcomers were government-sponsored. They were sent initially to hotels while more permanent accommoda-tions were found for them. The hotels and motels served as holding centers and distribution points for adjacent areas of Alberta. This was particularly so for privately sponsored refugees, who were sent wherever sponsors could be found.

In these early days there was enormous confusion surrounding the settlement of third wave immigrants. There was a near total ignorance of Southeast Asians among both bureaucrats and sponsors. Although a number of more established, second wave Vietnamese residents quickly volunteered as translators, communication problems were severe. This was especially so for many Chinese-Vietnamese, Lao, and Khmer who initally had few people to speak for them. The responsibility for the settlement of government-sponsored refugees at first fell largely to the Canada Employment Centers and private immigrant-settlement agen-cies—Edmonton Immigrant Services, Catholic Immigrant Services in Edmonton, Calgary Immigrant Aid, Calgary Catholic Immigration Society, and the Calgary Center for Indochinese Refugees. As the num-ber of refugees increased, workers in these organizations were swamped. In the most narrow sense the settlement of government sponsored refu-gees involved finding them housing, providing them with a minimum of furniture, clothing and food, placing their children in school, providing them with health services, deciding who was to receive ESL training, and most important, securing at least one family member a job. This was an enormous task, even though it left out the problems of social and psy-chological settlement entirely. It is much to their credit that the many individuals involved were able to cope at all.

The difficulties were compounded after the federal government desig-nated Griesbach Barracks in Edmonton as one of two national receiving and distribution centers for Southeast Asian refugees in Canada. To a certain extent work done at Griesbach Barracks lightened the load on other people in Alberta working with refugees, because the staff there gave the people permanent landing papers, clothing, a medical checkup and a brief explanation of the settlement process. At the same time, however, Griesbach Barracks recruited many people away from the more local settlement efforts; its presence also made refugees more conscious of Alberta, and hence brought more refugees to the province.

Slowly the private and public response to the challenge strengthened. By mid-1980 private sponsors were taking a substantial load off govern-mental and private agencies. Objectively, these individuals were in many ways rather ill-equipped to deal with refugees, since they had little knowledge of Southeast Asian cultures, history or language, were uncertain of their sponsorship responsibilities, and were limited in their

temporal and financial resources. Despite these handicaps most sponsorship situations were very productive—so much so that government-
sponsored refugees usually felt themselves to be disadvantaged.

The sponsorship program also dispersed refugees across the province
in a way that would not have occurred otherwise. Sponsorship was
available to all Albertans and many outside of Edmonton and Calgary
took up the challenge. By the end of 1980 about 30 percent of the
refugees had settled outside of Edmonton and Calgary. By then refugees
had been sent to virtually every town in Alberta. Larger population centers naturally took considerably more:

Location	1979	1980
Calgary	1,012	1,630
Edmonton	994	1,458
Lethbridge	182	155
Medicine Hat	77	108
Red Deer	59	194
Vegreville	71	18
Tofield	39	25
Lacombe	37	18
Camrose	35	41
Stony Plain	25	17
Neerlandia	22	11
Grande Prairie	21	21
Coaldale	21	1
Drumheller	19	9
St. Paul	19	22
Lloydminster	18	21
Brooks	17	39
Ponoka	16	23
Stettler	—	23
Other	500	483
Total	3,184	4,317

Table 2. Indochinese Refugees Arriving in Alberta 1979–80 [34]

Many of those who initially went to Alberta's smaller towns have since
left for Edmonton or Calgary, where they find themselves less isolated
from other refugees and more able to get jobs and find familiar items of
food and culture:

> I went to Peace River, where I was the only Lao. I was so lonely that for
> months I hated to stay home and spent a lot of time walking. Eventually I
> went to Edmonton, but I didn't know any Lao there. I was desperate for
> information about friends and family in Laos. It took a while before I found
> another Lao—I heard him speaking Lao with another person quite by chance.
> Through him I was introduced to many other people in the community.

At the same time, private settlement agencies began to more effectively assist in the settlement of government-sponsored refugees. This
was made possible chiefly by generous funding by Alberta's govern-

ment. In Edmonton the established agencies divided settlement tasks. Catholic Immigrant Services concentrated on housing and housing-related activities. With the support of the Mennonite Central Committee, Anne Falk addressed the many health-related problems of refugees. ESL classes were expanded by the Alberta Vocational Centre and the Catholic and Public School Boards. Edmonton Immigrant Services Association helped people find jobs and ran orientation courses for incoming refugees. Hundreds of unpaid volunteers helped these agencies to facilitate the settlement process. In Edmonton, St. Catherine's School quickly became a center for refugee activities. Soon the Vietnamese had an office in the school and were using the school's facilities for a number of recreational activities. Calgary Immigrant Aid Services and Catholic Immigration Society expanded to meet the challenge in that city. A number of organizations also arose there specifically in response to the Southeast Asian refugee situation. The earliest of these was the Calgary Center for Indochinese Refugees, organized by a group of concerned Chinese-Canadians in April 1979. This was at a time when most incoming refugees were ethnic Chinese. Language Training Services was established as a voluntary agency to coordinate ESL classes for refugees. In Edmonton similar organizations were developed, including Edmonton Area Refugee Services and Community Aid to Refugees Today.

There were few similar organizations outside of Edmonton and Calgary. In Lethbridge, Medicine Hat and Red Deer, Alberta Advanced Education and Manpower supported some services through community colleges. At Lethbridge Community College a program provided ESL classes and translation assistance. This was augmented by U-First Community Services, a Lethbridge-based settlement agency. Similar programs to that at Lethbridge Community College were also established in Medicine Hat and Red Deer. In addition to the Indochinese Refugee Services Program at Red Deer Community College, Red Deer and vicinity have also benefited from Central Alberta Refugee Effort (CARE) Committee, a community-sponsorship organization. In early 1980 these organizations were followed by the opening of a Catholic Immigrant Services office in Red Deer.

These associations and service organizations played a vital role in settling refugees, particularly those who were government-sponsored. As it was, many government-sponsored refugees were unable to use their services or were unaware of them. These individuals had to virtually go it alone—with no knowledge of English, or of Canadian customs and institutions. This produced a great deal of unnecessary suffering. People sat in houses in the winter without heat. Others went without food when their initial government allotment was used up. Active cases of tuberculosis and malaria went untreated. Refugees went from company to company looking for work without knowing a word of English.

Both Vietnamese pioneers from 1975-76 and more recent Chinese and Vietnamese arrivals provided vital assistance to their more recently arrived compatriots. Many of these people were willing to visit new arrivals, to help them find jobs and housing, and to translate for them. A number of these volunteers virtually became settlement agencies in themselves, often receiving twenty calls for assistance in a single night. In this the Vietnamese were at an advantage compared to refugees from other ethnic backgrounds, for only they had substantial existing communities. For the Chinese this was partially compensated for by the assistance of Chinese-Canadian volunteers and the ethnic Chinese churches, especially the Chinese Alliance and Pentecostal churches in Calgary and Edmonton. In Edmonton the Chinese Community Services Center also provided valuable assistance.

The Lao were not so well served. There were virtually no Lao in Alberta before 1978. By early 1980 Lao were able to provide some mutual aid to each other in Edmonton and Calgary. Again, the churches were extremely helpful, especially the Highland Baptist Church and a Mennonite Church in Edmonton, both of which had sponsored a number of Lao. Several ex-missionaries to Laos worked extensively with Lao refugees.

Because Lao and Khmer refugees were primarily "land people" rather than "boat people," it was their usual fate to wind up in Thai camps. There was a general feeling among countries that were receiving refugees that many Lao and Khmer would return to their countrties when things got better, so few attempts were made to resettle them in foreign countries. In addition, there was a feeling that, because many were farmers, they would not adapt well to Canadian life. Few Lao or Khmer were sponsored by the government when compared to others. If they were to come, they would have to be privately sponsored. Over fifty Lao refugees were sponsored by Mennonites in Tofield, where they were generously supported. Most of them found work in Edmonton. Others were scattered across the province. Even so, Lao outside of these two cities felt isolated and many of them have subsequently moved to either Calgary or Edmonton. For example, one family was sponsored on a farm which was twenty miles from the nearest town. The husband found work in the town, but had to stay in town during the week because he did not have a car. His family was left alone on the farm. His wife could neither speak to anyone nor go anywhere. Before they moved to the city she was suffering severe anxiety attacks. Others who settled in rural areas where there were other refugees usually suffered less psychological strain.

The comparatively few Khmer who have come to Alberta so far have been assisted primarily through regular social services' channels. In addition, they have also received some help from Mennonites in Edmonton and a Lutheran church in Calgary. Even so, the Khmer have been the least well served by public and private attempts at refugee assistance and have had to carry on primarily on their own. This has led to difficulties in finding employment, underuse of social and health services, social isolation, and a lack of public and government awareness of Khmer problems and concerns.

Despite the generous response of some Albertans to this third wave of

Southeast Asian immigration, numerous difficulties still remain which will take many years to resolve. Agencies, sponsors, and volunteers only do so much and have been able to address only the most obvious needs. Of the unresolved difficulties, the most important one is lack of English language fluency. As one refugee put it:

> They have eyes but cannot see (read)
> They have ears but cannot hear (understand)
> They have mouths but cannot speak.

Many refugees know little English and consequently feel isolated, unable to control their situation, and unable to communicate their needs and interests to others. There is a universal acknowledgement of the need for language training, yet occupational demands make it difficult for most to attend ESL classes. Throughout Alberta today, classes are filled with tired Indochinese, who, having worked all day and attended to the demands of their families, are struggling to learn a new language.

Other problems are not so easily resolved. Perhaps the most vital of these is the continuing and weak economic situation of refugees.[35] Third wave immigrants are typically less skilled, educated, and westernized than those who came before. Because they were hard-working and willing to take virtually any job, relatively few people were unemployed by 1980. At the same time, many were then severely underemployed. Many worked at low paying service jobs in restaurants, sewing factories, hotels, and hospitals. More fortunate ones found more remunerative jobs in manufacturing, janitorial work, and construction. Some of these people were quite highly skilled, but found it difficult to upgrade themselves because of financial pressure to work; most faced financial commitments which ate up virtually their entire paychecks. In addition, many refugees were forced to take two jobs or have a number of family members work in order to have a high enough income to sponsor the immigration of other family members.

Between 1975 and 1980 Alberta's strong economy provided many economic advantages to the province's Indochinese immigrants not enjoyed in other parts of the country. However, these advantages disappeared with the sharp downturn in the economy in 1980-81. Because of their short job tenure and lack of experience Indochinese immigrants were far more profoundly affected by the economic slowdown than most other Albertans. By 1983 it was commonly estimated that thirty to forty per cent of all adult Indochinese in the province were without work.

In a sense, problems resulting from this economic situation illustrate that the quickness with which Indochinese settlement proceeded during 1978 and 1979 obscured some very basic weaknesses in adaptation. This was particularly true with respect to English language facility and having sufficient knowledge of Canadian life to effectively "work the system" in economic hard times.

Another problem is the profound sense of cultural and social discontinuity felt by most of the refugees. A sense of anxiety exists about many aspects of life, for their hard-won establishment here is very tenuous.

Few people feel entirely at ease with their present life. Other problems relate to the situation of their relations and friends overseas. For example it is not unusual to visit a family who will tell you one of their brothers, sisters, aunts or uncles escaped from Vietnam six or more months ago and no one has heard from that person since; the mail delivery each day is a most important event in the life of each refugee. This worry about family members overseas is perhaps most extreme among the Khmer, many of whom have had their whole extended families exterminated:

> I have only been here three weeks. Before that I and my two sons were in a Thai camp for refugees from Kampuchea. We had walked 170 kilometers to get there with little to eat; the whole countryside was desolated. When we arrived in the camp we thought that we were the only ones in our entire extended family that were still living. It was only by accident that one of my sons saw a picture of my brother posted in the camp. He had survived and had been brought to Canada. Thereafter he had his picture distributed through all the camps in Thailand in the hope that some of the family might

The Nguyen family on the front steps of their home in Edmonton in 1979.

see it. My wife is dead and his is too. So are several of our brothers and sisters. Some other family members may still live but we can't be sure. I don't know what will happen to our country or its people.

Family life in Alberta has become a reservoir of security for those refugee individuals who have been fortunate enough to be living in families. Vietnamese, Chinese-Vietnamese, Lao, and Khmer families are hardly identical, but they nevertheless operate on some similar principles. The family is the fundamental social unit in their lives. Families are often considerably larger than the typical Canadian ones, chiefly because more than just parents and children live in them. Family, to most peoples of Southeast Asia, is the vehicle through which life flows; people come and go, but family remains forever. Therefore, male children are very important, for all groups emphasize patrilineal relations. Family, not the individual, is also the most important economic unit. No one has been fortunate enough to recreate family units in Alberta that completely perform all these functions, but to the extent that families exist, at the very least, they perform these functions symbolically. They give people a sense of place. To a certain extent they also help people to redefine who they are and to get their bearings in this new country.

Because of the severe traumas to which so many of the people have been exposed, other aspects of their culture have been severely disrupted by their relocation here. Broadly speaking, culture is a way of life, not something done in an ethnic celebration; in a real sense, the inability to act in terms of it undermines what a person is. Vietnamese, Chinese, Lao and Khmer cultures are very different from each other. Nevertheless, many Canadians treat refugees as if they were all the same: ethnically, nationally, and linguistically. People from these countries therefore feel very ill-defined in reference to other Canadians; this emphasizes the feelings they already have of a lack of grounding in their new country. Without doubt, this adds to an identity crisis and further alienation for many refugees.

The rise and development of Southeast Asian associations in Alberta is intelligible in the light of these profound needs. As noted, most refugees have arrived in Alberta with only their physical and intellectual resources at their disposal; consequently they enter Canadian society on very disadvantageous terms. Few have their families here intact, and many people are alone. All are divorced from community and society as they previously had known them. Most people, particularly those without families, have a profound need for some continuity with their home country and stability within their immediate environment. It is precisely this that associations offer to their members—a cultural and social grounding which provides some security and comfort to individuals while they are adapting to a completely new life situation. Although all refugees have these needs in common, associations and organizations vary with respect to ethnicity and to governmental and individual support.[36]

Two major Vietnamese associations have been started in Alberta: the Edmonton Viets Association and the Calgary Vietnamese Canadian

A group of young women of the Vietnamese community in Edmonton pictured as they perform a traditional courtship dance at a New Year's party. (Photo by Helen FitzPatrick)

Association. Both associations began at approximately the same time. After meeting for some time on an informal basis, both became formally registered in 1978. Both were started by Vietnamese who had arrived in Alberta between 1975-77 and arose as a result of the needs to coordinate important annual celebrations. The men who initially ran the associations were young, knew English, had stable jobs, and were becoming established. The officers of the association consisted of the "student" population, former naval and army officers, and a few government bureaucrats who could act as a middleman between government, the media, and the associations.

In both Calgary and Edmonton the first cultural events organized by the associations were Tet celebrations in 1977. Tet is the most important of all Vietnamese holidays and celebrates the lunar new year. Another very important holiday for Vietnamese for which the associations prepared is the Mid-Autumn Festival for children, celebrated on the fifteenth day of the eighth lunar month. A number of Canadians have been invited to these celebrations in the last few years. Vietnamese are most anxious that Canadians get to know who they are and to become familiar with their culture. It is their way of giving something back to Canadians. These celebrations are also very important meeting places for Vietnamese, who go to great efforts to attend. For instance, at the 1980 Tet banquet at the Edmonton Inn, some of the 700 people who attended came from as far away as British Columbia. In 1981, the community had grown so much in each city that there were two Tet celebrations.

Both the Calgary and Edmonton communities contain a large number of talented people. Both have their own rock groups: *The Seagull* in Calgary, and the Edmonton Viets Association's "*Mobile Music Group.*" There are a number of young contemporary singers and several traditional Viet folk singers and classical musicians, all of whom perform regularly at Vietnamese events. Several people have contributed articles, poetry, and art work to local and national Vietnamese publications. The Edmonton and Calgary associations are now in constant contact with each other and are beginning to take cultural and sports activities to people in outlying areas. For instance, members of the Edmonton association have gone to Red Deer to hold a singing concert for new arrivals; they also play soccer and ping pong (favorite Vietnamese sports) together. The Associations sponsor sports activities, and they have competitions across Alberta and in Saskatchewan. Such activities have done much to promote good will and solidarity among people and to bring them together to structure their time and identities positively.

In Edmonton the Vietnamese Association established a small drop-in center. Their center now employs one full-time and one part-time coordinator; they have expanded their activities to include cross-cultural communications, settlement assistance, and the publication of a monthly newsletter. The parallel association in Calgary at first established a drop-in center at St. Joseph's Cathedral Community Hall; they have subsequently moved to a new center. The Calgary association also publishes a newsletter, provides limited settlement assistance, and organizes a range of cultural and sports activities.

Other Vietnamese groups have arisen around religious concerns. In Calgary the Vietnamese Buddhist Association was formed at the end of 1979, sharing a hall with a Japanese group. A similar Vietnamese Buddhist association was founded in Edmonton somewhat later. Many Vietnamese in Calgary and Edmonton are Catholic, and they have generally congregated at a few churches in each city. There is presently a Vietnamese priest in Calgary. In Edmonton a number of Vietnamese attend the Christian Beulah Alliance Church, and there is one other Vietnamese Christian congregation.

Most refugees come to Canada as nominal Buddhists, but are quite flexible as far as religion is concerned. Many have found Christian contacts and services to be quite helpful to their social and psychological adjustment to Canada, especially when services are presented in their first language. Many sponsors have been members of church groups and have rather consistently brought refugees to services provided by these churches. Whether this will result in many long-term conversions is an open question. Church services nevertheless presently fill a spiritual vacuum for people, even when they do not entirely understand their content.

Vietnamese-Chinese associations have not developed as fully, a fact which reflects the group's relative lack of a long-term community, its fewer middle class organizationally-minded individuals, and perhaps its weaker sense of collective solidarity. It should be noted that while many Vietnamese-Chinese were involved in small-scale business, relatively few were highly educated or very active in Vietnamese government and politics. The same could not be said of the Vietnamese. The Vietnam Chinese Association was formed in Edmonton in 1979 shortly after the incorporation of the Vietnamese Association. The organization now produces a New Year's celebration and a limited number of recreational activities which include sports and musical performances.

Calgary also has a Vietnamese-Chinese association. Chinese in Calgary have also been assisted by other Chinese-Canadians, at first through the Calgary Centre for Indochinese Refugees and now more generally. Some have benefited from association with the First Alliance Church and the Chinese Alliance Church. The Chinese Community Centre has provided similar assistance in Edmonton.

The Lao and Khmer in Edmonton have been able to bring people together through their collective involvement in Theravada Buddhism; both are also associated with the Sinhalese (from Sri Lanka), who are also Theravada Buddhists. The Lao in Edmonton have had their own association since 1979.

The Future

It is very difficult to see what the future will hold for these new Canadians and new Albertans, for they are by no means all the same. Nor can one predict the way Alberta itself will change. Even so, a few things seem certain. First, most individual Southeast Asians will eventually adapt successfully to Alberta. Although some are presently limited economically by low-paying jobs, underemployment, and lack of consumer sophistication, they work hard, save money, and want to better themselves. A number are already buying homes. Second, these communities will continue to grow rapidly as they are augmented by people coming from overseas and from other provinces. By these processes each of these communities could easily double in numbers in the next ten years. Third, they will become Southeast Asian Canadians rather than Southeast Asian refugees in Canada. This process is already well established among the 1975-76 Vietnamese refugees and in the children of all origins. Finally, even as they become more established in Alberta much of their concern will continue to be with friends and relatives overseas. They may be in Alberta, but they are still an intimate part of those long-term social and political forces which have determined the course of life in Southeast Asia. Many of their relatives are still in peril, and the refugee camps remain full. Stability is far from achieved in Vietnam, Laos, and Kampuchea, and every shift of policy there has repercussions on people here. Most Southeast Asians in Alberta are here because of factors outside of their control. They are involuntary immigrants who would never have considered leaving under normal conditions. They are here, yet are not entirely reconciled to it; nor have they fully absorbed what has happened to them, to their kin and countries. At the same time they are also being subjected to the demands of Canadian life: they have to learn new ways of thinking and doing things, to find jobs, to learn English, and to obey the laws. Concerns here and overseas are difficult to resolve and sometimes contradictory. In this respect, Southeast Asians today are some of the province's most psychologically stressed people.

Southeast Asians in Alberta have met many challenges valiantly. Their accomplishments have been remarkable. They have survived incredible trials to begin life anew in Canada. Even so, only time, a brightening future in Alberta, and particularly a lessening of the turmoil in Southeast Asia will begin to remove the scars of their past.

Conclusion

The population of western Canada is made up of a fascinating mix of diverse peoples. Not only did many different nationalities and religious groups settle in western Canada, but many of these groups, such as the British, Americans, Scandinavians, and Germans who arrived during the first wave of immigration prior to World War I were themselves very heterogeneous.

Subsequent waves of immigration during the 1920s, the early post-World War II period, and since the late 1960s have increased the province's cultural, linguistic, and religious diversity. Attending ethnic festivals in the province's cities, one encounters dramatic diversity in the cultural expressions of widely different groups, such as Caribbeans, Ismailis, El Salvadoreans, Filipinos, Vietnamese, and Koreans, as well as the more familiar European and Asian ethnic groups.

Despite the present vitality of new immigrant groups in the larger urban centers, ethnic differences are not as important in Alberta society as they were prior to World War II. In each decade since 1920, the population of Alberta has been increasingly Canadian born; the percentage of immigrants has decreased steadily from 46 percent in 1921 to 16 percent in 1981: Alberta is not the immigrant society it was prior to the 1920s. Ethnicity is no longer a major feature of urban residential patterns in the largest cities, and rural evidences of ethnic diversity are muted, now more evident for many groups (with the exception of the Hutterites) in church architecture, roadside historical markers, and surnames in particular areas than in the day-to-day life of large numbers of people.

The once highly visible ethnic diversity of the prairie provinces, including Alberta, which was symbolized and preserved for decades in rural bloc settlements and in urban ethnic ghettoes, has eroded over time. With the exception of the Hutterites, who have undergone only minor changes, all groups have experienced a significant degree of acculturation or assimilation to prairie life. For most groups, the Great Depression and World War II diluted or broke up many of the isolated rural settlements. The rapid urbanization of the postwar era, coupled with the passing of the pioneer generation, further hastened the assimilation of minorities. Recent studies of rural ethnic groups, other than the Hutterites, have revealed substantial erosion of ancestral language use, high rates of intermarriage, and only limited retention of folk cultures. Nevertheless, the degree of assimilation differs from group to group, ranging from a high degree among Scandinavians and Germans to significantly lower degrees among Doukhobors, Mennonites, and Ukrainians.

The decline of ethno-cultural differences was the inevitable result of changing social circumstances on the Prairies. Common social pressures, mobility, the rise of populist political parties, public education, wartime military service, and eventually the mass media all served to mute ethnic differences. Changing agricultural technology, farm consolidation, and expectations of a rising standard of living also broke down the rural bloc settlements. The urban and frontier mining camp economies brought people together and made them socially similar in spite of lingering ethno-cultural differences. Assimilation was further hastened before the 1960s by deliberate provincial government policies which created a school system and curriculum that was hostile, or at best indifferent, to the maintenance of ethnic languages and cultures. But even a public educational system much more sympathetic to the maintenance of ethnic diversity could not have dramatically halted the erosion of cultural differences.

The erosion of group differences was not a simple one-way process whereby groups gave up Old World values and conformed to a pre-existing mold. The processes of integration and assimilation have been enormously complex, influenced by a myriad of social, demographic, economic, and political factors. The group-by-group organization of the book may have tended at times to oversimplify this complexity by indirectly implying that each group simply adjusted to a static host society which was at root British-Canadian and Protestant. But Alberta's society was never fixed or static, and many different groups shaped it. Newcomers from Britain and eastern Canada, who were overwhelmingly Anglo-Saxon and Protestant, indeed founded the major social, political, and educational institutions in the province during the era of settlement prior to World War I. Other immigrant groups determined the nature of the agricultural economy that developed in the same era: Americans introduced dryland and irrigated farming in southern Alberta; Scandinavians made a unique adaptation to mixed farming in central Alberta; central and eastern Europeans settled the northern fringes of the park belt through their ability to survive in a subsistence economy.

The diversity of Alberta's population was also gradually evident not only in economics, but also in politics and religion. American immigrants were important shapers of the political system in Alberta. They introduced populist ideas, which were a major force in changing the traditional two party system, and helped bring to power the UFA in 1921. Similarly, the history of the left wing political parties and radical labor unions in the province from the turn of the century through to the 1940s is tied intimately to the history of central and eastern Europeans in the province. The latter were instrumental in creating the political and labor organizations which arose in the mining camps and cities to challenge the economic and political status quo. Immigration also profoundly affected organized religion in the province. The tremendous diversity of Protestant denominations and sects, the diversity and strength of Catholicism, and the presence of Orthodox Christianity are all directly related to pre-1930 immigration patterns.

By the mid-1920s it had become difficult to think of Alberta as a predominantly Anglo-Saxon and Protestant society. Undeniably, central and eastern Europeans felt pressured to conform to a dominant society, but this dominant society now had both Scandinavian and American components and was only vaguely defined. In addition, the numbers and concentrations of central and eastern Europeans were sufficient to place an indelible stamp on the cultural, social, and religious life of north central Alberta. Immigrants from Europe, the United States, and Asia did not simply come to an Albertan society that was a fixed entity. They all played a part in shaping it. Thus, in a very real sense, the history of Alberta's diverse ethnic groups is not merely an interesting but peripheral dimension of the province's history; rather it is at its center.

What role will ethnic groups play in the future development of Alberta? Will governmental policies of multi-culturalism, support for heritage languages, or official bilingualism make any difference to overall trends toward assimilation? It is too early for a definitive answer, since policies of pluralism are relatively new and still in a tentative, testing stage. Public opinion is now more favorable to diversity than ever before, despite lingering traces of racism. Ethnic groups have emerged from church basements and ethnic halls, finding that they can share elements of their culture with a growing and appreciative public audience. The ethnic experience has ceased to be solely the preserve of the groups themselves and has now become part of the larger conception of what prairie Canada was and is.

Paradoxically, this greater degree of acceptance may make the maintenance of ethnicity more, rather than less, difficult, since it has removed many of the former barriers to assimilation and decreased the need for ethnic organizations. This is particularly true for groups such as the Germans and Scandinavians who have lived in Alberta for three or more generations. However, even though the institutional base of ethnicity has been eroded for such groups, there are still two important factors contributing to the continued vital presence of ethnicity in Alberta. First, even though third or fourth generation Albertans of Scandinavian origin, for example, may have little interest in ethnic institutions, they may have a keen interest in ethnicity as ancestry; they may find that exploring their ethnic roots at least partially fulfills their need for personal identity—a need which is often accentuated by the impersonality of modern urban society. Second, and perhaps more important for the continued visible presence of ethnic diversity, new immigrants are still coming to Alberta. Most of these recent immigrant groups, such as the Vietnamese and various South Asians, are still building their communities and establishing institutions that will be vital to them and to their children in the foreseeable future. So, while some of the once striking evidences of ethnicity in the province, such as the rural bloc settlements, have all but disappeared, many of the descendants of those who established those settlements still keep alive ethnic values and traditions, and new immigrants are meeting the contemporary challenge of adjusting to a new land.

Despite the many differences among them, ethnic groups in Alberta have shown a growing awareness of the commonality of the problems they face. The Alberta Cultural Heritage Council and local multi-cultural, citizenship, folklore, and heritage language councils have promoted common understandings among ethnic group leaders so that issues of language and cultural retention, education, and prejudice are now being discussed across ethnic groups. The unique history of native peoples and French Canadians, and their claims to unique status have at times limited their cooperation with other ethnic groups. Nevertheless, native, francophone, and immigrant minorities all share the common problems of minority groups struggling both for survival as distinct groups and for acceptance as a group as well as individuals. All have valued languages, cultures, and traditions they want to preserve, develop, and transmit to future generations. All share the conviction that they can make a contribution to Alberta and to Canada by keeping their languages and traditions alive.

All of the minorities, including French Canadians and native peoples, face the consequences of high rates of mobility and greater social mixing. These factors challenge the future survival of separate ethnic groups, whose continued existence will depend on conscious planning, effective leadership, and the use of modern educational techniques. Survival is no longer assured by isolation, prejudice, and group barriers. Governmental policies on culture, education, human rights, and immigration can have an impact on the future of minorities. But future survival will depend perhaps more than ever on the conscious desire to survive and on the dedicated work of the groups themselves.

Notes

Chapter One

1. J.G. MacGregor, *A History of Alberta* (Edmonton, 1972), chaps. 10, 11.
2. See the essay on Ontarians in this volume; Census of Canada, 1911.
3. A.I. Silver, "French Canada and the Prairie Frontier; 1870–1890," *Canadian Historical Review*, L (March 1969), pp. 11–36; A.I. Silver, *The French-Canadian Idea of Confederation. 1864–1900* (Toronto, 1982), chaps. 7, 10.
4. Norman Macdonald, *Canada: Immigration and Colonization 1842–1908* (Toronto, 1966).
5. *Ibid.*, chap. 11.
6. Paul F. Sharp, *Whoop-Up Country* (Minneapolis, 1955), p. 215; C.M. MacInnes, *In the Shadow of the Rockies* (London, 1930), chap. 14.
7. A.S. Morton, *History of Prairie Settlement* (Toronto, 1938), chap. 4; Gulbrand Loken, *From Fjord to Frontier: A History of the Norwegians in Canada* (Toronto, 1980), chap. 3; Lawrence Lee, "The Mormons Come to Canada, 1887–1902," *Pacific Northwest Quarterly*, 59, (1968), pp. 11–22.
8. Edmund Heier, "The Immigration of Russo-German Catholics and Lutherans Into Canada," *Canadian Slavonic Papers*, V (1960), pp. 160–175.
9. E. Gerwin, "A Survey of the German-Speaking Population in the Province of Alberta" (M.A. thesis, University of Alberta, 1938), p. 59; Morton, *History of Prairie Settlement*, p. 88.
10. A. Malycky, "A History of the German-speaking Population of Alberta," (Unpublished Ms., Calgary, 1983).
11. *Ibid.*; *A Heritage in Transition: Essays in the History of Ukrainians in Canada*, ed. Manoly Lupul (Toronto, 1982), p. 37.
12. H. Palmer, *Patterns of Prejudice* (Toronto, 1982), pp. 21–22.
13. *Ibid.*
14. Royal Commission on Bilingualism and Biculturalism, *The Cultural Contribution of the Other Ethnic Groups* (Ottawa, 1970), pp. 238–239; Census of Canada, 1911.
15. Thomas F. Gossett, *Race: The History of an Idea in America* (New York, 1965), chap. 7; Palmer, *Patterns*, pp. 23–24.
16. *Ibid.*; David Hall, "Clifford Sifton: Immigration and Settlement Policy, 1896–1905" in *The Settlement of the West*, ed. H. Palmer (Calgary, 1977), pp. 60–85.
17. David Breen, "The Canadian West and the Ranching Frontier, 1875–1922"

(Ph.D. diss., University of Alberta, 1972), pp. 29, 31, 136–137; Patrick Dunae, *Gentlemen Emigrants* (Vancouver, 1981), chaps. 5, 7.

18. *Ibid.*, pp. 382–459; David Breen, "The Turner Thesis and the Canadian West: A Closer Look at the Ranching Frontier," in *Essays on Western History*, ed. L. H. Thomas (Edmonton, 1976), pp. 147–158; M. Hopkins, *Letters From a Lady Rancher* (Glenbow, 1982); S. Evans, "Ranching in the Canadian West, 1882–1912" (Ph.D. diss., University of Calgary, 1976); L.G. Thomas, "The Rancher and the City: Calgary and the Cattlemen 1883–1914," in *Transactions of the Royal Society of Canada*, VI, ser. IV, June, 1968, pp. 203–215; S. Jamieson, "Women in the Southern Alberta Ranch Community 1881–1914," in *The Canadian West: Social Change and Economic Development*, ed. H.C. Klassen (1977).

19. Breen, "The Canadian West and the Ranching Frontier," pp. 191–204.

20. Helen Reid, *All Silent All Damned: The Search for Isaac Barr* (Toronto, 1969).

21. For discussions of the British role in the labor movement see David Bercuson, *Fools and Wise Men: The Rise and Fall of the One Big Union* (Toronto, 1978), pp. 37, 44; Ann Capling, "The Communist Party of Canada in Alberta, 1922–1929" (M.A. thesis, University of Calgary, 1983), p. 8; W.J. Cousins, "A History of the Crow's Nest Pass," (M.A. thesis, University of Alberta, 1951), p. 178.

22. Ross McCormack, "Cloth Caps and Jobs: The Ethnicity of English Immigrants in Canada, 1900–1914," in *Ethnicity, Power and Politics in Canada*, ed. Jorgen Dahlie and Tissa Fernando (Toronto, 1981), pp. 44–47; Max Foran, *Calgary. An Illustrated History* (Toronto, 1978), p. 86.

23. On Canadian government immigration promotion in the U.S. see Harold Troper, *Only Farmers Need Apply* (Toronto, 1972).

24. On the background to American immigration to the Canadian west see Troper, *Only Farmers*; Karel Bicha, *The American Farmer and the Canadian West, 1896–1914* (Lawrence, Kansas, 1968); Paul Sharp, "The American Farmer and the Last Best West," *Agricultural History* (April 1947), pp. 65–75; Paul Sharp, "When Our West Moved North" *American Historical Review* 55, 1950, pp. 286–300. There is considerable debate among these authors over the numbers of Americans who came to the Canadian west.

25. Sharp, "American Farmer"; Marcus Lee Hansen and John Brebner, *The Mingling of the Canadian and American Peoples* (Toronto, 1940).

26. Sharp, "When Our West"; Troper, *Only Farmers*, pp. 41–42.

27. For detailed references on black immigration see the chapter on blacks in this volume.

28. Lawrence Lee, "The Mormons Come to Canada"; John Lehr, "The Sequence of Mormon Settlement in Southern Alberta," *The Albertan Geographer* 10, 1974, pp. 20–29; H. Palmer, *Land of the Second Chance* (Lethbridge, 1972), chap. 10.

29. *Ibid.*; Carl Dawson, *Group Settlement* (Toronto, 1936), chap. 10; Leonard Arrington and Dean May, "A Different Mode of Life: Irrigation and Society in Nineteenth-Century Utah," *Agricultural History* (January 1975), pp. 3–20.

30. Local histories of central and southern Alberta contain accounts of the impact of American settlers on rural society. See for example, Lacombe Rural History Club, *Wagon Trails to Hard Top: History of Lacombe and Area* (Lacombe, 1973); Cleverville Pioneer Club History Book Committee, *Cleverville-Champion 1905–1970: A History of Champion and Area* (Champion, 1972); *Conquerville. A Growing Community*, ed. Margaret Dragland (Conquerville, 1964); *Silver Sage: Bow Island, 1900–1920*, comp. Jack Thomas (Bow Island, 1972); Foremost Historical Society, *Shortgrass Country: A History of*

Foremost and Nemiskam (Calgary, 1975). See also Sarah Roberts, *Of Us and the Oxen* (Saskatoon, 1968).

31. For discussions of the return of the settlers to the U.S., see local histories, Alberta Provincial Archives, Survey Board, Medicine Hat hearing, Hanna Hearing, and Premier's Papers, 69.289.

32. W.E. Mann, *Sect, Cult and Church in Alberta* (Toronto, 1955), chap. 1; Three Hills Rural Community Group, *As the Years Go By* (Altona, Manitoba, 1970).

33. W.L. Morton, *The Progressive Party in Canada* (Toronto, 1950); Paul Sharp, *The Agarian Revolt in Western Canada: A Survey Showing American Parallels* (Minneapolis, 1948); W.K. Rolph, *Henry Wise Wood of Alberta* (Toronto, 1950).

34. Sharp, *Agarian Revolt*, p. 20.

35. G.A.A., *Glimpses of the Past, Golden Anniversary Booklet, 1912–1962*, American Woman's Club of Calgary (n.p., n.d.); S.R. Nagy, "A Statistical Analysis of John Blue's Alberta Past and Present" (History 532 paper, University of Calgary, April 1979). Max Foran, *An Illustrated History of Calgary*, p. 88.

36. K.O. Bjork, "Scandinavian Migration to the Canadian Prairie Provinces, 1893–1914," *Norwegian-American Studies* 26 (1974), pp. 63–75; William Wonders, "Scandinavian Homesteaders in Central Alberta" in *The New Provinces: Alberta and Saskatchewan, 1905–1980*, ed. H. Palmer and D. Smith (Vancouver, 1980), pp. 131–171.

37. Loken, *From Fjord to Frontier*, chap. 5.

38. Frank Paulsen, *Danish Settlements on the Canadian Prairies: Folk Tradition, Immigrant Experiences and Local History* (Ottawa, 1974); J.B. Hedges, *Building the Canadian West*, pp. 208, 287, 376; Spruce View School Area Historical Society, *Grub Axe to Grain* (Calgary, 1973), pp. 29–68; Standard Historical Book Society, *From Danaview to Standard* (Calgary, 1979).

39. W.E. Mann, *Sect, Cult and Church in Alberta*, pp. 12, 19, 24, 34, 98, 154; M.E. Thompson, *The Baptist Story in Western Canada* (Calgary, 1974), pp. 320–336.

40. For a discussion of the background of Finnish immigration and causes of radicalism among the Finns see Alan Kuitunen, "The Finnish Canadian Socialist Movement, 1900–1914" (M.A. thesis, University of Calgary, 1982). On the Icelanders see the chapter in this volume.

41. Paul C. Nyholm, *The Americanization of the Danish Lutheran Churches in America* (Copenhagen, 1963), p. 467; G. Loken, *From Fjord to Frontier*, chap. 4.

42. For a general discussion of the cooperative movement in western Canada which mentions the Scandinavian contribution see Ian MacPherson, *Each For All: A History of the Cooperative Movement in English Canada, 1900–1945* (Toronto, 1978). The Scandinavian contribution to the cooperative movement is also evident in the local histories of several communities in central Alberta.

43. On the Dutch and French, see the chapters in this volume. Information on Belgians from interviews, Frank and Lucy Soulet, Blairmore, Aug. 1980; Celina Audenart, Raymond, Aug. 1980.

44. For the background on the Dutch see the Dutch chapter in this volume.

45. Malycky, "A History of the German-speaking Population of Alberta"; Gerwin, "A Survey," pp. 61–64.

46. Malycky, "A History of the German-speaking Population"; H. Palmer, "Nativism and Ethnic Tolerance in Alberta, 1880–1920" (M.A. thesis, University of Alberta, 1971), pp. 216–229.

47. Palmer, *Patterns*, pp. 26–27; Malycky, "A History."

48. Palmer, *Patterns*, pp. 47–49; Census of Canada, 1911, 1921.

49. Frank Epp, *Mennonites in Canada 1786–1920* (Toronto, 1974), chap. 13; A.A. Sawatzsky, "The Mennonites of Alberta and Their Assimilation" (M.A. thesis, University of Alberta, 1964), chap. 1; Palmer, *Land of the Second Chance*, chap. 7.

50. *Ibid.*

51. Palmer, *Patterns*, pp. 52–53; see also chapter on Hutterites in this volume. H. Palmer, "The Hutterite Land Expansion Controversy in Alberta," *Western Canadian Journal of Anthropology* II, #2, (July 1971), pp. 18–46.

52. For a general discussion of the causes of emigration see Johan Chmelar, "The Austrian Emigration, 1900–1914," in Bernard Bailyn, ed., *Dislocation and Emigration: The Social Background of American Immigration, Perspectives in American History* VII (1973), pp. 275–378. See also the chapters on Hungarians, Romanians, Poles, and Ukrainians in this volume.

53. Chmelar, "The Austrian Emigration," p. 319.

54. See chapter on Hungarians in this volume. On the Slovaks, see H. Palmer, *Land of the Second Chance*, chap. 14; John Gellner and John Smerek, *The Czechs and Slovaks in Canada* (Toronto, 1968), pp. 65, 69.

55. *Ibid.*; Herbert Collier, *Remeber When? A History of the Viking District* (Edmonton, 1937), pp. 12–17, 37; Viking Historical Society, *Let Us Not Forget, A History of Viking and District* (College Heights, Alberta, 1968), pp. 74–79.

56. John Lehr, "The Government and the Immigrant: Perspectives on Ukrainian Block Settlement in the Canadian West," *Canadian Ethnic Studies* 9, 2 (1977), pp. 42–52; J. Lehr, "The Landscape of Ukrainian Settlement in the Canadian West," *Great Plains Quarterly* 2, 2, 1982, pp. 94–105.

57. Orest Martynowych, "The Ukrainian Socialist Movement in Canada, 1900–1918" Part 1, *Journal of Ukrainian Graduate Studies* 1, 1, (Fall 1976), pp. 27–44; Part 2, *Ibid.*, (Spring 1977), pp. 22–31; G. Okulevich, *Russkie v Kanade* (Toronto, 1952); Donald Avery, *Dangerous Foreigners: European Immigrant Workers and Labour Radicalism in Canada 1896–1932* (Toronto, 1979).

58. Bercuson, *Fools and Wise Men*; Avery, *Dangerous Foreigners*.

59. Palmer, *Patterns*, pp. 47–50, 53–56.

60. See the chapter on Jews in this volume; Census of Canada, 1921.

61. George Woodcock and Ivan Avakumovic, *The Doukhobors* (Toronto, 1968), chap. 6.

62. *Ibid.*, chaps. 7, 9.

63. Palmer, *Land of the Second Chance*, chap. 15.

64. For Sifton's attitudes toward Italians and other non-agricultural immigrants see D.J. Hall, "Clifford Sifton: Immigration and Settlement Policy," pp. 77–78; Census of Canada, 1921.

65. Peter Chimbos, *The Canadian Odyssey: The Greek Experience in Canada* (Toronto, 1980); George Vlassis, *The Greeks in Canada* (Ottawa, 1942), pp. 16–25, 59–62, 104–106. Interview, James Condon, Calgary, 13 Dec. 1977; Interview, Nick Spillios, Edmonton, spring 1979; Census of Canada, 1921.

66. Baha Abu Laban, *An Olive Branch on the Family Tree: The Arabs in Canada* (Toronto, 1980); Mildred Duncanson, "Uncle Sam Jamha" in *Alberta History* 28, 3, (Summer 1980), pp. 18–25; *A Salute to the Arab Pioneers of Northern Alberta* (Edmonton, 1973); Provincial Archives of Alberta Phonotape 72:256, Alexander Hamilton (Ali Abouchdai).

67. *Ibid.*; Harold Barclay, "A Lebanese Community in Lac La Biche, Alberta" in *Minority Canadians: Immigrant Groups*, ed. Jean Elliott (Scarborough, 1971).

68. Palmer, *Land of the Second Chance*, chap. 12.

69. Crow's Nest Pass Historical Society, *Crowsnest and its People* (Calgary, 1979) and passim. Information on Italians in Calgary from interviews with Antho-

ny and Teresa Aiello, 29 May 1979; Norrie Macmillan, 20 Jan. 1978; Mario Grassi, 11 Feb. 1978; James Barbaro, 25 May 1979.

70. Barrhead and District Historical Society, *Trails Northwest: A History of the District of Barrhead, Alberta* (Edmonton, 1968), pp. 249–256; Barrhead Chamber of Commerce, *The Golden Years* (Calgary, 1978), pp. 50, 259; Freedom-Naples FWUA, *History of Freedom and Naples Communities* (Freedom, 1963); Lac La Biche Heritage Society, *Lac La Biche, Yesterday and Today* (Calgary, 1975), pp. 125, 165, 167–168; *Edmonton Journal* 29 August 1914; Provincial Archives of Alberta, Interviews, Mrs. Gisella Biollo, Mike Biollo Phonotape #74.106/2, 27 Oct. 1973; Mamie Meardi, Phonotape #106/11, 1973.

71. Ed Wickberg, ed., *From China to Canada: A History of the Chinese Communities in Canada* (Toronto, 1982), chap. 1; Ken Adachi, *The Enemy That Never Was* (Toronto, 1976), chap. 1.

72. Ban Seng Hoe, *Structural Changes of two Chinese Communities in Alberta, Canada* (Ottawa, 1976); H. Palmer, "Anti-Oriental Sentiment in Alberta, 1880–1920" in *Canadian Ethnic Studies* II, 2 (1970), pp. 31–57.

73. *Ibid,*; Brian Dawson, "The Chinese Experience in Frontier Calgary, 1885–1910" in *Frontier Calgary*, ed. A.W. Rasporich and H.C. Klassen (Calgary, 1975), pp. 124–140.

74. See the chapter on the Japanese in this volume.

75. H. Palmer, "Patterns of Prejudice: Attitudes toward Chinese and Japanese in Alberta, 1920–1950" in *Social History* 13, 25 (1980), pp. 137–160.

Chapter Two

1. For a discussion of these broad changes see H. Palmer and T. Palmer, "The Alberta Experience," *Journal of Canadian Studies* 17, 3 (1982), pp. 20–34.

2. For the debate over immigration in the 1920s, see Palmer, *Patterns*, chap. 2.

3. For background to the quota system in the United States, see John Higham, *Strangers in the Land* (New York, 2nd edition, 1967), chap. 11.

4. Census of Canada, 1931; W.A. Carrothers, *Emigration from the British Isles* (London, 1929), p. 261.

5. *Ibid.*; Robert England, *The Colonization of Western Canada* (Toronto, 1936); R.A. MacDonell, "British Immigration Schemes in Alberta" in *Alberta Historical Review* 6, (Winter 1958), pp. 5, 13; Norma Milton, "Essential Servants: Immigrant Domestic Servants on the Canadian Prairies, 1885–1930" (M.A. thesis, University of Calgary), pp. 45–48.

6. W.J.C. Cherwinski, "Misfits, Malingerers, and Malcontents: The British Harvester Movement of 1928," in *The Developing West*, ed. John Foster (Edmonton, 1983), pp. 271–302.

7. The local histories cited in chap. 1, fn. 32 contain accounts of return migration to the United States. Figures from Census of Canada, 1921, 1931.

8. On the Dutch settlement see the Dutch chapter in this volume. Information on Danish settlement at Tilley from Diane McInnes, "The Danish Colony in Tilley" (History 432 paper, University of Calgary, March 1982); on the Norwegians at Valhalla see Pioneer History Society of Hythe and Area, *Pioneer Round-Up* (Hythe, 1972), pp. 438–441, 531, 457, 460, 464, and passim. Interviews, Lavern Sorgaard, Bert Strand, Grande Prairie, July 1979.

9. Palmer, *Patterns*, pp. 94–95.

10. *Ibid.*

11. *Ibid.*
12. Dept. of Employment and Immigration, unpublished records, "Immigration to Canada by Province of Intended Destination, Alberta." Census of Canada, 1931.
13. Census of Canada, 1931. See also the chapters on Ukrainians, Poles, and Romanians in this volume.
14. Elizabeth Gerwin, "A Survey of the German-speaking Population of Alberta," p. 66; Edmund Heiler, "German Lutheran and Catholic Immigrants," p. 121.
15. Frank Epp, *Mennonite Exodus* (Altona, Manitoba, 1962); Frank Epp, *Mennonites in Canada, 1920–1940: A People's Struggle for Survival* (Toronto, 1982); Aron Sawatzsky, "The Mennonites of Alberta and Their Assimilation," chap. 3.
16. Ted Regehr, "Mennonite Change: The Rise and Decline of Mennonite Community Organizations at Coaldale, Alberta," *Mennonite Life* (December 1977), pp. 13–22; John Toews, *With Courage to Spare: The Life of B.B. Janz (1877–1964)* (Winnipeg, 1978), chaps. 6, 9.
17. Epp, *Mennonites in Canada*, p. 00; Palmer, *Patterns*, pp. 118–121.
18. On the Hungarians, see the Hungarian chapter in this volume. On Croatians, see A.W. Rasporich, *For a Better Life* (Toronto, 1982), pp. 121–123. On Czechs and Slovaks see Gelner and Smerek, *Czechs and Slovaks*, pp. 76–77; "The Acculturation of a Slovak Immigrant—Steve Kuryvial Tells His Story" in *Alberta Pioneers From Eastern Europe*, vol. 2, ed. J. Matejko and T. Yedlin (Edmonton, 1977), pp. 39–44; *Alberta's Pioneers From Eastern Europe: Reminiscences: The Story of Anthony Slezina*, ed. Jarmila Horna (Edmonton, 1979).
19. On the Estonians, see the Estonian chapter in this volume. On the Russians, see A. Balawyder, "Russian Refugees from Constantinople and Harbin, Manchuria Enter Canada (1923–1926)," *Canadian Slavonic Papers*, (April 1972), pp. 15–30. For general background on the situation of white Russians in Manchuria see John Stephan, *The Russian Fascists: Tragedy and Farce in Exile, 1925–1945* (New York, 1978), chap. 3. Eugene Rozvalaieff, "Russians from Harbin" in *Alberta's Pioneers from Eastern Europe: Reminiscences*, vol. 2, ed. J. Matejko and T. Yedlin (Edmonton, 1976), pp. 85–90; Maria von Rosenbach, *Family Kaleidoscope: From Russia to Canada* (Vancouver, 1976), pp. 145–159.
20. Glenbow Alberta Archives, CPR Papers, Box 89, file 749; Interviews, Mike Kosheiff, Fairview, Alberta, July 1979; John Sidoroff, Peace River, Alberta, July 1979; Mrs. Elizabeth Mishukoff, Edmonton, 5 April 1979.
21. Interviews; von Rosenbach, *Family Kaleidoscope; Calgary Herald*, 29 Mar. 1934, p. 5.
22. Information on Lithuanians from Dr. P. Gudjurgis, Edmonton, Feb. and Mar. 1980; Julius Tomas, Brooks, Mar. 1980; Andrew Nevada, Calgary, Feb. 1980; *Calgary Albertan*, 20 Feb. 1940.
23. Palmer, *Patterns*, pp. 127–132.
24. Palmer, *Patterns*, p. 127; Donald Avery, *Dangerous Foreigners*, pp. 111–112.
25. Irving Abella and Harold Troper, *None is Too Many, Canada and the Jews of Europe, 1933–1948* (Toronto, 1982); Palmer, *Patterns*, pp. 151–152.
26. For discussions of Ukrainian support for the communists see Myrna Kostash, *All of Baba's Children* (Edmonton, 1977), chaps. 11, 12; A. Makuch, "In the Populist Tradition: Organizing the Ukrainian Farmer in Alberta, 1909–1935" (M.A. thesis, University of Alberta), chap. 5. William Repka and Kathleen Repka, *Dangerous Patriots: Canada's Unknown Prisoners of War* (Vancouver, 1982), pp. 21–32. See also the chapter on Hungarians in this volume. Infor-

mation on Dutch and Danish voting patterns from federal election returns. For a general discussion of the appeal of Social Credit to non-Anglo-Saxon ethnic groups see Palmer, *Patterns*, pp.142–144.

27. For background on government deportation policy and practice see Henry Drystek, "The Simplest and Cheapest Mode of Dealing with Them: Deportation from Canada Before World War II," in *Social History* 15, 30 (1982), pp.407–43; Palmer, *Patterns*, pp. 130–132.

28. H. Palmer, "Ethnic Relations in Wartime: Nationalism and European Minorities in Alberta," *Canadian Ethnic Studies* 14, 3 (1982), pp. 1–23. On the Japanese, see the chapter in this volume. For a discussion of wartime anti-Semitism see H. Palmer, "Social Credit and Anti-Semitism" *The Jewish Star* (Calgary) 29 April-12 May 1983, pp. 4c–5c. On wartime attitudes toward the Germans, see also Patricia Koch, "Discrimination against Germans in the Calgary Area During World War II" (Honors' paper, University of Calgary, 1983).

29. H. Palmer, "Ethnic Relations in Wartime," pp. 1–23. H. Palmer "Patterns of Racism: Attitudes Towards Chinese and Japanese in Alberta, 1920–1950," *Social History* 13, 25, (May 1980), pp. 158–159; *From China to Canada: A History of the Chinese Communities in Canada*, ed. Edgar Wickberg (Toronto, 1982), chap. 14.

30. On general patterns of assimilation during this period, see statistical data compiled in W.B. Hurd, "Ethnic Origin and Nativity of the Canadian People" (Ottawa, 1941). On patterns of assimilation among the Norwegians see G. Loken, *From Fjord to Frontier*, pp. 188–200.

31. Chris Liebich, "The Coming of the Japanese Canadians to Alberta, 1942–1948: A Study in Public Policy and Public Attitude" (Honors' essay, University of Alberta, 1976); H. Palmer, "Patterns of Racism"; see also the chapter on Japanese in this volume.

32. For general discussions of postwar immigration see Freda Hawkins, *Canada and Immigration Public Policy and Public Concern* (Montreal, 1972); Jean Bruce, *After the War* (Toronto, 1982).

33. Figures form Department of Citizenship and Immigration, Annual Reports, 1946–1966.

34. Hawkins, *Canada and Immigration*, chap. 4; Bruce, *After the War*, chap. 1; Gerald Dirks, *Canada's Refugee Policy: Indifference or Opportunism* (Montreal, 1977), chaps. 5, 6.

35. *Ibid.*

36. On postwar attitudes in Alberta, see H. Palmer, "Nativism and Ethnic Tolerance in Alberta: 1920–1972" (Ph.D. diss., York University, 1973), pp. 274–278.

37. Dirks, *Canada's Refugee Policy*, pp. 151–164.

38. On postwar settlement patterns, see chapters on Poles, Estonians, and Hungarians in this volume. Between 1946 and 1955, 522 Czechs and Slovaks, 376 Estonians, 809 Hungarians, 535 Latvians, 449 Lithuanians, 4,955 Poles, 704 Russians, 3,869 Ukrainians, and 1,238 Yugoslavs gave Alberta as their intended destination. Department of Citizenship and Immigration, Ethnic Origin of Immigrants by Province of Intended Destination, 1946–1955.

39. Palmer, "Nativism and Ethnic Tolerance," p. 286.

40. For a general discussion of the Scottish impact on Canada see *The Scottish Tradition in Canada*, ed. Stanford Reid (Toronto, 1976).

41. On the Dutch, see the Dutch chapter in this volume. For background on German immigrants see Carol Morrison, "Post-World War II German Immigration to Calgary: the 1950's" (Honors' paper, University of Calgary, 1983).

42. Morrison, *ibid.*; Thomas Poetschke, "Reasons for Immigration and Ethnic Identity: An Exploratory Study of German Immigrants in Edmonton, Alberta" (M.A. thesis, University of Alberta, 1978); *Edmonton Journal* 6 Aug. 1976; Provincial Archives of Alberta, oral histories, Mr. and Mrs. W. Selb-staedt, 2 Oct. 1975 #75.521; Interview, Felix Koch, Calgary, Aug. 1979; Interviews, Adolf Kulpe, Rev. Art Brown, Alfred Degen, Medicine Hat, fall 1979 (with David Clarke). On the CCRR see Gerald Dirks, *Canada's Refugee Policy*, pp. 161–164.

43. *Ibid.* Interviews, Edmonton, Calgary, Medicine Hat, Lethbridge, 1969, 1979, 1980.

44. Interviews, James Gray, Nov. 1979; Jerry D'Arcy, 7 Dec. 1979; George Dunlap, 28 Nov. 1979; Ralph Will, 21 Nov. 1979 (all in Calgary). *Dusters and Gushers: The Canadian Oil and Gas Industry*, ed. James Hilborn (Toronto, 1968), p. 6.

45. *Ibid.*

46. Census of Canada, 1961.

47. M.C. Lawrence, "U.S. Expatriates in Calgary and Their Problems" (M.S.W. thesis, University of Calgary, 1972).

48. Robert Busch, "Edmonton's Recent Soviet-Jewish Immigrants": paper presented to Central and Eastern European Studies Association annual meetings, 1976; A. Levin, "A Soviet Jewish Family Comes to Calgary," *Canadian Ethnic Studies* 6 (1974), pp. 53–66; Jarmila Horna, "Adjustment of Refugees: A Case Study of Czechoslovak Refugees of 1968–69 in Edmonton, Alberta" (Edmonton, University of Alberta, Population Research laboratory Discussion Paper #3, February 1973); J. Horna, "The Czechs and Slovaks in Alberta: Some Issues and Problems of Research" in *Papers and Proceedings of Conferences and Meetings on Central and Eastern European Studies*, ed. T. Yedlin (Edmonton, 1976).

49. Freda Hawkins, *Canada and Immigration*, chap. 6.

50. Figures from annual reports, Department of Manpower and Immigration.

51. *Ibid.*

52. For the background on the Tibetans, Chileans, and Uganda Asians see Dirks, *Canada's Refugee Policy*, pp. 235, 238–244. Interviews with Tibetan refugees in Taber, Alberta, Aug. 1972. For detailed discussion of the Uganda Asians and Southeast Asian Immigrants, see the chapters on South Asians and Vietnamese in this volume.

53. Analysis of class background based on occupations as reported in annual reports Department of Manpower and Immigration, and interviews with West Indian, Korean, Filipino, and South Asian immigrants, Calgary and Edmonton, 1979, 1980; Isias Fernandes, Jr., *The History of Filipinos in Alberta* (Barrhead, 1974).

54. Interviews, *ibid.*

55. Interviews, Michael Lancaster, Edmonton, 4 Oct. 1978; Dolly Booth, Edmonton, 12 Oct. 1978; Horace Goodwin, Calgary, 12 June 1979; Stan Bernard, Calgary, 24 July 1979; Peter Gonzales, Calgary, 26 July 1979; Clarence Murdoch, 4 July 1979; Norma Ellis, 3 July 1979; George Henry, Calgary, 4 July 1979; Hugh Carter, Calgary, 11 July 1979; Ed Simpson and Delroy Ferrel, Calgary, 22 July 1979; Sam Kim, Calgary, 19 Nov. 1979; Sophia and Jorge Caso-Rohland, Edmonton, Oct. 1978. *Heritage*, Mar.-Apr. 1979.

56. *Heritage*, May-June 1978; *Heritage*, Sept-Oct. 1982. *Heritage* magazine contains interesting articles on the social and cultural activities of many of the new immigrant groups in the province.

57. For a comparative study of racism in Calgary, see Norman Buchignani, "Per-

ceptions of Racial Discrimination in Calgary: A Situation Report": Multicultural Directorate, Department of Secretary of State, 1982. See also Rick Ponting and Richard Wanner, "Blacks in Calgary: The Social and Economic Situation," A Research Report for the National Black Coalition of Canada, Calgary, 1983.

58. Besides the chapter on Vietnamese in this volume see also Yvette Knott, "A Case Study on the Canadian Policy and Calgary Community Response to the Southeast Asian Refugees, 1979–1980" (M.A. thesis, University of Calgary, 1981); and Joyce Arndt "The Private Sponsorship of the Indochinese Refugees" (M.S.W. thesis, University of Calgary, 1983).

59. Besides the discussion of South Asian and Vietnamese families in this volume, see also Helen Chan, "Family Organization and Change Among the Chinese in Calgary" (M.A. thesis, University of Calgary, 1980).

60. Wickberg, ed., *From China to Canada: A History of the Chinese Communities in Canada* (Toronto, 1982), pp. 245–246. Interview, Kim Hung and Raymond Pong, Edmonton, 21 Nov. 1978.

61. Bang Seng Hoe, *Structural Changes of Two Chinese Communities in Alberta, Canada* (Canada, 1976), pp. 312–318.

62. Wickberg, *From China to Canada*, chap. 18; Hoe, *Structural Changes*, chap. 6; Interviews, Rev. David Wen, Jose Khu, Dr. K.W. Chang, Dr. John Kong, Judy Lo, Calgary, fall 1979.

Chapter Three

1. My thanks to Hugh Dempsey, Chief Curator of the Glenbow Museum, Calgary; and Olive Dickason, Department of History, University of Alberta; for their comments on this article; and to John Friesen, Department of Educational Policy and Administrative Studies, Faculty of Education, University of Calgary, for his remarks on the final pages. Ian Getty of the Nakoda Institute, Morley, Alberta, kindly commented on a final draft of the paper. I learned a great deal from the students in my Canadian Studies class at Old Sun College, on the Blackfoot Reserve, Winter Term, 1983/84. Any errors or omissions are, of course, my responsibility. My thanks as well to Julia Harrison of the Glenbow Museum for allowing me to examine a draft of her book on Glenbow's Metis Exposition, held in 1985, I am indebted to Fred Lennarson of Edmonton for forwarding numerous photostats of articles and letters on the Lubicon Lake question. Susan Kooyman, formerly with the Provincial Archives of Alberta, Edmonton, assisted with the selection of photos from The Provincial Archives. My thanks to Susan Knox, Marjory McLean, and Joyce Woods, of the Department of History, University of Calgary, for typing the several drafts of this article.

2. An overview of the Alberta Indian tribes is provided by Hugh Dempsey in *Indian Tribes of Alberta* (Calgary: Glenbow-Alberta Institute, 1978). Another useful summary is W.B. Fraser's, "The Alberta Indian: His Past, His Present, His Future," published by The Friends of the Indians Society, Calgary, Alberta, 1959, available at the Glenbow Museum Library.

3. Joe Sawchuk, Patricia Sawchuk, and Theresa Ferguson, *Metis Land Rights in Alberta: A Political History* (Edmonton: Metis Association of Alberta, 1981), p. 1.

4. This figure is highly conjectural, see F.G. Roe, "The Numbers of the Buffalo: Some Suggestions toward the Total Aggregate," chap. 18 in *The*

North American Buffalo (Toronto: University of Toronto Press, 1970), pp. 489–520; see particularly p. 492.

5. A popular summary of the life of the Canadian Plains Indian is provided by Hope MacLean in "Indians of the Plains" in *Indians, Inuit, Metis* (Ottawa: Canadian Association for the Support of Native Peoples, 1976), pp. 25–33. An excellent account of the Blackfoot tribes' culture is: James Willard Schultz and Jessie Louise Donaldson, *The Sun God's Children* (Boston: Houghton Mifflin, 1930). Perhaps the best short summary of Blackfoot life is T.J.C. Brasser's kit, in Canada's Visual History, vol. 46 (Ottawa: National Museum of Man, n.d.).

6. Hugh Brody describes the way of life of the Beaver Indians today in *Maps and Dreams. Indians and the British Columbia Frontier* (Vancouver: Douglas and McIntyre, 1981). For an account of the Woods Cree in the 1950s see Roger Vandersteene, o.m.i., *Wabasca. Dix ans de vie indienne. Adapté du néerlandais par Jacques De Deken*, o.m.i. (Gemmich, Belgique: Editions O.M.I., 1960).

7. As there is no official registry or census of the Metis and nonstatus Indians (as there is for status Indians) it is extremely difficult to estimate their numbers. While accepting a conservative 60,000 as their working figure officials of the Metis Association of Alberta believe that in reality the Metis and nonstatus might well number as many as 100,000 to 120,000.

   Andrew Siggner and Chantal Locatelli, "An Overview of Demographic, Social and Economic Conditions Among Alberta's Registered Indian Population," 9 January 1980. Research Branch, P.R.E., Indian and Inuit Affairs Program, p. 3.

   Sam J. Sinclair, President of the Metis Association of Alberta, "The Challenge of the Constitution," 8 March 1982, mimeographed p. 3, available from the Metis Association of Alberta, Edmonton.

   The land areas are given in Richard T. Price, "Indian Land Claims in Alberta: Politics and Policy-Making (1968–77)" (M.A. thesis, University of Alberta, 1977), p. 20; and Daniel R. and Alda M. Anderson, *The Metis People of Canada: A History* (Toronto: Gage, 1978), p. 108.

8. Hugh Brody gives the Beaver Indians' reaction to the migration theory in *Maps and Dreams*, pp. 14–15. The Blackfoot interpretation of their origin appears in John C. Ewers, *The Blackfeet* (Norman: University of Oklahoma Press, 1958), pp. 3–4. Archaeological interpretations appear in: Thomas Y. Canby, "The First Americans," *National Geographic*, 156, 3 (September 1979): 330–363; Alan Bryan, "The First People," in *Alberta: A Natural History*, ed. W.G. Hardy (Edmonton: M.G. Hurtig, 1967), pp. 276–293; Olive Dickason, "A Historical Reconstruction for the North-western Plains," *Prairie Forum*, 5, 1 (1980): 19–37; Specific information on archaeological sites in Alberta can be obtained from H.M. Wormington and Richard G. Forbis' "Summary and Conclusions," *An Introduction to the Archaeology of Alberta, Canada* (Denver: Denver Museum of Natural History, 1965), pp. 183–201.

9. Richard G. Forbis, *A Review of Alberta Archaeology to 1964* (Ottawa: National Museum of Canada, 1970), p. 27, cited in Dickason, "Reconstruction," p. 28 (for the information on stone circles). R.O.K. Reeves, "Six Milleniums of Buffalo Kills," *Scientific American*, 249:4 (October 1983): 120 (for a full description of Head-Smashed-In).

10. For a popular account see Suzanne Zwarun, "Medicine Wheels Decoded. Shedding light on mysteries older than the Pyramids," *Weekend Magazine*, 25 June 1977, pp. 14–16, 18.

11. The periodization theory is outlined in "Northern Plains Periodization. Temporal Units," mimeographed, Department of Archaeology, University of Calgary. No author's name is listed.

12. My thanks to Barry Dau, graduate student, Department of Archaeology, University of Calgary, for his help with this paragraph. Reeves, "Buffalo Kills," *Scientific American*, p. 135.

13. John Ewers provides the classic account of the arrival, and the influence of the European horse on the Blackfoot in his *The Horse in Blackfoot Culture*, Smithsonian Institution, Bureau of American Ethnology, Bulletin 159 (Washington: Smithsonian Institution Press, 1955). The comparison of a horse's and a dog's efficiency appears in Ewers, The *Blackfeet*, p. 94. An excellent description of how the Plains Indians adjusted to the horse appears in Ruth Underhill, *Red Man's America* (Chicago: University of Chicago Press, 1971), pp. 152–153.

14. Ewers, *Horse*, pp. 299–316.

15. Frances Densmore, "Dakota and Ojibwe People in Minnesota," *Roots*, 5(1977):29. *The Gospel of the Redman*, comp. Ernest Thompson Seton and Julia M. Seton (Santa Fe: Seton, 1966. First published 1937), p. 47. Ewers, *Blackfeet*, p. 17.

16. For a complete review of the rise of the Indian middleman, consult Arthur J. Ray, *Indians in the Fur Trade* (Toronto: University of Toronto Press, 1974).

17. David G. Mandelbaum outlines the westward advance of the Cree in his section, "The Westward Movement," pp. 15–51, in *The Plains Cree* (Regina: Canadian Plains Research Center, 1979), originally published in 1940. Dempsey, *Indian Tribes of Alberta*, p. 54.

18. Brasser, *Blackfoot*, p. 3; Eric Ross, *Beyond the River and the Bay* (Toronto: University of Toronto Press, 1970), pp. 43–45.

19. See the sketches of the Chipewyan, Beaver and Slavey Indians in Dempsey, *Indian Tribes of Alberta*, pp. 65–86; and Brody, *Maps*, pp. 22–23. For northwestern Alberta consult the second chapter, "Early Contacts in Northwestern Alberta" in Gertrude Cecila Nicks, "Demographic Anthropology of Native Populations in Western Canada, 1800–1975" (Ph.D. diss., University of Alberta, 1980), pp. 9–68. In preparing the above two paragraphs of the text I found the lecture by Hugh Demsey, "Tribal Migrations in Western Canada," given on 30 Sept. 1980 (in his "Aboriginal Canada" course at the University of Calgary), most useful.

    For northeastern Alberta consult J.M. Parker and K.W. Tingley, "Historical and Geographical Overview," pp. 6–22, in *History of the Athabasca Oil Sands Region, 1890 to 1960's*, vol. 1: Socio-economic developments. Prep. for the Alberta Oil Sands Environmental Research Program (AOSERP) by the Boreal Institute for Northern Studies, The University of Alberta. AOSERP Report 80 (1980).

    The recently published vol. 6, *The Subarctic*, of the *Handbook of North American Indians* (Washington: Smithsonian Institution, 1981), contains many useful articles on the tribes of northern Alberta.

20. There are three good studies of the Iroquois in the Canadian West: Jack A. Frisch, "Some Ethnological and Ethnohistoric Notes on the Iroquois in Alberta," *Man in the Northeast*, 12 (1976): 51–64.

    Theodore J. Karamanski, "The Iroquois and the Fur Trade of the Far West," *The Beaver*, outfit 312:4 (Spring 1982): 4–13.

    Trudy Nicks, "The Iroquois and the Fur Trade in Western Canada," in *Old Trails and New Directions: Papers of the Third North American Fur Trade*

Conference, ed. Carol M. Judd and Arthur J. Ray (Toronto: University of Toronto Press, 1980): 85–101.

21. Dempsey, *Indian Tribes of Alberta*, p. 6.
22. Sylvia Van Kirk, *"Many Tender Ties." Women in Fur Trade Society, 1670-1870* (Winnipeg: Watson and Dwyer, 1980), pp. 53–65.
23. T.J. Brasser, "Metis Artisans," *The Beaver*, outfit 306:2 (Autumn 1975): 52–57.
24. D.B. Sealey, "A New Lifestyle Develops," chap. 2 in *The Metis: Canada's Forgotten Peoples*, ed. D.B. Sealey and Antoine S. Lussier (Winnipeg: Manitoba Metis Federation Press, 1975), pp. 13–30.
    Guillaume Charette, *Vanishing Spaces: Memories of Louis Goulet (Memoirs of a Prairie Metis)*, trans. Ray Ellenwood (Winnipeg: Editions Bois-Brûlés, 1980), pp. 77–78.
25. Ray, *Indians*, p. 205.
26. Donald Wayne Moodie, "The St. Albert Settlement: A Study in Historical Geography," (M.A. thesis, University of Alberta, 1965), p. 22.
27. Canby, "The Search," p. 342.
28. G. Graham-Cumming, "Health of the Original Canadians, 1867–1967," *Medical Services Journal* (February 1967), p. 118.
29. Ray, *Indians*, pp. 106, 187–190.
30. John Palliser, *The Journals, Detailed Reports, and Observations Relative to the Exploration* (London: G.E. Eyre and W. Spottiswoode, 1863), p. 200, quoted in Ray, *Indians*, p. 291.
31. Hugh Dempsey, *Crowfoot* (Edmonton: Hurtig, 1972), pp. 60–61.
32. A graphic account of the arrival of the whisky traders is contained in Paul Sharp, *Whoop-Up Country* (Norman: University of Oklahoma Press, 1973), pp. 40–54.
33. Dempsey, *Crowfoot*, pp. 74, 76.
34. Father Scollen quoted in Dempsey, *Indians*, p. 13.
35. Dempsey, *Crowfoot*, p. 81.
36. John Taylor, "Two Views on the Meaning of Treaties Six and Seven," in *The Spirit of the Alberta Indian Treaties*, ed. Richard Price (Toronto: Butterworth, 1979), p. 13.
37. Mandelbaum, *Plains Cree*, p. 42; Edward Athenakew, *Voices of the Plains Cree* (Toronto: McClelland and Stewart, 1973), p. 85.
38. "Extract of a Despatch — W.J. Christie, Esq., Chief Factor to Lieut. Gov. Archibald, bearing date, Edmonton House, 13th April, 1871, in Alexander Morris, *The Treaties of Canada with the Indians* (Toronto: Belfords Clarke, 1880), p. 171.
39. Taylor, "Views," p. 40.
40. The Treaties at Forts Carlton and Pitt, Number Six, in Morris, *Treaties*, p. 352. For an interesting discussion of native title by an Alberta Indian lawyer, see LeRoy Little Bear's testimony to the Berger Commission, 26 June 1976, in *The Past and Future Land. An account of the Berger Inquiry into the Mackenzie Valley Pipeline*, ed. Martin O'Malley (Toronto: Peter Martin Associates, 1976), pp. 238–243.
41. Part of a speech delivered at an Indian Council at Fort Carlton, August 1884, Riel Papers in the Confidential Papers of the Department of Justice relative to the Trial of Louis Riel, PAC, quoted in George F.G. Stanley, *The Birth of Western Canada* (Toronto: University of Toronto Press, 1961. First published in 1936), pp. 275–276.
42. Bleasdell Cameron quoted in J.W. Grant MacEwan, *Portraits from the Plains* (Toronto: McGraw-Hill, 1971), pp. 103-104. See also Rudy Wiebe's sketch

of "Mistahimaskwa (Big Bear) in *Dictionary of Canadian Biography. Volume II (1881-1890)* (Toronto: University of Toronto Press, 1982), pp. 597–601; and also John L. Tobias, "Canada's Subjugation of the Plains Cree, 1879–1885," *Canadian Historical Review*, 64, 4 (1983): 514–548. Hugh Dempsey's *Big Bear — The End of Freedom* (Vancouver: Douglas & McIntyre, 1984) is the first full biography of this important chief.

43. Dempsey, *Crowfoot*, p. 86; Hugh Dempsey, *Red Crow* (Saskatoon: Western Producer Prairie Books, 1980), p. 98.

44. Lynn Hickey, "Summary of Elders' Interviews" (paper prepared for the Indian Association of Alberta) quoted in Taylor, "Views," p. 42. The informants vary in terms of actual depth of the soil surrendered, but agree that it was from six inches to two feet.

45. Taylor, "Views," p. 44.

46. Father C. Scollen to Lieutenant Colonel A.G. Irvine, 13 April 1879, no. 14924 in the Indian Affairs Archives, Ottawa, quoted in Dempsey, *Crowfoot*, p. 105.

47. Dempsey, *Red Crow*, p. 98; Dempsey, *Crowfoot*, pp. 93–107.

48. Interview with Many Guns by Hanks, about 1939, quoted in Dempsey, *Crowfoot*, p. 102.

49. Lieutenant Governor Laird quoted in the Toronto *Globe*, 4 October 1877, printed in Morris, *Treaties*, p. 262.

50. Stanley, *Birth*, pp. 224–225.

51. *Ibid.*, p. 235.

52. John Tobias' article, "Protection, Civilization, Assimilation: An Outline History of Canada's Indian Policy," *Western Canadian Journal of Anthropology*, 6,2 (1976): 13-30, reprinted in *As Long as the Sun Shines and Water Flows*, ed. Ian A.L. Getty and Antoine S. Lussier (Vancouver: University of British Columbia Press, 1983), pp. 39-55, provides an overview of Canadian Indian Policy. George F.G. Stanley's, "As Long as the Sun Shines and Water Flows: An Historical Comment" in *Sun*, eds. Getty and Lussier, pp. 1–28 is also very helpful.

53. A short summary of Crowfoot's life is contained in Hugh Dempsey's article on the Blackfoot Chief in vol. 11 of the *Dictionary of Canadian Biography* (Toronto: University of Toronto, 1982), "Isapo-Muxika (Crowfoot)," pp. 442–445.

54. See the historian Robert Page's testimony at the Berger Inquiry, Yellowknife, 27 April 1976, reprinted in Martin O'Malley, *The Past and Future Land* (Toronto: Peter Martin Associates Limited, 1976), pp. 55–68. See also Hugh Dempsey's article on the impact of the CPR on the Plains Indian in *CPR West: The Iron Road and the Making of a Nation*, ed. Hugh A. Dempsey (Vancouver: Douglas and McIntyre, 1984).

55. Big Bear opposed the taking up of arms, but once trouble broke out he stayed with his people. See Rudy Wiebe, "Mistahimaskwa (Big Bear)," in vol. 11 of the *Dictionary of Canadian Biography*, pp. 599–600. For a new look at the rebellion consult: Bob Beal and Rod Macleod, *Prairie Fire: The 1885 Northwest Rebellion* (Edmonton: Hurtig, 1984). Older studies include: G.F.G. Stanley, *The Birth of Western Canada. A History of the Riel Rebellions* (Toronto: University of Toronto Press, 1961; originally published in 1936), and Desmond Morton, *The Last War Drum: The North West Campaign of 1885* (Toronto: Hakkert, 1972).

56. For the contribution of the Roman Catholic missionaries among the Cree of central Alberta consult, E.O. Drouin, *Hobbema. Ongoing Indian Mission of Central Alberta* (Edmonton: Imprimerie Laflamme, 1969), pp. 16–18, and C.

Scollen, o.m.i., letter dated Bear's Hill Reserve, 20 April 1885, Oblate Archives, Provincial Archives of Alberta; and for the Methodists, James Woodsworth, *Thirty Years in the Canadian North-West* (Toronto: McClelland, Goodchild and Stewart, 1917), pp. 94–97. See also the chapter by John W. Grant, "Range to Reservation," in his *Moon of Wintertime, Missionaries and the Indians of Canada in Encounter Since 1534* (Toronto: University of Toronto Press, 1984), pp. 143–166, which reviews missionary activity in the West.

57. Dempsey, *Crowfoot*, pp. 164–172, 189–193. Dempsey, *Red Crow*, pp. 149-155.
58. Jack Dunn, "The Alberta Field Force of 1885" (M.A. thesis, University of Calgary, 1979), pp. 62–63, 68–69.
59. F.C. Cornish, "The Blackfeet and the Rebellion, " *Alberta Historical Review*, 6(1958):21. Jas. W. Morrow, "Early History of Southern Alberta, " Lethbridge *Herald*, 15 Aug. 1931, p. 3.
60. John Jennings, "The Reservation System and Deteriorating Relations," chap. VII in " The North West Mounted Police and Indian Policy, 1874-96" (Ph.D. diss., University of Toronto, 1979), pp. 273–328. Archibald Oswald MacRae, *History of the Province of Alberta* (n.p.p.: The Western Canada History Co., 1912), p. 430.
61. Descriptions of Indian life at the turn of the century appear in Hugh Dempsey, *Charcoal's World* (Saskatoon: Western Producer Prairie Books, 1978), pp. 9, 13, and John Snow, *These Mountains are our Sacred Places* (Toronto: Samuel Stevens, 1977), pp. 50–64.
62. For an account of a Plains Metis woman in Alberta who did adjust consult: Jock Carpenter, *Fifty Dollar Bride, Marie Rose Smith—A Chronicle of Metis Life in the 19th Century* (Sydney, B.C.: Gray's Publishing Ltd., 1977).
63. Alvin Toffler, *Future Shock* (Toronto: Bantam Books, 1971. First published 1970), pp. 11–12.
64. There are two good secondary accounts of the making of Treaty Eight: Richard Daniel, "The Spirit and Terms of Treaty Eight," in The *Spirit of the Alberta Indian Treaties*, ed. Richard Price, pp. 47–100. Rene Fumoleau, *As Long As This Land Shall Last. A History of Treaty 8 and Treaty 11, 1870-1939* (Toronto: McClelland and Stewart, 1973), pp. 46–104.
65. Fumoleau, *Land*, pp. 19, 100.
66. Charles Mair, *Through the Mackenzie Basin: A Narrative of the Athabasca and Peace River Expedition of 1899* (Toronto: W. Briggs, 1908), p. 51.
67. M. Zaslow, *The Opening of the Canadian North, 1870–1914* (Toronto: McClelland and Stewart, 1971), p. 225.
68. For a Metis viewpoint on scrip consult: Anderson and Anderson, *Metis*, pp. 98–99; and Sawchuk *et al.*, *Metis Land Rights*, pp. 112–115, 137–140. Another viewpoint appears in: Thomas Flanagan, "The Half-Breed Land Grant," chap. 3 in *Riel and the Rebellion* (Saskatoon: Western Producer Prairie Books, 1983), pp. 58–74.
69. D.J. Hall, "The Half-Breed Claims Commission," *Alberta History*, 25, 2 (Spring 1977): 1–8.
70. For a short survey of the experience of the Metis at St. Paul see: Anderson and Anderson, *Metis*, pp. 101–103; and also, George F.G. Stanley, "Alberta's Half-breed Reserve. Saint-Paul-des-Métis, 1896-1909," in *The Other Natives. The/Les Metis*, vol. 2 (Winnipeg: Manitoba Metis Federation Press, 1978), pp. 75-108. As Stanley points out, there was a boarding school at St. Paul from 1903–1905, the year it burnt down, pp. 93, 96.

Sawchuk et al., "St. Paul des Métis: The First Metis Colony, 1896–1909," in Metis Land Rights, pp. 159–186.

71. These difficult years have been recorded by the following Western Canadian Indian writers: Edward Ahenakew, Voices of the Plains Cree (Toronto: McClelland and Stewart, 1973); Joe Dion, My Tribe the Crees (Calgary: Glenbow Museum, 1979); Mike Mountain Horse, My People The Bloods (Calgary: Glenbow-Alberta Institute, 1979); John Snow, These Mountains are our Sacred Places (Toronto: Samuel Stevens, 1977). There is a very good study of conditions on the Blackfoot reserve in the twentieth century. See: Lucien M. Hanks and Jane Richardson Hanks, Tribe Under Trust. A Study of the Blackfoot Reserve of Alberta (Toronto: University of Toronto Press, 1950). G. Graham-Cumming provides the best overview of the Indians' health problems in "Health of the Original Canadians, 1867–1967," Medical Services Journal, Canada (February 1967), pp. 115–163. See also, Tom Philip, "Pioneering Peacer Medicine. How Dr. Mary Percy Jackson Conquered the Wild and Healed the Sick," Alberta Report (26 December 1983), pp. 30–33 (My thanks to Nellie Carwell for this reference).

72. P.E. Breton, o.m.i., Hobbema. Une florissante mission indienne de l'Ouest (Edmonton: Editions de l'Ermitage, 1962), p. 35.

73. Hugh Dempsey, "The Place of Indians in Western Canadian History," mimeographed, p. 12. Text prepared in 1968.

74. "Indians Not Vanishing in West," Regina Leader, 19 Apr. 1927.

75. Rev. Charles Herbert Huestis, The Indian Problem in Alberta (n.p.p.: n.p., 1911), p. 5.

76. R.J. Carney, "Making Indian Children Stand Erect," The ATA Magazine, March 1978, pp. 7–12.

77. Price, "Land Claims," p. 20. For two specific studies of land surrenders see: Kenneth James Tyler, "A tax-eating proposition: the history of the Passpasschase Indian Reserve" (M.A. thesis, University of Alberta, 1979). David Lupul, "The Bobtail Land Surrender," Alberta History, 26,1 (Winter 1978): 29–39.

78. Hugh A. Dempsey, "One Hundred Years of Treaty Seven," in One Century Later, ed. Ian A.L. Getty and Donald B. Smith (Vancouver: University of British Columbia Press, 1978), p. 27.

79. James Dempsey, "The Indians and World War One," Alberta History, 31,3 (Summer 1983), pp. 3–7. The Parish Record of St. Paul's Church and School, Blood Reserve, Macleod, Alberta, 10,5 (May 1923). Mountain Horse, The Bloods, pp. 143–144. Duncan Campbell Scott, "The Canadian Indians and the Great World War," in Canada and the Great World War, vol. 3 (Toronto: United Publishers, 1919), pp. 312–313, 322–324.

80. Buffalo Child Long Lance, "Indians of the Northwest and West Canada," The Mentor, March 1924, p. 6.

81. Dudley McClean, "Sun Dance," Calgary Herald, 25 August 1923.

82. Dempsey, "Treaty Seven," p. 28.

83. Diamond Jenness, "Canada's Indians Yesterday. What of Today?" Canadian Journal of Economics and Political Science, 20 (1954): 96–97. Dempsey, "Treaty Seven," p. 28.

84. Stan Cuthand, "The Native Peoples in the 1920s and 1930s," in One Century Later, ed. Getty and Smith, pp. 31–35.

85. Dempsey, Indian Tribes, p. 70; Fumoleau, Land, pp. 250–254, 288–292.

86. For a biographical sketch of Joe Dion see Hugh Dempsey's introduction to Dion's book, My Tribe The Crees, pp. v–viii, and Dion's comments on the

Metis, pp. 182–187. Joe Dion's father was a French-speaking Metis, Gustav Dion, and his mother, Mary, a Cree Indian, L.G. Smith, Registrar, Dept. of Indian Affairs to Donald B. Smith, dated Ottawa, 14 February 1983.

87. Anderson and Anderson, *Metis*, pp. 104–105. Murray Dobbin, The *One-And-A-Half Men. The Story of Jim Brady and Malcolm Norris. Metis Patriots of the 20th Century* (Vancouver: New Star Books, 1981), pp. 58–65.

88. Dobbin *One-And-A-Half Men*, p. 77.

89. Anderson and Anderson, *Metis*, pp. 107–109. Sawchuk *et al.*, *Metis Land Rights*, pp. 187, 196.

90. Sealey, *The Metis*, p. 153; Paul Bilodeau, "Metis activism faltering, says former Metis leader," Kainai *News*, November 1, 1983. Sheila Pratt and Wendy Smith, "Metis will be given clear title to lease lands," Calgary *Herald*, June 1, 1985. Government of Alberta News Release, May 31, 1985.

91. Murray Dobbin's *One-And-A-Half Men* provides a complete account of Norris' life.

92. John Laurie "Mr. Johnny Callihoo. 'One of the *Greatest Indians* ever born in Alberta,' " *The Camsell Arrow*, 9,3 (September/October 1955): 9–11.

93. Dobbin, *One-And-A-Half Men*, pp. 145–161. Carney, "Indian children," p. 12.

94. A useful summary of the development of the Canadian social welfare system is, Irving J. Goffman, "Canadian Social Welfare Policy," in *Contemporary Canada*, ed. Richard H. Leach (Toronto: University of Toronto Press, 1968), pp. 191–224. A very valuable survey is provided by James Frideres, "Government Policies and Programs Relating to Urban People of Indian Ancestry in Alberta," in *The Dynamics of Government Programs for Urban Indians in the Prairie Provinces*, ed. Raymond Breton and Gail Grant (Montreal: The Institute for Research on Public Policy, 1984), pp. 321-518.

95. Siggner and Locatelli, "Overview," p. 5.

96. "Blood Education Control Closer than Ever," Kainai *News*, 1 June 1982, p. 19. John Eisenberg and Harold Troper, "Blue Quills: Community Control," in *Native Survival* (Toronto: Ontario Institute for Studies in Education, 1973), p. 68.

97. Statement by Elders at the Alberta Language Seminar, February 1974, quoted in *Selected Indian Perceptions of Human Resource Development on the Stoney Indian Reserve at Morley and the Cree Four-Band Reserve at Hobbema* (Calgary: Office of Educational Development, Native Student Services, University of Calgary, 1975), p. 3.

98. "Jim Gladstone of Blood Reserve is Named to Senate," Calgary *Herald*, Feb. 1, 1958; "First woman Chief Elected in Alberta," *Indian News*, 8,1 (March 1965), p. 7.

99. Hugh Dempsey, "75 years of callousness, neglect and short-sighted policies," Calgary *Herald*, 28 Aug. 1980, K18. Hugh Dempsey, "The centennial of Treaty Seven and why Indians think whites are knaves," *Canadian Geographical Journal*, 95,2 (October/November 1977), p. 19.

100. Dunnery Best, "Jacuzzis for some Indians — but not all," *The Financial Post*, 4 Oct. 1980.

101. Richard Daniel, "The Spirit and Terms of Treaty Eight," in Price, *Spirit of the Alberta Indian Treaties*, p. 92.

   In October 1975 these landless Indians living in seven isolated communities in northern Alberta, filed a caveat, claiming legal interest to an area close to 25,000 square miles, lying between the Athabasca and Peace Rivers. It had become apparent by early 1977 (after a decision in the Supreme Court of Canada on a caveat case in the Northwest Territories) that Alberta might lose in Court. At this point the provincial government moved to pass retroactive legislation through Bill 29. Section 141(1) of this bill stated that, "No caveat may be registered which affects land for which no certificate of title has been issued." As the Isolated Communities' caveat related to essentially unpatented Crown land, their court battle was legislated out of existence. While opposition arose both inside and outside the provincial legislature to this bill (which had retroactively removed the Indians' legal basis for filing the caveat), the government did not alter the legislation. Price, "Land Claims," pp. 181, 219.

102. I have taken this summary from two letters and a short summary prepared by the Edmonton Interchurch Committee on the North: R.M. Connelly, Director, Specific Claims Branch, Office of Native Claims, Ottawa, dated 21 March 1984 to Moira Hutchinson, Associate Researcher, Taskforce on the Churches and Corporate Responsibility, Toronto. The photostat of the letter was supplied to me by Fred Lennarson of Edmonton. Milt Pahl, Minister Responsible for Native Affairs, dated Edmonton, 20 June 1984, to Donald B. Smith. A short summary of the Lubicon Lake Crees' claim has been produced by the Edmonton Interchurch Committee on the North, 10765–98 Street, Edmonton, Alberta, T5H 2P2, November 1984.

103. Douglas Martin, "Caught Up in an Oil Rush, a Canadian Tribe Reels," New York *Times*, 5 June 1984, p. A2.

104. For the full background on their claim see the transcripts (over 6,500 pages), Court of Appeal of Alberta, on appeal from the Court of Queen's Bench of Alberta, available in the Archives of the Glenbow Museum, ask for the Lubicon Lake Cree Papers. Journalist John Goddard surveys the Crees' case in "Last Stand of the Lubicon," *Equinox*, May/June 1985, pp. 67–76.

105. H.B. Hawthorn, *A Survey of the Contemporary Indians of Canada*, 2 vols. (Ottawa: Indian Affairs Branch, 1966), I:147–148. Detailed studies of northern native groups, such as Patricia Alice McCormack's Ph.D. thesis (in anthropology), "How the North (West) was Won: Development and Underdevelopment in the Fort Chipewyan Region" (University of Alberta, 1984), are badly needed.

106. Indian Association of Alberta, "Economic Development and the Spirit of the Treaties," p. 1. Mimeographed, n.d.

107. Eugene Steinhauer, President of the IAA, quoted in a Newsrelease dated 17 February 1981, "Treaty Indians of Alberta Parley with Hon. H.A. 'Bud' Olson Concerning Economic Development of the Reserves," mimeographed, available from the IAA.

108. "Reserve Unemployment, Economic Control is the Way Out," *Elbow Drums. Calgary Friendship Centre*, March 1981. Consult also: Jack Beaver, *To Have What Is One's Own* (Ottawa: National Indian Socio-Economic Development Committee, 1979), and "Economic Development and the Spirit of the Treaties," Treaty and Aboriginal Rights Research of the IAA, mimeographed, no date.

109. The land claims in Alberta normally fall into one of the three basic categories:

a) Aboriginal land claims based on unextinguished Indian use and occupancy (for example, the case of the Lubicon Lake band).

b) Land entitlement claims based on the treaty formula of one square mile per family of five (several Alberta bands claim that the reserves allotted them were based on incorrect estimates of their population in the year of the treaty—or the year of the reserve survey).

c) Reserve land surrender claims based on improper or illegal reserve surrenders (the Peigans have such a claim). See Price, "Land Claims," p. 9.

Land claim cases involve both the federal and the provincial governments, as well as the respective Indian band. The province must agree to make the land available. Unfortunately Indian land claims are very low on the Alberta government's list of priorities, and very few have been settled in the province. Price, "Land Claims," p. 153. Linda Goyette, "Indians' Budget Permits No New Projects," Kainai *News*, May 1, 1982.

110. Siggner and Locatelli, "Overview," pp. 45, 47. The retention of students refers to students currently in Grade XII, who were enrolled in Grade II ten years earlier. Committee on Tolerance and Understanding. "Native Education in Alberta," Discussion Paper #2 (June 1984). The Northland school division has a "drop out rate of close to 85 percent," and in the division 95 percent of the 2400 students are native (p. 9). Hence, one out of six native students does not enrol in high school.

111. Siggner and Locatelli, "Overview," p. 13.

112. Unfortunately the story of those who have not adjusted is much better known than that of those who have. See Hugh Brody's study of Indians on Skid Row in a Western Canadian city, *Indians on Skid Row. The Role of Alcohol and Community in the Adaptive Process of Indian Urban Migrants* (Ottawa: Information Canada, 1971).

113. Joan Ryan, *Wall of Words. The Betrayal of the Urban Indian* (Toronto: Peter Martin Associates, 1978), p. 109.

114. Ryan, *Wall of Words*: reviews the experience of urban Indians in Calgary.

115. Siggner and Locatelli, "Overview," p. 47.

116. George K. Jarvis and Menno Boldt, "Native Indian Mortality: A Prospective Study," mimeographed, 1979.

"Suicide, Sociologists find Alberta Indians Killing Themselves at Five Time National Rate," Calgary *Herald*, 9 Dec. 1981, C12.

James H. Gray, "Chapter Eight, Where the Solution is the Problem," *Bacchanalia Revisited. Western Canada's Boozy Skid to Social Disaster.* (Saskatoon: Western Producer Prairie Books, 1982), pp. 116–136.

117. Statement of the Government of Canada on Indian Policy, 1969. Presented to the First Session of the Twentieth Parliament by the Honourable Jean Chretien, Minister of Indian Affairs and Northern Development. For a review of the background to the "White Paper," read Sally M. Weaver, *Making Canadian Indian Policy. The Hidden Agenda, 1968-1970* (Toronto: University of Toronto Press, 1981).

118. Dennis Bell, "Wild Radical or New Messiah, Harold Cardinal," *Indians Without Tipis*, ed. D. Bruce Sealey and Verna Kirkness (Vancouver: William Clare, 1973), pp. 242–244.

Cardinal outlines his position in *The Unjust Society. The Tragedy of Canada's Indians* (Edmonton, M.G. Hurtig, 1969). For the viewpoint of William I.C. Wuttunee, an Indian lawyer in Calgary who supported the government's position, see *Ruffled Feathers* (Calgary: Bell Books, 1971). Cardinal takes a more moderate stance in his second book, *The Rebirth of Canada's Indians* (Edmonton: Hurtig, 1977).

119. Price, "Land Claims," pp. 39–41.

120. *Ibid.*, pp. 49–50.

121. Indian Chiefs of Alberta, *Citizens Plus* (Edmonton: Indian Association of Alberta, 1970), p. 8.

122. Some Indian critics of the federal government argue that it is currently—

contrary to its promise—implementing many aspects of its "White Paper." Consult: Marie Smallface Marule, "The Canadian Government's Termination Policy: From 1969 to the Present Day," in *One Century Later*, ed. Getty and Smith, pp. 103–116.

For a recent survey of the operation of the Department of Indian Affairs see: J. Rick Ponting and Roger Gibbins, *Out of Irrelevance: A Socio-political introduction to Indian Affairs in Canada* (Toronto: Butterworths, 1980), pp. 1–192.

123. Sawchuk *et al.*, *Metis Land Claims*, pp. 66, 73, 110, 207, 246. My thanks to Ralph Sabey of Edmonton for pointing out the oil and gas issue. For a review of recent Metis history see: Murray J. Dobbin, "The Metis in Western Canada since 1945," in *The Making of the Modern West: Western Canada Since 1945*, ed. A.W. Rasporich (Calgary: Umiversity of Calgary Press, 1984), pp. 183–194.

124. Sealey, *The Metis*, pp. 143–158.

125. Kathryn Warden, " 'It's a man's world out there in Indian country,' " Calgary *Herald*, 29 Apr. 1980.

126. "Natives abandon sexist provision," Toronto *Globe*, 9 Apr. 1982.

"Gladue Opposes Munro's Stand on Indian Women's Rights," Kainai *News*, 1 May 1983. "Women to Regain Indian Status," *Globe*, 9 Mar. 1984.

127. Karen Large, "Alberta Bands Support AFN Split," Kainai *News*, 1 June 1984, p. 1.

128. Canada. Department of Indian Affairs, *Strengthening Indian Band Government* (Ottawa, 1982), quoted in House of Commons, Minutes of Proceedings of the Special Committee on Indian Self-Government, *Indian Self-Government in Canada* (Ottawa: Canadian Government Publishing Center, 1983), p. 17.

129. House of Commons, *Self-Government*, p. 41.

130. "Year of Decision. Native Rights to be Defined," Kainai *News*, 2 May 1982, p. 2.

131. "Rev. Fr. Lacombe is at Edmonton," Medicine Hat *News*, 20 Feb. 1908, p. 10. The text uses the old-fashioned term "Half breed" for which I have substituted "Metis."

Chapter Four

1. My thanks to Gratien Allaire of the Faculté Saint-Jean; Michel Boivin of the Bureau du Québec at Edmonton; Louiselle Daigneault, Directrice, Bureau de l'éducation, ACFA; Estelle Dansereau of the University of Calgary; Eloi DeGrâce then with the Provincial Archives of Alberta; Father Georges Durocher of the Faculté Saint-Jean; Gertrude Laing, a former Commissioner on the Royal Commission on Bilingualism and Biculturalism; Heather Lysons, Faculty of Education, University of Alberta; Ken Munro of the Department of History, University of Alberta; Alain Nogue, formerly Coordinateur en Education of the ACFA; for their help with the preparation of this essay. The opinions and any misunderstandings contained within are, of course, my responsibility. I am very grateful to: Joyce Woods, Marjorie McLean, and Nicole Tremblay-Julien, all of Calgary, for typing the several drafts of this article. Finally my thanks to Claudette Croteau for her assistance in the summer of 1979 with the preliminary research, and to all those members of the Franco-Albertan community in the Bonnyville and Falher areas that I interviewed in June and July 1979.

2. Father Lacombe to Archbishop Taché, 27 October 1887, Taché Papers quoted in M. Lupul, "Relations in Education between the State and the Roman Catholic Church in the Canadian North-West" (Ph.D. diss., Harvard University, 1963), p. 131.

3. For 1981 figures see: "Canada Update from the 1981 Census, 26 April 1983. Statistics Canada, pp. 3, 9.
   For 1971: La Fédération des Francophones hors Quebec Federation of Francophones outside Quebec. *The Heirs of Lord Durham. Manifesto of a Vanishing People,* trans. by Diane Norak (Toronto: Burns and MacEachern Limited, 1978), p. 24.

4. George F.G. Stanley, "French Settlement West of Lake Superior," *Transactions of the Royal Society of Canada,* vol. 48, ser. 3 (June 1954), p. 107. Allan R. Taylor, "Note Concerning Lakota Sioux Terms for White and Negro," *Plains Anthropologist,* 21 (1976), no. 71, p. 64. In Blackfoot the term is *nii?+sââpiikoan.*

5. Grace Lee Nute, *The Vovageur* (New York: D. Appleton, 1931), pp.13–14.

6. Benoît Brouillette, *La Pénétration du continent américain par les Canadiens-français 1763–1846* (Montreal: Fides, 1979. First published in 1939), pp. 75–76,79. Nute, *Voyageur,* p. 227

7. E.J. Hart, *Ambition and Reality. The French-speaking Community of Edmonton, 1795–1935* (Edmonton: Le salon d'histoire de la francophonie albertaine, 1980), p. 7.

8. George F.G. Stanley, "Marie-Anne Gaboury (Lagimodière)," *Dictionary of Canadian Biography,* vol. 10, 1871 to 1880 (Toronto: University of Toronto Press, 1972), pp. 296–297.

9. George F.G. Stanley, "French and English in Western Canada," in *Canadian Dualism. Studies of French-English Relations,* ed. Mason Wade (Toronto: University of Toronto Press, 1960), p. 314

10. Arthur J. Ray, *Indians in the Fur Trade* (Toronto: University of Toronto Press, 1974), p. 205.

11. Legal, Emile J. *Short Sketches of the History of the Catholic Churches and Missions in Central Alberta* (Edmonton: n.p., 1915), pp.9–12.
    Champagne, Joseph-Etienne. *Les missions catholiques dans l'ouest canadien (1818–1875)* (Ottawa: Editions des Etudes Oblates, 1949) pp. 65, 86–87.
    James G. MacGregor's *Father Lacombe* (Edmonton: Hurtig, 1975) is the most recent biography of the famous priest. The phrase the "Black-Robe Voyageur" comes from the title of Katherine Hughes' earlier study of Lacombe, published in 1911.

12. C.A. Dawson, *Group Settlement Ethnic Communities in Western Canada* (Toronto : Macmillan, 1936), p. 342.
    Donald Wayne Moodie, "The St.Albert Settlement: A Study in Historical Geography" (M.A. thesis, University of Alberta, 1965), pp.iii–iv.
    Emile Tardiff, *Saint Albert* (Edmonton: La Survivance Printing Limited, n.d.), pp. 10, 35, 37, 39.

13. Marcel Giraud, "The Western Metis after the Insurrecion," *Saskatchewan History* 9 (1956): 3–4.
    Joe Sawchuk, Patricia Sawchuk, Theresa Ferguson. *Metis Land Rights in Alberta: A Political History* (Edmonton: Metis Association of Alberta, 1981), p. 87.
    Thomas Flanagan, *Riel and the Rebellion. 1885 Reconsidered* (Saskatoon: Western Producer Prairie Books, 1983), pp. 41, 72–73.

14. George F.G. Stanley, "Alberta's Half-breed Reserve Saint-Paul-des-Métis,

1896–1909," in *The Other Natives. The/Les Metis*. vol. 2 (Winnipeg: Manitoba Metis Federation Press, 1978), pp. 75–108, particularly pp. 105–107.

15. Michel Mabru, "Les Francophones de l'Alberta," Université de Poitiers, 1978, thèse de troisième cycle, p. 56.

16. Denise Stocco, "French-Canadian Colonization in Alberta," Provincial Museum and Archives of Alberta (August 1973), p. 31.

17. Hart, *Ambition and Reality*, p. 18.

18. Hugh A. Dempsey, "Brisebois: Calgary's Forgotten Founder," in *Frontier Calgary*, ed. Anthony W. Rasporich and Henry C. Klassen (Calgary: McClelland and Stewart West, 1975): 28–40.
Max Foran and Heather MacEwan Foran, *Calgary, Canada's Frontier Metropolis* (n.p.p.: Windsor Publications, 1982), p.39.

19. John Hawkes, *The Story of Saskatchewan*, vol. 1 (Chicago: S.J. Clarke Publishing Company, 1924), p. 646.

20. The population estimate appears in Manoly R. Lupul, *The Roman Catholic Church and the North-West School Question* (Toronto: University of Toronto Press, 1974), p.3. Sir John A. Macdonald to Sir Adolphe Chapleau, 1888, cited in Eugene A. Forsey, "Languages and the Law," *Language and Society*, 2 (September 1980) : 20.

Macdonald's intentions as to the status of the French language in the West have been vigorously debated. Donald Creighton has argued that originally Macdonald did not wish to protect French in Manitoba and the Northwest: see his "John A. Macdonald, Confederation, and the Canadian West," *Historical and Scientific Society of Manitoba*, ser. 3, no. 23 (1966–67), reprinted in *Canadian History since Confederation*, ed. Bruce Hodgins and Robert Page (Georgetown: Irwin-Dorsey, 1979), pp.44–52. Ralph Heintzman takes the contrary view that the first governments of Manitoba and the Northwest Territories were established in the 'spirit of confederation'; "The Spirit of Confederation: Professor Creighton, Biculturalism, and the Use of History," *Canadian Historical Review*, 52 (1971): 245–275. D.J. Hall enters the debate essentially on Creighton's side. In his article, " 'The Spirit of Confederation': Ralph Heintzman, Professor Creighton, and the Bicultural Theory," *Journal of Canadian Studies* 9,4 (1974): 24–43 (reprinted in *History*, ed. Hodgins and Page, pp. 53–77). Basically Heintzman argues what was the position of the Macdonald-Cartier Conservatives in the Union of the Canadas in the 1850s, and Hall presents the viewpoint of the Clear Grits.

A fascinating development concerning French language rights in Alberta and Saskatchewan is the current court case of Yvon Lefebvre, a Franco-Albertan engineer. In 1981, Lefebvre contested the legality of the Northwest Territorial Assembly's elimination in 1892 of French from the legislature and the courts. He argues that the resolution never became law because it was not proclaimed by Joseph Royal, the Territories' French Canadian Lieutenant Governor. (An amendment in 1891 to the Northwest Territories Act required any resolution of the assembly to be embodied in a proclamation before becoming law.) This means, if Lefebvre's interpretation is held to be correct by the courts, that a person still has the right to a trial in either French or English in Alberta. The court case of the Franco-Albertan engineer, and a similar case in Saskatchewan, will probably reach the superior provincial courts in the near future. These cases parallel the struggle in Manitoba to restore French language rights in that province, denied in 1890.

For more information on the Lefebvre and Mercure cases in Saskatchewan see: Aileen McCabe, "French fight moves west," Calgary *Herald*, 17 Nov. 1981; Pat Crone, "Man demands French trial of $22 traffic ticket," Calgary *Herald*, 29 Nov. 1981; Pat Crone, "French rights battler had Legal training," Calgary *Herald*, 5 Dec. 1981; Emile Arcand, "Au conseil général 'Le cas Lefebvre,' " *Le Franco*, le 2 juin 1982; "Le cas Lefebvre revient au conseil général," *Le Franco*, le 1 juin 1983; and "En Saskatchewan, le statut du français," *Le Franco*, le 4 janvier 1984.

For the comments of the Bilingualism and Biculturalism Commission on this question see: The Report of the Royal Commission on Bilingualism and Biculturalism, vol. 1 (Ottawa: Queen's Printer, 1967), pp. 51–52, ". . . there seems to be some doubt as to the constitutionality of this abolition" (p. 51).

For a review of French Canada's position toward emigration westward, consult A.I. Silver, *The French-Canadian Idea of Confederation, 1864–1900* (Toronto: University of Toronto Press, 1982).

21. Charles Nolin quoted in the Regina *Leader*, 26 Jan. 1892, quoted in Lewis H. Thomas, "Government and Politics in Manitoba and the Northwest Territories," in *The Prairie West to 1905*, ed. Lewis G. Thomas (Toronto: Oxford University Press, 1975), pp. 116–117.

For a short review of the schools question in the Northwest Territories see: Keith A. McLeod, "Politics, Schools and the French Language, 1881–1931," in *Shaping the Schools of the Canadian West*, ed. David C. Jones *et al.* (Calgary: Detselig, 1979), p. 63. The article originally appeared as a chapter in *Politics in Saskatchewan*, ed. Norman Ward and Duff Spafford (Don Mills: Longmans, 1968).

22. Stocco, "Colonization," p. 2
Mabru, "Francophones," pp. 38–39.

23. *L'Ouest Canadien*, 22 juin 1899, quoted in Hart, *Ambition and Reality*, p. 24.

24. Roger Motut, "The French Fact in Alberta," address given at the University of Calgary, 1 February 1978, in the Quebec and Confederation lecture series. Stocco, "Colonization," pp. 17, 30, 34, 35, 45, 50, 52, 54, 57.

25. *Ibid.*, pp. 16, 19, 30, 25.

26. *Ibid.*, pp. 24, 26; *Histoire de Girouxville History*, ed. Lucie St. André, vol. 1, 1911–1930 (Altona, Manitoba: Société historique de Girouxville, 1977), p. 13.

27. Mabru, "Francophones," p. 42

28. *Ibid.*, p.43.
Stocco, "Colonization," p. 7.

29. Robert Painchaud, "Les origines des peuplements de langue française dans l'Ouest canadien, 1870–1920: mythes et réalités," *Mémoires de la Société royale du Canada*, série 4, tome 13 (1975), p. 112.

30. Canada, Bureau of Statistics, *Census of the Prairie Provinces*, 1916, p. 222, quoted in Hart, *Ambition and Reality*, p. 78.

31. Stanley, "French and English," pp. 327, 329, 331.; *Soixante-cinq Années de Luttes* éd. René Rottiers (Regina: L'Association Culturelle Franco-Canadienne de la Saskatchewan, 1977), pp. 5–19.

32. "Ses écrits resteront," *Le Franco*, le 23 janvier 1981. "La littérature d'expression française en Alberta—Les romans," *Le Franco*, 16 novembre 1979.
E.K. Brown, "A Fine Novel of the West," Winnipeg *Free Press*, 27 Sept. 1947, in E.K. Brown, *Responses and Evaluations: Essays on Canada* (Toronto: McClelland and Stewart, 1977), p. 292.
Donatien Frémont, *Les Français dans l'ouest canadien* (Saint Boniface: Les Editions du Blé, 1980. First published in 1959), p. 135.

33. Mabru, "Francophones," p.52; Howard Palmer informed me of the large

number of Belgians in the Saint Albert area. For information on René Richard, see Jean-Guy Quenneville, "Deux Personnalités francophones de l'ouest," in *L'état de la recherche et de la vie française dans l'ouest canadien* (Saint-Boniface: CEFCO, 1982), pp. 47–50.

34. Stocco, "Colonization," p.35.
Sheilaugh S. Jameson, "The Story of Trochu," *Alberta Historical Review*, 9,4 (Autumn 1961), pp.1–9.

35. Lettre du Rév. Père H. Voisin á Msgr. H.J. O'Leary, Red Deer, le 14 octobre 1924. Copy in library, Faculté Saint-Jean, Edmonton.
Frémont, *Les Français*, pp.131–132.
Stocco, "Colonization," p.44.

36. Frémont, *Les Français*, p. 131.
Stocco, "Colonization," p. 55; A.W. Rasporich, "Utopian Ideals and Community Settlements in Western Canada 1880–1914," in *The Canadian West*, ed. Henry Klassen (Calgary: Comprint Publishing Company, 1977), pp. 51–52.

37. Marcel Sexé, *Two Centuries of Fur-Trading 1723–1923. Romance of the Revillon Family* (Paris: Draeger Frères, 1923), pp. 75, 81–83.
Stocco, "Colonization," pp. 15, 33.

38. Jack Peach, "Looking Backward. Mission District was once the French Quarter of Calgary," Calgary *Herald*, 9 Aug. 1980.
Robert Stamp, "French and Catholic," *Calgary Magazine*, May 1980, pp. 68–70, 86–89.
Max Foran, *Calgary* (Toronto: Jack Lorimer, 1978), p. 178.
Stanley, "French and Engish," p. 345.

39. Hart, *Ambition and Reality*, pp. 29–32, 52, 78. The successors of *L'Ouest canadien* included: *Le Courrier de l'Ouest* (1905–1916); *Le Progrès* (1909–1913); *L'Etoile de Saint Albert* (1912–1914); *Le Progrès albertain* (1914–1915); *L'Union* (1917–1929); *La Survivance* (1928–1967), now published as *Le Franco* (formerly *Le Franco-Albertain*).

40. *Ibid.*, pp. 57–58.

41. Motut, "The French Fact," p. 8. Robert Choquette, "Problèmes de moeurs et de discipline ecclésiastique: les catholiques des Prairies canadiennes de 1900 à 1930," *Histoire Sociale/Social History*, 8 (1975), pp. 108–113.
Personal information, Eloi DeGrâce, Provincial Archives of Alberta, 12 Nov. 1981.

42. Hart, *Ambition and Reality*, p. 48.

43. *Ibid.* pp. 47–52. The goal of the *ACJC* is quoted on p. 49.

44. *Ibid.*, pp. 39, 52, 65–67. See also André M. Déchene, "La participation des Canadiens-Français à la vie politique de l'Alberta," in *Aspects du passé franco-albertain*, éd. A. Trottier, K.J. Munro, G. Allaire (Edmonton: Le Salon d'histoire de la francophonie albertaine, 1980), pp. 9–20.

45. Hart, *Ambition and Reality*, pp. 69–72, 118.

46. Choquette, "Problèmes," p.103.

47. Gilles Boileau, "L'homme et le sol chez les Canadiens-français de Rivière-la-Paix," *Revue de géographie de Montréal*, 20 (1966): 11–12.

48. Mabru, "Francophones," p. 40.

49. Choquette, "Problèmes," pp. 102–103.

50. Robert Choquette, "John Thomas McNally et l'érection du diocèse de Calgary," *Revue de l'Université d'Ottawa*, 45 (1975), pp. 406, 411, 414–415.

51. Hart, *Ambition and Reality*, p. 99.

52. *Ibid.*, pp. 117–120.

53. Hart, *Ambition and Reality*, pp. 122–123.

Déchêne, "Participation," in *Aspects*, éd. A. Trottier *et al.*, p.15.

J.A. Irving, *The Social Credit Movement in Alberta* (Toronto: University of Toronto Press, 1959), pp. 215–216.

54. Hart, *Ambition and Reality*, pp. 98, 109, 120, 125–126, 128.

55. *Ibid.*, pp. 87–90.

56. The exact passage reads in French: "Détruire le complexe d'infériorité qui trop souvent existe chez les Canadiens-français de l'Alberta comme d'ailleurs chez les groupes minoritaires." Roger Motut, ACFA *50 ans d'histoire* (Edmonton: Le Secrétariat de l'ACFA, 1976), p. 5.

57. Hermas Bastien, *Le bilingualisme au Canada* (Montréal, 1938), pp. 128–129, quoted in O. Silla, "Pour une sociologie de l'éducation bilingue des minorités franco-canadiennes," *Projet de recherche. Ecole Bilingue ou Unilingue pour les Franco-Albertains?*, 2 vols., éd. Ousmane Silla (Edmonton: n.p., 1974), 2:40. Louis-Philippe Pigeon, " Impressions d'Alberta," *Le Canada Français*, 20 (juin 1933): 925.

58. Joseph P. Moreau, "Le Collège des Jésuites (1913–1942)" in *Aspects*, éd. A. Trottier *et al.*, pp. 21–34.

59. Royal Commission on Bilingualism and Biculturalism, bk. II, sec. 449, recommendation 19. *Report*, vol. 2, pp. 174–175.

60. Motut, *50 ans*, p. 17. In 1975 the Oblate Fathers sold the College to the University.

61. Stanley, "French and English," p. 348.
Motut, "The French Fact," p. 10.

62. "Mt. Rév. Henri Routhier," *The Canadian Who's Who*, vol. 12 (1970/72), p. 969.

63. Irving, *Social Credit*, p. 215.

64. *Canadian Parliamentary Guide* (1982/83), p. 335; Dave Bowes, "Dieppe Man New Speaker," *Red Deer Advocate*, 24 Sept. 1962; Arthur Blakely, *The Montreal Gazette*, "The forgotten Francophone," *Edmonton Journal*, 8 Dec. 1972; Robert Sheppard, "After 27 years in House, Lambert loses nomination," *Globe*, 14 Mar. 1984.

65. Motut, *50 ans*, p. 7.
Hart, *Ambition and Reality*, pp. 100–101.
Personal information, Father G. Durocher, Faculté Saint-Jean, Edmonton, 19 Nov. 1981.

66. The circulation of *La Survivance* appears in Guy Lacombe, "Paul-Emile Breton, journaliste français de l'Alberta," (Thèse de M.A., Université Laval, 1966), p. 60.
Motut, *50 ans*, pp. 15–16. The four *caisses populaires* in existence in 1939 had expanded to twelve by 1981.

67. High River *Times* reproduced in the *Edmonton Journal*, 30 Nov. 1944.

68. See also: "French-Canadian Bill Withdrawn in Legislature," Calgary *Herald*, 23 Mar. 1945.

69. *La Survivance*, 28 mars 1945 quoted in Céline Bélanger, "La Fondation de CHFA," trans. Nicole Clériot in Trottier *et al.*, *Aspects*, p. 142. In French the passage reads:
Certains de ceux qui se sont opposés avec violence à l'incorporation de l'ACFA ont dévoilé clairement leur pensée: ils ne veulent pas de radio française, car disent-ils cela empêcherait l'anglicisation de notre population et donc nuirait à l'unité du pays. Ceux qui parlent ainsi feraient bien de se rappeler une chose: c'est que nous sommes catholiques et français et, quoiqu'ils fassent, nous le resterons . . . Nous n'accepterons jamais d'être traités en étrangers dans notre propre maison, le Canada.

L'incident de la semaine dernière est une nouvelle preuve que nous devons compter sur nous-mêmes, d'abord et avant tout. Une fois de plus, on nous a prouvé que nous n'avons pas à nous fier aux déclarations de bonne entente, au fair play, aux principes britanniques et démocratiques de nos concitoyens anglo-saxons.

I have followed the English translation of the passage which appears on pp. 141–142 of *Glimpses of the Franco-Albertan Past*, ed. A. Trottier, K.J. Munro, G. Allaire (Edmonton: Le Salon d'histoire de la francophonie albertaine, 1981). *Glimpses* is the English translation of *Aspects*.

70. For a good review of the struggle to obtain a French language radio station consult: Bélanger, "La Fondation de CHFA," in Trottier *et al., Aspects,* pp. 123–146. A complete account of the establishment of French language radio stations in western Canada appears in Rossel Vien, *Radio française dans l'Ouest* (Montreal: Hurtubise HMH, 1977).

71. Robert S. Patterson, "Progressive Education: Impetus to Educational Change in Alberta and Saskatchewan," in *The New Provinces: Alberta and Saskatchewan, 1905–1980,* ed. Howard Palmer and Donald Smith (Vancouver: Tantalus Research Limited, 1980), p. 182.

72. Stanley, "French and English," pp. 337–338.

73. "Conférence du Président de l'ACFA donnée à la Chambre de Commerce d'Edmonton," *Le Franco,* 27 février 1981.

74. For a good review of this subject see: Richard Jones, "The Recent Evolution of French Canada," *The Quarterly of Canadian Studies,* 4, 2 (1976): 105–114.

75. A Brief prepared for submission to the Royal Commission on Bilingualism and Biculturalism by the Alberta Bilingual Teachers' Association. Manuscript 80.283, folder 22, Provincial Archives of Alberta, Edmonton.

76. Midge Nicholochuk, " Legal Aspects and Structure of the Department of Education," in *Project,* vol. 2, éd Silla, p. 44.

77. La Fédération des Francophones hors Québec, *The Heirs of Lord Durham,* p. 47.

78. Alain J. Nogue, "The Alberta Education Football. Can Alberta carry it?" Speech delivered at the Teachers' Convention, 23 Feb. 1979, mimeographed. Available from the ACFA, Edmonton.

79. William F. Mackey, "Safeguarding language in schools," *Language and Society,* 4 (Winter 1981): 13–14. "Ecole française à Edmonton. Les anglophones ne comprennent pas," *Le Franco,* le 7 décembre 1983, p.1. "L'Ecole française catholique à Edmonton," pamphlet. ACFA. *Les Etudiants franco-albertains et l'éducation au palier secondaire.* Edmonton: ACFA (juin 1984). Available from ACFA, Edmonton.

80. "Education Française plus accessible," *Le Franco,* 20 mai 1981. "Federal Government's new Constitutional Resolution," Calgary *Herald,* 20 Nov. 1981, p. 7. The quote is taken from the Canadian Charter of Rights and Freedoms, pt. 1, Clause 23,3b.

81. G. Pariseau, "Canadian Broadcasting Corporation—Radio-Canada, C.H.F.A. . . . La Voix Française de Radio-Canada en Alberta," in *Conference Proceedings of Bilingual School Administrators Seminar* (Edmonton: Faculté Saint-Jean, 1978), p. 126.

82. Mabru, "Francophones," p. 179.

83. J. Boucher, "Canadian Broadcasting Corporation—Radio-Canada. The Role of French Television in a Bilingual Education System," in *Conference Proceedings,* p. 123. Mabru, "Francophones," p. 188.

84. Robert Painchaud, "The Franco-Canadian Communities of Western Canada since 1945," in *Eastern and Western Perspectives,* ed. David Jay Bercu-

son and Philip A. Buckner (Toronto: University of Toronto Press, 1981): 4–6.

85. Alberta Education, "Le fait français en Alberta (septième année)," in *French Canadian Culture/La culture canadienne–française,* interim edition (1979), pp. 4–5.

86. Jack Spearman, "As a businessman, J. Louis Lebel has something to offer new post," Calgary *Herald,* 9 Dec. 1978, E27. "Jean-Louis Lebel à Dome Canada," *Le Franco,* le 26 janvier 1983. "The 'Doc' sells out Allarco," *Alberta Report,* 1 Aug. 1980.

87. Mabru,"Francophones," p. 98.

88. Luce Bosé, "Est-il possible de vivre en français à Edmonton," *Le Franco,* 25 janvier 1980.

89. St. John's United Church, "Pastoral Charge of Dr. Duclos, 1916–1930: His Remarkable Experiences at Bonnyville and Cold Lake in fourteen years," mimeographed manuscript. Provincial Archives of Alberta, Edmonton.

90. Lacombe, "Breton," pp. 27, 81–90.

91. Painchaud, "Franco-Canadian Communities," pp. 10–12.

92. Hart, *Ambition and Reality,* p. 135.

93. "Editorial. Venir en aide aux nouveaux arrivés francophones," *Le Franco,* le 14 mars 1980. Christian Côté, "Les Québécois, un oiseau migrateur?" *Le Franco,* 28 novembre 1980.

94. Diane Gallager-McVey, "La population francophone albertaine a augmenté," *Le Franco,* le 1 septembre 1982.

95. Boucher, "French Television" in *Conference Proceedings,* p. 124.

96. Wayne Jackson, "Ethnicity and Areal Organization among French Canadians in the Peace River District, Alberta" (M.A, thesis, University of Alberta, 1970), p. 115.

97. Alain J. Nogue. Notes for Speech given at the Symposium on Bilingual Education in Calgary, on 22 Apr. 1978. Mimeographed, p. 4. Available from the ACFA, Edmonton.
   In the past both the Franco-Albertans' level of education and their personal income have been below the provincial average, see La Fédération des Francophones hors Québec, *The Heirs of Lord Durham,* pp. 33, 35.

98. Nogue, "Alberta Education," p. 4.

99. My thanks to Gertrude Laing of Calgary for these observations, 2 Dec. 1983. " French as a Job Factor," Toronto *Globe,* 14 Nov. 1983.

100. "French Education Double in Alberta," Calgary *Herald,* 16 Sept. 1980.

101. Nogue, "Alberta Education," p. 4.

102. Richard Gwyn, *The Northern Magus* (Markham, Ontario: Paperjacks, 1981), p.225.

103. Dr. Ousmane Silla, *Ecole bilingue ou unilingue pour les franco-albertains?* The University of Alberta, 1974, cited in Association canadienne-française de l'Alberta, *Mémoire présenté au Comité de la Tolérance et de la Compréhension* (Edmonton: février 1984). The English translation appears in the English text of the submission. Both documents are available from the ACFA in Edmonton. For a good summary of several Calgary francophones' wishes, consult: Yvonne Zacharias, "Families fight to keep French alive," Calgary *Herald,* 4 Feb. 1984, Section D, p. 1.
   The assimilation rate of Franco-Albertans is currently at least 50 percent, and maybe as high as 70 percent, see—
   "L'école française: le débat continue," *Le Franco,* le 29 juin 1983. The memoir that "Le Comitè ad hoc en éducation de l'ACFA," presented to the

Roman Catholic School Board in Edmonton, 6 June 1983, is reprinted.

The estimate is made in this passage: "De fait, nous avons appris dernièrement que le taux d'assimilation des Franco-Albertans s'élève à plus de 51% et nous savons qu'il n'a pu se maintenir à ce taux déjà alarmant que parce qu' il y a eu une immigration massive de francophones venus d'autres provinces. Cela revient à dire que le taux réel d'assimilation des Franco-Albertains dépasse très probablement 70%." The statistic is based on the results of the federal census of 1981. See Linguistic Transfer Rates, A note to the Regional Director from Director, P.C.L.O., Government of Canada, Marcel Saint-Onge, 26 August 1983, supplied to the author by Louiselle Daigneault, Directrice du Bureau de l'éducation, ACFA, Edmonton.

Chapter Five

1. Eliane Allen Mitchell, "The Scot in the Fur Trade," *The Scottish Tradition in Canada,* ed. W. Sanford Reid, Generations Series (Toronto: McClelland and Stewart, 1976), pp. 27–49.
2. The phrase "custom of the country" is the euphemism commonly used in the Red River Settlement to describe a common-law relationship. "Scotch-Metis" has been used to distinguish the offspring of Scot-Indian marriages from those of French-Canadian-Indian or English-Indian marriages since the early 1800s in Red River. See Douglas Hill, *The Opening of the Canadian West* (Don Mills, Ont.: Longman Canada Ltd., 1967), chap. 2. Scotsmen are somewhat sensitive about the word used to designate their ethnic origin. 'Scotch' is a famous Scottish alcoholic drink and a 'Scot' is a person born in Scotland. 'Scotch' used to identify someone born in Scotland seems to have begun in Ontario among Scottish immigrants or the host society and tends to be widely used by the Canadian-born not of Scottish origin. John Kenneth Galbraith entitled his book on Scottish-Ontarians *The Scotch.*
3. *Census of Canada* 1901, 1911, 1921.
4. *Ibid.,* 1931, Table 24.
5. *Ibid.,* 1941, Table 26.
6. E. Luxton Interviews, Glenbow Alberta Institute (GAA); Eva Delday, *Between the Red Deer and the Bow* (Brooks and District Museum and Historical Society, 1975), pp. 111–112.
7. GAA, C.P.R. Immigration and Colonization Papers.
8. GAA, C.P.R. Immigration and Colonization Papers. Report by Father Mac-Donell.
9. Sims, "Clandonald: A Rural Catholic Community."
10. David Breen, "The Canadian West and the Ranching Frontier, 1875–1932" (Ph.D. diss. University of Alberta, 1972).
11. Interview with Mrs. Kay Mabb, Red Deer, July 1980.
12. Interview with Mrs. Jemima Day, Calgary, July 1980. GAA City of Calgary Subdivision Map 1916.
13. Day Interview.
14. John Blue, *Alberta Past and Present*, 3 vols., (Chicago: Pioneer Historical Publishing Co., 1924). Blue solicited a fee and biographical data from those who wanted to be included in this publication, vol. 3, p. 405.
15. *Ibid.,* vol. 3, p. 541.
16. *Ibid.,* vol. 2, p. 144.

17. *Ibid.*, vol. 2, p. 142.
18. *Ibid.*, vol. 2, p. 459.
19. S. Nagy, "A Statistical Analysis of *Alberta Past and Present*," seminar paper, University of Calgary, 1979.
20. M.L. Malliah, "A Socio-historical Study of the Legislators of Alberta 1905–1967" (Diss., University of Alberta, 1970), Table II–7, p. 33.
21. *Ibid.*, Table V-2, pp. 76, 73.
22. *Census of Canada*, 1921, 1931, 1961.
23. Malliah, Table II-4, p. 27; J.M. Reid, *Scotland Past and Present* (London: Oxford University Press, 1959), chap. 5.
24. E.G. Mardon, *Who's Who in Federal Politics from Alberta* (Lethbridge: University of Lethbridge, 1972), p. 65.
25. *Ibid.*, p. 43; *Canadian Parliamentary Guide* 1926; *Back Over the Trail: A History of the Huxley Area* (Huxley, Alberta: The Acadia Women's Institute, 1967), p. 94.
26. Mardon, p. 75; *Canadian Parliamentary Guide* 1926; GAA, Phonotape RCT 99–1.
27. Mardon, *op. cit.; Canadian Parliamentary Guide* 1922; GAA, File D9712.234.H127.
28. David Jay Bercuson, *Fools and Wisemen: The Rise and Fall of the One Big Union* (Toronto: McGraw-Hill Ryerson, 1978), p. 65; GAA, File B.E.24.U58AC18. Elizabeth A. Taraska, "The Calgary Craft Union Movement" (M.A. thesis, University of Calgary, 1970), p. 40.
29. GAA, File B.E.24.U58AC18. *Canadian Parliamentary Guide:* 1921, p. 491.
30. Anthony Mardiros, *William Irvine: The Life of a Prairie Radical* (Toronto: J. Lormier & Co., 1979), chap. 1.
31. *Ibid.*, p. 11.
32. *Ibid.*, p. 21.
33. *Ibid.*
34. *Ibid.*, p. 54. For details of the Non-Partisan League See W. L. Morton, *The Progressive Party of Canada* (Toronto: University of Toronto Press, 1950), pp. 44–48, 87–90.
35. Mardiros, *op. cit.*, p. 54; Mardon, *op. cit.*
36. GAA, File A.N398; Catherine O'Neill, "One Big Family," *Western Producer*, 13 Nov. 1953.
37. See for example, William Malcolm, *The Days Before Yesterday*, p. 521; David Anderson, *Mosquito Creek Round Up*, p. 549; Albert Campbell, *Still God's Country: The Early History of Byemoor and Area*, ed., Marie J. Campbell (1975), p. 92; Alex Galloway, *Vermilion Memories* (Vermilion Old Timers, n.d.), p. 46.
38. GAA, File A.N.398 copy of article in *Western Producer*, 27 Nov. 1952.
39. James G. MacGregor, *North West of Sixteen* (Edmonton: Hurtig Publishing, 1968), chap. 1.
40. Interviews in Edmonton, Red Deer, and Calgary, 1980.
41. *Edmonton Journal*, 24 Aug. 1909.
42. Andy Baxter, "History of the Calgary United Scottish Games," Souvenir program, Canadian Interprovincial Championships (Calgary: Alberta Highland Dance Association, 1980).
43. Baxter. For more on Ralph Connor see *Postscript to Adventure: The Autobiography of Ralph Connor*, ed. J. King Gordon (Charles W. Gordon) (London: Hodder and Stoughton Ltd. 1938) and Edward H. Wood, "Ralph Connor and the Canadian West" (M.A. thesis, University of Saskatchewan, 1975).
44. George M. Stanley, "The Scottish Military Tradition," *The Scottish Tradition*

in Canada, p. 150; Major Roy Farran, D.S.O., M.C., *The History of the Calgary Highlanders,* 1921–54 (Calgary: The Bryant Press Limited, n.d.).

45. Interview with Pipe Major Don Maxwell and members of the band, July 1980. .
46. Interview with Mrs. Marlene O'Brien, Edmonton, May 1980.
47. *Ibid.*
48. *Ibid.*
49. *Edmonton Journal,* 3 Aug. 1907.
50. Interview with Mrs. Seller, Calgary, July 1980.
51. Interview with Mr. Donald MacFarlane, Red Deer, July 1980.

Chapter Six

1. I wish to acknowledge my thanks to Howard Palmer, Donald Smith, and Herman Ganzevoort of the Department of History, University of Calgary; Hugh Dempsey of the Alberta-Glenbow Institute, Calgary; Jean Burnet of the Department of Sociology, Glendon College, York University; and Peter Oliver of the Department of History, York University, for their constructive criticisms of this chapter. Any errors, omissions, and limitations are, of course, my own responsibility.
2. Through the paper, I have standarized the reference to people of Ontario by referring to them as "Ontarians" even though Ontario did not exist as a province until 1867. Present-day Ontario did not exist as a separate colony until 1791. It was known as Upper Canada from 1791 to the Union of the Canadas in 1840. Thereafter it was known as Canada West until Confederation in 1867.
3. For an interesting discussion of the impact of a mature society on a new area of colonization see *The Founding of New Societies,* ed. Louis Hartz (New York, 1964). For the application of the Hartzian model to western Canada see J.E. Rea, "The Roots of Prairie Society," in *Prairie Perspectives,* ed. D. Gagan (Toronto, 1970), pp. 46–57.
4. For a discussion of the nationalistic nature of the Methodist Church see George Emery, "Methodism on the Canadian Prairies, 1896 to 1914: The Dynamics of an Institution in a New Environment" (Ph.D. diss., University of British Columbia, 1970).
5. M.E. Jordan, "Henry Bird Steinhauer and His Whitefish Lake Mission," *Alberta Historical Review,* 3 (Autumn 1955), pp. 11–12.
6. On the McDougalls, see M.E. Jordan, "George Millward McDougall, Missionary and Nation-Builder," *Alberta Historical Review,* 3 (Winter 1955), pp. 24–33; and J.W. Friesen, "John McDougall: The Spirit of a Pioneer," *Alberta Historical Review,* 22 (Spring 1974), pp. 9–17.
7. For a biographical sketch see "Elizabeth Boyd McDougall: First in the Southwest" in Grant MacEwan, . . . *And Mighty Women Too: Stories of Notable Western Canadian Women* (Saskatoon, 1975), pp. 42–51.
8. For a discussion of the changing image of the West in the mid-nineteenth century see Douglas Owram, *A Promise of Eden: The Canadian Expansionist Movement and the Idea of the West, 1856–1900* (Toronto, 1980).
9. A very good sampling of Brown's writings on the West from his Toronto *Globe* can be found in F.H. Underhill, "Some Aspects of Upper Canadian Radical Opinion in the Decade before Confederation," Canadian Historical Association *Report* (1927), pp. 46–61.
10. Thomas McMicking, "The Overlanders in Alberta, 1862," ed. Hugh Demp-

sey, *Alberta Historical Review*, 14 (Summer 1966), pp. 1–12.

11. R.C. Macleod, *The NWMP and Law Enforcement 1873–1905* (Toronto, 1976), p. 81.

12. On the nature of ranching in early Alberta see David Breen, "The Canadian West and the Ranching Frontier: 1875–1922" (Ph.D. diss., University of Alberta, 1972); and L.G. Thomas, "The Rancher and the City: Calgary and the Cattlemen, 1883–1914," *Transactions of the Royal Society of Canada VI*, 4 (June 1968), pp. 203–215.

13. W.S. Waddell, "Frank Oliver and the Bulletin," *Alberta Historical Review*, 5 (Summer 1961), pp. 7–12.

14. Thomas Braden, "When the Herald Came to Calgary," *Alberta Historical Review*, 9 (Summer 1961), pp. 1–5.

15. For information on James Lougheed's life see John Blue's *History of the Province of Alberta* (Chicago, 1924), vol. II, p. 517. Also see W.K. Regular, "Regionalism, Nationalism and the Canadian Character: The Senate Career of James A. Lougheed 1890–1905" (B.A. Honors thesis, Memorial University of Newfoundland, 1978).

16. R.S. Patterson, "F.G. Haultain and Education in the Early West" (M.Ed. thesis, University of Alberta, 1961); W.E. Edmonds, "F.W.G. Haultain: Premier of the North-West Territories," *Alberta Historical Review*, 5 (Autumn 1957), pp. 11–17; and Neil G. McDonald, "The School as an Agent of Nationalism in the North West Territories: 1884–1905" (M.Ed. thesis, University of Alberta, 1971).

17. *Report of the Council of Public Instruction* (1900), quoted in McDonald, "The School as an Agent of Nationalism," p. 142.

18. Government of Alberta, Department of Education, *Annual Report* (1906), p. 29.

19. Quoted in B.E. Batchelor, "The Agrarian Frontier Near Red Deer and Lacombe, Alberta: 1882–1914" (Ph.D. diss., Simon Fraser University, 1978), p. 102.

20. Mary E. Inderwick, "A Lady and Her Ranch," *Alberta Historical Review*, 15 (Autumn 1967), p. 1.

21. "The North-West: Letters from an Ontario Farmer," *Toronto Globe*, 15 Aug. 1895, p. 9.

22. For an excellent discussion of immigration patterns in North America see Marcus L. Hansen, *The Mingling of the Canadian and American Peoples* (New York, Arno Reprint, 1970).

23. There are numerous local histories in Alberta. Of special interest on Ontarians are: *Where the Wheatland Meets the Range*, by the Claresholm History Book Club (Claresholm, 1974); *Mosquito Creek Roundup*, by the Nanton and District Historical Society (Nanton, 1971); *Trails to Highways*, by the Eastway Ladies' Club (Vulcan, 1972); and *Seventy Five Years Along the Red Deer River*, ed. H.D. Howe (Calgary, 1971).

24. "Adamville Academy, Teacher and Class 44 Years Ago," *Barrie Examiner*, 10 Aug. 1933. I am indebted to Donald Smith for drawing my attention to this material.

25. G. Edmund Kelly, "The Man from Glengarry: A Letter to My Grandchildren," *Alberta Historical Review*, 6 (Winter 1958), pp. 10–15.

26. Georgina Thomson, "Some Early History of Parkland, Alberta," *Alberta Historical Review*, 3 (Autumn 1955), pp. 5–11.

27. On the Parry Sound Colonists see R. Douglas Francis, "Establishment of the Parry Sound Colony," *Alberta History*, 29 (Winter 1981), pp. 23–29; Lawrence Rye, "Reminiscences of a Parry Sound Colonist," *Alberta His-*

torical Review, 10 (Autumn 1962), pp. 18–27; and Peter R. Ream, *The Fort on the Saskatchewan: A Resource Book on Fort Saskatchewan and District* (Edmonton, 1974).

28. W.C. Pollard, *Pioneering in the Prairie West: A Sketch of the Parry Sound Colonies that settled Near Edmonton, N.W.T. in the Early Nineties* (Toronto, 1926).

29. Ida M. Reid, "Good Hope Days," *Alberta Historical Review,* 9 (Spring 1961), pp. 22–25.

30. A.A. den Otter, "Urban Pioneers of Lethbridge," *Alberta Historical Review,* 25 (Winter 1977), p. 16. The material on C.A. Magrath is from "Charles A. Magrath was 'Big Canadian'," *Lethbridge Herald,* 31 Oct. 1949.

31. I am indebted to Carl Betke for this material on Edmonton from his dissertation "Urban Social Developments in Edmonton: 1898–1929" (Ph.D. diss., University of Alberta, 1981).

32. Paul Voisey, "In Search of Wealth and Status: An Economic and Social Study of Entrepreneurs in Early Calgary," in *Frontier Calgary,* ed. A. W. Rasporich and H. C. Klassen (Calgary, 1975), pp. 221–241.

33. A good study of the oil industry is Philip Smith, *The Treasure-Seekers: The Men Who Built Home Oil* (Toronto, 1978).

34. H.C. Klassen, "Life in Frontier Calgary," in *Western Canada: Past and Present,* ed. A. W. Rasporich (Calgary, 1975), pp. 42–75.

35. Greg Thomas and Ian Clarke, "The Garrison Mentality and the Canadian West," *Prairie Forum,* 4 (Spring 1979), pp. 83–104. See also J. Warkentin, "Time and Places in the Western Interior," *Artscanada,* 196/170/171 (1972), pp. 20–37.

36. See Howard Palmer, "Nativism and Ethnic Tolerance in Alberta, 1920–1972" (Ph.D. diss., York University, 1973).

37. Douglas R. Babcock, *A Gentleman of Strathcona: Alexander Cameron Rutherford,* Historic Sites Services Occasional Paper no. 8 (Alberta, 1980).

38. Biographical material on Arthur L. Sifton is from A. O. Macrae, *History of the Province of Alberta* (Western Canadian History Company, 1912), vol. II, p. 1000; and E.G. Mardon, *Who's Who in Federal Politics from Alberta* (n.p. 1972). For Charles Stewart see "Charles Stewart," *Lethbridge Herald,* 7 Dec. 1946; Sharleen Chevraux, *The Ten Dollar Bets: A History of Killam and District* (Winnipeg, 1967), p. 58.

39. The statistics on cabinet ministers and legislators in this chapter are from H.L. Malliah, "A Socio-Historical Study of the Legislators of Alberta: 1905–1967" (Ph.D. diss., University of Alberta, 1970).

40. Warren Caragata, *Alberta Labour: A Heritage Untold* (Toronto, 1979), p. 35.

41. Paul Voisey, "The 'Votes for Women' Movement," *Alberta Historical Review,* 23 (Summer 1975), p. 10.

42. Una MacLean, "The Famous Five," *Alberta Historical Review,* 10 (Spring, 1962), pp. 1–5. For brief biographical sketchs of Murphy, McKinney and McClung, see Grant MacEwan, . . . *And Mighty Women Too.*

43. Sheilagh S. Jamieson, "Give Your Other Vote to the Sister," *Alberta Historical Review,* 15 (Autumn 1967), pp. 10–16.

44. John Thompson, "Bringing in the Sheaves: The Harvest Excursionists, 1890–1929," *Canadian Historical Review,* 59 (December 1978), pp. 467–489; and Roy W. Hay, "Recollections," *Alberta Historical Review,* 18 (Autumn 1970), pp. 26–27.

45. Quoted in John Irving, *The Social Credit Movement in Alberta* (Toronto, 1959), p. 12.

46. Calgary *Herald,* 21 Mar. 1981, p. 1.

Chapter Seven

1. The authors gratefully acknowledge the assistance of Norma Milton, Joanna Matejko, and Betty Wulff for conducting interviews. Herman Ganzevoort was also most helpful in providing copies of immigrant memoirs and discussing the chapter.
2. Herman Ganzevoort, "Dutch Immigration to Canada, 1892–1940" (Ph.D. diss., University of Toronto, 1975), chap. 1.
3. For a good overview of the Dutch-American experience see Robert P. Swierenga, "Dutch," in *Harvard Ethnic Encyclopedia* (Cambridge, Massachusetts, 1980).
4. H. Palmer, "Nativism in Alberta, 1880–1920" (M.A. thesis, University of Alberta), 1971, chap. 2.
5. Ganzevoort, *op. cit.*, chap. I.
6. Ganzevoort, *ibid.*
7. Nobleford Monarch History Book Club, *Sons of Wind and Soil* (Calgary, 1976), p. 233; "Recollections, Mrs. John Hofman, Sr. (nee Gertie Veldhuis)," 1970, p. 1.
8. Unpublished manuscript by Ted Reitsma on history of Dutch in Alberta in possession of authors, p. 1; Granum History Committee, *Leavings by Trail, Granum by Rail* (Granum, 1977), pp. 258, 475, 415.
9. *Sons of Wind and Soil*, p. 74; Census of Canada, 1921.
10. H. Ganzevoort, *op. cit.*, pp. 169–173; *Sons of Wind and Soil*, pp. 233, 383, 359–360, 380, 225, 204, 309, 393, 329, 386.
11. *Ibid., Shortgrass Country: A History of Nemisam and Foremost* (Calgary, 1975), p. 302.
12. Ganzevoort, *op. cit.*, pp. 173–174; *Sons of Wind and Soil*, pp. 70, 73–76; *Leavings by Trail, Granum by Rail*, p. 409; *Shortgrass Country*, pp. 302, 317–318, 391–394, 452–453.
13. *Sons of Wind and Soil*, pp. 70–75.
14. *Ibid.*, p. 254; A. E. Palmer, *When the Winds Came* (Lethbridge, 1972), p. 13.
15. *Leavings By Trail, Granum By Rail*, p. 407; *Sons of Wind and Soil*, pp. 383, 394.
16. *Sons of Wind and Soil*, pp. 233, 329–330, *Shortgrass Country*, p. 302.
17. Ganzevoort, *op. cit.*, p. 176.
18. J. B. Hedges, *Building the Canadian West* (New York, 1939), pp. 167, 209–210, 284–285; Ganzevoort, *ibid.*, pp. 122–124, 179; History Committee, Nightingale Community Association, *The English Colony: Nightingale and District*, pp. 64, 196–197, and *passim; Edmonton Bulletin*, 12 Sept. 1907; *Calgary Daily News*, 23 Mar. 1909.
19. Dutch families remaining in the area included the Bartelens, Lauweryssens, Pals, Van Wenzels, Willms, Kiemays, Vergouwens, Damens, Voermans, Ver Weires, Den Boers and Kiemenys. At the time of the 1921 census, there were 270 people of Dutch origin in the Strathmore area. *The English Colony;* Census of Canada, 1921.
20. Generalizations based on analysis of *The English Colony* and *passim;* and interviews Tony Bartelen, Aug. and Sept. 1979, Lyalta, Alberta.
21. Ted Reitsma, "Neerlandia" Unpublished Ms., p. 2; Ganzevoort, *op. cit.*, pp. 185–188; Barrhead and District Historical Society, *Trails Northwest. A History of the District of Barrhead, Alberta* (Barrhead, 1967), chap. 25.
22. *Ibid.; Edmonton Bulletin*, 4 Apr. 1911.
23. Reitsma, *ibid.;* Census of Canada, 1921.
24. Reitsma, Ganzevoort, *Trails Northwest.*

25. Public Archives of Alberta, Oral History Tapes, 73, 81, Interview with Ted Reitsma, 17 Feb. 1973; Ted Reitsma, "The Struggles of a Dutch immigrant" (Unpublished Ms.). Reitsma subsequently played an important role in the community of Neerlandia.

26. Trails Northwest, p. 276; Ganzevoort, op. cit., p. 187.

27. Reitsma, "Neerlandia," Trails Northwest, p. 275; Ganzevoort, ibid., p. 187.

28. Reitsma, ibid., p. 5; Reitsma, "Struggles of a Dutch Immigrant," p. 25.

29. Reitsma, "Neerlandia," pp. 5-6; Trails Northwest, p. 276.

30. Mennonites in Alberta form a distinctive ethno-religious group and their "Dutch" origins have no real social meaning. Mennonites came to Alberta from Russia, and the group had not lived in Holland for several hundred years. Not all Mennonites registered with the census takers as Dutch; some gave "German" and "Russian" as their ethnic origin.

31. Calgary Herald, 27 May 1979.

32. Ganzevoort, op. cit., chap. 6.

33. Ibid.

34. Ibid., Sons of the Soil, and passim.

35. Coyote Flats Historical Society, Coyote Flats (Lethbridge, 1976), pp. 238-239.

36. Ganzevoort, op. cit., p. 137.

37. Among the early families in the settlement were the Ten Hoves, Nienhuis, Weeninks, Bruinsmas, Brouwers, Bajemas, Prins, Martenas, Hoeves, Siebengas, Tymstras, Salomons, Miendersmas, and Wierengas. Lacombe Rural History Club, Wagon Trails to Hard Top. History of Lacombe and Area (Calgary, 1972), pp. 621-664; Interview, Frank Prins, Lacombe, Sept. 1979.

38. Census of Canada, 1931.

39. Ganzevoort, op. cit., chap. 7; Interview, Mr. A. Noy, 26 July 1979, Rockyford, Alta.

40. Big Hill Country: Cochrane and Area (Calgary, 1977), pp. 429, 562-563. Reitsma, "Neerlandia," "Struggles of a Dutch Immigrant."

41. Federal Election Returns, 1935.

42. Census of Canada, 1941.

43. William Peterson, Planned Migration (Berkeley, 1955), chap. 5; Antony Sas, "Dutch Migration to and Settlement in Canada. 1945 to 1955" (Ph.D. diss., Clark University, 1957), chap. 1.

44. Sas, "Dutch Migration," pp. 5-7.

45. Ibid., p. 9.

46. Peterson, chap. 6; Sas, p. 112; Interview, Ria Van Holten, Calgary, Sept. 1979; K. Ishwaran, Family Kinship and Community (Toronto, 1977), p. 3.

47. Sas, "Dutch Migration," p. 1.

48. Sas, ibid., pp. 37-44.

49. Sas, ibid., p.67; Census of Canada, 1951, 1961; Canada Immigration Division, Dept. of Manpower and Immigration Annual Statistics, 1956-69.

50. Sas. ibid., p. 57; Interview, Bernard Nieboer, Lethbridge, Summer, 1967; Interviews, Lacombe, Red Deer, Sept. 1979; Census of Canada, 1971; Tabulations by authors from 1 percent sample.

51. Sas, ibid., pp. 19-21.

52. Interview Nieboer, ibid. Many of the Dutch families who came to the Lethbridge area were exceptionally large since sugar beet farming required intensive labor and large families were difficult to place elsewhere. For example, one family was as large as nineteen children, and many had between ten and fifteen.

53. Census of Canada, 1961; Interview, Simon Bennik, Calgary, Sept. 1979.

54. Interview, Nieboer; Interview, Margaret de Witt, Calgary, 1979; Sas, *op. cit.*
55. Interview, Nieboer, *ibid.*
56. Peterson, *op. cit.;* Interview, Gerald Snow, Lethbridge, Summer 1967; Canadian Sugar Factories, Ltd., Lethbridge, 1966, "Acreage Analysis of Labor Working Beets, 1950–1965," Information provided by Gerald Snow.
57. Interviews, Lethbridge, Coaldale.
58. Interviews, Red Deer, Sept. 1979; *Atlas of Alberta* (Edmonton, 1967), pp. 60–61.
59. Census of Canada, 1951, 1961, 1971. Figures on 1971 occupations from special tabulations, 1 percent sample.
60. For a good discussion of the religious organizational basis of Dutch society see K. Ishwaran, *Family, Kinship and Community*, chap. 2.
61. Peterson, *op. cit.*, chap. 9; Church membership figures calculated from *Yearbook*, 1979, Christian Reformed Church (Grand Rapids, 1979), pp. 10–13.
62. Interviews, Calgary, Edmonton, Red Deer, Lethbridge.
63. For a lengthy discussion of the role of religion and families in a Dutch Christian Reformed community in Ontario see K. Ishwaran, *Family*, chap. 5.
64. Membership figures calculated from *Yearbook*, Reformed Church in America, 1978. Peterson, *Planned Migration*, chap. 9; Interviews, Lethbridge, Calgary.
65. On conflict between farm hands and farmers in the northern provinces, see K. Ishwaran, *op. cit.*, p. 27; D. de Jong, "Canadian and Reformed: Cause and Calling of the Canadian Reformed Churches" (Unpublished Ms., Calgary, 1979); Interviews, D. de Jong, Calgary, Sept. 1979; Rev. W.W.J. Vanoene, "Inheritance Preserved: The Canadian Reformed Churches," in *Historical Perspective* (Winnipeg, 1975).
66. Interviews, Lethbridge, 1967, 1979; Rev. M. Heerschap, Lethbridge, July 1980.
67. Peterson, *op. cit.*, chap. 9; Census of Canada, 1971; The reason for their under-representation in the postwar immigration is that the southern Catholic provinces were more highly industrialized than most other parts of Holland so could absorb excess population. Also, Catholics were generally less concerned than Calvinists over the potential social and spiritual "dangers" of industrialization.
68. Interview, Peter Vanderlinden, Calgary, 26 June 1979.
69. Census of Canada, 1971; *Official Language and Language Most often Spoken at Home*, pp. 23–24, 28; Ken O'Bryan *et. al.*, *Non-Official Languages: A Study in Canadian Multiculturalism* (Ottawa, 1976), pp. 74–155, 192; Interviews, Red Deer, Calgary, Summer 1979; Maria Goossens, "Degree of Bilingualism among Dutch Immigrants in Calgary," in *Canadian Languages in the Social Context*, ed. Regna Darnell (Edmonton, 1973).
70. Interview, John Van Dam, Redcliff, Sept. 1979; *Sons of Wind and Soil*, p. 265; *Canadian Parliamentary Guide* (Ottawa, 1978). Cornelius Van der Swan was elected mayor in Sundre, John Olthius in Lacombe, John Van Dam in Redcliff, and Arnold Lubbers in Nobleford.

Chapter Eight

1. Jakob Benediktsson, "Icelandic Emigration to America," *Le Nord* (Copenhagen) 5: 1942: 40–50; W.J. Lindal, *The Icelanders in Canada* bk. 2 (Winnipeg, Viking Printers, 1967); Jane McCracken, *Stephan G. Stephansson: The Poet of the Rocky Mountains* (Edmonton, Alberta Culture, 1982), chap. 1.

2. *Ibid.*

3. For a detailed account of the trip, see the English version of Stephansson's memoirs, "Westward Ho," trans. Axel Vopnfjord, *Icelandic Canadian,* 32 (Winter 1973), pp. 18–21; on the Canadian government response, see Norman Macdonald, *Canada: Emigration and Colonization. 1841–1903* (Toronto, Macmillan, 1966), pp. 207–208.

4. Lindal, *The Icelanders,* pp. 102–103; Jean Elford, "The Icelanders—Their Ontario Year," *Beaver,* outfit 304, no. 4 (Spring 1974), pp. 53–58.

5. Lindal, *The Icelanders,* pp. 111–112; Elford, "The Icelanders," p. 56.

6. McCracken, *Stephansson,* chap. 3; Lindal, "The Icelanders"; W. Kristjanson, *The Icelandic People in Manitoba* (Winnipeg, Wallingford Press, 1965), pt. 4.

7. McCracken, *Stephansson,* chap. 3; "The Icelandic Community in Pembina County, North Dakota," *Icelandic Canadian,* 33, no. 1 (Autumn 1974), pp. 42–50; "Icelandic Settlements in Dakota," *Icelandic Canadian,* 35, no.3 (Spring 1977), pp. 18–24.

8. McCracken, *Stephansson,* chaps. 2, 3; interview with Rosa Benediktson (daughter of Stephan Stephansson), Red Deer, Alberta, 18 Oct. 1979.

9. Kristjanson, *The Icelandic People,* chaps. 20, 21; V. Emil Gudmundson, "North American Influences on the Beginnings of Unitarianism Among Icelanders in the United States and Canada" (Paper delivered to Collegium Conference on Unitarian History, Collegeville, Massachusetts, September 1979); Phillip Hewett, *Unitarians in Canada* (Don Mills, Ont., Fitzhenry & Whiteside, 1978), pp. 130–134.

10. For extended discussions of Stephansson's religious thought, see Gudmundson, "North American Influences," and McCracken, *Stephansson,* chap. 4. The statement of objectives is quoted in Gudmundson, "North American Influences," pp. 13–14.

11. Gudmundson, "North American Influences," Jane McCracken, *Stephansson,* chap. 4.

12. McCracken, *ibid.,* chap. 5.

13. Sadie Lee, "Pioneering in Alberta: A History of Markerville," *Lur,* Summer 1974, p. 3.

14. Quoted in *ibid.,* pp. 3–4.

15. *Ibid.*

16. Bruce Batchelor, "The Agrarian Frontier Near Red Deer and Lacombe, Alberta, 1882–1914" (Ph.D. diss., Simon Fraser University, 1978).

17. Lee, "Pioneering in Alberta," pp. 4–5; E.L. Meeres, *The Homesteads That Nurtured a City* (Red Deer, n.p., 1978), pp. 97–99.

18. *Calgary Herald,* 27 Jan. 1892, 4 Dec. 1889. For a more detailed account of press reaction see Meeres, *The Homesteads* pp. 101–102. For a general discussion of attitudes toward immigration in general and Scandinavians in particular, see H. Palmer, *Patterns,* pp. 26–27.

19. Carl Morkeberg, *Markerville Story* (Innisfail Alta., Innisfail Province, 1967); Interviews, Markerville, Oct. 1979; Personal communication, Rosa Benediktson, 29 Dec. 1979.

20. Spruce View School Area Historical Society, *Grub-Axe to Grain* (Calgary, Friesen, 1973), p. 109.

21. *Ibid.,* pp. 148–163; Interview, Rosa Benediktson, Dec. 1979.

22. Interviews, Carl Morkeberg, Joe Johannson, Markerville, Oct., 1979.

23. Carl Morkeberg, *Markerville Story,* pp. 16–18, 75–77, 84–86; Carl Morkeberg, "Markerville" and "The History of the Morkeberg Family of Markerville," in Spruce View Area Historical Society. *Grub-axe to Grain,* pp. 132,

151–152; J.A. Ruddick et. al., *Dairying in Canada* (Toronto, Ryerson Press, 1937), pp. 40, 104–105.

24. Carl Morkeberg, *Markerville Story*, pp. 9–11.
25. *Ibid.*,pp 7–9, 208–209.
26. *Grub Axe*, pp. 107, 132.
27. See discussion of the term "West Icelanders" in Magnus Einarsson, "Oral Tradition and Ethnic Boundaries; West Icelandic Verses and Anecdotes," *Canadian Ethnic Studies*, vol. 7., no. 2, 1975, pp. 19–32; For comment on the original intentions of the Icelandic settlers see W.J. Lindal, *The Icelanders*, pp. 100–102. For further analysis of Stephan Stephansson as a West Icelander, see Jane McCracken, "Stephan G. Stephansson: Icelandic-Canadian Poet and Freethinker," *Canadian Ethnic Studies*, 15, 1, 1983, pp. 33–54.
28. *Grub Axe*, p. 139.
29. Carl Morkeberg, *Markerville Story*, pp. 7–9; *Grub Axe*, pp. 107, 163; McCracken, *Stephansson*, chap. 6.
30. *Grub Axe*, p. 107; Lee, "Pioneering in Alberta," *Lur*, Summer 1974, p. 6.
31. *Grub Axe*, p. 107; *Innisfail Free Lance*, 7 Aug. 1902, p. 4; 8 Aug. 1907, p. 4; *Innisfail Province* 2 Aug. 1906.
32. Lindal, *The Icelanders*, p. 195; *Grub Axe*, p. 146.
33. Interview, Carl Morkeberg, Markerville, Oct. 1979. In 1901, before the arrival of a new wave of Icelandic settlers to Markerville, there were only 153 people who had been born in Iceland in all of Alberta, and not all of them lived in the Markerville area. This number did not include the children of the settlers, most of whom had been born either in the United States or in Canada rather than in Iceland (Census of Canada, 1901).
34. Burnt Lake Historical Society, *Along the Burnt Lake Trail* (Calgary, Friesen, 1977), pp. 172–174, 269–278; Provincial Archives of Alberta, 73.523 Icelandic pioneers at Burnt Lake; Memoirs of Johan Sveinson, Samuel Anderson, Ofeigier Sigurdson, Sam Johnson, Sigurdur Grimson, Chris Johnson; *Grub Axe*, pp. 69–105, 159–176; Carl Morkeberg, *Markerville Story*, pp. 54–55; Personal Communication, Rosa Benediktson, 29 Dec. 1979; McCracken, *Stephansson*, chap. 6.
35. Carl Morkeberg, "Markerville," in *Grub Axe*, p. 133; Census of Canada, 1916.
36. Interviews, Markerville, Oct. 1979; Carl Morkeberg, *Markerville Story*, pp. 21–23. For mention of the conflict between Danes and Icelanders see *Innisfail Province*, 28 Apr. 1924.
37. *Ibid.*
38. W.J. Lindal, *Icelanders in Canada*, pp. 224–230; Census of Canada, 1916.
39. Jakob Benediktsson, "Icelandic Emigration to America," *Le Nord*, vol. 5, no. 1, 1942, p. 49; Watson Kirkconnell, "Canada's Leading Poet: Stephan G. Stephansson, 1853–1927," *University of Toronto Quarterly*, vol. V, no. 32, January 1936, pp. 274–276; McCracken, *Stephansson*, chap. 8.
40. Kirkconnell, "Stephansson."
41. Kirkconnell, "Stephansson"; Sharleen M. Chevraux, "Stephan G. Stephansson," *Heritage*, vol. 3, no. 4, 1974, pp. 5–7; Rosa Benediktson, "Stephan G. Stephansson," *Lur*, Summer 1974, p. 7; McCracken, *Stephansson*, chap. 9.
42. Interviews, Markerville, Oct. 1979; *Grub Axe*, p. 134; Priscilla Popilchak, "Markerville: A Village of Yesterday, Today and Tomorrow" (History Paper, University of Calgary, 1978).
43. Interview, I. Hanse, Calgary, 19 July 1979; W.J. Lindal, *ibid.*, pp. 162–163, 198–199.

44. *Ibid.;* Census of the Prairie Provinces, 1936.
45. Interview, B. Sigurdson, Calgary, 26 June 1979.
46. Department of Manpower and Immigration, Annual Statistics, 1946–1977. Interviews, Calgary, Edmonton, Fall 1979.
47. Interviews, Fretha Stephansson, Joe Johannson, Carl Morkeberg, Markerville, Oct. 1979; Rosa Benediktson, Red Deer, Oct. 1979.
48. For general background on Scandinavians in Alberta see K.O. Bjork, "Scandinavian Migration to the Canadian Prairie Provinces," *Norwegian American Studies,* 26, 1974, pp. 63–75; H. Palmer, *Land of the Second Chance* (Lethbridge, 1972), chap. 11; William Wonders, "Scandinavian Homesteaders in Central Alberta," in *The New Provinces, Alberta and Saskatchewan, 1905–1980,* ed. H. Palmer and Donald Smith (Calgary, 1980), pp. 131–171; Jorgen Dahlie, "Learning on the Frontier: Scandinavian Immigrants and Education in Western Canada," *Canadian and International Education,* vol. 1, no. 2, December 1972, pp. 56–66.

Chapter Nine

1. V. Raud, *Estonia: A Reference Book* (New York, 1953), pp. 20–23; *Homesteads and Happiness* Eckville and District Historical Society (Eckville, 1979), and passim.
2. *Homesteads and Happiness,* p. 558; Interview Nick Kingsep (son of Henry Kingsep), Calgary, Mar. 1980.
3. PAC, RG 76, vol. 25, File 651, Pedley to Smart, 9 September 1899.
4. A. Kurlents, *Eestlased Kanadas* (Toronto, 1975), pp. 21–26; *Homesteads and Happiness,* p. 558; Diary, August Posti, 23 Mar. 1902; in possession of Medicine Valley Estonian Society.
5. Kurlents, *ibid.; Homesteads and Happiness,* p. 558.
6. Kurlents, *ibid.,* pp. 26–37; *Homesteads and Happiness,* p. 587. The earliest Estonian settlers in the area besides the Kingsep family were the Kinna, Koot, Muru, Langer, Matteus (Mathews), Mottus, Pihuoja, Posti, Raabis, and Sestrap families.
7. Kurlents, *ibid.; Homesteads and Happiness,* p. 574.
8. *Homesteads and Happiness,* pp. 13, 21–26, 548–549; Interview, Nick Kingsep, *op. cit.*
9. *Homesteads and Happiness,* pp. 542–543; Kurlents, *op. cit.,* p. 575.
10. *Ibid.,* pp. 559, 903.
11. Minute Book, Medicine Valley Estonian Society, 24 April 1910.
12. *Homesteads and Happiness,* pp. 360, 560; Kurlents, *op. cit.*
13. Selma Pallo, "Free Land Attracted Henry Kingsep to Sylvan Lake, *Red Deer Advocate,* 28 June 1967; Interview, Nick Kingsep, *op. cit.;* Minute Book, Medicine Valley Estonian Society, 6 November 1910, 11 May 1912, 25 January 1913, and September 1915.
14. *New World Jubilee Album* 1909–1934 (New York, New World Printing, 1934(?)), pp. 61–63; *Red Deer Advocate,* 2 Jan. 1920.
15. *Homesteads and Happiness,* p. 40.
16. Kurlents, *op. cit.; Homesteads and Happiness,* p. 588; Federal Election Returns, 1921.
17. Minute Book, Medicine Valley Estonian Society, 11 May 1912, 25 January 1913.
18. *Homesteads and Happiness,* pp. 559–560, 588–589, 903; Interview, Nick Kingsep.

19. *Homesteads and Happiness,* and passim. Interview, Nick Kingsep.
20. *New World Jubilee Album,* pp. 61–63.
21. Kurlents, *op. cit.;* Edith Clark, *Trails of Tail Creek Country* (n.p., n.d.), pp. 130–131; Joseph Tipman, "Estonians Came to Stettler," *Stettler Independent,* 18 May 1977.
22. *Ibid.;* Quote from *Stettler Independent,* 18 May 1977; For a description of off-farm work see *Stettler Independent,* 29 June 1977. Among the earliest settlers, besides the Neithals, Oros and Rahuus, were the Hennel, Kelu, Kerbes, Kets, Klaus, Kroon, Kutras, Olower, Reinglas, Saar and Tipman families.
23. Kurlents, *op. cit.;* Joe Tipman, "Two Estonian Homestead Seekers," *Stettler Independent,* 1 June 1977; Interview, Joe Tipman, Stettler, 5 Aug. 1980.
24. Kurlents, *ibid.;* Clark, *op. cit.;* Interviews, Phelix Leew, Calgary, 14 Mar. 1980; Joe Tipman, *ibid.*
25. *Ibid.*
26. Kurlents, *op. cit.;* Quote from Barons History Book Club, *Heart of the West* (Calgary, 1972), p. 236.
27. *Ibid.,* pp. 236–240; Interview Oscar Erdman, Calgary, 25 Mar. 1980.
28. Foremost Historical Society, *Shortgrass Country* (Foremost, 1975), pp. 419, 371, 329–331, 324–325; Schuler History Committee, *Saga of Schuler Stalwarts* (n.p., 1973), pp. 36, 135.
29. Emanuel Nodel, *Estonia: Nation on the Anvil* (New York, 1963), p. 172.
30. Kurlents, *op. cit.; Homesteads and Happiness,* pp. 180, 580.
31. Kurlents, *ibid.; Homesteads and Happiness,* p. 556.
32. Kurlents, *ibid.;* Interview with Kinna in *Red Deer Advocate,* 19 Dec. 1924; *New World Jubilee Album,* pp. 61–63; Interview, Nick Kingsep.
33. *Homesteads and Happiness,* and passim.
34. Quote from Villibald Raud, *Estonia: A Reference Book* (New York, 1953), p. 31; *A Case Study of a Soviet Republic. The Estonian SSR,* ed. Tone Parming and Elmar Jarvesoo (Boulder, Colorado, 1978), p. 25.
35. *Ibid.*
36. *Ibid.;* Gerald Dirks, *Canada's Refugee Policy: Indifference or Opportunism?* (Montreal, 1977), pp. 164–166.
37. Dirks, *Canada's Refugee Policy,* chap. 7; Kurlents, *op. cit.;* Department of Citizenship and Immigration, "Ethnic Origin of Immigrants by province of Destination," mimeographed report, Ottawa, 1956; Census of Canada, 1951, 1961.
38. On the social origins of the postwar immigrants see Parming, *A Case Study,* p. 25; Information on Alberta from interviews Lydia Pals, Edmonton, Jan. 1980; Andres Pilt, Edmonton, Dec. and Jan. 1980; Mr. and Mrs. Rouk, Calgary, 5 Jan. 1980; Mrs. Eva Weir, Edmonton, Dec. 1979; Mrs. Ludmilla Kowalski, Edmonton, Dec. 1979.
39. Kurlents, *op. cit.;* Interviews, Pals, Pilt, Rouk.
40. *Ibid.;* 60th Anniversary, Immanuel Church, (Lethbridge, 1969).
41. Interviews, Census of Canada, 1971; *Wheat Heart of the West,* p. 513.
42. Interviews.

Chapter Ten

1. The writer gratefully acknowledges the comments and suggestions of George Richardson and W. Roman Petryshyn.
   There is an abundance of literature on the Ukrainian Canadians and the

notes have been prepared to direct the interested reader to additional information on specific topics.

2. See Vladimir J. Kaye, *Early Ukrainian Settlements in Canada 1895–1900* (Toronto: University of Toronto Press, 1964). Pt. I of Kaye's study examines in detail Dr. Oleskiw's role in the settlement of the Canadian northwest.

3. All figures in this section are based on *A Statistical Compendium on the Ukrainians in Canada, 1891–1971*, ed. William Darcovich (Edmonton: University of Alberta Press, 1977) I, ser. 20.41–64, pp. 33–38; and III, ser. 50.24–38, pp. 485–486. This manuscript has since been published (1980) by the University of Ottawa Press.

4. The 1981 Canada Census differed from its predecessors in that it gave respondents the option of single (specific) or multiple origin to identify their ethnic background. This change in format complicates direct comparison with earlier census findings. All 1981 data in this chapter are based on single origin (Ukrainian) responses only.

5. For an account of the formative years of the Edna-Star colony, see Kaye, *Early Ukrainian Settlements*, pp. 318–360. James G. MacGregor, *Vilni Zemli/Free Lands: The Ukrainian Settlement of Alberta* (Toronto: McClelland and Stewart, 1969) is a more popular account.

6. This thesis is developed by John C. Lehr in "The Government and the Immigrant: Perspectives on Ukrainian Block Settlement in the Canadian West," *Canadian Ethnic Studies*, IX, 2 (1977), pp. 42–52, and "The Process and Pattern of Ukrainian Rural Settlement in Western Canada, 1891–1914" (Ph.D. diss., University of Manitoba, 1977).

7. The North Saskatchewan River was a barrier to settlement as well as a major transportation artery in the early years. The establishment of several ferry crossings affected both the east-west and north-south movement of people and goods. For example, after the Shandro Ferry opened in 1909, settlers north of the river could travel south to Mundare for supplies rather than to Bruderheim or Lamont to the west.

8. See Timothy C. Byrne, "The Ukrainian Community in North Central Alberta" (M.A. thesis, University of Alberta, 1937), for a pioneer effort to break down the bloc according to area of origin. More recently, Alexander Royick in "Ukrainian Settlements in Alberta," *Canadian Slavonic Papers*, 10, 3, (1968), pp. 278–297, has analyzed Ukrainian distribution throughout the province according to both district of origin in Ukraine and dialect areas in Alberta.

9. See Charles W. Hobart, *et. al.*, *Persistence and Change: Alberta Ukrainians* (Edmonton: University of Alberta Press for the Department of Sociology, 1966), pp. 122–123.

10. See, for example, *Lamont Tribune*, 18 Feb. 1915, where the Pakan correspondent rallied to an insult from nearby Andrew.

11. *Lamont Gazette*, 16 Jan. 1919.

12. For a fictional account of Ukrainian pioneer life in the Vegreville bloc, see Illia Kiriak, *Sons of the Soil* (Toronto: Ryerson Press, 1959). John C. Lehr discusses Ukrainian cottage architecture in, for example, *Ukrainian Vernacular Architecture in Alberta*, Historic Sites Service Occasional Paper no. 1, (Edmonton, Alberta Culture, Historical Resources, 1976).

13. They include such widely divergent institutions as the Ukrainian Bookstore, St. Josaphat's Ukrainian Catholic Cathedral, the provincial headquarters of the Association of United Ukrainian Canadians, the Ukrainian National Federation Hall, the Ukrainian Canadian Archives and Museum and Ukrainian News Publishers.

14. Darcovich, *Statistical Compendium*, I, ser. 21.243–294, p. 67.
15. For an elaboration of the Ukrainian stereotype that emerged in contemporary Anglo-Canadian literature, see Frances Swyripa, "A Survey of Anglo-Saxon Concepts of the Character and Background of the Ukrainian in Canada" (B.A. Honors' thesis, University of Alberta, 1973), and *Ukrainian Canadians: A Survey of Their Portrayal in English-Language Works* (Edmonton: University of Alberta Press for the Canadian Institute of Ukrainian Studies, 1978), pp. 1–25.
16. W.D. Reid, "The Non-Anglo-Saxons in Canada—Their Christianization and Nationalization," *Addresses Delivered at the Presbyterian Pre-Assembly Congress* (Toronto: Board of Foreign Missions of the Presbyterian Church in Canada, 1913), p. 126.
17. The annual reports of the supervisor of schools for foreigners, published in the *Annual Report of the Department of Education for the Province of Alberta* between 1907 and 1916, outline departmental policy and problems in this regard.
18. Robert Fletcher, "Report of the Supervisor of Schools among Foreigners," *Annual Report of the Department of Education for 1915*, p. 78.
19. Peter Svarich, "Organizing for Education," in *Land of Pain, Land of Promise*, trans. Harry Piniuta (Saskatoon: Western Producer Prairie Books, 1978), p. 124.
20. *Ibid.*
21. *Ibid.*, pp. 124–125, and Vasyl' A. Chumer, *Spomyny* (Memoirs) (Edmonton: The Author, 1942), pp. 124–126, for two Ukrainian accounts of the crisis. The "official" version is found in Fletcher, "Annual Report of the Supervisor of Schools among Foreigners," *Annual Report of the Department of Education for 1914*, pp. 66–70.
22. They did not totally capitulate; two years later, for example, Leshniw School District near Innisfree advertised in the Ukrainian press for a Ukrainian-English teacher, offering $65 a month salary. See *Ukrains'kyi holos* (Ukrainian Voice), 31 Mar. 1915.
23. This type of thinking is illustrated in Miriam Elston, "Making Ruthenians into Canadians: An Interesting Experiment in Education," *The Graphic* (4 April 1914) n.p., and "English Schools for Foreigners in Alberta," *The Westminster* (n.d.), pp. 430–431. These and others of Elston's articles on the Alberta Ukrainians are located in the Provincial Archives of Alberta (Acc. 65.55).
24. See, for example, Claude Hill Robinson, "A Study of the Written Language Errors of 1238 Pupils of Ukrainian Origin" (B.Ed. thesis, University of Alberta, 1934); David M. Sullivan, "An Investigation of the English Disabilities of Ukrainian and Polish Students in Grades IX, X, XI, XII of Alberta" (M.Ed. thesis, University of Alberta, 1946); and Michael Skuba, "An Analysis of English Errors and Difficulties Among Grade Ten Students in the Smoky Lake School Division" (M.Ed. thesis, University of Alberta, 1955).
25. The two churches were also active among Ukrainians in Alberta mining centers as well as Edmonton and Calgary, approaching evangelization through adult Bible and evening English classes and Sunday School for children. For several years the Methodist Ruthenian Girls' Home in Edmonton provided room and board for Ukrainian girls flocking to Edmonton in search of jobs, lessons in Canadian housekeeping and English, and assistance in locating employment. [The present Bissell Centre in Edmonton had its origins in Presbyterian and Methodist activity among Ukrainians in the city.]

26. Robert H. Warden, "Report of the Home Mission Committee, Western Section, 1902–03," *Acts and Proceedings of the Twenty-Ninth General Assembly of the Presbyterian Church in Canada* (1903), p.5.

27. Rev. Dr. Charles Lawford at the Pakan mission, for example, was said to have disliked the Ukrainians, and it was not until 1909 that the Methodists in Alberta acquired their first Ukrainian missionaries in Metro Ponich and Tarranty Hannochko. See G.N. Emery, "Methodist Missions Among the Ukrainians," *Alberta History* (Spring 1971), pp. 10–18.

28. W. Roman Petryshyn, "The Ukrainian Canadians in Social Transition," in *Ukrainian Canadians, Multiculturalism, and Separatism: An Assessment*, ed. M. R. Lupul (Edmonton: University of Alberta Press for the Canadian Institute of Ukrainian Studies, 1978), p. 94. An additional 0.8 and 1.3 percent of Ukrainian Canadians supported the Presbyterian Church in 1931 and in 1971 respectively. *Ibid.*, the 1981 figure is based on Bohdan S. Kordan, "Ukrainians and the 1981 Canada Census: A Data Handbook" (Unpublished Ms., Canadian Institute of Ukrainian Studies, University of Alberta, 1985), Table 4.5.

29. Fears for the defeat of conscription if enemy aliens were allowed to vote were felt to be substantiated by Liberal electoral victories in Alberta and Saskatchewan that year. In Alberta the provincial Conservatives had argued unsuccessfully for the disfranchisement of enemy aliens.

30. *Postup* (Progress), 22 Feb. 1916.

31. Budka's stand was understandable in light of his background, for the Ukrainian Catholic Church in Galicia had been strongly pro-Hapsburg since the reforms of Maria Theresa and Joseph II, but it revealed his naiveté regarding Canadian affairs.

32. See, for example, *Vegreville Observer*, 30 May 1917.

33. *Manitoba Free Press*, 17 July 1916. The signing editors included M. Bellegay, editor of the Edmonton-based Methodist newspaper, *Kanadyiets'* (Canadian).

34. At Rabbit Hills, for example, a group of Russophile Ukrainians passed a series of such resolutions which were then translated and sent to the Edmonton papers. See *Russkii golos* (Russian Voice), 21 Sept./4 Oct. 1915. A similar denunciation of the Ukrainians was widely distributed in 1918 and provoked a heated controversy in the *Vegreville Observer*. See *Vegreville Observer*, 29 May, 5 June, 26 June, and 10 July 1918.

35. *Saskatoon Phoenix*, 30 Nov. 1916.

36. See *The Canadian Patriotic Fund: A Record of Its Activities from 1914 to 1919*, ed./comp. Philip H. Morris (n.p.: n.d.), p. 57.

37. Kaye, *Ukrainian Settlements in Canada*, p. 324.

38. *Ibid.*, p. 350.

39. Maria Yureichuk, "Our Trip by Raft" in Piniuta, *Land of Pain, Land of Promise*, p. 81.

40. C.H. Speers, Winnipeg, to Edounard [*sic*] Schultze, Imperial Consul, Austria, 11 August 1900 (Archives of the University of Alberta, 80–20–6/A.107).

41. See Helen Potrebenko, *No Streets of Gold: A Social History of Ukrainians in Alberta* (Vancouver: New Star Books, 1977), pp. 206–212, for a sympathetic account of the Ukrainian role in the march.

42. *No Streets of Gold* and Myrna Kostash's *All of Baba's Children* (Edmonton: Hurtig, 1977) are particularly rich on the Depression, the Ukrainian left, and labor unrest. See also Andrij Makuch, "The 'Kryza' in Alberta: Com-

munists, Ukrainians and the UFA" (B.A. Honors' thesis, University of Alberta, 1978).
43. Chumer, *Spomyny*, p. 25.
44. In Galicia, taverns and shops were run by Jews and many Ukrainians felt comfortable with similar arrangements in Canada in spite of widespread dislike of the Jewish moneylender. Jews came to operate much of Vegreville's business section.
45. Fletcher, "Report of the Supervisor of Schools for Foreigners," *Annual Report of the Department of Education for 1916*, p. 97.
46. One of the leading figures behind the Ukrainian farmers' organization was Toma Tomashevsky, editor and publisher of several Ukrainian newspapers, including *Postup* in Mundare. For the constitution of the Canadian Ukrainian Farmers' Union, see *Postup*, 15 Mar. 1917.
47. The 1931 and 1971 percentages are based on Darcovich, *Statistical Compendium*, II, ser. 40.213–238, pp. 406–407. The 1981 percentages are derived from Kordan, "Ukrainians and the 1981 Canada Census," Table 7.3.
48. A Ukrainian-Canadian sociologist has pointed out that, having achieved over-equality in the manufacturing sphere, Ukrainian Canadians are entering the last of three socio-economic stages with greater participation in trade, sales, finance, administrative and professional occupations. See W.W. Isajiw, "Occupational and Economic Development" in *A Heritage in Transition: Essays in the History of Ukrainians in Canada*, ed. M. R. Lupul (Toronto: McClelland and Stewart for the Multiculturalism Directorate, Department of the Secretary of State, 1982), p. 80; the Isajiw article is an overview of socio-economic development among Ukrainian Canadians.
49. Based on Darcovich, *Statistical Compendium*, II, ser. 40.161–172, pp. 394–395. From less than .025 percent in 1931, the proportion of the Ukrainian-Canadian work force in these occupations had increased to .23 percent (physicians and surgeons), .74 percent (professional engineers) and .13 percent (lawyers), in 1971; the national figures were .33 percent, .89 percent, and .19 percent respectively.
50. In 1961, on an average Canadian index of 100, Jewish and British Canadians received the highest income (166.9 and 109.8 respectively), while at the opposite end of the scale Ukrainians (86.9) ranked above only the Indians and Inuit (not reported), the French (85.8) and the Italians (81.0); the 1971 census indicated that in the intervening ten years Ukrainians fell below the French and Italians. Petryshyn, "The Ukrainian Canadians in Social Transition," pp. 86–98.
51. See Darcovich, *Statistical Compendium*, III, ser. 42.34–43, pp. 454–455.
52. See Oleh Wolowyna, "Trends in the Socio-Economic Status of Ukrainians in Canada 1921–1971," in *Changing Realities: Social Trends Among Ukrainian Canadians*, ed. W. R. Petryshyn (Edmonton: Canadian Institute of Ukrainian Studies, 1980), pp. 53–77.
53. See Sidney I. Pobihushchy, "The Development of Political Socialization of Ukrainians in Alberta," *Slavs in Canada*, II (1968), pp. 20–30, for a cursory examination of the differences in integration among the three immigrations and the Canadian-born.
54. When he died in 1975, Hawrelak had been exonerated by the courts and the citizens of Edmonton; he had been reelected as mayor in 1974 with 49.2 percent of the vote in a seven-way race. See *Edmonton Journal*, 2 Nov. 1975.
55. See Thomas E. Flanagan, "Ethnic Voting in Alberta Provincial Elections, 1921–1975," in *Society and Politics in Alberta: Research Papers*, ed. Carlo Caldarola (Toronto: Methuen Publications, 1979), pp. 304–21. Like many

westerners, the Ukrainians had been favorably disposed toward the federal Conservatives since Diefenbaker's term as leader; they also applauded his anticommunism and appointment of a Ukrainian Canadian (Michael Starr) to cabinet.

56. Roman March, "Political Mobility of Ukrainians in Canada," in Petryshyn, *Changing Realities*, pp. 215, 218; and Darcovich, *Statistical Compendium*, II, ser. 33.1–208, pp. 325–35. The figures refer to successful candidatures, not different individuals. A "Ukrainian" candidate was defined as someone having at least one Ukrainian parent.

57. Russification has included official and public subordination of the Ukrainian language and culture to Russian and the appointment of ethnic Russians to important positions in Ukraine. *Internationalism or Russification? A Study in the Soviet Nationalities Problem* (London: Weidenfeld and Nicolson, 1968) is a revealing study of the problem by a Soviet Ukrainian, Ivan Dzyuba; a disillusioned Ukrainian-Canadian communist, John Kolasky, exposed Russification in *Two Years in Soviet Ukraine* (Toronto: Peter Martin Associates, Ltd., 1970).

58. Miriam Elston, "A Ruthenian Day of Days," *Canadian Courier* (n.d.), p. 13.

59. *Ibid.*

60. A number of Ukrainian Baptists emigrated from Russian Ukraine and the Baptist Church in Canada worked among them, but they were not significant in Alberta.

61. This rule was relaxed with the arrival of married Ukrainian Catholic priests in the third immigration. At present, married Ukrainian Catholic priests ordained in Europe can serve in Canada, but Canadian Ukrainian Catholic bishops can ordain married men only under special circumstances.

62. For many years Mundare was the headquarters of the Canadian Province of the Ukrainian Basilian Fathers, and both the OSBM and SSMI have had a great impact on the village. The Sisters Servants, for example, operated a school, orphanage, and hospital in addition to their own novitiate.

63. See Paul Yuzyk, *The Ukrainian Greek Orthodox Church of Canada 1918–1951* (Ottawa: University of Ottawa Press, 1981) for an in-depth examination of the issue.

64. The 1931 and 1971 percentages are based on Darcovich, *Statistical Compendium*, II, Table 30.2, p. 181, and Table 30.1–12, pp. 185–86. The 1981 percentages are derived from Kordan, "Ukrainians and the 1981 Canada Census," Table 4.5; his data did not provide a detailed breakdown of Ukrainian religious affiliation by province, although Table 4.3 gave provincial figures for Eastern Orthodox, Ukrainian Catholic, and all other for Ukrainian ethnic origin.

65. James S. Woodsworth (dir.), "Ukrainian Rural Communities" (Winnipeg, 1917), pp. 73–94. The report of an investigation by the Bureau of Social Research for the governments of Alberta, Saskatchewan and Manitoba, the Woodsworth survey provides detailed information on social and economic conditions in the Mundare, Chipman, Shandro, and Lamont districts in Alberta.

66. See Editorial Committee, *Ukrainians in Alberta* (Edmonton: Ukrainian Pioneers' Association of Alberta, 1975), pp. 161–169, for an excellent summary of the life cycle of two national halls (Myrnam and Pruth) in the Vegreville bloc.

67. Because of space limitations, women's and youth affiliates will not be discussed, although most organizations had them. Youth affiliates naturally attempted to educate the young in the ideological principles of their elders,

as well as in Ukrainian history and culture, and often had an entertainment component. Women's organizations were concerned with museums, handicrafts, culture, child-rearing and language preservation.

68. Some indication of the comparative strength of ULFTA in Alberta can be seen from the location of labor temples in 1940: Nova Scotia 2, Quebec 2, Ontario 22, Manitoba 20, Saskatchewan 12, Alberta 39, and British Columbia 4. John Kolasky, *The Shattered Illusion* (Toronto: Peter Martin Associates, Ltd., 1979), p. 244.

69. That they had some success was demonstrated by uneasiness in official Canadian circles early in World War II as to Ukrainian-Canadian loyalty. The OUN leadership in Europe believed that Ukraine's independence rested on the simultaneous destruction of Poland and the USSR, which only Germany had the military power to achieve; to 1939 various sectors of Hitler's regime let it be thought that he was interested in an independent Ukraine.

70. See Byrne, "The Ukrainian Community in North Central Alberta," pp. 63–81.

71. William Halina, "What CANADA Thinks of Hlynka!" (Published by Vegreville Constituency Committee, Labor Progressive Party, n.d.). In his pamphlet Halina included excerpts from Edmonton and Calgary newspapers to indicate that other Canadians also questioned Hlynka's statements.

72. For example, see M.R. Lupul, "Ukrainian Canadians: Their Precarious Situation Today," *Ukrainian Canadian Review* (1972–73), pp. 3–10, for a discussion not only of the problems facing the organized community, but also of one attempt to inject new blood into the executive of the Edmonton branch of the Ukrainian Canadian Committee.

73. Although it is now outdated, a survey among students of Ukrainian origin at the University of Alberta in 1968 revealed that less than 9 percent could correctly name at least one Ukrainian organization, and that membership in both Ukrainian and other organizations was low. Only 69.1 percent of those surveyed thought Ukraine was oppressed and 32.0 percent professed indifference. Concern among immigrants, as compared with the Canadian-born, however, was markedly higher. See Bohdan Bociurkiw, "Ethnic Identification and Attitudes of University Students of Ukrainian Descent: The University of Alberta Case Study" (Unpublished Ms., Ottawa, 1970), pp. 11, 14, 19. Bociurkiw's study also corroborated many trends discussed earlier.

74. A recent estimate placed membership in Ukrainian organizations in Canada between 30,000 and 60,000. See Ol'ha Woycenko, "Community Organizations" in Lupul, *A Heritage in Transition*, p. 192.

75. In 1971 only 48.1 percent of Ukrainians in Alberta reported Ukrainian as their mother tongue; based on Darcovich, *Statistical Compendium*, II, ser. 31.21–39, p. 234. The 1981 figure was derived from Kordan, "Ukrainians and the 1981 Canada Census," Table 5.9.

76. In the Bociurkiw study, 52.8 percent of the sample identified themselves as "Canadian only" (p. 12). The recent Ottawa-sponsored Non-Official Languages Study that looked at attitudes among Ukrainians in Montreal, Vancouver, Winnipeg, Toronto and Edmonton, found similar results: 44.5 percent of those polled identified themselves as "Canadian" and in the third generation this jumped to 55.3 percent. See Olga Kuplowska, "Profile of Ukrainian Canadians re Language Retention," *Review* (May 1977), p.15.

77. A 1973 university study showed that Alberta school students in grades 4 to 8, asked to apply descriptive adjectives to different ethnic groups, tended to

have an increasingly negative stereotype of the Ukrainians. See Rosemary McVicar, "Children's Concepts of Ethnic Groups" (M.Ed. thesis, University of Alberta, 1973).

78. Kuplowska, "Profile of Ukrainian Canadians," p. 13. The Non-Official Languages Study, on which Kuplowska's data is based, also found that in contradiction to the low instance of Ukrainian as a mother tongue in the 1971 Canadian census, three-quarters of the respondents in the five cities favored the retention of the Ukrainian language in Canada: Kuplowska, p. 14.

Chapter Eleven

1. For background on Romania see Ian M. Matley, *Romania, A Profile* (New York, 1970); *The History of the Romanian People*, ed. Andrei Otetea (Bucharest, 1970); Stephen Fischer Galati, *Twentieth Century Rumania* (New York, 1970); *Social Change in Romania. 1860–1940*, ed. Kenneth Jowitt (Berkeley, 1977).

2. Quote from G. James Patterson, *The Romanians of Saskatchewan: Four Generations of Adaptation* (Ottawa, 1977), p.10. On gypsies in the early pioneering period in High River see Bert Sheppard, *Spitzee Days* (High River, 1971?) pp. 195–196. Hungarians came primarily from the province of Transylvania, while the Germans were mostly from Bessarabia. While it is true that census data with regard to Romanians can only be a rough approximation, when used with care the census can provide invaluable information on the whereabouts of Romanians in the province and some of the major demographic characteristics of the group.

3. Emily Balch, *Our Slavic Fellow Citizens* (New York, 1910), pp. 429–439; John Paul Himka "The Background to Emigration: Ukrainians of Galicia and Bukovyna, 1848–1914," in *A Heritage in Transition: Essays in the History of Ukrainians in Canada*, ed. M.R. Lupul (Toronto, 1982), chap. 1, and Johann Chmelar, "The Austrian Emigration, 1900–1914," in *Dislocation and Emigration, Perspectives in American History*, vol. 5, ed. Donald Fleming and Bernard Bailyn, 1973, pp. 328–332.

4. Ukrainian Pioneers Association of Alberta, *Ukrainians in Alberta* (Edmonton, 1975), pp. 23–27. For a discussion of, and maps showing, rural concentrations of Bukovinians see T.C. Byrne, "The Ukrainian Community in North Central Alberta" (M.A. thesis, University of Alberta, 1937); John Lehr, *Ukrainian Vernacular Architecture in Alberta* (Edmonton, 1976), p. 6. Graph showing rate of Ukrainian immigration in John Lehr, "The Government and the Immigrant: Perspectives on Ukrainian Bloc Settlement in the Canadian West," *Canadian Ethnic Studies* 9, 2, 1977, p. 43.

5. Patterson, *The Romanians of Saskatchewan*, pp. 12–17.

6. M.G. Toma, "From Boian, Bukovina to Boian, Alberta," *Calendarul Ortodox Credinta* (Detroit, 1974), pp. 102–104; Information on villages contributing Ukrainian immigrants from Isidore Goresky, personal communication, Nov. 1979.

7. For first person accounts of leaving Boian and the journey to Canada see "From Boian in Bukovina to Boian in Alberta: Raveta Toma: Reminiscences of A Romanian Pioneer"; Petrea Mihalchan, "Starting a New Life in Alberta," in *Alberta's Pioneers from Eastern Europe: Reminiscences*, ed. T. Yedlin and J. Matejko (Edmonton, 1976), pp. 19–24; Mike Toma, "From Boian, Bukovina to Boian, Alberta," *Calendarul Ortodox* (Detroit, 1974), p. 102.

8. Locations of early settlements from interviews and G. James Patterson, *The Romanians of Saskatchewan: Four Centuries of Adaptation* (Ottawa, 1977), pp. 71–73. List of families supplied by Martin Hauca, Edmonton, 1979. List of eighty-two men who donated to Romanian Orthodox church in January 1901 supplied by Ted Prescott, Willingdon, Alberta.

9. Calgary *Albertan*, 18 May 1909.

10. Interviews, Martin Hauca, Edmonton, 18 Nov. 1979; Isidore Goresky, Edmonton, 9 Nov. 1979. Bukovina had at one time been part of the larger province of Moldavia.

11. Anne B. Woywitka, "A Roumanian Pioneer," *Alberta Historical Review*, Autumn 1973, pp. 20–27.

12. John Lehr, *Ukrainian Vernacular Architecture*; Patterson, *The Romanians of Saskatchewan*, pp. 76–79.

13. Woywitka, "A Roumanian Pioneer"; Toma, "From Boian, Bukovina."

14. *Ibid.*; Census of Canada, 1921.

15. Michael Toma, "St. Mary's Romanian Orthodox Church at Boian," in *The History of Willingdon 1928–1978*, ed. Myrtle Charuk (St. Paul, 1978), pp. 100–103; Gerald Gordey, "Boian Church," *Heritage*, vol. 2, pp. 9–14.

16. Account of events in Rev. M. Panciuk, "The Romanian Orthodox Church of Hairy Hill, Alberta," *Calendarul Ortodox*, 1974, pp. 105–107.

17. Information on Cohan based on interviews plus biographical information supplied by Rev. Valerian D. Trifa, Romanian Orthodox Episcopate of America to Authors, 26 Feb. 1980. List of priests at Hairy Hill in Panciuk, *ibid.*; List of priests at Boian provided by Michael Toma, Ardrossan, Alberta, 11 June 1979. For a discussion of the overall pattern of priest transiency in Romanian-Orthodox parishes across North America, see Gerald Bobango, *The Romanian Orthodox Episcopate of America: The First Half Century, 1929–1979* (Jackson, Michigan, 1979), p. 28.

18. Nick Svekla, "Boian Marea School District Nr. 1779," in *Saints Constantine and Helen 22nd Anniversary Booklet*, Edmonton, 1970, pp. 27–28. Interviews.

19. *Ibid.*

20. For general background on living conditions in mining camps see David Bercuson, *Wise Men and Fools* (Toronto, 1978), chap. 1; Donald Avery, *Dangerous Foreigners: European Immigrant Workers and Labour Radicalism in Canada, 1896–1932* (Toronto, 1979), chap. 1. For an in depth account of a mixed Ukrainian-Romanian family in Hardieville mining camp see oral history Interview #124, Eliane Silverman collection, University of Calgary, 109p. For accounts of Slavic working class life in mining camps see *Pioneer Polish Settlers in Alberta*, ed. Joanna Matejko (Toronto, 1980).

21. *Ibid.*; Interview, Mrs. N. Rohove, Lethbridge, July 1980.

22. *Ibid.*; Census of Canada, 1921; On role of immigrant boarding houses see Emily Balch, *Our Slavic Fellow citizens*, pp. 349–353; Robert Harney, "Boarding and Belonging: Thoughts on Sojourner Institutions," *Urban History Review*, 2, 1978, pp. 8–37; and Gerald Bobango, *The Romanian Orthodox Episcopate*, pp. 11–12.

23. Interviews, Lethbridge, 1968, 1979.

24. Sir William Otter, *Internment Operations, 1914–1920* (Ottawa, 1921), p. 6; Desmond Morton, "Sir William Otter and Internment Operations in Canada during the First World War," *Canadian Historical Review* (March 1974), pp. 32–58; University of Calgary Eliane Silverman collection, Interview #124, p. 42; H. Palmer, *Patterns*, chap.1.

25. *Ibid.*; Public Archives of Canada (PAC), RG 13 A2, vol. 213, File #1008 contains correspondence on Romanians at Field, B.C.

26. Discussion of Railways Agreement in H. Palmer, "Nativism in Alberta, 1920–1972" (Ph.D. diss., York University, 1973), chap. 2; Interviews: Michael Toma, *ibid.*; Eli and Alice Malin, Calgary, 7 Nov. 1979. In 1936, of the 1,714 immigrants from Romania in Alberta, 1,100 had immigrated prior to 1920; 588 had immigrated between 1921 and 1930; and 21 had arrived between 1931 and 1935, Census of Alberta, 1936.

27. *Ibid.*

28. Michael Toma, "From Boian, Bukovina to Boian, Alberta"; Interviews: Toma, Malin, Doris and Steve Bezovie, Calgary, Nov. 1979; Mrs. Lena Soprovich, Edmonton, 13 and 18 June 1979; Mrs. Mary Romanko, Edmonton, 7 June 1979.

29. Toma, "From Boian," pp. 103–104.

30. For discussion of the impact of the arrival of the railway, see Frances Swyripa, "The Ukrainian Bloc in East Central Alberta," a report submitted to the Director, Ukrainian Cultural Heritage Village, 1976; Swyripa, "Urban Points: The Canadian Pacific Railway, 1927–1928," *ibid.*; Swyripa, "Rural Communities," *ibid.*

31. Personal Communication, Mike Toma, April 1980; *The History of Willingdon, 1928–1978*, ed. Myrtle Charuk.

32. Interviews Toma, Martin Hauca, Edmonton, June 1979; Isidore Goresky, 20 Nov. 1979; *Canadian Parliamentary Guide* (Ottawa, 1928), p. 354; *Edmonton Journal*, 5 Oct. 1956; "George Maftei Mihalcheon, 1892–1956," *Saints Constantine and Helen 22nd Anniversary Booklet*, pp. 23, 25.

33. *Ibid.*

34. Federal Election Returns.

35. Census of Canada, 1931; Interview, Martin Hauca, Edmonton, May 1979.

36. Interview, Doris Bezovie.

37. Interviews, Soprovich, Toma.

38. Federal Election returns; Interviews. In Boian, during the 1935 federal election, the Social Credit candidate received sixty-six of the ninety-five votes cast, the Conservative one, the Liberal four, the CCF eighteen and the Communist six. However, in nearby, predominantly Ukrainian Hairy Hill, the Communist candidate, well-known Ukrainian radical, Mathew Popovich and the CCF candidate, first Ukrainian-Canadian Member of Parliament in Canada, Michael Luchkovich, each received more votes than the Social Credit candidate.

39. Interview, Mrs. N. Rohove, Lethbridge, July 1980. Census of Canada, 1931, 1941; Census of Alberta, 1936. For a discussion of the impact of the depression on mining in Alberta see A.A. den Otter, "Railways and Alberta's Coal Problem, 1880–1960," in *Western Canada: Past and Present*, ed. A. W. Rasporich (Calgary, 1975), pp. 84–98.

40. Interviews, Veronica Paulence, Marian Burke, Calgary, Nov. 1979.

41. Census of Canada, 1921, 1931, 1941. Rural areas around Medicine Hat and Hanna included many Germans from Roumania and many of these people indicated they were of Romanian origin; certainly most of the 437 people of "Romanian" origin who indicated to the census takers that they were Lutherans were in fact of German origin. For example, the "Romanians" at Hanna and Delia were Germans from Romania. See the Delia and District Historical Society, *The Delia Craigmyle Saga* (Lethbridge, 1970), pp. 805–809. In 1941, there was no advantage for people of German origin to

claim they were Romanian since Romania had entered the war on the side of Germany.

42. Census of Canada, 1941.

43. Palmer, "Nativism in Alberta," chap. 4; Interviews.

44. Matley, *Romania*, pp. 124–129.

45. The History Committee, *Tales from Two Townships: The Story of Dalemead and Shepard* (n.p., 1967), pp. 29–31; Lethbridge *Herald* 26 Dec. 1963; Department of the Secretary of State, *The Canadian Family Tree* (Toronto, 1979), pp. 185–186.

46. *International Yearbook and Statesman's Who's Who* (London, 1971), p. 625; Interview, Trajan and Florica Nitescu, Calgary, 6 Nov. 1979. Department of the Secretary of State, *The Canadian Family Tree* (Ottawa, 1967).

47. Interviews; Census of Canada, 1941, 1951.

48. On ethnic relations in Edmonton during the 1950s, see Palmer, "Nativism in Alberta," chap. 5; On Ukrainian mobility patterns, see W.W. Isajiw, "Participation of Ukrainians in Business Occupations in Canada," in *Changing Realities: Social Trends Among Ukrainian Canadians*, ed. W. R. Petryshyn (Edmonton, 1980), pp. 97–103; and Norbert Hartmann and W.W. Isajiw, "Ethnicity and Occupation: An Assessment of the Occupational Structure of Ukrainian Canadians in the 1960s," in *Canadian Ethnic Studies*, 12, 2, 1980, pp. 55–73.

49. Palmer, *ibid.*; Interviews.

50. Fr. Mircea Panciuk, "Past—Present—Future," *Saints Constantine and Helen 21st Anniversay Booklet*, p. 11.

51. *Ibid.*, pp. 11–19; Interviews, Michael Toma, Lena Soprovich, Mary Romanko, Edmonton, 7 June 1979.

52. *Ibid.*, Interviews, Ileana Panciuk, Edmonton, 14 June 1979; Anna Toma, Ardrossan, 11 June 1979.

53. Interview, Dan and Sophie Boghean, Calgary, 7 Nov. 1979; Also interviews, Calgary, 1979.

54. For a discussion of the origins and continuing significance of the division between the two groups see, Gerald J. Bobango, *The Romanian Orthodox Episcopate of America: The First Half Century*. For detail on the origins and development of the Calgary parish see *Romanian Orthodox Episcopate of America, Historical Anniversary Album, 1929–1979* (Jackson, Michigan, 1979), pp. 121–122.

55. *Ibid.*; Interview, Bill Juravel, Calgary, 6 Nov. 1979.

56. Department of Manpower and Immigration, Immigration Statistics, 1970–1977.

57. Interviews, Vasile Matache, Edmonton, 27 June 1979; Petru Ilica, Edmonton, 15 June 1979; Also Interviews conducted in Calgary.

58. *Ibid.*; quote from Vasile Matache, "Impressions and Problems of An immigrant From Romania," *Second Banff Conference on Central and East European Studies* (Edmonton, 1978), p. 107.

59. For data on demographic trends in the area, see *Atlas of Alberta* (Edmonton, 1969), pp. 51, 54–55.

60. *The History of Willingdon. 1928–1978*, ed. Myrtle Charuk, pp. 9, 15, 19, 21, 33, 35, 60, 61, 67. In Willingdon, N.W. Svekla was the village secretary-treasurer from 1960 to 1970 and Nick Hauca has been the mayor since 1971.

61. Census of Canada, 1971.

62. Distribution of Ukrainians and Romanians by Census Division, 1941.

Division	Romanians (4,200)	Percentage of total of Romanians in census dist.	Ukrainians (72,000)	Percentage of total of Ukrainians in census dist.
1	223	5.3	254	0.3
2	179	4.2	1477	2.0
3	58	1.4	200	0.27
4	49	1.2	166	0.23
5	122	2.9	474	0.65
6	514	12.2	2139	2.90
7	164	3.9	615	0.85
8	160	3.8	1579	2.2
9	90	2.1	533	0.70
10	1466	34.9	26686	37.1
11	427	10.2	11234	15.6
12	51	1.2	1472	2.0
13	235	5.6	9372	13.0
14	250	5.9	11710	16.2
15	23	0.5	1142	1.6
16	130	3.1	2376	3.3
17	65	1.5	430	0.6

The two groups are within 3 percent of each other in all but six census divisions.

63. In 1941, the last year in which detailed breakdowns are available for Romanians the comparative figures for Romanians and Ukrainians were:

	Romanian	Ukrainian
rural percentage	74	81
Canadian-born percentage	70	67

64. M.G. Toma, "From Boian," p. 104.

Chapter Twelve

1. Statistical sources used in this chapter include: *Census of Canada, 1901–1981, Census of the Prairie Provinces, 1906–1936, Report of the Royal Commission on Bilingualism*, bk. IV; *Cultural Contribution of the Other Ethnic Groups* (Ottawa: Information Canada, 1970); *Statistical Compendium on the Ukrainians in Canada, 1881–1976*, ed. William Darcovich and Paul Yuzyk (Ottawa, 1977); Unpubl. Mss.; *Historical Statistics of Canada*, ed. M. C. Urquhart and K. A. H. Buckley (Toronto, 1965).

2. Father Anthony Sylla, OMI (1881–1897) came to Alberta in 1909 and spent eighteen years among Polish and Slavic Roman Catholics in southern and central Alberta serving miners, farmers, and other Polish immigrants.

3. P.E. Breton, *Forgeron de Dieu* (Montreal, 1954). This book was translated into English and Polish. It describes the life of Brother Antoni Kowalczyk.

4. Polish rural settlements in Alberta were well described by Father Anthony Sylla in his unpublished *Memoir*, based on his own experience and many interviews with his parishioners. He also used Father Paul Kulawy's unpublished diary. Many reminiscences of Alberta's pioneers are included in the book: *Polish Settlers in Alberta: Reminiscences and Biographies*, ed. Joanna Matejko, *et. al.* (Toronto, 1979). The early Polish missions are described by

Bishop Emile J. Legal, *Short Sketches of the History of the Roman Catholic Churches in Central Alberta* (Winnipeg, 1914). Statistical data and information on distribution of the Polish settlers in Alberta are presented in Roman Mazurkiewicz, *Polskie wychodzctwo i osadnictwo w Kanadzie* (Warsaw, Naukowy Instytut Emigracyjny, 1929). See also: "Polish Farmers in Alberta, 1896–1939" by J. Matejko in *The Polish Presence in Canada and America*, ed. Frank Renkiewicz (Toronto, 1982), pp. 47–62.

5. "Cairn Honors Polish Pioneers of Nisku—Rabbit Hills," *Western Catholic Reporter*, 16 Nov. 1957. Interviews, Mrs. Kacper Halwa, Edmonton, Mar. 1981; Mr. Ernie Sarnecki, Edmonton, Apr. 1981; Mr. Peter Hamula, Edmonton, Apr. 1981.

6. More information on the Skaro Polish settlement is available in two booklets: *50th Anniversary—Skaro Shrine—Star, Alberta* (Edmonton, 1969); *Wachowicz Centennial Project* (Edmonton, 1967). Father A. Sylla gives a very detailed description of the Skaro settlement and mission in 1897–1927. See also, J. Matejko, *ibid.*, pp. 202–206, 314–316.

7. Joanna Matejko and Alexander Matejko, "Polish Pioneers in the Canadian Prairies," *Ethnicity*, 1978, no. 5, pp. 351–369; *Township General Register* — T. 48, R.18 M4 and R.19 M4; A. Sylla, *Memoir*, vol. 2. Interviews, Mrs. Sophie Kalawsky, Round Hill, Apr. 1981; Mr. Peter Hamula, Edmonton, Apr. 1981. *St. Stanislaus Church—Round Hill, Alberta, 75th Anniversary, 1905–1980* Mss. (Round Hill, Alberta, 1980). Until 1971, St. Stanislaus mission was served by Polish priests in Polish and in English. Later, Polish priests would come only occasionally to celebrate special occasions such as the 70th or 75th anniversary of the church. Only thirty families of Polish origin still live in the Round Hill area, two-thirds of whom are of the third generation. The majority live on mixed farms, where they raise wheat, flax, rapeseed, vegetables, and pigs. The second generation speaks Polish quite well, but the third generation only understands a few Polish words.

8. Father Francis (Franciszek) Olszewski (1896–1955) was a very colorful person. At the turn of the century he travelled extensively all over central Alberta visiting Polish settlers. He farmed his homestead at Krakow to support a Polish boarding school and the congregation of "The Auxiliaries of the Apostolate" which he established himself. The nuns, farmers' daughters from central Alberta, left for the United States in 1911.

9. J. Matejko, *et. al.*, *ibid.*, pp. 279–290; Interview, Father Tadeusz Rataj, Holden, Sept. 1976.

10. More information on the Polish settlers in the Athabasca area in reminiscences of John Liss in J. Matejko, *et. al.*, *ibid.*, pp. 298–299; Memoir of Tomasz Gorski in *Biuletyn Kongresu Polonii Kanadyjskiej—Okreg Alberta*, Edmonton, 1968, no. 22; Article about the visit of a Polish emigration commissioner from Warsaw to the Polish settlers in Athabasca in *Edmonton Journal*, 2 Oct. 1929.

11. *Daily Herald-Tribune*, Grande Prairie, 2 Nov. 1976; *Rural Route*, Grande Prairie, 30 Nov. 1977, p. 12; *Biuletyn Kongresu Polonii Kanadyjskiej—Okreg Alberta*, Edmonton, 1961, No. 10, p. 7; Interview, Mr. Antoni Wozniak, Grande Prairie 19 July 1977; Rev. Joachim Michalowski, Edmonton, 21 Sept. 1977.

12. The Tide Lake Polish community was described by Father A. Sylla. Part of his description was published in J. Matejko, *et. al.*, *ibid.*, pp. 106–109; see also H. Palmer, *Land of the Second Chance* (Lethbridge, 1972), p. 65. Interview, Mr. Donald Olekszyk, Ardmore, 15 Oct. 1973.

13. M.B. Venini Byrne, *From the Buffalo to the Cross. A History of the Roman*

Catholic Diocese of Calgary (Calgary: Calgary Archives and Historical Publishers, 1973), pp. 298–300, 465.

14. Excerpt from Father Sylla's *Memoir* published in *Alberta's Pioneers from Eastern Europe: Reminiscences.* vol. 1, ed. T. Yedlin and J. Matejko (Edmonton, Division of East European Studies, University of Alberta, 1976), pp. 25–35.

15. The miners' community of the Crow's Nest Pass is well represented in the reminiscences of Walter Chuchla, Albert Kolber, and the families of Jakubiec, Klish and Pieronek, in J. Matejko, *et.al., ibid.*

16. Leon Garczynski *Co to jest Kanada?* (Warszawa, 1930); *Wskazowki dla wychodzcow do Kanady* (Warszawa, 1927); *Wiadomosci o Kanadzie dla uzytku uchodzcow* (Warszawa, 1937).

17. Interview, Mr. Andy Solikoski, for many years a President of the Polish Canadian Society, Edmonton, Sept. 1980; *Golden Anniversary: Polish-Canadian Society, Edmonton Alberta, 1927-1977* (Edmonton, 1977).

18. Warren Caragata, *Alberta Labour: A Heritage Untold* (Toronto, 1979), p. 96.

19. Interview, Mr. Antoni Szydlik, Ardmore, Oct. 1973.

20. *Pamietniki emigrantow—Kanada* (Warszawa, 1971), pp. 308–309. This collection of memoirs includes several memoirs from Alberta.

21. Henry Radecki, *Ethnic Organizational Dynamics: The Polish Ethnic Group in Canada* (Waterloo, 1979), p. 9.

22. J. Matejko, *et al., ibid.,* p. 236.

23. Andrew Wolodkiewicz, *Polish Contribution to Arts and Sciences in Canada* (London, 1969); this book includes several biographies of Polish Albertans.

24. Research on Polish professionals and businessmen in Calgary was done by Mrs. Alicja Szulc of Calgary in 1979. Interesting characteristics of the Polish community of Calgary are presented in Kathryn Anne Watts, "Calgary's Polish Community: Social Factors Contributing to its Formation and Persistence" (M.A. thesis, University of Calgary, 1976).

25. For more information on Polish organizations see Henry Radicki, *Ethnic Organizational Dynamics: The Polish Ethnic Group in Canada* (Waterloo, 1979).

26. Interview, Mr. Antoni Andrzejewski, one of the most active and devoted leaders in the Polish Scouts Association in Canada, Edmonton, Sept. 1980.

27. *History of the Polish-Canadian Women's Federation in Edmonton, 1958–1978,* ed. Joanna Matejko (Edmonton, Polish-Canadian Women's Federation, Branch no. 3, 1978); Records of this organization.

28. Interview, Dr. T. I., Edmonton, Mar. 1980.

29. Interview, Dr. Bronislaw Bochinski, President of the Polish-Canadian Academic and Businessmen's Club, Edmonton, Sept. 1980.

30. The Polish Culture Society of Edmonton was established in December of 1971 by a group of academics. Instrumental in organizing the Society were Dr. A. Matejko (the first president) and Joanna Matejko, at that time recent arrivals in Canada, and two representatives of the previous wave of immigrants: Dr. K. Kowalewski and Dr. C. Rodkiewicz. The Society organized many lectures including such an event as *Milosz Days* (a two-day program of lectures, discussions, and a reading of poetry by the 1980 Nobel Laureate in Literature, Czeslaw Milosz) held at the University of Alberta in September 1981; sponsored a theater spectacle about Poland in the Northern Alberta Jubilee Auditorium in July 1983; participated in "Heritage Days," and in various cultural activities. Up to the end of 1983, the Society has published, in Polish, sixteen issues of its bulletin "Okolnik."

Chapter Thirteen

1. Fred Dreisziger, *et al.*, *Struggle and Hope: The Hungarian Canadian Experience* (Toronto, 1982), chap. 2. For an overview of the Hungarian experience in Ontario which has many parallels with the Alberta experience see the special issue of *Polyphony, The Bulletin of the Multicultural History Society of Ontario*, vol. 2, nos. 2–3, 1979–1980. For a fuller account of the history of Hungarians in Alberta, see Howard and Tamara Palmer, "The Hungarian Experience in Alberta," in *Hungarian Studies Review*, vol. VIII, no. 2, Fall 1981, pp.149–208.

2. Paul Body, "Emigration from Hungary," in Fred Dreisziger, *et al.*, *Struggle and Hope*.

3. Martin Kovacs, *Esterhazy and Early Hungarian Immigration to Canada* (Regina, 1974); Norman Macdonald, *Canada, Immigration and Colonization: 1841–1903* (Toronto, 1966), pp. 224–228; Martin Kovacs, "From Industries to Farming," *Hungarian Studies Review*, vol. VIII, no. 1, Spring 1981, pp. 45–60.

4. *Ibid.*; Andrew Marchbin, "The Origin of Migration from Southeastern Europe to Canada," *Canadian Historical Association Report*, 1934, pp. 110–123; *Medicine Hat Times*, 25 Dec. 1886.

5. Kovacs, *ibid.*; Merle Storey, "Hungarians in Canada," *Canadian Geographical Journal*, August 1957, p. 48; Martin Kovacs, "The Saskatchewan Era: 1885–1914," in Dreisziger, *et al.*, *Struggle and Hope*, chap. 3; The 1911 census figure included an undetermined number of non-Magyars from the Austro-Hungarian Empire.

6. A.A. den Otter, "Sir Alexander T. Galt and the Northwest" (Ph.D. diss., University of Alberta, 1975), pp. 230–232; H. Palmer, "Nativism in Alberta, 1880–1920" (M.A. thesis, University of Alberta, 1971), pp. 39–41; A.A. den Otter, "Urban Pioneers of Lethbridge," *Alberta History*, Winter 1977, pp. 15–24. Information on Hungarian farmers from Pennsylvania and from Esterhaz arriving in Lethbridge from Martin Kovacs, "A Comparison of Hungarian Communities in Early Alberta and Saskatchewan," in *The New Provinces: Alberta and Saskatchewan 1905–1980*, ed., H. Palmer and D. Smith (Vancouver, 1980), pp. 101–130.

7. Dreisziger, *op. cit.*, chap. 4; Jeno Ruzsa, *A Kanadai Magyarsag Tortenete* (Toronto, 1940); Paula Benkart, "Hungarians," in *Harvard Encyclopedia of American Ethnic Groups*, ed. Stephen Thernstrom (Cambridge, Mass., 1980), p. 466.

8. See Kovacs, "Hungarian Communities in Early Alberta," pp. 114–116, for a discussion of the significance of the boardinghouse in the Lethbridge area. See also Benkart, "Hungarians," p. 466.

9. Alice A. Campbell, *Milk River Country* (Lethbridge, 1959), pp. 363, 390–392, 396–397, 400, 404, 406; Women's Institute, *Drybelt Pioneers of Sundial, Enchant Retlaw* (Lethbridge, 1967), pp. 250, 264, 274, 275–276, 301–302; Census of the Prairie Provinces, 1916.

10. Mecca Glen Centennial Committee, *Mecca Glen Memories* (Ponoka, 1968), pp.235, 236, 237, 243, 244, 272–273. Quote from p. 236.

11. *Ibid.* Interviews, Mrs. Rosie Toth, Bashaw, 15 Feb. 1980, August 1980. Mr. Julius Mraz, Edmonton, 12 Feb. 1980.

12. *Ibid.* pp. 243, 235, 272–273; Interview, Julius Mraz, formerly of Bashaw; Edmonton, 12 Feb. 1980.

13. H. Palmer, "Nativism in Alberta, 1880–1920," chap. 3; Lethbridge *Herald*, 18 Nov. 1914.

14. Dreisziger, *op. cit.*, chaps. 2, 4, 5.
15. In 1936, by which time most families who were going to be reunited had been, among Hungarian immigrants men outnumbered women more than 2:1—2,464:1,048. Census of the Prairie Provinces, 1936, vol.1, p. 1025.
16. Census of Canada, 1931.
17. Dreisziger, *op. cit.*, chap. 1.
18. *Ibid.*, chap. 2. One-fourth of the 150,000 Hungarians who emigrated abroad during the 1920s and 1930s came from outside the postwar boundaries of Hungary.
19. *Ibid.* Information on regional origins of Hungarians in Alberta in Ruzsa, *op. cit.*
20. J.B. Hedges, *Building the Canadian West* (New York, 1939), pp. 361–362. H. Palmer, "Nativism in Alberta, 1920–1972" (Ph.D. diss., York University, 1972), chap. 2.
21. Donald Avery, *Dangerous Foreigners* (Toronto, 1979), p. 102; Glenbow Archives, CPR Colonization Papers, Files 291, 438, 523, 728, 829–933, 836, 839, 1001, 1017, 1035, 1823, 1824.
22. Magrath District Historical Society, *Irrigation Builders* (Lethbridge, 1974), p. 347; CPR Colonization Papers, File 682.
23. For an account of the life of sugar beet growers see John Thompson and Allen Seagar, "Workers, Growers and Monopolists: The 'Labour Problem' in the Alberta Beet Sugar Industry During the 1930s," *Labour*, 1978, p. 154. For a more detailed account of Hungarian settlement in southern Alberta during the 1920s, see L.M. Panulics, *The Long Road: Hungarians in Southern Alberta* (Calgary, 1983), pp. 19–43.
24. Glenbow Archives, CPR Colonization papers.
25. Lethbridge *Herald*, 8 Oct. 1925. See also Lethbridge *Herald*, 21 May, 17 July 1925.
26. Interview, Father Steven Molnar, Calgary, Dec. 1979; Interviews, Lethbridge, 1967.
27. Census of Canada, 1931.
28. Rusza, *op. cit.*; Interview, Joe Molnar, Calgary, 18 Jan. 1980.
29. *The History of the Eastern Irrigation District* (Brooks, 1960).
30. Glenbow Archives, CPR Papers, Nominations Repayment Papers, fn. 835. Quotes from Memorandum, William Schwartz to H.S. Kent, 11 Jan. 1933; "Report for Mr. H.S. Kent," Brooks, 24 Nov. 1932.
31. Interview, Rev. Steven Molnar, Calgary, Dec. 1979.
32. J.B. Hedges, *Building the Canadian West*, p. 317; Warburg and District Historical Society, *Golden Memories* (Warburg, Alberta, 1977); CPR Colonization Papers, File 760.
33. *Golden Memories*, pp. 179, 214, 226–227, 253–254, 258–259, 260–264, 279, 282–285, 330–333, 347, 353–356, 380–381, 412–413, 417–418, 428, 451, 452, 455, 462; Interviews, Charlie and Rose Kovacs, Calgary, Dec. 1979, Mr. and Mrs. John Fritz, Edmonton, Jan. 1980.
34. *Ibid.*; J.B. Hedges, *Building the Canadian West*, p. 319.
35. *Golden Memories*, p. 259. Interviews, Charlie Kovacs, John Fritz.
36. *Golden Memories*, pp. 323, 50, 353.
37. *Ibid.*, pp. 48–49.
38. *Ibid.*; Interviews, Kovacs and Fritz.
39. On the Heatherdown settlers see Hills of Hope Historical Committee, *Hills of Hope* (Spruce Grove, 1976), pp. 259, 482–484.
40. Sangudo District History Society, *The Lantern Era* (Winnipeg, 1979). See pp. 85, 581–582, 611–613, 629–631, 669–670, 686–688, 802–803.

41. Interview, Mr. V. Varyu, Edmonton, Alberta, 23 Jan. 1980; Greenlawn Centennial Committee, *In Retrospect, 1967* (Winnipeg, 1968), p. 239.

42. Census of Canada, 1941; Interview, Father Steven Molnar, Calgary, Dec. 1979.

43. Drumheller Valley Historical Association, *The Hills of Home: Drumheller Valley* (Calgary, 1973), p. 454–459; Calgary *Herald,* 1 Nov. 1930; Special section of *Edmonton Journal,* 30 Dec. 1933; Interviews, Father Steven Molnar, Rose and Charlie Kovacs, Arthur Roberts, Calgary, Jan. 1980.

44. Interviews.

45. *Ibid.*

46. *Ibid.*

47. For a discussion of the social order of the boardinghouse in North America, see Robert Harney, "Boarding and Belonging," *Urban History Review,* no. 2, pp. 8–37.

48. Interviews.

49. Census of Canada, 1921, 1931.

50. Interviews, Ann Lazlock, Calgary, June and Dec. 1979; Father Steven Molnar, June 1979.

51. *Ibid.;* Interview, Margaret Lorincz, Calgary, June 1979; Jeno Ruzsa, *op. cit.* For discussion of Hungarian ethnic "colonies" in other urban centers in North America during the 1930s, see John Kosa, "Hungarian Immigrants in North America; Their Residential Mobility and Ecology," *Canadian Journal of Economics and Political Science,* August 1956, pp. 358–365.

52. Interviews, Ann Lazlock, Father Steven Molnar, Mrs. Gyula Koronghy, Calgary, Dec. 1979; Ruzsa, *op. cit.*

53. Ruzsa, *ibid.;* Interview, Charlie Kovacs.

54. Dreisziger, *op. cit.,* chap. 4; Istvan Szoke, *We Are Canadians* (Toronto, 1954), pp. 64–68, 71–72, 76–82. Interviews, Kovacs and Molnar; Bela Eisner, "A Survey of Selected Canadian-Hungarian Communities," Department of Citizenship and Immigration, 1942. (located in library of the Department of the Secretary of State, Ottawa), pp. 34–37.

55. Allan Seagar, "A History of the Mine Workers Union of Canada, 1925–1936" (M.A. thesis, McGill University, 1977).

56. Interview, Arthur Roberts, Calgary, Jan. 1980. For a discussion of the connection between support for the left and discrimination among immigrants generally in Alberta during the 1930s, see H. Palmer, "Nativism in Alberta, 1920–1972," chap. 3. For the background on pre-1930 ethnic relations in the Drumheller Valley see James Gray, *Roar of the Twenties* (Toronto, 1975), pp. 288–289; David Bercuson, *Wise Men and Fools* (Toronto, 1978), chap. 8; James Gray, *Red Lights on the Prairies* (Toronto, 1971), pp. 207–212. Interviews, East Coulee, Drumheller, Calgary.

57. Allan Seagar and John Thompson, "Workers, Growers and Monopolists," pp. 159–171. Glenbow Archives, Interview, Peter Meronik, Coleman, Alberta, 19 June 1977, pp. 17–22.

58. Victor Hoar, *The Mackenzie-Papineau Batallion* (Toronto, 1969); Szoke, *We Are Canadians,* p. 80; Interview, Charlie Kovacs. For the life history of one of the volunteers see *The Delia and District Historical Society* (Lethbridge, 1970), pp. 470–471.

59. Material on Csávossys from two interviews and their own account in a local history. Glenbow Archives, G.A. Dunsmore (collector) "An Interview with Baron Josef and Endre Csávossy," 17 Apr. 1973; Interview, Marianne Fedori with Endre Csávossy, 4 Jan. 1980; Foothills Historical Society, *Chaps and*

Chinooks, A History of West Calgary (Calgary, 1976), pp. 543–544; See also *Calgary Albertan*, 8 Oct. 1928, and Calgary *Herald*, 8 Oct. 1928.

60. Interview, Endre Csávossy, 4 Jan. 1980.
61. Dreisziger, *op. cit.*, chaps. 1, 6. For the overall context of ethnic relations in the province during World War II, see Palmer, "Nativism in Alberta, 1920–1972," chap. 4.
62. Interview, Joe Molnar.
63. Interviews; Quote from John Marlyn, *Under the Ribs of Death* (Toronto, 1957).
64. Census of Canada, 1941, 1951.
65. For the general pattern of the breakup of Hungarian urban/ethnic "colonies" in the early postwar era, see John Kosa, "Hungarian Immigrants in North America," p. 361; Other generalizations based on Dreisziger, *op. cit.*, chap. 6, and Interviews. Some of the leftists who had gone back to Hungary returned to Canada disillusioned.
66. John Kosa, "A Century of Hungarian Emigration, 1850–1950," *The American Slavic and East European Review* (December 1957), pp. 511–513. According to data from the International Refugee Organization, 57 percent of the refugees were from the Hungarian middle class and 16 percent were from the working class.
67. Dreisziger, *op. cit.*, chap. 2; Department of Immigration, Annual Statistics, 1946–56; Gerald Dirks, *Canada's Refugee Policy: Indifference or Opportunism* (Montreal, 1977), p. 153.
68. Interviews, Les Bondar, John Zold, Calgary, June 1979; Tibor Rada, Albert Siebert, Calgary, June 1979.
69. Interviews, Dr. Bela Biro, Dr. Eugene Szekely, Edmonton, 2 Jan. 1980; Father Steven Molnar; Dreisziger, *op. cit.*, chap. 7. For details on the Hungarian-Catholic Parish in Calgary, see M.B. Byrne, *From the Buffalo to the Cross* (Calgary, 1973), pp. 177–179.
70. Dreisziger, *ibid.*, chap. 7; Dirks, *Canada's Refugee Policy*, chap. 9.
71. Dreisziger, *ibid.*, chaps. 2, 7; Census of Canada, 1961.
72. Interviews, Calgary *Herald*, 12 amd 29 Aug. 1957.
73. Interviews; Calgary *Herald*, 18 May, 28 March, 15 June, 12 Sept. 1957; Editorials in Calgary *Herald* 30 June and 3 Aug. 1957.
74. Interviews; Farkas, Molnar, Biro; Sandor Zsitvay, Calgary, June 1979; M. Hajnal, Edmonton, Jan. 1980.
75. Census of Canada, 1951, 1961.
76. Interviews, Tom Kennedy, Calgary, June 1979; Arpi Burdin, Calgary, Dec. 1979.
77. Dreisziger, *op. cit.*, chap. 2. Interviews, Calgary, Edmonton, Lethbridge; Evidence of the fact that Hungarians are more assimilation prone than other eastern European groups like Ukrainians and Poles can be found in Ken O'Bryan, *et al.*, *Non-Official Languages: A Study in Canadian Multiculturalism* (Ottawa, 1976).
78. Rev. K.C. Doka and Rev. B.D. Nagy, "Calvin Hungarian Church—Calgary," in Synod History Committee, *Growth: A History and Anthology of the Synod of Alberta of the Presbyterian Church in Canada* (n.p., 1968), p. 124.
79. For an overview of the range of activities which exists within the Hungarian community in Edmonton and Calgary see the entire issue of *Heritage*, May-June, 1977; *Edmonton Journal*, 5 May 1979.
80. In the under-fifteen category, 24 percent of those of Hungarian background in the province compared to 34 percent of the total population were in this category. A number of factors have created this demographic structure. The

postwar refugees tended to have small families; also, many of the men from the 1920s' immigration did not marry or re-establish families in Canada.

Chapter Fourteen

1. E. Kallen, *Spanning the Generations* (Toronto, 1971), p. 21.
2. Author's interview with Judah Shumiatcher, 9 Dec. 1979 in Calgary.
3. A. J. Arnold, "The Earliest Jews in Winnipeg, 1874–1881," *The Beaver* (Autumn 1974) p. 4.
4. J. Belkin, *Through Narrow Gates* (Montreal, 1966), p. 27. L. Greenberg, *The Jews in Russia*, vol. 2 (New York, 1976), p. 55.
5. B. Sack, *History of Jews in Canada*, vol. 1 (Montreal, 1945), p. 55.
6. A. D. Hart, *The Jew in Canada* (Montreal, 1926), p. 1
7. Lethbridge *Herald*, "Jews," 1 June 1960. *Gronlunds' Calgary Directory*, 1902, p. 49. A. D. Hart, *ibid.*, p. 147.
8. *The Macleod Gazette* "A Questionable Benefit," 23 June 1893.
9. Calgary *Herald* "Those Jews Again," 5 July 1893.
10. Public Archives of Canada (PAC), External Affairs Branch, RG25 A1, vol. 96. Memorandum.
11. *Ibid.*, A. M. Burgess to J. G. Colmer, 10 Dec. 1893.
12. *Ibid.*
13. A. D. Hart, *op. cit.* Also Glenbow-Alberta Institute (GA), Shumiatcher Papers, file 1184. Provincial Archives of Alberta (PAA) Phonotape 73.461. Interview with Mrs. Louis Podersky, July 1973.
14. A. W. Cashman, *The Best Edmonton Stories* (Edmonton, 1976), pp. 116–117.
15. H. L. Feingold, *Zion in America* (New York, 1974), pp. 148–149.
16. *Henderson's Directory*, 1906.
17. PAA Phonotape 73.449. Interview, Hyman Goldstick.
18. *The Albertan*, 11 Sept. 1912.
19. L. Greenberg, *The Jews in Russia* (New York, 1976), p. 44.
20. H. Gutkin, *Journey Into Our Heritage* (Toronto, 1980), p. 55.
21. PAC, MG3O C119, vol. 20, Rosenberg Papers, P. Waterman to the Jewish Colonization Association, Montreal, 29 April 1908.
22. *Ibid.*
23. *Ibid.*, M. Heppner to P. Waterman, 3 April 1909. *Ibid*, the Winnipeg agent to Jewish Colonization Association, Montreal, 17 April 1911.
24. Author's interview with Judah Shumiatcher (grandson), 9 Dec. 1979.
25. *Ibid.*
26. Glenbow Alberta Archives (GAA), Shumiatcher Papers, file 1184. The following table shows the decline of the colony during its thirty year span:

Rumsey
Agricultural Population

	1915	1925	1933
No. of Colonists	46	28	10
Jewish Population	138	102	53
Farms	48	26	10
Acreage	10,600	12,400	4,520
Value of Machinery	$8,800	$43,800	$10,663
Average Value of Livestock per farmer	$656	$2,806	$1,465

27. PAC MG30, C119, vol. 20, Rosenberg Papers, Agent to Jewish Colonization Association, Montreal, 19 July 1916. GAA Interview with Bella Singer,

1971. PAA Phonotape 73.464, interview with Fred Swartz, *ibid.* Phonotape 73.462 interview with Simon Simons, *ibid.* Phonotape 73.458 interview with Abe Estrin.

28. PAC MG30 C119 vol. 20 Rosenberg Papers, Mr. Rosenthal to Ellman, Agent for Jewish Colonization Association, 8 July 1921.

29. *Ibid.* Memorandum, 11-12 Nov. 1922.

30. PAA Phonotape 73.450. Interview with Helen Sanders Olin.

31. Author's interview with Ben Roginsky 18 Nov. 1979.

32. GAA, Sibbald Agricultural Society File; The Sibbald Women's Institute, *The Sibbald Community History* (Hanna, 1962).

33. GAA Sibbald Agricultural Society File.

34. PAC MG30 C1219 vol. 20, Rosenberg Papers. E. Sengans to L. Rosenberg, 11 May 1934.

35. PAA "History of the Jewish Community in Vegreville," Phonotape 73.456 interview with Harry Bloomfield.

36. *Ibid.*

37. *Canadian Jewish Reference Book*, ed. Eli Gottesman (1965).

38. *Who's Who in Canadian Jewry* (1963). PAA Phonotape 73.449 interview with Hyman Goldstick.

39. GAA D. Spindel Collection, file 3939; PAA Access No. 76.27, "Jews in Alberta."

40. J. Kage, *With Faith and Thanksgiving* (Montreal, 1962), pp. 83–85.

41. H. M. Sacher, *The Course of Modern Jewish History*, revised edition (New York, 1977), p. 348.

42. *Ibid.*, pp. 356–357.

43. B. Baskerville, *The Polish Jew* (London, 1906), pp. 8, 18. See also GAA Phonotape interview with Bella Singer, 1971.

44. GAA Phonotape interview with Bella Singer, 1971.

45. PAA Phonotape 73.464. interview with Fred Swartz. Phonotape 75.322 interview with Ralph Bernstein. Phonotape 73.453 interview with Katie Baltzan Saslow. See also H. M. Sacher, *The Course of Modern Jewish History*, p. 214.

46. Confidential interviews, 1979–1980, in Calgary.

47. H. Gutkin, *Journey Into Our Heritage*, p. 95.

48. PAA Phonotape 73.462 interview with Simon Simons. Phonotape 73.5453 interview with Katie Baltzan Saslow.

49. PAA Phonotape 75.311 interview with Ralph Bernstein. Phonotape 73.458 interview with Abe Estrin. Phonotape 73.453 interview with Katie Baltzan Saslow.

50. Irving Abella and Harold Troper, *None is Too Many* (Toronto, 1982).

51. S. Belkin, *Through Narrow Gates*, p. 201, fn. 8.

52. H. L. Feingold, *Zion in America*, p. 182.

53. PAA Phonotape 73.463 interview with Moses Lieberman. *Calgary Jewish News*, "Centennial Edition," June 1975.

54. Confidential conversations, 1978–1979, in Calgary with community leaders.

55. H. Palmer, "Nativism in Alberta, 1925–1930," *Canadian Historical Association Papers*, 1974, p. 201; interview with Ben Roginsky, 18 Nov. 1979.

56. Interviews of A. Eichler and Z. Lubinsky by M. Fedori, July 1979.

57. Confidential Interviews, Oct. 1979.

58. *Atlas of Alberta*, 1969, pp. 60–61.

59. *Ibid.*

60. Interview with Rowena Pearlman, July 1979; A. Eichler, Oct., 1979.

61. H. Rich, "The Vertical Mosaic and Canada's Jews," *Viewpoints*, Spring 1980, p. 37; *Census of Canada*, 1971, 5.1 Profile Studies, Table 24, pp. 73, 23. And *ibid.*, CT-26B.
62. Confidential interviews with author, June and July 1979.

Chapter Fifteen

1. These figures have been supplied by Simon Evans, partly from the Hutter-rites' own self-census and from the 1981 Canadian census.
2. John Hostetler, *Hutterite Society* (Baltimore, The John's Hopkins Press, 1974), pp. 7–8.
3. Victor Peters, *All Things in Common: the Hutterite Way of Life* (New York, 1965), p. 76.
4. Their nonconformity in dress has caused them to argue that if their children were sent to regular schools, they would be subjected to discrimination much like the American Negro has been.
5. This submissiveness is based on Ephesians 5:22-24.
6. In a handwritten manuscript, *Hutterite Brethren, Life and Religion*, Paul S. Tschetter of Fairview Colony indicates that they are prepared to oppose all orders, rules and regulations which are against God and His command-ments and scripture. "God's word says obey God more than sin."
7. John Hostetler indicates that a study published in the 1950s suggested an average family of ten, *Hutterite Society*, p. 203. A recent study of Edward Boldt, "The Recent Development of a Unique Population: The Hutterites of North America," *Prairie Forum*, vol. 8, no. 2 (Fall 1983), pp. 235–240, has suggested that the trend is to considerably smaller families.
8. See Edward Boldt, "The Recent Development of a Unique Population," and John Bennett, "Change and Transition in Hutterian Society," in A.W. Rasporich, *Western Canada: Past and Present* (Calgary, McClelland and Stewart West, 1975), pp. 120–132. Karl Peters in an article in the latter book, "The Instability of the Community of Goods in the Social History of the Hutterites," pp. 99–119, points out this possibility.
9. Hutterite children were taken from their parents and imperial troops often quartered in Hutterite homes.
10. Some Hutterites did not settle communally and they integrated with nearby Mennonites.
11. U.F.F. Ziegelschmid, *Das Klein-Geschichtsbuch der Hutterischen Bruder* (Phil-adelphia: The Carl Schurz Memorial Foundation, 1947), p. 631: a colony was established near Dominion City Manitoba, but it was later abandoned due to flooding.
12. In 1927–8 in the Pincher Creek area, groups opposed Hutterite plans to withdraw their lands from the larger school district in the area. Moreover, the local residents wanted to use the school to assimilate the Hutterites. However, Hutterites were allowed by School Law to establish a school on the colony because of the distance children would have to go to attend the existing public school.
13. In the Magrath area, the school inspector reported that the only people not in arrears were the Hutterites, Alberta, *Department of Education Annual Report*, 1935, p. 75.
14. The mayor and business groups of Raymond petitioned Prime Minister Bennet to relax restrictions on immigration, stressing the ability to pay bills and their honesty, Victor Peters, *All Things in Common*, p. 53.

15. Brief of the Hutterian Brethren to the Alberta Legislative Committee on the Hutterite Problem, 10 February 1947, p. 3.
16. In 1950 this was amended to 6,400 to 12,800 acres, depending on which of the soil and moisture zones of the province it was located.
17. As a consequence of the pressure on the Brethren, who had hitherto been registered individually as religious societies, the federal government persuaded the Hutterites to agree to the incorporation of the group as a whole. The legislation, encouraged by a French Canadian member from Manitoba, established an administrative structure headed by "bishops" or senior ministers from each of the groups and defined the tenets of the faith and the rights of individuals within the community. This move helped to regularize the formal contacts with the federal government, later very important in the controversy over paying income tax. The significance of the move was that it provided a more precise framework and formal mechanism for control of colonies, to prevent breakaways such as had occurred at Monarch and Brocket in the 1940s and later at Felger in the 1950s.
18. It should be noted that children are perceived to be gifts from God.
19. Brief to the Executive Council on Behalf of Alberta's 51 Hutterite Colonies, 13 January 1950; Submission to the Agricultural Committee of the Legislature of the Province of Alberta on Behalf of Alberta's 51 Hutterite Colonies, 29 March 1960. They objected to the lack of appeal in the decisions which affected their life.
20. A liaison office was established in Calgary to advise the Hutterites about difficulties. There was also an advisory committee with Hutterian and non-Hutterian participation. During the three years the liaison office existed, an elders' committee of Hutterites displayed excellent cooperation, seeking advice about land acquisition and plans for new colonies.
21. A pamplet published by Wilson Colony near Lethbridge suggested that to transport children to off-colony schools where they would be tempted by the spirit of anti-Christ, would be like throwing them as lambs to the wolves, *The Hutterite Brethren of America* (1968), pp. 15–16. At a public meeting in January 1973, Reverend Jacob Waldner implored the non-Hutterians to understand why he could not allow his children to be exposed to such temptations of contemporary Alberta society.
22. Some colonies also established daughter colonies in Saskatchewan and Montana, as a reaction to unfavorable political conditions in Alberta.
23. The more profitable enterprises seem to have easier times in modernizing.
24. They form about 7,400 out of Alberta's 1981 census of 2,213,000.

Chapter Sixteen

1. Hudson's Bay Co. Records Society, *Saskatchewan Journals and Correspondence*, vol. XXXVI, 1967, p. 200, fn. 1 for career of Joseph Lewis. Born in New England, came to Canada in 1795, served in fur trade across western Canada, killed by Blackfoot Indians in 1870. See also Hugh Dempsey, "Black White Man," *Alberta Historical Review*, vol. 6, no. 3, Summer 1958, pp. 7–11.
2. Peter Freuchen, *The Legend of Daniel Williams* (New York, 1956); Robin Winks, *The Blacks in Canada* (New Haven, 1971), p. 302; Colin Thomson, *Blacks in Deep Snow* (Don Mills, 1979), pp. 61–69.
3. Kenneth Porter, *The Negro on the American Frontier* (New York, 1971), p. 495.

4. For information on the life of John Ware see Grant MacEwan, *John Ware's Cow Country* (Edmonton, 1960); High River Pioneers and Old Timers Assoc., *Leaves from the Medicine Tree* (Lethbridge, 1960), pp. 369–371; PAA Phonotape 67.194, interview, Janet (Nettie) Ware; "The Story of Janet (Nettie) Ware," *Heritage*, vol. 2, no. 4, pp. 7–8.
5. Editorial from *Macleod Gazette*, 23 June 1885.
6. Sir George Simpson, *Narrative of a Journey Round the World, 1847*, vol. 1, p. 80. On the Mills see Winks, *Blacks in Canada*, p. 302; Thomson, *Blacks in Deep Snow*, pp. 69–71; and Dempsey, *op. cit.*
7. Florette Henri, *Black Migration* (New York, 1975), p. 19; R. Bruce Shepard, "Black Migration as a Response to Repression: The Background Factors and Migration of Oklahoma Blacks to Western Canada, 1905–1912, as a Case Study" (M.A. thesis, University of Saskatchewan, 1976), chap. 1.
8. *Ibid.*
9. Shepard, "Black Migration," chap. 2; Stewart Grow, "The Blacks of Amber Valley," *Canadian Ethnic Studies*, vol. VI, 1974, pp. 18–20.
10. *Ibid.*
11. Harold Troper, *Only Farmers Need Apply* (Toronto, 1972); Shepard, *Black Migration*, chap. 4; Winks, *Blacks*, pp. 306–313.
12. Troper, *Only Farmers*, pp. 127–128; For evidence of hostile opinion on the part of Edmonton's mayor to the Mitchell proposal, see report in *Coleman Miner*, 5 June 1908.
13. There is a good deal of material on the response to the Oklahoma blacks in Canada. See Shepard, "Black Migration," chap. 4; Stewart Grow, "Blacks of Amber Valley," pp. 25–26; Harold Troper, "The Creek Negroes of Oklahoma and Canadian Immigration, 1909–1911," *Canadian Historical Review*, September 1972, pp. 272–288; Thomson, *Blacks*, pp. 76–86; Winks, *Blacks*, pp. 308–313.
14. Board of trade petition printed in *Edmonton Capital*, 25 Apr. 1911. IODE petition in Public Archives of Canada, Laurier Papers, 184085, Edmonton IODE to Oliver, 31 Mar. 1911.
15. Shepard, "Black Migration," chap. 4.
16. *Ibid.*, chap. 5.
17. Sources which suggest that isolation was chosen to avoid prejudice are PAA Phonotape 73.48, interview with William Chesser, interview, Boadie Bowen, *op. cit.; The Window of Our Memories*, ed. Velma Carter (Edmonton, 1981), pp. 57, 68.
18. Interview, Boadie Bowen, Calgary, 10 Aug. 1979; Carter, *ibid.*, p. 37.
19. For press accounts of the groups' arrival in Canada see Winnipeg *Free Press*, 17 and 20 Mar. 1908. Winks, *Blacks*, p. 305; GAA, F.F. Parkinson Papers, summary of Wildwood settlement and interview, Tony Payne; *The Communicant*, vol. 2, no. 8, December 1974, p. 11.
20. Carter, *op. cit.*, pp. 28–29.
21. *Ibid.*, pp. 37, 44.
22. Winks, *Blacks*, p. 305; PAA, *ibid.*; Interview with William Chesser; *The Communicant, ibid.*, p. 9; Berrymore Carnwood Historical Society, *Forests to Grainfields* (Calgary, 1977), p. 123.
23. *The Ladder of Time: A History of Breton and District* (Edmonton, 1980), pp. 13, 15, 25, 26, 29, 45, 47, 52, 53, 337, 397, 423, 426, 554; Interview, Emma King, Breton, Oct. 1980; Carter, *op. cit.*, p. 66–70.
24. *The Communicant, ibid.*, p. 10; Barrhead District Historical Society, *Trails Northwest: A History of the District of Barrhead, Alberta* (Barrhead, 1967), pp. 121–122; Interview, Rev. Andrew Risby, Calgary, Alberta, 11 Aug. 1979.

25. *Ibid.; Trails Northwest*, pp. 121–122. Census of Canada, 1921.
26. Interview, Rev. A. Risby, *ibid.*; Carter, *op. cit.*, pp. 55, 57; Judith Hill, "Alberta's Black Settlers: A Study of Canadian Immigration Policy and Practice" (M.A. thesis, University of Alberta, 1981), p. 142.
27. S.D. Clark, *Church and Sect in Canada* (Toronto, 1948), pp. 368–378, 417–418, 429–440; E.T. Clark, *The Small Sects in America* (Nashville, 1937), chaps. 3, 4; Joseph Washington, *Black Sects and Cults* (Garden City, 1972), chap. 4.
28. Interview, Rev. A. Risby, *ibid.*
29. On the first arrival of blacks in the area see Stewart Grow, "The Blacks of Amber Valley," p. 22; *Calgary Albertan*, 24 Mar. 1911; and William A. Oppen, "Athabasca Landing" (B.A. essay, University of Alberta, Department of History), p. 67; Interview, Boadie Bowen, *ibid.*
30. John Hope Franklin, *From Slavery to Freedom*, 3rd edition (New York, 1974), pp. 164, 226, 406; For a list of published material on the black Freemasons and Oddfellows see James M. McPherson, *et. al.*, *Blacks in America* (New York, 1971), p. 158.
31. Winks, *Blacks*, p. 306; GAA Parkinson Papers', Summary on Amber Valley and interviews with Jeff Edwards, Thomas Mapp, Mrs. Nettie Murphy, 1963; Carter, *op. cit.*, p. 19.
32. For a statistical analysis of the timing and extent of blacks taking up land in the region see Judith Hill, "Alberta's Black Settlers," pp. 126–132; and C.C. Irby, "Northeast Alberta: A Marginal Agricultural Situation" (Ph.D. diss., Simon Fraser University, 1978), pp. 165–167.
33. Grow, "Blacks of Amber Valley," pp. 29–33; Interviews; for discussions of work as freighters see Carter, *op. cit.*, pp. 19, 22.
34. *Ibid.*
35. On the self-sufficiency of the pioneers see Carter, *ibid.*, pp. 13–14. On the early farming problems, see Judith Hill, "Alberta's Black Settlers," pp. 130–131.
36. Judith Hill, *ibid.*, p. 131.
37. On prejudice in Athabasca, see Judith Hill, *ibid.*, p. 140.
38. Interviews, Boadie Bowen. On attempts by Alberta blacks to get into the armed forces and government response, see Robin Winks, *Blacks*, pp. 314, 317–318; Public Archives of Canada, RG24, C10, vol. 4739, file 448-14-259.
39. *Ibid.*, Census of Canada, 1921, 1931; *Western Producer*, 1 Dec. 1949, Calgary *Herald*, 15 Sept. 1961, Calgary *Herald*, 16 Aug. 1974. Ina Burns, "Kind Hearts and Gentle People," *Family Herald*, 25 June 1959; Carter, *op. cit.*, pp. 13, 23. For statistical evidence of farm abandonment in the Amber Valley area, see C.C. Irby, "Northeast Alberta," pp. 253–255.
40. *Edmonton Journal*, 8 July 1975.
41. Census of Canada, 1911–1971.
42. List of occupations of Calgary blacks supplied by Richard Bellamy; list for Edmonton in *The Communicant*, vol. 2, no. 2, July 1974, pp. 19–20. On urban occupations, see also Carter, *op. cit.*, p. 35, 46. For discussion of black entrepreneurship see J.H. Franklin, *From Slavery to Freedom*.
43. Interviews, Burt Proctor, Calgary, 22 Mar. 1978; Boadie Bowen, *op. cit.*; Richard Bellamy, *op. cit.*; Headley Tulloch, *Black Canadians, A Long Line of Fighters* (Toronto, 1975), pp. 126–128.
44. For a list of entertainment groups and prominent athletes in the Edmonton area see *The Communicant*, vol. 2, no. 3, July 1974, pp. 20–27.
45. *Ibid.*, *Edmonton Journal*, 11 Jan. 1979.

46. *The Communicant, ibid.,* pp. 26–27; Interview, Boadie Bowen, 4 Dec. 1979; E.J., 2 Dec. 1978.

47. For Jones' own account see Carter, *op. cit.,* pp. 54–55.

48. For press accounts of discriminatory practises, see Calgary *Herald,* 17 Dec. 1938, 22 Mar. 1947, 23 Apr. 1947, 1 Dec. 1947, 24 Aug. 1948, 8 May 1951. For a discussion of general patterns of discrimination in Edmonton and elsewhere in Canada during the 1930s and 1940s, see Robin Winks, *The Blacks in Canada,* p. 325–420.

49. GAA, City Clerk Papers, 31 March 1920 (Petition), Percentage of households calculated from Henderson City Directory, 1920. For the development of the controversy see Calgary *Herald,* Apr. 27, 29, 30, May 22, 1920.

50. Mention of Negro residential segregation in Calgary *Herald* and *Calgary Albertan,* Apr. 1920. See also *Calgary Albertan,* 8 Apr. 1940.

51. Robin Winks, *Blacks,* pp. 320–325; H. Palmer, "Nativism in Alberta, 1925–1930," *Canadian Historical Association Papers,* 1974, pp. 188–212; Interview Boadie Bowen, 4 Dec. 1979.

52. Census of Canada, 1931; Interviews, Edith Huston, Edmonton, Alberta, 23 Sept. 1978; Burt Proctor, *op. cit.* For further detail on Shiloh see Carter, *op. cit.,* p. 35. For information on the African Methodist Episcopal Church see *Edmonton Journal,* 4 June, 30 July, 2 Aug., and 3 Sept. 1921. For a discussion of the role of the black church in Canada see Winks, *Blacks,* chap. 11.

53. Calgary *Herald,* Oct. 1910, Apr., 1920; *Edmonton Journal,* 24 Sept. 1921. For a discussion of the difficulties facing black organizations in Canada see Winks, *Blacks,* pp. 333, 335, and passim.

54. *Calgary Albertan,* 8 Apr. 1940.

55. Interviews, Ruth Heslep, Velma Carter, St. Albert, Spring 1979; Bowen, Proctor, Risby, *op. cit., Calgary Albertan,* 8 Apr. 1940; Winks, *Blacks,* pp. 420, 424, 425.

56. *Ibid.*

57. Calgary *Herald,* 22 Mar. and 23 Apr. 1947; Glenbow Archives, City Clerk Papers, CCF club to city council, 31 March 1947; D.S. Moffat, City Solicitor to City Clerk, 28 March 1947; *Ibid.,* 8 April 1947; Personal communication from ex-mayor J.C. Watson, 24 May 1979.

58. Information on the AAACP from interviews, Bowen, Risby; Headley Tulloch, *Black Canadians,* p. 128; On Grizzle's role see Calgary *Herald,* 23 Apr. and 1 Dec. 1947; For background on Randolph see Jervis Anderson, *A. Philip Randolph* (New York, 1973), and for information on Grizzle see Winks, *Blacks,* pp. 425–426.

59. Interviews, Calgary, Summer 1979.

60. Winks, *Blacks,* p. 461; Calgary *Herald,* 8 Dec. 1955; *Edmonton Journal,* 25 Nov. 1978. Interviews, Calgary, Edmonton, Summer 1979.

61. Morris Davis and Joseph Krauter, *The Other Canadians* (Toronto, 1971), Table 7.

62. Calgary *Herald,* 3 Oct. 1969; Interview, Virnetta Anderson, Calgary, 16 May 1979.

63. Boadie Bowen provided a great deal of information for this chapter in four lengthy interviews in 1979 and January 1980. Bowen's life history is an archetype of the black Alberta experience. Bowen was born in Alabama in 1900 and migrated with his family, which included fourteen children to Texas, Oklahoma, Washington, and British Columbia before arriving in Amber Valley in 1911. He grew up in Amber Valley, and in 1926 married a daughter of Thomas Mapp, one of the original pioneers in Amber Valley. He began farming, worked in Edmonton, and in 1930 began work out of

Calgary as a railway porter. Bowen retired from the railway in the 1970s and continued to work as a shoeshine man until his death in 1981.

64. *The Communicant*, Feb. 1975, p. 5.

65. Calgary *Herald*, 1 May 1979.

66. The Glenbow Archives photographic collection contains several pictures of minstrel shows in Nanton, Calgary, and Trochu. See also Cardston and District Historical Society, *Chief Mountain Country* (Cardston, 1978), p. 40. Programs from the Rotary Club Minstrel shows in Rotary Club Papers, Glenbow Archives, are very revealing. Transcriptions of Aberhart's speeches which include Negro jokes are located in Glenbow Archives, Norman Smith Papers, CFCN Broadcast, 30 June 1935, p. 7; 7 July 1935, p. 5. On Racial theory concerning Negroes see Thomas Gossett, *Race: The History of an Idea in America* (New York, 1965); For discussion of the place of nonwhites in Albertans' ethnic and racial hierarchy see H. Palmer, "Nativism in Alberta, 1880–1920" (M.A. thesis, University of Alberta, 1971), pp. 187–220.

67. For a discussion of Negro civil rights in Montana see Michael Malone and Richard Roeder, *Montana. A History of Two Centuries* (Seattle, 1976), pp. 75–76.

68. For further discussion of the tie between noncodified restrictions and the weakness of black organizations see Winks, *Blacks*, p. 335.

Chapter Seventeen

1. David Iwassa, "Canadian Japanese in Southern Alberta, 1905–1945" (Research Paper, University of Lethbridge, 1972), p. 1. Later in his career, Inamasu became an owner breeder of race horses.

2. *Ibid.*, pp. 3, 11.

3. *Ibid.*, pp. 7, 8, 13, 14.

4. *Ibid.*, pp. 4–5. For a full account of Japanese in Canada see Ken Adachi, *The Enemy That Never Was* (Toronto: McClelland and Stewart, 1976). For the life of itinerant single men in this period see Edmund Bradwin, *The Bunkhouse Man: A Study of Work in the Camps in Canada* (Toronto: University of Toronto Press, reprinted 1974) and Rolf Knight and Maya Koizumi, *A Man of Our Times: The Life-History of a Japanese Canadian Fisherman* (Vancouver: New Star Books, 1976).

5. A good study of racism in Alberta *vis-a-vis* Asians is Howard D. Palmer, "Patterns of Racism, Attitudes to Chinese and Japanese in Alberta, 1920–1950," *Social History*, vol. XIII, no. 25, May 1980.

6. Iwassa, *op cit.*, p. 7.

7. Census of Canada, 1911.

8. Iwassa, *op. cit.*

9. *Ibid.*, pp. 16–17; *Memories: Redwater and district* (Calgary, 1972), p. 26.

10. Kazuo Ito, *Issei: A History of Japanese Immigration in North America* (Seattle: Hokubei Hyakunen Sakura Jikkoiin-Kai, 1973), pp. 110, 112–115, 123–124; Iwassa, *op. cit.*, p. 26.

11. Iwassa, *ibid.*, p. 29.

12. For the point of view of the brides see Ito, *op. cit.*, pp. 247–288 and Iwassa, *ibid.*, pp. 29–32.

13. Iwassa, *ibid.*, pp. 37–38.

14. For a discussion of Japanese culture and its compatibility with North

American culture see Harry H. L. Kitano, *The Japanese Americans: The Evolution of a Subculture* (Englewood Cliffs, N.J.: Prentice-Hall, 1969).

15. Iwassa, *op. cit.*, p. 37.
16. *Ibid.*, pp. 45, 48.
17. *Ibid.*, pp. 50–51.
18. *Ibid.*, pp. 46–47, 57.
19. See Adachi, *op. cit.*, pp. 189–190, 192–193.
20. Palmer, *op. cit.*, p. 149.
21. *The New Canadian*, 12 Dec. 1941; Adachi, *op. cit.*, p. 200.
22. *The Vancouver Daily Province*, 8 Dec. 1941, p. 6.
23. For a complete account of the uprooting of Japanese Canadians in World War II see Ann Sunahara, *The Politics of Racism: The Uprooting of Japanese Canadians in World War II* (Toronto: Lorimer, 1981).
24. Iwassa, *op. cit.*, p. 149.
25. For local reaction to the B.C. Japanese see Report, Const. V. Carter, Lethbridge CID, 5 March 1945, Premiers Papers, Acc 69.209, PAA; *Raymond Recorder*, 20 Mar. 1942; Lethbridge *Herald*, 10, 12, and 14 Mar. 1942; *Taber Times*, 19 Mar. 1942.
26. Iwassa, *op. cit.*, p. 66.
27. *Raymond Recorder*, 20 Mar. 1942, p. 1.
28. Interviews in Alberta by the author.
29. For negotiations and agreements with the provinces see Canada, House of Commons, Sessional Paper 1261, 1943/44.
30. Austin C. Taylor to Wm. Andrews and Chas. Graham, April 1942, BCSC Papers, RG 36/27, vol. 29, file 1603, PAC.
31. Iwassa, *op. cit.*, pp. 71–73; and interviews by the author.
32. Forest E. LaViolette, *Canadian Japanese in World War II* (Toronto: University of Toronto Press, 1948), pp. 131–134.
33. Interview by the author with Asano Shigehiro, Calgary, Alberta.
34. *The New Canadian*, 10 April 1943, p. 1.
35. Interview by author with Seiku Sakumoto; Report, J.D. Bird, Supt., "K" Division CID, 20 Dec. 1943, BCSC Papers, RG 36/27, vol. 30, file 1613, PAC.
36. La Violette, *op. cit.*, pp. 130–131; *The New Canadian*, 5 Mar. 1943, p. 4.
37. For a full discussion of the schooling issue see Christopher Liebich, "The Coming of the Japanese Canadians to Alberta, 1942–1948: A Study of Public Policy and Public Attitudes" (B.A. Honors' Essay, Department of History, University of Alberta, 1976).
38. Interviews by author; Iwassa, *op. cit.*, p. 84.
39. Order-in-Council, PC 8173, 8 Sept. 1942.
40. For records of requests to buy land see Department of Labour Papers, RG 27, vol. 642, file 23-2-2-12-1, PAC.
41. For the details of the dispossession and dispersal and attempted deportation of Japanese Canadians see Sunahara *supra*.
42. See House of Commons, *Debates*, November 1945, pp. 2429–2431.
43. Ernest Manning, Premier of Alberta, to Rev. C.C. Kitney, 17 April 1945, Premiers' Papers, 69.289, file 1207, PAA.
44. As quoted in Liebich, p. 106.; Calgary *Herald*, 26 July 1946.
45. Report of J.S. Connors, CIB Lethbridge, 21 June 1946, BCSC Papers, RG 36/27, vol. 30, PAC.
46. Report of J.S. Connors, CIB Lethbridge, 2 Feb. 1947, BCSC Papers, RG 36/27, vol. 30, PAC.
47. Palmer, *op. cit.*, p. 158.

48. *Ibid.*
49. Between 1947 and 1950 a Royal Commission investigated losses by Japanese Canadians in sales by the Custodian of Enemy Property made at less than the "fair market value" or of goods stolen while in the custody of the Custodian. In June 1950, the government announced that $1.2 million would be paid on 1,434 claims totalling over $5 million. For details see Sunahara, *op. cit.*
50. Ted Aoki, as quoted in Japanese Canadian Centennial Project, *A Dream of Riches: The Japanese Canadians: 1877–1977* (Vancouver, 1977), p. 141.
51. T.M. Nakayama, "Anglican Missions to the Japanese in Canada," *Canadian Church Historical Society Journal*, vol. 8, no. 2, June 1966, p. 40.
52. Gordon Hirabayashi, Lecture given to the Conference on the Japanese Experience in North America, Lethbridge, Alberta, October 1976.
53. David F. Sunahara, "Alberta Japanese Canadian Youth Conference," *Canadian Ethnic Studies*, vol. X, no. 1, 1978, pp. 124–125.

Chapter Eighteen

1. I would like to thank the many South Asian Albertans who provided information used in this paper. I would also like to thank Norma Milton and Dr. Doreen Indra, who interviewed people in Calgary and Edmonton, respectively.
2. For an excellent survey of historical India see A.L. Basham, *The Wonder That Was India* (New York, 1959).
3. H. Tinker, *A New System of Slavery* (London, 1974).
4. A.L. Basham, *op. cit.*, pp. 10–43.
5. See W.P. Ward, *White Canada Forever* (Vancouver: UBC Press, 1978). See also N. Buchignani and D. Indra, *Continuous Journey: A Social History of South Asians in Canada* (Toronto, 1985).
6. S. Andracki, *The Immigration of Orientals into Canada with Special Reference to Chinese* (New York: Arno Press, 1978).
7. K. Adachi, *The Enemy That Never Was* (Toronto: McClelland and Stewart, 1976).
8. N. Buchignani and D. Indra, "The Political Organization of South Asians in Canada," in *Ethnicity, Power and Politics in Canada*, ed. J. Dahlie and T. Fernando (Toronto: Meuthen, 1981), pp. 202–232. For an extensive bibliography of South Asians in Canada see N. Buchignani, "A Review of the Historical and Sociological Literature on East Indians in Canada," *Canadian Ethnic Studies* 9, 1:86-108.
9. H. Sugimoto, "Japanese Immigration, the Vancouver Riots, and Canadian Diplomacy" (M.A. thesis, History, University of Washington, 1966.)
10. T. Ferguson, *A White Man's Country: An Exercise in Canadian Prejudice* (Toronto: Doubleday, 1975).
11. Khalsa Diwan Society of Victoria, *Report on Dominion, Provincial and Municipal Franchise* (Victoria: Khalsa Diwan Society, 1947).
12. R. Pannu, "A Sociological Survey of Teachers from India Teaching in Alberta, 1958–65" (M.Ed. thesis, University of Alberta, 1966).
13. Interviews based on confidential conversations with author.
14. N. Buchignani, "South Asians and the Ethnic Mosaic: An Overview," *Canadian Ethnic Studies* 11, 1:48-68.
15. In 1969 an umbrella organization was begun in Calgary, the India Canada

Society. By 1976 this organization (renamed the India Canada Association of Calgary) represented the interests of nine smaller South Asian organizations:

Group	Basis of Association
Bengali Cultural Association of Calgary	regional Bengali Indian cultural groups
Fiji Indian Society	all Indians from Fiji
Gujarati Mandel	religious Hindus of Gujarati Indian origin
Hindu Society of Calgary	Hindu religion
India Student's Association	university students from India
Indo-Canadian Artists Association	interest in South Asian music and arts
Asio-Canadians Musicians' Guild of Alberta	interest in South Asian music and arts
Raga-Mala Society of Calgary	interest in South Asian music and arts
Singh Society	Sikh religion

A similar umbrella organization has arisen in Edmonton, the Council of India Societies of Edmonton. It includes:

Group	Basis of Association
Sikh Society of Alberta	
Siri Guru Singh Sabha	Sikh religion
Nanaksar	
Sant Nirangari Association	
Tamil Cultural Association	regional Madrasi Indian cultural origins
Alberta Malayalee Association	regional Kerala Indian cultural origins
Andhra Cultural Association	regional Andhra Pradeshi Indian cultural origins
Kerala Samajam	regional Kerala Indian cultural origins
Kannada Cultural Association	regional Mysore Indian cultural origins
Alberta Gujarati Association	religious Hindus of Gujarati Indian origin
Jhankaar	Indian arts and music
Hindu Society of Alberta	Hindu religion
Elam	Ceylon Tamil cultural origins

16. These figures were derived from two sources—estimates of community size by members of these groups and by adjusting these in the light of national averages. They are very approximate.

17. For an extensive history of the Sikhs see K. Singh, *A History of the Sikhs* (Princeton: Princeton University Press, 1966).

18. For more detail on Pakistanis in Canada see "A History of People of Pakistani Origin in Canada (1976)" published by the Canada Pakistan Association of Ottawa-Hull. See also M. Siddique, "Patterns of Familial Decision Making and Division of Labor: A Study of the Immigrant Indian and Pakistani Community in Saskatoon" (M.A. thesis, University of Saskatchewan, Saskatoon).

19. On the large Arab Sunni Muslim population in Canada see B. Abu Laban, *An Olive Branch on the Family Tree: Arabs in Canada* (Toronto, 1980).

20. For more details on Ismailis in East Africa see H. Tinker, *Separate and Unequal: India and the Indians in the British Commonwealth, 1920–1950* (London: Hurst, 1976) and H. Tinker, *The Banyan Tree: Emigrants from India, Pakistan amd Bangladesh* (Oxford: Oxford University Press, 1977).

21. U. Tandon, *Problems of A Displaced Minority: The Position of East Africa's*

Asians (London: Minority Rights Group, 1977); R. Moudgil, "From Stranger to Refugee: A Study of the Integration of Ugandan Asians in Canada" (Ph.D. diss., SUNY at Buffalo, 1977); T. Fernando, "East African Asians in Western Canada: the Ismaili Community," *New Community* 7, 3:361–368.

22. K. Gillon, *Fiji's Indian Migrants: A History to the End of Indenture in 1920* (Melbourne: Oxford University Press, 1962). On Fijians in British Columbia, see N. Buchignani, "Immigration, Adaptation, and the Management of Ethnic Identity: An Examination of Fijian East Indians in British Columbia" (Ph.D. diss., Simon Fraser University, 1977).

23. On recent Sri Lankan political history see R. Kearney, *The Politics of Ceylon* (New York: Cornell University Press, 1973). On Sri Lankans in Canada see E. Appathurai, *The Sri Lankans in Eastern Canada* (Ottawa: Secretary of State, 1980).

Chapter Nineteen

1. I would like to thank the many Khmer, Lao, Vietnamese, and Vietnamese Chinese whose assistance made this short history possible; they are too numerous to mention here without doing a disservice to those left out. I would also like to acknowledge the contribution of: Yvette Knott (Calgary Immigrant Aid), Eva Burton (Calgary Sponsor & Refugee Society), Anne Falk (Mennonite Centre for Newcomers in Edmonton), Dr. Norman Buchignani (University of Lethbridge), Ron Selin (Canada Employment and Immigration, Edmonton), Maureen Stewart (CARE, Red Deer), Rhonda Beveridge (Indochinese Refugee Services, Red Deer), Mina Wong (Chinese Community Centre, Edmonton) and Wei Diep (Edmonton Immigrant Services).

2. Rodolphe De Konick, "The Tropical, Agricultural Corner of Asia; An Introduction to Southeast Asia," in *Southeast Asian Exodus: From Tradition to Resettlement*, ed. Elliot L. Tepper (Ottawa, 1980), pp. 83–96.

3. N.H. Chi, "Vietnam: The Culture of War," in Elliot L. Tepper, *ibid.*, pp. 15–30.

4. *Ibid.*, p. 20.

5. Phat Wu and Hong Tai Au, "Facts About Ethnic Chinese from Vietnam," in *Refugees from Indo-China: Their Background* (Ottawa, 1979), p. 16.

6. David Wurfel, "Indochina: The Historical and Political Background," in Elliot L. Tepper, *op. cit.*, pp. 97–114.

7. Margaret MacMillan, "Indo-China: A History," in *Refugees from Indo-China: Their Background* (Ottawa, 1979), p. 33; J.F. Cady, *Postwar South East Asia* (Cleveland, 1974).

8. Robert Garry, "Cambodia," in Elliot L. Tepper, *op. cit.*, p. 35.

9. *Ibid.*

10. N.H. Chi, *op. cit.*, p. 19.

11. Robert Garry, *op. cit.*, p. 35.

12. David Wurfel, *op. cit.*, pp. 97–114.

13. *Laos: War and Revolution*, ed. Nina S. Adms and Alfred W. McCoy (New York, 1970).

14. Ontario Ministry of Culture and Recreation, Citizenship Division, *Ontario Ethnocultural Profiles: Vietnamese* (Toronto, 1977).

15. Gail Kelly, *From Vietnam to America* (Boulder, 1977).

16. *Ibid.*

17. *Ibid.*, pp. 11–39.
18. Canada Employment and Immigration, "Newsletter—Indochinese Refugees" (Ottawa: mimeographed, 16 July 1979).
19. Hoanh T. Ngo, "The Vietnamese Refugees in Toronto: Their Problems and Aspirations," in *Visible Minorities and Multiculturalism: Asians in Canada*, ed., K.V. Ujimoto and G. Hirabayashi (Toronto, 1980).
20. Norman Buchignani, "The Economic Adaptation of Southeast Asian Refugees in Canada," in Elliot L. Tepper, *op. cit.*, p. 193.
21. Canada Employment Centre, Edmonton, *Report of the Viets in Edmonton, 1978*, p. 3.
22. N. Buchignani, *op. cit.*
23. In Calgary, for instance, Mr. Ted Friesen, Special Needs Councilor, continues to be held in extremely high regard by refugees for his assistance and humanity shown to them. During the TET festival of 1980 the Calgary Vietnamese honored him with a plaque for his work with them. In Edmonton, a special project called "The Viet Outreach Project" was initiated by the Canada Employment Centre under the supervision of Al Fitzpatrick. He, too, is remembered kindly by some of the first Vietnamese pioneers.
24. See Matthew Suh, "Psychiatric Problems of Immigrants and Refugees," for an elaboration of these problems in Elliot L. Tepper, *op. cit.*, pp. 207–220.
25. The Calgary figure is a personal estimate; the Edmonton one from a Canada Employment Centre Report, 11 Feb. 1979.
26. Bruce Grant, *The Boat People: An "Age" Investigation* (London, 1979), p. 122.
27. Paul Ferner, "Special Report: South East Asia Perspective," Development Education Primate's World Relief and Development Fund (Toronto, 1980).
28. William Shawcross, *Sideshow: Kissinger, Nixon and the Destruction of Cambodia* (New York, 1979).
29. Howard Adelman, Charles Le Blanc and Jean-Philippe Therien, "Canadian Policy on Indochinese Refugees," in Elliot L. Tepper, *op.cit.*, p. 141.
30. Alberta Advanced Education and Manpower, Planning Secretariat, "Report on the Movement of Indochinese Refugees to Alberta in 1979," prepared for the Interdepartmental Committee on Indochinese Refugees, mimeographed, January 1980, p. 1. The actual figure quoted is 3,050 but see fn. 32.
31. Employment and Immigration Canada, mimeographed 8 Feb. 1981. The actual figure quoted is 4,717 but see fn. 32.
32. Included in the Lao and Khmer figures are some people of Chinese or part Chinese origin: these figures are my own estimates.
33. I would like to thank Ron Selin, Public Affairs, Canada Employment and Immigration, Edmonton for these preliminary figures. Inasmuch as statistics on incoming refugees are collected through several sources, some of which have not produced final figures, annual totals for 1979–80 should be considered approximate.
34. At St. Catherine School, for instance, ESL classes leapt from an enrollment of approximately 25 students in April 1979 to over 200 in the fall of 1979.
35. Norman Buchingani, *op. cit.*
36. Doreen Indra, "Community and Inter-Ethnic Relations of Southeast Asian Refugees in Canada," in Elliot L. Tepper, *op. cit.*, pp. 173–190; Penny Van Esterik, "Cultural Factors Affecting the Adjustment of Southeast Asian Refugees," in Elliot L. Tepper, *op. cit.*, pp. 151–172.

Contributors

NORMAN BUCHIGNANI is an Associate Professor of Anthropology at the University of Lethbridge. He has been involved in research on South Asians and other Canadian visible minority groups for over a decade and is the coauthor of *Continuous Journey: A Social History of South Asians in Canada* (1985), and the author of *Cultures in Canada: Strength in Diversity* (1984).

DOUGLAS FRANCIS was born in Ontario and educated at York University and the University of Toronto. He presently teaches Canadian and Western Canadian intellectual history at the University of Calgary. He has completed a biography of Frank H. Underhill, a noted Canadian intellectual and social critic, and is presently working on a book on *Images of the Canadian West*.

DOREEN INDRA has been involved in practical and research aspects of ethnocultural group settlement in Canada for many years. She was the Director of one of Alberta's major immigrant settlement agencies during the time when tens of thousands of Indochinese refugees came to Canada, and since then has been continuously active in research on their settlement in the province. She is the coeditor of *Uprooting, Loss and Adaptation: The Resettlement of Indochinese Refugees in Canada* (1985), the coauthor of *Continuous Journey: A Social History of South Asians in Canada*, and the author of numerous articles on ethnic groups and ethnic relations. She is currently an Assistant Professor of Anthropology at the University of Lethbridge.

ROBERT J. MACDONALD was born in Regina. He has studied in Saskatchewan, France, at Queen's and the University of Calgary. After teaching school in Alberta, he taught courses in History, Education, and Canadian Studies at Lethbridge, Mount Royal College, Calgary, Saskatchewan, and Camrose Lutheran College. His publications include research on Hutterites, Quebec, and Saskatchewan History, while his reports include work for Alberta Historic Sites. His research interests include studies in circumpolar areas and ethnic studies.

JOANNA MATEJKO, nee Grzeskowiak, was born in Poland. During World War II her family was deported to the Soviet Union. Joanna's father joined the Polish Army of General W. Anders, left for the Middle East, and fought with the Allies in Italy. His family of seven children had been rescued from starvation by the Polish Army and followed the route of thousands of Polish families to Iran, India and British Africa. Joanna completed her junior high education in Iran and her secondary education in Lusaka, Northern Rhodesia (now Zambia). She took an M.A. in history at the Jagiellonian University of Cracow and until 1968 worked for the Institute of History of the Polish Academy of Sciences in Warsaw. She coauthored and edited several books. In 1970, Joanna immigrated to Canada and settled in Edmonton together with her family. Since then she has been involved in Polish community activities. She has published several articles in both Polish and English on Poles in Alberta and has edited a book *Polish Settlers in Alberta* (1979).

NORMA MILTON is a graduate of the University of Calgary, with an M.A. in Canadian History. She specialized in immigration and ethnic history. She is currently working as an independent researcher and consultant.

HOWARD PALMER is a Professor in the Department of History at the University of Calgary. He is former editor of *Canadian Ethnic Studies* and author of many books and articles on ethnic studies and Alberta's politics. His books include *Land of the Second Chance* (1972), *Immigration and the Rise of Multiculturalism* (1975), and *Patterns of Prejudice* (1982).

TAMARA PALMER received an M.A. in English from York University, specializing in Canadian ethnic literature. She has worked as a free-lance editor and writer and is currently teaching in the faculty of general studies at the University of Calgary.

MAX RUBIN, an M.A. graduate of the University of Regina, is presently working on a social history of the Jews of Ontario. He has contributed articles to the *Calgary Jewish News* and to Saskatchewan weeklies dealing with the Jewish experience in western Canada.

DONALD B. SMITH was born in Toronto in 1946. He received his university education at the University of Toronto (B.A. and Ph.D.) and at Universite Laval in Quebec City (M.A.). In 1974 he came to the University of Calgary to teach Canadian History, where he now is an Associate Professor specializing in the history of French Canadians and native peoples. He is the author of *Long Lance: The True Story of an Impostor* (1982).

DAVID SUNAHARA was born in Slocan City, British Columbia, in 1944. He attended the University of Western Ontario (B.A., M.A.) and the University of Alberta (Ph.D.). He is presently employed by the government of Alberta.

M. ANN SUNAHARA was born in Toronto in 1946. She attended the University of Toronto (B.Sc.), the University of Calgary (M.A.) and the University of Alberta (LL.B.). She is the author of *The Politics of Racism: The Uprooting of Japanese Canadians During The Second World War* (1981), and is presently practising law in Edmonton, Alberta.

FRANCES SWYRIPA, a research associate of the Canadian Institute of Ukrainian Studies, University of Alberta, from 1977 to 1983, is currently completing her Doctorate in history at the University of Alberta. Among her publications are *Ukrainian Canadians: A Survey of their Portrayal in English-Language Works* (1978), and *Loyalties in Conflict: Ukrainians in Canada During the Great War* (1983), of which she is coeditor.

Index

Place names in Alberta are indexed separately, beginning on p. 549.

Place Names in Alberta